Fodor's 1st Edition

Barcelona to Bilbao

By George Semler

The complete guide, thoroughly up-to-date

Packed with details that will make your trip

The must-see sights, off and on the beaten path

What to see, what to skip

Mix-and-match vacation itineraries

City strolls, countryside adventures

Smart lodging and dining options

Essential local dos and taboos

Transportation tips, distances and directions

Key contacts, savvy travel tips

When to go, what to pack

Clear, accurate, easy-to-use maps

Fodor's Travel Publications • New York, Toronto, London, Sydney, Auckland
www.fodors.com

Fodor's Barcelona to Bilbao

EDITOR: Robert I.C. Fisher

Editorial Contributors: George Semler, James C. Townsend, Katherine Semler

Editorial Production: Kristin Milavec

Maps: David Lindroth, *cartographer;* Bob Blake and Rebecca Baer, *map editors*

Design: Fabrizio La Rocca, *creative director;* Guido Caroti, *art director;* Jolie Novak, *senior picture editor;* Melanie Marin, *photo editor*

Cover Design: Pentagram

Production/Manufacturing: Angela L. McLean

Cover Photograph: 143-®-RAGA-Spain/The Stock Market (Guggenheim Museum Bilbao)

Copyright

Special Sales

Fodor's Travel Publications are available at special discounts for bulk purchases for sales promotions or premiums. Special editions, including personalized covers, excerpts of existing guides, and corporate imprints, can be created in large quantities for special needs. For more information, contact your local bookseller or write to Special Markets, Fodor's Travel Publications, 280 Park Avenue, New York, NY 10017. Inquiries from Canada should be directed to your local Canadian bookseller or sent to Random House of Canada, Ltd., Marketing Department, 2775 Matheson Boulevard East, Mississauga, Ontario L4W 4P7. Inquiries from the United Kingdom should be sent to Fodor's Travel Publications, 20 Vauxhall Bridge Road, London SW1V 2SA, England.

PRINTED IN THE UNITED STATES OF AMERICA

10 9 8 7 6 5 4 3 2 1

Important Tip

Although all prices, opening times, and other details in this book are based on information supplied to us at press time, changes occur all the time in the travel world, and Fodor's cannot accept responsibility for facts that become outdated or for inadvertent errors or omissions. So **always confirm information when it matters,** especially if you're making a detour to visit a specific place.

CONTENTS

Maps

ON THE ROAD WITH FODOR'S

THE TRIPS YOU TAKE THIS YEAR and next are going to be significant trips, if only because they'll be among the first in the new millennium. Acutely aware of that fact, we've pulled out all stops in preparing *Barcelona to Bilbao*. To guide you in putting together your experience in northern Spain, we've created multiday itineraries and neighborhood walks. And to direct you to the places that are truly worth your time and money in these important years, we've rallied the team of endearingly picky know-it-alls we're pleased to call our writers. Having seen all corners of the regions they cover for us, they're real experts. If you knew them, you'd poll them for tips yourself.

George Semler fell in love with Europe on a boat train to Paris in 1960 and says he hasn't yet recovered and doesn't want to. "It was the flat fish knives, the capers, and the snowy tablecoths that did it . . . I knew I was home."

"Later, Spain and the Mediterranean seemed even more exciting than Paris to me: the light, the decibel level, the sharpness of everything. A normal Monday morning in Spain seems to me about as festive as New Year's Eve north of the Pyrenees."

Since the initial coup de foudre, Semler has been out of his native United States nearly constantly, traveling and working in France, Greece, Vietnam, China, Morocco, Cuba and Spain—among other destinations—over the last 35 years. After settling in Madrid with his wife Lucie Hayes in 1970, Semler worked as a movie extra, hockey player-coach, translator and freelance journalist while completing Masters and Doctoral studies in Spanish language and literature (to go with his Yale BA in French) and writing articles for publications ranging from the *International Herald Tribune* to the *Los Angeles Times,* from *Forbes fyi* to *Sky* and *Saveur.* Along with magazine pieces on food, travel, art, and sport he has published two books of his own—*Barcelonawalks* and *Madridwalks*—and contributed to Fodor's Morocco, Cuba, Spain, and France titles over the last decade.

Presently at work on a book about a seven-week, 270-mile hike from Atlantic to Mediterranean along the crest of the Pyrenees, Semler, a Barcelona resident for the past 25 years, is also completing a memoir on bringing up his polyglot family of four (see Katherine, below) through the final five years of the Franco regime, the democratic transition years, and into the modern and ebullient Spain of today.

With an American father and a Catalan mother, **James Townsend** has lived with a foot on either side of the Atlantic. His mission has long been getting the best of both worlds—and as his chapter on Catalonia (Costa Brava to Tarragona) proves—Fodor's is much the winner. His mother's family fled Spain in 1939 during the Spanish Civil War—members of that family were deeply involved in the liberal Republican government, including his great-uncle, Carles Pi i Sunyer, who was mayor of Barcelona and his grandfather, Santiago Pi i Sunyer, who was under-secretary of education in the Spanish Republican goverment—but he returned *en familia* to Catalonia in 1962 as a child to live in a small village in the foothills of the Pyrenees, mixing with the children his age and polishing his Catalan and Spanish. This was all to serve him well in later years as a writer and translator. After receiving degrees from Marquette and Boston universities, he became a permanent resident of Barcelona, where he works as a freelance journalist, writer, and translator. He often writes for *La Vanguardia,* Barcelona's major daily newspaper, and stays in touch with the U.S. via the internet.

Raised in Madrid, San Sebastián, and Barcelona, **Katherine Semler**—the author of our Smart Travel Tips section—attended preschool in Euskera (the Basque language), kindergarten in Spanish, elementary school in French, and secondary school in the United States in English. She went on to earn a B.A. in French and

Russian literature at Vassar and a graduate degree in French and Catalan literature at Dartmouth. (We are not making this up.) Along with her husband, she currently resides in Barcelona.

Don't Forget to Write

Keeping a travel guide fresh and up-to-date is a big job. So we love your feedback—positive and negative—and follow up on all suggestions. Contact the Barcelona to Bilbao editor at editors@fodors.com or c/o Fodor's, 280 Park Avenue, New York, New York 10017. And have a wonderful trip!

Karen Cure

Karen Cure
Editorial Director

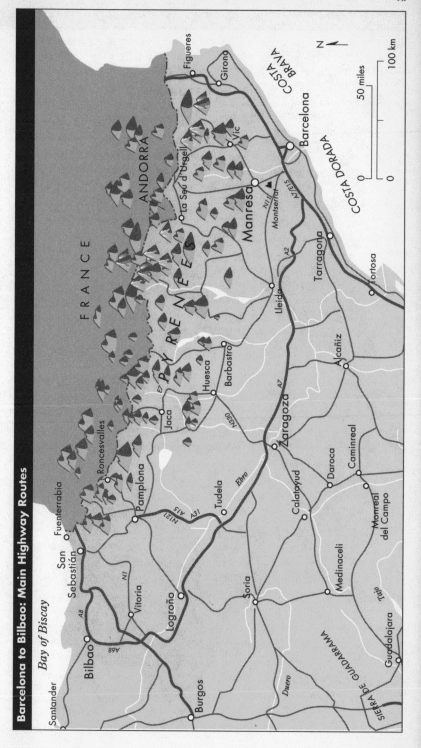

Barcelona to Bilbao: Main Highway Routes

Spain and Its Provinces

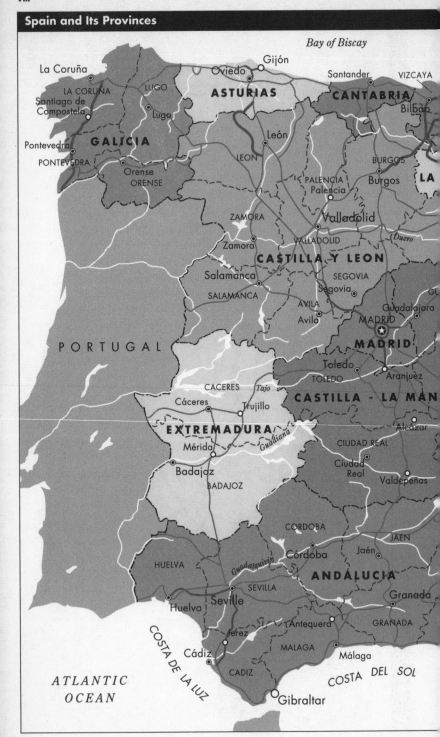

Bay of Biscay

La Coruña
LA CORUÑA
Santiago de
Compostela
Pontevedra
PONTEVEDRA
GALICIA
Orense
ORENSE

LUGO
Lugo

Oviedo
ASTURIAS
Gijón

León
LEON

Santander
CANTABRIA
VIZCAYA
Bilbao

BURGOS
Burgos
LA

PALENCIA
Palencia

Valladolid
VALLADOLID

Duero

ZAMORA
Zamora

CASTILLA Y LEON

Salamanca
SALAMANCA

SEGOVIA
Segovia

AVILA
Avila

Guadalajara

MADRID
MADRID

GU

PORTUGAL

Toledo
TOLEDO

Aranjuez

CASTILLA - LA MAN

CACERES
Cáceres
Trujillo
Tajo

EXTREMADURA
Mérida
Badajoz
BADAJOZ

Guadiana

CIUDAD REAL
Ciudad
Real
Valdepeñas

Alcázar

CORDOBA
Córdoba

JAEN
Jaén

HUELVA

Guadalquivir

SEVILLA
Seville

Huelva

ANDALUCIA

Granada

GRANADA

Jerez

Antequera

MALAGA
Málaga

Cádiz
CADIZ

COSTA DE LA LUZ

COSTA DEL SOL

Gibraltar

ATLANTIC
OCEAN

PAIS VASCO
(EUSKADI)
San
Sebastián
GUIPUZCOA
Victoria
ALAVA   Pamplona
TREVINO   NAVARRA
Logroño
RIOJA
Soria
SORIA   Zaragoza
Ebro
JADALAJARA   ARAGON
ZARAGOZA
Tajo
TERUEL
Cuenca
Teruel
CUENCA   CASTELLON
CHA
Jucar   Castellón
de la Plana
Valencia
Requena
VALENCIA
Albacete
Játiva
ALBACETE   ALICANTE
Segura   Alicante
MURCIA
Murcia
Lorca
Cartagena
COSTA
CALIDA
ALMERIA
Almería
COSTA DE
ALMERIA

FRANCE

ANDORRA

HUESCA
Huesca   LERIDA   GERONA

CATALUNYA   Gerona
(CATALONIA)   COSTA
BRAVA
Lérida   BARCELONA
Barcelona
TARRAGONA   Tarragona
Tortosa
COSTA
DORADA   Balearic
Sea
Menorca →

COSTA DEL AZAHAR

Palma

Mallorca

Ibiza   BALEARIC
ISLANDS
Eivissa
Formentera

COSTA BLANCA

Menorca
Ciudadela
Mahón

KEY
—·—· Regions
——— Provinces
◉ Provincial
capitals

Mediterranean
Sea

N

ALGERIA

0   50 miles
0   75 km

SMART TRAVEL TIPS A TO Z

Basic Information on Traveling in Spain, Savvy Tips to Make Your Trip a Breeze, and Companies and Organizations to Contact

Half the fun of traveling is looking forward to your trip—but when you look forward, don't just daydream. There are plans to be made, things to learn about, serious work to be done. The following information will give you helpful pointers on many of the questions that arise when planning your trip and on the road. In addition, the organizations listed in this section will supplement the information in this guide book. Note that much of the information in the section is Spain-wide; for specific details about the various topics covered below *within* the regions covered in this book—Catalonia, Navarra, Aragón, La Rioja, and Euskadi (the Basque Country) —additionally consult the A to Z sections at the end of each regional chapter in this book.

AIR TRAVEL

There are regular nonstop flights connecting the eastern United States with Spain. Flying from other cities in North America usually involves a stop. Flights from the U.K. to a number of destinations in Spain are very frequent and offered at very competitive fares. If you are traveling from North America, consider flying a British or other European carrier, especially if you are traveling to a destination in Spain other than Madrid or Barcelona, as the savings can be significant. Be warned, however, that this usually entails an overnight stop in London or other European city on the return flight. There are no direct flights to Spain from Australia or New Zealand.

For air travel within the regions covered in this book there are numerous regular flights, but rates tend to be high, so consider alternative ways of getting around (☞ Transportation, *below*). Bilbao, Girona, Pamplona, and San Sebastián all have small airports and flights do run from

Barcelona to each of them. However, flights between those cities are less common because of the short distance and, in most cases, train or car travel is more prevalent.

BOOKING YOUR FLIGHT

When you book, **look for nonstop flights** and **remember that "direct" flights stop at least once.** Unless there are considerable savings to be had, avoid connecting flights, which require a change of plane.

CARRIERS

American, Continental, US Airways, Air Europa, Spanair, and TWA fly to Madrid; Delta and Iberia fly to Madrid and Barcelona. Within Spain, Iberia is the main domestic airline; two independent airlines, Air Europa and Spanair, fly a number of domestic routes at somewhat lower prices.

➤ FROM NORTH AMERICA: AeroMéxico (☎ 800/237–6639). **Air Europa** (☎ 888/238–7672). **American** (☎ 800/433–7300). **Continental** (☎ 800/231–0856). **Delta** (☎ 800/221–1212). **Iberia** (☎ 800/772–4642). **Spanair** (☎ 888/545–5757). **TWA** (☎ 800/892–4141). **US Airways** (☎ 800/622–1015).

➤ FROM THE U.K.: **British Airways** (☎ 0345/222–111). **Iberia** (☎ 020/7/830–0011).

➤ WITHIN SPAIN: **Iberia** (902/400500). **Air Europa** (☎ 902/401501). **Spanair** (☎ 902/131415).

CHECK-IN & BOARDING

Assuming that not everyone with a ticket will show up, airlines routinely overbook planes. When that happens, airlines ask for volunteers to give up their seats. In return these volunteers usually get a certificate for a free flight and are rebooked on the next flight out. If there are not enough volunteers, the airline must choose who will be denied boarding. The first to get bumped are passengers who checked in late and those flying on discounted tickets, so **get to the gate and check in as early as possible,** especially during peak periods.

Always **bring a government-issued photo ID to the airport,** as it may be required for check-in.

CUTTING COSTS

The least-expensive airfares to Spain must usually be purchased in advance and are nonrefundable. When you're quoted a good price, book it on the spot—the same fare may not be available the next day. Always **check different routings** and look into using different airports. Travel agents, especially low-fare specialists (☞ Discounts & Deals, *below*), are helpful.

Consolidators are another good source. They buy tickets for scheduled international flights at reduced rates from the airlines, then sell them at prices that beat the best fares available directly from the airlines, usually without restrictions. Sometimes you can even get your money back if you need to return the ticket. Carefully read the fine print detailing penalties for changes and cancellations, and **confirm your consolidator reservation with the airline.**

➤ CONSOLIDATORS: **Cheap Tickets** (☎ 800/377–1000). **Discount Airline Ticket Service** (☎ 800/576–1600). **Unitravel** (☎ 800/325–2222). **Up & Away Travel** (☎ 212/889–2345). **World Travel Network** (☎ 800/ 409–6753).

DISCOUNT PASSES

If you buy a round-trip transatlantic ticket on **Iberia** (☞ *above*), you might want to purchase a Visit Spain pass, good for four domestic flights during your trip. The pass must be purchased before you arrive in Spain, all flights must be booked in advance, and the cost is $260, or $350 if you want to include flights to the Canary Islands. Prices are $20 to $50 less if you travel between October 1 and June 14.

On certain days of the week, Iberia also offers minifares (*minitarifas*), which can save you 40% on domestic flights. Tickets must be purchased in advance, and you must stay over at the destination Saturday night (☞ Discounts & Deals, *below*).

ENJOYING THE FLIGHT

Because Spain is one of the most popular destinations in the world, flights to and within the country are often packed. To take the edge off the discomfort, some Spanish airlines are now serving a nice selection of Spanish wines and it has recently become customary to show two in-flight movies. All flights to Spain are no-smoking. Smoking is not allowed on any domestic flights in Spain either.

FLYING TIMES

Transatlantic flying time is seven hours from New York. As there are no direct flights from the United States to Barcelona, an additional flight is required from Madrid, involving a connecting flight lasting 1 hour to Barcelona or 40 minutes to Bilbao.

HOW TO COMPLAIN

If your baggage goes astray or your flight goes awry, complain right away. Most carriers require that you **file a claim immediately.**

➤ AIRLINE COMPLAINTS: U.S. Department of Transportation **Aviation Consumer Protection Division** (✉ C-75, Room 4107, Washington, DC 20590, ☎ 202/366–2220). **Federal Aviation Administration Consumer Hotline** (☎ 800/322–7873).

AIRPORTS

Most flights arriving in Spain from the United States and Canada pass through Madrid's Barajas (MAD), but the major gateway to Catalonia and other regions in this book is Spain's second-largest airport, Barcelona's El Prat de Llobregat (BCN). This airport gets scheduled routes from numerous international carriers, but Catalonia also has two other airports that handle other air traffic, including a great number of charter flights. One is Girona, 90 km (56 mi) north of Barcelona and highly convenient to the resort coast of the Costa Brava. The other is at Reus, 110 km (68 mi) south of Barcelona and a gateway to Tarragona and the coastal towns of the Costa Daurada.

From the U.K. and elsewhere in Europe, there are also regular flights to Alicante (ALC), Málaga (AGP), Palma de Mallorca (PMI), and the Canary Islands.

➤ AIRPORT INFORMATION: Madrid: **Barajas** (☏ 91/305–8343). Barcelona: **El Prat de Llobregat** (☏ 93/298–3838). Girona: **Aeroport de Girona** (☏ 972/186600). Reus: **Aeropuerto de Reus** (☏ 977/779800).

DUTY-FREE SHOPPING

Duty-free items are available on your flight as well as in international terminals. Duty-free is not available to passengers traveling within the European Union only.

BIKE TRAVEL

Traveling on two instead of four wheels and under your own power is a great way to see Spain. Bike travel is especially popular in northern Spain, where fiendly little *pellotons* (groups of bikers) rise and fall over and around the green hills of the Basque Country and the Pyrennees. Most Spanish biking is done on road bikes. Itineraries from town to town on bikes offer a great way to see the countryside and to work up enough of an appetite for all the food there is to sample. Remember that roadside stops in Spain can offer top-quality gourmet meals hardly betrayed by the attractiveness of the building or location of the restaurant. Do beware of the lack of a shoulder on many Spanish roads. Cars travel very fast and though drivers are used to encountering bikers they do not go out of their way to make you feel safe and cared for. Spain's numerous nature areas are perfect for mountain biking; in many cases there are specially marked trails.

It is better to rent a bike locally, rather than facing the logistics and complications of bringing your own bike with you. Note, for instance, that bikes are usually not allowed on trains; they have to be packed and checked in as luggage. Most Spanish nature areas have at least one agency offering mountain bikes for rent and, in many cases, guided biking tours. Check with the individual park visitors' center for details. In addition,

hotels located in rural areas often have bikes available for guests, either for rent or for free.

BIKES IN FLIGHT

Most airlines accommodate bikes as luggage, provided they are dismantled and boxed. Bike boxes are often free at bike shops and cost about $5 (at least $100 for bike bags) from airlines. International travelers can sometimes substitute a bike for a piece of checked luggage at no charge; otherwise, the conveyance cost is about $100. Domestic and Canadian airlines charge $25–$50.

BOAT & FERRY TRAVEL

There are regular ferry services between the U.K. and northern Spain. Brittany Ferries sails from Portsmouth to Santander, and P&O European Ferries sails from Plymouth to Bilbao. Spain's major ferry line, Transmediterránea, connects mainland Spain to the Balearics and the Canary Islands. If you are traveling from Spain to Morocco with a car, there are ferries from Málaga, Algeciras and Tarifa, run by Transmediterránea and Buquebus. Note that in both cases the fast catamaran service takes half the time as the standard ferry, but catamarans are often cancelled due to seas as they can only navigate in very calm waters.

➤ FROM THE U.K.: **Brittany Ferries** (☏ 0752/221–321 or 0990/360360). **P&O European Ferries** (☏ 0990/980555).

➤ IN SPAIN: **Buquebus** (☏ 902/414242). **Transmediterránea** (☏ 902/454645).

BUS TRAVEL

Within Spain, an array of private companies provide bus services, with service that ranges from knee-crunchingly basic to luxurious. Depending on your destination you will be able to choose more direct routes on more comfortable buses for higher fares or more basic local buses that are cheaper. Fares are lower than the corresponding train fares, and service is more extensive: if you want to reach a town not served by train, you can be sure a bus will go there. Smaller towns don't usually have a central bus depot, so ask the tourist office where to wait for the bus to your destination (usually a local café or central square). Spain's major national long-haul company is **Enatcar**. See individual chapters for companies serving the different regions. Note that there are fewer services during the weekend.

You can get to Spain by bus from London and Paris. It is a long journey, but the buses are modern and it is an inexpensive way to travel to Spain from the U.K. Eurolines is the main carrier and connects many European cities with Barcelona, which has two main bus terminals, Estació de Sants (for long-distance and international routes) and Estació del Nord (for inter-Spain routes)—for further information on these terminals, *see* Barcelona A to Z *in* Chapter 2.

BUS INFORMATION

➤ WITHIN SPAIN: **Enatcar** (✉ Calle Mendazábal, Madrid, ☎ 902/ 422242).

➤ BUS TERMINALS: **Estació del Nord** (✉ Carrer d'Ali Bei 80, Barcelona, ☎ 93/265–6508). **Estació de Sants** (✉ Carrer de Viriat, Barcelona, ☎ 93/490– 0202). **Termibus** (✉ Calle Gurtubai 1, Bilbao, ☎ 94/439–5077) **Estación de Autobuses** (✉ Av. del Calle Conde Oliveto 8, Pamplona, ☎ 948/221026).

➤ BUS TOURS: **Marsans** (✉ Gran Via 59, Madrid, ☎ 902/306090). **Pullmantur** (✉ Plaza de Oriente 8, Madrid, ☎ 91/541–1805).

➤ FROM THE U.K.: **Eurolines/National Express** (☎ 01582–404511 or 0990–143219).

BUSINESS HOURS

BANKS & OFFICES

Banks are generally open weekdays 9–2, Saturday 8:30 or 9–1, but in the summer most banks close at 2 PM weekdays and stay closed on Saturday. Currency exchanges at airports and train stations stay open later. Traveler's checks can also be cashed at El Corte Inglés department stores until 9 PM. Most government offices open mornings only, 9–2.

GAS STATIONS

In major towns and on main routes, gas stations are open 24 hours a day.

It is often hard to tell whether it is self-serve or not except through observation.

MUSEUMS & SIGHTS

Most museums are open from 9:30 to 2 and 4 to 7 and are closed one day a week, usually Monday; but opening hours vary widely, and there are often (slightly) different opening hours in summer and winter, with winter hours being curtailed in some way. A few large museums, such as Barcelona's Picasso Museum, stay open all day and do not close for the midday hours. Note that many churches and historic houses in smaller villages are often kept closed; to gain entrance, you need to obtain the key (*la clau*), often kept by a caretaker (in an adjacent house), at the local town hall (*ajuntament*), or even at the corner bar.

PHARMACIES

Pharmacies open normal business hours (9–1:30 and 5–8), but there is always a duty pharmacy open at other times in each village and city neighborhood.

SHOPS

When planning a shopping trip, **keep in mind that almost all shops in Spain close at midday** for at least three hours, except for the department-store chain El Corte Inglés and large supermarkets. Stores are generally open from 9–10 to 1:30 and from 5 to 8. Most shops are closed on Sunday, and in several other places they're also closed Saturday afternoon. That said, larger shops in tourist areas may stay open Sunday in summer and during the Christmas holiday.

CAMERAS & PHOTOGRAPHY

Spain lends itself to memorable photographs. It is practically impossible to take bad pictures there, short of leaving the lens cap on. Note that you are not allowed to take photographs of military installations, nor should you take pictures of police. Spaniards generally do not object to having their photo taken, but **always ask their permission first.** Bear in mind, too, that many museums and monuments ban photography. Others prohibit the use of flash or a tripod. The best pictures are to be had in the early morning and in the evening. The harsh midday sun can result in over-contrasty photos. On the beach, bear in mind that the reflected glare can confuse your camera's light meter.

EQUIPMENT PRECAUTIONS

It can be difficult and expensive to locate new batteries for your camera so come prepared with a new one.

FILM & DEVELOPING

All the major brands of film are readily available in Spain, but it is more expensive than in the United States (a color-print roll of 36 exposures costs around 700 ptas./€421), so take a good supply of film with you. If you buy film in Spain, use only large stores or photography shops. Film sold in smaller outlets may be out of date or stored in poor conditions.

Film developing in Spain is expensive, and the quality is unreliable except at major laboratories, which take longer to process film. Look for shops displaying the Kodak Q-Lab sign, which is a guarantee of quality. If you are in a real hurry, larger towns and resorts have shops that will develop film in a few hours. In general, though, it is preferable to have your film developed at home. X-ray machines in Spanish airports are claimed to be film-safe.

➤ PHOTO HELP: **Kodak Information Center** (☎ 800/242–2424). *Kodak Guide to Shooting Great Travel Pictures,* available in bookstores or from Fodor's Travel Publications (☎ 800/533–6478; $16.50 plus $5.50 shipping).

VIDEOS

Spain uses the PAL system for videos. Tape in other systems is hard to come by, so take a good supply with you.

CAR RENTAL

Currently, one of the best ways to rent a car, whether you arrange it from home or during your travels, is through an internet website—the rates are the best and the arrangements the easiest. Generally, chances of getting a better deal are higher if you book your car back home, *before* arriving in Spain (in fact, if you are already in Spain, you may wish to

have a family member or friend book a car for you back in your home country). That noted, Avis, Hertz, Budget, and the European agency Europcar all have agencies at the airports of Barcelona and Bilbao and in other cities where you can book *un cotxe de lloguer* (rental car). National companies work through the Spanish agency, Atesa. Smaller local companies offer lower rates. All agencies have a wide range of models, but cars with automatic transmission are less common. Rates in Barcelona begin at the equivalents of U.S. $55 a day and $240 a week for an economy car with air-conditioning, manual transmission, and unlimited mileage. This does not include the tax on car rentals, which is 16%.

➤ MAJOR AGENCIES: **Alamo** (☎ 800/522–9696; 020/8759–6200 in the U.K.). **Avis** (☎ 800/331–1084; 800/331–1084 in Canada; 02/9353–9000 in Australia; 09/525–1982 in New Zealand). **Budget** (☎ 800/527–0700;0870/607–5000 in the U.K., through affiliate Europcar). **Dollar** (☎ 800/800–6000; 0124/622–0111 in the U.K., through affiliate Sixt Kenning; 02/9223–1444 in Australia). **Hertz** (☎ 800/654–3001; 800/263–0600 in Canada; 020/8897–2072 in the U.K.; 02/9669–2444 in Australia; 09/256–8690 in New Zealand) **National Car Rental** (☎ 800/227–7368; 020/8680–4800 in the U.K., where it is known as National Europe).

➤ LOCAL AGENCIES: **National Atesa** (☎ 902/100101).

➤ WEBSITE: Most car rental web sites offer information along the same lines; a good site is www.autoeurope.com.

CUTTING COSTS

To get the best deal **book through either the Internet or a travel agent** who will shop around. Also **look into wholesalers,** companies that do not own fleets but rent in bulk from those that do and often offer better rates than traditional agencies. Prepayment is required.

Wholesalers: AUTO EUROPE (☎ 207/842–2000 OR 800/223–5555, FAX 800/235–6321). EUROPE BY CAR (☎ 212/581–3040 OR 800/223–1516, FAX 212/246–1458). DER TRAVEL SERVICES (✉ 9501 W. DEVON AVE., ROSE-

MONT, IL 60018, ☎ 800/782–2424; FAX 800/282–7474 FOR INFORMATION; 800/860–9944 FOR BROCHURES). KEMWEL HOLIDAY AUTOS (☎ 914/835–3000 OR 800/678–0678, FAX 914/835–5126).

INSURANCE

When driving a rented car you are generally responsible for any damage to (or loss of) the vehicle. Before you rent see what coverage your personal auto-insurance policy and credit cards already provide. Collision policies that car-rental companies sell for European rentals usually do not cover theft.

REQUIREMENTS & RESTRICTIONS

Your own driver's license is valid in Spain, but you may want to get an International Driver's Permit for extra assurance. If you are stopped you will be asked to present your license and passport (or photocopy). It's available from the American or Canadian automobile association, or, in the United Kingdom, from the Automobile Association or Royal Automobile Club. In Spain, anyone over 18 with a valid license can drive; however, some rental companies will not rent a car to drivers under 21.

SURCHARGES

Before you pick up a car in one city and leave it in another **ask about drop-off charges or one-way service fees,** which can be substantial. Note, too, that some rental agencies charge extra if you return the car well *before* the time specified in your contract. To avoid a hefty refueling fee **fill the tank just before you turn in the car.**

CHILDREN

In Spain, kids are treated like royalty. You'll see children accompanying their parents everywhere, including bars and restaurants, so bringing yours along should not be a problem. Shopkeepers will shower your child with *caramelos* (sweets), and even the coldest waiters tend to be friendlier when you have a youngster with you. But although you won't be shunted into a remote corner when you bring kids into a Spanish restaurant, **you won't always find high chairs or special children's menus.** Children are expected to eat what their parents do,

and it is perfectly acceptable to ask for an extra plate and share your food. Be prepared for late bedtimes, especially in summer; it's surprisingly common to see under-fives playing cheerfully outdoors until midnight. Because children are expected to go with their parents everywhere, few hotels provide baby-sitting services, but can often put you in ouch with an individual baby-sitter (*canguro*).

FLYING

On most carriers children ages 2–12 can obtain a 30% discount on the regular fare. Children under 2 do not have to pay for a seat but will be charged 10% of a full fare ticket plus taxes. Most airlines provide bassinets for infants but make sure you order it in advance and reconfirm a day or two prior to your flight. Some aircrafts do not have the attachments for bassinets so if the airline changes the planned aircraft at the last minute you could end up without your bassinet.

FOOD

Children may turn up their noses at some of the regional specialities offered in Spain, but although there are rarely special menus for children available most restaurants are happy to provide simple dishes for children, such as plain grilled chicken, steak, or fried potatoes. Local kids often eat *sopa de fideos* (noodle soup) or a plain *tortilla francesa* (omelette). Familiar fast-food chains including McDonalds, Burger King, and Pizza Hut are well represented in Barcelona and other major cities and popular resorts.

LODGING

Most hotels in Spain allow children under a certain age to stay in their parents' room at no extra charge, but others charge them as extra adults. **Ask the cutoff age for children's discounts.**

SIGHTS & ATTRACTIONS

Museum admissions and bus and metro rides are generally free for children up to age five. Many museums and historic sights feature special prices for children; note that this guide book only lists adult admission prices. We indicate places that children might especially enjoy with a ♻ rubber duck in the margin.

SUPPLIES & EQUIPMENT

Disposable diapers (*pañales*), formula (*leche de continuación*), and bottled baby foods are readily available at supermarkets and pharmacies. Be aware however that most baby food in Spain contains a fair amount of sugar and some additives.

CONSUMER PROTECTION

Whenever shopping or buying travel services, **pay with a major credit card** so you can cancel payment or get reimbursed if there's a problem. If you're doing business with a particular travel company for the first time, **contact your local Better Business Bureau and the attorney general's offices** in your state and the company's home state to see if any complaints have been filed. If you're buying a package or tour, always **consider travel insurance** that includes default coverage (☞ Insurance, *below*).

➤ LOCAL BBBS: **Council of Better Business Bureaus** (✉ 4200 Wilson Blvd., Suite 800, Arlington, VA 22203, ☎ 703/276–0100, FAX 703/525–8277).

CRUISE TRAVEL

Barcelona is the cruise capital of Spain, with many Mediterranean cruises originating there. Royal Caribbean, Holland America Line, Renaissance Cruises, the Norwegian Cruise Line, Princess Cruises are among the lines that call in at Spain. Popular ports of call are Gibraltar, Málaga, Alicante and Palma de Mallorca.

➤ MAJOR CRUISE LINES: **Costa Cruises** (☎ 800/462–6782). **Holland America** (☎ 800/426–0329). **Norwegian Cruise Line** (☎ 800/327–7030). **Princess Cruises** (☎ 800/774–6237). **Renaissance Cruises** (☎ 800/525–5350). **Royal Carribean** (☎ 800/327–6700).

CUSTOMS & DUTIES

Keep receipts for all purchases. Upon reentering your home country, **be ready to show customs officials what you've bought.** If you feel a duty is incorrect, or you object to the way your clearance was handled, note the inspector's badge number and ask to see a supervisor. If the problem isn't resolved, write to the appropriate authorities, beginning with the port director at your point of entry.

SPAIN

From countries that are not part of the European Union, visitors age 15 and over are permitted to bring into Spain duty free up to 200 cigarettes or 50 cigars, up to one liter of alcohol over 22 proof, and up to two liters of wine. Dogs and cats are admitted as long as they have up-to-date vaccination records from their home country.

AUSTRALIA

Australia residents who are 18 or older may bring home $A400 worth of souvenirs and gifts (including jewelry), 250 cigarettes or 250 grams of tobacco, and 1,125 ml of alcohol (including wine, beer, and spirits). Residents under 18 may bring back $A200 worth of goods. Seeds, plants, and fruits need to be declared upon arrival. Prohibited items include meat products.

➤ INFORMATION: **Australian Customs Service** (Regional Director, ✉ Box 8, Sydney, NSW 2001, ☎ 02/9213–2000, FAX 02/9213–4000).

CANADA

Canadian residents who have been out of Canada for at least 7 days may bring home C$500 worth of goods duty-free. If you've been away less than 7 days but more than 48 hours, the duty-free allowance drops to C$200; if your trip lasts 24–48 hours, the allowance is C$50. You may not pool allowances with family members. Goods claimed under the C$500 exemption may follow you by mail; those claimed under the lesser exemptions must accompany you. Alcohol and tobacco products may be included in the 7-day and 48-hour exemptions but not in the 24-hour exemption. If you meet the age requirements of the province or territory through which you reenter Canada, you may bring in, duty-free, 1.14 liters (40 imperial ounces) of wine or liquor *or* 24 12-ounce cans or bottles of beer or ale. If you are 16 or older you may bring in, duty-free, 200 cigarettes and 50 cigars. Check ahead of time with Revenue Canada or the Department of Agriculture for policies regarding meat products, seeds, plants, and fruits.

You may send an unlimited number of gifts worth up to C$60 each duty-free to Canada. Label the package UNSOLICITED GIFT—VALUE UNDER $60. Alcohol and tobacco are excluded.

➤ INFORMATION: **Revenue Canada** (✉ 2265 St. Laurent Blvd. S, Ottawa, Ontario K1G 4K3, ☎ 613/993–0534; 800/461–9999 in Canada).

NEW ZEALAND

Homeward-bound residents 17 or older may bring $700 worth of souvenirs and gifts. Your duty-free allowance also includes 4.5 liters of wine or beer; one 1,125-ml bottle of spirits; and either 200 cigarettes, 250 grams of tobacco, 50 cigars, or a combination of the three up to 250 grams. Prohibited items include meat products, seeds, plants, and fruits.

➤ INFORMATION: **New Zealand Customs** (Custom House, ✉ 50 Anzac Ave., Box 29, Auckland, New Zealand, ☎ 09/359–6655, FAX 09/359–6732).

UNITED KINGDOM

If you are a U.K. resident and your journey was wholly within the European Union (EU), you won't have to pass through customs when you return to the United Kingdom. If you plan to bring back large quantities of alcohol or tobacco, check EU limits beforehand.

➤ INFORMATION: **HM Customs and Excise** (✉ Dorset House, Stamford St., Bromley Kent BR1 1XX, ☎ 020/7/202–4227).

UNITED STATES

U.S. residents who have been out of the country for at least 48 hours (and who have not used the $400 allowance or any part of it in the past 30 days) may bring home $400 worth of foreign goods duty-free. U.S. residents 21 and older may bring back 1 liter of alcohol duty-free. In addition, regardless of your age, you are allowed 200 cigarettes and 100 non-Cuban cigars. Antiques, which the U.S. Customs Service defines as objects more than 100 years old, enter duty-free, as do original works of art done entirely by hand, including paintings, drawings, and sculptures.

You may also send packages home duty-free: up to $200 worth of goods for personal use, with a limit of one parcel per addressee per day (and no alcohol or tobacco products or perfume worth more than $5); label the package PERSONAL USE and attach a list of its contents and their retail value. Do not label the package UNSOLICITED GIFT or your duty-free exemption will drop to $100. Mailed items do not affect your duty-free allowance on your return.

➤ INFORMATION: **U.S. Customs Service** (inquiries, ✉ 1300 Pennsylvania Ave. NW, Washington, DC 20229, ☎ 202/927–6724; complaints, ✉ Office of Regulations and Rulings, 1300 Pennsylvania Ave. NW, Washington, DC 20229; registration of equipment, ✉ Resource Management, 1300 Pennsylvania Ave. NW, Washington, DC 20229, ☎ 202/927–0540).

DISABILITIES & ACCESSIBILITY

Unfortunately, Spain has done little to make traveling easy for visitors with disabilities. Only newer museums, such as Bilbao's Guggenheim, have wheelchair-accessible entrances or elevators. Most of the churches, castles, and monasteries on a sightseer's itinerary involve quite a bit of walking, often on uneven terrain.

LODGING

When discussing accessibility with a reservations agent, **ask hard questions.** Are there any stairs, inside *or* out? Are there grab bars next to the toilet *and* in the shower/tub? How wide is the doorway to the room? To the bathroom? Older buildings or ships may have more limited facilities. For the most extensive facilities meeting the latest legal specifications **opt for newer lodgings.**

➤ COMPLAINTS: **Disability Rights Section** (✉ U.S. Department of Justice, Civil Rights Division, Box 66738, Washington, DC 20035-6738, ☎ 202/514–0301; 800/514–0301; 202/514–0301 TTY; 800/514–0301, FAX 202/307–1198) for general complaints. **Aviation Consumer Protection Division** (☞ Air Travel, *above*) for problems with airlines.

THE GOLD GUIDE / SMART TRAVEL TIPS

TRAVEL AGENCIES

In the United States, the Americans with Disabilities Act requires that travel firms serve the needs of all travelers, but some agencies specialize in working with people with disabilities.

➤ TRAVELERS WITH MOBILITY PROBLEMS: **Access Adventures** (✉ 206 Chestnut Ridge Rd., Rochester, NY 14624, ☎ 716/889–9096). **CareVacations** (✉ 5-5110 50th Ave., Leduc, Alberta T9E 6V4, ☎ 780/986–6404 or 780/986–8332). **Flying Wheels Travel** (✉ 143 W. Bridge St., Box 382, Owatonna, MN 55060, ☎ 507/451–5005 or 800/535–6790, FAX 507/451–1685).

➤ TRAVELERS WITH DEVELOPMENTAL DISABILITIES: **New Directions** (✉ 5276 Hollister Ave., Suite 207, Santa Barbara, CA 93111, ☎ 805/967–2841 or 888/967–2841, FAX 805/964–7344).

DISCOUNTS & DEALS

Be a smart shopper: **compare all your options** before making decisions. A plane ticket bought with a promotional coupon from travel clubs, coupon books, and direct-mail offers may not be cheaper than the least expensive fare from a discount ticket agency. And remember that what you get is just as important as what you save.

DISCOUNT RESERVATIONS

Look into discount reservations services, which use their buying power to get better prices on hotels, airline tickets, even car rentals. Ask about special packages or corporate rates.

When shopping for the best deal on hotels and car rentals **look for guaranteed exchange rates,** which protect you against a drop in your home currency. With your rate locked in, you won't pay more even if the price goes up in the local currency.

➤ AIRLINE TICKETS: ☎ 800/FLY–4–LESS. ☎ 800/FLY–ASAP.

➤ HOTEL ROOMS: **International Marketing & Travel Concepts** (☎ 800/790–4682). **Steigenberger Reservation Service** (☎ 800/223–5652). **Travel Interlink** (☎ 800/888–5898).

PACKAGE DEALS

Don't confuse packages and guided tours. When you buy a vacation package through a travel agent, you travel on your own, just as though you had planned the trip yourself. Fly/drive packages, which combine airfare and car rental, are often a good deal.

DRIVING

Driving is the best way to see Spain's rural areas and get off the beaten track. The country's main cities are well-connected by a network of four-lane *autovías* (freeways). *Autopista* is a toll road. At the toll booth plazas (the Spanish term is *peaje*; in Catalan, *peatge*), there are three systems to choose from—*Automàtic,* with machines for credit cards or coins; *Manual,* with an attendant; or *Telepago,* an automatic chip-driven system mostly used by native regulars. The letter N stands for a national route (*carretera nacional*), either four- or two-lane. Towns and villages are covered by a network of secondary roads maintained by regional, provincial and local governments.

Major routes in Spain bear heavy traffic, especially in peak holiday periods, so be extremely cautious. Spain's roads are shared by a mixture of local drivers, Moroccan immigrants traveling between northern Europe and northern Africa, and non-Spanish holiday-makers, some of whom are more accustomed to driving on the left hand side of the road. Watch out, too, for heavy truck traffic on national routes. Expect many difficult parking conditions on the streets of major cities. Parking garages are common and affordable and provide added safety to your vehicle and possessions.

AUTO CLUBS

➤ IN AUSTRALIA: **Australian Automobile Association** (☎ 02/6247–7311).

➤ IN CANADA: **Canadian Automobile Association** (CAA, ☎ 613/247–0117).

➤ IN NEW ZEALAND: **New Zealand Automobile Association** (☎ 09/377–4660).

➤ IN THE U.K.: **Automobile Association** (AA, ☎ 0990/500–600). **Royal Automobile Club** (RAC, ☎ 0990/722–722 for membership; 0345/121–345 for insurance).

➤ IN THE U.S.: **American Automobile Association** (☎ 800/564–6222).

➤ IN SPAIN: **Real Asocaición de Carreteras** (RACC, ✉ José Abascal 10, Madrid, ☎ 900/200093).

EMERGENCIES

The rental agencies Hertz and Avis have 24-hour breakdown service. If you belong to an auto club (AAA, CAA, or AA), you can get emergency assistance from their Spanish counterpart, RACC (☎ 900/112222). There are emergency telephones on all *Autopistes* (toll highways), located every 2 km (1¼ mi), with service stations generally found every 40 km (25 mi).

GASOLINE

Gas stations are plentiful, and those on major routes are open 24-hours. Most stations are self-service, though prices are the same as those at full-service stations. You punch in the amount of gas you want (in pesetas, not in liters), next unhook the nozzle, pump the gas, and then pay. At night, however, you must pay before you fill up. Most pumps offer a choice of gas, including leaded, unleaded and diesel, so **be careful to pick the right one** for your car. All newer models of cars in Spain use unleaded gas (*gasolina sin plomo*), which is available in two grades, 95 and 98 octane. Regular 97-octane leaded gas (*super*) is gradually being phased out. Although prices were decontrolled in 1993, they vary little between stations, and were at press time (summer 2000) 133 ptas./€0.80 a liter for *super*; 127 ptas./€0.76 a liter for *sin plomo* (unleaded; 95 octane); and 140 ptas./€0.84 a liter for unleaded, 98 octane. Credit cards are widely accepted.

ROAD CONDITIONS

Spain's highway system now includes some 6,000 km (3,720 mi) of super-highways. Still, you'll find some stretches of major national highways that are only two lanes wide, where traffic often backs up behind heavy trucks. *Autopista* tolls are steep.

Most Spanish cities have notoriously long morning and evening rush hours. Traffic jams (*atascos*) are especially bad in and around Barcelona. If possible, **avoid the morning rush hour, which can last from 8 until noon, and the evening rush hour, which lasts from 7 to 9.**

ROAD MAPS

Detailed road maps are readily available at bookstores and gas stations.

RULES OF THE ROAD

Spaniards drive on the right. Horns are banned in cities, but that doesn't keep people from blasting away. Children under 10 may not ride in the front seat, and seat belts are compulsory everywhere.

Speed limits are 50 kph (31 mph) in cities; 100 kph (62 mph) on N roads; 120 kph (74 mph) on the *autopista* (toll highways) or *autovía* (freeways); and, unless otherwise signposted, 90 kph (56 mph) on other roads, such as *carreteres nacionals* (main roads) and *carreteres comarcals* (secondary roads). Many Spaniards drive much faster than the speed limit, however, so beware of the left lane. Right turns on red are not permitted. In the cities, people are more often stopped for petty rule-breaking such as crossing a solid line or doing a U-turn than for speeding. However, Spanish highway police are especially vigilant regarding speeding and illegal passing; fines start at 15,000 ptas./€90.36, and, in the case of foreign drivers, police are empowered to demand payment on the spot. Beware of unclear directions on road signs. Indications are often confusing or insufficient.

Drunk driving tests are becoming more prevalent. It is illegal to drive with alcohol levels that excede 0.5% BAC or 0.25 on a breath test. Fines vary from one region of Spain to another.

Parking can be very difficult in Spanish cities, especially Barcelona. Parking tickets (for fines) range between 5,000/€30 and 15,000 ptas./€90. Barcelona's street parking system runs from 9 AM to 2 PM and 4 PM to 8 PM Monday to Friday and all day Saturday. Park in the specially marked blue spaces (about 300 ptas./€1.80 per hour), with tickets valid for two hours, but renewable. There are also underground garages (called "Parking" and symbolized by a white P on a blue background). On the streets, do not park where the pavement edge is yellow or where there is a private entry (*gual* or *vado*). No-parking signs, "1–15" or "15–30," signify you can park on those dates in the month on the side of the street where indicated. Towing is common. If your car is towed in Barcelona call a special number (☎ 93/428–4595); you will have to pay 15,000 ptas./€90 to get your car back. On top of that you will be presented with a fine, which you can pay at any police station at your convenience. If your car is towed in Bilbao contact the Ayuntamiento, or town hall (☎ 94/424–1700).

ELECTRICITY

To use your U.S.-purchased electric-powered equipment in Spain, **bring a converter and adapter.** Spain's electrical current is 220 volts, 50 cycles alternating current (AC); wall outlets take Continental-type plugs, with two round prongs.

If your appliances are dual-voltage you'll need only an adapter. Don't use 110-volt outlets, marked FOR SHAVERS ONLY, for high-wattage appliances such as blow-dryers. Most laptop computers operate equally well on 110 and 220 volts, so they require only an adapter.

EMBASSIES

➤ EMBASSIES: **Australia** (Plaza Descubridor Diegos de Ordas 3, ☎ 91/441–9300). **Canada** (Calle Nuñez de Balboa 35, ☎ 91/423–3250). **New Zealand** (Plaza Lealtad 2, ☎ 91/523–0026). **United Kingdom** (Calle Fernando el Santo 16, ☎ 91/319–0200). **United States** (Calle Serrano 75, ☎ 91/587–2200).

EMERGENCIES

You can expect Spaniards to be helpful if you have an emergency. The pan-European **emergency phone number 112** is operative in some parts of Spain, but not all. Otherwise, dial the emergency numbers below for national police, local police, fire department or medical services. On the road, there are emergency phones at frequent regular intervals on freeways (*autovías*) and toll highways (*autopistas*). They are marked S.O.S.

If your documents are stolen, contact both police and your embassy

(above). If you lose a credit card, phone the issuer immediately (☞ Money, *below*).

➤ EMERGENCY NUMBERS: **National Police** (☎ 091). **Local Police** (☎ 092). **Fire Department** (☎ 080). **Medical Services** (☎ 061).

ENGLISH-LANGUAGE MEDIA

In cities and major resorts you will have no trouble finding newspapers and magazines in English. U.K. newspapers are available on the same day; in some cases, special editions are printed in Spain for early distribution. You will also find major U.S. magazines, along with *USA Today* and the *International Herald Tribune*.

BOOKS

Books in English, including the latest paperback bestsellers, are on sale at airports. There are also bookshops selling English-language books in Barcelona and some other large cities.

NEWSPAPERS & MAGAZINES

There are local English-language publications in major Spanish cities and resorts, including Barcelona (*Barcelona Metropolitan,* monthly).

El País is the most neutral and reputable newspaper in Spain. This publication was born with the democratic era that began after Franco's death in 1976, and has a more socialist bent. *ABC* was the newspaper of the Franco era and remains more conservative and right wing. *La Vanguardia* competes with *El País* in Catalonia, while Catalonia's most widely read newpaper is *El Periódico,* published in both Spanish and Catalan. *El Mundo* was created when the social and political climate of government scandals broke out in the 1980's and, along with *El Periódico,* is a more popular newspaper than *La Vanguardia* or *El País.*

Spain's leading magazine is *Hola!* (*Hello!*), a fascinatingly glossy full-color orgy of style and gossip, much taken with gala parties, the doings of Spanish royalty, and Hollywood heavyweights. Many international magazines have Spanish editions, such as *Vogue* and *Elle*; such publications are always helpful when you want to learn about the latest Spanish style or the newest boutique in Barcelona. The leading cultural events publication is *Guia del Ocio,* though each paper also publishes news and listings about cultural events.

TELEVISION & RADIO

Spain is served by two state-owned national channels, two private networks, plus regional channels in some parts of Spain, as well as local channels serving individual towns. Many hotels have satellite television, which generally includes at least one news channel in English (CNN, Sky News, or BBC World).

ETIQUETTE & BEHAVIOR

Spaniards are very tolerant of foreign visitors and their strange ways, but you should always act with politeness. Be respectful when visiting churches; casual dress is all right, as long as it is not too gaudy, unkempt, or skimpy. Spaniards object to men going bare-chested anywhere other than the beach or swimming pool, and they do not look kindly on public displays of drunkenness.

When addressing Spaniards you are not well acquainted with, use the formal *usted* rather than the familiar *tu.* When meeting people for the first time it is appropriate to shake hands. Women often give a kiss on each cheek when meeting men or other women.

FOOD & DRINK

Spaniards love to eat out, and restaurants in Spain have evolved dramatically thanks to the favorable economic climate and to tourism. A new generation of chefs have transformed classic Spanish dishes to suit modern tastes, and they have some of the freshest ingredients in Europe to work with.

Similarly, Spain's wines have enjoyed a boom and are among the best in Europe. They are very favorably priced, too. In addition to the traditional sherries of Andalusia and the aged reds of Rioja, there are new, modern style wines produced all over Spain. Look for reds from Navarra, Ribera del Duero and Somontano, and whites from Rueda and Galicia, particularly AlbariÒos from the RÌas Baixas of Galicia.

The restaurants featured in this guide include the best in each price range. Restaurants are identified with a crossed knife-and-fork icon ✕ ; establishments denoted by a ✕🖫 symbol are hotels with restaurants which stand out for their cuisine and which are open to nonguests.

In addition to the standard menu, restaurants offer a daily lunchtime menu (*menú del día*) consisting of two courses plus coffee or dessert, at a very attractive price. If the waiter does not volunteer the daily menu when you are seated, on the assumption that foreigners will order a la carte, ask for it (*hay menú del día, por favor?*). In addition to eating at regular restaurants, you can always grab something to eat at a *cafería* or one of the many fast food outlets, both American franchises and local chains such as Pans & Co (sandwiches) and Tele-Pizza. The best way to have a light snack, though, is to enjoy a sampling of *tapas* (small appetizers) at a bar. These are available in an amazing variety.

MEALS

Most restaurants in Spain do not serve breakfast (*desayuno*). Instead, head for a café-bar or cafeteria. Outside the major hotels, which serve buffet breakfasts, breakfast in Spain is usually limited to coffee and toast or a roll. Lunch (*almuerzo* or *comida*) traditionally consists of a starter, a main course, and a dessert, followed by coffee and perhaps a liqueur. Dinner (*cena*) is somewhat lighter, with perhaps only one course.

MEALTIMES

Mealtimes in Spain are among the latest in Europe. Lunch starts at 2–2:30, and dinner starts between 8 and 10, more usually between 9 and 11 in Barcelona and other urban centers. However, in areas which cater to foreign visitors, particularly the Costa Brava, restaurants open for lunch and dinner much earlier (noon–1 for lunch, 7–8 for dinner). Unless otherwise noted, restaurants listed in this guide are open for lunch and dinner.

PAYING

Credit cards are widely accepted in Spanish restaurants. If paying by credit card, always leave the tip in cash (☞ Tipping, *below*).

RESERVATIONS & DRESS

It is generally a good idea to make reservations if you don't want to wait a long time for your table. However, a good number of places may not take reservations, in which case you can plan to have a drink and a tapa at the bar while you wait for a table.

WINE, BEER, & SPIRITS

Aside from its famous wines, Spain produces many brands of lager. The most popular are San Miguel, Cruzcampo, Aguila and Mahou. Spain is also Europe's biggest producer of brandy, and the world's major producer of sparkling wine (called *cava*). Spanish law prohibits the sale of alcohol to persons under 16.

GAY & LESBIAN TRAVEL

Since the end of Franco's dictatorship, the situation for gays and lesbians in Spain has improved dramatically: the paragraph in the Spanish civil code that made homosexuality a crime was repealed in 1978. Violence against gays does exist, but it is generally restricted to the rougher areas of very large cities. In the summer, the beaches of the Costa Brava (Sitges and Lloret del Mar) are gay and lesbian hot spots.

➤ LOCAL RESOURCES: **Gai Inform** (✉ Fuencarral 37, 28004, Madrid, ☎ 91/523–0070). **Teléfono Rosa** (✉ Calle Finlandia 45, 08014, Barcelona, ☎ 900/601601).

➤ TOUR OPERATORS: **Olivia** (✉ 4400 Market St., Oakland, CA 94608, ☎ 510/655–0364 or 800/631–6277).

➤ GAY- AND LESBIAN-FRIENDLY TRAVEL AGENCIES: **Different Roads Travel** (✉ 8383 Wilshire Blvd., Suite 902, Beverly Hills, CA 90211, ☎ 323/651–5557 or 800/429–8747, FAX 323/651–3678). **Kennedy Travel** (✉ 314 Jericho Turnpike, Floral Park, NY 11001, ☎ 516/352–4888 or 800/237–7433, FAX 516/354–8849). **Now Voyager** (✉ 4406 18th St., San Francisco, CA 94114, ☎ 415/626–1169 or 800/255–6951, FAX 415/626–8626). **Skylink Travel and Tour** (✉ 1006 Mendocino Ave., Santa Rosa, CA 95401, ☎ 707/546–9888 or 800/

225–5759, FAX 707/546–9891) serves lesbian travelers. **Yellowbrick Road** (✉ 1500 W. Balmoral Ave., Chicago, IL 60640, ☎ 773/561–1800 or 800/642–2488, FAX 773/561–4497).

HEALTH

If you require medical attention, ask for assistance from the hotel front desk or go to the nearest public **Centro de Salud** (day hospital). For serious cases, you will be referred to the regional hospital. Medical care is good in Spain, but nursing is perfunctory; in Spain, relatives are expected to look after patients' needs while in the hospital.

Sunburn and sunstroke are real risks in summertime Spain. On the hottest sunny days, even those who are not normally bothered by strong sun should cover themselves up; carry sunblock lotion; drink plenty of fluids; and limit sun time for the first few days.

Spain was recently documented as having the highest number of AIDS cases in Europe. Those applying for work permits will be asked for proof of HIV-negative status.

MEDICAL PLANS

No one plans to get sick while traveling, but it happens, so **consider signing up with a medical-assistance company.** Members get doctor referrals, emergency evacuation, or repatriation, hot lines for medical consultation, cash for emergencies, and other assistance.

➤ MEDICAL-ASSISTANCE COMPANIES: **International SOS Assistance** (✉ 8 Neshaminy Interplex, Suite 207, Trevose, PA 19053, ☎ 215/245–4707 or 800/523–6586, FAX 215/244–9617; ✉ 12 Chemin Riantbosson, 1217 Meyrin 1, Geneva, Switzerland, ☎ 4122/785–6464, FAX 4122/785–6424; ✉ 331 N. Bridge Rd., 17-00, Odeon Towers, Singapore 188720, ☎ 65/338–7800, FAX 65/338–7611).

OVER-THE-COUNTER REMEDIES

Over-the-counter remedies are available at pharmacies (*farmacias*). Some brands will be familiar to you, such as aspirin (*aspirina*), while other medications are sold under different brand names. If you regularly take a nonprescription medicine, take a sample box or bottle with you; the Spanish pharmicist will be able to provide you with its local equivalent. You will generally be allowed to buy much more potent medicine over the counter than in the United States, such as antibiotics and strong pain killers. Pharmacists are qualified to help you decide what to take if you describe your particular ailment, so in some cases a visit to a doctor can be avoided by simply asking a good pharmacist what to do.

HOLIDAYS

In 2001, Spain's national holidays include: January 1, January 6 (Epiphany), April 13 (Good Friday), May 1 (May Day), August 15 (Assumption), October 12 (National Day), November 1 (All Saints), December 6 (Constitution), December 8 (Immaculate Conception), and December 25.

In addition, each region, city, and town has its own holidays honoring political events and patron saints. Madrid holidays include May 2 (Madrid Day), May 15 (St. Isidro), and November 9 (Almudena). Barcelona celebrates April 23 (St. George), September 11 (Catalonia Day), and September 24 (Mercy).

If a public holiday falls on a Tuesday or Thursday, remember that **many businesses also close on the nearest Monday or Friday** for a long weekend called a *puente* (bridge). If a major holiday falls on a Sunday, businesses sometimes close on Monday.

LANGUAGE

Although Spaniards exported their language to all Central and South America, you may be surprised to find that Spanish is not the principal language in all of Spain. In Catalonia, you'll hear Catalan, while the Basques speak Euskera; west of the Basque Country, in Galicia, the natives speak Gallego; while south of Catalonia, in Valencia, the locals speak Valenciano. Franco outlawed all of these local languages and dialects in 1939, thinking it fomented regional extremism. With Franco's death in the 1960s, a renaissance of Catalan

thought and literature began in Catalonia, and similar movements have gathered momentum in other regions with local languages. While Barcelona, for the most part, is bilingual, many natives—even the proud *catalanoparlants*—opt to read their newspapers and books in mainstream Spanish. Of the city's five newspapers, three are published in Spanish, two in Catalan; however, the Spanish papers publish some 2 million copies, while the Catalan ones publish only about 300,000. When it comes to speaking, however, Catalans prefer their regional language—local radio and television stations may broadcast in these languages. Road signs may be printed (or spray-painted over) with the preferred regional language. Spanish is referred to as Castellano, or Castilian.

Fortunately, **Spanish is fairly easy to pick up, and your efforts to speak it will be graciously received.** Learn at least the following basic phrases: *buenos días* (hello—until 2 PM), *buenas tardes* (good afternoon—until 8 PM), *buenas noches* (hello—after dark), *por favor* (please), *gracias* (thank you), *adiós* (good-bye), *sí* (yes), *no* (no), *los servicios* (the toilets), *la cuenta* (bill/check), *habla inglés?* (do you speak English?), *no comprendo* (I don't understand). See the Spanish Vocabulary *in* Chapter 6 or, better yet, pick up a copy of *Fodor's Spanish for Travelers* for more helpful expressions.

If your Spanish breaks down, you should have no trouble finding people who speak English in major cities and coastal resorts, but you won't necessarily be able to count on the bus driver or the passerby on the street. Those who do speak English may speak the British variety, so don't be surprised if you're told to queue (line up) or take the lift (elevator) to the loo (toilet). Many guided tours offered at museums and historic sites are in Spanish; ask about the language that will be spoken before signing up.

LANGUAGES STUDY PROGRAMS

There are a number of private schools offering Spanish courses for foreigners, of various durations. **Don Quijote** is one network with schools in several locations around Spain. The international network **Inlingua** has 30 schools in Spain. Some Spanish universities, including that of Barcelona, have Spanish study programs, but these are over longer periods, usually two months or more. The state-run **Cervantes Institute**, devoted to promoting the Spanish language, organizes courses at their centers world wide, and can provide information on courses in Spain.

➤ LANGUAGE STUDY PROGRAMS: **Cervantes Institute** (✉ 122 East 42nd St., Suite 807, New York, NY 10168, ☎ 212/689–4232). **Don Quijote** (✉ Calle Placentinos 2, Salamanca, 37998, ☎ 923/268860). **Inlingua International** (✉ Belpstrasse 11, Berne, CH-3007, Switzerland, ☎ 4131/388–7777).

LANGUAGES FOR TRAVELERS

A phrasebook and language-tape set can help get you started.

➤ PHRASE BOOKS & LANGUAGE-TAPE SETS: *Fodor's Spanish for Travelers* (☎ 800/733–3000 in the U.S.; 800/668–4247 in Canada; $7 for phrasebook, $16.95 for audio set).

LODGING

Unlike many other areas of Spain, the regions covered in this guide book have been economic powerhouses, led by the two hubs of Barcelona and Bilbao. Because of this, Catalonia and (to a lesser extent) the Basque country have been relatively well provided with commercial hotels and, therefore, there has been little need for the famous government-subsided *paradores* (often renovated castles) and *albergues* that pepper most other regions. Many of Barcelona's hotels are relatively new high-rises, though there is a growing trend toward the restoration of historic buildings. Barcelona is an extremely popular convention city and when the biggest conventions arrive, nearly every one of the city's hotel rooms is booked solid—we're not joking!—so be sure to make your reservations as far in advance as possible. The same goes for the peak season along the Costa Brava, a particularly popular vacation

spot for Spaniards. In some years, by the end of April, the most popular resort hotels in Cadaqués, Tossa del Mar, and Lloret de Mar are booked to capacity into October.

By law, hotel prices must be posted at the reception desk and should indicate whether or not tax (IVA of 7%) is included. Breakfast is *not* usually included in the room price. The lodgings we review are the cream of the crop in each price category. We always list the facilities available, but we don't specify whether they cost extra; so when pricing accommodations, always ask what's included and what's not—in particular, breakfast (usually its the very fanciest or very cheapest hotels that charge extra) and private garage parking.

For information on hotel consolidators, *see* Discounts, *above*.

APARTMENT & VILLA RENTALS

If you want a home base that's roomy enough for a family and comes with cooking facilities **consider a furnished rental.** These can save you money, especially if you're traveling with a group. Home-exchange directories sometimes list rentals as well as exchanges.

➤ INTERNATIONAL AGENTS: **El Sol** (✉ P.O. Box 329, Wayne, PA 19087, ☎ 610/353–2335, FAX 610/353–7756). **Hideaways International** (✉ 767 Islington St., Portsmouth, NH 03801, ☎ 603/430–4433 or 800/843–4433, FAX 603/430–4444; membership $99). **Hometours International** (✉ Box 11503, Knoxville, TN 37939, ☎ 423/690–8484 or 800/367–4668). **Interhome** (✉ 1990 N.E. 163rd St., Suite 110, Miami Beach, FL 33162, ☎ 305/940–2299 or 800/882–6864, FAX 305/940–2911). **Rent-a-Home International** (✉ 7200 34th Ave. NW, Seattle, WA 98117, ☎ 206/789–9377, FAX 206/789–9379). **Vacation Home Rentals Worldwide** (✉ 235 Kensington Ave., Norwood, NJ 07648, ☎ 201/767–9393 or 800/633–3284, FAX 201/767–5510). **Villas and Apartments Abroad** (✉ 420 Madison Ave., Suite 1003, New York, NY 10017, ☎ 212/759–1025 or 800/433–3020, FAX 212/755–8316). **Villas International** (✉ 950 Northgate Dr., Suite 206, San Rafael, CA 94903, ☎

415/499–9490 or 800/221–2260, FAX 415/499–9491).

CAMPING

Camping in Spain is not a wilderness experience. The country has more than 500 campgrounds, and many of them have excellent facilities, including hot showers, restaurants, swimming pools, tennis courts, and even nightclubs. But in summer, especially in August, be aware that **the best campgrounds fill with Spanish families, who move in with their entire households:** pets, grandparents, even the kitchen sink and stove. You can pick up an official list of all Spanish campgrounds at the tourist office.

It can be difficult to find a spot for independent camping outside the established campsites. For safety reasons, you cannot camp next to roads, rivers, or on the beach. Nor can you camp in urban areas, nature parks (except in designated camping areas), and it is illegal to camp within one kilometer of an established campsite. The best bet is to seek the owner's permission to camp on a private farm.

HOME EXCHANGES

If you'd like to exchange your home for someone else's temporarily, **join a home-exchange organization,** which will send you updated listings of available exchanges for one year and will include your own listing in at least one of them. It's up to you to make specific arrangements.

➤ EXCHANGE CLUBS: **HomeLink International** (✉ Box 650, Key West, FL 33041, ☎ 305/294–7766 or 800/ 638–3841, FAX 305/294–1448; $88 per year). **Intervac U.S.** (✉ Box 590504, San Francisco, CA 94159, ☎ 800/756–4663, FAX 415/435–7440; $83 per year).

HOSTELS

No matter how old you are, you can **save on lodging costs by staying at hostels** (*albergue juvenil,* and not a *hostal,* a popular term for a modest hotel without major facilities, which is signaled by a small "s" next to the "H" on the hotel's doorway blue plaque). In some 5,000 locations in more than 70 countries around the world, Hostelling International (HI),

the umbrella group for a number of national youth-hostel associations, offers single-sex, dorm-style beds and, at many hostels, couples' rooms and family accommodations. Membership in any HI national hostel association, open to travelers of all ages, allows you to stay in HI-affiliated hostels at member rates (one-year membership is about $25 for adults; hostels run about $10–$25 per night), and assures you priority on the waitlist if the hostel is full. Members are also eligible for other discounts worldwide, even on rail and bus travel in some countries.

➤ ORGANIZATIONS: **Australian Youth Hostel Association** (✉ 10 Mallett St., Camperdown, NSW 2050, ☎ 02/ 9565–1699, FAX 02/9565–1325). **Hostelling International–American Youth Hostels** (✉ 733 15th St. NW, Suite 840, Washington, DC 20005, ☎ 202/783–6161, FAX 202/783–6171). **Hostelling International–Canada** (✉ 400–205 Catherine St., Ottawa, Ontario K2P 1C3, ☎ 613/237–7884, FAX 613/237–7868). **Youth Hostel Association of England and Wales** (✉ Trevelyan House, 8 St. Stephen's Hill, St. Albans, Hertfordshire AL1 2DY, ☎ 01727/855215 or 01727/845047, FAX 01727/844126). **Youth Hostels Association of New Zealand** (✉ Box 436, Christchurch, New Zealand, ☎ 03/379–9970, FAX 03/365–4476). Membership in the United States is $25, in Canada C$26.75, in the United Kingdom £9.30, in Australia $44, and in New Zealand $24.

HOTELS

Spanish hotels are rated by the government with one to five stars. While quality is a factor, **the rating is technically only an indication of how many facilities the hotel offers.** For example, a three-star hotel may be just as comfortable as a four-star hotel but lack a swimming pool.

Hotel entrances are marked with a plaque bearing the letter H and the number of stars. The letter R (standing for *residencia*) after the letter H indicates an establishment with no meal service. The designations *fonda* (F), *pensión* (P), *hostal* (Hs) and *casa de huéspedes* (CH) indicate budget accommodation. In most cases, especially in smaller villages, the rooms will be clean but basic. In larger cities they can be downright dreary.

Spain's major private hotel groups include the Sol-Meliá, Tryp, Hotusa, with establishments all over Spain of different categories. The NH chain, with hotels in the main cities, appeals to business travelers. (Chains listed below with a ☜ symbol indicate websites offering online booking.) Dozens of reasonably priced beachside highrises along the various coasts cater to package tours. Note that high-season rates prevail not only in summer but also during Holy Week and local fiestas.

Although single rooms (*habitación sencilla*) are usually available, they are often on the small side and you might prefer to pay a bit extra for single-occupancy in a double room (*habitación doble uso individual*). All hotels we review have private baths unless otherwise noted.

➤ MAJOR SPANISH HOTEL CHAINS: **Hotusa** (☎ 93/319–9062). **NH Hoteles** (☎ 902/115116, www. nh-hoteles.es). **Sol Melia** (☎ 902/ 144444, www.solmelia.es). **Tryp** (☎ 901/116199).

PARADORS

Spain runs more than 80 paradors, with several of them located in the regions covered in this book (most, however, are based in central and southern Spain). Some are in castles on a hill with sweeping views; others are in historic monasteries or convents filled with art treasures; still others are in modern buildings on choice beachfront property. Rates are reasonable, considering that most paradors are four- and five-star hotels. The paradors are invariably immaculate and tastefully furnished, often with antiques or reproductions. All have restaurants that serve some regional specialties, and you can stop in for a meal or a drink without spending the night. Breakfast, however, is an expensive buffet; you'll do better to go down the street for a cup of coffee and a roll.

Because paradors are extremely popular with foreigners and Spaniards alike, **make reservations well in advance.**

➤ INFORMATION: In Spain: **Paradores de España** (✉ Central de Reservas, Requena 3, 28013 Madrid, ☎ 91/ 516–6666, FAX 91/516–6657, www. parador.es). In the United States: **Marketing Ahead** (✉ 433 5th Ave., New York, NY 10016, ☎ 212/686– 9213 or 800/223–1356). In the United Kingdom: **Keytel International** (✉ 402 Edgeware Rd., London W2 1ED, ☎ 020/7/402–8182).

RURAL B&BS

A growing number of *casas rurales* (country houses similar to B&Bs) offer accommodation in rural areas, either in guest rooms or on a self-catering basis. The comfort and conveniences vary widely, and it is always best to book through one of the associations offering this type of accommodation in the various Spanish regions. Ask at the local tourist information offices for casas rurales available in the area.

MAIL & SHIPPING

The postal system in Spain, called *Correos,* does work, but delivery times can vary widely. An airmail letter to the United States may take four days, or it may take two weeks. Delivery to other worldwide destinations is equally unpredictable. Sending letters by special-delivery (*urgente*) will ensure speedier delivery.

POSTAL RATES

Airmail letters to the United States and Canada cost 115 ptas./€0.69 up to 20 grams. Letters to the United Kingdom and other EU countries cost 70 ptas./€0.42 up to 20 grams. Letters within Spain are 35 ptas./€0.21. Postcards are charged the same rate as letters. You can buy stamps at post offices and at licensed tobacco shops.

RECEIVING MAIL

Because mail delivery in Spain can often be slow and unreliable, it's best to have your mail sent to American Express. You can also have mail held at a Spanish post office; have it addressed to **Lista de Correos** (the equivalent of Poste Restante) in a town you'll be visiting. Postal addresses should include the name of the province in parentheses, e.g., Figueres (Girona).

You can pick up mail at **American Express** (☎ 800/528–4800 for a list of overseas offices).

OVERNIGHT SERVICES

When speed is the essence or when sending valuable items or documents, you can use a courier (*mensajero*), although it is expensive to ship items from Spain abroad, especially if you want overnight service. The major international agencies, such as Federal Express and UPS, have representatives in Spain. The biggest Spanish courier service is Seur.

➤ INFORMATION: **DHL** (☎ 902/122424). **Federal Express** (☎ 900/100871). **MRW** (☎ 900/300400). **Seur** (☎ 902/101010). **UPS** (☎ 900/102410).

MONEY

Spain is no longer the cheap destination it used to be, but prices still compare favorably to those elsewhere in Europe, especially as regards lodging, food, and drink. Coffee in a bar: 125 ptas./€0.75 (standing), 150 ptas./€0.90 (seated). Beer in a bar: 125 ptas./€0.75 (standing), 150 ptas./€0.90 (seated). Small glass of wine in a bar: 100 ptas./€0.60. Soft drink: 150–200 ptas./€0.90–1.20 a bottle. Ham-and-cheese sandwich: 300 ptas./€1.80. Two-kilometer (1-mile) taxi ride: 400 ptas./€2.40, but the meter keeps ticking in traffic jams. Local bus or subway ride: 135–150 ptas./€0.81–0.90. Movie ticket: 500–800 ptas./€3.01–4.81 Foreign newspaper: 300 ptas./€1.80. In this book we quote prices for adults only, but note that **children, students, and senior citizens almost always pay substantially reduced fees.** For information on taxes in Spain, *see* Taxes, *below.*

ATMS

Before leaving home, **make sure your credit cards are programmed for ATM use in Spain.** All decent-size towns have ATM's; although tiny villages in the Pyrenees do not offers these facilities, plenty of slightly larger Pyrenean towns do have them. It's a good idea to warn your credit card company that you're going abroad—sometimes they see exotic destinations on charges and suspend service for security reasons. Local bank cards often do not work overseas or can access only your checking account; **ask your bank about a MasterCard/Cirrus or Visa debit card,** which works like a bank card but can be used at any ATM displaying a MasterCard/Cirrus or Visa logo. These cards, too, may tap only your checking account; check with your bank.

CREDIT CARDS

We use the following abbreviations: **AE,** American Express; **DC,** Diner's Club; **MC,** MasterCard; and **V,** Visa. Note that Discover is rarely accepted outside the United States. If your card is lost or stolen, ring the applicable phone number below.

➤ REPORTING LOST CARDS: **American Express** (☎ 900/941413). **Diners** (☎ 901/101011). **Master Card** (☎ 900/974445). **Visa** (☎ 900/971231).

CURRENCY

As of January 1, 1999, Spain's official currency is the European monetary unit, the euro. Prices are often quoted in both pesetas and Euros—convenient for Americans, as the euro is practically equal to a U.S. dollar—but until the year 2002 the euro will be used only on the level of trade and banking. The first euro notes and coins will not go into circulation until then, so the peseta (pta.) continues to be legal tender. You can, however purchase traveler's checks in Euros, convenient if you'll be traveling to more than one of the Euro-denominated countries (Austria, Belgium, Finland, France, Germany, Ireland, Italy, Luxembourg, the Netherlands, Portugal, and Spain). Peseta bills are 10,000, 5,000, 2,000, and 1,000 ptas. Coins are 500, 200, 100, 50, 25, 10, 5, and 1 pta. Be careful not to confuse the 100- and 500-ptas. coins—they're the same color and almost the same size. Five-ptas. coins are called *duros.* At press time the exchange rate was 168 ptas. to the U.S. dollar, 116 ptas. per Canadian dollar, and 267 ptas. to the pound sterling. One euro was worth 0.98 U.S. dollars.

Up to January 1, 2002, the peseta (pta.) will remain the main unit of currency in Spain; after that date, however, the new single European Union (EU) currency, the euro, will take over. Until then, people will use the peseta in their day-to-day transactions and travelers will continue to exchange their money for banknotes and coins. At press time (summer 2000), the exchange rate was about 180 pesetas to the U.S. dollar. As of 1999 the euro (ECU) began to be quoted; at press time, 1 ECU equaled about 170 pesetas. For the euro denomination, the exchange rate was about 0.95 euros to the U.S dollar, 0.62 to the pound sterling, 1.40 to the Canadian dollar, 1.61 to the Australian dollar, 2.06 to the New Zealand dollar, and 0.78 to the Irish punt. These rates can and will vary.

At this point, any transaction not involving cash may currently be transacted in euros. Pesetas will stay in circulation up to July 1, 2002, the date of their final demise. After January 1, 2002, participating European national currencies will no longer be listed on foreign exchange markets. The rates of conversion between the euro and local currencies have already been irrevocably fixed (1 euro = 168 pesetas), eliminating commission charges in currency exchange. Please note that prices in euros correspond generally to the U.S. dollar as their exchange rates are relatively close.

Slowly but surely, the euro is becoming a part of daily European life; for every item purchased—be it a candy bar or a car—the price in both pesetas and euros has to be, by law, listed to familiarize people to this monumental change. Under the euro system, there are eight coins: 1 and 2 euros, plus 1, 2, 5, 10, 20, and 50 euro cent, or cents of the euro. All coins have one side that has the value of the euro on it and the other side with each countries' own unique national symbol. There are seven banknotes: 5, 10, 20, 50, 100, 200, and 500 euros. Banknotes are the same for all EU countries.

CURRENCY EXCHANGE

For the most favorable rates, **change money at banks.** Although ATM transaction fees may be higher abroad than at home, ATM exchange rates are excellent because they are based on wholesale rates offered only by major banks. You won't do as well at exchange booths in airports or rail and bus stations, in hotels, in restaurants, or in stores. To avoid lines at airport exchange booths, **get some local currency before you leave home.**

➤ EXCHANGE SERVICES: **International Currency Express** (☎ 888/842–0880 on East Coast; 888/278–6628 on West Coast). **Thomas Cook Currency Services** (☎ 800/287–7362 for locations and phone orders).

TRAVELER'S CHECKS

Traveler's checks are accepted in cities. If you'll be staying in rural areas or small towns, take extra cash just in case. Lost or stolen checks can usually be replaced within 24 hours. To ensure a speedy refund, buy your own traveler's checks; don't let someone else pay for them. Irregularities like this can cause delays. The person who bought the checks should make the call to request a refund.

OUTDOOR ACTIVITIES & SPORTS

Spain's fair weather is especially suited to outdoor sports, practically year-round, although in summer you should restrict your physical activity to early morning or late afternoon. Spain has more golf courses than anywhere else in Europe, and is also a paradise for hikers, water sports enthusiasts and—believe it or not—snow skiers. Spain's sports federations can provide information, and local tourist offices (☞ Visitor Information, *below*) can also be helpful.

GOLF

Many golf courses are private and green fees can be on the high side (they are cheaper in summer), but many hotels linked to golf courses offer attractive all-inclusive deals.

➤ GOLF: **Real Federación Española de Golf** (✉ Capitán Haya 9, 28020 Madrid, ☎ 91/555–2682).

SAILING & WATER SPORTS

With 1,200 miles of coastline, there is no shortage of water sports in Spain. Sailing is available at the many yacht harbours dotting the Costa Brava coast; leading anchorages would be Palamós and Cadaqués on the Mediterranean and San Sebastián and Getaria on the northern coast in the Basque Country. The northern Spanish coast offers good surfing while the Mediterranean is good for windsurfing, sailing and swimming. If you have an internationally recognized scuba diver's license, you can contact one of the scuba clubs in Catalonia.

➤ WATERSPORTS INFORMATION: **Federación Española de Vela** (✉ Spanish Sailing Federation, Luís de Salazar 12, 28002 Madrid, ☎ 91/519–5008). **Federación de Actividades Subacuáticas** (✉ Spanish Underwater Activities Federation, Santaló 15, 08021 Barcelona, ☎ 93/200–6769).

HIKING

Spain's nature parks (*parques naturales*) are perfect for hiking and rock climbing, and there is usually plenty of information available from local clubs and from the park visitors centers.

➤ HIKING: **Federación Española de Montañismo** (✉ Alberto Aguilera 3, 28015 Madrid, ☎ 91/445–1382).

SKIING

Not everyone thinks of sunny Spain as a skier's paradise, but the country—the second most mountainous in Europe after Switzerland— has 28 ski stations. The best ones are located in the Pyrenees; some of the best are Puigmal, Baqueira Beret, and Candanchú.

➤ SKIING: **Federación Española de Deportes de Invierno** (✉ Arroyo Fresno 3 A, 28035 Madrid, ☎ 91/ 376–9930). **Tourism and Ski-run Information Line** (☎ 91/350–2020).

PACKING

Pack light. Although baggage carts are free and plentiful in most Spanish airports, they're rare in train and bus stations. On the whole, Spaniards dress up more than Americans or the British. Summer will be hot nearly everywhere; visits in winter, fall, and spring call for warm clothing and, in winter, boots. It makes sense to wear casual, comfortable clothing and shoes for sightseeing, but you'll want to **dress up a bit in large cities, especially for fine restaurants and nightclubs.** American tourists are easily spotted for their sneakers—if you want to blend in, wear leather shoes. On the beach, anything goes; it's common to see females of all ages wearing only bikini bottoms, and many of the more remote beaches allow nude sunbathing. Regardless of your style, **bring a cover-up** to wear over your bathing suit when you leave the beach.

Label each of your bags with your name, address, and phone number, and **pack a copy of your itinerary** inside each one. At check-in **make sure that each bag is correctly tagged** with the destination airport's three-letter code. If your bags arrive damaged or fail to arrive at all, file a written report with the airline before leaving the airport.

PASSPORTS & VISAS

Make two photocopies of your passport's data page—one for someone at home and another for you, carried separately from your passport. If you lose your passport, promptly call the nearest embassy or consulate and the local police.

ENTERING SPAIN

Visitors from the United States, Australia, Canada, New Zealand, and the U.K. need a valid passport to enter Spain. Australians, in addition, require a visa for stays of over a month. You should obtain it from the Spanish Embassy before you leave.

PASSPORT OFFICES

The best time to apply for a passport, or to renew your old one, is in the fall or winter. Before any trip, check your passport's expiration date.

➤ AUSTRALIAN CITIZENS: **Australian Passport Office** (☎ 131–232).

➤ CANADIAN CITIZENS: **Passport Office** (☎ 819/994–3500 or 800/ 567–6868).

➤ NEW ZEALAND CITIZENS: **New Zealand Passport Office** (☎ 04/494– 0700 for information on how to apply; 04/474–8000; 0800/225–050 in New Zealand for information on applications already submitted).

➤ U.K. CITIZENS: **London Passport Office** (☎ 0990/210–410) for fees and documentation requirements and to request an emergency passport.

➤ U.S. CITIZENS: **National Passport Information Center** (☎ 900/225– 5674; calls are 35¢ per minute for automated service, $1.05 per minute for operator service).

REST ROOMS

There are public rest rooms in some locations, and in some cities, such as Barcelona, you'll have to use small coin-operated booths. But the best option is to use the facilities at a bar or cafeteria, although it is customary to order a drink. The cleanliness of the establishment is a good indication of the conditions of their toilets. Gas stations have rest rooms, but you sometimes have to request the key to use them.

SAFETY

Petty crime is a perennial problem in Spain's most popular destinations. Pickpocketing and thefts from cars are the more usual offenses. Certain areas in Barcelona and other large cities are also to be avoided. Check the individual chapters of this guide for trouble spots.

If your rented car should happen to break down, be especially wary of anyone who stops to help you: it is not uncommon for robbers to puncture your tires and then steal your belongings while pretending to offer assistance. Use ATM's with the same caution you would at home. Be especially cautious in train and bus stations and in Barcelona on the Ramblas, where masses of people sometimes offer camouflage for petty thieves. If you do encounter a problem with theft, go to the police to file your claim. Give them your hotel name and room number as often stolen purses or bags are recovered after their contents are taken.

WOMEN IN SPAIN

The traditional Spanish custom of the *piropo* (a shouted "compliment" to women walking in the street) is fast disappearing, but women traveling on their own are still likely to encounter it on occasion. The piropo is harmless, if annoying, and simply ignoring the perpetrator is the best tactic.

SENIOR-CITIZEN TRAVEL

While there are few early bird specials or movie discounts, senior citizens generally enjoy discounts at museums in Spain. Spanish social life encom-

passes all ages—it's very common to see senior citizens having coffee next to young couples or families at late-night cafés.

To qualify for age-related discounts **mention your senior-citizen status up front** when making hotel reservations (not when checking out) and before you're seated in restaurants (not when paying the bill). When renting a car, ask about promotional discounts, which can be cheaper than senior-citizen rates. Senior citizens in Spain are referred to as members of the "Tercera Edad" (literally, third age bracket).

➤ EDUCATIONAL PROGRAMS: **Elderhostel** (✉ 75 Federal St., 3rd fl., Boston, MA 02110, ☎ 877/426–8056, FAX 877/426–2166). **Interhostel** (✉ University of New Hampshire, 6 Garrison Ave., Durham, NH 03824, ☎ 603/862–1147 or 800/733–9753, FAX 603/862–1113).

STUDENTS IN SPAIN

Students can often get discounts when visiting museums and other sites.

➤ STUDENT IDs & SERVICES: In the U.S.: **Council on International Educational Exchange** (CIEE, ✉ 205 E. 42nd St., 14th fl., New York, NY 10017, ☎ 212/822–2600 or 888/268–6245, FAX 212/822–2699). In Canada: **Travel Cuts** (✉ 187 College St., Toronto, Ontario M5T 1P7, ☎ 416/979–2406 or 800/667–2887).

TAXES

VALUE-ADDED TAX (V.A.T.)

Value-added tax (similar to sales tax) is called IVA (for *Impuesto sobre el valor añadido*) in Spain. It is levied on services, such as hotels and restaurants, and on consumer products. When in doubt about whether tax is included, ask, *Está incluido el IVA* ("ee-vah")?

The IVA rate for hotels and restaurants is 7%, regardless of their number of rated "stars" or "forks." Menus will generally say at the bottom whether tax is included (*IVA incluido*) or not (*más 7% IVA*).

While food and basic necessities are taxed at the lowest rate, most consumer goods are taxed at 16%. Global Refund is a V.A.T. refund service that makes getting your money back hassle-free. The service is available Europe-wide at 130,000 affiliated stores. In participating stores, **ask for the Global Refund form** (called a Shopping Cheque). Have it stamped like any customs form by customs officials when you leave the European Union. Then take the form to one of the more than 700 Global Refund counters—conveniently located at every major airport and border crossing—and your money will be refunded on the spot in the form of cash, check, or a refund to your credit-card account (minus a small percentage for processing).

Global Refund (✉ 707 Summer St., Stamford, CT 06901, ☎ 800/566–9828, FAX 203/674–8709, taxfree@us. globalrefund.com, www.globalrefund. com).

TELEPHONES

Spain's telephone system is efficient, and direct dialing is the norm everywhere. Numbers within Spain now require dialing nine digits (two digit regional code always beginning in 9, followed by a 7-digit number), even within the same area code. Only cell phones conforming to the European GSM standard will work in Spain.

COUNTRY & AREA CODES

The country code for Spain is 34. Phoning home: 00 gets you an international line; country codes are 1 for the United States and Canada, 61 for Australia, 64 for New Zealand, and 44 for the United Kingdom.

DIRECTORY & OPERATOR INFORMATION

For general information in Spain, dial 1003. The operator for international information and assistance is at 025 (some operators speak English).

INTERNATIONAL CALLS

International calls are awkward from public pay phones because of the enormous number of coins needed, and they can be expensive from hotels, which often add a surcharge. The best way to phone home is to use a public phone that accepts phone cards (available from tobacconists and most newsagents) or go to the local telephone office. Every town has one, and major cities have several. When your call is connected, you'll be sent to a quiet cubicle and charged according to the meter. If the price is 500 ptas. or more, you can pay with Visa or MasterCard.

To make an international call yourself, dial 00, then the country code, then the area code and number. In Barcelona you can phone overseas from the office at Carrer de Fontanella 4, off Plaça de Catalunya; in Bilbao, there is a *Locutorio* (phone center) on Calle Licenciado Poza 53 in the Indaucho area of Bilbao (the one in the center of town has closed).

Before you go, **find out your long-distance company's access code in Spain.**

LOCAL CALLS

All area codes begin with a 9; for instance, Barcelona is 93 and Bilbao is 94. The 900 code indicates a toll-free number. Numbers starting with a 6 indicate a cellular phone; note that calls to cell phones are significantly more expensive. To call within Spain—even locally—dial the area code first.

LONG-DISTANCE SERVICES

AT&T, MCI, and Sprint access codes make long-distance calls relatively convenient, but you may find the access code blocked in many hotel rooms. Ask your hotel operator to connect you; if he or she cannot, ask for an international operator or dial the international operator yourself. One way to improve your odds of getting connected to your long-distance carrier is to travel with more than one company's calling card (a hotel may block Sprint, for example, but not MCI). If all else fails, use a pay phone.

➤ Access Codes: AT&T USADirect (☎ 900–99–00–11). MCI Call USA (☎ 800/444–4444). Sprint Express (☎ 800/793–1153).

➤ Access Codes in Spain: AT&T (☎ 900/990011). MCI (☎ 900/990014). Sprint (☎ 900/990013).

PHONE CARDS

Newer pay phones work on special phone cards (*tarjeta telefónica*), which you can buy at any tobacco shop or newsagent for 1,000 or 2,000 ptas./€5.89.

PUBLIC PHONES

You will find plentiful pay phones in booths (*cabina telefónica*) and also in many bars and restaurants. Most have a digital readout, so you can see your money ticking away. If using coins, you need at least 25 ptas./€.07 for a local call, 75 ptas./€.22 to call another province; simply insert coins and wait for a dial tone. (At older models, you line coins up in a groove on top of the dial, and they drop down as needed.)

TIME

Spain is on Central European Time, one hour ahead of Greenwich Mean Time, six hours ahead of Eastern Standard Time. In other words, when it is 3 PM in Barcelona, it is 2 PM in London, 9 AM in New York City, and 6 AM in Los Angeles. Spain, like the rest of the European Union, switches to daylight saving time on the last weekend in March and switches back on the last weekend in October.

TIPPING

Pride keeps Spaniards from acknowledging tips, but waiters and other service people expect to be tipped, and you can be sure that your contribution will be appreciated. On the other hand, if you experience bad or surly service, don't feel obligated to leave a tip.

Restaurant checks almost always include service, but **do not tip more than 10% of the bill** in any case, and leave less if you eat tapas or sandwiches at a bar—just enough to round out the bill to the nearest 100. Tip cocktail servers 75 ptas./€.22 a drink, depending on the bar. The bill most often does not tell you that the service is included, but it is. In a fancy establishment, leave 10%—likewise if you had a great time.

Tip taxi drivers about 10% of the total fare, but more for long rides or extra help with luggage. Note, though, that there is an official surcharge for airport runs and baggage.

Tip hotel porters 100 ptas./€.22 a bag, and the bearer of room service 100 ptas. A doorman who calls a taxi for you gets 100 ptas. If you stay in a hotel for more than two nights, tip the maid about 100 ptas. per night. A concierge should receive a tip for any additional help he or she provides.

Tour guides should be tipped about 300 ptas., ushers in theaters 50 ptas./€.04, barbers 100 ptas., and women's hairdressers at least 200 ptas./€.58 for a wash and style. Restroom attendants are tipped 25 ptas./€.07

TOURS & PACKAGES

On a prepackaged tour or independent vacation everything is prearranged, so you'll spend less time planning—and often get it all at a good price.

WORKING WITH AN AGENT

Travel agents are excellent resources, but it's smart to collect brochures from several: some agents' suggestions may be influenced by relationships with tour and package firms that reward them for volume sales. If you have a special interest **find an agent with expertise in that area**; the American Society of Travel Agents (ASTA; ☞ Travel Agencies, *below*) has a database of specialists worldwide.

Make sure your travel agent is familiar with the rooms and other services in any hotel he or she recommends. Ask about location, room size, beds, and whether the hotel has whatever specific amenities you need. Has your agent been there in person or sent others whom you can contact?

BUYER BEWARE

Each year consumers are stranded or lose their money when tour operators—even large ones with excellent reputations—go out of business. So **check out the operator.** Ask several travel agents about its reputation, and try to **go with a company that has a consumer-protection program.** (Look for information in the company's brochure.) In the United States, members of the National Tour Association and United States Tour Operators Association are required to set aside funds to cover your payments and travel arrangements in case the company defaults. It's also a good idea to choose a tour company that participates in the American Society of

Travel Agent's Tour Operator Program (TOP); ASTA will act as mediator in any disputes between you and your operator.

Remember that the more your package or tour includes, the better you can predict the ultimate cost of your trip. **Beware of hidden costs.** Are taxes, tips, and transfers included? Entertainment and excursions? These can add up.

➤ TOUR-OPERATOR RECOMMENDATIONS: **American Society of Travel Agents** (☞ Travel Agencies, *below*). **National Tour Association** (NTA, ✉ 546 E. Main St., Lexington, KY 40508, ☎ 606/226–4444 or 800/682–8886). **United States Tour Operators Association** (USTOA, ✉ 342 Madison Ave., Suite 1522, New York, NY 10173, ☎ 212/599–6599 or 800/468–7862, FAX 212/599–6744).

TRAIN TRAVEL

International overnight trains to Barcelona from many of the leading cities of Europe, including Paris, Grenoble, Geneva, Zurich, and Milan; the route from Paris takes 11½ hours. International trains pull into three Barcelona train terminals: Estació de Sants (✉ Plaza dels Països Catalans); Estació de França (✉ Avinguda Marqués d'Argentera 6); and Passeig de Gràcia (✉ Intersection of Passeig de Gracia/Aragó).

The bulk of Spain's inter-city services (along with some of Barcelona's *rodalies,* or local train routes) are handled by the government-run railroad system—RENFE (*Red Nacional de Ferrocarriles Españoles*); the company's routes include many towns in Aragon, Navarre, and the Basque Country regions. While their fast TALGO service (which includes Bilbao on its itinerary) is very efficient, most RENFE service remains below par by European standards. Local train travel can be tediously slow, and most long-distance trips run at night. RENFE trains runs on two types of schedules, express—*Catalunya Exprés,* with express stops to major towns, and local—either the *Regional* or *Delta* trains, which have rural routes with innumerable local stops. While overnight trains have comfortable sleeper cars, first-class

fares that include a sleeping compartment are comparable to airfares. In addition to RENFE, the Catalan's government's FGC (*Ferrocarrils de la Generalitat de Catalunya*) also provides train service, notably to the regions surrounding Barcelona.

For most journeys, trains are the most economical way to go. First- and second-class seats are reasonably priced, and you can get a bunk in a compartment with five other people for a supplement of about $25. There is train service connecting Barcelona with most other major cities in Spain; in addition, there are some special routes, such as a high-speed Euromed route that connects Barcelona to Tarragona and the Valencia coast.

Most Spaniards buy train tickets in advance by standing in long lines at the station *taquilla* (ticket office). The overworked clerks rarely speak English, however, so if you don't speak Spanish, you're better off going to a travel agency that displays the blue-and-yellow RENFE sign. The price is the same. For a one-way ticket, ask for *anada;* for a round-trip ticket, *anada i tornada.* In Catalan, the term is *ida y vuelta.*

CUTTING COSTS

If you purchase a same-day round-trip ticket while in Spain, you'll get a 20% discount; if you purchase a different-day round-trip ticket, a 10% discount applies. There are 20% discounts on long-distance tickets if you buy a round-trip ticket, and there are 20% discounts for students and senior citizens (though they usually have to carry cards issued by the local government, the Generalitat, so they are not intended for tourists). Anyone can obtain Interrail passes at similar prices to Eurail; there is no longer an age limit. For information, contact the Young People's Tourist Office (☎ 902/252575).

If you're planning extensive train travel, **look into rail passes.** If Spain is your only destination, consider a **Spain Flexipass.** Prices begin at U.S.$150 for three days of second-class travel within a two-month period and $190 for first class. Other passes cover more days and longer periods.

Spain is one of 17 European countries in which you can use **Eurailpasses,** which buy you unlimited first-class rail travel in all participating countries for the duration of the pass. If you plan to rack up the miles, get a standard pass; these are available for 15 days ($544), 21 days ($718), one month ($890), two months ($1,260), and three months ($1,558), prices subject to change. If your needs are more limited, **look into a Europass,** which costs less than a Eurailpass and buys you a limited number of travel days, in a limited number of countries (France, Germany, Italy, Spain, and Switzerland), during a specified time period.

In addition to standard Eurailpasses, Rail Europe sells the Eurail Youthpass (for those under age 26), the Eurail Saverpass (which gives a discount for two or more people traveling together), a Eurail Flexipass (which allows a certain number of travel days within a set period), the Euraildrive Pass, and the Europass Drive (which combines travel by train and rental car). Whichever pass you choose, remember that you must **buy your pass before you leave** for Europe.

Many travelers assume that rail passes guarantee them seats on the trains they wish to ride. Not so: you need to **reserve seats in advance** even if you're using a rail pass. Seat reservations are required on some European trains, particularly high-speed trains, and are wise on any train that might be crowded. You'll also need a reservation if you want sleeping accommodations.

➤ GENERAL INFORMATION: **RENFE** (☎ 902/240202; International Information ☎ 93/490–1122). **FGC** (93/205–1515).

➤ INFORMATION AND PASSES: **Rail Europe** (✉ 226–230 Westchester Ave., White Plains, NY 10604, ☎ 914/682–5172 or 800/438–7245; ✉ 2087 Dundas E, Suite 105, Mississauga, Ontario, Canada L4X 1M2, ☎ 416/602–4195). **DER Tours** (✉ Box 1606, Des Plaines, IL 60017, ☎ 800/782–2424, FAX 800/282–7474). **CIT Tours Corp.** (✉ 342 Madison Ave., Suite 207, New York, NY 10173, ☎ 212/697–2100; 800/248–8687; 800/248–7245 in western U.S.).

FROM THE U.K.

Train services to Spain from the United Kingdom are not as frequent, fast, or affordable as flights, and you have to change trains (and stations) in Paris. It's worth paying extra for a Talgo express or for the Puerta del Sol express to avoid having to change trains again at the Spanish border. Journey time to Paris (from the U.K.) is around six hours; from Paris to Barcelona, it's an additional 7 hours. Allow at least two hours in Paris for changing trains. If you're under 26 years old, Eurotrain has excellent deals.

➤ FROM THE U.K.: **British Rail Travel Centers** (☎ 020/7/834–2345). **Eurotrain** (✉ 52 Grosvenor Gardens, London SW1W OAG, England, ☎ 020/7/730–3402). **Transalpino** (✉ 71–75 Buckingham Palace Rd., London SW1W ORE, England, ☎ 020/7/834–9656).

➤ RESERVATIONS: **Marketing Ahead** (✉ 433 5th Ave., New York, NY 10016, ☎ 212/686–9213 or 800/223–1356). **DER Tours** (✉ Box 1606, Des Plaines, IL 60017, ☎ 800/782–2424, FAX 800/282–7474).

➤ IN SPAIN: **Iberrail** (✉ Capitán Haya 55, 28020 Madrid, ☎ 91/571–6692).

TRANSPORTATION AROUND SPAIN

Spain is the second largest country in Western Europe after France, so seeing any more than a fraction of the country involves considerable distances. If you want to enjoy the landscape and the freedom of stopping wherever your fancy takes you or straying from your fixed itinerary, a car is a good choice. The main roads in Spain are generally good, although traffic can be heavy on major routes (☞ Driving, *above*), and parking is a problem in towns and cities.

Spain is well served by domestic flights, but the fares are high and traveling by train can be preferable. The Spanish train service between the major cities is fast, efficient, and punctual (☞ Train Travel, *above*), but can be slow and involve frequent changes of train on secondary, regional routes, in which case a bus is the more convenient alternative (☞ Bus Travel, *above*).

TRAVEL AGENCIES

A good travel agent puts your needs first. Look for an agency that has been in business at least five years, emphasizes customer service, and has someone on staff who specializes in your destination. In addition **make sure the agency belongs to a professional trade organization.** The American Society of Travel Agents (ASTA), with 27,000 agents in some 170 countries, is the largest and most influential in the field. Operating under the motto "Integrity in Travel," it maintains and enforces a strict code of ethics and will step in to help mediate any agent-client disputes if necessary. ASTA also maintains a website that includes a directory of agents. (Note that if a travel agency is also acting as your tour operator, *see* Buyer Beware *in* Tours & Packages, *above*.)

➤ LOCAL AGENT REFERRALS: American Society of Travel Agents (ASTA, ☎ 800/965–2782 24-hr hot line, ᖴᴀX 703/684–8319, www.astanet.com). Association of British Travel Agents (✉ 55–57 Newman St., London W1P 4AH, ☎ 020/7/637–2444, ᖴᴀX 020/7/637–0713). Association of Canadian Travel Agents (✉ 1729 Bank St., Suite 201, Ottawa, Ontario K1V 7Z5, ☎ 613/521–0474, ᖴᴀX 613/521–0805). Australian Federation of Travel Agents (✉ Level 3, 309 Pitt St., Sydney 2000, ☎ 02/9264–3299, ᖴᴀX 02/9264–1085). Travel Agents' Association of New Zealand (✉ Box 1888, Wellington 10033, ☎ 04/499–0104, ᖴᴀX 04/499–0786).

VISITOR INFORMATION

➤ TOURIST OFFICE OF SPAIN: U.S.–General (✉ 666 5th Ave., 35th floor, New York, NY 10103, ☎ 212/265–8822, ᖴᴀX 212/265–8864). Chicago (✉ 845 N. Michigan Ave., Chicago, IL 60611, ☎ 312/642–1992, ᖴᴀX 312/642–9817). Los Angeles (✉ 8383 Wilshire Blvd., Suite 960, Beverly Hills, CA 90211, ☎ 213/658–7188, ᖴᴀX 213/658–1061). Miami (✉ 1221 Brickell Ave., Suite 1850, Miami, FL 33131, ☎ 305/358–1992, ᖴᴀX 305/358–8223). Canada (✉ 2 Bloor St. W, 34th floor, Toronto, Ontario

M4W 3E2, Canada, ☎ 416/961–3131, ᖴᴀX 416/961–1992). United Kingdom (✉ 22–23 Manchester Sq., London W1M 5AP, England, ☎ 020/7/486–8977; ᖴᴀX 020/7/486–8034).

WEB SITES

Do check out the World Wide Web when you're planning. You'll find everything from weather forecasts to virtual tours of cities. Fodor's Web site, www.fodors.com, is a great place to start your online travels; if you log on to its Barcelona mini-guide section, there is an extensive and very helpful Web Links listing, with many site addresses offered, including www.bcn.es, the main web site for the city of Barcelona. For information on Spain try www.okspain.org, www.tourspain.es, www.cyberspain.com, and www.red2000.com/spain.

WHEN TO GO

May and October are the optimal times to come to Spain, as the weather is generally warm and dry. May gives you more hours of daylight, while October offers a chance to enjoy the harvest season, which is especially colorful in the wine regions.

In April you can see some of Spain's most spectacular fiestas, particularly Semana Santa (Holy Week); and by then the weather in southern Spain is warm enough to make sightseeing comfortable.

Spain is the number-one destination for European travelers, so **if you want to avoid crowds, come before June or after September.** It's crowded and more expensive in summer, especially along the coasts. The Mediterranean is usually too cold for swimming the rest of the year, and the beach season on the Atlantic coast is shorter still. Spaniards themselves vacation in August, and their annual migration to the beaches causes huge traffic jams on August 1 and 31. Major cities are relaxed and empty for the duration; small shops and some restaurants shut down for the entire month, but museums remain open.

CLIMATE

Summers in Spain are hot: temperatures frequently hit 100°F (38°C), and air-conditioning is not widespread.

Try to **limit summer sightseeing to the morning hours.** That said, warm summer nights are among Spain's most pleasant experiences.

Winters in Spain are mild and rainy along the coasts, especially in Galicia.

Elsewhere, winter blows bitterly cold. Snow is infrequent except in the mountains, where you can ski from December through March in the Pyrenees and other resorts near Granada, Madrid, and Burgos.

The following are average daily maximum and minimum temperatures for major cities in Spain.

BARCELONA

Jan.	55F	13C	May	70F	21C	Sept.	77F	25C
	43	6		57	14		66	19
Feb.	57F	14C	June	77F	25C	Oct.	70F	21C
	45	7		64	18		59	15
Mar.	61F	16C	July	82F	28C	Nov.	61F	16C
	48	9		70	21		52	11
Apr.	64F	18C	Aug.	82F	28C	Dec.	55F	13C
	52	11		70	21		46	8

➤ FORECASTS: **Weather Channel Connection** (☎ 900/932–8437), 95¢ per minute from a Touch-Tone phone.

1 DESTINATION: BARCELONA TO BILBAO

BARCELONA AND BILBAO: BOOKENDS OF THE PYRENEES

TRAVELERS TO SPAIN HAVE often followed one "ruta turistica" or another: the trail of Don Quixote, the pilgrimage to Santiago de Compostela, medieval castles, wine routes. Conveniently, the 21st century comes equipped with yet another: Barcelona "to" Bilbao, a trip connecting the two major metropoli of Spain's northern Mediterranean and Atlantic coasts, two dazzling architectural masterpieces, and two of Iberia's most important cultural entities, the Basque Country and Catalonia. Passionate Mediterraneans versus dour Atlantic seafarers; sprightly, sardana-dancing Catalans versus sturdy, stone-lifting Basques; colorful Surrealists paintings versus massive stone sculpture: at first glance, Barcelona and Bilbao may seem mutually antithetical. Yet, upon introspection, the things they share may be more important than the things that separate them.

As Spain's traditional alternate capital (a millennium older than Madrid, and equally populous), Barcelona has long been an architectural tour de force with its medieval Gothic Quarter, the elegant Moderniste Eixample district, the colorful Rambla promenades, a wealth of museums, a fleet of superbly designed shops and clubs, and the celebrated buildings of Antonio Gaudí. Capital of the contentious region of Catalonia, the richest province in Spain, and the traditional vanguard of modern Spanish art and style (this is a city where urban planners go on pilgrimages), Barcelona is the planet's principal repository for late 19th-early-20th-century Art Nouveau (Moderniste) architecture.

How fitting, then, that at the other end of the Pyrenees, Bilbao—capital of the anthropologically mysterious Basque Country—has become one of the first great magnets of 21st-century art and architecture, thanks largely to the Frank Gehry-designed Museo Guggenheim Bilbao, acclaimed as one of modern architecture's seminal structures. Together, these two cities offer Spain's most stylish and design-driven postmodern face: playful, daring, flamboyant, the quintessential marriage of form and function, art and architecture, urbanism and humanism.

From Barcelona to Bilbao, from Gaudí to Gehry, this book charts the most recent and exciting new chapters in Spain's history and traces it, point to point, as the book flies, across northern Spain—if indeed this is Spain at all, for Barcelona and Bilbao are the centers of two of the Iberian Peninsula's most *un*Spanish *Comunidades Autónomas* (Autonomous Communities).

Sturdy Atlantic Basques from what is invariably known around the peninsula as "the north" and fiery Mediterranan Catalans from what the rest of the country sometimes snidely refers to as "Poland" (i.e., the east, northeast, or, in any case, someplace very different), these two peoples have long been characterized by their industrial might, though in very different ways. Bilbainos are brash, proud, somewhere between London and Chicago, rough-and-ready coal miners, steel workers, shipbuilders: hard hats. Catalans are equally proud, though less aggressive and pugnacious, more accommodating, successful at light industry and trade, a mix of Milan and Paris, textile makers and merchants, skillful and patient in business. The standard wisdom and perennial joke about Basques and Catalans is that if you call a Basque a son of a something-or-other he hits you in the nose whereas a Catalan will negotiate some peaceful solution, an agreement, consensus, a pact. Known as *pactistas*, or negotiators, the cosmopolitan Catalans are proud to be descended from Greeks, Romans, Phoenicians, and all of Mediterranean culture, whereas proto-Basques are fiercely defensive about their ethnic and cultural "purity," their territorial integrity, and the fact that neither Greeks nor Romans nor French nor even Castilians have ever completely succeeded in subduing their independent spirit.

Bilbao, with its traditional heavy industry—steel and shipbuilding—and Barcelona, with its textile mills, were each enormously wealthy northern industrial and commercial giants at the end of the 19th century when Madrid was in the throes of losing the last of its vast 16th-century empire. More importantly, industrial development in Catalonia and the Basque country created a large (and eventually well organized) working class in environments with long histories of democratic rule and a commitment to the rights and liberties of the individual. Basques were studied by early Marxists for their naturally collective social structure, while Barcelona's Consell de Cent (Council of the 100), founded in 1279, was Western Europe's first democratic parliament. Freedom, individualism, prosperity: needless to say, art was not far behind.

Basques speak Euskera, a somewhat rudimentary non–Indo-European language short on lyrical nuance and long on consonants, with words such as *eskerrik-asko* for "thank-you" and *mendigoikoetxea* for "house on top of the mountain." Catalans speak Catalan, one of the most Latinate of Romance languages, a version of Provençal French closer to Occitanian or Langue d'Oc, the language of the French southwest, with lovely archaisms such as *Deu vos guard* (God guard you) for "goodbye" and the very Gallic *Si us plau* for "please." Less than 15% of Euskera is Latin-based, while Catalan is only slightly touched by the Arabic influence that eight centuries of Moorish presence on the Iberian Peninsula imprinted thoroughly into Castilian Spanish. Whereas Euskera is absolutely unintelligible to non-Euskerophones, Catalan, though morphologically closer to French shares (as a result of many years of intimate cohabitation), a certain amount of vocabulary and usage (much of it horrifying to Catalan purists) with Castilian Spanish. Those skeptical of the important difference between Catalan and Spanish need only refer to the famous Catalan tongue-twister: "*Setze jutges d'un jutjat menjen fetge d'un penjat,*" which in Castilian Spanish comes out as "*Dieciseis jueces de un juzgado comen el higado de un ahorcado,*"—all of which adds up to the information that "Sixteen courtroom judges eat a hanged man's liver."

Catalans dance the delicate *sardana,* with light and dainty cat's-paw movements and so much arithmetic that the rest of Spain chuckles about them, topically famous for their commercial acumen, "counting even while they dance." Basques dance the *jota* or the *aurresku,* dances involving vigorous athleticism and an endless succession of impossible leaps.

Since it could be argued that there are no two peoples in all Iberia more different than Basques and Catalans (well, okay, maybe Andalusians and Asturians) and, especially, Bilbainos and Barcelonins, it is ironic that both cities are headed into the 21st century as Spain's prime tourist destinations and great repositories of art and architecture, especially when Spain's capital, Madrid, already has even more famous paintings per capita than . . . bars.

Barcelona was already prospering, a boomtown since the 1992 Olympics blew the lid off this steamy Mediterranean fleshpot, a city so sensual and sybaritic that even the buildings seem to wink at you. But Bilbao, always a secret oasis of culture and cuisine for those who knew and understood her, only charged onto the international stage in 1997 when Frank Gehry's Guggenheim became the world's most exciting piece of architecture. So traditionally wealthy and culture-hungry that in 1890 Bilbao constructed a 1,500-seat opera house for a population of 30,000, Flaviobriga (as the Romans knew it) has spearheaded an unprecedented economic and social recovery in the Basque country, a turnaround especially notable for being based on nothing more substantial than aesthetics: art and architecture. Even in 1890, Bilbao's hard-core industrial "realists" protested bitterly when the Arriaga opera house was projected to occupy prime dock and factory space along the river, so perhaps a century later when Thomas Krens (director of New York City's Guggenheim Museum) and Frank Gehry (one of America's most written-about architects) offered to replace the rusting remains of Bilbao's long-extinct shipyards with a glimmering titanium whale full of paintings and sculptures, the scheme already sounded strangely familiar to the town elders.

While Barcelona's Olympic refurbishing brought about a gleaming Richard Meier–designed Contemporary Art Museum, a port filled with bright structures of glass and steel, dizzying ringroads for the city's chronically chaotic traffic system, and a general cleaning and face-lifting for the city's many architectural treasures, Bilbao has gone on to add the Norman Foster–designed subway that has become the pride and joy of the "Metropoli" of greater Bilbao, the

Santiago Calatrava footbridge over the river, and the Euskaldun music and convention center (just several minutes downstream from the Guggenheim). Now projected is Cesar Pelli's immense Abandoibarra riverside garden and commercial center scheduled to be finished by late 2002, while Bilbao churches and buildings long blackened by industrial soot are emerging, resplendent, and blinking into the new light reflecting up and down the not-so-bright waters of the Nervión estuary (though at Bilbao's present clip don't bet against a run of Atlantic salmon within the decade).

Though Barcelona, 2,000 years old, offers a uniquely rich anthology of architecture running through Roman, Romanesque, Gothic, Renaissance, Baroque, neoclassical, Art Nouveau, and contemporary design (starting with Mies van der Rohe and continuing through Meier and Rafael Moneo), Bilbao also has a full panoply of treasures beyond the Guggenheim to enjoy. From the early 16th-century Gothic Santiago Cathedral to the austere Baroque and Neoclassical structures of the 700-year-old Casco Viejo, Bilbao's leap across the river in 1876 produced a wealth of late-19th and early 20th-century Art Deco and rationalist architecture in its *ensanche* (widening). Meanwhile, Barcelona's unfinished Gaudí masterpiece, the Sagrada Família, is one of the few buildings in the world as absorbing and exciting as Gehry's Guggenheim.

Modern and contemporary artists from Barcelona and Bilbao parted ways around the time of the late-19th-century Impressionists, with Catalan artists developing, guided by Picasso, Miró and Dalí, into more radical and vanguardist tendencies such as Cubism and Surrealism while La Escuela Vasca (The Basque School), inspired by Jorge Oteiza's seminal *Quosque Tandem* (Until When, Until When), sought a more retro-reaching ethnocultural aesthetic rooted in the essential Basque spirit. Today's international giants Eduardo Chillida and Antoni Tàpies reflect these trends, the former in powerful, compact forms reminiscent, in some way, of the 4,000-year-old Mikeldi monolith in Bilbao's Museo Vasco; the latter in daringly playful combinations of form, texture, and color. Oteiza's "I reject all that is not essential . . . ornamentation" would seem to strike directly at much of Barcelona's late-19th-century Art Nouveau move-

ment in which, as in Domènech i Montaner's Palau de la Música, ornamentation seems very much to *be* the essence. Even typical Basque calligraphy tends toward blocky rune-like characters, whereas the Catalan aesthetic is typified in the Joan Miró Caixa symbol, a colorful abstract, light and playful, a flourish.

Whereas both cities are seaports flanked by green hills, Bilbao is actually surrounded by them; you can spot livestock grazing up on Artxanda from inside the atrium of the Guggenheim. Barcelona's beaches in Barceloneta and nearby at Castelldelfells, Sitges, and north along the Costa Brava are countered by Vizcaya's rich coast, from the beaches of Getxo and Gorliz to the world-class half-mile-long left-curling surfing wave at Mundaca in the mouth of the Ría de Guernica. While Barcelona is two hours from the Pyrenees and 30 minutes from the Montseny nature preserve, Bilbao is less than a half an hour from the limestone peaks of Amboto and the rolling green hills of the valley of Atxondo.

Debating Basque versus Catalan cuisine could actually cause brain damage, so beware. It is said that Bilbao concentrates within a small area, traversable on foot in less than 30 minutes, the greatest number of first-rate dining establishments in Spain. This is almost certainly true. When so many chefs reach such a high level of excellence, it becomes very difficult for their sphere of influence not to expand exponentially. At the same time, staying in business becomes impossible for restaurants that cannot compete: culinary Darwinism. The Basque country is known for supreme gastronomic quality, and Bilbao offers the most consistently serious and sober approach to fine ingredients perfectly prepared. Products fresh from the Atlantic and the inland and upland delicacies brought to Bilbao's immense Mercado de la Ribera daily provide the base while fine cooking traditions ensure the rest.

Catalan cuisine—lighter and more Mediterranean than Bilbao's powerful Atlantic codfish-heavy repertory—is more eclectic and cosmopolitan, more experimental and less tradition-bound. Combinations of tastes such as sweet and salty have found their way into Catalan cuisine from the Moorish tenure in the Balearic Islands, while French influence from what was once northern Catalonia makes duck and rabbit more prevalent in Barcelona than Bilbao's beef and cod. All in all, though everything from Japanese to Cuban cuisine is available in Barcelona, expect a more radical and innovative range of tastes and ingredients in Catalonia, and more straight-up fine Basque dining in Bilbao.

Between these two Basque and Catalan hubs of art and industry stretch the Pyrenees of Catalonia, Aragón, and Navarra, with the vineyard-heavy region of La Rioja conveniently just south along the Ebro as a virtual wine cellar and buffer zone against Castilla's arid expanse. Each Pyrenean valley offers a complete subtreasury of destinations loaded with landscapes, history, memorable towns, and wining and dining experiences of every kind. Catalonia, Spanish-speaking Aragón, and the Basque country are the three main language and cultural groupings, though nearly every valley and village has its own traditions, typical dress, dishes, and even dialects such as Aranés from the Vall d'Aran, Patués from Benasque, Chistavino from Upper Aragón's Gistain, and Belsetá from Bielsa.

Either way you cross, from east to west or (more generally) west to east, the changes in language, climate, cuisine, and terrain as you move from one valley to another are welcome and dramatic variations on this highland theme of peaceful peaks and valleys, pure and rushing water, and wide open spaces.

South of Navarra, La Rioja is a microcosm of plains, river valleys, and mountains, all wedged in between the edge of the Castilian meseta and the Ebro River. Bilbainos consider La Rioja and its vineyards to be little more than Vizcaya's wine cellar, as many of the bodegas in La Rioja were founded by Basque families, and Bilbao founder Don Diego Lopez de Haro was in fact from La Rioja Alta's wine capital at Haro. A sweep across northern Spain wouldn't make sense without including La Rioja, part of which is actually in the Basque province of Alava.

The only serious problem is how to do it all in a lifetime, much less a week or two. A week in Barcelona, another in and around Bilbao, and 10 days in between is still probably not enough time to see all the riches of these regions. No matter. One thing remains certain: Stationed at opposite ends of the Iberian Peninsula's high-land nexus to—and barrier against—the rest of the European continent, Barcelona and Bilbao are now unlikely bedfellows in the new Gaudí-Guggenheim alliance that is rewriting travelers' itineraries across the north of Spain.

— George Semler

WHAT'S WHERE

This slice of geography across the north of Spain from Barcelona to Bilbao includes some of the most dramatically varied urban and natural landscapes anywhere on the Iberian Peninsula. Mediterranean Barcelona and Atlantic Bilbao connected by some 300 mi of Pyrenees all drained by the mighty Ebro River, with La Rioja thrown in for Bacchian relief and recourse, adds up to an all but unbeatable beat to explore.

The contrasts and contradictions are extreme and exquisite: from the heights of Gaudí's Sagrada Família church you can nearly see the Pyrenean heights you might be skiing down or the Costa Brava underwater park you could be finning through a couple of hours later. Bilbao's Guggenheim offers views of sheep grazing on Artxanda. From a summer dawn encounter with Mundaca's famous nonpareil left-rolling surfing wave, you can be in the Aragonese Pyrenees glacier-skiing the peak of Aneto that evening.

The Iberian Peninsula's northernmost edge, the one that connects it to the rest of Europe, is anchored at either end by the heavyweight industrial giants and art and architecture hotbeds of Barcelona and Bilbao. The Pyrenees in between these two seaports are composed of a series of 22 valleys and 23 peaks, the highest of which are in the central Pyrenees in what was once the realm (now Autonomous Community) of Aragón. The Catalan Pyrenees ascend sharply from the Mediterranean while the Pyrenees of Navarra roll moistly down to the Atlantic coast at the Bay of Biscay. La Rioja, south of Navarra on the Ebro River, is Spain's best wine country and a close cousin to its Basque and Navarran neighbors to the north. La Rioja Alavesa is the Rioja wine country that falls north of the Ebro in the Basque province of Alava.

Barcelona: Capital of Catalonia

Two thousand years of history have made the early Barcino into an amalgam of many Barcelonas, from the Laie of the first Iberian peoples who populated the hilltops overlooking the fertile lowlands between the mouths of the Llobregat and Besòs rivers to the cosmopolitan Barcelona of the 20th and early 21st centuries still busily building east out into the Mediterranean and up and down the coastline. In between, there are the historical neighborhoods and enclaves inhabited by Romans, Visigoths, Franks, and Jews; a second and third set of city walls around, respectively, the eastern suburbs of Sant Pere and La Ribera and the western *arrabal* (slum) now known as El Raval; outlying villages gradually incorporated into the urban fabric such as Gràcia and Sarrià; and the Eixample (widening), a vast post-1860 urban development composed of a grid system of square city blocks that is one of Europe's most spectacular manifestations of the Art Nouveau style. The headliners here, of course, are the eye-popping buildings designed by Antonio Gaudí, virtually a separate chapter, and his still-under-construction Sagrada Família church, another theme of its own within Gaudí studies. Add to all this Barcelona's ongoing adventures in design, from Norman Foster's communications tower to Frank Gehry's goldfish, Richard Meier's contemporary art museum, or Rafael Moneo's Auditori and the result is an overwhelming array and variety of architectural sights to explore.

Although Barcelona is an ocean of a city, many of its most historic sights are conveniently grouped in the sector of the old town, or La Ciutat Vella, which extends from the harborfront about 2 km (1 mi) up to the border of the 19th-century Eixample neighborhood. The heart of La Ciutat Vella is the Barri Gòtic (Gothic Quarter)—the medieval kernel of the metropolis—where narrow streets draped in rich, velvety darkness, stage-set with famous churches, and graced with elegant patios (courtyards) compose one of Barcelona's most venerable neighborhoods. Leading sights here include the landmark Catedral de la Seu and Plaça Sant Jaume, once the Roman forum and now the seat of both the Catalan and the Barcelona governments. Dividing the old town at the Barri Gòtic's western edge is the famous Rambla, which terminates at the vast Plaça de Catalunya to the north (although leafy Rambla Catalunya continues up to the Diagonal) and the harbor to the south (though the wooden Rambla de Mar boardwalk crosses the harbor). Adorned with flower markets, bird stalls, and a torrent of humanity, this is the city's most famous thoroughfare and a never-ending fiesta unto itself. Must-dos here include the Boqueria—one of Europe's most spectacular food markets; the Gran Teatre del Liceu opera house; the medieval, magnificent Drassanes Reiales shipyards; and the sumptuous Palau Güell, one of Antoni Gaudí's earliest masterpieces.

The area to the west of the Rambla, on the right as you walk toward the port, is El Raval—originally a slum and now an increasingly gentrified quarter, thanks in good part to the Richard Meier–designed Museu d'Art Contemporánea de Barcelona. Once notorious for its Barri Xinès (or Barrio Chino) red-light district—whose Gypsies, saltimbanques, and prostitutes once inspired Picasso's most memorable Blue- and Rose-period paintings (not to say his *Demoiselles d'Avignon*) (even though Carrer D'Avinyó is not, strictly speaking, in the Raval), today's Raval is still a steamy jumble of raw life and emotion. The medieval hospital, Plaça del Pedró, the Mercat de Sant Antoni, and Sant Pau del Camp are highlights of this helter-skelter, rough-and-tumble part of Barcelona. As you move to the north and east of the Gothic Quarter you'll find the neighborhoods of Sant Pere and La Ribera. Sant Pere is Barcelona's old textile neighborhood and is centered on church of Sant Pere; that extravaganza of Modernisme, the Palau de la Música Catalana theater, is located here. Set between the lower reaches of the Via Laietana and the Parc de la Ciutadella, the adjacent Barri de la Ribera remains one of the city's best waterfront districts; the district surrounds the basilica of Santa Maria del Mar—the masterpiece of Catalan Gothic architecture—and includes Carrer Montcada, Barcelona's most aristocratic early thoroughfare, lined with 14th- to 18th-century Renaissance palaces, several of which now house the celebrated Museu Picasso.

To the south of La Ribera and east of the main harbor is the waterfront village of Barceloneta— a relentlessly picturesque quarter where sophisticated *barcelonins* love to escape to enjoy a Sunday paella on the beach and a stroll through some of the city's most romantic streets. Just to the north is Barcelona's central downtown park, La Ciutadella. In the park you'll find the zoo, home to Snowflake, the albino gorilla; the Umbracle, a deliciously 19th-century cast-iron greenhouse; and streets lined with graceful seaside houses. Fast-forward to the present by strolling over to the Port Olímpic and its Frank Gehry goldfish sculpture and the postmodern Port Vell complex and mall.

A cable car connects Barceloneta with Montjuïc, the towering hill overlooking the south side of the port that is home to some of the city's most famous museums, such as the Miró Foundation, the Romanesque collection of Pyrenean murals and frescoes in the Palau Nacional, the Mies van der Rohe Barcelona Pavilion, and the lush gardens of the Jardins de Mossèn Cinto Verdaguer. Bus or funicular will take you back down to the city center, where the centerpiece of Barcelona's urban drama awaits—L'Eixample, a dazzling, dizzying grid above Plaça de Catalunya studded with many of the city's most famous examples of Moderniste (Art Nouveau) architecture, three of which can be found on the Manzana de la Discordia "city block" where Domènech i Muntaner, Puig i Cadafalch, and Gaudí went head to head to design three of the greatest Moderniste buildings: Casa Lleó Morera, Casa Amatller, and Casa Batlló, one of Gaudí's most jaw-dropping creations. The Ruta del Modernisme will take you past many other important structures, climaxing in Gaudí's legendary, emblematic, and unfinished fantasy, the church of the Sagrada Família—the veritable icon of Barcelona—for which you should plan a full half-day visit. The Eixample's principal thoroughfares are Rambla de Catalunya and Passeig de Gràcia, where the city's most elegant shops rub shoulders with more great Moderniste buildings.

More Moderniste delights lay in Parc Güell—a phantasmagorical park created by Gaudí at the upper edge of Gràcia, a hip and happening district that lies north of the Diagonal thoroughfare. Above and west of Gràcia is what is universally referred to as *la parte alta* (the upper part) of Barcelona: La Bonanova (around the top of Calle Balmes and Calle Muntaner), Sant Gervasi (between Sarrià and Calle Mandri), the onetime country village of Sarrià, aristocratic Pedralbes, the Tibidabo promontory, and the Collserola hills above and behind the city. Sarrià is a lively nucleus filled with antiques shops and restaurants; Pedralbes is a hillside enclave of sprawling aristocratic mansions and a stunning triple-cloistered Gothic monastery (now housing part of the excellent Thyssen-Bornemisza collection of paintings); Tibidabo towers over Barcelona with its amusement park, its Disneyesque church, and Sir Norman Foster's gigantic communications spire; and the Collserola hills comprise an almost 20,000 acre wild boar–infested park of forestland around and northwest of the hilltop town of Vallvidrera.

Catalonia: From the Costa Brava to Montserrat

Barcelonins are undeniably lucky: few populaces enjoy such glorious—and easily accessible—options for day-tripping. Of course, many of them, along with foreign travelers in the region, spend weeks touring the magnificent sights of Catalonia. For many, the first destination is the the Catalan Riviera—the famed Costa Brava, which stretches north from Blanes (67 km/42 mi north of Barcelona) to Cadaqués and the French border, comprising a delightful series of tiny *calas* (inlets) and rocky shores only occasionally marred by massive development. The name means "brave coast"—a description belied by its hospitality to holiday makers but not by its terrain, indented and capriciously sketched with innumerable coves. It has long been colonized by sleek hotels, sun worshipers, and celebrated artists, the most noted of whom was Salvador Dalí, who was born in Figueres (now the site of amazing Teatre-Museu Dalí), lived in a storybook chalet at nearby Port Lligat, and immortalized the whitewashed houses and golden sands of Cadaqués. Figueres is an excellent point from which to visit the beautiful Gulf of Rosas, the ancient Roman ruins of Empúries, and even the French towns of Matisse country. Head into the hinterland to discover fabled Girona, a historic treasure-house home (along with Krakow) to one of Europe's two best-preserved Jewish quarters, fine Roman walls, and pastel-colored 19th-century houses along the Riu Onyar.

Returning south to Barcelona through the mountain retreat of Montseny, the traveler can head into southern Catalonia, beginning with a pilgrimage to the legendary "serrated mountain," Montserrat, still the holiest shrine in Catalonia, famous for its "Black Virgin" and spectacular geologic backdrop (funiculars provide breathtaking vantage points). Your religious or art historical pilgrimage can then continue on to three noted 12th-century Cistercian monasteries in Catalonia: Santes Creus, Santa Maria de Poblet, and Vallbona de les Monges. Farther afield is the magnificent provincial city of Tarragona, known for its Roman legacy. More worldly pleasures await in Sitges, the prettiest and most popular beach town near Barcelona.

The Pyrenees

Barcelona and Bilbao (Catalonia and the Basque Country) are linked by the Pyrenees, which stretch east–west along the border with France, while, below Navarra, La Rioja nestles south of the Ebro river in Spain's finest wine country. The N260 is the main Pyrenean route connecting the Atlantic and Mediterranean coasts, while the A2 and, west of Zaragoza, A68 toll road freeways are the high speed, lowland highway. Logroño and Pamplona are a mere four hours from Barcelona traveling at standard Spanish freeway speeds of 75 amd 80 mph, and a six o'clock departure from Barcelona can have you at Navarra's Parador de Olite, for example, in plenty of time for a 9:30 dinner.

The optimum way of exploring the spectacular and highly recommendable mountain range of the Pyrenees is on foot, but to do so from Atlantic to Mediterranean would take seven weeks. Take heart— you can enjoy its well-marked trails, romantic retreats and monasteries, and charming inns with much shorter excursions. Pedestrian crossings are usually run from west to east, though road trips can go either way. If you drive west you'll need to start early to avoid hours of late afternoon sun in your eyes.

The Catalan Pyrenees offer four main valleys to explore, from the easternmost valleys of the rivers Ter and Ritort in the Vall de Camprodón through the wide and luminous Cerdanya Valley straddling the French border due north of Barcelona; the upper Garonne valley, Vall d'Aran, on Catalonia's northwestern edge; and, at the western border of Catalonia and Aragón, the Boí valley with its rich Romanesque treasures.

Aragon's Pyrenees form the highest part of the range, with Aneto and the Maladeta Massif all rising to above 11,000 ft. From Aragon's easternmost valley of Benasque through the massive and magic valleys and villages of upper Huesca, the Grand Canyon of the Pyrenees at Ordesa and Monte Perdido national park, Jaca and the valley of Canfranc, and west through the valleys of Hecho, Ansó, and Roncal, Aragón is the loftiest, wildest, and ruggedest terrain in the Pyrenees.

Navarra and the Atlantic Pyrenees are a moist relief after the scorching Mediterranean heat and the central Pyrenean rocky heights. The Irati beech forest is one of Europe's most extensive woodlands, once the source of beams and mainmasts for the "Invincible" Spanish Armada and today a highland retreat and hiking preserve. Roncesvalles and the Baztán Valley descend gently down through the valley of the Bidasoa River to the watering spots of Fuenterrabía and nearby San Sebastián.

Bilbao and the Basque Country

Once a sightseeing backwater, northern Spain and the Basque Country's suddenly bright, newly "must-see" industrial city of Bilbao—centered on its gleaming titanium Museo Guggenheim Bilbao and surrounded by green summits—is even experiencing a change in its traditional weather patterns: locals swear (and can statistically prove) that the grimy *siri-miri* drizzle that has perennially characterized Bilbao and the Basque country has miraculously lifted. Whether or not it's *el niño*, Frank Gehry, or a collusion between the Guggenheim's Thomas Krens and higher powers, it seems to be a fact. The rainy Basque country is now the sunny Basque country, or at least a lot more so. With two good art museums, a half dozen (if not a dozen) culinary standouts, and an old quarter that's getting better every day, Bilbao is now much more than a one-night stand. Three days is a minimum, and, with the Guggenheim to delight in, a week there is even better.

What do you do with a week in the Bilbao region? Go to the Museo Guggenheim at least three times, the Museo de Bellas Artes (Fine Arts Museum) once, spend a day touring the fishing ports of Mundaka and Bermeo by train, another at the beaches of Getxo and Bakio by car, a sixth at Axpe in the verdant upland reaches of the Atxondo valley, and the seventh out in the highland villages of Las Encartaciones west of Bilbao. In between there's the Bilbao's medieval quarter, the Casco Viejo, and the late-19th-century Ensanche to explore.

Moving away from Bilbao, the lush patchwork of hills and valleys (with the Atlantic coast never far away) that is the Basque Country is a delight to all the senses, especially after the aridity of the Castilian steppe or the granite and limestone heights of the central Pyrenees. When you hear your first few sentences of the staccato Basque language, Euskera, you'll be sure you really are in another country bound to Spain by the national soccer league and the *tortilla de patatas* (potato omelet) more than by any natural cultural affinity. Shepherds and fishermen, Basques have a solid and sometimes taciturn reserve that makes the boisterous booming of a Basque bar even more effusive and infectious then ever when the time comes for what is probably the most important element in Basque life and culture: food and drink. Pamplona's Fiestas de San Fermin prove over and over again that Basques are peerless revelers, but the smaller fiestas in mountain hamlets or fishing villages are equally joyous events.

Navarra, southeast and inland of Bilbao and San Sebastián, covers a wide gamut of peoples and countrysides from the high valleys of the Pyrenees to the scorched southwestern villages along the northern banks of the Ebro river. Guipúzcoa, forming a corner with France, is the province of San Sebastián, Euskadi's traditional summer watering spot for Madrid aristocrats ever since Queen Eugenie was prescribed the cold waters of the Atlantic in the mid-19th century. The Basque coast all the way from the French border to the Nervión estuary west of Bilbao is a series of beaches and fishing ports of great color and robustness, an important blast of North Atlantic wind and weather that seems to produce a ruddy and salubrious aura of power in locals and visitors alike. Look at the complexions, bones, and sinews in an Ignacio Zuloaga painting and you'll get an idea of how a few days or weeks of the Basque coast can make you feel.

The uplands of the Basque provinces of Vizcaya and Guipúzcoa, from Oñate to Axpe to Gordexola and Carranza, are wilder and more rustic than easily imaginable so close to the major industrial hub of Bilbao, while the Basque capital at Vitoria, the Plain of Alava, and, especially, Laguardia, and the Rioja Alavesa offer yet another distinct range and variety of landscapes, from windswept steppes to fertile vineyards.

Another highlight is La Rioja, southeast of Vitoria and southwest of Pamplona, famed as Spain's finest traditional winegrowing district. Logroño and Haro are the main towns to visit here, with Nájera and Calahorra next, but the real gems of La Rioja are hidden away in the seven river valleys that drain the mountains stretching from the Sierra de la Demanda in the west to the Sierra de Alcarama at the eastern end of this Ebro river watershed. Wine tasting your way through La Rioja Alta is the best way to become part of the countryside, with the ambrosial produce of the limestone clay soil flowing through your bloodstream. People from La Rioja live and move comfortably through every detail of Bacchian lore and endeavor, from glass blowing to barrel making to wine tasting, and are conversant on the tiniest nuances of oenology in the way that the Inuit of Alaska are said to appreciate dozens of different kinds and qualities of snow.

PLEASURES AND PASTIMES

Architecture: 2,000 Years of Genius

If Madrid is about paintings, Barcelona and Bilbao are about architecture, the former mainly Art Nouveau and Gaudí and the latter Gehry and the Guggenheim. For Barcelona's comprehensive Gaudí treatment, the unmissable sights are the following: Parc Güell in upper Gràcia; Gaudí's first house, Casa Vicens, in the adjacent village of Gràcia; the Palau Güell, off the lower Rambla; the rippling-around-the-corner Casa Milà, known as La Pedrera ("Stone Quarry"), with its roof garden of veiled and hooded warrior-maidens and its Gaudí study center and museum in the attic; Casa Batlló, Gaudí's allegory on the St. George and the dragon theme; and Casa Calvet, near the Hotel Ritz on Carrer de Casp. The most important of all of Gaudí's works is the still-growing Temple Expiatori de la Sagrada Família.

As a backdrop to the city's ample Art Nouveau patrimony, Barcelona's Roman, Romanesque, and Gothic legacy is also extensive. The famous Rambla—the promenade that Federico García Lorca called the only street in the world that he wished would never end—separates the Gothic Quarter and its Roman core from the Raval, where the medieval hospital, the shipyards, and Sant Pau del Camp, Barcelona's oldest church, are the main attractions, along with the Richard Meier's modern MACBA (Museu d'Art Contemporani de Barcelona) and the CCCB (Centre de Cultura Contemporanea de Barcelona) next door.

Throughout the Pyrenees, Romanesque chapels and hermitages and the characteristic highland village architecture will keep your eyes entertained, even delighted, but for highlights look for the church at Beget, Santa Maria de la Seu at Seu d'Urgell, and the matching set of gemlike Romanesque churches and chapels in the Vall de Boí in western Catalonia.

In Aragón don't miss the magnificent ancient and noble town houses of Benasque, the heavy porticoed town hall of Bielsa, the 11th-century cathedral at Jaca, and the ancient bridges and farmhouses in the Hecho and Roncal valleys. Navarra and the Basque Country's long, sloping-roofed *caseríos* (farmhouses) exude a rustic sense of home and well-being, while the emblazoned town houses of Laguardia and Haro and the fortified manor houses of Las Encartaciones west of Bilbao look like places to repair to for a final stand.

Nájera's Santa María la Real, with its Claustro de los Caballeros (cloister) and Laguardia's polychrome portal, Santa María de los Reyes, are two memorable gems in La Rioja on either side of the Ebro. And, of course, Bilbao is much more than the Guggenheim, though even if it weren't, the Guggenheim alone would emphatically justify a visit.

Gastronomy:
The Delights of Dining

Gastronomically, Catalonia is scoring stratospherically well with the likes of one of the most talked-about restaurants

in the world today—Ferran Adrià's El Bullí in Roses—along with a flotilla of other remarkable spots in Barcelona: Santi Santamaria's Racó de Can Fabes, Fermín Puig and his recently opened Drolma in Hotel Majestic, and Xavi Pellicer's cutting-edge Abac near Passeig del Born are three that top the list. Other top Barcelona gourmet enclaves would include Can Gaig, Neichel, El Racó d'en Freixa, and Jean Luc Figueras, not to forget Ca L'Isidre, Leopoldo, and Tram-Tram. For tapas, there's Cal Pep, La Estrella de Oro, Quimet i Quimet, and a growing legion of Basque bars whose success leaves little room for doubt about their quality. Strong in seafood, Barcelona's top places range from Gràcia's Botafumeiro to Barceloneta's Can Majó, with many excellent alternatives in between.

The cooking across the Pyrenees specializes in roasts and thick bean soups usually welcome even in the dead of summer when, no matter how hot the days, nights are cool, and the altitude begets appetites. Llívia's Can Ventura is a place to seek out, as is the deluxe Torre del Remei just west of Puigcerdà. La Seu d'Ugell's El Castell offers another inventive and authentic mountain cuisine with international overtones, as does Ca l'Irene in Vall d'Aran's Arties (6 km/4 mi east of Vielha). Just outside of Benasque in Anciles, the Restaurante Ansils is the place to find. Jaca's famous La Cocina Aragonesa is worth waiting for, as is Hecho's Gaby-Casa Blasquico or, in Pamplona, either Josetxo or Rodero, both experts at putting products from Navarra's varied landscapes together in original ways.

San Sebastián, Bilbao, and the Basque country in general have long been considered culinary pilgrimages, while La Rioja, with its well-developed wine palate and rich reserves of game and garden produce also offers a staggeringly consistent level of memorable cuisine. Ramon Roteta (or the Hermandad) in Hondarribia, Casa Camara (or Txulotxo) in Pasajes de San Juan, Arzak in San Sebastián, Kaia Kaipe (or Iribar) in Guetaria, Mendi Goikoa in Axpe, Jolastoki in Getxo, either Guria or Perro Chico (among many) in Bilbao, and La Posada Mayor de Migueloa in Laguardia—all masters of the Basque Country's expertise in preparing fresh Atlantic fish and homegrown beef and vegetables in simple yet sophisticated ways—would rank among the most embarrassing places to have to admit not having visited on a tour of this gastronomically gifted corner of Spain.

Markets: Cornucopiae— The Urban Horns of Plenty

"Collecting" markets of different kinds is a rewarding passion—many veteran travelers consider this the best way, in fact, to get to know people and places. So, if you want to dive into Barcelona headfirst, there's no better way than a visit to its Boqueria market on the Rambla—the oldest and last still-functioning market of its kind in Europe, a colorful cornucopia of produce ranging from apples and pears to partridges, chanterelles, scallops, and sea snails. As if wandering through this erotic display of raw materials weren't enough, there are fine dining opportunities stacked in there, from Pinotxo—a famous counter (only eight bar stools) serving the best jumbo shrimp and scrambled eggs with wild mushrooms in town—to the Kiosco Universal, with more places to sit and excellent fare as well. La Gardunya, at the back of the Boqueria, is the traditional post-opera, onion-soup refuge (in the grand tradition of the old Parisian Les Halles).

Barcelona's other produce markets are scattered throughout the city. The markets of Gràcia, Barceloneta, and Sarrià, to name just a few, will make you feel like part of the neighborhood. For the mother market of them all, and very much off the tourist beaten track, head out to one of the main supply points for southern Europe, Mercabarna (where there is an excellent restaurant, Boviscum—get it? serves bovines?), off the Ronda Litoral toward the airport. The Mercat de Sant Antoni— a food market and much more—rages on weekends; Els Encants, Barcelona's flea market, not far from the Sagrada Família at Plaça de le Glòries, is always a colorful collection of odds and ends; the Thursday antiques market in front of the cathedral is a good browse, and the natural produce market of cheeses, honeys, and herbs open alternate Saturdays in Plaça del Pi is like a miniature Sant Ponç festival, an oasis of farm-fresh fragrance in downtown Barcelona.

Markets in the Pyrenees start with Puigcerdà's Sunday vegetable, fruit, wild mushroom, and clothing bazaar; or with the wild mushroom stands in Guardiola and Bagà on the way up to the Tunel del Cadí. Markets across the Pyrenees are generally held on Sundays—social as well as commercial events, they offer a chance to catch a glimpse of everyone in town and then some. Check for Puigcerdà's early November horse traders' market or, near Bilbao, Gordexola's December Feria de San Andres livestock exchange, colorful fall events even if you're not in the market for anything ovine, bovine, or equine.

San Sebastián's two markets, La Bretxa in La Parte Vieja and the Mercado de San Martín near the cathedral, display a brilliant selection of the ingredients that have made local chefs famous. Finally, Bilbao's Mercado de la Ribera is the largest market of its kind (open, hangarlike, semioutdoor) in Europe, three floors of produce from fish at river level to meat on the top floor—paradise, in advance, for all cooks.

Music and Music Festivals

If, as St. Augustine wrote, music and architecture are twin arts, it should be no surprise that Barcelona's musical offering rivals its architectural patrimony. The Liceo Opera House on the Rambla reopened in 1999 after five years of reconstruction following the 1994 fire that left little more than a gutted shell; the Palau de la Música (with its stampeding cavalry sculptures erupting from the wings and its immense stained-glass chandelier overhead) is a strong candidate for the world's most unusual music hall, while the new Auditori, if lacking the warmth of the Palau, is ample and acoustically impeccable, a space deliberately antithetical to the Palau where, as the name of the place suggests, what you hear is what's at center stage. Meanwhile, look for concerts held in the lovely triple-tiered Monasterio de Pedralbes or in the medieval shipyards at Drassanes or in other extraordinary Gothic spaces ranging from Plaça del Rei to the San Felip Neri chapel, where you might have a chance to hear Jordi Savall, Europe's most prestigious researcher, restorer, and performer of early music with his Hesperion chorus and orchestra.

Summer music festivals are held all across the Pyrenees, from the Spanish enclave at Llívia near Puigcerdà, through La Seu d'Urgell, Ansils (next to Benasque), Lanuza (where the stage floats on the surface of a lake) and Jaca.

San Sebastián's late-July jazz festival features some of the world's greatest performers, while Bilbao's classical music scene is now split between the Palacio Euskalduna and the traditional Teatro Arriaga from early October through May. Music festivals in and around Bilbao begin with the capital's February choral festival and continue through Getxo's mid-June blues festival, early July jazz festival, and late-August festival of sea chanties.

Pyrenees Hiking

Walking the 800 km (496 mi) HRP, GR-10, or GR-11 trail (or a combination thereof) from one end of the Pyrenees to the other, a seven-week trek, might be more than you're looking for, but day walks in and out of natural resources such as the Parque Nacional de Ordesa y de Monte Perdido or even up to the peak of Aneto and back are immensely rewarding. The two-day Alberes walk from Le Perthus up to Puig Neulós and across the last Pyrenean heights to Banyuls sur Mer or Cap de Creus is one of the most spectacular. From Roncesvalles, take two days and walk over to Saint Jean Pied de Port and back along the well-marked GR-65 across the spot where Roland fell on August 15, 778; the Camino de Santiago's most dramatic leg, this walk is a beauty both ways with excellent dining and lodging at either end. Other walks to consider include the walk up the Basque coast between Zumaya and Hendaye, passing through Guetaria, Zarauz, Orio, San Sebastián, Pasajes, and Hondarribia; and the walk around the periphery of the Urdaibai wetlands, a 75 km (47 mi), four- or five-day trek along the GR-98 with stops in villages overlooking the Ría de Guernica.

Pyrenean Natural History

Collecting flora and fauna across the Pyrenees is potentially an altogether life-consuming project. In the Catalan Pyrenees in the Nuria Valley, a family of eagles and a family of Belgians have been keeping an eye on each other for several generations. Snow partridge in and around the Ulldeter refuge and ski resort above the Vall de Camprodon's ski area are censed annually in early May, when a pre-dawn commando of biologists takes positions to await the sunrise and the mating rituals of the *perdiz nival* (snow partridge). Different strains of butterflies, mountain goats, wild mushrooms, and alpine gentians, not to mention blueberries, raspberries, blackberries, strawberries, wild plums, pears, and peaches are found all along the wildest heights of the Pyrenees, while native Pyrenean trout make this region a paradise for fly-fishermen. Brown bears, lynx, otter, foxes, wild boar, and wolves are also present in the Pyrenees, though rarely seen. Capercaillie (*Tetrao urogallus*) or, in Spanish, *urogallo,* is a rare giant grouse and a great prize to observe anywhere in Spain, including the Pyrenees. Atlantic salmon migrate up the rivers of the Pyrenees to spawn, notably Navarra's Bidasoa. But the two Pyrenees residents most sought and seen are the wary *isard* (izard, Pyrenean chamois, wild goat, *sarrio,* in Spanish) and the comic *marmota* (marmot), roly-poly groundhogs. The *isard* is easily observed by staying at high altitudes until dusk, especially after an evening cloudburst when they descend to feed near trails they don't dare approach during the day. The marmot's shrill warning whistle echoes through high Pyrenean meadows, giving him away as entire communities scramble for their burrows.

Wine Country: Rich Wines, Rich Past

Wine routes across the north of Spain are another superb way to get to know different parts of the country from the soil up. La Rioja is the most important and best region. El Priorat, west of Reus, also has a rugged but exciting wine trail through the terraced vineyards once tended by the monks of the local priory. The Empordá, north of Figueres, in the shadow of the Alberes mountain range, has some innovative new vintners such as Jordi Oliver of the Oliver Conti vineyards producing excellent new-wave brews. Farther west, between Huesca and Barbastro, the D. O. (Denominación de Origen) Somontano produces the only wine of the Pyrenees, a highly respected series of high-tech modern winemakers such as Enate and Viñas del Vero. Haro is the wine capital of La Rioja, with its—to wine lovers—legendary Barrio de la Estación (railroad station quarter) winemakers offering tasting tours. Across the Ebro River, Laguardia is the heart of the Rioja Alavesa's wine country, with the key villages of Cenicero and Elciego en route. In the Basque country, Guetaria is the cradle and traditional home of the fresh young txakolí. Txomin Etxaniz is Guetaria's most famous vintner, though txakolí is made throughout both Guipúzcoa and Vizcaya provinces. Astigarraga, just outside of San Sebastián, is the Basque country's cider center, with dozens of *sidrerías* open year-round for testing anything from cider to applejack.

GREAT ITINERARIES

Attempting to tour Barcelona, Bilbao, the Pyrenees, and La Rioja in a three-day whirlwind may seem the height of folly but, time being of the essence, this may be the only option available. Below are some suggestions on ways to cull the best of these various worlds on limited time. Overnight train rides can make your sleeping time into travel time and are highly recommended.

If You Have 3 Days

In three days, with an hour's flight from Barcelona to Bilbao, you can do more than you think. First discover the splendors of Barcelona—promenade down the **Rambla,** tour the **Boqueria market** and Gaudí's **Palau Güell** before taxiing to L'Eixample, Barcelona's celebrated Art Nouveau district, and visiting the **Manzana de la Discòrdia**—the famous block featuring three noted Moderniste buildings. Then feast your eyes on "faith, in frozen lava" (as one critic put it): Gaudí's emblematic church of **La Sagrada Família.** From the Sagrada Família taxi to the picturesque seaside "village" of **La Barceloneta** for lunch followed by a look at **Santa Maria del Mar**—the purest of the Catalan Gothic churches—when it opens after the mid-day hiatus at 4:30. A quick visit to the **Museu Picasso** precedes another taxi to another Gaudí extravaganza, his magnificent park, **Parc Güell.** From Parc Guell, taxi to Gaudí's first house, **Casa Vicens,** in Carrer de les Carolines, before finishing the day at Gaudí's most renowned domestic structure, **Casa Milà,** nicknamed La Pedrera ("The Stone Quarry"), for a spectacular sunset surrounded by the architect's most phantasmal chimneys. You might still find time to catch a concert at Barcelona's (and the world's?) most splendiferous music

hall, the **Palau de la Música** before a late dinner at Botafumeiro, serving until 1 AM.

On day two, try to get a glimpse of the **Miró Foundation** or of the **Monestir de Pedralbes**—a venerable monastery virtually wallpapered with great Old Masters from the Thyssen-Bornemieza Collection—on your way to the airport to fly to Bilbao in time for a late lunch at El Perro Chico or a tapa in the **Casco Viejo** (old town) at Xukela. After lunch walk down the river, cross Santiago Calatrava's **Zubi-Zuri footbridge**—you virtually "walk on water," thanks to the transparent (though badly scuffed) walkway—and report in to the Gehry landmark **Museo Guggenheim** (with tickets bought in advance to avoid lines). Spend the afternoon and evening exploring the museum before dining someplace simple but perfect, such as Guria or Goizeko Kabi. Day three ought to include a walk through **Parque Doña Casilda de Iturrioz,** a visit to the surprisingly impressive painting collection of the **Museo de Bellas Artes,** and another hour or two in the Guggenheim before walking up the river for a look at the **Mercado de la Ribera,** Bilbao's main food market. Explore the **Casco Viejo** and **Museo Vasco**—the city's fascinating Museum of Basque Archaeology, Ethnology, and History —before returning to the **Guggenheim** until the sunset to catch the fire sculpture in the reflecting pool at closing time. Then dine at the Guggenheim's excellent Martín Berasategui restaurant, or walk down the river to the little ramp up from the Zubi-Zuri footbridge to Zortziko for one of Bilbao's top gourmet experiences.

If You Have 7 Days

In a full week you can do all the things you would have done in three days at a more relaxed pace, as well as make a road trip into the Pyrenees or out to the Costa Brava at the Mediterranean end. At the Atlantic end of the process you can drive around the Vizcayan coast, to San Sebastián, or into the upland Basque hills. In the final analysis you may have to decide whether the city or the countryside interests you more. In Barcelona, walk the **Rambla,** touring the **Boqueria market** and Gaudí's **Palau Güell** before taxiing to the L'Eixample district to stroll along the Ruta del Modernisme, climaxing at Gaudí's amazing church of **La Sagrada Família.**

From the Sagrada Família taxi to **La Barceloneta** for a harborside lunch followed by a look at the Gothic masterpiece that is **Santa Maria del Mar** (it opens at 4:30). Visit the **Museu Picasso**, and then have a coffee in the patio of the **Museu Textil** across the way. Later, back near Santa Maria del Mar, visit the **Casa Gispert** store—one of the city's most aromatic and picturesque shops, bursting with spices, chocolates, and nuts—and have a tapa in the Barri de la Ribera on Carrer Banys Vells before a concert at the famous **Palau de la Música** and a late dinner at Botafumeiro. On day two in Barcelona, use the morning to see Gaudí's extraordinary park, **Parc Güell,** then the architect's first house commission, **Casa Vicens,** in Carrer de les Carolines and then his domestic masterpiece, **Casa Milà**; lunch at Cal Pep (for the city's finest tapas) and visit the **Miró Foundation** and the Romanesque collection in the **Palau Nacional** in the afternoon. In the evening, check listings for musical events at the **Auditori** or the **Liceu** opera house. On day three, try to have an early look at the **Monestir de Pedralbes** on your way out for a day either in the Pyrenees around Bellver de Cerdanya, Puigcerdà, and Llívia or up the Costa Brava to Figueres and Cadaqués, especially noted for their links with the great Surrealist artist Salvador Dalí.

Get back to Barcelona in time for the 10:30 PM overnight train to Bilbao and you'll be there at 7:50 in the morning, or, if sleeping on trains isn't your thing, get an early flight on day four. In Bilbao, start at Gehry's **Guggenheim** before taking a walk up the river over Santiago Calatrava's shimmering **Zubi-Zuri footbridge** to the **Mercado de la Ribera** before diving into the old town, or **Casco Viejo,** for tapas at Xukela or Victor Montes (or both!). While you're there, go through the **Museo Vasco**—the Museum of Basque Archaeology, Ethnology, and History, housed in an austerely elegant 16th-century convent—and then take the **Norman Foster–designed subway** from the Casco Viejo stop to the Sabino Arana stop and walk back through the **Parque Doña Casilda de Iturrioz** to the **Museo de Bellas Artes** to take in its fine Old Masters and Basque collection. On day five, visit the **Guggenheim** again before making a loop out to the beach town and suburb of **Getxo** for lunch at Jolastoki and con-

tinuing the tour around the Basque coast through Bakio, Bermeo, Mundaca, and Guernica—a comfortable, low-speed, two- to three-hour drive depending on stops. Dine at Gehry's favorite, Bilbao-blue Perro Txiko or Goizeko Kabi, famed for its *patata rellena de centollo* (horseshoe crab-stuffed potato). On the sixth day, have another morning at the Guggenheim, this time concentrating on the permanent collection, before heading east to the elegant seaside resort town of **San Sebastián,** with a stop at the mountain town of Axpe for lunch at Mendi Goikoa. Or opt instead for a walk through Guetaria—known as *la cocina de Guipúzcoa,* (the kitchen of Guipúzcoa province) for its surfeit of good restaurants and taverns—and a feast of *besugo a la parrilla* (sea bream roasted over coals) at Iribar. Continue on to San Sebastián, then take a run up the wide, yellow beach at Zarauz. In San Sebastián get in an evening stroll along La Concha on the way into the La Parte Vieja for the *txikiteo* (wine and tapa grazing) and eventual dinner. On your seventh day, see **Pasajes de San Juan**—an extremely photogenic hamlet—and **Fuenterrabia,** the last fishing port before the French border, with a final night at the Parador El Emperador or the Caserío Artzu.

If You Have 8 to 12 Days

If you have close to two weeks, you can do the seven-day tour above and then continue on to Navarra, Pamplona, Vitoria, and La Rioja. On day eight drive up the Bidasoa River and down through Navarra from Irún to Pamplona, on the N121 road, stopping to explore the **Valle del Baztán** on the way. In **Pamplona,** stay at the Hotel Perla (Hemingway's room was No. 217) if you can. On day nine, swing down from Pamplona through **Vitoria** for a walk through its lovely old town before continuing to **Haro** for tapas in La Herradura and a night at Los Agustinos. On day 10 move over to **Laguardia** for a look through this fortified promontory and spend the night at the Posada Mayor Migel de Migueloa. Next day, drive up the **Najerilla Valley** to Anguiano and the Monasterio de Valvanera before, on the the 12th and final day, visiting **Logroño** and engineering one of the Iberian Peninsula's greatest txikiteos through Calle del Laurel. With a third week on your hands, consider a drive, allowing time to stop for hikes, across the Pyrenees.

FODOR'S CHOICE

No two people will agree on what makes a perfect vacation, but it's fun and helpful to know what others think. Here's a compendium drawn from the must-see lists of our regional experts. We hope you'll have a chance to experience some of these great memories-in-the-making yourself while visiting Spain. For detailed information about entries, refer to the appropriate chapters within this guidebook.

Places

★ **Beget, Catalan Pyrenees.** Above Camprodón off the road to France this tiny village has earned the reputation as the *més bufó* (cutest) in Catalonia. The 30 houses are each miniature and memorable stone devisings, as is the 12th-century Romanesque Sant Cristófol church.

★ **Cap de Creus, Costa Brava.** Famous as a New Year's Eve sunrise gathering point for revelers eager to be the first to greet the year's first sun, this is the Iberian Peninsula's easternmost point and the official end of the Pyrenees. The rocky promontory over the Mediterranean, with a lighthouse and an excellent restaurant, is a bracing walk through the rosemary and thyme-scented hiking trails from Cadaqués or El Port de la Selva.

★ **Laguardia, La Rioja.** Overlooking La Rioja from the Alava side of the Ebro, this walled promontory has a dense concentration of noble facades emblazoned with coats of arms, a good hideout for wine-tasting and a cozy sense being aboard some landlocked ocean liner.

★ **Mundaca, Vizcaya.** Overlooking the ochre sands at the mouth of the Ría de Guernica, this little fishing village has become Vizcaya's number one surfing destination, home of Europe's longest left-curling wave, as well as several cozy hotels and restaurants.

★ **Pasajes de San Juan, San Sebastián.** Walk to Pasajes de San Pedro and take the tiny launch over to Pasajes de San Juan, a picture-perfect hamlet, with its flower-covered balconies and three excellent restaurants at the edge of the channel leading up to Rentería, San Sebastián's freight port.

★ **San Juan de Gaztelugatxe, Vizcaya.** This tiny Romanesque chapel perched on a rock off the coast of Bakio in Vizcaya rises across a thread of land and 231 stairs from the mainland. Sir Francis Drake once "conquered" the little island, a magic spot alleged to fulfill wishes and cure insomnia.

★ **San Juan de Plan, Central Pyrenees.** Nestled under the 12,124-ft Posets peak in Aragón's Chistau Valley, this tiny village of 150 inhabitants has an excellent ethnological museum, a fine hotel and restaurant, and an ancient weaving industry and loom restored by the local women.

★ **Vallvidrera, Barcelona.** Overlooking Barcelona from the Collserola hills behind the city, Vallvidrera is a two-hour walk from Sarrià on the Carretera de les Aïgues or a 10-minute funicular ride from the Peu Funicular stop on the FFCC train line. On a clear day, views of Montserrat to the west and Barcelona below to the east are spectacular.

Churches

★ **Monestir de Pedralbes, Pedralbes, Barcelona.** With its triple-tiered cloister, gardens, convent kitchen, and dining room, and the Rubens, Tiepolos, and Zurbarans of the Thyssen-Bornemisza Collection, this one of Barcelona's best secrets.

★ **Sagrada Família, L'Eixample, Barcelona.** Antoni Gaudí's mad scheme rises ever higher above the city, his early 20th-century calculations now computer-confirmed. Predicted to be completed by mid-century, the structure is now taking shape rapidly as economic problems ease and technology improves.

★ **Sant Climent de Taüll, Boí Valley, Catalan Pyrenees.** The best of the 10 Romanesque churches of the Boí Valley in western Catalonia, this church has a slender six-story bell tower, which, along with the miniature rounded apses below, create a perfectly balanced and universally acclaimed feast for the eye.

★ **Sant Pau del Camp, El Raval, Barcelona.** This tiny pre-Romanesque gem dwarfed by the Raval raging around it is Barcelona's oldest church, originally outside the city walls, as the *del camp* (in the fields) suggests. The cloister is a cool and soothing oasis of peace.

⭐ **Santa Maria de la Seu, La Seu d'Urgell, Catalan Pyrenees.** The intimate, east-facing rose window may be small, but the light of the Pyrenees makes the colors come startlingly alive. The 50 sculpted capitals of the cloisters are filled with ribald humor and satire.

⭐ **Santa Maria del Mar, Barrio de la Ribera, Barcelona.** The best 14th-century Mediterranean Gothic church of all, "the seafarers' basilica" is noted for its clean lines and upsweeping elegance—actually, the result of a stonemason's design and the 1936 anticlerical holocaust that burned out 500 years of choir stalls and clutter.

⭐ **Santa María la Real, Nájera, La Rioja.** One of the most graceful churches in La Rioja, Najera's 11th-century Monasterio de Santa María la Real is distinguished for its Plateresque Claustro de los Caballeros (Nobleman's Cloister), its choir stalls, and choir loft.

Dining

⭐ **Botafumeiro, Gràcia, Barcelona.** The best Galician restaurant in Barcelona, this features a curving wooden bar in the front room where you can cruise around the menu with half rations of anything from *bellota* (acorn-fed Iberian pig) to *kokotxas de bacalao* (cod jaw) is the best spot for people-watching and economy alike. *$$$$*

⭐ **Drolma, L'Eixample, Barcelona.** Fermín Puig has jumped to the forefront of Barcelona's gourmet scene after waiting 20 years for the moment to make his move. Every ingredient and each detail is carefully worked out, while the cuisine is inventive, traditional, and always, in the final analysis, food. Try the *foie gras a la ceniza amb ceps* (foie gras cooked in tinfoil over coals with wild mushrooms)—a childhood memory from Fermin's grandmother. *$$$$*

⭐ **El Bullí, Roses, Costa Brava.** Whether you describe him as a mad scientist, a poet, or a Dalí of the kitchen, superchef Ferrán Adrià makes your palate his playground with concepts like *escuma de fum* (foam of smoke)—no joke—and a bevy of other dazzling dishes. All in all, this is not only Spain's top restaurant but one of Europe's hottest culinary shrines. Anyone for chocolate caramel tuiles garnished with pink peppercorns? *$$$$*

⭐ **Guria, Bilbao.** Genaro Pildain is the dean of Bilbao chefs, a self-described culinary perfectionist with classical tastes. Everything that comes out of Guria's kitchen is impeccable, from *alubias* (beans) to potato and leek soup to codfish. *$$$$*

⭐ **La Torre del Remei, Bolvir (Puigcerdà), Catalan Pyrenees.** The top gourmet solution in the Pyrenees, José Maria and Lola Boix have put together a superb dining experience in this graceful estate near Puigcerdà. The cuisine defies categorization: French, Catalan, international? It doesn't matter: it's exquisite. *$$$$*

⭐ **Can Majó, Barceloneta, Barcelona.** ⭐ The top seafood place nearest the beach in Barceloneta, this is the spot to sit under a full moon between early June and early October. The *calderosa de bogavante,* a bouillabaisse-paella hybrid, with one of the house Albariño white wines from Galicia adds up to an unbeatable combination. *$$$–$$$$*

⭐ **Casa Leopoldo, El Raval, Barcelona.** Rosa Gil's famous place at the edge of the darkest Raval continues to be one of Barcelona's favorite dining spots. Always booming with internationals and locals having a hilariously good time, this place is first-rate and the ambience relaxed. *$$$*

⭐ **Casa Cámara, Pasajes de San Juan (Donibane), San Sebastián.** The point here is to go to Pasajes de San Juan, preferably on foot from San Sebastian along the well-marked trail from the end of the Zurriola beach. Fish soup and *Besugo* (sea bream) is always excellent. *$$*

⭐ **Cal Pep, Barrio de la Ribera, Barcelona.** Barcelona's premier tapas joint, Pep takes good care of anyone who comes through the door. The counter is the place to be and very much worth waiting for—only an arm's reach from the flames, grill, and hot olive oil cooking what you are about to devour. *$–$$*

Lodging

⭐ **Claris, Eixample, Barcelona.** Widely considered Barcelona's best hotel, the Claris combines antique pieces of furniture with contemporary lines and designs in an original way. Near the center of the Eixample, the hotel offers taste, comfort, and impeccable service as well as a rooftop pool and a fine-tuned Japanese water-garden. *$$$$*

⭐ **Parador El Emperador, Fuenterrabía, Guipúzcoa.** This elegant 10th-century bastion overlooking the estuary of the Bidasoa river border with France has lovely views out to sea and over to Hendaye. Filled with chivalric armor and coats of arms, it's not difficult to imagine Carlos V, who launched the Spanish Empire to its apogee in the 16th century, arriving with his entourage. The rooms are ample arrangements of wood and stone. *$$$$*

⭐ **Mendigoikoa, Axpe, Vizcaya.** This lovely farmhouse, restaurant and inn at the foot of Amboto—Vizcaya's magic mountain—overlooks the rolling green hills of the Atxondo valley and the village of Axpe. A favorite of national leaders and luminaries from the king and queen of Spain to the Basque *lehendakari* (president), every stone and wood beam in this 400 year old *caserío* (farmhouse) is a work of art. *$$$–$$$$*

⭐ **Carleton, Ensanche, Bilbao.** There may be more luxurious accommodations in Bilbao, but for sheer old-world ambience and a sense of what the town is all about, the Carleton is peerless. Walking distance from everything in town, this historic building has hosted Orson Welles, Ava Gardner, Ernest Hemingway, and the Basque Government during the ill-fated Second Spanish Republic overthrown by Franco in 1936–39. *$$$*

⭐ **Hostería del Monasterio de San Millán, San Millán de la Cogolla, La Rioja.** Nestled in the lower monastery, El Monasterio de Yuso—where the 13th Spanish poet Gonzalo de Berceo first wrote in *roman paladino,* the early Latin dialect that became modern Spanish—this site is as comfortable and esthetically perfect as it is historic. *$$$*

⭐ **Posada Mayor de Migueloa, Laguardia, Rioja Alavesa.** The best of Laguardia's hotels and restaurants, this delicious stone and wood-beam masterpiece has food to match, all accompanied by the full-bodied local wines of La Rioja Alavesa. The rooms are cozy nests under heavy wood beams. *$$–$$$*

Natural Resources

⭐ **Alberes Range, Girona, Catalan Pyrenees.** Northern Catalonia's Alberes range—the easternmost stretch of the Pyrenees—coasts down a spectacular grassy crest from the 4,112-ft Puig Neulós peak to the 3,237-ft Sallefort promontory two hours above sea level at Banyuls sur Mer.

⭐ **Benasque, Huesca, Central Pyrenees.** Jumping-off point for the climb to the 11,233-ft Aneto, highest peak in the Pyrenees, the town of Benasque can also pack you off to one of the greatest natural hydraulic phenomena in the Pyrenees at the disappearing river of Aiguallits or west up the pristine Estós valley toward the 11,124 ft Posets peak.

⭐ **Najerilla, La Rioja.** The Najerilla River draining La Rioja's Sierra de la Demanda runs 72 km (45 mi) from the upper Najerilla valley and the Sierra de San Lorenzo to join the Ebro at Torremontalbo. One of Europe's best limestone-based chalk streams, the Najerilla is a world-class trout river.

⭐ **Ordesa, Huesca, Central Pyrenees.** The Parque Nacional de Ordesa y Monte Perdido is Spain's Grand Canyon. Start from Torla and walk up the Arazas River into the park to the Refugio de Goriz and on to Brèche de Roland and the Serradets refuge in France, the most spectacular and dramatic three-day hike in the Pyrenees.

⭐ **Parque Nacional de Aigüestortes, Lleida, Catalan Pyrenees.** The Parque Nacional de Aigüestortes i Estany de Sant Maurici is a highland aquatic marvel honeycombed with Pyrenean tarns, lakes, and streams on the high ground between the Noguera Pallaresa and Noguera Ribagorçana valleys, some of the Pyrenees' best terrain.

FESTIVALS AND SEASONAL EVENTS

Fiestas throughout Spain are all but infinite in number and nature, with all manner of bizarre practices ranging from wild bulls stampeding through the streets to caballeros hanging from dead geese suspended over water. Most of northern Spain's festivals, fiestas, and annual highlights revolve around the liturgical calendar, with Christmas and Easter logically in the forefront. Then again, certain obscure saints (San Fermín comes to mind) have become associated with massive international blowouts, while others—witness Haro's annual June 29 *batalla del vino* (Wine Battle)—were originally associated with pagan rites marking the solstice, with the local saints subsequently superimposed during the Christian era.

it's especially wild in Sitges and in Bielsa the holiday is a spectacular display of *trangas*: ram-horned, potato-toothed, black-faced, blood-soaked monsters.

➤ MARCH: **Alimentaria, Barcelona.** Barcelona's big convention show for food and gourmet novelties, this is a biennial event held at the main Barcelona convention venue, the Fira de Barcelona (☎ 93/233–2000; 🏷️).

SPRING

➤ LATE APRIL: **La Diada de Sant Jordi, Barcelona.** Held on St. George's Day, April 23rd, this delightful Barcelona occasion celebrates the Rose Festival and International Book Day on the anniversary of the deaths of both Cervantes and Shakespeare in 1616.

WINTER

➤ LATE DECEMBER: **Día de San Sebastián, San Sebastián.** This holiday celebrates the city's patron saint on January 20th with the famous *tamborradas*—drum processions of what seems to be the entire population dressed in either soldiers' or chefs' attire and pounding drums and wooden percussion instruments called *barriles* with sticks.

➤ MID-FEBRUARY: **Carnaval.** This moveable feast precedes Lent; while celebrated in Barcelona,

SUMMER

➤ THURSDAY BEFORE EASTER: **Danza de la Muerte, Verges.** This small town near Girona has become known for its macabre Dance of Death, held on Maundy Thursday to commemorate and ward off the medieval decimation of the populace by the bubonic plague; dancers dressed in black with skeletons painted on their tights seem to hover in midair as

they dance eerily through the streets.

➤ LATE JUNE: **La Verbena de Sant Joan.** In the Pyrenees, Mediterranean coast especially, but also in La Rioja and parts of the Basque Country, this fête is held to celebrate Midsummer's Eve, June 24th, when bonfires extend the light of the year's longest day until dawn.

➤ LATE JUNE: **Fiesta Mayor, Jaca.** Falling on June 25th and in honor of Santa Orosia, this is a series of processions and *romerías* (festive pilgrimages) that last for a week beginning on the 23rd; the first Friday in May is Jaca's other typical fiesta, celebrating victory over the Moors with parades of *moros y cristianos* and gatherings at the hermitage on the edge of town.

➤ LATE JUNE: **Alarde de Irún, Irún.** Twenty kilometers (12 miles) northeast of San Sebastián, this town celebrates the 1522 victory over its French neighbors across the Bidasoa estuary every June 30th; a.k.a Alarde de San Marcial, the celebration includes no fewer than 18 companies, some 3,000 men, who assemble uniformed, armed, and wearing red *boinas* (berets) in Plaza de San Juan at dawn to await the "General's" command to fire their weapons and march to the San Marcial chapel, all amid abundantly flowing txakolí and high comedy.

➤ LATE JUNE: **Fiestas de Sant Joan, Isil.** This holiday is one of the more lively Pyrenean festivities, celebrated in this Noguera Pallaresa valley village by young men bearing torches—*els fallaires*; they descend from the surrounding peaks on the June 23rd midsummer's eve to be received by the young women who reward their bravery with wine before making a bonfire and dancing the sardana.

➤ LATE JUNE: **Fiestas de San Juan, Laguardia.** This fiesta begins on June 23rd and continues until the Fiesta de San Pedro on the 29th; in between, bulls (or, to be exact, wild cows) are run through the streets in a local version of Pamplona's famous event and the whole town dances wildly for days.

➤ LATE JUNE: **Batalla del Vino, Haro.** This Wine Battle falls suspiciously close to the solstice, though the saint officially responsible for the June 29rd wine waterfight is San Felices de Bilibio, tutor of San Millán del Cogollo, and Sts. Peter and Paul, whose fiestas begin and end the weeklong celebration; Haro's other great festive event is the September 8th celebration of La Virgen de la Vega.

➤ LATE JUNE–EARLY JULY: **Fiestas de San Marcial, Benasque.** Held between June 29th and July 2nd, these five days of midsummer revelry feature the traditional *Bal de Benas,* an ancient folklorical dance practiced and prepared by the young men of this Pyrenean town.

➤ EARLY JULY: **Moda Barcelona, Barcelona.** Barcelona's big blow-out for the fashion world is held twice yearly—July 1st to 15th and February 1st to 15th—in the Salón

Gaudí of the convention center, the Fira de Barcelona (☎ 93/233–2000; ✆).

➤ MID-JULY: **Sanfermines, Pamplona.** Known worldwide since the 1926 publication of Hemingway's first novel, *The Sun Also Rises,* Pamplona's legendary "Running of the Bulls" begins with daily *encierros* (enclosings, somewhat ironically meaning releasing or running of bulls through the streets in order to enclose them under the bullring), and then moves on to *corridas* (the bullfights themselves); with 24-hour hilarity reigning, this a wonderfully loony fiesta if you're in the right mood (incidentally, Jake Barnes and his buddies in *The Sun Also Rises* didn't really get it, and Hemingway never even ran with the bulls). The holiday runs July 6–15.

➤ MID-JULY: **Sanfermines, Lesaka.** In this Pyrenean village north of Pamplona, the Fiestas de San Fermín is celebrated every July 7, when *dantzaris* (dancers) leap along the parapets along the river Onín that separates the town's two neighborhoods. Bulls are released in the central square, and the flavor of this mini–San Fermín is probably closer to that of the pre-1926 Pamplona than the present debacle in the big city. The entire holiday is celebrated July 6–15.

➤ MID-JULY: **Tributo de las Tres Vacas, Roncal Valley.** This "Tribute of the Three Cows" has been celebrated every July 13 since 1375 in honor of a treaty settling high pasture and passage rights that concluded years of bloody

conflict between the French Barétous and the Spanish Roncal valleys.

➤ LATE JULY: **Danza de los Zancos, Anguiano.** On July 22, in this tiny La Rioja town, the "Dance of the Stilts" brings thousands to Anguiano to watch men on stilts hurtle down through the village's steep stone streets into the arms of the townspeople.

➤ EARLY AUGUST: **La Virgen Blanca, Vitoria.** This town celebrates this fiesta every August 4th with a week of revelry initiated by a curious ritual in which an umbrella-carrying dummy called Celedón is lowered from the church to a neighboring house from which an identically dressed man emerges, whereupon everyone lights up a cigar and the party begins.

➤ EARLY AUGUST: **Fiestas de San Lorenzo, Huesca.** Huesca's patron saint, San Lorenzo, is venerated every August 1st through 9th during the Fiestas de San Lorenzo, another San Fermín–like blowout with more authentic local tradition; the three or four different dances to the local saint are odd and interesting in their idiosyncratic, different way (green is the reigning color for sash and neckerchief, commemorative of *albahaca,* or basil, Huesca's symbolic herb).

➤ EARLY AUGUST: **Fiestas de Guetaria,** Guertaria's annual fiestas are unleashed the first week of August, a charming small-town affair with an extraordinary sense of well-being and hilarity; every fourth year (the next will be in 2003) the fiesta commemorates the return of Juan Sebastián Elcano from his circumnavagation of the globe with a moving pageant featuring a procession of exhausted and weather-beaten sailors arriving from the sea and staggering up from the port.

➤ LATE AUGUST: **Semana Grande, Bilbao and San Sebastián.** Bilbao's biggest fiesta is this "Grand Week," or Aste Nagusia, held during the third week of August; while it's famous for bullfights featuring mammoth bulls, true tests of nerve, as Basques and especially *bilbainos* would have it, there are also culinary contests and processions of "giants." Another Semana Grande is held in San Sebastián and falls a few days on either side of the August 15th celebration of La Virgen de la Asunción—a week of outdoor concerts, processions, and general animation.

AUTUMN

➤ SEPTEMBER: **Euskal Jayak, San Sebastián.** San Sebastián's best fiestas are the Euskal Jayak ("Basque Fiestas", as in jai-alai, translated as *fiesta alegre*, or joyous fiesta), a week

of Basque rural sports such as wood chopping and stone lifting that begin with cider tasting on the first Saturday in September, the eve of the first of two *trainera* (whaleboat) races held on the first two Sundays of September.

➤ MID-SEPTEMBER: **Fiesta de la Virgen de Mijaran, Vielha.** The annual September 7th to 11th celebration of the fiesta of La Virgen de Mijaran is a chance to let loose with the locals in this Haute Garonne, Atlantic-oriented, and drained valley. Folklorical costumes, dances, and processions keep the full five-day affair festive.

➤ LATE SEPTEMBER: **Las Fiestas de la Mercé, Barcelona.** This is one of Barcelona's main fiestas and is held in honor of the city's patron saint, Our Lady of Mercy.

➤ LATE SEPTEMBER: **Film Festival, San Sebastián.** San Sebastián's annual Film Festival is held during the last 10 days of September and remains Spain's most glamorous film festival.

➤ LATE SEPTEMBER: **Fiesta de la Vendimia, Logroño.** Logroño's most important fiesta celebrates the grape harvest and coincides with the September 21st feast of San Mateo; from the September 20th to 26th,

Logroño is even more of a celebration than it normally is anyway—the main event is the blessing of the first *mosto* (must, unfermented grape juice) by La Rioja's patron saint La Virgen de la Valvanera in the city's central Plaza del Espolón (also note Logroño's second fiesta: the feast of San Bernabé, celebrated June 9–12, and marking the Día de La Rioja—the survival of a 1521 siege by French troops, with wine, bread, and fish passed around to commemorate the way the city outlasted the siege.

➤ OCTOBER: **Día del Pilar, Zaragoza.** Every October 12th, Zaragosa honors the city's and Spain's patron saint, La Virgen del Pilar (Our Lady of the Pillar), affectionately dubbed La Pilarica; processions of giants and *cabezudos* (big heads) and, especially, a gigantic floral offering to the Virgin are the main events, while *la jota*, the typical dance of Aragón, is performed all over town for the full 7- to 10-day day fiesta.

➤ LATE NOV.–EARLY DEC.: **Salón Náutico, Barcelona.** Barcelona's popular boat show is an annual event and attracts major crowds to the city's big convention venue, the Fira de Barcelona (☎ 93/233–2000; ✆).

2 BARCELONA

Capital of Catalonia, Barcelona has long been dubbed "La Gran Encisera"—the Great Enchantress. Little wonder: With its steamy seaport, the medieval romance of its Gothic Quarter, and a feast of Catalan Art Nouveau buildings—including the great creations of Antonio Gaudí—Barcelona remains one of the most eye-knocking cities in Europe. A cradle of art, architecture, and design—the indelible marks left by Picasso, Miró, and Dalí are never far away—this Mediterranean metropolis is now generating a renaissance of Catalan culture. Much better than flawless, Barcelona remains unforgettably exciting, relentlessly alive.

By George
Semler

THE THRONGING RAMBLA, THE REVERBERATION OF A GUITAR in the silence of the medieval Gothic Quarter, riotous ceramic color splashed across Moderniste facades, waves breaking over a sandy beach: one way or another, though always sensually, Barcelona will find a way to grip your heart. The Catalonian capital is boiling into the new millennium in the throes of a cultural and industrial rebirth only comparable to the late 19th-century *Renaixença* that filled the city with flamboyant Modernismo architecture. Wedged tightly along the Mediterranean coast between the forested Collserola hills and Europe's busiest seaport, Barcelona has now catapulted to the rank of Spain's most visited city, a 2,000-year-old master of the legerdemain of perpetual novelty.

First of all a visual feast, Barcelona is a city that means color: the stained-glass glow of the Barri Gòtic; the flamboyant, even theatrical, mosaic-encrusted monuments of Antonio Gaudí; Picasso's "blue period" paintings on view in the Barcelona museum dedicated to the 20th century's most famous artist; Miró's now universal blue and crimson shooting stars. Then, of course, there is the physical setting of the city, crouched cat-like between Montjuïc and Tibidabo, between the verdant Collserola hills and the 4,000 acre harbor. Obsessed with playful and innovative interpretations of everything from painting to theater to urban design and development, Barcelona consistently surprises itself in its constant quest for emotion and self-renewal: an improvisational fling always on the brink of something new.

Indeed, Barcelona never sleeps. So palpably passionate you can *feel* the city vibrating around you, Barcelona is wired with a vitality that is never intimidating. Just about the time you begin to drop into an ethylic coma at two in the morning, *barcelonins* are just setting out as the city's night scene begins to kick in for real. Relentlessly alive, creative, acquisitive, and playful in about equal doses, Barcelona never stops. No matter which outside governmental regime pulled the strings in the past, Catalans just kept working, scheming, playing, and building. Now, with its recent past as provincial Madrid outpost well behind, Barcelona is charging into the future with more creativity and raw energy than ever.

Barcelona's latest boom mode began on October 17, 1987, when Juan Antonio Samaranch, president of the International Olympic Committee, announced that his native city had been chosen to host the 1992 Olympics. After repeated attempts and near misses in 1924 and 1936, this single masterstroke allowed Spain's so-called "second city" to throw off the shadow of Madrid and the 40-year "internal exile" of the Franco regime and resume its rightful place as one of Europe's most dynamic destinations. Not only did the Catalan administration lavish untold zillions in subsidies from the Spanish government for the Olympics, they then used the Games as a platform to broadcast the news about Catalonia's culture and national identity from one end of the universe to the other. Spain who? Calling Barcelona a second city of anyplace is playing with fire; modern Spain has always been fundamentally bicephalous, even though official figures always counted Madrid's suburbs, but not Barcelona's, in order to feed the illusion that the Catalan capital was little more than another minor provincial port.

More Mediterranean than Spanish, historically more akin to Marseille or Milan than Madrid, Barcelona has always been ambitious, decidedly modern (even in the 2nd century), and quick to accept the most recent innovations. Its democratic form of government harks back to the so-called Usatges Laws, which were instituted by Ramon Berenguer

I in the 11th century and amounted to a constitution. This code of privileges represented one of the earliest known examples of democratic rule, while Barcelona's Consell de Cent (Council of 100), constituted in 1274, was Europe's first parliament and is the true cradle of western democracy. More recently, the city's electric light system, public gas system, and telephone exchange were among the first in the world. The center of an important sea-faring commercial empire with colonies spread around the Mediterranean as far away as Athens when Madrid was still a Moorish outpost marooned on the arid Castilian steppe, Barcelona traditionally absorbed new ideas and styles first. Whether it was the Moors who brought navigational tools, philosophers and revolutionaries from nearby France spreading the ideals of the French Revolution, or artists like Picasso and Dalí who bloomed in the city's air of freedom and individualism, Barcelona has always been a law unto itself.

Artistically Speaking

In fact, this independent and individual outlook has been spectacularly reflected in the city's feast of art and architecture, which covers 2,000 years of history from classical Roman, Romanesque, Gothic, Renaissance and Baroque, Neoclassical, and Moderniste (Catalan Art Nouveau) to the rationalist, minimalist, and Postmodern solutions of Richard Meier, Santiago Calatrava, and Rafael Moneo. There's even a gilt-scaled Frank Gehry fish presiding over the Olympic Port, Barcelona's own tiny fragment of Bilbao's Guggenheim, Gehry's masterwork (Bilbao has a puppy; Barcelona, a minnow).

Indeed, if Madrid is about paintings (the Prado Museum's staggering collection of canvases is just one of the many treasures of the Spanish capital), Barcelona is about architecture, mainly Antonio Gaudí (1852–1926), whose buildings are the most startling statements of Modernisme—the Spanish, and mainly Catalan, chapter of the late-19th-century Art Nouveau movement. Other leading Moderniste architects include Lluís Domènech i Muntaner and Josep Puig i Cadafalch. Painters Joan Miró (1893–1983), Salvador Dalí (1904–89), and Antoni Tàpies (born 1923) are also strongly identified with Barcelona. Pablo Picasso spent his formative years here—the city's poorer quarters inspired his great paintings of acrobats and saltimbanques—and one of the city's treasures is a museum devoted to his works.

If there are innumerable design and architectural opportunities in Barcelona, the most famous area is L'Eixample—"The Widening"—a vast post-1860 urban development composed of a grid system of square city blocks. Developed during a moment of economic prosperity and nationalistic fervor, Barcelona's Eixample claimed as its own the artistic movement called Art Nouveau in France, Modern Style in England, Sezessionstil in Austria, Jugendstil in Germany, Liberty or Floreale in Italy, and Modernisme in Spain. Scanning all of these different terms, in fact, provides a good overview of what Art Nouveau, as it has come to be most widely known, is all about: new, modern (in the late 19th century), playful, flowery, revolutionary, and free. In fact, Art Nouveau was a reaction to the misery and massification brought about by technology and the industrial revolution, a "Greening" of Europe a century before the "Greening of America" movement popular in the '60s in the United States. Art Nouveau is, with a doubt, what most characterizes Barcelona: whereas many European cities have excellent Roman and medieval quarters, only Barcelona has 50 monumental buildings as well as more than 250 private houses with Art Nouveau facades, interiors, or other elements, with with the works of Gaudí providing virtually a separate chapter of its own.

As a backdrop to the city's ample Moderniste fleet, Barcelona's Roman and medieval legacy is equally as interesting and extensive. The famous Rambla—the promenade that Federico García Lorca called the only street in the world that he wished would never end—separates the Gothic Quarter and its Roman core from the Raval, where the medieval hospital, the shipyards, and Sant Pau del Camp, Barcelona's oldest church, are the main attractions, along with Richard Meier's modern MACBA (Museu d'Art Contemporani de Barcelona) and the CCCB (Centre de Cultura Contemporanea de Barcelona) next door.

Like a kaleidoscope, then, Barcelona is ever-changing. The medieval intimacy of the Gothic Quarter balances the grace and distinction of the wide boulevards in the Moderniste Eixample, while Roman walls and columns play counterpoint to sleek new 21st-century structures in the Raval or the Olympic Port. A visit to Gaudí's Temple of the Sagrada Família followed by a quick hop over to the Mediterranean Gothic gem Santa Maria del Mar will leave your senses reeling with the gap between Catalan Art Nouveau ornamentation and the early Gothic's classical economy and elegance. Even more dramatically, proceed from Domènech i Montaner's Moderniste showstopper, the Palau de la Música, to Mies van der Rohe's minimalist masterpiece, the Barcelona Pavilion: from more and more to less and less.

Catalan First, Spanish Second

Through a tumultuous history of political ups and downs, prosperity never abandoned Barcelona, as it continued to generate energy and creativity no matter which power attempted to impose authority from afar: Romans, Visigoths, Charlemagne, Moors, the Crown of Aragón, Felipe V, Napoléon, or Franco. It never mattered: in Barcelona life and commerce continued to forge ahead. The city's history, synonymous with Catalonia's, hinges on four key dates: the 801 Frankish conquest by Charlemagne that wrested Catalonia away from the Moorish empire on the Iberian Peninsula, the 988 independence from the Franks, the 1137 alliance through marriage with Aragón, and the 1474 marriage alliance of Aragón with the Castilian realms of Leon and Castile.

The Roman Empire annexed the city built by the Iberian tribe known as the Laietans and established, in 133 BC, a colony called Colonia Favencia Julia Augusta Paterna Barcino, which, somewhat liberally translated from the Latin, means "Favored Colony of Julius Augustus the Father of Whom was Barca." Hamilcar Barca, the great Carthaginian general, father of Hannibal, had founded the city that would someday bear his name just after the First Punic War, in 237 BC. After Rome's 4th-century decline and the beginning of its disintegration, Barcelona enjoyed one of its early golden ages as the Visigothic capital under the rule of Ataulf and the Roman Empress of the West, Galla Placidia (388–450), daughter of Theodosius I and one of the most influential and fascinating women of early European history. Ataulf, assassinated in Barcelona in 415, was succeeded by Visigothic rulers who moved their capital to Toledo, leaving Barcelona to a secondary role through the 6th and 7th centuries. The Moors invaded in the 8th century; and in 801, in what was to be a decisive moment in Catalonia's and Barcelona's history, the Franks under Charlemagne captured the city and made it a buffer zone at the edge of Al Andalus, the Moors' empire on the Iberian Peninsula. Moorish rule extended to the Garraf Massif just south of Barcelona, while Catalonia became the Marca Hispanica (Spanish March or, really, "edge") of the Frankish empire.

Over the next two centuries the Catalonian counties, ruled by counts originally appointed by the Franks, gained increasing autonomy until

985, when the Franks failed to reinforce their Catalonian counties against a Moorish attack. As of 988 Catalonia declared itself an independent federation of counties with Barcelona as its capital. The marriage, in 1137, of Sovereign Count Ramon Berenguer IV to Petronella, daughter of King Ramiro II of Aragón, united Catalonia through marriage with the House of Aragón. The Crown of Aragón made Barcelona its capital and controlled the Mediterranean until the 15th century. Yet another marriage, that of Ferdinand II of Aragón and Isabella of Castile (who was also queen of León) in 1474, brought Aragón and, as a result, Catalonia as well into a united Spain. As the capital of Aragón's Mediterranean empire, Barcelona had grown in importance between the 12th and the 14th centuries and only began to falter when maritime emphasis shifted to the Atlantic after 1492.

Despite the establishment of Madrid as the seat of Spain's Royal Court in 1562, Catalonia continued to enjoy autonomous rights and privileges until 1714, when, in reprisal for having backed the Austrian Habsburg pretender to the Spanish throne during the War of the Spanish Succession (1700–1714), all institutions and expressions of Catalan identity were suppressed by the triumphant Felip V of the French Bourbon dynasty. Not until the mid-19th century would Barcelona's industrial growth bring about a *Renaixença* (renaissance) of nationalism and a cultural flowering that recalled Catalonia's former opulence.

Catalan nationalism and Barcelona's power and prosperity continued to gain strength in the early 20th century. After the abdication of Alfonso XIII and the establishment of the Spanish Republic in 1931, Catalonia, with Barcelona leading the way at full throttle, enjoyed a high degree of autonomy and cultural freedom. Once again backing a losing cause, Barcelona was a Republican stronghold and a hotbed of antifascist sentiment and Catalan nationalism during the Spanish civil war, with the result that, when, in the phrasing of Franco critics, "peace broke out," the Catalan language and identity were once again brutally suppressed by such means as book burning, the renaming of streets and towns, and the banning of the Catalan language in schools and in the media. This repression or, as some historians termed it, "internal exile" of Catalonia's identity lasted until Franco's death in 1975, at which point it became evident that the Catalans had once again, more stubbornly than ever, managed to keep their language and culture alive despite El Caudillo's unity-oriented *Movimiento Nacional*. Although there are varying degrees of Catalonian nationalism now in play ranging from radical Terra Lliure *independentists* (pro-independence militants) to arch-conservative Spain-firsters, the vast majority of today's Catalans think of themselves as Catalans first and Spanish citizens, if at all, second.

Catalonian home rule was granted after Franco's death in 1975, and Catalonia's parliament, the ancient Generalitat, was reinstated in 1980. Catalan is now Barcelona's co-official language, along with Castilian Spanish, and is eagerly promoted through free classes funded by the Generalitat. Street names are signposted in Catalan, and newspapers, radio stations, and a TV channel publish and broadcast in Catalan. The circular Catalan *sardana* is danced regularly all over town. The triumphant culmination of this rebirth was, of course, the staging of the Olympics in 1992—stadiums and pools were renovated, new harborside promenades created, and an entire set of train tracks moved to make way for the Olympic Village. Not content with this onetime project, Barcelona's last two mayors have presided over an urban renewal and the creation of postmodern structures that have made the city a perennial field trip for architecture students.

When, in a recent interview, a foreign economist lamented Barcelona's Catalan nationalism, observing that speaking Catalan "certainly doesn't broaden Catalonia's economic base," he was reminded that the local economy seems about as healthy as it needs to be and that "the Catalan language is about our cultural identity, not about economics." Critics, including prize–winning novelist and onetime Barcelona resident Mario Vargas Llosa, have charged that today's Barcelona, considered Spain's most cosmopolitan city when the Franco regime was asphyxiating Madrid and the rest of the country, has become more provincial, more concerned with its own identity than with reaching out to the world beyond. While this may be true to some degree, other voices counter that Barcelona, while developing and reinforcing its Catalan identity, has lost little if any of its cosmopolitan vocation.

Either way, the fact remains that, despite Catalan-only captions in certain museums, Barcelona is thriving, vibrant with tourism, conventions, and visitors representing a wide range of interests. As art critic and Barcelona historian Robert Hughes put it in his Fiestas de la Mercé 2000 inaugural speech, "Culture, always self-critical, in perpetual debate with itself, is not the butter on the bread of life, but the bread itself, and in Barcelona this has always been recognized as a fact."

Barcelona, in the end, is a feast for all the senses, though perhaps mainly the visual one. Not far behind are the pleasures of the palate, while Orphic delights are prospering as never before. The air temperature is almost always about right, more and more streets are pedestrianized, tavern after tavern burrows elegantly into medieval walls, and every now and then the fragrance of the sea in the port or in Barceloneta reminds you that this is, after all, a giant seaport and beach city with an ancient Mediterranean tradition that is, at the outset of its third millennium, flourishing—and seducing visitors, as it has for centuries.

Pleasures and Pastimes

Dining

The post-Franco renaissance of Catalan culture brought with it an important renewal of Catalan cuisine. A city where not so long ago the best policy was to look for Italian or French food, or the odd faux-Castilian roast, is now filled with exciting restaurants celebrating local produce from the sea as well as from inland and upland areas. Catalans are great lovers of fish, vegetables, rabbit, duck, lamb, game, and natural ingredients from the Pyrenees or the Mediterranean. The *mar i muntanya* (sea and mountain—that is, surf and turf), a recipe combining seafood with inland or highland products, is a standard specialty on most menus. The influence of nearby France seems to ensure finesse, while Iberian ebullience discourages pretense. The now-fashionable Mediterranean diet featuring "good" (anticholesterol) virgin olive oil, seafood, fibrous vegetables, onions, garlic, and red wine is nowhere better exemplified than in Catalonia. Catalan cuisine is wholesome and served in hearty portions. Spicy sauces are more prevalent here than elsewhere in Spain; you'll find plenty of *allioli*, for example—pure garlic and virgin olive oil (nothing else)—beaten to a (deceptively) mayonnaise-like consistency and used to accompany a wide variety of dishes, from rabbit to lamb to potatoes and vegetables. *Romescu* (olive oil, garlic, almonds, and red pepper) is another standard sauce used notably on *calçots,* the long-stemmed spring onions consumed especially in late winter and early spring. Typical entrées include *habas a la catalana* (a spicy broad-bean stew), *escudella* (a thick vegetable and sausage stew with pasta and, often, chicken added), and *espinacas a la catalana* (spinach cooked with oil, garlic, pine nuts, raisins, and bits of bacon). Bread is often doused with olive oil and spread with tomato to make *pa amb tomaquet,* delicious on its own or as an accompaniment to nearly anything. Read Colman Andrews's classic *Catalan Cuisine—Europe's Last Culinary Secret,* which is found on nearly every Catalan gourmet's nightstand, for a more detailed rundown of the products and practices of Catalan chefs.

Catalan wines from the nearby Penedès region, especially the local *méthode champenoise* (sparkling white wine known in Catalonia as *cava*) more than adequately accompany all regional cuisine, and the new wave of modern, artisanal wine makers in the Priorat, Ampurdan, and Costers del Segre regions are producing exciting alternatives.

Lodging

There are two basic lodging choices here: the Gothic Quarter and the Eixample (the late-19th-century "widening"). Two secondary options are the Port or upper Barcelona. Each choice has its advantages. The port (basically the Hotel Arts) offers splendid views over the Mediterranean and proof positive that you are indeed in a maritime city. The Gothic Quarter places you just a few minutes' walk from nearly everything you need to see and do in the old part of town. The Eixample surrounds you with Art Nouveau architecture and is halfway from uptown attractions such as Parc Güell and Gaudí's Sagrada Família and downtown sights such as the Palau de la Música and the Picasso Museum. Upper Barcelona offers better air, cooler temperatures in summer, and a sense of refuge, but it's a $10 taxi ride home after the Sarrià train (FFCC de la Generalitat) closes shortly before midnight. Bargains are scarce in Spain these days, but hotels will negotiate room rates if they're not full. Business travelers may get a 20%–40% break. Faxing for reservations may also get you a better rate. Ask about weekend rates, which are often half price.

Modernisme

More than any other city in the world, Barcelona is filled with buildings and other works of the late-19th-century artistic and architectural movement known as Art Nouveau in France, Modernismo in the rest of Spain, and modernism in English-speaking countries. The curved line replaced the straight line; flowers and fruits and wild mushrooms were sculpted into facades. Colored facades became fashionable, along with undulating roofs and flora and fauna of all sorts. The pragmatic gave way to ornamental profusion. Barcelona's Palau de la Música Catalana by Lluís Domènech i Montaner, widely considered the flagship of the movement, is a stunning compendium of Art Nouveau resources and techniques ranging from acid-etched glass to stained glass, polychrome ceramic ornamentation, carved wooden arches, and a plethora of sculptures scattered into any open space available on the facade or inside the music hall itself. Gaudí has become, of course, the most famous of the Moderniste architects, but his personal style, as evidenced in the intensely naturalistic treatments of La Pedrera and the Sagrada Família, his last two buildings, took off in a direction all his own. Modernisme is everywhere in Barcelona, not only because it tapped into the playfulness of the Catalan artistic impulse (as evidenced in the works of Picasso, Miró, Dalí, and others) but because it coincided with Barcelona's late-19th-century industrial prosperity and an upsurge of nationalistic sentiment.

Museums

The Museu Picasso is probably Barcelona's best-known museum, but bear in mind that the city has far superior permanent collections of art, the finest of which is the Romanesque exhibit at the Palau Nacional on Montjuïc. Other lesser-known gems are the Thyssen-Bornemisza Collection at the Monestir de Pedralbes, above Sarrià, filled with works by, among others, Canaletto, Tintoretto, Tiépolo, Rubens, Zurbarán; and the works of Catalan impressionists such as Nonell, Casas, and Russinyol at the Museu d'Art Modern in the Ciutadella. The Fundació "la Caixa," at Passeig de Sant Joan 108, frequently offers excellent itinerant shows that have ranged from Kandinsky to William Blake. Gaudí's famous Pedrera (Casa Milà), on the Passeig de Gràcia, now features a superb permanent exhibit on the architect's life and work in the Gaudí-designed attic, as well as a model apartment and rotating exhibitions in the Sala Gaudí. The Museu d'Art Contemporani de Barcelona (MACBA), in the Raval west of the Rambla, has an excellent and well-guided collection of contemporary art featuring works by Calder, Tàpies, Oteiza, Rauschenberg, and Brossa. The Centre de Cultura Contemporànea offers shows, lectures, concerts, book openings, and events of all kinds. Other museums with excellent displays are the Museu d'Història de la Ciutat in the Plaça del Rei, the Museu d'Història de Catalunya in the Port Vell's Palau de Mar, and the Museu de la Ciencia in upper Barcelona. For a secret museum in a superb building, look for the Museu de Belles Arts de la Reial Acadèmia de Belles Arts de Sant Jordi in the Llotja near Santa Maria del Mar. For an out-of-town excursion take the train 15 minutes out under the Collserola hills to the Baixador de Vallvidrera and walk up to the Museu Verdaguer in the Vil.la Joana, the house where the great romantic priest-poet, Jacint Verdaguer, author of *Canigó,* died in 1902. From there, trails lead two hours back over the hills to Barcelona.

Music

With the restored Liceu Opera House and the new Auditori joining the Palau de la Musica in the city's triumvirate of gorgeous music venues, Barcelona's music offerings have become one of the city's great resources. In addition, churches such as Santa Maria del Mar, Santa Maria del Pi, Sant Pau del Camp, Sant Felip Neri, and others hold world-class choral events, especially prior to Christmas and Easter, that should not be missed. Historic monuments such as the medieval shipyards at Drassanes and the Monestir de Pedralbes also schedule exquisite early music concerts. With a tapa before and a light dinner or an onion soup afterward (plenty of good restaurants remain open until 1 AM), musical events—especially combined with memorable architectural settings—make a nearly unbeatable evening on the town. Jazz and popular music are also in good supply here, with top world figures from saxophonists Maceo Parker and Kenney Garrett to up-and-coming stars like Ben Waltzer, Billy McHenry, and Barcelona's own Jordi Rossy playing at jazz clubs such as the Jamboree, the Harlem Jazz Club, and La Cova del Drac. James Taylor, the Cranberries, and Enya have been heard in Barcelona recently, along with Cuban bolero master Ibrahim Ferrer, the Buena Vista Social Club, and classical-folk "fusion" standouts such as Lisbon's Madredeus. Rare is a Barcelona month without a music festival of one kind or another: the fall jazz festival, the winter guitar festival, the spring early music festival, and the summer *Grec* performing arts festival chief among them. Barcelona isn't Vienna, but on the other hand, across the full breadth of the global music-scape, it may be better.

Grazing

Perhaps nothing is as satisfying and exciting in Barcelona as spontaneous wandering, tippling, and tapa-hunting. Never does *la gran encisera* (the great enchantress), as the city has been called, disappoint. Whether during the day or after dark, wandering semi-aimlessly through the Gothic Quarter, Gràcia, Barceloneta, or La Ribera offers an endless selection of taverns, cafés, bars, and restaurants where wines, beers, *cava* (Catalan sparkling wine), or *txakolí* (a fresh young

Basque white wine served in the increasingly popular Basque taverns) accompany little morsels of fish, sausage, cheese, peppers, wild mushrooms, or tortilla (potato omelet). If you find yourself stuck on Passeig de Gràcia or the Rambla, be warned: you're missing out. The areas around Passeig del Born, Santa Maria del Mar, Plaça de les Olles, and the Picasso Museum are the prime *tapeo* (tapa-tasting) and *txikiteo* (tippling) preserves. Around Plaça de la Virreina in Gràcia is another, while the Eixample has its share of lively saloons as well, though the in-between ambling and rambling are not as interesting. Art gallery openings, outdoor concerts, and events of one kind or another ranging from festive processions to troupes of *castellers* (castlers), Catalonia's human pyramids, are easy to work into these wanderings; between the scenery, the fare and the walking, this is about the best way to make the most of this moveable feast of a city.

EXPLORING BARCELONA

Barcelona is made up of three main zones. The old city (Ciutat Vella) lies between Plaça de Catalunya and the port and breaks down into the Rambla, the Barri Gotic (Gothic Quarter), Barri de la Ribera (Waterfront Quarter), el Raval (medieval "outskirts" west of the Rambla), and Barceloneta (the old fishing quarter). Above it is the grid-patterned expansion built after the city's third set of walls was torn down in 1860. Known as the Eixample ("Widening"), this area contains most of Barcelona's Moderniste architecture. Farther out are the former outlying towns of Gràcia, Sarrià, and Pedralbes, and looming up behind are Tibidabo and the Collserola hills.

Barcelona's main cross-town traffic arteries are the Diagonal (so called as it runs diagonally to the meridian or longitudinal line going through the city), and the mid-town speedways, Carrer d'Aragó, and Gran Via de les Corts Catalanes, both cutting northeast-southwest through the heart of the city. Passeig de Gràcia, which becomes Gran de Gràcia above the Diagonal, runs all the way from Plaça Catalunya up to Plaça Lesseps, but the main up and down streets, for motorists, are Balmes, Muntaner, Aribau, and Comtes d'Urgell. For pedestrians (which you are strongly encouraged to be in Barcelona), it all changes. Because of general noise and air pollution you should avoid walking these streets (with the possible exception of Passeig de Gràcia, which is unavoidable because of its dense endowment of Moderniste architecture) and walk the charming and leafy Rambla de Catalunya, the upper extension of the Rambla between Plaça Catalunya, and the Diagonal.

The main bus and subway hub is Plaça Catalunya, with the principal entrance at the top of the Rambla in front of the Café Zurich. Become familiar (especially) with the ultradeluxe, air-conditioned, and comfortable Ferrocarrils (FFCC) de la Generalitat, a separate train or subway line run by the Generalitat (Government of Catalonia) connecting Plaça Catalunya with Sarrià and, beyond the Collserola hills behind the city, the suburban towns of San Cugat, Terrassa, and Sabadell. Between the FFCC de la Generalitat and the regular subway system, the odd taxi (a longish trip across town rarely exceeds $10 on the meter), and walking, Barcelona is easy to navigate. Buses are also available, of course, day and night, Plaça Catalunya being the principal nerve center. If you don't object to being bused around town with a few dozen (other) tourists, the **Barcelona BusTurístic** offers two 3½-hour tours, north and south, covering all the major sights. A two-day ticket costing 2,500 ptas/€15.03 allows you to get on and off at any of the 26 stops as often as you want and provides a card worth important discounts at most of Barcelona's museums and attractions.

But for independent operators, Barcelona's a breeze on foot, with a taxi now and then, and the Sarrià train as your main up and downtown connection. Since Barcelona's street signs are printed in Catalan, note should be made of the most prevalent signage: *carrer* (street); *plaça* (square); *passeig* (boulevard); *rambla* (avenue promenade); *avinguda* (avenue); and *passatge* (passage).

Numbers in the margin correspond to points of interest on the neighborhood maps.

Great Itineraries

The Rambla, the Gothic Quarter, the Raval, the Barri de Ribera, Barceloneta, and all of old Barcelona hold constant surprises, even for longtime residents. Markets such as the Rambla's Boqueria, the Raval's Mercat de Sant Antoni, and the Els Encants flea market near Plaça de les Glories are always good browsing grounds, well seeded with cafés, bars, patios, and terraces for mid-itinerary breaks. The mystifying numberless grid square of the Eixample is somewhat noisier and more vehicular than the old part of town, but the Champs-Elysées–like Passeig de Gràcia and leafy Rambla de Catalunya are sprinkled with Moderniste treasures ranging from Gaudí's Casa Battló or La Pedrera to Art Nouveau–period pharmacies and grocery stores. Design emporiums such as Vinçon and BD are other targets of opportunity to break up the midtown maze, while boutiques and shops from Armani to Loewe are dangerous places to enter with a live credit card in your pocket. The formerly outlying towns of Gràcia and Sarrià, as well as the stately mansions and Pedralbes Monastery, are a mere 15 minutes away by train. Montjuïc is yet another world of things to see—a week's worth of museums, gardens, and stadiums ranging from the Mies van der Rohe Pavilion to the Isozaki-designed Palau Sant Jordi to the Miró Foundation or the Romanesque collection in the Palau Nacional. Final call might be Tibidabo—landmarked by the Norman Foster Communications tower—and a highland hike through the Collserola hills up behind the city. Don't forget to get lost: planned visits are always enhanced by the joys of aimless wandering, and Barcelona is not nearly as vast as it seems at first. In fact, a walk from Pedralbes to the port can be completed in under two hours.

Three days would be sufficient to explore the Rambla and the Gothic Quarter, see the Sagrada Família and the main Moderniste sights, go to one or two important museums, and perhaps take in a concert. Five days would allow a more thorough exploration of the same, as well as more museums and the chance to explore Barceloneta, Gràcia, and Sarrià, and even the Collserola hills above and behind the urban sprawl. A week to 10 days would give you time to learn the city's authentic rhythms and resources; check the daily papers for gallery openings and concerts; make a side trip to Sitges, Montserrat, Montseny Girona, or the Costa Brava (☞ Chapter 3); and generally begin to get a feel for what makes this the biggest and busiest city on the Mediterranean.

IF YOU HAVE 3 DAYS

Stroll the Rambla and the **Boqueria** ⑧ market; then cut over to the city's main medieval landmark, the **Catedral de la Seu** ㉑. Detour through the **Plaça del Rei** ㉕ before cutting back to the **Plaça Sant Jaume** ㉛, where the Catalonian government, the Palau de la Generalitat, stands across the square from the *ajuntament* (city hall). From there it's a 10-minute walk to the **Museu Picasso** (54), from which another, even shorter stroll leads past that shining example of Catalan Gothic, the church of **Santa Maria del Mar** (59), to Cal Pep, in Plaça de les Olles (for the best tapas in Barcelona). Try to catch an evening concert at the spectacular **Palau**

de la Música ㊾. Day two might be a Gaudí day: spend the morning marveling at his uniquely Moderniste masterpieces, starting with his magnum opus, the **Temple Expiatori de la Sagrada Família** (87), midday at **Parc Güell** (94), and, after catching Gaudí's first house, **Casa Vicens** (98), on the way down through Gràcia from Parc Güell, spend the afternoon touring **Casa Milà** (83)—with some of Gaudí's most incredible chimneys—and the celebrated **Manzana de la Discordia** (80) block, which include the extraordinary **Casa Batlló** and **Casa Lleó Morera,** on Passeig de Gràcia. **Palau Güell** ⑯, just off the lower Rambla, is another important Gaudí visit. On day three, climb Montjuïc for the world's best Romanesque art collection, at the **Museu Nacional d'Art de Catalunya** (114), in the Palau Nacional. While on Montjuïc, investigate the **Fundació Miró** (112)—along with the artist's colorful painting, there are nice vistas here over the city—**Poble Espanyol** (117), and the 1992 Olympic facilities, especially Arata Izosaki's superb Palau Sant Jordi, Santiago Calatrava's gleaming sculptural tower, the Galería Olímpica museum, and the restored Olympic Stadium. Take the cable car across the port for a late paella at Can Manel la Puda in Barceloneta, once Barcelona's most pungent, picturesque fishing port.

IF YOU HAVE 5 DAYS

Walk the Rambla, the **Boqueria** ⑧ market, the Plaça del Pi, and the Barri Gòtic, including the **Catedral de la Seu** ㉑, on the first day. The next day, take a few hours to see the **Museu Picasso** (54) and the church of **Santa Maria del Mar** (59). Walk through Barceloneta and down to the **Port Olimpic** (77) or out onto the *rompeolas* (breakwaters) and back. On the third morning you can explore the Raval, to the west of the Rambla, and visit Richard Meier's **Museu d'Art Contemporànea** (MACB) ㊵, the **Centre de Cultura Contemporànea** (CCCB) ㊷, and the medieval **Hospital de Sant Pau** ㊹, as well as Barcelona's oldest church, **Sant Pau del Camp** ㊽. If you have time, have a look through the **Museu Marítim** ⑳ and the adjacent medieval shipyards, the **Reial Drassanes.** In the early afternoon (until 3:30) you can take a guided tour of the **Palau de la Música Catalana** ㊾ and pick up tickets to a concert. From the Palau de la Música taxi across town to the minimalist **Mies van der Rohe Barcelona Pavilion** (116) above Plaça Espanya for Barcelona's most radical architectural contrast. At the top of the stairs is the **Museu Nacional d'Art de Catalunya** (114) and the Romanesque collection. The fourth day can be devoted to Gaudí, with the **Temple Expiatori de la Sagrada Família** (87) in the morning and **Parc Güell** ⑯ at midday. In the afternoon, walk down through Gràcia past Gaudí's first house, **Casa Vicens** (98), and continue down the Passeig de Gràcia past **Manzana de la Discordia** (80): **Casa Ametller, Casa Batlló,** and **Casa Lleó Morera** in the heart of the city's grid-patterned Eixample. The **Palau Güell** ⑮, just off the Rambla, will complete the comprehensive Gaudí tour of Barcelona. On the morning of day five, take the train out to **Sarrià** and **Pedralbes** to see the **Monestir de Pedralbes** (104), one of Barcelona's finest hidden gems—a medieval landmark now home to part of the celebrated Thyssen-Bornemisza collection of paintings. In the afternoon, explore the mountain massif of Montjuïc: revisit the **Museu Nacional d'Art de Catalunya** (114), in the Palau Nacional, or continue directly on to the **Fundació Miró** (112). **Poble Espanyol** (117), the restored **Estadi Olimpic** (113), and the adjacent Arata Izosaki's superb **Palau Sant Jordi** are the main attractions, along with Santiago Calatrava's gleaming sculptural tower, the Galería Olímpica museum. Take the cable car across the port for an outdoor paella at Can Manel la Puda in Barceloneta.

IF YOU HAVE 7–10 DAYS

Basically, more time would allow doing the five-day plan at a more leisurely pace, as well as exploring the museums more thoroughly. Start

PEDRALBES

SARRIÀ

Ronda del General Mitre

Avda. Diagonal

Avda. de Pedralbes

Passeig de Manuel Girona

C. de les Escoles

C. de Modolell

C. Via Augusta

Plaça Pius XII

Plaça Prat de la Riba

Plaça de la Reina Maria Cristina

Via de Carles III

C. de Numància

Avda. de Sarrià

C. de Calvet

C. de Muntaner

Travessera de les Corts

Pl. de Francesc Macià

Avda. de Madrid

C. d'Entença

C. del Brasil

C. de Joan Güell

C. del Vallespir

C. de Berlin

Avda. de Josep Tarradellas

C. de París

C. de Villarroel

Avda.

C. de Sants

C. de Corsega

C. de Muntaner

C. d'Aribau

Estació Sants

Pl. Països Catalans

C. del Rossello

Casanova

C. de P

C. d'Antoni de Capmany

C. de la Creu Coberta

Avda. de Roma

C. de Provença

C. del Comte Borrell

C. de Villarroel

C. de Mallorc

C. de Valencia

Rocafort

C. de Viladomat

C. del Comte d'Urgell

C. de

C. d'Arago

Entença

C. de Calabria

C. de la Diputació

Plaça Universitat

Gran Vía de les Corts Catalanes

Plaça d'Espanya

C. de Vilamarí

Plaça Universitat

C. de Sepulveda

Avda. Reina M. Cristina

C. de Floridablanca

Joaquin Costa

RA

Plaça de Sant Jordi

Pl. de les Cascades

Avda. de Mistral

C. de Tamarit

C. de Ile·ida

Avda. del Paral·lel

C. de Manso

C. del

Pg. de les Cascades

Palau Nacional

Rda. de Sant Pau

C. de Hospital

MONTJUÏC

Jardins de Joan Maragall

C. de Blai

C. de Magalhaes

Carretes

C. de Sant Pau

Les Flores

C. la Unió

Estadi Olimpic

Avda. de Miramar

C. Nou de la Rambla

Camí dels Tres Pins

Pg. de Montjuïc

Plaça Portal de la Pau

Parc de Montjuïc

C. dels Mondials

Jardins de Miramar

Castell de Montjuïc

Moll de Sant Bertrán

TORRE DE JAUME

N

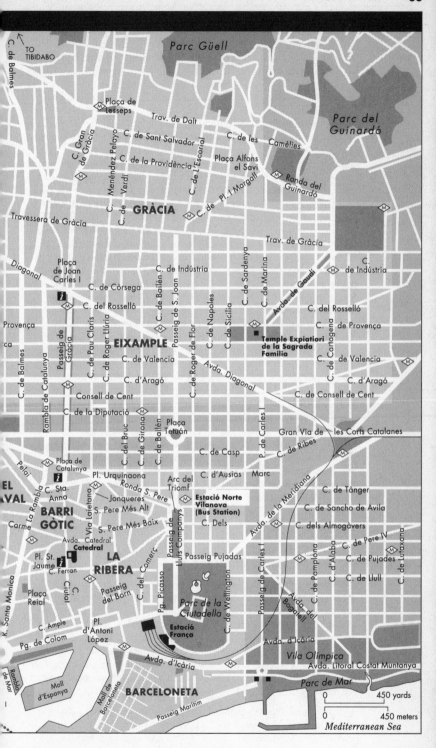

C. de Balmes

TO TIBIDABO

Parc Güell

Plaça de Lesseps

Trav. de Dalt

C. de Sant Salvador

C. Gran de Gràcia

Menéndez Pelayo

Verdi

C. de la Providència

C. de l'Escorial

C. de les

Camèlies

Parc del Guinardó

Plaça Alfons el Savi

C. de Pl. i Margall

Ronda del Guinardó

GRÀCIA

Travessera de Gràcia

C. de

Trav. de Gràcia

Diagonal

Plaça de Joan Carles I

C. de Còrsega

C. de Bailèn

C. de Indústria

C. de Sardenya

C. de Marina

C. de Indústria

Avda. de Gaudí

C. del Rosselló

C. de Provença

C. del Rosselló

C. de Pau Claris

C. de Roger Llúria

Passeig de S. Joan

C. de Napoles

C. de Sicília

C. de Cartagena

Provença

Passeig de Gràcia

EIXAMPLE

C. de Roger de Flor

Temple Expiatori de la Sagrada Família

C. de Valencia

C. de Valencia

C. de Balmes

Rambla de Catalunya

C. de Valencia

C. d'Aragó

Avda. Diagonal

C. d'Aragó

C. d'Aragó

Consell de Cent

C. de la Diputació

C. de la Diputació

C. de Consell de Cent

Plaça Tetuán

C. del Bruc

C. de Girona

C. de Bailèn

P. de Carles

Gran Vía de les Corts Catalanes

C. de Ribes

Pelai

Plaça de Catalunya

C. de Casp

C. de Casp

Pl. Urquinaona

Arc del Triomf

C. d'Ausias Marc

EL RAVAL

C. Sta. Anna

La Rambla

Ronda S. Pere

Jonqueres

S. Pere Més Alt

Estació Norte Vilanova (Bus Station)

Avda. de la Meridiana

C. de Tànger

C. de Sancho de Avila

BARRI GÒTIC

Carme

Via Laietana

S. Pere Més Baix

C. Dels

C. dels Almogàvers

C. de Pere IV

Avda. Catedral

Catedral

LA RIBERA

Passeig de Lluís Companys

Passeig Pujadas

Passeig de Carles I

C. de Pamplona

C. d'Alaba

C. de Pujades

C. de Llull

C. de Lutxana

Pl. St. Jaume

C. Ferran

C. Ciutat

Passeig del Born

C. del Comerç

Pg. Picasso

Avda. del Bogatell

Plaça Reial

C. Ample

Pl. d'Antoni López

Parc de la Ciutadella

C. de Wellington

Pg. de Colom

Estació França

Avda. d'Icària

Vila Olímpica

Avda. Litoral Costat Muntanya

Rambla de Mar

Moll d'Espanya

Moll de Barceloneta

BARCELONETA

Avda. d'Icària

Parc de Mar

Passeig Marítim

0   450 yards

0   450 meters

Mediterranean Sea

with the Rambla, Barcelona's best-known and most characteristic promenade. Wander the **Boqueria** ⑧ market, the **Plaça del Pi,** and the Barri Gòtic, including the **Catedral de la Seu** ㉑, on the first day. The next day, take a few hours to see the **Museu Picasso** ㊴ and the church of **Santa Maria del Mar** ㊾ and the area around the **Born.** On day three, walk through Barceloneta and down to the **Port Olympic** ⑦ or out onto the *rompeolas* (breakwaters) and back. Go to the beach and have a paella in Barceloneta at Can Majó. On the fourth day you can explore the Raval, to the west of the Rambla, and visit Richard Meier's **Museu d'Art Contemporànea** (MACB) ㊵, the **Centre de Cultura Contemporànea** (CCCB) ㊷, and the medieval **Hospital de Sant Pau** ㊻, as well as Barcelona's oldest church, **Sant Pau del Camp** ㊽. Look through the **Museu Marítim** ⑳, the medieval shipyards, the **Reial Drassanes,** and explore the new **World Trade Center** complex in the port. On the fifth day (until 3:30) you can take a guided tour of the **Palau de la Música Catalana** ㊾ and pick up tickets to a concert. From the Palau de la Música taxi across town to the minimalist **Mies van der Rohe Barcelona Pavilion** ⑯ above Plaça Espanya for Barcelona's most radical architectural contrast. At the top of the stairs is the **Museu Nacional d'Art de Catalunya** ⑭ and the Romanesque collection. The sixth day can be devoted to three very different Gaudí works spanning more than 40 years: his last project, the wild-and-woolly **Temple Expiatori de la Sagrada Família** ㊧, in the morning; Gaudí's first house, **Casa Vicens** ㊨, in Gràcia at midday; and **Parc Güell** ㊤ in the late afternoon. On the seventh day, explore the onetime village of Gràcia, taking time for browsing through Gràcia's markets and shops. On the eighth day concentrate on the Passeig de Gràcia's treasures—**Casa Milà** ㊤ with its Gaudí museum, **Casa Batlló,** and **Casa Lleó Morera** in the heart of the city's grid-patterned Eixample, and, if you haven't seen it yet, **Palau Güell** ⑯, just off the Rambla. On the morning of day nine, take the train out to **Plaça Sarrià** ⑨ and **Pedralbes** to see the **Monestir de Pedralbes** ㊃, one of Barcelona's finest hidden gems. In the afternoon explore Montjuïc: revisit the **Museu Nacional d'Art de Catalunya** ⑭, in the Palau Nacional, or continue directly on to the **Fundació Miró** ⑫. A 10th day would offer a chance to complete Montjuïc. Go through **Poble Espanyol** ⑰; the restored **Olympic Stadium** and Arata Izosaki's superb **Palau Sant Jordi** are the main attractions, along with Santiago Calatrava's gleaming sculptural tower, the Galería Olímpica museum. Take the cable car across the port for an outdoor paella at Can Manel la Puda in Barceloneta.

The Rambla: The Heart of Barcelona

The central pedestrian artery and people-watching event in the city, La Rambla is Barcelona's best-known and most historic promenade. Lined with a succession of newspaper and magazine kiosks, bird merchants and outdoor florist stands, festooned with colorful signs and lurid paraphernalia of every description, the Rambla is a rainbow of a street roaring just over a kilometer through the heart of the Ciutat Vella—the Old City—from Plaça de Catalunya past the Boqueria market and the Liceu Opera House to the Christopher Columbus monument at Portal de la Pau.

Centuries ago, the avenue was a (usually dry) watercourse, a sandy arroyo called *rmel* (Arabic for sand), from which the word Rambla evolved. Today, medieval seasonal hydraulics have been replaced by a constant and colorful flood of humanity flowing past flower stalls, bird vendors, newspaper kiosks, and outdoor cafés. No wonder Federico García Lorca famously called this street the only one in the world he wished would never end: the show is always raging here with buskers of every stripe and spot, from painted human statues to mimes, acrobats, jugglers, musicians, puppeteers, portraitists, break dancers, rappers, and rockers, all hard at work beneath the canopy of the giant plane trees that line the Rambla. A central pedestrian island between two traffic lanes, the Rambla is a thoroughfare where the rolling stock pales beside the colorful and endless deluge of locals and travelers tumbling down its middle promenade.

The crowd seethes and dawdles, at once busy and nonchalant. Couples sit at tiny café tables no bigger than tea trays sipping glasses of anything from coffee to cognac while the neverending parade files by. Nimble-footed waiters dodge traffic, bringing trays of coffee to tables along the promenade. Peddlers, kiosk owners, parrots and parakeets along the stretch called the Rambla dels Ocells (Bird Market) all contribute a polycaphony of singsong calls over the din of taxis and motorbikes, each note contributing to the greater urban symphony. Here, in busy, frantic Barcelona, the Rambla is perenially plugged with squads of laughing, walking revelers, often more animated at 1 AM than at 3 PM.

The Rambla's original sandy expanse followed the course of an old riverbed flowing down from the Collserolla hills along the edge of the pre-13th-century second-city walls that encircled the Gothic Quarter and the Barri de la Ribera. When, in the late 13th century, walls enclosing the Raval were erected along what are now the Rondas de Sant Antoni and Sant Pau, the open space outside the second set of walls was left as a mid-city promenade and forum. For over a thousand years the Rambla has been a meeting place for peddlers, workers in search of jobs, farmers selling produce or livestock, and your occasional thief and beggar.

Collectively known as La Rambla, each section has its own title and-personality: Rambla Santa Monica at the southeastern or port end was named for an early convent; Rambla de les Flors in the middle is named for its traditional flower merchants; and Rambla dels Estudis at the top leading down from Plaça de Catalunya is so called for the Barcelona university located there until the early 18th century. From the universal rendezvous point at the head of the Rambla at Café Zurich to the Boqueria produce market, the Liceu opera house, or the seamy, steamy denizens of the night on the Rambla's lower reaches, there is something for everyone at any hour along this hub of Barcelona street life.

An even more comprehensive macro-Rambla trek could begin at the Diagonal (at the bizarre reclining giraffe bronze sculpture) and continue down leafy Rambla de Catalunya through the Rambla proper, between Plaça de Catalunya and the Columbus monument at Portal de la Pau and across the port on the wooden Rambla de Mar boardwalk to the Maremagnum and the Port Vell (Old Port). In the end, a visitor might come to know Barcelona quite well without ever even straying far from the Rambla—Barcelona's all-purpose promenade, forum, boardwalk, boulevard and runway.

Numbers in the text correspond to numbers in the margin and on the Rambla map.

A Good Walk
Start at one of the landmarks of the **Plaça de Catalunya** ①, a standard meeting point astride the city's central metro and bus stops: the **Café Zurich** ②, situated at the head of the Rambla. Just down the Rambla on the right is the **Font de les Canaletas** ③ (Canaletas Fountain), with a small brass plaque explaining (in Catalan) that if you drink the water from this fountain, one of the earliest canals bringing water from the

upper Llobregat river directly to the city center, you will fall under the spell of Barcelona and always return. This section of the Rambla is the **Rambla dels Estudis,** so named for the early university located here until Felipe V banished the unruly and revolutionary students to the town of Cervera, some 100 km (62 mi) west of Barcelona. Next is the **Rambla dels Ocells** (Rambla of the Birds), where all manner of fowl from parrots to partridges are sold, a practice carried down from the days when markets and conglomerations of peasants looking for work gathered outside the city walls, making the sandy arroyo into the popular meeting point it has remained to this day. At Carrer Portaferrissa check out the Baroque-era landmarks of **Betlem** ④ church on the right, the **Palau Moja** ⑤ on the left, along with the **Portaferrisa fountain** ⑥ on the right as you turn left into Carrer Portaferrissa.

The **Rambla de les Flors** is aromatically unmistakable, famous among 19th-century Catalan impressionists as a source of beautiful flower vendors who frequently became their models and, often, their wives. After a look through the historic **Palau de la Virreina** ⑦—now an exhibition center—stroll through the spectacular **Boqueria** ⑧ food market. Back on the Rambla, note the colorful Joan Miró mosaic underfoot at Pla de la Boqueria and the bizarre Art Nouveau–neo-Egyptian **Casa Bruno Quadros** ⑨ house, complete with its parasol-toting Chinese dragon. From Pla de la Boqueria, cut in to the Plaça del Pi and the church of **Santa Maria del Pi** ⑩, with its celebrated rose window. Explore this area, especially **Carrer Petritxol** ⑪; why not stop in for a time-out at one of this historic street's *chocolaterias* (hot-chocolate shops) before continuing down the Rambla? Take a look at the leafy Plaça and unusual church of **Sant Agustí** ⑫ just down Carrer Hospital to the right before continuing past the Art Nouveau **Hotel Espanya** ⑬ on Carrer de Sant Pau and the **Gran Teatre del Liceu** ⑭, Barcelona's famous opera house, with its original facade, and the rest of the block filled with its new offices and dressing rooms. Off to the left of the Rambla is **Plaça Reial** ⑮, an elegantly neoclassical square that's been an address to the rich and famous as well as a ragtag contingent of street people.

Gaudí's spectacular **Palau Güell** ⑯, on Carrer Nou de la Rambla, is the next stop and a stunning introduction to the work of Barcelona's architectural genius. **Carrer Escudellers** ⑰—lined with fascinating sights, from an Art Nouveau saloon to one of Barcelona's most historic shops—goes left at Pla del Teatre. Continue down the Rambla toward the port to the towering column honoring Christopher Columbus, the **Monument a Colom** ⑱, and the **Port** ⑲, accessed by the Rambla de Mar (from here consider making a brief probe—or not—into the unprepossessingly modern Port Vell complex, with its shopping center, IMAX theater, and aquarium). Back at the Columbus monument, investigate the medieval **Drassanes Reiales** ⑳ shipyards and the **Museu Marítim,** with its fascinating exhibits devoted to Barcelona's great maritime history. For a fitting finale, retire to a Rambla café to watch the passing parade before dinnertime.

TIMING

This walk covers about 5 km (3 mi). Including stops, allow three to four hours. The best time to find things open and the Rambla rollicking is between 9 and 2 in the morning and 4 and 8 in the evening, although this populous runway has a life of its own 24 hours a day. Some museums remain open through the lunch hour but others close—check hours. Most church hours are 9 AM to 1:30 PM and 4:30 PM to 8 PM; there is usually a midday closing.

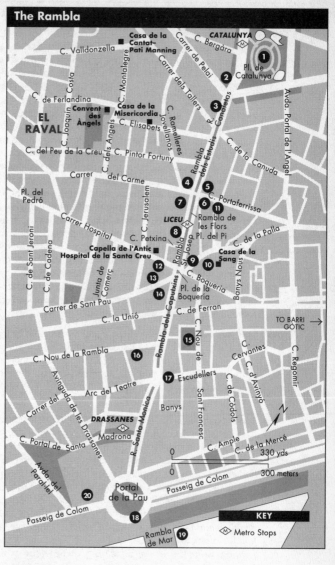

Sights to See

4 **Betlem.** The Betlem (Bethlehem) church is one of Barcelona's few Baroque buildings and hulks stodgily on the Rambla just above the Rambla de les Flors. Burned out completely at the start of the Spanish Civil War in 1936, the church lacks much opulence within these days, whereas the outside, recently spruced up, is made of what looks like quilted stone. If you find this one of the world's more unsightly churches, feel no guilt: you're in the company of all of Barcelona with the possible exception of Betlem's parishioners. This was where Viceroy Amat claimed the hand of the young Virreina-to-be when she was left in the lurch by the Viceroy's nephew so, in a sense, Betlem has compensated the city for itself with the half century of good works La Virrein (☞ Palau de la Virreina, *below*) was able to accomplish with her husband's fortune. The nativity scenes on display down the stairs at the side entrance on the Rambla at Christmastime are an old tradition here, allegedly begun by St. Francis of Assisi, who assembled the world's first in Barcelona in the early 13th century. ⊠ *Xuclà 2,* ☎ *93/ 318–3823.*

❽ Boqueria. Barcelona's most spectacular food market, also known as the Mercat de Sant Josep, is an explosion of life and color sprinkled with delicious little bar-restaurants. Set within a steel hanger, it's placed in the middle of a Neoclassical-style square built in 1840 by architect Francesc Daniel Molina (without the hangar the space would resemble Plaça Reial just down the Rambla). The Ionic columns visible around the edges of the market will soon be freestanding, as renovations designed to reveal the original 19th-century design are currently under way. Highlights include the sunny greengrocer's market outside (to the right if you've come in from the Rambla), along with **Pinotxo**— Pinocchio, just inside to the right—which has won international acclaim as a gourmet sanctuary, and, without a doubt, owner Juanito and his family serve some of the best food in Barcelona. (The secret? "Fresh, fast, hot, salty, and garlicky.") If Pinotxo—landmarked by a ceramic portrait of the wooden-nosed prevaricator himself—is overbooked (which it usually is), try the Kiosko Universal over toward the port side of the market. Don't miss herb and wild-mushroom supplier and expert Petràs (ask anyone for the location), with his anthological display of wild mushrooms, herbs, nuts, and berries ("Fruits del Bosc"—Fruits of the Forest). ⊠ *Mercat de Sant Josep (La Boqueria), Rambla 91.* ☉ *Open Mon.–Sat. 8–8.*

❷ Café Zurich. At the head of the Rambla, over the metro station, and ever of key importance to Barcelona rank-and-file society, this classic café has long been one of the city's most popular meeting points. The outdoor tables offer peerless people-watching; the interior is high-ceilinged and elegant. ⊠ *Plaça Catalunya 1,* ☎ *93/317–9153.* ☉ *Daily 9 AM–2 AM.*

⑰ Carrer Escudellers. Named for the *terrissaires* (earthenware potters) who traditionally worked here making *escudellas* (bowls or stew pots), this colorful loop is an interesting sub-trip off the Rambla. Go left at Plaça del Teatre and you'll soon reach (appropriately) Barcelona's most comprehensive ceramics display at **Art Escudellers** at No. 5 Escudellers. Across the street is the **Grill Room**, a lovely Art Nouveau saloon that, though generally listless and underbooked, if not actually empty, has graceful wooden decor in curving modernist loops and arches. Next on the right is **Los Caracoles**, a landmark restaurant specializing in Catalan, Castilian, and international cuisine. Speaking of the cuisine, take a swing through the mouthwatering kitchen—the owners are invariably pleased to let you do so—and out the side door for an aromatic preview. Another hundred yards down Carrer Escudellers, you will come to **Plaça George Orwell**, named for the author of *Homage to Catalonia* and a space created in the last decade in order to create light and air for this traditionally squalid neighborhood. A little flea market hums along on Saturday, a place to have a browse-through—especially if you've been mugged recently by one of the street prowlers around here (you might be able to buy something of your own back cheap!).

Take a right on Carrer de la Carabassa and walk down this pretty cobbled alley with graceful bridges between several houses and their former gardens. At the end of the street, looming hugely atop her own basilica, is **Nostra Senyora de la Mercè** (Our Lady of Mercy). This giant representation of Barcelona's patron saint is a 20th-century (1940) addition to the roof of the 18th-century Església de la Mercè; the view of La Mercè gleaming greenly in the sunlight, babe in arms, is one of the Barcelona waterfront's most impressive sights. As you arrive at Carrer Ample, the **15th-century door** with a winged St. George delivering

LA DIADA DE SANT JORDI: BARCELONA'S LOVERS' DAY

BARCELONA'S BEST DAY? Easy. April 23rd, Saint George's day, La Diada de Sant Jordi, Barcelona's Valentine's day, a day when kissometer readings go off the charts, a day so sweet and playful, so goofy and romantic, that 6 million Catalans go giddy from dawn to dusk.

Patron Saint of Catalonia, international knight-errant Saint George allegedly slew a dragon about to devour a beautiful princess south of Barcelona. From the dragon's blood sprouted a rosebush, from which the hero plucked the prettiest for the princess. Hence, the traditional Rose Festival celebrated in Barcelona since the Middle Ages to honor chivalry and romantic love, a day for men and mice alike to give their true loves roses. In 1923, the lovers' fest merged with International Book Day to mark the anniversary of the all but simultaneous April 23, 1616 deaths of Miguel de Cervantes and William Shakespeare.

Over four million roses and half a million books are sold in Catalonia on Sant Jordi's Day, men giving their inamoratas roses and the ladies giving books in return. Bookstalls run the length of the Rambla, and despite being an official workday, nearly all of Barcelona manages to play hooky and wander. In Barcelona, Saint George is everywhere, beginning on the facade of the Catalonian seat of government, the Generalitat. Art Nouveau master Eusebi Arnau sculpted Sant Jordi skewering the unlucky dragon on the facade of the Casa Amatller as well as on the corner of Els Quatre Gats café, while Gaudí dedicated an entire house, Casa Batlló, to the Sant Jordi theme with the cross of Saint George implanted in the scaly roof and the bones of the dragon's victims framing the windows of the main facade.

A Roman soldier martyrized for his Christian beliefs in the 4th century, Saint George is one of the most venerated of all saints, patron of England, Greece, and Rumania, among others. Associated with springtime and fertility, Sant Jordi roses include a spike of wheat and a little red and yellow "senyera," the Catalonian flag. And the books? Besides the Shakespeare and Cervantes anniversary, Barcelona is the publishing capital of the Spanish-speaking world. Language and love have, in any case, always been closely associated, to the point that contemporary evolutionary psychologists identify the cerebral cortex as both the erotic and linguistic center of the human brain . . . and don't affairs of the heart inevitably lead to exchanges of letters, books, poetry?

In Barcelona and all of Catalonia, Sant Jordi's day erupts joyfully. The spring air is sweet and filled with promise. Lovers are everywhere. There is a 24-hour reading of *Don Quixote*. Authors come to bookstalls to sign books. In Sarrià, a floral artisan displays 45 kinds of roses representing 45 different kinds of love, from impossible to unrequited to filial and maternal. The sardana is reverently performed in Plaça Sant Jaume, while the Generalitat, its patio filled with roses, opens its doors to the public. Choral groups sing love songs in resonant corners of the Gothic Quarter while jazz combos play in Plaça del Pi. The Rambla is solid humanity from the Diagonal to the Mediterranean, two miles of *barcelonins* basking in the warmth of spring and romance. Rare is the roseless woman on the streets of Barcelona, schoolgirls to *avias* (grandmothers), all aglow with bashful smiles.

By midnight, the Rambla, once a watercourse, is again awash with flower water and covered with rose-clippings and tiny red-and-yellow-striped ribbons with diminutive letters spelling "Sant Jordi" - "Diada de la Rosa" - "Day of the Rose" -"t'estimo" - "I love you."

a perfect squash backhand to another pesky dragon is unique in Barcelona (all the rest are forehands). The door was added to the basilica when the Sant Miquel church was torn down in the early 19th century. From the Mercè, a walk out Carrer Ample leads back to the Rambla. Don't miss the grocery store on the corner of Carrer de la Carabassa—**La Lionesa**, at Carrer Ample 21, is one of the best-preserved 19th-century shops in Barcelona. Farther along at No. 7 is the **Solé** shoe store, with handmade shoes from all over the world. You might recognize Plaça Medinaceli, next on the left, from Pedro Almodovar's film *Todo sobre mi Madre* (*All about My Mother*); the scene featured the heroine's dog and her senile father.

⑪ Carrer Petritxol. Hard by the Rambla and one of Barcelona's most popular streets, lined with art galleries, *chocolaterías,* and bookstores, this narrow passageway dates back to the 15th century when it was used as a shortcut through the backyard of an eponymous property owner. Working up Petritxol from Plaça del Pi, stop to admire the late-17th-century *sgraffito* (contrasting ground ornamentation), some of the city's best, on the facade over the **Roca** knife store, *the* place for cutlery in Barcelona. Next on the right at Petritxol 2 is the 200-year-old **Dulcinea** hot-chocolate refuge, with a portrait of the great Catalan playwright Àngel Guimerà (1847–1924) over the fireplace and plenty of cozy nooks for conversation and the house specialty, the *suizo* (literally, "Swiss": hot chocolate and whipped cream). Also at Petritxol 2 is the **Llibreria Quera**, one of the city's best two or three hiking and mountaineering bookstores with maps, guides, and literature on all aspects of trekking through (especially) the Pyrenees and the rest of the world as well.

Note the plaque to Guimerà over No. 4 and the Art Box gallery at No. 1–3 across the street. At No. 5 Petritxol is **Sala Parès**, founded in 1840, the dean of Barcelona's art galleries and the site for many of the most important art shows ever held in Barcelona, featuring artists like Nonell, Russinyol, and Picasso, among others. Farther up are the galleries **Trama** at No. 8 and the **Galeria Petritxol** at No. 10. **Xocoa** at No. 9 is another popular chocolate spot. Look carefully at the "curtains" carved into the wooden door at No. 11 and the floral ornamentation around the edges of the ceiling inside. **Granja la Pallaresa**, yet another enclave of chocolate and *ensaimada* (a light-looking but, be warned, deathly sweet Majorcan roll in the shape of a snail with confectioner's sugar dusted on top). Finally on the left at No. 17 is the Rigol fine arts supply store.

⑨ Casa Bruno Quadros. Like something out of an amusement park, this whimsically eclectic exercise designed (assembled is more like it) by Josep Vilaseca in 1885 includes a Chinese dragon with a parasol, Egyptian balconies and galleries, and a Peking lantern—exotic touches all very much in vogue at the time of the Universal Exposition of 1888. Now housing the Caixa de Sabadell bank, this prankster of a building is theoretically in keeping with Art Nouveau's eclectic playfulness, though it has never been taken very seriously as an expression of Modernisme and, consequently, is generally omitted from most studies of Art Nouveau architecture. ⊠ *La Rambla* 99.

Casa de la Sang (House of Blood). To the right as you look up at the rose window of the church of Santa Maria del Pi is the appropriately blackened face of the seat of the 14th-century religious brotherhood charged with the preparation of the last spiritual rites, psychological comfort, and burial of prisoners condemned to death. In the famous Ramon Casas painting *Garrote Vil* (1894)—depicting the execution of the anarchist who bombed the Liceu Opera House (the painting can be seen in Barcelona's Museu d'Art Modern)—the penitent monks dressed in long black cassocks and conical headgear are from this order, the *Casa de la Congregació de la Puríssima Sang* (House of the Congregation of the Purest Blood). The house was first built in 1342 and was renovated in 1613 and 1789. ⊠ *Placa del Pi. Interior closed to the public.*

👆 ⑳ **Drassanes Reials and the Museu Marítim.** The superb Maritime Museum is housed in the 13th-century **Drassanes Reials** (Royal Shipyards), to the right at the foot of the Rambla adjacent to the harborfront. This vast covered complex begun in 1378 built and launched the ships of Catalonia's powerful Mediterranean fleet directly from its yards into the port (the water then reaching the level of the eastern facade of the building). Today, these are the world's largest and best-preserved medieval shipyards; centuries ago, at a time (1377–1388) when Greece was a province of the House of Aragón, they were of crucial importance to the sea power of Catalonia (then allied with Aragón). On the Avinguda del Paral.lel side of Drassanes is a completely intact section of the 14th- to 15th-century walls—Barcelona's third and final ramparts—that encircled the Raval along the Paral.lel and the Rondas de Sant Pau, Sant Antoni, and Universitat. (*Ronda* was originally used to specify streets or circumvolutions running around the outside of the city walls.) The earliest part of Drassanes is the section farthest from the sea along Carrer de Portal de Santa Madrona. Subsequent naves were added in the 17th and 18th centuries. The section housing the restaurant, for example, was built in the 17th century.

Though the shipyards seem more like a cathedral than a naval construction site, the Maritime Museum is filled with ships, including a spectacular collection of ship models that will enchant children, as well as a jaw-dropping, life-sized reconstructed galley; figureheads; nautical gear of all kinds; and early navigational charts. Headphones and infrared pointers provide a fascinating self-guided tour. Keep an eye on Barcelona's musical agenda as concerts, often featuring early music master and viola de gamba virtuoso Jordi Savall, are occasionally held in this acoustical gem. The cafeteria is Barcelona's hands-down winner for dining in the midst of medieval elegance. Don't miss the monument of a sailing ship, commemorating the 1571 Battle of Lepanto, out on the Rambla corner nearest the port. ⊠ *Plaça Portal de la Pau 1,* ☎ *93/301–1871.* 🎫 *850 ptas./5.11; free 1st Sat. of month after 3.* ⊙ Daily 10–7.

❸ **Font de les Canaletas.** This fountain is a key spot in Barcelona, being the place where all great sports victories are celebrated by jubilant *Barça* fans. It was originally known for the best water in Barcelona, brought in by *canaletas* (small canals) from the mountains. The bronze plaque on the pavement in front of the fountain explains that if you drink from its waters, you will fall under Barcelona's spell and forever return . . . so beware. ⊠ *Top of Rambla.*

★ ⑭ **Gran Teatre del Liceu.** Barcelona's opera house has long been ranked among the most beautiful in Europe. First built in 1848, burned and restored once in 1861, bombed by anarchists in 1893, the splendid and heroic Liceu was a cherished cultural landmark until finally gutted once and for all by a raging fire of mysterious origins in early 1994; soprano Montserrat Caballé stood on the Rambla in tears as her beloved opera house was consumed by the flames. The five-year restoration process has been judged a complete success—indeed, a great improvement. The auditorium is majestic in size, with five golden parterre rings rising one above the other; boxes have two levels, with those in the back sitting on a high rise. Even if you don't see an opera, inquire about tours of the building; some of the Liceu's oldest and most spectacular halls and rooms (including the glittering lobby foyer known as the Saló dels Miralls, or Room of Mirrors) were unharmed by the fire of 1994, including those of Spain's oldest social club, El Círculo del Liceu, where if indeed you can get in at all, you'll need a necktie (which they supply). ⊠ *La Rambla 51–59,* ☎ *93/485–9900.* ☞ *Guided tours 800 ptas./ €4.81.* ☉ *Daily 9:45–10:15.*

⑬ Hotel Espanya. A cut alongside the jagged edge of the Sant Agustí church leads straight to the Hotel Espanya, built by Lluís Domènech i Montaner in 1900 and notable for its Art Nouveau decor. The hotel is, at the moment, not recommendable, but the Eusebi Arnau chimney in the breakfast room to the left and the Ramon Casas murals in the dining room (making this one of the most beautiful of all Modernista rooms) make this an important compendium of turn-of-the-20th-century art and architecture. ⊠ *Carrer Sant Pau 9–11,* ☎ *93/318–1758.*

⑱ Monument a Colom (Columbus Monument). This Barcelona landmark to Christopher Columbus sits grandly at the foot of the Rambla along the wide harborfront promenade of the Passeig de Colom, not far from the very shipyards (☞ Drassanes Reials, *above*) that constructed two of the ships of his tiny but immortal fleet. Standing atop the 150-ft-high iron column—the base of which is aswirl with gesticulating angels—Columbus seems to be looking out at "that far-distant shore," which he was able to discover thanks to the patronage of Ferdinand and Isabella. In truth, he is facing the opposite direction and is pointing—with his 18-inch-long finger—in the general direction of Sicily. The monument was erected for the 1888 Universal Exposition to commemorate the "Discoverer's" commissioning, in Barcelona, by the Catholic Monarchs in 1491. Since the royal court was at that time (and, until 1561, remained) itinerant, Barcelona's role in the discovery of the New World is, at best, circumstantial. In fact, Barcelona was consequently excluded from trade with the Americas by Isabella, so Catalonia and Columbus have never really seen eye to eye. For a bird's-eye view over the Rambla and the port, take the elevator to the top of the column. (The entrance is on the harbor side.) ⊠ *Portal de la Pau s/n,* ☎ *93/302–5224.* ☞ *300 ptas./€1.80.* ☉ *Weekdays 10–1:30 and 3–6:30, weekends 10–6:30.*

NEED A BREAK?	Along this walk, opt for two of Barcelona's favorite hangouts: the **Café de l'Opera**(⊠ La Rambla 74) across from the Liceu opera house or the quiet **Café del Pi** (⊠ Carrer del Pi 1), next to the Santa Maria del Pi church.

⑦ Palau de la Virreina. The Neoclassical Virreina Palace, built by a viceroy to Peru in 1778, is now a major exhibition center for paintings, photography, and historical items; find out what's on while you're here. The building also houses a bookstore and a municipal tourist office. The exterior has beautiful accents, including the portal doorway and pediments carved with elaborate floral designs. ⊠ *Rambla de les Flors 99,* ☎ *93/301–7775.* ☉ *Tues.–Sat. 10–2 and 4:30–9, Sun. 10–2, Mon. 4:30–9.*

★ **⑯ Palau Güell.** Disneyesque chimneys, a flying-bat weather vane, parabolic arches, neo-Byzantine salons, and post-Mudéjar ornament all accent this imposing mansion—one of the first and greatest masterpieces built by that genius of Barcelonan Modernismo, Antoni Gaudí, and one of the few private Gaudí houses open to public view. He built this mansion in 1886–89 for textile baron Count Eusebi de Güell Bacigalupi, the architect's main patron and promoter. Gaudí's principal obsession in this project was to find a way to illuminate this seven-story house tightly surrounded by other buildings in the cramped quarters of the Raval. The prominent *quatre barras* (four bars) of the Catalan *senyera* (banner) on the facade between the parabolic entrance arches attest to the nationalist fervor that Gaudí shared with Güell. The dark facade is a dramatic foil for the treasure house inside, where spear-shaped Art Nouveau columns frame the windows and prop up a series of minutely detailed and elaborately carved wood ceilings.

Begin downstairs in the stables with the "fungiform" (fungus- or mushroom-like) columns supporting the whole building. Note Gaudí's signature parabolic (looping) arches between the columns and the way the arches meet overhead, forming an oasislike canopy of palm fronds, probably little consolation for political prisoners (such as Andreu Nin, who was never seen again) held there during the 1936–39 Spanish Civil War when the space was used as the *checa* (Republican secret-police headquarters). The patio where the horses were groomed receives light through a skylight, one of many Gaudí devices and tricks used to create, or seem to create, more light: mirrors, skylights, even frosted-glass windows over artificial lighting giving the impression of exterior light. Don't miss the faithful hounds in the grooming room with rings for hitching horses, or the pine blocks (up above) used as cobblestones to deaden the sound of horses' hooves in the entrance. The chutes on the Nou de Rambla side of the basement were for loading feed straight in from street level overhead; the catwalk and spiral staircase were for the servants to walk back up into the main entry.

Upstairs are three successive receiving rooms, the wooden ceilings progressing from merely spectacular to complex to byzantine in their richly moulded floral and leaf motifs. The third receiving room, the one farthest in with the most elaborate ceiling ornamentation, has a jalousie in the balcony over the room, a double grate through which Güell was able to inspect and, almost literally, eavesdrop on his arriving guests. The main hall, with the three-story-tall tower reaching up above the roof, was the room for parties, dances, and receptions. Musicians played from the balcony, and the overhead balcony window was for the main vocalist. A chapel of hammered copper with retractable kneeling pads and a small bench for two built into the right side of the altar is enclosed behind a double door able to completely remove the liturgical part of the room for more festive occasions. Around the corner is a small organ, the flutes in rectangular tubes climbing the mansion's central shaft.

The dining room is dominated by a beautiful mahogany banquet table seating 10, an Art Nouveau fireplace in the shape of a deeply curving horseshoe arch, and walls with floral and animal motifs. Note the Star of David in the woodwork over the window and the Asian religious themes in the vases on the mantelpiece. From the outside rear terrace, the polished Garraf marble of the main part of the house is exposed and visible, while the brick servants' quarters rise up on the left; Gaudí, no doubt as per instructions from the owners, used less expensive materials for the servants' quarters. The passageway built toward the Rambla was all that came of a plan to buy an intervening property and connect three houses into a major structure, a scheme that never materialized, as the intermediate owners refused to sell.

Gaudí is most himself on the roof, where his playful, polychrome ceramic chimneys seem right at home with later works such as Parc Güell and La Pedrera. Look for the flying-bat weather vane over the main chimney, symbol of Jaume I el Conqueridor (James I, the Conqueror), who brought the House of Aragón to its 13th-century imperial apogee in the Mediterranean. Jaume I's affinity for bats is said to have stemmed from his Majorca campaign when, according to one version, he was awakened by the fluttering *rat penat* (literally, "condemned mouse") in time to stave off a Moorish night attack. Another version attributes the presence of the bat in Jaume I's coat of arms to his gratitude to the Sufi sect who helped him successfully invade Majorca, using the bat as a signal indicating when and where to attack. See if you can find the hologram of COBI, Javier Mariscal's 1992 Olympic mascot on a restored ceramic chimney (hint: the all-white one at the Rambla end of the roof terrace). ⊠ *Nou de la Rambla 3–5,* ☎ *93/317–3974.* ⊠ *450 ptas./€2.70 with guided tour.* ⊙ *Weekdays 10–2 and 4–7:30.*

❺ **Palau Moja.** The first palace to occupy this corner on the Rambla was built in 1702 and inhabited by the Marquès de Moja. The present austere palace was completed in 1790 and, with the Betlem church across the street, forms a small Baroque-era bottleneck in the onetime watercourse now known as the Rambla. If there are temporary exhibitions on view in the Palau Moja, getting inside will also give you a look at the handsome mural and ceiling paintings by Francesc Pla, known as *el Vigatà* (with reference to his native town of Vic). In the late 19th century, the Palau Moja was bought by Antonio Lopez y Lopez, Marquès de Comillas, and it was here that Jacint Verdaguer, Catalonia's national poet and chaplain of the Marquès's multi-million-dollar Compania Transatlántica shipping company, wrote his famous patriotic epic poem "L'Atlàntida." ⊠ *Portaferrissa 1,* ☎ *93/316–2740.* ⊙ *On rare occasions for temporary exhibits.*

❶ **Plaça de Catalunya.** Barcelona's main transport hub, Plaça de Catalunya is the frontier between the old city and the post-1860 Eixample. Comparable in size to Paris's Place de l'Étoile or to Rome's St. Peter's Square, although at 165,000 square ft considerably smaller than Moscow's 198,000-square-ft Red Square, Plaça de Catalunya is generally an unavoidable place to scurry across at high speed on your way to somewhere quieter, shadier, and generally gentler on the senses. The only relief in sight is the **Café Zurich**, at the head of the Rambla and the mouth of the metro, which remains the classic Barcelona rendezvous point. The block behind the Zurich, known as El Triangle, houses a strip of megastores, including FNAC and Habitat, among others. Corte Inglés, the monstrous ocean-liner look-alike department store on the northeast side of the square, offers a wide range of Spanish goods at standard prices and good quality.

The underground tourist office on the northeast corner is the place to pick up free maps of the city and check on walking tours, some in English, that originate there. The most interesting items in this large but mostly uncharming square are the sensual and exuberant sculptures. Starting from the corner nearest the head of the Rambla, have a close look at, first, the blocky Subirachs monument to Francesc Macià, president of the Generalitat (Autonomous Catalan government) from 1934 to 1936. In the center of the reflecting pool is Clarà's stunning *Déesse* (Goddess), kneeling gracefully in the surface film. At the northwest corner is Gargallo's heroic bronze of men, women, and oxen hauling in the grape harvest, while at the northeast corner across from the Corte Inglés is the Federic Marès bronze of a buxom maiden on horseback holding a model of the ship with which Columbus discovered the New World.

⓯ **Plaça Reial.** Colombian Nobel prize–winning novelist Gabriel García Marquez, prestigious architect and urban planner Oriol Bohigas, and once-mayor of Barcelona and future-president of the Catalonian Generalitat Pasqual Maragall are among the many famous people known to have acquired apartments overlooking this potentially stunning square, a chiaroscuro masterpiece where formal Neoclassical elegance clashes with everyday big-city street squalor. Somewhat reminiscent of Seville, the elegant, symmetrical 19th-century arcaded Plaça Reial is bordered by elegant ocher facades with balconies overlooking the wrought-iron **Fountain of the Three Graces** and treelike, snake-infested lampposts designed by Gaudí in 1879. Sidewalk cafés line the square, though in recent years the Plaça has earned a reputation for hosting squads of drug pushers, purse snatchers, and the homeless, who occupy the benches on sunny days. The place is most colorful on Sunday morning, when crowds gather to sell and trade stamps and coins; after dark it's a center of downtown nightlife for the jazz-minded, the young, and the adventurous (it's best to be street-wise touring this somewhat-safe nabe in the late hours). Bar Glaciar, on the uphill corner toward the Rambla, is a booming beer station for young international travelers. The Taxidermist, across the way, is the only good restaurant in the plaza; Tarantos has top flamenco performances; and Jamboree, the Taxidermist, and the Barcelona Pipa Club are venues for world-class jazz.

⑲ Port. Beyond the Columbus monument—behind the ornate Duana, or former customs building, now headquarters for the Barcelona Port Authority—is the **Rambla de Mar,** a boardwalk with a drawbridge designed to allow boats in and out of the inner harbor. The Rambla de Mar extends out to the **Moll d'Espanya,** with its Maremagnum shopping center, IMAX theater, and new aquarium. Next to the Duana, you can board a Golondrina boat for a tour of the port or, from the Moll de Barcelona on the right, take a cable car to Montjuïc or Barceloneta. You can also take a boat to the end of the *rompeolas* (breakwater), 3 km (2 mi) out to sea, and walk back into Barceloneta. Trasmediterranea and the fleeter Buquebus passenger ferries leave for Italy and the Balearic Islands from the Moll de Barcelona, down to the right. At the end of the quay is Barcelona's new World Trade Center, a complex of offices, convention halls, restaurants, and a hotel.

⑥ Portaferrissa. Both the fountain and the ceramic representation of Barcelona's second set of walls and the early Rambla are set just across the street from Palau Moja (on the right where Carrer de Portaferrissa leads left away from the Rambla), and both are worth studying carefully. If you can imagine pulling out the left side of the ceramic scene and looking broadside at the amber yellow 13th-century walls that ran down this side of the Rambla, you will see a clear picture of what this spot looked like in medieval times. The sandy Rambla ran along outside the walls, while the portal looked down through the ramparts into the city. As the inscription on the fountain explains, the Porta Ferrica, or "iron door," was named for the iron measuring stick attached to the wood and used in the 13th and 14th centuries to establish a unified standard for measuring goods. ✉ *Rambla and Carrer Portaferrissa.*

⑫ Sant Agustí. This unfinished church is one of Barcelona's most unusual structures, with jagged stone sections projecting down the left side and the upper part of the front entrance on Placa Sant Agustí waiting to be covered with a facade. Begun in 1728 and abandoned 20 years later, the projected facade, designed by Pere Costa, was to be Baroque in style but funding stopped and so did the construction. Inside are some large-format early 19th-century paintings by Claudi Lorenzale. ✉ *Plaça Sant Agustí,* ☎ 93/318–6231.

⑩ Santa Maria del Pi. Sister church to Santa Maria del Mar and to Santa Maria de Pedralbes, this early Catalan Gothic is perhaps the most fortresslike of all three, hulking dark and massive and perforated only by the main entryway and the mammoth (especially in the diminutive Plaça del Pi) rose window, said to be the world's largest—try to see it from inside in the late afternoon to get the best view of the colors. Named for the lone pine tree (*pi*) that once stood in what was a marshy lowland outside the 4th-century Roman walls, an early church dating back to the 10th century preceded the present Santa Maria del Pi, begun in 1322 and finally consecrated in 1453. Like Santa Maria del Mar, the church of Santa Maria del Pi is one of Barcelona's finest examples of Mediterranean Gothic architecture, though the aesthetic distance between Santa Maria del Pi and Santa del Mar is substantial. The church's interior is disappointingly cluttered after the clean and lofty lightness of Santa Maria del Mar (☞ Sant Pere and La Ribera, *below*), but the creaky choir loft and the Ramón Amadeu painting of the La Mare de Deu dels Desamparats (Our Lady of the Helpless), for which the artist reportedly used his wife and children as models for the Virgin and children portrayed, are interesting to note. The lateral facade of the church, around to the left in Plaça Sant Josep Oriol, bears a plaque dedicated to the April 6, 1806, fall of the portly parish priest José Mestres, who slipped off the narrow catwalk visible high above circling the outside of the apse. The priest survived the fall unhurt, and the event was considered a minor miracle, thus the plaque.

The adjoining squares, **Plaça del Pi** and **Plaça de Sant Josep Oriol,** are two of the liveliest and most appealing spaces in the old quarter, filled with much-frequented outdoor cafés and used as a venue for markets selling natural products or paintings or as an impromptu concert hall for musicians. The handsome entryway and courtyard at No. 4 Plaça de Sant Josep Oriol across from the lateral facade of Santa Maria del Pi is the **Palau Fivaller,** now seat of the Agricultural Institute, an interesting patio to have a look through. From Placeta del Pi, behind the church, you can see the bell tower and the sunny facades of the apartment buildings on the north side of Plaça Sant Josep Oriol, which was once the cemetery for the blind (as commemorated in the little street leading in, Carrer Cecs de la Boqueria, or Blind of the Boqueria), has tables and is a cozy place to spend some time. ⊠ *Plaça del Pi s/n,* ☎ *93/318–4743.* ☉ *Daily 9–1:30 and 4:30–8.*

Medieval Splendor: The Barri Gòtic

No other city in Spain can boast an ancient quarter that rivals Barcelona's Barri Gòtic in either historic atmosphere or sheer wealth of monumental buildings. The Gothic Quarter—a jumble of medieval buildings, squares, and streets—is the name given to that area around the Catedral de la Seu, still packed with glorious Gothic structures of the late Middle Ages, that marked the zenith of Barcelona's power in the 15th century. On certain corners, you feel as if you're making a genuine excursion back into time, in which it is the 20th century, not the 15th, that suddenly seems fantastic.

To understand Gothic Barcelona you need to understand the city's own special style. The Gothic was first created in France (a mere 100 mi away) in the 13th century, but Catalan Gothic is directly related to the variants created in southern France. Of an almost biblical simplicity, with (some say) more dignity than charm, this is Gothic that is less Spanish than Aquitainian, French, and German. Gloom, energy, and medieval romance are the keynotes—in fact, it takes several minutes for your modern eyes to adjust to the velvety darkness of the city cathedral. Because of the glaring southern light of Aquitaine windows in southern France, churches were often small, with stained-glass windows providing the only light, and these were often set high up on the wall.

Even when there were rose windows, traceries were often heavy. All this may have served to cut down on the illumination, but it also, in turn, heightened the mysticism of the religious experience. Even when packed with people, the cathedral allows congregants to feel alone and emphasizes individual communication with spiritual matters—all very much in the mystical tradition of the greatest Spanish saints.

The Gothic Quarter actually sits upon the first ancient Roman settlement of the city. Sometimes referred to as the *rovell d'ou* (egg yoke), this high ground the Romans called Mons Taber coincides almost exactly with the early 1st- to 4th-century Roman Barcino. Plaça del Rei (considered one of Barcelona's best), the Roman underground beneath the City History Museum, Plaça Sant Jaume, and the area around the onetime Roman Forum, the medieval Jewish Quarter or Call, and the ancient Plaça Sant Just complete this tour. All in all, this nearly completely pedestrianized area remains rich in Roman, Gothic, and even Moderniste—the Els Quatre Gats restaurant (once a Picasso haunt)—treasures.

Numbers in the text correspond to numbers in the margin and on the Barri Gòtic map.

A Good Walk

Start out by jumping feet first into the 15th-century past by visiting the famous city cathedral, the **Catedral de la Seu** ㉑. Drink in its crepuscular shadows, and then step back out into the light of its beautiful Gothic cloister, still home to a flock of "canonical" geese legendarily brought over to the city by the ancient Romans and descended from the famous flock of Rome's Capitoline Hill. Don't miss the cathedral's Capilla de Santa Llúcia (St. Lucie Chapel) or the inside of the Roman wall visible in the Arxiu Històric de la Ciutat in the **Casa de l'Ardiaca** ㉒ across the street. Back to the left (northeast) of the cathedral is the **Museu Frederic Marès** ㉓, with some superb masterpieces of devotional medieval sculpture (also enjoy the little terrace café, surrounded by Roman walls). Next, pass the patio of the Arxiu de la Corona d'Aragó (Archives of the House of Aragón) in the **Palau del Lloctinent** ㉔; then turn left again and down into **Plaça del Rei** ㉕, the oldest and most evocative square of the Gothic Quarter.

As you leave Plaça del Rei, the **Museu d'Història de la Ciutat** ㉖ is on your left. Here you can peruse the Roman city underground, one of Barcelona's most fascinating sites. Returning to the rear of the apse of the cathedral, walk left up Carrer Paradís to No. 4, Barcino's highest point and home of the Centre Excursionista de Catalunya and the perfectly preserved 2,000-year-old pillars of the Roman **Temple d'August** ㉗. Farther around the back of the cathedral are **Plaça de Garriga Bachs** ㉘—with murals about the 1818 Catalan resistance movement—outside the cloister; **Plaça San Felip Neri** ㉙, a picturesque nook; and **La Baixada de Santa Eulàlia** ㉚, a unique overhead monument honoring the city's patron saint. Cutting back to the cathedral cloister, go right on Carrer del Bisbe and walk under the neo-Gothic bridge over the street to **Plaça Sant Jaume** ㉛. Here, the seats of Catalonian and Barcelona government face each other across what was once part of the Roman Forum in, at the moment, political discord: the municipal government is socialist while the Autonomous Catalan government is Convergencia i Unió, a conservative coalition of Catalan nationalists and Christian Democrats. Both the **Generalitat de Catalunya** ㉜ and the **Casa de la Vila** ㉝ (town hall) are superb places to visit, among the best concentrations of art and architecture in Barcelona.

48

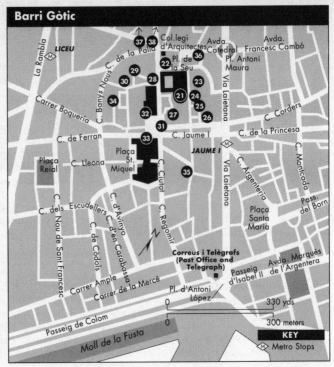

For a walk through Barcelona's **El Call** ㉞ (medieval Jewish quarter, from the Hebrew *qahal,* "meeting"), leave the Plaça Sant Jaume on Carrer del Call, turn right on Sant Domènech del Call, and proceed to the next corner: a synagogue once stood across the intersection on the left, at the corner of Carrer Marlet. Now turn left on Carrer Marlet and proceed to the next corner, Arc de Sant Ramón del Call—high on the right, a stone with Hebrew inscriptions and a transcript on a glass plaque mark all that remains of the Jewish community that prospered here until a 1391 pogrom virtually wiped out Barcelona's Jews a century before the 1492 expulsion. Back in Plaça Sant Jaume walk to the left of the Casa de la Vila and take your first left on Carrer d'en Hércules down to **Plaça Sant Just** ㉟, another square filled with fascinating sights. Now walk outside the Roman walls, through Plaça del Àngel and Carrer Tapineria to the front of the cathedral, past the **Casa de la Pia Almoina** ㊱ and its Museo Diocesá, and make your way through Plaça Nova past the Col.legi d'Arquitectes (with the Picasso drawing of Sardanas on the facade facing the cathedral) and the **Reial Cercle Artistic** ㊲ with its beautiful Gothic voussoir, or keystone arch, over the door, down to Carrer Montsió, where a right takes you to the 20th century and the **Casa Marti** ㊳, a.k.a. **Els Quatre Gats**—from 1897 to 1903 a famous haunt for Barcelona's artistic, literary, and musical elite. Pablo Picasso had his first solo exhibition here in 1900.

TIMING

This walk covers some 3 km (2 mi) and should take about three hours, depending on stops. Allow another hour or two for the City History Museum.

Sights to See

③⓪ Baixada de Santa Eulàlia (Slope of Santa Eulàlia). Straight out from the side door of the cathedral cloister down Carrer Sant Sever past the Església de Sant Sever is the tiny overhead chapel dedicated to Santa Eulàlia, the most honored martyr of the city. Down this hill, or *baixada* (descent), Eulàlia was rolled in a barrel filled with—as the Jacint Verdaguer verse in ceramic tile on the wall reads—*glavis i ganivets de dos talls* (swords and double-edged knives), the final of the 13 tortures to which the martyr was subjected before her crucifixion at Plaça del Pedró. ⊠ *Baixada de Santa Eulàlia.*

㉒ Casa de l'Ardiaca (Archdeacon's House). Across from the Santa Llúcia chapel, this diminutive but lovely leafy courtyard with its fountain and, on the day of Corpus Christi, one of the most impressive dancing eggs (L'Ou Comballa, or "dancing egg"—literally, "the egg how it dances"—refers to the ancient Barcelona tradition of placing an egg atop the spurts of water from the city's fountains to celebrate Corpus Cristi every June) and floral arrangements in town, is the seat of the Municipal archives (upstairs) and affords some of the premier views of the inside of the 4th-century Roman watchtowers and walls. Look at the Montjuïc sandstone carefully and you will see blocks clearly taken from other buildings, carved and beveled into decorative shapes, proof of the haste of the nervous Romans as the Visigoths approached from the north. The marble letterbox by the front entrance was designed in 1895 by Lluís Domènech i Montaner for the Lawyer's Professional Association and, as the story goes, is meant to symbolize, in the images of the doves, the lofty flight to the heights of truth and justice and, in the images of the turtles, the plodding pace of administrative procedures. ⊠ *Carrer de Santa Llúcia 1,* ☎ *93/318–1342.* ☉ *Mon.–Sat. 10– 2 and 4–8, Sun. 10–2.*

㊱ Casa de la Pia Almoina—Museu Diocesá (Diocesan Museum). Behind the massive iron floral grate in the octagonal Roman watchtower to the left of the stairs of the Catedral de la Seu, this museum houses, along with temporary art exhibits, a permanent collection of religious sculptures and a potpourri of liturgical paraphernalia, from monstrances to chalices to the paintings from the apse of the Sant Salvador de Polinyà chapel, which constitute one of the few 12th-century works visible outside of Barcelona's Romanesque collection in the Palau Nacional (☞ Montjuïc, *below*). Anyone beginning a tour of the Roman walls should drop in for a look at the excellent relief map/scale model of Roman Barcelona (sold in the city history museum) on display in the vestibule. Inside, original Roman stones are clearly visible in this much-restored structure, the only octagonal tower of the 82 that ringed the 4th-century *Barcino.* Look for the Romanesque *Mares de Deu* (Mother of God) wood sculptures such as the one from Sant Pau del Camp church in Barcelona's Raval. ⊠ *Avinguda de la Catedral 4,* ☎ *93/315– 2213.* ▨ *350 ptas./€2.10.* ☉ *Mon.–Sat. 10–2 and 5–8, Sun. 11–2.*

㉝ Casa de la Vila—Ajuntament de Barcelona. The 15th-century Casa de la Vila—Ajuntament de Barcelona (city hall), located on the Plaça Sant Jaume, has an impressive black-and-burnished-gold mural (1928) by Josep Maria Sert and the famous Saló de Cent, from which the Council of One Hundred ruled Barcelona between 1372 and 1714. To visit the interior, which is lavishly endowed with art (especially the sensual sculptures by all of the great Catalan masters from Maillol to Gargallo to Clarà to Subirachs), you need to make arrangements with the office ahead of time (ask for the *protocolo,* the protocol office). Check listings for free concerts or open events here, the only way to get in.

✉ *Plaça Sant Jaume 1,* ☎ *93/402–7000.* ☉ *Mon.–Sat. 10–2 and 4–8, Sun. 10–2.*

★ ㊳ **Casa Martí–Els Quatre Gats.** Just three minutes' walk from the Cathedral, this Art Nouveau house built in 1896 by Josep Puig i Cadafalch for the Martí family houses the famous Quatre Gats café and restaurant, a good place for a coffee or even a meal if the spot strikes your fancy. The exterior is richly decorated with Eusebi Arnau sculptures, featuring the scene of St. George and the dragon that no Puig i Cadafalch project ever failed to include. The interior is even more spectacularly hung with reproductions of some of the most famous Ramon Casas paintings, such as the prominently displayed scene of the Toulouse Lautrec–ish Casas and the rangy Pere Romeu comedically teamed up on a tandem bicycle—one of the most iconic images of Barcelona. The recently restored (Nov. 2000) Joseph Llimona sculpture of St. Joseph and the Infant Jesus gleaming whitely over St. George and the dragon was torn down in the anticlerical violence of July 1936. Picasso had his first opening here on February 1, 1900, and Antoni Gaudí hung out here with Moderniste painters from Casas to Russinyol to the likes of Nonell and Anglada Camarassa, so the creative reverberations ought to be strong. *Quatre Gats* means "four cats" in Catalan, a euphemism for "hardly anybody," but the original four—Casas, Russinyol, and Utrillo, hosted by Pere Romeu—were all definitely somebodies. ✉ *Carrer Montsió 3 bis,* ☎ *93/302–4140.* ☉ *Daily 9 AM–2 AM (closed Aug. 2–20).*

★ ㉑ **Catedral de la Seu.** Barcelona's Cathedral, named for La Seu, or See, the seat of the bishopric is, if falling short as a memorable work of art, still impressive and filled with many centuries of Barcelona history and legend. Imposing, if not altogether aesthetically felicitous, this Gothic monument was built between 1298 and 1450, with the spire and neo-Gothic facade added in 1892. Historians are not sure about the cathedral architect—one name much bandied about is Jaume Fabre, a native of Majorca. The plan of the church is cruciform, with transepts standing in as bases for the great tower—a design also seen in England's Exeter Cathedral. Floodlit in striking yellow beams at night with the stained-glass windows backlit from inside and ghostly seagulls soaring over the spiky Gothic spires, Barcelona's main ecclesiastical structure, while only a bronze medalist behind Santa Maria del Mar and La Sagrada Família, is a fine place to explore Gothic Barcelona.

This is reputedly the darkest of all the world's great cathedrals—even at high noon, the nave is enveloped by shadows, which give it magically much larger dimensions than it actually has—so it takes a while for eyes to adjust to the rich, velvety darkness of the cathedral, but once they do, there are many sights here worth seeking out: the beautifully carved choir stalls of the Knights of the Golden Fleece; the intricately and elaborately sculpted Plateresque organ loft over the door out to Carrer Comtes (complete with a celebrated Saracen's Head sculpture); the series of 60-odd wood sculptures of men and women along the outside lateral walls of the choir in a nearly animated succession of evangelistic poses; the famous cloister; and, in the crypt, Santa Eulàlia's tomb.

St. Eulàlia, originally interred at Santia Maria del Mar—then known as Santa Maria de les Arenes (St. Mary of the Sands)—was moved to the cathedral in 1339 and is the undisputed heroine and patron of the Barcelona cathedral. *Eulalistas* (St. Eulàlia devotees, as opposed to followers of La Mercé) celebrate the fiesta of *La Laia*—as all Eulàlias are affectionately nicknamed—from February 9 to 15, and they would prefer that the cathedral be named for their favorite martyr. For the moment, the cathedral remains a virtual no-name cathedral, known universally as La Catedral and more rarely as La Seu.

Appropriately, once you enter the front door (there are also lateral entrances through the cloister and from Carrer Comtes down the left side of the apse), the first thing you see are the high relief sculptures of the **story of St. Eulàlia**, Barcelona's co-patroness (along with La Mercé, Our Lady of Mercy, the official titleholder), on the near side of the choir stalls. The first scene, on the left, shows St. Eulàlia in front of a bored and bemused Roman Consul Decius with her left hand on her heart and her outstretched right hand pointing at a cross in the distance. In the next scene to the right, Eulàlia is tied to a column and being flagellated by Decius-directed thugs. To the right of the door into the choir the senseless Eulàlia is being hauled away, and in the final scene on the right she is being lashed to the X-shape cross upon which she was crucified in mid-February of the year 303. To the right of this high relief is a sculpture of St. Eulàlia, standing with her emblematic X-shaped cross, resurrected as a living saint.

Surrounded by two dozen ornate and gilded chapels dedicated to all the relevant saints of Barcelona and beyond, one chapel to seek out is the **Capilla de Lepanto** containing the **Santo Cristo de Lepanto** in the far right corner coming through the front door. This 15th-century polychrome wood sculpture of a somewhat battle-scarred and bedraggled dark-skinned Christ, visible on the altar of this 100-seat chapel behind a black-clad Mare de Deu dels Dolors (Our Lady of Sorrow), was, according to oral legend, the bowsprit of the commanding Spanish galley at the battle fought between Christian and Ottoman fleets in the Gulf of Patras off Lepanto, Greece on October 7, 1571. The fleet of the Holy League was composed of 200 galleys from Spain, Venice, the Papacy, and other Italian states, carrying some 30,000 soldiers and sailors. The Turkish force was evenly matched and, though considered invincible, was routed by the Christian fleet (at least nominally) commanded by John of Austria (d. 1578). In the battle—considered decisive in halting Turkish encroachment and hegemony in the Mediterranean—10,000 Christian galley slaves were freed, 15,000 Turks were killed or captured, 7,000 Spanish and Italians died, and a 24-year-old-marine lieutenant and novelist-to-be named Miguel de Cervantes was grievously wounded and lost the use of his left arm. Lepanto is considered the high-water mark of Spain's golden era; after the 1588 disaster of the Spanish Armada in the English Channel Spain began to lose power and colonies one by one all the way down to the final 1898 Spanish-American War, in which the remaining imperial possessions, Cuba and the Philippines, were taken over by the United States.

It is interesting to note that the explanatory plaque next to the alms box at the right front of the chapel states that, though John of Austria was the commander-in-chief of the Holy League's fleet, the fleet captain and main battle commander was Lluís de Requesens (1528–76), a local Catalan aristocrat and prominent Spanish general during the reign of Felipe II.

Outside the main nave of the cathedral to the right is the leafy, palm-tree-shaded **cloisters** surrounding a tropical garden and pool filled with 13 show-white geese, one for each of the tortures inflicted upon St. Eulalia in an effort to break her faith. Legend has it that they are descendants of the flock of geese of Rome's Capitoline Hill, whose honking alarms roused the city to ward off invaders during the ancient days of the Roman Republic. Don't miss the fountain with the bronze sculpture of an equestrian St. George hacking away at his perennial sidekick, the dragon, on the eastern corner of the cloister. On the Day of Corpus Christi this fountain is one of the more spectacular floral displays, featuring the *ou com balla* (dancing egg). The intimate **Santa Llúcia chapel** is at the front right corner of the block (reached by a separate entrance or from the cloister). Another Decius victim (though in this version Decius merely wanted her body, in contrast to the Eulalia drama in which it was her mind he was after), St. Llúcia allegedly plucked out her eyes to dampen the Roman Consul's ardor, whereupon new ones were miraculously generated. Patron saint of seamstresses, of the blind, and of the light of human understanding, St. Lucía is portrayed over the altar in the act of presenting her plucked-out eyes, sunny-side-up on a salver, to an impassive Decius.

In front of the cathedral is the grand square of the Plaça de la Seu, where, on Saturday from 6 PM to 8 PM, Sunday morning, and occasional evenings, Barcelona folk gather to dance the *sardana,* the somewhat dainty and understated circular dance, a great symbol of Catalan identity. Watch carefully: mixed in with heroic septuagarians bouncing demurely are some young *esbarts* (dance troupes) with very serious coaches working on every aspect of their performance, from posture to the angle of arms to the velvet-smooth footwork. Observing the throng of sardana dancers, scores of foreigners and locals take photographs or just watch in rapt amazement as these rings of dancers deep in concentration repeat the surprisingly athletic movements and steps that represent a thousand years of tradition. Also check out the listings for the annual series of evening organ concerts held inside the cathedral. ⊠ *Plaça de la Seu,* ☎ *93/315–2213.* ☉ *Daily 7:45–1:30 and 4–7:45.*

㉗ Centre Excursioniste de Catalunya (CEC)—Columnes del Temple d' August (Outing Center of Catalunya—Columns of the Temple of Augustus). The highest point in Roman Barcelona is marked with a circular millstone at the entrance to the Centre Excursionista de Catalunya. Inside this entryway on the right are some of the best-preserved 1st- and 2nd-century Corinthian Roman columns in Europe. Massive, fluted, and crowned with the typical Corinthian acanthus leaves in two distinct rows under eight fluted sheaths, these columns remain only because Barcelona's early Christians elected, atypically, not to build their cathedral over the site of the previous temple. The Temple of Augustus, dedicated to the Roman Emperor Caesar Augustus, occupied the northwest corner of the Roman Forum, which coincided approximately with today's Plaça Sant Jaume. ⊠ *Carrer Paradis 10,* ☎ *93/315–2311.* ☉ *Mon.–Sat. 10–2 and 5–8, Sun. 11–2.*

Col.legi d'Arquitectes. Barcelona's architects' college, constructed in 1961 by Xavier Busquets, houses three important gems: a superb library (across the street) where for a small fee the full range of the college's bibliographical resources are placed at your disposal for architectural research purposes; a book store specializing in architecture, graphics, design, and drafting supplies; and a nonpareil restaurant (one of the city's great secrets), where you can either pull up to a merely excellent ten-dollar lunch menu or go for the gourmet à la carte recipes that chef Manel Martí collects from all over Catalonia. And let's not forget the Picasso friezes just above the college's windows. Designed by Picasso in 1960 and reproduced by the Norwegian Carl Nesjar using a sandblasting technique, the frieze on the eastern facade (Carrer de Capellans) represents typical groups of Sant Medir celebrants, the popular choral groups of Antoni Clavé, and animals from l'Arrabassada hill behind Barcelona. The central frieze portrays giants in popular processions and dances, while the frieze on Carrer dels Arcs evokes children and the joy of living. Inside the building are two more Picasso friezes, one a vision of

Barcelona and the other a poem dedicated to the *sardana,* Catalunya¥s national dance. ⊠ *Plaça Nova 5,* ☎ *93/306–7801.* ☉ *Mon.–Sat. 10– 8..*

㉞ El Call. Its name derived from the Hebrew word *qahal* (meeting place, or place to be together), Barcelona's Jewish Quarter is just to the Rambla side of the Palau de la Generalitat. Carrer del Call, Carrer de Sant Domènec del Call, Carrer Marlet, and Arc de Sant Ramón del Call mark the heart of the 9th- to 14th-century Jewish quarter, today distinguished only by the reproduction of a plaque bearing Hebrew text on the corner of Carrer Marlet and Arc de Sant Ramón del Call. The sad saga of Barcelona's historic Jewish community came to its culminating moment in August of 1391 when a nationwide outbreak of anti-Semitic violence reached Barcelona with catastrophic results: nearly the entire Jewish population was murdered or forced to convert to Christianity. The Expulsion Decree of 1492 came 100 years too late for many Catalonian Jews, who had either been murdered or had fled or converted in 1391.

㉜ Generalitat de Catalunya. Housed in the Palau de la Generalitat, opposite the Casa de la Vila–Ajuntament de Barcelona (☞ *above*), this is the seat of the autonomous Catalan government. Through the front windows of this ornate 15th-century palace, the gilded ceiling of the Saló de Sant Jordi (St. George), named for Catalonia's dragon-slaying patron saint, gives an idea of the lavish decor within. The Generalitat only opens to the public on the Día de Sant Jordi (St. George's Day), April 23, during the Fiesta de la Mercé in late September, and on various other city or Catalonian holidays; check with *protocolo.* The Generalitat hosts carillon concerts on Sundays at noon, another opportunity to see the inside of this splendid building. ⊠ *Plaça de Sant Jaume 4,* ☎ *93/402-4600.* ☉ *On special occasions only. Check with Protocol office.*

㉖ Museu d'Història de la Ciutat (City History Museum). Just off the Plaça del Rei, this fascinating museum traces the evolution of Barcelona from its first Iberian settlement to its founding by the Carthaginian Hamilcar Barca in about 230 BC to Roman and Visigothic times and beyond. Antiquity is the focus here: Romans took the city during the Punic Wars, and the striking underground remains of their *Colonia Favencia Julia Augusta Paterna Barcino* (Favored Colony of the Father Julius Augustus Barcino), through which you can roam on metal walkways, are the museum's main treasures. Archaeological finds range from parts of walls and fluted columns to recovered busts and vases. Aboveground, off the Plaça del Rei (☞ *below*), the **Palau Reial Major,** the splendid **Saló del Tinell,** the chapel of **Santa Àgata,** and the **Torre del Rei Martí,** a lookout tower with views over the Barri Gòtic, complete the self-guided tour. ⊠ *Palau Padellàs, Carrer del Veguer 2,* ☎ *93/315– 1111.* 🖃 *750 ptas./€4.51.* ☉ *Tues.–Sat. 10–2 and 4–8, Sun. 10–2.*

OFF THE BEATEN PATH

MUSEU DEL CALÇAT – Hunt down the tiny Shoe Museum, in a hidden corner of the Gothic Quarter between the cathedral and Carrer Banys Nous. The collection includes a pair of clown's shoes and a pair worn by Pablo Casals. The tiny square, originally a graveyard, is just as interesting as the museum, with its bullet- and shrapnel-pocked walls and quiet fountain. ⊠ *Plaça de Sant Felip Neri,* ☎ *93/301–4533.* 🖃 *300 ptas./€1.80.* ☉ *Tues.–Sun. 11–2.*

㉓ Museu Frederic Marès (Frederic Marès Museum). Here, off the left (north) side of the cathedral, you can browse for hours among the miscellany assembled by the early 20th-century sculptor-collector Frederic Marès.

COLONIA FAVENCIA JULIA AUGUSTA PATERNA BARCINO

FOR A TOUR OF PROTO-BARCELONA, the 2,000-year-old Roman city of Barcino (pronounced *Bark*-ino), start at the freestanding bronze letters 50 yards to the right of the cathedral steps in Plaça Nova spelling BARCINO. Roman Barcelona was originally enclosed by a 1st-century ritual (decorative) wall built during the Pax Romana, when Roman hegemony in the Mediterranean was uncontested. In the 4th century, with the Visigoths encroaching southward, the city was hurriedly surrounded by a 1,270-yard defensive wall of heavy sandstone blocks cut from Montjuïc. This is the wall visible today from outside the Roman ramparts.

Eighty-two watchtowers, most of them rectangular, guarded this wall, which was 30 ft high and 12 ft thick. In Plaça Nova you can see one of the cylindrical watchtowers used to guard corners, as well as small segment of the aqueduct that used to carry water in from the mountains. Walk inside the walls up Carrer del Bisbe, turn left on Santa Llúcia, and go into the building housing the Municipal Archives, the Arxiu Històric de la Ciutat, for a look at the wall from the inside. Returning to the left side of the cathedral steps, find the 16th-century Casa Pia Almoina (House of Pious Charity), now the Diocesan Museum, in its unique octagonal tower. At the entrance to the museum is an excellent reproduction of Barcino. Walk down Carrer de la Tapineria (named for *tapins*, the medieval wooden shoes once made by cobblers here). To your right, rectangular towers, or parts of them—large stones surrounded by 20th-century brick restoration—are discernible every 50 ft or so.

Guiding along from one watchtower to the next, walk around the left side of the cathedral through Plaça Ramon Berenguer el Gran, down Carrer Tapineria, through Plaça de l'Angel, and across Carrer Jaume I into Carrer Sots-tinent Navarro.

A right turn on Carrer Pom d'Or brings you to the Plaça dels Traginers. The cylindrical towers here were command posts placed at the corners of the enclosure to enhance visibility. Continue straight ahead through Carrer Correu Vell and you'll see more sections of Roman wall to your right. Take a right on Carrer Regomir. A few steps up is Barcino's eastern portal, with pedestrian doors on either side of the central carriage port. The pedestrian door seems low because the city has risen some 11½ ft over the last 2,000 years.

Now cut left through Carrer Comtessa de Sobradiel and turn right on Carrer d'Avinyó. Look for No. 19, the Pakistani restaurant El Gallo Kiriko. Here, one side of the back dining room is a section of the Roman wall with two perfect watchtowers—not a bad place for a meal. Next door, still at No. 19, the Asociació Excursionista, Expedicionari, i Folkloric (AEEF; Hiking, Expeditionary, and Folklorical Association) offers a free walk between the 1st-century ritual wall and the 4th-century defensive wall from 7 to 9 PM every weekday except Thursday.

Back out on Carrer d'Avinyó, continue right across Carrer de Ferran and take your first right into Carrer del Call. Continue up Carrer del Call into Plaça Sant Jaume—once part of the Roman Forum. To the right of the Generalitat, across Carrer del Bisbe, Carrer Paradis 4 is your last stop: Here, at the highest point in the Roman Mons Taber (Barcelona's equivalent of Athens's Acropolis), stood the Roman Temple of Augustus. These massive columns, surrounded and concealed for hundreds of years by medieval structures, were finally uncovered during the 19th century and now stand in the entryway to the CEC, Catalonia's most important mountaineering organization. For a walk through the Roman underground, pop into the Museu d'Història de la Ciutat, around the corner off Plaça del Rei.

Everything from paintings and polychrome wood carvings—such as Juan de Juní's 1537 masterpiece *Pietà* and the Master of Cabestany's late-12th-century *Apparition of Christ to His Disciples at Sea*—to Marès's personal collection of pipes and walking sticks is stuffed into this surprisingly rich potpourri. ⊠ *Plaça Sant Iu 5,* ☎ *93/310–5800.* 🖬 *350 ptas./€2.10.* ☉ *Tues.–Wed. and Fri.–Sat. 10–7, Thurs. 10–5, Sun. 10–3.*

㉔ Palau del Lloctinent (Lieutenant's Palace). On the corner between the cathedral and Plaça del Rei, the Palau del Lloctinent's three facades face the Carrer dels Comtes de Barcelona on the cathedral side, the Baixada de Santa Clara, and the Plaça del Rei. Typical of late Gothic, early Renaissance Catalan design, the building was constructed by Antoni Carbonell in 1557. The heavy stone arches over the entry, the central patio, the intricately carved roof over the stairs are all fine examples of noble 16th-century architecture. The door on the stairway, which replaced an equestrian Sant Jordi sculpture identical to the one over the door of the Generalitat, is a 1975 Antoni Subirachs work portraying scenes from the life of Sant Jordi. The Palau del Lloctinent was inhabited by the King's official emissary or viceroy to Barcelona during the 16th and 17th centuries and is now open to the public for occasional concerts and for the Corpus Christi celebration when an egg is made to "dance" on the fountain amidst an elaborate floral display in the center of the patio. ⊠ *Carrer dels Comtes de Barcelona s/n,* ☎ *93/485–4285.*

㉘ Plaça de Garriga Bachs. This little space just outside the cathedral cloister is flanked by ceramic murals depicting executions of heroes of the Catalan resistance to the invasion of Napoleonic troops in 1809. In the first three scenes we see the five resistance leaders waiting their turns to be garroted or hanged (the *garrote vil,* or vile garrote, was reserved for the clergymen, as hanging was considered a lower and less humane form of execution). The fourth scene shows the surrender of three agitators who attempted to rally a general Barcelona uprising to save the first five by ringing the cathedral bells. The three are seen here, pale and exhausted after 72 hours hiding in the organ, surrendering after being promised amnesty by the French. All three were subsequently executed.

㉕ Plaça del Rei. This plaza is widely considered the oldest and most beautiful space in the Gothic Quarter. Long held to be the scene of Columbus's triumphal return from his first voyage to the New World—the precise spot where Ferdinand and Isabella received him is purportedly on the stairs fanning out from the corner of the square (though new evidence indicates that the Catholic monarchs were at a summer residence in the Empordá)—the **Palau Reial Major** was the official royal residence in Barcelona. The main room is the **Saló del Tinell**, a magnificent banquet hall built in 1362. Other elements around the square are, to the left, the **Palau del Lloctinent** (Lieutenant's Palace); towering overhead in the corner is the dark 15th-century **Torre Mirador del Rei Martí** (King Martin's Watchtower); the 14th-century **Capilla Reial de Santa Àgueda** (Royal Chapel of Saint Agatha) is on the right side of the stairway; and behind and to the right as you face the stairs is the **Palau Clariana-Padellàs**, moved to this spot stone by stone from Carrer Mercaders in the early 20th century and now the entrance to the Museu d'Història de la Ciutat (☞ *above*).

㉙ Plaça San Felip Neri. A tiny square just behind Placa Garriga Bachs off the side of the cathedral cloister, this space was once the cemetery for Barcelona's executed heroes and villains. A favorite spot for early music concerts, the square is centered around a fountain, whose delightful trickling—a constant E-flat major—fills the square with its own water music. The large pock marks on the walls of the San Felip Neri church were caused by the explosion of a bomb during the Spanish Civil War.

㉛ Plaça Sant Jaume. This central square behind the city cathedral houses both the government buildings of Catalonia, the **Palau de la Generalitat** (☞ *above*) and that of Barcelona, the **Casa de la Vila—Ajuntament de Barcelona** (☞ *above*). This was the site of the Roman forum 2,000 years ago. The plaça was cleared in the 1840s, but the two imposing government buildings facing each other across it are much older.

㉟ Plaça San Just i Pastor. Off to the left side of town hall down Carrer Hèrcules (named for the mythical founder of Barcelona) is the site of the Església de Sant Just i Pastor, one of the oldest Christian churches in Barcelona, dating from the 4th century. Christian catacombs are reported to have been found beneath Plaça Sant Just. The Gothic fountain is the oldest in Barcelona and bears an image of St. Just and city and Sovereign Count-King's coats of arms. The excellent entryway and courtyard to the left of Carrer Bisbe Caçador is the Palau Moixó, the town house of an important early Barcelona family, while down Carrer Bisbe Caçador is the Academia de Bones Lletres, the Catalan Arts and Letters Academy. The fine restaurant on the corner, Café de l'Academia, fills with workers from the town hall and the Generalitat at lunchtime. The church is dedicated to the boy martyrs, Just and Pastor; the Latin inscription over the door translates into English almost in reverse syntax as "Our pious patron is the black and beautiful Virgin, together with the sainted children Just et Pastore."

NEED A BREAK? If you feel inclined to take a breather in a Pakistani restaurant at a table set between two 4th-century Roman watchtowers, seek out **El Gallo Kiriki** (⊠ Carrer d'Avinyó 19), just a block west of Plaça Sant Jaume, for either lunch or a beverage. **Cafè de l'Acadèmia** (⊠ Carrer Ledó 18) is another good choice for lunch. If a coffee is all you need, look for the **Mesón del Café** (⊠ Carrer Llibreteria 16), where a deep breath is nearly as bracing as a cappuccino.

㊲ Reial Cercle Artístic. This private fine arts society has two art galleries and a restaurant and bar open to the public and offers drawing and painting classes to artists. The main entrance with its heavy keystone arch, the stone carvings inside to the right in the Sala Güell at the upper part of the gallery walls, and the sculptures along the stairway are all elegant and graceful Gothic details worth stopping for. The restaurant is acceptable, if undistinguished. ⊠ *Carrer dels Arcs 5*, ☎ *93/318–7866.* ⊙ *Mon.–Sat. 10–7, Sun. 10–3.*

El Raval: West of the Rambla

El Raval (from *arrabal*, meaning suburb or slum) is the area to the west of the Rambla, on the right as you walk toward the port. Originally a rough outskirt of town stuck outside Barcelona's second set of walls, which ran down the left side of the Rambla, the Raval used to be notorious for its Barri Xinès (or Barrio Chino) red-light district, whose attractions often lured the young Pablo Picasso to end his nights here. Gypsies, circus acrobats, and saltimbanques who made this area their home soon found immortality in the many canvases Picasso painted of them during his Blue Period, now considered some of the most memorable and poignant works of the artist. In fact, it was other denizens not far from the Barri Xinès—ladies of the night—who wound up inspiring one of the 20th-century's most famous paintings, Picasso's *Demoiselles d'Avignon*, which singlehandedly opened the door to Cubism. Not bad for a city slum.

But the Raval is a slum no longer, having been gentrified and much improved over the last 20 years, largely as a result of becoming the home of the Museo de Arte Contemporáneo de Barcelona (MACBA) and the other cultural institutions nearby such as the Centro de Cultura Contemporánea (CCCB) and the Convent dels Àngels. The Rambla del Raval has been opened up between Carrer de l'Hospital and Drassanes, and light and air are pouring into the streets of the Raval for the first time in a thousand years. The medieval hospital, Plaça del Pedró, the Mercat de Sant Antoni, and Sant Pau del Camp are highlights of this helter-skelter, rough-and-tumble part of Barcelona. The only part to consider avoiding is the lower section between Carrer de l'Hospital and Drassanes, and, of course, it's safer if you can avoid carrying a tote or hangbag.

Numbers in the text correspond to numbers in the margin and on the Raval map.

A Good Walk

Starting from Plaça Catalunya, take an immediate right after the Font de les Canaletas into **Carrer Tallers,** named for butchers, tailors, or small textile factories (shops) depending whether you're using Catalan or Spanish. Go left through Carrer de les Sitges past to Plaça del Bonsuccés and take a right on Elisabets at the picturesque and generally excellent Bar Castells, with its convenient marble counter outside on the corner. Stay on Elisabets past El Llar del Llibre, now a bookstore and once the chapel for the **Casa de Misericordia** ㊴, a former center for wayward or orphaned women, next door. Walk out into Plaça dels Àngels, where the medieval penumbra is suddenly brightened by Richard Meier's gleaming **Museu d'Art Contemporánea de Barcelona** ㊵ (MACBA). To the left is the **Convent dels Àngels** ㊶, while behind the MACBA is the **Centre de Cultura Contemporánea de Barcelona** ㊷ (CCCB), with its fine collection of contemporary masters, such as Chillida, Calder, and Rauschenberg. Beyond that is the **Casa de la Caritat— Pati Manning** ㊸, yet another cultural institution. Take Carrer de Ferlandina out to Joaquin Costa, where on the corner you will see Bar Almirall, a landmark Art Nouveau bar. Go left all the way down Joaquin Costa to Carrer del Carme and turn left past an even more beautiful Art Nouveau bar, Bar Muy Buenas, a nearly irresistible arrangement of curving wooden arches, acid-etched glass, and marble former codfish-salting basins.

Continuing down Carrer del Carme, you will reach the back entrance to the medieval **Antic Hospital de la Santa Creu i de Sant Pau** ㊹. Cut to the right into this entrance. The first door and patio to your right is the former **Casa de la Convalescencia** (Convalescents House), now the Institut d'Estudis Catalans. Continue through the patio of the medieval hospital where you will pass the doors, on your right, to the **Biblioteca de Catalunya** and, to the left, the children's library. Continue through the orange trees in the patio of the hospital, leaving the **Escola Massana** art school on your right, and you will emerge through the massive wooden doors into Carrer Hospital. First go left to look at the **Capilla de l'Antic Hospital de la Santa Creu** ㊺, now used as a space for art exhibits; then turn around and walk back down Carrer Hospital, past the tempting Passatge Bernardí Martorell (with two good restaurants at the end of it: El Cafetí and Casa Leopoldo) to **Plaça del Pedró** ㊻. From here, walk out Carrer de Sant Antoni Abat past the gorgeous colonial furniture store La Maison Coloniale at No. 54, formerly the Sant Antoni chapel, to the **Mercat de Sant Antoni** ㊼, a combination flea, food, clothes, and (on Sunday) stamp market. From here follow the Ronda de Pau east toward the port, cut left on Carrer de les

58

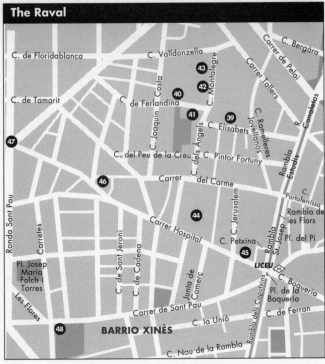

Flors, and you will pass the excellent Cal Isidre restaurant before reaching Barcelona's oldest church, **Sant Pau del Camp** ㊽. From here it's just 200 yards to Drassanes, Barcelona's medieval shipyard, and the bottom of the Rambla.

Sights to See

㊹ **Antic Hospital de la Santa Creu i de Sant Pau.** Approached through either the Casa de la Convalescencia entry on Carrer del Carme or through the main door on Carrer Hospital, this cluster of medieval architecture surrounds a garden courtyard and a midtown orange grove. Considered one of the first medical complexes in the world, founded in the 10th century, most of the present buildings and courtyards were built in the 15th and 16th centuries. As you approach from Carrer del Carme, the first door on the left is the **Reial Acadèmia de Cirurgia i Medecina** (Royal Academy of Surgery and Medicine), a Neoclassical 18th-century building of carved stone. On the right is the 17th-century Casa de la Convalescencia and straight ahead is the simple 15th-century Gothic facade of the hospital itself, with the light of the inner cloisters gleaming through the heavy, arched portal. The Royal Academy of Surgery and Medicine—open for visits until 2 PM on weekdays—contains a circular amphitheater originally used for the observation of dissections. Across the way is the door into the patio of the **Casa de Convalescència** (Convalescence House), with its Renaissance columns and its brightly decorated scenes of the life of St. Paul in the vestibule. The primarily blue and yellow *azulejos* (ceramic tiles) start with the image to left of the door into the inner courtyard portraying the moment of the saint's conversion: SALVE, SALVE, QUID ME PERSEGUERIS (Be saved, be saved, and in return follow me). The ceramicist, Llorenç Passolas, was also the author of the late-17th-century tiles around the inner patio. The image of St. Paul in the center of the courtyard over what was once a well is another homage to the building's initial benefactor, Pau Ferran. Look for the horseshoes, two of them around the keyholes, on the double wooden doors in the entryway, wishing good luck to the convalescent and, again, in reference to benefactor Ferran, from *ferro* (iron), as in *ferradura* (horseshoe).

Continuing toward the hospital patio, look carefully to your left toward the back of the Boqueria market and you might see, protected from the sun by their typical flimsy shelters, the last example or two of a vanishing breed: the amanuensis. Derived from the Latin *manus* (hand), these scribes traditionally used the space behind the market to write everything from wills to love letters for the illiterate. If you see nothing of their kind, it's because the last of them is finally gone, though the profession lives on elsewhere in the Raval as immigrants pour into Barcelona.

Inside the archway, on the right is the 1½-million-volume **Biblioteca de Catalunya**, national library of Catalunya and second in scope only to Madrid's Biblioteca Nacional in Spain. The wide Gothic arches and vaulting of what was once the hospital's main nave were designed in the 15th century by the architect of Santa Maria del Pi church, Guillem Abiell, who was clearly seeking light and space here, using a very different formula than the one he applied to the gloomy and all but unrelieved enclosure of Santa Maria del Pi. Opposite the library is the door to the **Biblioteca Infantil**, the children's library.

The hospital patio centered on a Baroque cross, filled with orange trees, and usually filled with students from the **Escola Massana** art school at the far end on the right. The stairway under the arch on the right was built in the 16th century, and the Gothic well to the left of the arch is from the 15th century, as is the romantic little Romeo-and-Juliet balcony in the corner to the left of the Escola Massana entry. Leaving through the heavy wooden door out to Carrer Hospital, from the far sidewalk you can see the oldest section of the medieval hospital, part of the old Hospital de Colom founded by the canon Guillem Colom in 1219 to the left of the door. The facade itself is from the 16th century.

Every May 11, Carrer Hospital is the main site for the celebration of the **Fira de Sant Ponç,** a much beloved holiday in Barcelona. Sant Ponç was the patron saint of herbalists and beekeepers and his feast day is when, so to speak, the "forest comes to Dunsinane" or, at least, all of the Catalonian hinterland comes to Barcelona laden with every natural product it can lug, haul, or carry. Camomile, rosemary, thyme, laurel, lavender, basil, Maria Louisa, pollens, mint, honeys of every kind, and even bees in glass cases working away at their honeycombs, candied fruits, snake oil, tiger toenail powder, headache remedies, aphrodisiacs, and every imaginable condiment and savoury from fennel to saffron to tarragon: The slightest mention of Sant Ponç to any *barcelonin* will invariably elicit a backward inclination of the head, closing (perhaps even fluttering) of the eyelids, and a deep and luxuriant nasal inhalation.

Everyone in Barcelona including Mayor Joan Clos seems to find a moment, especially if the weather is good, to disappear from work and to take a walk from the Rambla out to Carrer Hospital to browse through the artisanal sausage, goat cheese, wild mushrooms, cakes, jams, jellies, anti-tobacco licorice sticks, herbal olive oils, homemade wines, pies, cheesecakes, fig bread, crepes, hand-carved wooden spoons, knives and forks, teas, coffees, and a thousand medicinal herbal potions, lotions, unguents, and concoctions guaranteed to cure what ails you or, at least, smell good in the attempt. In medieval times, the days when farmers cleared their larders for the harvest soon to come—a sort of late spring cleaning—medicinal herbalists and the sorceress fringe soon hijacked this tradition and set up stalls along the walls of the 15th-century hospital (where, presumably, there was a heightened interest in remedial products). Today Sant Ponç is the official start of the Catalonian summer and one of Barcelona's sweetest days.⊠ *Carrer Hospital 58 and Carrer del Carme 45.*

Barrio Chino (Chinese Quarter). Sandwiched between Barcelona's Pigalle-like Avinguda del Paral.lel—complete with its La Molina knock-off of the Parisian Moulin Rouge—and the lower Rambla (always a combat zone), Barcelona's most notorious district, the Barrio Chino, has raged raucous and unrepentant for centuries, long more emblematic and characteristic of the city than, say, Gaudí or the Gothic Quarter. After all, Genet set a novel here, and the area denizens inspired many of Picasso's greatest paintings of circus acrobats and gypsies; its brothels were the kernel that resulted in the artist's celebrated *Les Demoiselles d'Avignon.* Though all of the Raval has been confused and commingled with the Barrio Chino (Barri Xinès in Catalan; Chinese Quarter in English, but known universally and eternally as the Barrio Chino), the authentic, hard-core "Chino" is everything between Carrer Hospital and the port on the bottom right side of the Rambla. As you walk from Plaça Reial toward the sea, Barcelona's notorious red-light district is on your right in the lower part of the Raval.

China never had anything to do with this; the quarter's name is a generic reference to all foreigners, as the area was traditionally inhabited by immigrants from other parts of Spain or from abroad. This is still the case, perhaps more so. In Plaza dels Àngels in front of the Macba, children playing soccer can be heard, usually in separate groups, speaking Arabic, Urdu, and Tagalog, among other languages, as well as in Spanish and Catalan. The U.S. Navy's Sixth Fleet, rarely seen here these days, used to consider Barcelona's Barrio Chino all but home and even rented a nearby locale for use as an on-shore base of operations until it was bombed in the early '80s and subsequently closed. French novelist Jean Genet wrote a novel (*La Marge*) about Barcelona's Barro Chino as did other European writers such as Pierre de Mandariargues; the prostitutes, transvestites, pimps, gypsies, and common thieves provided rough and colorful textures ideal for literature. The fact that the elegant and aristocratic Liceu opera house perched precariously at the edge of all this steamy and sordid squalor made *la Lírica,* the world of opera, all the more pungent and poignant. (El Raval and "el Chino" had, in fact, a faithful group of opera fans, who would be hoisted, with their two-buck tickets, in a creaky wooden elevator, from a separate entrance on Carrer Hospital to the fifth-tier, limited-or-no-view seats, dressed in jeans and T-shirts, to avidly follow, with binoculars and even recording devices, the same opera the white-tied and betailed Barcelona bourgeoisie were yawning their way through down below.)

The world of "el Chino" was entirely alien to the straight world beyond its borders. Barcelona journalist Quim Calvet described "el chino" as a simple matter of appetites and necessities: "You had one group with these . . . appetites and money and another group that needed to do whatever it could to survive." Rival chiefs of groups of drug pushers and prostitutes habitually collected protection money from local establishments. When an aspiring extortionist challenged the presiding gangster, there were duels, complete with rules and an elaborate code of conduct having nothing to do with conventional law and order.

Though there are pockets and places still used as a haven for prostitutes, drug pushers, and street thieves, today's Barrio Chino is not nearly as dangerous as it once was. In fact, the reinforced police presence here may even make it safer than the Rambla or parts of the Gothic Quarter—but don't count on it. The recently opened constructed Rambla del Raval runs through the middle of what used to be no-man's-land, bringing light and fresh air into what was until recently the most insalubrious and unsafe part of Barcelona.

45 Capilla de l'Antic Hospital de la Santa Creu (Chapel of the Old Hospital of the Holy Cross). This quiet refuge is between the Carrer Hospital entrance to the medieval hospital and the Rambla. Now an art gallery, the chapel is generally open for a browse through an art or photography exhibit and a look at the lovely vaults and arches of the chapel. The sculpture over the chapel door is a Baroque 18th-century representation of Charity by Pere Costa, who also did the lower part of the facade of the unfinished Sant Agustí church just down from Carrer Hospital toward the Rambla. Don't miss the ancient wooden choir loft at the back of the chapel or a look up into the cupola towering over the central nave. ⊠ *Carrer Hospital 54.*

43 Casa de la Caritat—Pati Manning. The Centre d'Estudis i Recursos Culturals de la Diputació de Barcelona (Study Center for Cultural Resources of the Disputation of Barcelona) is one of the three cultural entities (the others are the MACBA and the CCCB) that occupy this felicitously restored 14th-century Carthusian convent. A library, training courses, and cultural initiatives of all kinds are organized at the Pati Manning. ⊠ *Carrer de Montalegre 5–9,* ☎ *93/402–2565.* ⊙ *Weekdays 11–7, Sat. 10–8, Sun. 10–3.*

39 Casa de la Misericordia. This pretty courtyard, densely vegetated with palm trees and vines, was once a school and a home for female orphans and the children of the destitute. Founded in 1581 by theologian Don Diego Pérez de Valdivia as a home for the poor, the Casa dels Àngels, as it was initially called, soon found itself overwhelmed with the homeless and redirected its efforts solely toward girls from the city of Barcelona. The Llar del llibre bookstore next door was the former chapel of the Casa de la Misericordia. Around the corner on Carrer dels Ramelleres at No. 17 a ring of wood in the wall just above waist level is all that remains of the ancient *torno,* or turntable, a standard feature in early orphanages and convents. Alms, groceries, and unwanted babies alike were placed in this opening slot, to be spun anonymously into the Casa de la Misericorda. ⊠ *Carrer Elisabets 6,* ☎ *93/412–0781.*

42 Centre de Cultura Contemporània de Barcelona (CCCB). This museum, lecture hall, and concert and exhibition space is worth checking out no matter what's on the schedule. Housed in the restored and renovated Casa de la Caritat, a former medieval convent and hospital, the CCCB is, like the Palau de la Música Catalana, one of Barcelona's best combinations of contemporary and traditional architecture and design. A smoked-glass wall on the right side of the patio, designed by architects Albert Villaplana and Helio Pinon, reflects out over the rooftops of the Raval to Montjuïc and the Mediterranean beyond. ⊠ *Montalegre 5,* ☎ *93/412–0781.* ▦ *650 ptas./€3.91 (450 ptas./€2.70 Wed.; entry to the patio and bookstore free).* ⊙ *Tues.–Fri. 11–2 and 4–8, Wed. and Sat. 11–8, Sun. 11–7.* ✎

41 Convent dels Àngels. This former Augustinian convent built by Bartolomeu Roig in the middle of the 16th century has recently been restored and converted into a general cultural center with an exhibition hall (El Forum dels Àngels) directly across from the main entrance to the MACBA, a design and bookstore, a 150-seat auditorium, and a restaurant and bar. Once the Monestir de Nostra Senyora dels Àngels

Peu de la Creu (Monastery of Our Lady of the Angels of the Foot of the Cross), the FAD (Foment dels Arts Decoratives) now operates this handsome new Raval resource. The Forum dels Àngels is an impressive space with beautifully carved and restored sculptures of angels in the corners and at the top of the walls. ☒ *Plaça dels Àngels,* ☎ *93/ 443–7520.* ⊙ *Mon.–Sat. 9–9, Sun. 10–2.*

㊼ Mercat de Sant Antoni. At the far edge of the Raval at the junction of Ronda de Sant Antoni and Comte d'Urgell, this mammoth steel hangar was designed in 1882 by Antoni Rovira i Trias, the winner of the competition for the planning of Barcelona's Eixample. A combination food, clothing, and flea market, it becomes a book, comics, stamp, and coin fest on Sundays. Considered Barcelona's greatest masterpiece of ironwork architecture, this entire city block covered by the Greek cross-shape Mercat de Sant Antoni is, strictly speaking, on the edge of the Eixample, though it fits naturally into a tour of the Raval. An interesting spot to browse through, as much for its artistic value as for the potpourri of produce on sale there, the Sant Antoni market is one of Barcelona's most fundamental and characteristic gems. ☒ *Carrer Comte d'Urgell,* ☎ *93/443–7520.* ⊙ *Mon.–Sat. 9–9, Sun. 10–2.*

㊵ Museu d'Art Contemporani de Barcelona (Barcelona Museum of Contemporary Art). Designed by American architect Richard Meier in 1992, this gleaming explosion of light and geometry in the darkest Raval houses a permanent collection of contemporary art as well as traveling exhibits. With barely a nod (via the amorphous tower in front of the main facade) to Gaudí, Meier's exercise in Minimalism (resembling, to some degree, a bathroom turned inside-out) has been much debated in Barcelona. Basque sculptor Jorge Oteiza's massive bronze *La Ola* (The Wave) on the MACBA's front porch is popular with skateboard surfers, while Eduardo Chillida's *Barcelona* climbs the wall to the left of the main entrance. The MACBA's 20th-century contemporary art collection (Calder, Rauschenberg, Oteiza, Chillida, Tàpies) is excellent, as is the guided tour carefully introducing the philosophical bases of contemporary art as well as the pieces themselves. ☒ *Plaça dels Àngels,* ☎ *93/412–0810.* ▣ *800 ptas./€4.81.* ⊙ *Mon. and Wed.–Fri. 11– 7:30, Sat. 10–8, Sun. 10–3.*

㊻ Plaça del Pedró. This landmark in medieval Barcelona was the dividing point where ecclesiastical and secular paths parted and in some ways remains an important fork on the way in from the Mercat de Sant Antoni and points south. The high road, Carrer del Carme, leads to the cathedral and the seat of the bishopric, whereas the low road, Carrer de l'Hospital, heads down to the medieval hospital and the Boqueria market, a clear choice between body and soul. Named for a stone pillar or *pedró* (large stone) marking the fork in the road, the Plaça became a cherished landmark for Barcelona Christians after St. Eulàlia, co-patron of Barcelona, was crucified there on her distinctive X-shape cross after suffering the legendary 13 ordeals designed to persuade her to recant, which she, of course, heroically refused to do. As the story goes, an overnight snowfall chastely covered her nakedness with virgin snow. Destroyed and replaced on various occasions over the centuries, the present version of Eulàlia and her cross was sculpted by Barcelona sculptor Frederic Marés and erected in 1951. The bell tower and vacant alcove at the base of the triangular plaça are the **Sant Llàtzer** church, originally built in the open fields in the mid-12th century and used as a leper hospital and place of worship after the 15th century when Sant Llàtzer was officially named patron saint of lepers. Presently in the process of being rescued from the surrounding buildings that once completely obscured the church, Sant Llàtzer's has a tiny antique patio and apse that are visible from the short Carrer de Sant Llàtzer, which cuts behind the church between Carrer del Carme and Carrer Hospital.

48 **Sant Pau del Camp.** Barcelona's oldest church was originally outside the city walls (*del camp* means "in the fields") and was a Roman cemetery as far back as the 2nd century, according to archaeological evidence. A Visigothic belt buckle found earlier this century suggests that the Visigoths may have used it as a cemetery between the 2nd and 7th centuries. What we see now was built in the 12th century and is the earliest Romanesque structure in Barcelona, suggestive even of some of the pre-Romanesque Asturian churches or of the pre-Romanesque Sant Michel de Cuxà in Catalunya Nord (Catalonia North, a.k.a. southern France). Elements of the church (the classical marble capitals atop the columns in the main entry) are thought to be from the 6th and 7th centuries. The hulking mastodonic shape of the church is a reminder of the fortress or refuge it must have served as through Moorish invasions and sackings. Check carefully for masses or musical performances here, as the church is otherwise nearly always closed. The cloister is Sant Pau del Camp's best feature, one of Barcelona's semi-secret gems most natives have never seen and few even know of. The right side of the altar leads out into the tiny garden, surrounded by porches or arcades, a moist and verdant sanctuary and a gift from the ages as the busy Paral.lel roars by only a few yards away. ✉ *Sant Pau 101,* ☎ *93/441–0001.*

Sant Pere and La Ribera: The Medieval Textile and Waterfront Districts

Barcelona has rarely, if ever, laid fallow architecturally, as these two districts prove. A medley of artistic styles going back centuries, this area is studded with some of the city's most iconic buildings, ranging from the light and elegant 14th-century basilica of Santa Maria del Mar—a church of the purest Catalan Gothic—to that great flagship of the city's Moderniste architecture, the extraordinary Palau de la Música. Past and present definitively collide at the Museu Picasso, where works of the great 20th-century master are ensconced in an elegantly medieval palace.

Sant Pere is Barcelona's old textile neighborhood and is centered on church of Sant Pere. Set between the lower reaches of the Via Laietana and the Parc de la Ciutadella, the adjacent Barri de la Ribera—the hub of Catalonia's great maritime and economic expansion in the 13th and 14th centuries—remains one of the city's best waterfront districts; the district surrounds the basilica of Santa Maria del Mar and includes Carrer Montcada, Barcelona's most aristocratic early thoroughfare, lined with 14th- to 18th-century Renaissance palaces; Carrer Flassaders and the area around the early mint, La Seca, behind Carrer Montcada; the shop- and restaurant-rich Carrer Banys Vells; Plaça de les Olles; and La Llotja, Barcelona's early maritime exchange.

La Ribera began a revival in the 1980s and with its intimate bars, cafés, taverns, and shops continues to gain ground as one of the more fashionable quarters of the city. El Born, the onetime central market of Barcelona, will soon become a library, and the Passeig del Born, considered the Rambla of medieval Barcelona —*Roda al mon i torn al Born* (Go around the world but return to the Born) went the saying—may once again take its place as one the city's hubs of dining, shopping, and art-gallery browsing.

Numbers in the text correspond to numbers in the margin and on the Sant Pere, La Ribera, La Ciutadella, and Barceloneta map.

A Good Walk

Sant Pere and La Ribera lie, respectively, generally to the north and east of the Gothic Quarter across Via Laietana. From the central Plaça de Catalunya, it's no more than a 15-minute walk through Porta del Àngel and Carrer Comtal, past the sgraffiti-covered Casa Gremial dels Velers to the architectural extravaganza that is the **Palau de la Música Catalana** ㊾. After taking in (and getting over) the Palau music hall (guided tours in English are available until 3), continue along Carrer Sant Pere Més Alt (literally, Upper St. Peter's Street) to the Plaça Sant Pere on your way past the spirit-haunted church of **Sant Pere de les Puelles** ㊿. From here, cut back along Carrer Sant de Pere Més Baix (Lower St. Peter's Street) to the **Biblioteca Popular de la Dona Francesca Bonnemaison** (51) at No. 7 before walking through Carrer Beates and across to the historic (and presently being restored) marketplace of **Mercat de Santa Caterina** (52). Walk through Carrer Semoleres into Plaça de la Llana, named for the wool (*llana*) industry once centered here, and turn left on Carrer Corders, named for the makers of rope (*corda*) who once worked here. The **Capella del Marcús** (53) is the curious little chapel stuck in against neighboring structures at the end of Carrer Montcada.

Down Carrer Montcada across Carrer Princesa is one of the city's greatest cultural treasures, the **Museu Picasso** (54), housed in three of the noble merchant mansions of the Calle Montcada. Across the street at No. 12 is the **Palau de los Marqueses de Llió—Museu Textil** (55), featuring one of Carrer Montcada's best two patios, along with **Palau Dalmases** (56). Continue through Carrer Montcada's treasury of Renaissance palaces to the tunnel-like Arc de Sant Vicenç, where a loop through Carrer de la Seca, Carrer Cirera, **Carrer Flassaders** (57), and back along **Passeig del Born** (58) will get you back to Placeta Montcada and the back door of the noted sailors' church of **Santa Maria del Mar** (59). Walk up the right side of the church on Sombrerers (named for the medieval makers of, you guessed it, sombreros) and make an aromatic stop at the Gispert dry-goods (nuts, teas, coffees, spices, herbs) store, one of Barcelona's oldest and loveliest shops. Walk around the church's eastern side through the **Fossar de les Moreres** (60) (Cemetery of the Mulberry Trees) to **Plaça de les Olles** (61).

Another side trip from Santa Maria del Mar begins on the other (west) side of the church on **Carrer Banys Vells** (62), lined with a series of beautiful shops and restaurants. At the end of Bany Vells, turn left on Carrer Barra de Ferro and work your way back through Carrer de la Carassa, noting the sculpted *carassa* (a stone face announcing a medieval brothel) over the corner of Carassa and Mirallers. Walk down Mirallers, taking a right on Grunyí out to Argenteria, where a left will take you back to the main facade of Santa Maria del Mar and the excellent wine-tasting bar La Vinya del Senyor. Duck through the brief 30 ft or so of Carrer Anissadeta (Barcelona's shortest street) and go left on Carrer Canvis Vells past the excellent Moroccan shop Baraka to the early maritime exchange **La Llotja** (63). Then go through Trompetas past the tiny door under the heavy wooden 15th-century beams and stone pillars at No. 14, said to have been an early residence of the Picasso family, to Carrer Agullers, home of two of Barcelona's best emporiums of wines and cheeses, the Viniteca, and the little Vila grocery store on the corner opposite, all run and owned by the friendly and knowledgeable Vila family.

TIMING

Depending on the number of stops, this walk can take a full day. Count on at least four hours of actual walking time. Catching Santa

Sant Pere, La Ribera, La Ciutadella, and Barceloneta

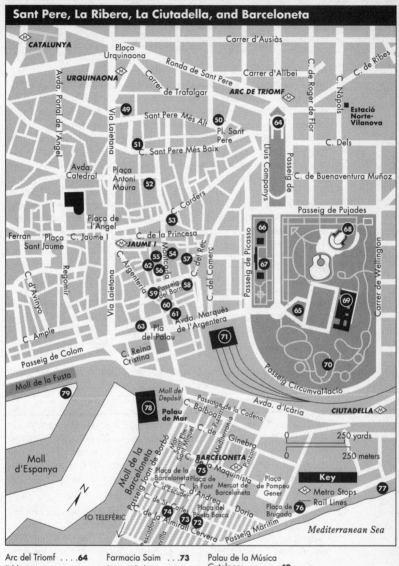

Maria del Mar open is key (it's closed from 1:30 to 4:30). If you make it to that tapas mecca Cal Pep before 1:30 you might get a place at the bar, but if you don't, waiting's a pleasure. The Picasso Museum is at least a two-hour visit.

Sights to See

⑤ Biblioteca Popular de la Dona Francesca Bonnemaison (Women's Public Library). Barcelona's (and probably the world's) first library exclusively for women, this lovely spot was founded in 1909 as a female sanctuary, evidence of Barcelona's early 20th century progressive attitudes and tendencies. Over the opulently coffered main reading room, the stained-glass skylight reads TOTA DON VAL MES QUAN LETRA APREN ("Any woman's worth more when she learns how to read"), the first line of a song by the 13th-century Catalan troubadour Severí de Girona. Once the Franco Spain of church, army, and aristocracy had restored order after the Spanish Civil War, the center was taken over by Spain's one legal political party, the Falange, and women's activities were reoriented toward more domestic pursuits. ⊠ *Sant Pere més Baix 7,* ☎ *93/268–0107.* ◷ *Tues.–Wed. and Fri. 4–9, Thurs. 10–10, Sat. 11–2.*

㉝ Capella del Marcús (Marcús Chapel). This Romanesque hermitage looks as if it had been left behind by some remote order of hermit-monks who meant to take it on a picnic in the Pyrenees. Nearly swallowed up by surrounding buildings, this tiny chapel, possibly—along with Sant Llàtzer—Barcelona's smallest religious structure, was originally built in the 12th century on the main Roman road into Barcelona, the one that would become Cardo Maximo just a few hundred yards away as it passed through the walls at Porta del Àngel. Bernat Marcús, a wealthy merchant concerned with public welfare and social issues, built a hospital for the poor. The chapel today known by his name was built as the hospital chapel and dedicated to the Mare de Déu de la Guia (Our Lady of the Guide). As a result of its affiliation, combined with its location on the edge of town, the chapel became linked with the *Confraria del Correus a Cavall* (Pony Express Guild), also known as the *troters* (trotters), and for two centuries (13th and 14th) made Barcelona the key link in overland mail between the Iberian Peninsula and Europe. ⊠ *Carrer Carders 2 (Placeta d'En Marcus).* ◷ *Open for mass only.*

㉒ Carrer Banys Vells. This little pedestrian-only alleyway paralleling Carrer Montcada just gets better and better. Exploring Bany Vells is a delight, from the two beautifully appointed and supplied Teresa Ferri restaurants, **L'Ou Comballa** and **El Pebre Blau**, all the way down the street past various and sundry shops and the stunningly beautiful, stone-vaulted **Va de Vi** (which means, in Catalan, "It's about wine") wine-tasting tavern to the **La Habana Vieja** Cuban cuisine oasis and the **Tarannà** design and general bric-a-brac shop on the corner at No. 4 Carrer Barra de Ferro. Banys Vells, by the way, means "old baths," referring to the site of the early public baths. Later baths were on the street Banys Nous (New Baths) in the Gothic Quarter near the cathedral. While you're in the neighborhood grab a beer and pick up your E-mail at the **Internet Gallery Café** (15-minute minimum for 250 ptas./€1.50) at No. 3 Barra de Ferro; have a look at the medieval-vintage, exquisitely restored **La Cua Corta** restaurant (where you can roast your filet mignon at your table) on Carrer de la Carassa; and have a single malt or a beer from Scotland at the **Clansmen** opposite Carrer Mirallers on Barra de Ferro.

㉗ Carrer Flassaders. The Carrer Flassaders (named for blanket makers) loop begins on Carrer Montcada opposite La Xampanyet, one of La Ribera's favorite bars (specializing in a sticky sparkling wine best avoided—but otherwise an excellent place for tapas and ambience). Duck into the short, dark Carrer Arc de Sant Vicenç. At the end you'll find yourself face to face with **La Seca**, the Barcelona mint where money was manufactured until the mid-19th century. Coins bearing the inscription, in Castilian, *Principado de Cataluña* (Principality of Catalonia) were minted here as late as 1836. Directly ahead is the studio and showroom of the internationally prestigious sculptor Manel Alvarez, look for announcements of openings on the door across from the end of Arc de Sant Vicenç. The interior of La Seca is an exquisitely restored split-level maze of wooden beams and pillars. Up above to the right is the enormous redbrick chimney over the mint's furnace.

Moving left to Carrer de la Cirera, look up overhead to the left for the niche with the image of **Santa Maria de Cervelló,** one of the patron saints of the Catalan fleet, on the back side of the Palau Cervelló on Carrer Montcada. Out on **Carrer dels Flassaders** walk left past several impressive shops—**Re-Born** at Flassaders 23; the café, restaurant, and design store **Café de la Princesa** at the corner of Carrer Sabateret—and then turn back down Flassaders past the main entry to La Seca at No. 40, with the gigantic royal Bourbon coat of arms over the imposing archway. At No 42 is the wide-vaulted and beautiful **La Maison de l'Eléphant,** an antiques dealer specializing in furniture from Morocco, Thailand, and India, also occupying part of La Seca. A right on Passeig del Born will take you back to Placeta Moncada and Santa Maria del Mar.

60 **Fossar de les Moreres** (Cemetery of the Mulberry Trees). This low marble monument runs across the open space along the eastern side of the church of Santa Maria del Mar. It honors those defenders of Barcelona who gave their lives in the 1714 siege that ended the War of the Spanish Succession and established Felipe V on the Spanish throne. The inscription (EN EL FOSSAR DE LES MORERES NO S'HI ENTERRA CAP TRAIDOR, or IN THE CEMETERY OF THE MULBERRY TREES NO TRAITOR LIES) refers to the story of the graveyard keeper who refused to bury those who had fought on the invading side, even when one of them turned out to be his son.

The traditional gathering place for the most radical elements of Catalonia's nationalist (separatist) movement, Terra Lliura (Free Land), the September 11 Catalonian national holiday, tends to be emotional here and, until Franco's death in November of 1975, was a guaranteed free-for-all between students and the *grises* (grays), the feared Franco riot police. From the Fossar de les Moreres, one of Santa Maria del Mar's most interesting peculiarities is easily visible. The lighter-colored stone on the lateral facade was left by the 17th-century Pont del Palau (Palace Bridge), erected to connect the Royal Palace (later military headquarters) in the nearby Pla del Palau with the Tribuna Real (Royal Box) over the right side of the Santa Maria del Mar altar so that kings, queens, viceroys, and generals could get to mass without risking their lives in the streets of not-so-pacific Barcelona. The offending bridge, always regarded as a symbol of imperialist oppression, passing as it did over the Fossar de les Moreres, was finally dismantled in 1987.

63 **La Llotja** (Maritime Exchange). Barcelona's Llotja, or trade center, like those of the other main commercial centers of the Corona de Aragón (Crown of Aragon, the Catalano-Aragonese confederation that dominated Mediterranean trade between the 14th and 17th centuries), was designed to be the city's finest example of civic architecture. Perpignan, Castelló d'Empúries, Tortosa, Valencia, Palma de Mallorca, and Zaragoza all have splendid *llotjas* dating from the 14th and 15th centuries, all built at the height of the flamboyant Gothic architectural style. Originally little more than a roof to protect merchants and their wares from the elements, Barcelona's present llotja was constructed in the Gothic style between 1380 and 1392. At the end of the 18th century the facades were (tragically) covered in the Neoclassical uniformity of the time, but the interior, the great Saló Gòtic (Gothic Hall), was left unaltered and was Barcelona's great venue for balls and celebrations throughout the 19th century. During this century, the Gothic Hall was used as the Barcelona stock exchange until 1975 and, still today, as the grain exchange.

The Escola de Belles Arts (Fine Arts School) occupied the southwestern corner of the Llotja from 1849 until 1960; Picasso, in fact, studied here, where his father was an art teacher. The Picasso family reportedly lived across the street under the 15th-century beams and porches at Consolat de Mar 35 (corner of Carrer Trompetes), where a half-width wooden door opens into four floors of ancient apartments with exposed ceiling beams. The Reial Academia de Belles Arts de Sant Jordi (Royal Academy of Fine Arts of St. George) still has its seat here, and its Museu de les Belles Arts (Fine Arts Museum) is one of Barcelona's secret (and free) sites, open daily until 2 PM. At the Cámara de Comercio (Chamber of Commerce) offices in the llotja, arrange for a guided tour of the stunningly grand Gothic Hall. ⊠ *Consolat de Mar 2–4,* ☎ *93/319–2412.* ⊘ *Weekdays 10–2.*

❺❷ **Mercat de Santa Caterina.** This former 13th-century church and convent became a market in the mid-19th century and retained what Alexandre Cirici i Pellicer—one of Barcelona's greatest chroniclers—identified as a certain air and aura of a North African souk. Presently being restored, the Neoclassical walls have been left standing to form part of the renovated marketplace. Meanwhile, underneath the market, Roman and Visigothic foundations have been discovered, so the final result is anybody's guess: a market with glass floors? Barcelona City History Museum underneath, and Moroccan souk up above? Only time will tell. ⊠ *Av. Francesc Cambo s/n,* ☎ *93/319–2135.*

★ ❺❹ **Museu Picasso.** The Picasso Museum is north of Via Laietana, down Carrer de la Princesa, and right on Carrer Montcada—a street known for Barcelona's most elegant medieval palaces, of which the museum occupies three. Picasso spent several of his formative years in Barcelona (1901–06), and this collection, while it does not include a significant number of the artist's best paintings, is particularly strong on his early work. Displays include childhood sketches, works from Picasso's Rose and Blue periods, and the famous 1950s Cubist variations on Velázquez's *Las Meninas.* Originally begun in 1962 on the suggestion of Picasso's marchand and crony Jaume Sabartés, the museum's initial donation was from the Sabartés collection. Later Picasso donated his early works and in 1981 his widow, Jaqueline Roque, added 141 pieces. The lower-floor sketches, oils, and schoolboy caricatures and drawings from Picasso's early years in La Coruna are perhaps the most fascinating and telling part of the whole museum, showing the facility the artist seemed to possess almost from the cradle. His *La Primera Communión (First Communion)*, painted at the age of 16, gives an idea of his early accomplishment. On the second floor we meet the beginnings of the mature Picasso and his Blue Period in Paris, a time of loneliness, cold, and hunger for the artist. The most famous series of paintings in the museum are in Rooms 22 to 26, where Picasso takes on Velázquez in his 1957 series based on the painting *Las Meninas (Ladies-in-Waiting)*. ⊠ *Carrer Montcada 15–19,* ☎ *93/319–6310.* 🎟 *750 ptas./€4.51; free 1st Sun. of month.* ⊘ *Tues.–Sat. 10–8, Sun. 10–3.*

⑤⑤ Museu Textil i de l'Indumentària–Palau de los Marqueses de Lló. One of Carrer Montcada's best two courtyards (the other is the Palau Dalmases at No. 20), this peaceful spot has a handy café where you can admire the 14th- to 16th-century loggia, stairway, and windows. The display inside includes every imaginable piece of clothing worn from prehistoric times through the late-19th-century Art Nouveau frenzy of decorative excess. ⊠ *Carrer Montcada 12–14,* ☎ *93/319–7603.* ✆ *500 ptas./€3.01; 1st Sat. of the month free 3–8.* ☉ *Tues.–Sat. 10–8, Sun. 10–3.*

NEED A BREAK?

The patio of **El Café Textil** (⊠ Carrer Montcada 12) is one of the two or three best in Barcelona and an ideal spot for anything from a tea to a light meal. In the winter the sun manages to find its way into this quiet space, while in summer you can always find shade unless Apollo's directly overhead. The adjacent store offers interesting books and artifacts, all related to the textile industry that made medieval Barcelona prosper.

⑤⑥ Palau Dalmases. Barcelona's best 17th-century Renaissance patio is showcased here, built into a 15th-century palace. First note the heavy wooden doors leading into the patio; then take a careful look at the evocation of the Rape of Europa represented in high relief running up the Baroque facade of the elegant stairway cutting across the end of the patio. Neptune's chariot, cherubic putti, naiads, dancers, tritons, and myriad musicians accompany Europa's mythological abduction by Zeus, who, in the form of a bull, carries her up the stairs and off to Crete (where she winds up bearing him three sons). On either side of the door leading up the stairs, look for the minuscule representations of either putti or maidens covering their nakedness with their arms. These, along with the 15th-century Gothic chapel, with its reliefs of musical angels, and the vaulting in the reception area and in the main salon, are the only remnants of the 15th-century palace originally built here. Now seat of the Omnium Cultural, a center for the diffusion of Catalan culture, there are lectures, book presentations, and multiple events open to the public here. The Espai Barroc, on the ground floor, is a café with Baroque-era flourishes, period furniture, and occasional musical performances. ⊠ *Carrer Montcada 20.* ✆ *Free.* ☉ *Daily 9– 2, 4:30–7. Café: Tues.–Sun. 7 PM–1 AM.*

★ **㊾ Palau de la Música Catalana.** One of the world's most extraordinary music halls, with facades that are a riot of color and form, the Palau de la Música (Music Palace) is a landmark of Carrer Amadeus Vives, set just across Via Laietana, a five-minute walk from Plaça Catalunya. From its polychrome ceramic ticket windows on the Carrer de Sant Pere Més Alt side to its overhead busts of (from left to right) Palestrina, Bach, Beethoven, and (around the corner on Carrer Amadeus Vives) Wagner, the Palau is a flamboyant tour de force designed by Lluís Domènech i Montaner in 1908 and is today considered the flagship of Barcelona's Moderniste architecture. Originally conceived by the Orfeó Català musical society as a revindication of the importance of music at a popular level—as opposed to the Liceu opera house's identification with the Catalan (often Castilian-speaking and monarchist) aristocracy—the Palau and the Liceu were for many decades opposing cross-town forces in Barcelona's musical as well as philosophical discourse.

The exterior is remarkable in itself. The Miquel Blay sculptural group over the corner of Amadeu Vives and Santa Pere Més Alt is Catalonia's popular music come to life, with everyone included from St. George the dragon slayer (at the top) to women and children, fishermen with oars over their shoulders, and every strain and strata of popular life and music, the faces of the past fading into the background.

The parish church of Sant Francese de Paula torn down in late 1999 has opened up the southwest corner of the Palau over Plaça Lluís Millet while the earlier glass facade over the present ticket window entrance is one of the city's best examples of nonintrusive (in fact, enhancing) modern construction over traditional structures.

The Palau's interior is, well, a permanent uproar before the first note of music is ever heard. In a tribute to international music, Wagnerian cavalry explodes from the right side of the stage over a heavy-browed bust of Beethoven, while Catalonia's popular music is represented by the flowing maidens of Lluís Millet's song *Flors de Maig* (*Flowers of May*) on the left. Overhead, an inverted stained-glass cupola seems to offer the divine manna of music straight from heaven; painted rosettes and giant peacock feathers explode from the tops of the walls; and even the stage is populated with muse-like Art Nouveau musicians all across the back wall. The visuals alone make music sound different here, and at any important concert the excitement is palpably thick (☞ Nightlife and the Arts, *below*). If you can't attend one, take a tour of the hall, offered daily at 10:30, 2, and 3 (in English) for 700 ptas./€4.21. ✉ *Ticket office: Sant Francesc de Paula 2 (just off Via Laietana, around a corner from the hall itself)*, ☎ 93/268–1000.

❸ Passeig del Born. Once the site of medieval jousts and Inquisitional autos-de-fé, the Passeig is at the end of Carrer Montcada behind the church of Santa Maria del Mar. Early Barcelona's most important square, the narrow, elongated plaza is now lined with late-night cocktail bars and miniature restaurants with tiny spiral stairways and intimate corners. The numbered cannon balls under the public benches are the work of the so-called poet of space—a 20th-century specialist in combinations of letters, words, and sculpture—the late Joan Brossa, harking back to the post-1714 era when Felipe V's conquering forces obliged residents of the Barri de la Ribera (Waterfront District) to tear down nearly 1,000 of their own houses to create fields of fire (so termed as the occupying army of Felipe V trained their guns on the conquered populace of Barcelona following the War of the Spanish Succession) for the batteries of cannon in the Ciutadella fortress designed to repress nationalist uprisings. Walk down to the Born itself—a great iron hangar, once a major produce market and soon to become a public library.

❻ Plaça de les Olles. This pretty little square named for the makers of *olles*, or pots (as in *olla podrida*, the, literally, "rotten pot Spanish stew"), has been known to host everything from topless sunbathers to elegant Viennese waltzers to tapa grazers stacked in three ranks deep at Cal Pep, where Barcelona's best delicacies are served up. The balconies at No. 6 over the Café de la Ribera are, somewhat oddly, decorated with colorful blue and yellow tile on the second and top floors. The house with the turret over the street on the right at the corner leading out to Pla del Palau (at No. 2 Plaça de les Olles) is another of Enric Sagnier i Villavecchia's retro-moderniste works. This one, a neo-Gothic heap of conical towers and balconies, is an improvement on white elephants such as the neo-Disney Temple Expiatori del Sagrat Cor that gleams relentlessly over Barcelona 365 days a year from the top of Tibidabo.

❺ Sant Pere de les Puelles (St. Peter of the Novices). One of the oldest medieval churches in Barcelona, this one has been destroyed and restored so many times that there is little left to see except the beautiful stained-glass window, which illuminates the stark interior. The word *Puelles* is from the Latin *puella* (girl)—the convent here was known for the beauty and nobility of its young women and was the setting for some of medieval Barcelona's most tragic stories of impossible love.

Legend has it that the *puellae,* when threatened with rape and murder at the hands of the invading Moors under Al-Mansur in 986, disfigured themselves by slicing off their own ears and noses in an (apparently futile) attempt to save themselves. ⊠ *Lluís El Piadós 1,* ☎ *93/ 268–0742.* ☉ *Open for mass only.*

★ ❺❾ **Santa Maria del Mar.** Ever since Jaume I el Conqueridor's 1229 conquest of the Moors in Mallorca to the battle cry of "Santa Maria!", his *ex voto* (pledge)—a major seafarers' church in the waterfront district then known as Vilanova—was a project awaiting its moment. The most sweepingly symmetrical and classical of all Barcelona's churches is on the Carrer Montcada off of Passeig del Born (or at the end of Carrer Argenteria if you approach it from Via Laetana). Simple and spacious, Santa Maria del Mar is a stunning contrast to the ornate and aesthetically complex architecture of later Gothic and Moderniste Barcelona. Built in a record 54 years (1329–1383), Santa Maria del Mar was the work of a stonemason who limited his design to the barebones specifications for a basilica of this kind. Santa Maria del Mar was intended to bless and protect the mighty Catalan fleet at a time when Catalonia so controlled the Mediterranean that, as the saying went, "not a fish dared swim in Mare Nostrum (Our Sea) without displaying the *quatre barras*" (the four stripes of the Catalan flag). Fishermen, merchant marines, and all other seafarers were included under the patronage of Santa Maria del Mar (St. Mary of the Sea). Alfons III placed the initial stone of the long-awaited Iglesia de la Ribera (Waterfront Church) exactly 100 years after his great-grandfather, Jaume I el Conqueridor, had promised to construct a church to watch over his navy at sea.

The finest existing example of early Catalan (or Mediterranean) Gothic architecture, Santa Maria del Mar is extraordinary for its unbroken lines, simplicity of form, symmetry, and elegance. The upsweeping verticality and lightness of the interior are especially surprising considering the blocky exterior surfaces. The site, originally outside the 1st- to 4th-century Roman walls at what was then the water's edge, was home to a Christian cult from the late 3rd century. In the year 303 the Christian martyr St. Eulàlia was buried at Santa Maria de las Arenas (St. Mary of the Sands). Her remains were later hidden in 713 when Moors sacked the city and, after being recovered in 878, relocated to the Barcelona cathedral in 1339. The size and strength of the Christian community after the mid-4th-century conversion of Emperor Constantine and the Roman Empire's official tolerance of the Christian religion after the XVI Concilio de Toledo in 693 eventually made a larger parish and church necessary.

Berenguer de Montagut, *magister opus* (contractor), stonemason and sculptor, carefully selected, fitted, and carved each stone hauled down from the same Montjuïc quarry that provided the sandstone for the 4th-century Roman walls. In all, the 16 octagonal towers, some five feet in diameter, spread out into vaulting arches at a height of 53 ft. The keystones are, in turn, 104 ft from the floor. The symmetry is relentless, at least if you go by the metric rule: eight-sided columns, 16 columns, 1.60 m in diameter, up to 16 m from the floor, and another 16 m to the keystones. Adding to the lightness is the height of the lateral naves, at 27 m just 5 fewer than the central nave.

It is, of course, ironic that Santa Maria del Mar owes much of its present formal grace and soaring spirituality to the anticlerical fury of the anarchists who on July 18, 1936, upon learning of the military rebellion led by generals named Sanjurjo and Franco, burned nearly all of Barcelona's churches as a reprisal against the alliance of army, church, and oligarchy that had ended Spain's democratic experiment begun in 1931. The basilica, filled with immense side chapels and great wooden choir stalls, burned for 11 days and nearly crumbled as a result of the intense heat. Restored after the 1939 end of the Spanish Civil War by a series of post-Bauhaus architects, all of whom understood the formal purity of the original design, Santa Maria del Mar remains one of the city's most cherished architectural gems.

The interior, which should be seen when illuminated, is especially rich in detail. The paintings in the keystones (where the arches meet overhead) represent, from the front, the Coronation of the Virgin, the Nativity, the Annunciation, the equestrian figure of the father of Pedro IV King Alfonso, and the Barcelona coat of arms. The 34 lateral chapels are dedicated to different saints and images. The first chapel to the left of the altar (No. 20) is the Capilla de Santo Cristo (Chapel of the Holy Christ), its stained-glass window an allegory of the 1992 Olympic Games held in Barcelona with names of medalists and key personalities of the day in tiny letters. An engraved stone to the left of the side door onto Carrer Sombrerers commemorates the spot where San Ignacio de Loyola, founder of the Jesuit Order, begged for alms in 1524–55.

The best and most beautiful example of Mediterranean Gothic architecture, the basilica has a stark beauty that is enhanced by a lovely southwest-facing rose window (built in 1425 and restored in 1485 after an earthquake destroyed the original) and unusually wide vaulting. Often compared to the German *Hallenkirche,* or single-naved church, the basilica is often used for choral events and especially for performances of early music, much of which was written precisely for this kind of space. The six-second acoustic delay, which can create mayhem in more modern compositions, was planned into most medieval musical scores designed to be sung or played in large spaces. This church is a much-sought-after wedding spot, so you're likely to see a hopeful couple exchanging vows here on a Saturday afternoon. Note that every Monday at 6 PM, there is a tour of the church with organ music and a brief explanation of the building's religious, social, and artistic significance; the presentation, given in Spanish, is entitled "Santa María del Mar, Luz y Misterio" (☎ 93/215–7411). For information on the church's most famous celebrations, see the Close-Up box on "Santa Maria del Mar: The Song of the Sibyl," *below.* ✉ *Plaça de Santa Maria.* ⊙ *Weekdays 9–1:30 and 4:30–8.*

NEED A BREAK? At Santa Maria del Mar, you're just a step from the best tapas in Barcelona at **Cal Pep** (✉ Plaça de les Olles 8). Try the *gambitas* (baby shrimp), *pulpo gallego* (octopus), or *garbanzos con espinacas* (garbanzos with spinach), and don't forget to order *pan de coca* (crunchy toast with oil and fresh tomato paste). Worry not if you have to wait for a while; it's part of the fest. Pep and company (somehow) always know exactly who's next and will serve you wine while you wait.

Near the Port: La Ciutadella and Barceloneta

Now Barcelona's central downtown park, La Ciutadella was originally the site of a fortress built by the conquering troops of the Bourbon monarch Felipe V after the fall of Barcelona in the 1700–1714 War of the Spanish Succession. Barceloneta and La Ciutadella fit together historically and urbanistically as some 1,000 houses in the Barrio de la Ribera, then the waterfront neighborhood around Plaça del Born, were ordered dismantled by their owners to create fields of fire for La Ciutadella's can-

SANTA MARIA DEL MAR: THE SONG OF THE SIBYL

EVERY BARCELONA Christmas Eve just prior to the celebration of the traditional midnight mass, Santa Maria del Mar is the scenario for an ancient Mediterranean tradition, the Cant de la Sibil.la or Song of the Sibyl. This pre-Christian tradition, performed only in Barcelona, in Mallorca, and in the still Corona de Aragón-influenced S'Alguer, Sardinia, is typically sung by a countertenor and has to do with the last judgement, the apocalypse and subsequent chaos while also predicting the birth and death of Christ as a sign of hope for the future.

In ancient Greece the Sibylla was a prophetess or witch reputed to possess powers of divination. The Delphic Oracle, for example, was delivered by a priestess seated on a golden tripod who uttered unintelligible sounds in a frenzied trance; a trained priest translated the prophecies to the questioner, usually speaking in verse. The Sybelline Oracles are included in the list of pseudepigrapha (false or "uncanonical" writings of a biblical type). Specifically described as Jewish apocalyptic pseudepigrapha, the 200 BC–200 AD Sybelline Oracles consisted of a series of Messianic prophecies predicting the birth of a Saviour.

The Catalan and Mediterranan Cant de la Sibil.la, in the Santa Maria del Mar version, is delivered by a senior countertenor carrying a great scepter and singing in a wheezy falsetto. Traced directly back to the 6th-century BC Temple of Apollo, the refrain to each of the many verses repeats *il giorn del judici, l'infern a servici* (the judgement day, hell is served), while the choir changes positions various times, choreographed to move to different stations on the altar. The combination of the ethereal goddesslike register of countertenor and the slow and dreamy movements of the choir transmit an eerie foreboding in utter contrast to the warm and fuzzy "a babe is born" concept that will dominate the Christian mass soon to follow. The chords and polyphonies are discordant, redolent of the shady musical territory Bach and Mozart use to create a sense of mystery and anxiety.

The standing-room-only Santa Maria del Mar audience is, year after year, completely absorbed and fascinated. There is no fidgeting, no coughing, no one leaves. No one moves. It is not uncommon to see people with hands over their faces, only eyes showing, a gesture of fascination and fear. Many heads are cocked, as if straining to hear the truth, to understand the Sybelline message, the future. Expressions of rapt attention are everywhere, while the tones are very eastern, African, Mediterranean.

Mediterranean music specialist Maria del Mar Bonet occasionally sings the same Sibyl song in the Santa Monica church on the Rambla, accompanied by a small organ and a tiny standing medieval zither that she occasionally strums. Bonet's voice is a deep Sephardic contralto, a virtual baritone, a low, womanly voice, a lament, waling, even more oriental and semitic than the countertenor.

non keeping watch over the rebellious Catalan independentists. Barceloneta was finally filled in and built almost four decades later in 1753 to compensate families who had lost their homes in La Ribera.

Barceloneta has always been a beloved and mavericky departure from the formality of cosmopolitan city life, an urban fishing village *barcelonins* sought for Sunday paella on the beach and a stroll through what feels like a freer, more Bohemian ambience than the one along the Passeig de Gràcia or even the Rambla. With its tiny original houses, its abundant laundry flapping brightly over the streets, and its history of seafarers, gypsies, and all manner of other colorful characters, Barceloneta continues to be a world apart, an anthology of Mediterranean romance, exuding a more spontaneous carpe diem kind of joy than Catalans are generally known for.

Open water in Roman times and gradually silted in only after the 15th-century construction of the Barcelona port, Barceloneta is Barcelona's traditional fishing and stevedores' quarter. Originally composed of 15 longitudinal and 3 cross streets and 329 two-story houses (either to allow easy access of sun and air or to avoid masking the Ciutadella's fields of fire, depending on whom you talk to, soldier or civilian), Barceloneta was Europe's earliest urban development, built by the military engineer Juan Martin Cermeno under the command of El Marquès de la Mina, Juan Miguel de Guzmán Dávalos Spinola (1690–1767).

Numbers in the text correspond to numbers in the margin and on the Sant Pere, La Ribera, La Ciutadella, and Barceloneta map.

A Good Walk

Starting at the **Arc del Triomf** ⓺₄, on Passeig de Sant Joan, built as the grand entryway for the Universal Exposition of 1888, walk down Passeig Lluis Companys and into el **Parc de la Ciutadella** ⓺₅, the green "lung" of downtown Barcelona. The **Castell dels Tres Dragons** ⓺₆, which houses the Museu de Zoología, is on your right. The next buildings on the right are the **Hivernacle,** a spectacular greenhouse converted into a restaurant and concert hall; the **Museu de Geologia** ⓺₇; and the **Umbracle,** a delicious shady iron structure with a collection of jungle plants that grow best in penumbra. Turn left at the Castell dels Tres Dragons to the **Cascada** ⓺₈—the floridly triumphal monument-cum-waterfall designed by Josep Fontseré i Mestres (with rocks sculpted by the young Antoni Gaudí) in 1881. The large building farther in to the left was the Ciutadella's arsenal (ammunition dump) and is now the home of the Parlament de Catalunya (Parliament of Catalonia) and the excellent **Museu d'Art Modern** ⓺₉. La Plaça de les Armes, a former parade ground, is the space in front of the Parliament with the graceful 1906 Josep Llimona sculpture *Desconsol* in the center of the pond.

To the right and behind the Parliament is Barcelona's first-rate **Zoo** ⑦₀, home of Snowflake, the city's unique and much-celebrated captive albino gorilla. Leaving the Parc de la Ciutadella on Marquès d'Argentera, you should not miss the **Estació de França** ⑦₁, Barcelona's last authentic old-world railroad station, even if it's difficult to find a train leaving it for anyplace you want to go. Past the station, turn left and walk 300 yards across the wide Carrer Doctor Aiguader into the minidistrict of Barceloneta and down Passeig de Joan de Borbó, the main thoroughfare paralleling the port. Carrer Maquinista is the third street on the left. Walk down to the **Mercat de Barceloneta,** a lofty hangar with an important fish market and the Alcaide *chiringuito* (café–bar) in the center. Don't miss Can Ramonet, the picturesque pink house on the left as you enter the market, the oldest restaurant in La Barceloneta. As you leave the market, the open square on the other side has two interesting buildings on the left: No. 47 is a freshly restored 18th-century house with a tiny no-name café on the ground floor, while No. 51 has a colorfully engraved late-19th-century facade.

Crossing to the right side of the square, look for La Cova Fumat at No. 56, a tiny restaurant and tapas sanctuary with an authentic fishing village ambience. Leave this delicious place through the back door into Carrer de Sevilla and turn left into Carrer de Sant Carles, where you will find a series of Barceloneta's most interesting buildings. At No. 12 is a typical early Barceloneta house of only two stories, crowned with elaborate Baroque floral ornamentation and scrolls—look for the shanty on the roof. At Sant Carles 9 is the 1918 **Cooperative Obrera La Fraternitat** 72, Barceloneta's best Art Nouveau building and the home of one of the city's first workers' organizations. At No. 7 is the ornate **Farmacia Saim** 73, a stone house built over an original Barceloneta structure in 1902. On the left at **Carrer Sant Carles No. 6** 74 is the only completely original Cermeño-designed house left in Barceloneta, consisting only of the ground floor, originally designed for boats, nets, and equipment, and an upper floor used as a living space. At No. 4 is Can Solé, a famous restaurant that is one of Barceloneta's oldest and best. Turn right into Plaça de la Barceloneta, where you will see the Baroque church of **Sant Miquel del Port** 75.

Return to Carrer de Sant Carles and take a left, walking all the way down to the beach, past several interesting houses with engraved facades at No. 19 and 32, to the **Fuente de Carmen Amaya** 76, a fountain and bas-relief sculpture dedicated to the famous Gypsy flamenco dancer, who was born in Barceloneta in 1913. Climb the stairs and cross the Passeig Maritim to the walkway over the beach. From here, to your left you will see the **Port Olímpic** 77 and the **Frank Gehry goldfish,** looking a lot better post-Guggenheim (which is really just an even bigger fish). From here you will see the Olympic Port's twin skyscrapers: the Hotel Arts, and the Mapfre office building looming over it. Farther left is another important Barceloneta landmark, the **Catalana de Gas water tower,** a colorful conical spire built by Art Nouveau architect Domènech i Estapà.

Now walk to your right up the beach past the tempting Chiringuito Silvestre, a summer (Apr.–Oct.) event serving acceptable paellas at tables on the beach. A few steps farther along on the right is Can Majó, Barceloneta's premier seafood restaurant, a good place for lunch or dinner. Continue up the boardwalk past sculptress Rebecca Horn's curious tower of rusting boxes to Plaça de Mar and turn right into Passeig Joan de Borbó, where you will pass a number of excellent dining spots, principally Can Costa, Suquet de l'Almirall, and Can Manel la Puda, all worthy choices for a late-afternoon or early evening paella. Return to the Gothic Quarter via the Moll de la Fusta side of the Passeig Joan de Borbó, leaving the Palau de Mar and the **Museu d'Historia de Catalunya** 78 on your right. The Roy Lichtenstein sculpture *Barcelona Head* is the colorful roosterlike monument in front of the central post office on Passeig de Colom, while the **Port Vell** 79 is to the left up the grassy, usually lover-covered hill.

TIMING

This is a three- to four-hour walk. Add another hour or two for the Museu d'Art Modern and lunch or dinner. Try to time your arrival in Barceloneta so you catch the local market in full activity at midday (until 2) and get a chance to graze through the neighborhood on your way to a beachside table for paella. Can Manel la Puda serves paella until 4:30 in the afternoon.

Sights to See

64 **Arc del Triomf.** This imposing, exposed-redbrick arch was built by Josep Vilaseca as the grand entrance for the 1888 Universal Exhibition. Similar in size and sense to the traditional triumphal arches of ancient Rome, this one refers to no specific military triumph anyone can recall. In fact, Catalunya's last military triumph of note may have been Jaume I El Conqueridor's 1229 conquest of the Moors in Mallorca—as suggested by the bats, always part of Jaume I's coat of arms, on either side of the arch itself. The Josep Reynés sculptures adorning the structure represent Barcelona hosting visitors to the Exhibition on the west (front) side, while the Josep Llimona sculptures on the east side depict the prizes being given to outstanding contributors to the Universal Exhibition.

74 **Carrer Sant Carlos No. 6.** The last Barceloneta house left standing in its original 1755 two-story entirety, the structure was originally planned as single-family dwellings with shop and storage space on the ground floor and the living space above. Overcrowding soon produced split houses and even quartered houses, with workers and their families living in tiny, cramped spaces. After nearly a century of military jurisdiction over Barceloneta, house owners were given permission to expand vertically and houses of as many as five stories began to tower over the lowly original dwellings. ⊠ *Carrer Sant Carles 6.*

66 **Castell dels Tres Dragons** (Castle of the Three Dragons). Built by Domènech i Montaner as the café and restaurant for the 1888 Universal Exposition, the building was named in honor of a popular mid-19th-century comedy written by the father of the Catalan theater Serafí Pitarra. An arresting building that greets you on the right entering the Ciutadella from Passeig Luí Companys, it features exposed brickwork and visible iron supports, both radical innovations at the time. Domènech i Muntaner's building later became an arts-and-crafts workshop where Moderniste architects met to experiment with traditional crafts and to exchange ideas. It now holds Barcelona's **Museu de Zoologia** (Zoology Museum). ⊠ *Passeig Picasso 5,* ☎ *93/319–6912.* 🖾 *350 ptas./€2.10.* ☉ *Tues.–Sun. 10–2.*

72 **Cooperativa Obrera La Fraternitat** (Brotherhood Workers Cooperative). This strikingly ornate building in this otherwise humble fishermen's quarter, the only Art Nouveau building in Barceloneta, housed the progressive workers' organization, La Fraternitat, founded in 1879. Begun as a low-cost outlet to help supply workers and their families with basic necessities at cut-rate prices, the cooperative soon became a social and cultural center with a chorus, a theater and meeting room, a café, and a public library. The present cooperative building was inaugurated in 1918 and is now being restored and converted, once again, to Barceloneta's library. ⊠ *Carrer Sant Carles 9.*

71 **Estació de França.** The elegantly restored Estació de França, Barcelona's main railroad station until about 1980 and still the stopping point for some trains to and from France and points along the Mediterranean, is outside the west gate of the Ciutadella. Tragically no longer very active, this is a pleasant place to visit to get a sense of the charm and romance of Europe's traditional old-world railroads. Sometimes used as an exhibition hall and always a breath of fresh air, the station has a café that is a good place for an espresso and breakfast. ⊠ *Marquès de l'Argentera s/n,* ☎ *93/319–6416.*

73 **Farmacia Saim.** This ornate house with floral trim around the upper balconies, griffons over the door, and the pharmacist's insignia (the serpent and amphora symbolic of the curative properties of snake oils mixed in the apothecary vial) is the successor of Barceloneta's first pharmacy. Originally situated across the street, the present house was built in 1902. One of the sturdiest houses in Barceloneta, Farmacia Saim was used as a bomb shelter during the 1936–39 Spanish Civil War when Franco's bombers, in an attempt to paralyze the Barcelona port to slow down Republican resupply, frequently dumped misdirected bombs on Barceloneta. ⊠ *Carrer Sant Carles 7.*

76 Fuente de Carmen Amaya (Carmen Amaya Fountain). Down at the eastern end of Carrer Sant Carles where Barceloneta joins the beach is the monument to the famous Gypsy flamenco dancer Carmen Amaya (1913–63), born in the Gypsy settlement known as Somorrostro, part of Barceloneta until 1920. A prodigious dancer from the age of 12, Amaya achieved universal fame at the age of 16, in 1929, when she performed at Barcelona's International Exposition. After traveling to Paris with Raquel Meller's troupe, Amaya made triumphal tours of America and starred in films such as *La hija de Juan Simón* (1934) and *Los Tarantos* (1962), only a year before her death. The fountain, and its high-relief representations of cherubic children in the throes of flamenco, has been punished and poorly maintained since it was placed here in 1959, but it remains an important reminder of Barceloneta's roots as a rough-and-tumble, romantic enclave of free-living sailors, stevedores, gypsies, and fishermen. Palpable and much beloved by *barcelonins* in the *chiringuitos* (ramshackle beach restaurants specializing in fish and rice dishes) that used to line the Barceloneta beach, this Gypsy ambience all but disappeared when the last of the chiringuitos fell to the wreckers' ball shortly after the 1992 Olympics.

68 La Cascada (The Waterfall). The sights and sounds of Barcelona seem far away by this monumental, faintly bombastic *Cascada*, by Josep Fontserè, designed in 1881 and presented as part of the 1888 Universal Exhibition. The waterfall's rocks were the work of a young architecture student named Antoni Gaudí—his first public works, appropriately natural and organic, and certainly a hint of things to come.

69 Museu d'Art Modern. (Museum of Modern Art). Once the arsenal for the Ciutadella—as evidenced by the thickness of the building's walls—this is the only surviving remnant of Felipe V's fortress and is presently shared by the Catalan parliament and the Museum of Modern Art. This collection of late-19th- and early 20th-century Catalan paintings and sculptures by such artists as Isidro Nonell, Ramon Casas, Marià Fortuny, Josep Clarà, and Pau Gargallo forms one of Catalonia's most important artistic treasures. Often overlooked in favor of other Barcelona standouts such as the Picasso Museum or the Romanesque collection at the MNAC in the Palau Nacional, the Museu d'Art Modern is a reminder that Catalonia's most emblematic and universal artists—Picasso, Dalí, Miró—emerged from an exceptionally rich artistic tradition. ⊠ *Plaça d'Armes, Parc de la Ciutadella,* ☎ *93/319–5728.* ☜ *500 ptas./ €3.01.* ☉ *Tues.–Sat. 10–7, Sun. 10–2.*

67 Museu de Geologia. The Museum of Geology is next to the Castell dels Tres Dragons, not far from the beautiful *Umbracle* (meaning, a shaded place for plants), a magnificently graceful 19th-century greenhouse that showcases a collection of jungle plants that grow best in penumbra; iron bars help create jungle lighting for the museum's valuable collection of tropical plants. Barcelona's first public museum, the Museu de Geologia displays rocks, minerals, and fossils along with special exhibits on Catalonia and the rest of Spain. ⊠ *Parc de la Ciutadella,* ☎ *93/319–6895.* ☜ *500 ptas./€3.01; free 1st Sun. of month.* ☉ *Tues.–Sun. 10–2.*

㉘ Museu d'Història de Catalunya. Built into what used to be a port warehouse, this state-of-the-art, interactive museum makes you part of Catalonian history from prehistoric times through more than 3,000 years and into the contemporary democratic era. Explanations of the exhibits appear in Catalan, Castilian (Spanish), and English. Guided tours are available on Sundays at noon and 1 PM. The cafeteria offers excellent views over the harbor. ⊠ *Plaça Pau Vila 1,* ☎ *93/225–4700.* ⊒ *500 ptas./€3.01; free 1st Sun. of month.* ⊗ *Tues.–Sat. 10–7, Sun. 10–2:30.*

㉕ Parc de la Ciutadella (Citadel Park). Once a fortress designed to consolidate Madrid's military occupation of Barcelona, the Ciutadella is now the city's main downtown park. The clearing dates from shortly after the War of the Spanish Succession, when Felipe V demolished some 2,000 houses in what was then the Barri de la Ribera (Waterfront District) to build a fortress and barracks for his soldiers and "fields of fire" (used for target practice) for his artillery. The fortress walls were pulled down in 1868 and replaced by gardens laid out by Josep Fontserè. Within the park are a cluster of museums, the Catalan parliament, and the city zoo.

㉗ Port Olímpic. Choked with yachts, restaurants, and tapas bars of all kinds, the Olympic Port is 2 km (1 mi) up the beach, marked by the mammoth **goldfish sculpture by Frank Gehry** (designer of Bilbao's famous Guggenheim Museum) in front of Barcelona's first real skyscraper, the Hotel Arts. The port rages on Friday and Saturday nights, especially in summer, with hundreds of young people of all nationalities circling and grazing until daybreak.

㉙ Port Vell. From Pla del Palau, cross to the edge of the port, where the Moll d'Espanya, the Moll de la Fusta, and the Moll de Barceloneta meet. Just beyond the colorful Roy Lichtenstein sculpture in front of the post office, the modern Port Vell complex—the IMAX theater, aquarium, and Maremagnum shopping mall—looms seaward on the Moll d'Espanya. The Palau de Mar, with its five (somewhat pricey and impersonal) quayside terrace restaurants, stretches down along the Moll de Barceloneta (try Llevataps or, on the far corner, the Merendero de la Mari; even better is El Magatzem around the corner by the entrance to the Museu de Historia de Catalunya in the Palau de Mar). Key points in the Maremagnum complex are the grassy hillside (for lovers, especially, on or around April 23, Sant Jordi's Day, Barcelona's variant of Valentine's Day); the **Ictineo II** replica of the Narcis Monturiol (1819–1885) submarine, the world's first, launched in the Barcelona port in 1862; and the Blue Note Café, which can be found in the lackluster (to say the least) Maremagnum mall.

㉕ Sant Miquel del Port. Stop in Plaça de la Barceloneta and have a close look at the Baroque church of Sant Miquel del Port with its new (somewhat body-builder) version of the winged archangel himself, complete with sword and chain, in the alcove on the facade. One of the first buildings to be completed in Barceloneta, Sant Miquel del Port was begun 1753 and finished by 1755 under the direction of architect Damià Ribes, who was in turn supervised by the military engineer Francisco Paredes under the command of Pedro Martín Cermeno, the military engineer charged with the construction of Barceloneta. Due to strict orders to keep Barceloneta low enough to fire La Ciutadella's cannon over, Sant Miquel del Port had no bell tower and only a small cupola until Elies Rogent added a new one in 1853. Along with the image of Sant Miquel, Sant Elm and Santa Maria de Cervelló, patrons of the Catalan fleet, also appeared on the Baroque facade. All three images were destroyed at the outbreak of the Spanish Civil War in 1936.

Interesting to note are the metopes, palm-size, gilt bas-relief sculptures around the interior cornice and repeated outside at the top of the facade. These 74 Latin-inscribed allegories each allude to different attributes of St. Michael: e.g., the image of a boat and the inscription IAM IN TUTO (I am in everything), alluding to the protection of St. Michael against the perils of the sea. Elsewhere on the facade, the furrowed-browed faces in the Baroque scrolls seem to be providing wind for the fleet, while the tiny bell in its rack, visible from the left side of the square, is another archaic detail. To the right of Sant Miquel del Port at No. 41 Carrer de Sant Miquel is a house decorated by seven strips of floral sgraffiti and a plaque commemorating Fernando de Lesseps, the engineer who built the Panama and Suez canals, who had lived in the house when serving as French Consul to Barcelona. In the square itself, take a close look at the fountain with its freshly painted Barcelona coat of arms and Can Ganassa, on the east side, a tapas bar with a comprehensive display of delicacies, featuring *torrades,* slabs of toast with tomato and anything from anchovies to peppers to guacamole.

NEED A
BREAK?
Friendly **Can Manel la Puda,** on Passeig de Joan de Borbó, is always good for a tasty, inexpensive feast in the sun. Serving lunch until 4 and starting dinner at 7, it's a handy and popular place for *suquets,* (fish stew), paella, and *arrós a banda* (rice with shelled seafood). ⊠ *Passeig Joan de Borbó 60–61,* ☎ *93/221–5013. AE, DC, MC, V. Closed Mon.*

Telefèric (cable car). This hair-raising ride over the Barcelona harbor from Barceloneta to Montjuïc (with a midway stop in the port) is spectacular, though it is not always clear whether the great views are the result of the vantage point or the adrenaline. The cable car leaving from the tower at the end of Passeig Joan de Borbó connects the Torre de San Sebastián on the Moll de Barceloneta, the tower of Jaume I in the port boat terminal, and the Torre de Miramar on Montjuïc. Cable-car naysayers claim the Telefèric is expensive, not very cool, and actually pretty scary. ☎ *93/225–2718.* ▨ *1,300 ptas./€7.81 round-trip, 1,100 ptas./€6.61 one-way.* ۝ *Oct.–June 21, weekends 10:30–5:30; June 22–Sept., daily 10:30–8:30.*

☝ ⑳ **Zoo.** Barcelona's excellent zoo—home of Snowflake, the world's only captive albino gorilla—occupies the whole bottom section of the Parc de la Ciutadella. There's a superb reptile house and a full complement of African animals. The dolphin show is a favorite and usually plays to a packed house. ⊠ *Parc de la Ciutadella,* ☎ *93/225–6780.* ▨ *1,600 ptas./€9.62.* ۝ *Oct.–Apr., daily 10–6; May–Sept., daily 9:30–7:30.*

The Eixample: Moderniste Barcelona

Barcelona's most famous neighborhood, this gracious late-19th-century urban development is known for its dizzying unnumbered grid and dazzling Art Nouveau architecture. The district encompasses an elegant checkerboard above Plaça de Catalunya and is called the Eixample, which means "widening" in Catalan. Somewhat wide and noisy for the most comfortable walking and wandering, the area, nevertheless, has so much superlative architecture that you'll find it easy to spend considerable time exploring this virtual living Moderniste museum. With its hard-line street grid—though softened a bit by the *xaflanes* (chamfers), the bevelled block corners at intersections—the Eixample is oddly labyrinthical for a Cartesian network (they forgot to number it) and many longtime Barcelona residents find it easy to get lost here, though it might be because it's so entertaining.

The Eixample was created with the dismantling of the city walls in 1860, when Barcelona embarked upon a vast expansion scheme fueled by the return of rich colonials from America, by an influx of provincial aristocrats who had sold their country estates after the debilitating second Carlist War (1847–49) and by the city's growing industrial power. The street grid was the work of urban planner Ildefons Cerdà, while much of the building here was done at the height of Modernisme by a virtual who's who of the greatest Art Nouveau architects, including many landmarks by Gaudí, Domènech i Muntaner, and Puig i Cadafalch. In the amazing architectural feast these masters serve up, the pièce de résistance, of course, is Gaudí's amazing Sagrada Família complex. The Eixample's principal thoroughfares are Rambla de Catalunya and Passeig de Gràcia, where the city's most elegant shops vie for space among its best Moderniste buildings.

For information on the Ruta del Modernismo (Modernism Route), a tour of nine major Art Nouveau sites (☞ Special-Interest Tours *in* Barcelona A to Z, *below*), inquire at your hotel or the tourist office (☞ Visitor Information *in* Barcelona A to Z, *below*), or purchase tickets directly at the **Casa Amatller** (☞ *below*) (✉ Passeig de Gràcia 41, ☎ 93/488–0139), open Monday–Saturday 10–7, Sunday 10–2. The price, 600 ptas./€3.61, gets you 50% discounts at all nine locations.

Numbers in the text correspond to numbers in the margin and on the Eixample map.

A Good Walk

Starting in the Plaça de Catalunya, walk up Passeig de Gràcia until you reach the corner of Consell de Cent. Take a deep breath: you are about to enter something resembling the eye of Barcelona's hurricane of Moderniste architecture, the **Manzana de la Discordia** ⑧⓪. This is the "city block," or "apple of discord" (the pun only works in Spanish), where the three great figures of Barcelona's late-19th-century Moderniste (Art Nouveau) movement—Domènech i Muntaner, Puig i Cadafalch, and Gaudí—went head to head and toe to toe with three very different, and very important, buildings: **Casa Lleó Morera, Casa Amatller,** and **Casa Batlló,** one of Gaudí's most jaw-dropping creations. The **Tàpies Foundation** ⑧①, with its distinctive wire sculpture *Núvol i cadira* (Cloud and Chair) by Antoni Tàpies himself, is just west, around the corner on Carrer Aragó. Swing by **Casa Domènech i Estapà** ⑧② on your way up to Gaudí's greatest (although most criticized) private commission, **Casa Milà** ⑧③, known as *La Pedrera* (*The Stone Quarry*), three blocks farther up Passeig de Gràcia; after seeing the roof (with its astonishing chimneys), the Gaudí museum, and the typical apartment here, pop into Vinçon for a look through one of Barcelona's top design stores, with views into the back of Casa Milà. Just around the corner at Diagonal 373 is Puig i Cadafalch's intricately sculpted **Casa Quadras** ⑧④, just two minutes from his Nordic castle–like **Casa de les Punxes** ⑧⑤ at No. 416–420. From here it's only a 10-minute hike to yet another Puig i Cadafalch masterpiece, **Casa Macaia** ⑧⑥, home of the culturally hyperactive Fundació la Caixa. By this time you're only three blocks from Gaudí's emblematic **Temple Expiatori de la Sagrada Família** ⑧⑦, for which you should plan a full half-day visit. After a tour of Gaudí's unfinished fantasy, stroll over to Domènech i Muntaner's **Hospital de Sant Pau** ⑧⑧— another major monument of the Moderniste movement. Other Eixample spots to visit, though they're widely scattered and not easily fitted into a single walking tour, can be seen if you head back south and to the west, and include Gaudí's **Casa Calvet** ⑧⑨, **Passatge Permanyer** ⑨⓪, the **Universidad Central** ⑨①, the chaletlike **Casa Golferichs** ⑨② by Rubió i Bel-

81

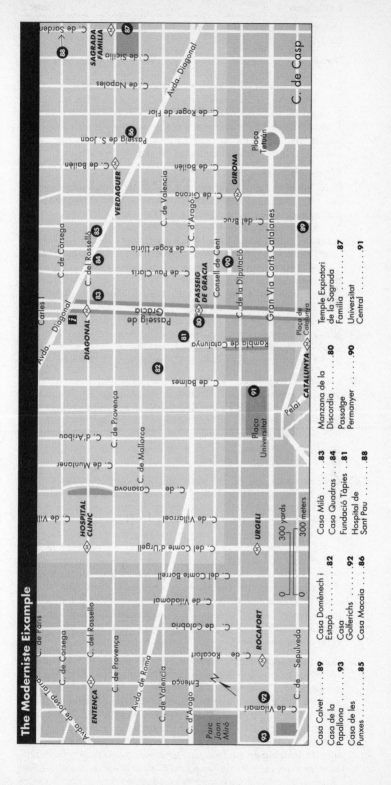

The Moderniste Eixample

lver, and the **Casa de la Papallona** ⑨, one of the most spectacular Art Nouveau buildings in town.

TIMING

Depending on how many taxis you take, this is at least a four-hour walk. Add another three hours to explore the Sagrada Família. Look for the *passatges* (passageways) through some of the Eixample blocks; Passatge Permanyer, Passatge de la Concepció, and Passatge Mendez Vigo are three of the best. Beware of the tapas emporiums lining Passeig de Gràcia (you'll note none are recommended here); they microwave previously prepared tapas and are not the best.

Sights to See

⑧⑨ **Casa Calvet.** As if working the thin end of the wedge, this exquisite but (for Gaudí) more conventional town house was the architect's first commission in the Eixample; the second was the dragonlike Casa Batlló, and the third (and last—he was never asked to do another) was the stone quarry–esque Casa Milà. Peaked with baroque scroll gables over the unadorned (no ceramics, no color) Montjuïc sandstone facade, Casa Calvet compensates for its structural conservatism in its details, from the doorhandles to the benches, chairs, vestibule, and spectacular glass-and-wood elevator. For a true taste of Gaudí, dine in the building's **Casa Calvet restaurant** (☞ Dining, *below*), a sensorial banquet. The only way to see the vestibule, elevator, and stairway of the actual house is to wander in as if on business. (Leave quietly if the doorman busts you, hiding this book as you retire. The doorman's lunch hour, by the way, is between 2 and 4.) ✉ *Carrer Aragó 255,* ☎ *93/487–0315.*

⑨③ **Casa de la Papallona.** This extraordinary apartment house crowned with an enormous yellow butterfly (*papallona*) made of *trencadis* (broken ceramic chips used by the Modernistes to add color to curved surfaces) was built in 1912 by Josep Graner i Prat. Next to Plaça Espanya, directly overlooking the Arenes de Barcelona bullring, the building displays lines of a routine, late-19th-century design—that is, until you reach the top of the facade. ✉ *Llançà 20.*

⑧⑤ **Casa de les Punxes** (House of the Spikes). Also known as Casa Terrades for the family that owned the house and commissioned Puig i Cadafach to build it, this extraordinary cluster of six conical towers ending in impossibly sharp needles is another of Puig i Cadafalch's northern European inspirations, this one rooted in the Gothic architecture of Nordic countries. One of the few freestanding Eixample buildings, visible from 360 degrees, this erst-Bavarian or Danish castle in downtown Barcelona is composed entirely of private apartments. Some of them are built into the conical towers themselves and consist of three circular levels connected by spiral stairways, about right for a couple or very small family. Interestingly, Puig i Cadafalch also designed the Terrades family mausoleum, albeit in much more sober and respectful style. ✉ *Diagonal 416–420. Closed to the public.*

⑧② **Casa Domènech i Estapà.** This less radical example of Eixample Art Nouveau architecture is interesting for its balconies and curved lines on the facade, for its handsome doors and vestibule, and for the lovely acid engravings on the glass of the entryway. Built by and for the architect Domènech i Estapà (1858–1917) in 1908–1909, this more sober and placid interpretation of the aesthetic canons of the epoch was finished only eight years before the death of the architect most known for his hostility to the Art Nouveau movement in architecture. Domènech i Estapà built more civil projects than any other architect of his time (Real Academia de Ciencias y Artes, Palacio de Justicia, Sociedad Catalana de Gas y Electricidad, Hospital Clínico, Observatorio Fabra) and was the author of the Carcel Modelo (Model Prison), considered a state-of-the-art example of penitentiary design when it was built in 1913. ⊠ *Valencia 241.*

OFF THE
BEATEN PATH

Museu Egipci de Barcelona (Fundació Arqueòlogica Clos). Even though you came to Barcelona to peruse, presumably, Catalonia, not ancient Egypt, you might be making a mistake by missing this major collection of art and artifacts. Housing what is probably Spain's most comprehensive exhibition on Egypt, this excellent museum opened to the public in this new expanded venue in spring 2000, so the state-of-the-art museological techniques are nearly as interesting as the subject matter. ⊠ *Valencia 284,* ☎ *93/488–0188.* ☞ *400 ptas./€2.40.* ☉ *Mon.–Sat. 10–2 and 4–8, Sun. 10–2; guided tour with Egyptologists Sat. at noon and 2.*

92 **Casa Golferichs.** Gaudí disciple Joan Rubió i Bellver built this extraordinary house for the Golferichs family when he was not yet 30. Known as El Xalet (The Chalet), house has an interior that is especially Gaudí-esque, with its cavernous verticality. The top floor, with its rich wood beams and cerulean walls, is often used for intimate small-format concerts, while the ground floor exhibits paintings and photographs. ⊠ *Gran Via 491,* ☎ *93/487–0315.* ☉ *Weekdays 9–2 and 4–8, Sat. 9–2.*

86 **Casa Macaia.** This graceful Puig i Cadafalch building constructed in 1901 is the seat of the ubiquitous Centre Cultural Fundació "La Caixa," a deep-pocketed, far-reaching cultural entity funded by the Caixa Catalana (Catalan Savings Bank). In addition to the two downstairs exhibition halls there is also an excellent design and architecture bookstore, a library, and a UNESCO-funded music and video library. Look for the Eusebi Arnau sculptures over the door depicting, somewhat cryptically, a man mounted on a donkey and another on a bicycle, reminiscent of the similar Arnau sculptures on the facade of Puig i Cadafalch's Casa Amatller on Passeig de Gràcia. Check listings for concerts, lectures, and art exhibits here for some of Barcelona's best cultural events. ⊠ *Passeig Sant Joan108,* ☎ *93/458–8907.* ☉ *Tues.–Sat. 11–2, 4–8; Sun. 10–3.*

★ **83** **Casa Milà.** Gaudí's Casa Milà, usually referred to as **La Pedrera** (The Stone Quarry), is one of Gaudí's most celebrated yet reviled designs, with a remarkable, curving stone facade that undulates around the corner of the block and topped by Gaudí's most unforgettable chimneys, so spooky they were nicknamed the *espantabruxes,* or witch-scarers. When the building was unveiled in 1910, local residents were horrified by the appearance of the cavelike balconies on their most fashionable street and coined the "Stone Quarry"—or, better, "Rockpile"—nicknames as rueful jibes; references were made to the gypsy cave dwellings outside Granada. Other critics were undone by the undulations of the facade. As one critic put it, the rippling, undressed stone made one feel as "though you are on board a ship in an angry sea." Seemingly defying the laws of gravity, there are no straight lines in the exterior, which is adorned with winding balconies covered with wrought-iron seaweedlike foliage sculpted by Josep Maria Jujol.

Originally meant to be dedicated to the Mother of God and crowned with a sculpture of the Virgin Mary, the initial design was altered by owner Pere Milà i Camps, who decided that after the anticlerical violence of the Setmana Tràgica (Tragic Week) of 1909 the religious statuary would be nothing short of an invitation for a new outbreak of mayhem. Barcelona writer Josep Maria Carandell published an article in May 2000 in *El País* suggesting that, in fact, the disagreement between Gaudí and Milà was more important, alleging that, in fact, Gaudí's intent in the alternating light and dark produced by the undulating facade was to make a heretical dualistic statement based on his Manichean beliefs. The sculptor of the Virgin Mary intended to center the facade was, like the founder of Manicheanism, named Carles Mani (1866–1911), and Carandell interprets the sculpture that never appeared as a dualistic exercise, and Gaudí as, far from a Catholic saint, a probable heretic.

No matter what his religious beliefs may have been, Gaudí's rooftop chimney park, alternately interpreted as veiled Saharan women or helmeted warriors, is as spectacular as anything in Barcelona, especially in late afternoon when the sunlight slants over the city into the Mediterranean. The handsome **Espai Gaudí** (Gaudí Space) in the attic has excellent critical displays of Gaudí's works from all over Spain, as well as explanations of theories and techniques, including a spectacular upside-down model (a reproduction of the original in the Sagrada Família museum) of the Güell family crypt at Santa Coloma made of weighted hanging strings. This hanging model is based on the "Theory of the Reversion of the Catenary," i.e., a chain suspended from two points will spontaneously hang in the exact shape of the inverted arch required to convert the stress to compression, thus support. The **Pis de la Pedrera** apartment flat is an interesting look into the life of a family that lived in La Pedrera in the early 20th century. Everything from the bathroom to the kitchen is filled with reminders of how rapidly life has changed in the last 75 years. ⊠ *Passeig de Gràcia 92,* ☎ *93/484–5995.* ▣ *Espai Gaudí 650 ptas./€3.91, Pis de la Pedrera 650 ptas./€3.91, combined ticket 1,100 ptas./€6.61.* ☉ *Daily 10–8; guided tours weekdays at 6 PM, weekends at 11 AM.*

84 **Casa Quadras.** Built in 1904 for Baron Quadras, this neo-Gothic and Plateresque (intricately carved in silversmithlike detail) facade is one of the most spectacular collections of the Eusebi Arnau sculptures present all over town (Palau de la Música, Quatre Gats, Casa Amatller, and Casa Lleó Morera are other Arnau sites). Look for the theme of St. George slaying the dragon once again, this one in a spectacularly vertiginous rush of movement down the facade. Don't miss the intimate-looking row of Alpine chalet–like windows across the top floor. Presently home of the **Museu de la Música** (Museum of Music—although it's planning to move to the Auditori within two years), the collection displays 16th- to 20th-century instruments from around the world and the scores and correspondence of Catalan musicians such as Enric Granados (1867–1916) and Isaac Albeniz (1869–1909). ⊠ *Diagonal 373,* ☎ *93/416–1157.* ▣ *400 ptas./€2.40; free first Sun. of month.* ☉ *Tues.–Sat. 10–2 and 5–8, Sun. 10–2.*

81 **Fundació Tàpies–Casa Montaner i Simó.** This former publishing house— built in 1880 and the city's first building to incorporate iron supports—has been handsomely converted to hold the work of preeminent contemporary Catalan painter Antoni Tàpies, as well as temporary exhibits. Tàpies is an abstract painter, although influenced by Surrealism, which may account for the sculpture atop the structure—a tangle of metal entitled *Núvol i cadira* (*Cloud and Chair*). The modern, airy, split-level Fundació Tàpies also has a bookstore that's strong on both Tàpies, Asian art, and Barcelona art and architecture. ⊠ *Carrer Aragó 255,* ☎ *93/487–0315.* ▣ *750 ptas./€4.51.* ☉ *Tues.–Sun. 10–8.*

88 **Hospital de la Santa Creu i de Sant Pau.** Certainly one of the most beautiful hospital complexes in the world, visible down Avinguda Gaudí from the Sagrada Família's Nativity facade, the Hospital de Sant Pau is notable for its Mudejar motifs and sylvan plantings. The hospital wards are set among lush gardens under exposed brick facades intensely decorated with mosaics and abundant polychrome ceramic tile. Begun in 1900, this monumental production won Lluís Domènech i Montaner his third Barcelona "Best Building" award, in 1912. (His previous two prizes were for the Palau de la Música and Casa Lleó Morera.) The Moderniste enthusiasm for nature is apparent here, as the architect believed patients were more apt to recover surrounded by trees and flowers than in sterile hospital wards. Domènech i Montaner also believed in the therapeutic properties of form and color and decorated the hospital intensely with Pau Gargallo sculptures and colorful mosaics. ⊠ *Carrer Sant Antoni Maria Claret 167,* ☎ *93/291–9000.* ⊙ *Daily 9–2 and 4–7.*

NEED A
BREAK?

If you're near Rambla Catalunya don't hesitate to report in to the semi-subterranean **La Bodegueta** (⊠ Rambla de Catalunya 100) for some *pa amb tomaquet* (bread moistened with tomato squeezings) and bits of cheese or ham. Most of the tapas places along the Passeig de Gràcia are sub-par, but for a quick drink or a coffee, you can't go wrong.

★ ⑧⓪ **Manzana de la Discordia.** The name is a pun on the Spanish word *manzana,* which means both city block and apple, alluding to the architectural counterpoint on this block and to the classical myth of the Apple of Discord (which played a part in that legendary tale about the Judgment of Paris told in ancient times). The houses here are spectacular and encompass three monuments of Modernisme—Casa Lleó Morera, Casa Amatller, and Casa Batlló. The ornate **Casa Lleó Morera** (No. 35) was extensively rebuilt (1902–06) by Palau de la Música architect Domènech i Montaner and is a treasure house of Catalan Modernisme. The facade is covered with ornamentation and sculptures depicting female figures using the modern inventions of the age: the telephone, the telegraph, the photographic camera, and the victrola. The inside is even more astounding, another anthology of Art Nouveau techniques assembled by the same team of glaziers, sculptors, and mosaicists Domènech i Montaner directed in the construction of the Palau de la Música. The Eusebi Arnau sculptures around the top of the walls on the main floor are based on the popular Catalan lullaby *La Dida de l'Infant del Rei* (The Nurse of the King's Baby), while the beautiful stained-glass scenes in the old dining room of Lleó Morera family picnics resemble Moderniste versions of Impressionist paintings. The house is closed to the public.

The neo-Gothic, pseudo-Flemish **Casa Ametller** (No. 41) was built by Josep Puig i Cadafalch in 1900 when the architect was 33 years old. Eighteen years younger than Doménech i Montaner and 15 years younger than Gaudí, Puig i Cadafalch was one of the leading statesmen of his generation, mayor of Barcelona, and, in 1917, president of Catalonia's first home-rule government since 1714, the Mancomunitat de Catalunya. Puig i Cadafalch's architectural historicism sought to recover Catalonia's proud past, in combination with eclectic elements from Flemish or Netherlands architectural motifs. The Eusebi Arnau sculptures (like those on the corner of the Quatre Gats in the Casa Martí at Carrer Monsió 3) range from St. George and the dragon to the figures of a handless drummer with his dancing bear. The flowing-haired "Princesa" is thought to be Ametller's daughter, while the playful animals up above are pouring chocolate, a reference to the source of the Ametller family fortune. The Casa Ametller is closed to the public, but an office on site dispenses tickets for the tour "La Ruta del Modernismo" (☞ Special Interest Tours *in* Barcelona A to Z, *below*).

Next door, to the right of Casa Ametller, is Gaudí at his giddiest: the eyepopping **Casa Batlló,** with its mottled facade, resembling anything from an abstract pointillist painting to a rainbow of colored sproodles sprinkled over an ice cream cone. Nationalist symbolism is at work here: the astonishing scaly roof line represents the Dragon of Evil impaled on St. George's cross, and the skulls and bones on the balconies are the dragon's victims. These motifs are allusions to Catalan Gothicism, for Gaudí was a passionate admirer of the Spanish Middle Ages and its codes of *hidalgueria* (chivalry) and religious fervor. Of the three competing buildings (four if you count Sagnier i Villavecchia's comparatively tame 1910 Casa Mulleras at No. 37) of the Manzana de la Discordia, Casa Batlló is clearly the star, as the mobs of camera-clicking tourists can tell without being told. Gaudí is said to have directed the chromatic composition of the facade from the middle of Passeig de Grácia, calling instructions to workmen on scaffolding equipped with baskets of multicolored fragments of ceramic tiling. The Casa Batlló is closed to the public. ⊠ *Passeig de Gràia 35, 41, and 43 (between Consell de Cent and Aragó). Interiors closed to the public.*

⑩ Passatge Permanyer. Cutting through the middle of the block bordered by Pau Claris, Roger de Llúria, Consell de Cent, and Diputació, this charming, leafy mid-Eixample respite is one of 46 *passatges* (alleys or passageways) that cut through the blocks of Barcelona's gridlike widening. Inspired by Nash's Neoclassical Regent's Park terraces in London (with their formal and separate town houses), Ildefons Cerdà originally envisioned many more of these utopian mid-block gardens, but Barcelona never regarded Cerdà benevolently. Having replaced the local candidate for the design of the Eixample through the machinations of the crown, the army, and local sympathizers, Cerdà was systematically and gleefully subverted at every opportunity. Once an aristocratic enclave and hideaway for pianist Carles Vidiella and poet, musician, and illustrator Apel.les Mestre, Passatge Permanyer is, along with the nearby Passatge Méndez Vigo, the best of these through-the-looking-glass downtown Barcelona alleyways. ⊠ *Carrer Pau Claris 118.*

★ ⑧ Temple Expiatori de la Sagrada Família (Expiatory Temple of the Holy Family). Barcelona's most emblematic and unforgettable landmark, Antoni Gaudí's Sagrada Família, is still under construction 118 years after it was begun. This striking and surreal creation was conceived as nothing short of a bible in stone, a gigantic representation of the entire history of Christianity, and continues to cause consternation, wonder, howls of protest, shrieks of derision, and cries of rapture. Whatever your reaction, there is no doubt that this landmark has earned a major place in the Great Book of Art History, and it is considered by historians to be one of the most important architectural creations of the 19th to 20th centuries (as for the 21st century, we will have to wait and see how the added structures work out). No building in Barcelona and few in the world—Frank Gehry's Bilbao Guggenheim for one—are more deserving of investing at least a full day in getting to know well. In fact, a quick visit can often be more tiring than an extended one. Nothing is so exhausting as admiration, and with Gaudí's masterpiece, there are too many things to see at one time. You find your eyes roving wildly from lacy walls, cobwebbed ceilings, and scintillating towers to mulitcolored pinnacles and gold mosaics. You revive sufficiently to return to the realm of little columns, festooned arches, and mysterious inscriptions. Many leave the church dazzled and enchanted. Its delights are not grasped in one visit. Like a Beethoven symphony or a Botticelli fresco, the Sagrada Família increases with closer acquaintance.

At first glance, it looms, hulks, towers, soars over Barcelona like some magical mid-city massif of needles and peaks left by endless eons of wind erosion and fungal metastasis. Stacks of caves and grottoes

GAUDÍ: BARCELONA'S EVANGELIST IN STONE

PERHAPS NO ARCHITECT has ever marked a major city as comprehensively and spectacularly as Antoni Gaudí (1852–1926). The great Moderniste (or Art Nouveau) master's still unfinished Temple Expiatori de la Sagrada Família (Expiatory Temple of the Holy Family) has become Barcelona's most emblematic structure, while another dozen-odd buildings, parks, gateways, and other works in and around Barcelona provide a constant Gaudí presence throughout the Catalonian capital.

Joan Bassegoda i Nonell, Barcelona's leading Gaudí expert and director of the Cátedra Gaudí, a Gaudí library and study center open to the public (✉ Av. Pedralbes 7, ☎ 93/204–5250), described, in a recent article, the evolution of Gaudí's unique approach to architecture. Noting that Gaudí's "originality is a return to origins," Bassegoda explains Gaudí's conviction that, throughout the history of architecture, architects had become prisoners of the forms they were able to create with the tools of their trade: the compass and the T-square. Ever since the Parthenon and before, all buildings had been composed of shapes these instruments could draw: circles, triangles, squares, and rectangles that in three dimensions became prisms, pyramids, cylinders, and spheres used for the construction of pillars, planes, columns, and cupolas.

Gaudí observed that in nature these shapes are unknown. Admiring the structural efficiency of trees, mammals and the human form, Gaudí noted that ". . . neither are trees prismatic, nor are bones cylindrical, nor are leaves triangular." A closer study of natural forms revealed that bones, branches, muscles, and tendons are all composed of and supported by fibers. Thus, though a surface curves, it is supported from within by a fibrous network that Gaudí translated into what he called "ruled geometry," a system of inner reinforcement he designed to construct hyperboloids, conoids, helicoids, or parabolic hyerboloids, all complicated terms for simple forms and familiar shapes: the femur is hyperboloid; the way shoots grow off a branch is helicoidal; the web between your fingers is a hyperbolic paraboloid.

Gaudí, then, was more than a sculptor playing with form; he was an engineer experimenting with construction. His parabolic (naturally looping) arches were functional techniques first and formal exercises on a second level. Gaudí's evolution away from the T-square and the compass can be traced from his first project, Casa Vicens (1883–85), colorful and daring though angular and rectilinear; through Palau Güell (1885–89), where only his rooftop chimneys hint at what's to come; Casa Calvet (1898-1900), where the vestibule, elevator, and stairwell are beginning to warp and heave into organic suggestions; Casa Mila (La Pedrera) (1905), with its undulating stone facade; Casa Batlló (1907), with its scaly dragon back of a roof and its tibias, femurs, and skulls; and, finally, the project that consumed the last 20 years of his life, the phantasmagorical Sagrada Família, a virtual midtown massif and forest that Gaudí himself once compared, in conversation with the German architect Ernst Neufert, to the "spires and needles of Montserrat, the famous religious shrine."

In the end, though, as Bassegoda recounts, Gaudí's innocent and playful nature, the student Gaudí who sculpted the rocks in Josep Fontseré's 1878 La Cascada (waterfall) in the Parc de la Ciutadella, prevailed. The great master's finest accolade, as reported by Bassegoda, came from the mother of a childhood friend from Reus who, upon seeing Barcelona and Gaudí's architecture for the first time, commented that the famous Moderniste was, after all, "just doing the same things he always did as a kid."

heaped on a labyrinth of stalactites, stalagmites, flora and fauna of every stripe and spot, the sheer immensity of it all, and the energy flowing from it are staggering. The scale alone is staggering: the current towering transept facades will one day be dwarfed by the main Glory facade and central spire—the **Torre del Salvador (Tower of the Savior)**, which will be crowned by an illuminated polychrome ceramic cross and one day soar to a final height 1 yard shorter than the Montjuïc mountain (567 ft) guarding the entrance to the port (Gaudí felt it improper for the work of man to surpass that of God). Today, for a 200-pta. additional charge, you can take an elevator skyward to the top of the bell towers for some spectacular views. Back down on ground, visit the **museum,** which displays Gaudí's scale models; photographs showing the progress of construction; and photographs of Gaudí's multitudinous funeral. In fact, the architect is buried to the left of the altar in the **crypt,** which has its own entrance.

Soaring spikily skyward in intricately twisting levels of towers, caverns, and spires, part of the Nativity facade is made of stone from Montserrat, Barcelona's cherished mountain sanctuary and home of Catalonia's patron saint, La Moreneta, the Black Virgin of Montserrat. Gaudí himself was fond of comparing the Sagrada Família to the flutes and pipes of the sawtoothed massif 50 km (30 mi) west of town, while a plaque in one of Montserrat's caverns reads LLOC D'INSPIRACIÓ DE GAUDÍ (Place of Inspiration of Gaudí).

History of Construction and Design. "My client is not in a hurry," Gaudí was fond of replying to anyone curious about the timetable for the completion of his mammoth project . . . and it's a lucky thing, because the Sagrada Família was begun in 1882 under architect Francesc Villar, passed on to Gaudí in 1891 (who worked on the project until his death in 1926), and in the year 2001 is still thought to be a half-century from completion, despite the comparative alacrity of today's computerized construction techniques. After the church's neo-Gothic beginnings, Gaudí added Art Nouveau touches to the crypt (the floral capitals) and in 1893 went on to begin the Nativity facade of a new and vastly ambitious project. Conceived as a symbolic construct encompassing the entirety of the history and scope of the Christian faith, the Sagrada Família was intended by Gaudí to impact the viewer with the full sweep and force of the gospel. For the last 15 years of his life, Gaudí actually became a recluse and took up residence in the church grounds. His life was cut short when, with just one tower finished, he was run over by a tram and, unrecognized for several days, died in a pauper's ward in 1926, just short of his 74th birthday.

Gaudí's plans called for three immense facades, the lateral (Nativity and Passion) facades presently, and respectively, visible on the northeast and southwest sides of the church, and the even larger Glory facade (as yet unbegun) designed as the building's main entry, facing southeast over Carrer de Mallorca. The four bell towers over each facade would represent the 12 apostles, a reference to the celestial Jerusalem of the Book of Revelation, built upon the 12 apostles. The four larger towers around the central Tower of the Savior will represent the evangelists Mark, Matthew, John, and Luke, while between the central tower and the reredos at the northwestern end of the nave will rise the 18th and second-highest tower in honor of the Virgin Mary. The naves are not supported by buttresses but by treelike helicoidal (spiraling) columns. The first bell tower, in honor of Barnaby, the only one Gaudí lived to see, was completed in 1921. Presently there are eight towers standing: Barnaby, Simon, Judas, and Matthias (from left to right) over the Nativity facade and James, Bartholomew, Thomas, and Phillip over the Passion facade.

Meaning and Iconography. Reading the existing facades is a challenging refresher course in Bible studies. The three doors on the **Nativity facade** are named for Charity in the center, Faith on the right, and Hope on the left. As explained by Joan Serra, vicar of the parish of the Sagrada Família and Gaudí scholar, the architect often explained the symbology of his work to visitors though never wrote any of it down. Thus, much of this has come directly from Gaudí via the oral tradition. In the Nativity facade Gaudí addresses nothing less than the fundamental mystery of Christianity: Why does God the Creator become, through Jesus Christ, a creature? The answer, as Gaudí explained it in stone, is that God did this to free man from the slavery of selfishness, symbolized by the iron fence around the serpent of evil (complete with an apple in his mouth) at the base of the central column. The column is covered with the genealogy of Christ going back to Abraham. To the left is a sea tortoise at the base of the parabolic arch, while to the right is a land turtle with flora and fauna from Catalonia above and behind.

Above the column is a portrayal of the birth of Christ, while above that is the Annunciation flanked by a grottolike arch of water in a solid state: ice, another element of nature. Overhead are the constellations in the Christmas sky at Bethlehem: if you look carefully (a pair of binoculars is an idea to take seriously) you'll see two babies representing the Gemini and the horns of a bull for Taurus.

To the right, the **Portal of Faith**, above Palestinian flora and fauna, shows scenes of Christ's youth: preaching at the age of 13 and Zacharias prophetically writing the name of John. Higher up are grapes and wheat, symbols of the eucharist, and a sculpture of a hand and eye, symbols of divine providence.

The left-hand **Portal of Hope** begins at the bottom with flora and fauna from the Nile; the slaughter of the innocents; the flight of the Holy Family into Egypt; Joseph, surrounded by his carpenter's tools, contemplating his son; the marriage of Joseph and Mary flanked by Mary's parents, grandparents of Jesus, Joaquin and Anna. Above this is a sculpted boat with an anchor, representing the Church, piloted by St. Joseph assisted by the Holy Spirit in the form of a dove. Overhead is a typical peak or spire from the Montserrat massif.

Gaudí, who carefully studied music, planned these slender towers to house a system of tubular bells (still to be created and installed) capable of playing more complete and complex music than standard bell-ringing changes had previously been able to perform. At a height of one-third of the bell tower are the seated figures of the apostles. The peaks of the towers represent the apostles' successors in the form of miters, the official headdress of a bishop of the Western Church.

The **Passion facade** on the Sagrada Família's southwestern side over Carrer Sardenya and the Plaça de la Sagrada Família is a dramatic contrast to the Nativity facade. As Vicar Joan Serra notes, Gaudí, whose plans called for nearly everything that appears on the Passion facade, intended to emphasize the abyss between the birth of a child and the crucifixion and death of a man. Ironically, Josep Maria Subirachs, the sculptor chosen in 1986 to execute Gaudí's plans, initially known to be an atheist, author of statements such as "God is one of Man's greatest creations . . ." now confesses to nothing more virulent than a respectful agnosticism, while rumors circulate that, in fact, Subirachs may be undergoing a profound spiritual transformation.

Known for his easy-to-identify hard-edged and geometrical interpretations of the human form, Subirachs has stated that he was "born nine months after the death of Gaudí." When multitudinous demonstrations of artists, architects, and religious leaders called for his resignation in 1990, Subirachs replied, "My work has nothing to do with Gaudí." The *casus belli* at the moment was the anatomically complete rendering of a naked Christ on the cross, which Subirachs defended as part of the stark realism of the scene he intended to portray. Contracted on the two conditions that he be allowed complete artistic freedom and living space at the work site, Subirachs eventually prevailed and his work is now virtually undebated. "I intended a contrast with Gaudí's more baroque style," explains Subirachs, "with a harder vision and a brutalization of the stone itself."

Subirachs, in fact, pays double homage to the great Moderniste master in the Passion facade: Gaudí appears over the left side of the main entry making notes or drawings, the evangelist in stone, while the Roman soldiers are modeled on Gaudí's helmeted, *Star Wars*–like warriors from the roof of La Pedrera.

Framed by leaning tibia-like columns, the bones of the dead, and following an S-shaped path across the facade, the scenes represented begin at the left with the Last Supper, the faces of the disciples contorted in confusion and dismay, especially that of Judas clutching his bag of money behind his back over the figure of a reclining hound, symbol of fidelity in contrast with the disciple's perfidy. The next sculptural group to the right represents the prayer in the Garden of Gethsemane and Peter awakening, followed by the kiss of Judas. The square numerical cryptogram behind contains 16 numbers offering a total of 310 combinations all adding up to 33, the age of Christ at his death.

In the center, Jesus is lashed to a pillar during his flagellation, a tear track carved into his expressive countenance. Note the column's top stone akilter, reminder of the stone soon to be removed from Christ's sepulcher. The knot and the broken reed on the base of the pillar symbolize the physical and psychological suffering in Christ's captivity and scourging. Look for the fossil imbedded in the stone on the back left corner of the pedestal, taken by Sagrada Família cognoscenti as an impromptu symbol of the martyr's ultimate victory. To the right of the door is a rooster and Peter lamenting his third denial of Christ "'ere the cock crows." Farther to the right are Pilate and Jesus with the crown of thorns, while just above starting back to the left is Simon of Cyrene helping Jesus with the cross after his first fall. Over the center is the representation of Jesus consoling the women of Jerusalem (cf. Book of Revelation): "Don't cry for me; cry for your children . . ." and a faceless (because her story is considered legendary, not historical fact) St. Veronica with the veil she gave Christ to wipe his face with on the way to Calvary, which was miraculously imprinted with his likeness. The veil is torn in two overhead and covers a mosaic that Subirachs disliked and elected to conceal. To the left is the likeness of Gaudí taking notes and farther left is the equestrian figure of a centurion piercing the side of the church with his spear, the church representing the body of Christ. Above are the soldiers rolling dice for Christ's clothing and the naked, crucified Christ at the center. The moon to the right of the crucifixion refers to the darkness at the moment of Christ's death and to the full moon of Easter; to the right are Peter and Mary at the sepulcher, Mary with an egg overhead symbolizing the resurrection of Christ. At Christ's feet is a figure with a furrowed brow, perhaps suggesting the agnostic's anguished search for certainty, thought to be a self-portrait of Subirachs characterized by the sculptor's giant hand and an "S" on his right arm.

Over the door will be the 16 prophets under the cross of salvation. Apostles James, Bartholomew, Thomas, and Phillip appear at a height of 148 ft on their respective bell towers. Thomas, the apostle who demanded proof of Christ's resurrection (thus the expression "doubting Thomas"), is visible pointing to the palm of his hand, asking to inspect Christ's wounds, while Bartholomew, on the left, is turning his face upward toward the culminating element in the Passion facade, not yet in place, the 26-ft-tall gold metallic representation of the resurrected Christ that will be placed on a bridge between the four bell towers at a height of 198 ft.

Future of the project. Architect Jordi Bonet, director of the work on the Sagrada Família, at press time (fall 2000) predicted that the nave would be covered by the end of the year 2000. Son of one of Gaudí's assistants, Bonet remembers playing among the rocks and rubble of the construction site as a child. Indeed, with Bonet's brother Lluís as head parish priest, the Sagrada Família is virtually a Bonet family project. Within 10 years, predicts Bonet, the inside of the entire apse will be covered and Barcelona will have a covered space with a capacity for 15,000 people, an area large enough to encompass the entire Santa Maria del Mar basilica. In another 50 years, the great central dome, resting on four immense columns of Iranian porphyry said to be the hardest of all stones, will soar to a height of 568 ft over what will be Barcelona's tallest building, the culmination of more than 170 years of construction in the tradition of the great medieval and Renaissance cathedrals of Europe.

The line from John (13:27) carved into a corner of the Passion facade by Josep Maria Subirachs, who like the Bonet brothers is now in his seventies, will have an even more ominous meaning by the time the project is completed: EL QUE ESTÁS FENT, FES-HO DE PRESSA (Whatever you are doing, do it quickly). ⊠ *Plaça de la Sagrada Família,* ☎ 93/207–3031. ⊡ *900 ptas./€5.41; 50% discount at this and other Moderniste venues with the Ruta del Modernismo Ticket available at Casa Ametller (*☞ *above, and Special-Interest Tours in Barcelona A to Z, below).* ☉ *Sept.–Mar., daily 9–6; Apr.–Aug., daily 9–8. Guided tours daily at 11:30, 1, 4, and 5:30 (English tours can be arranged with the guide organization Guiart),* ☎ 669–48–24–04. ✑

⑨ **Universitat Central.** Barcelona's Universitat Central was built in 1889 by Elies Rogent. In its neo-Romanesque style alluding, no doubt, to classical knowledge, the university's two-tiered Pati de Lletres (literary patio) is its most harmonious element, along with the vestibule, gardens, and Paraninfo (main assembly hall). Originally founded as a medical school in 1401 by King Martí I (el Humà, dubbed "the humane" for his preoccupation with medicine and social welfare), the university was exiled to the town of Cervera 100 km (62 mi) west of Barcelona in 1717 by Felipe V as part of his general program to dismantle Catalonia in reprisal for supporting the Habsburg contender in the War of the Spanish Succession. Cervera, an island of Bourbon support in a sea of Habsburgist Catalans, had been promised a multitude of riches, including (allegedly) a seaport, for supporting the Bourbon contender, but did at least become Catalonia's version of Oxford or Cambridge until the university was invited back to town in 1823. ⊠ *Gran Via 585.*

Gràcia: Radical Chic

Gràcia is a state of mind. More than a neighborhood, a village Republic that has periodically risen in armed rebellion against city, state, and country, Gràcia is a jumble of streets with names (Llibertat, Fraterni-tat, Progrès, Venus) that suggest the ideological history of this fierce little nucleus of working-class citizens and sentiment. Once home to Barcelona's first collectivized manufacturing operations (i.e., factories), this proved a dangerous precedent as workers organized and developed into radical groups ranging from anarchists to feminists to esperan-tists. Once an outlying town that joined the municipality of Barcelona only under duress, Gràcia attempted to secede from the Spanish state in 1856, 1870, 1873, and 1909.

Lying above the Diagonal from Carrer de Córsega all the way up to Parc Güell, Gràcia's lateral borders run along Via Augusta and Balmes to the west and Carrer de l'Escorial and Passeig de Sant Joan to the east. Today, it's filled with appealing and compelling bars and restau-rants, movie theaters, and outdoor cafés—always alive and usually thronged by young and hip couples in the throes of romantic ecstasy or agony of one kind or another. Mercé Rodoreda's famous novel *La Plaça del Diamant* (translated by David Rosenthal as *The Time of the Doves*) begins and ends in Gràcia's square of the same name during the August Festa Major, a festival that fills the streets with the rank-and-file residents of this always lively yet intimate little pocket of gen-eral resistance to Organized Life.

Numbers in the text correspond to numbers in the margin and on the Gràcia map.

A Good Walk

Starting in **Parc Güell** ⑨④—a fantastic Gaudí extravaganza of a park—find your way down through upper Gràcia to **Plaça Rovira i Trias** ⑨⑤, where a bronze effigy of architect Antoni Rovira i Trias is seated ele-gantly on a bench in the middle of the square. From there, continue over to **Plaça de la Virreina** ⑨⑥—picturesque location of several imposing Moderniste buildings by Francesc Berenguer, Gaudí's most famous as-sistant—and then over to **Plaça del Diamant** ⑨⑦, Plaça Trilla, and across Gran de Gràcia to Carrer de les Carolines and Gaudí's first house, **Casa Vicens** ⑨⑧, a spectacular homage to Mudejar architecture. Next stop is the **Mercat de la Llibertat** ⑨⑨, one of Gràcia's two food produce markets. Cut east past another exercise in Mudejar taste, the **Centre Moral Instructiu de Gràcia** ⑩⓪, and on to **Plaça del Sol,** one of Gràcia's most popular squares, and then farther east through Gràcia's other mar-ket, **Mercat de la Revolució** ⑩① (now officially known as Abaceria Cen-tral), before coming three blocks back over to **Plaça Rius i Taulet** ⑩②, Gràcia's main square with its emblematic clock tower. From Plaça Rius i Taulet cut out to **Gran de Gràcia** for a look at more elegant Art Nou-veau buildings by Berenguer, on your way to Botafumeiro for some of Barcelona's best Galician seafood. Back down near the bottom of Grà-cia, just above Carrer Còrsega is Jean Luc Figueras, an exquisite restau-rant just a few steps from the Gaudí-esque facade of another Art Nouveau gem, **Casa Comalat** ⑩③.

TIMING
This is a three- to four-hour outing that could take five with lunch in-cluded or an entire day really to get the feel of Gràcia. Evening ses-sions at the popular (v. o.—showing films in their original language) Verdi cinema usually get out just in time for a late-night bite at Bota-fumeiro, which closes at 1 AM. Güell Park is best in the afternoon when the sun spotlights the view east over the Mediterranean. Exploring Grà-

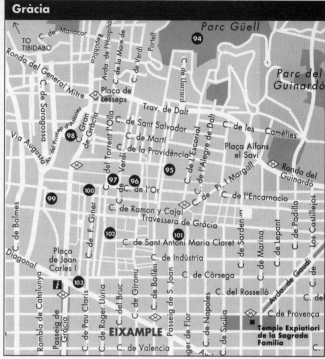

cia with the Llibertat and Revolucío markets closed is a major loss, so plan to reach the markets before 2 PM.

Sights to See

★ ⑩ **Casa Comalat.** At the bottom of Gràcia between the Diagonal and Carrer Còrsega, this often overlooked Moderniste house is a good one to add to your collection. For a look at the best side of an almost-Gràcia Art Nouveau tour de force, cut down past Casa Fuster at the bottom of Gran de Gràcia, take a left on Bonavista, then a right on Santa Teresa past Jean Luc Figueras's excellent restaurant at No. 10 to Casa Comalat across Carrer Còrsega at No. 316. This Salvador Valeri i Pupurull creation is one of Barcelona's most interesting Moderniste houses, especially this side of it, with its bulging polychrome ceramic balconies and its melted wax underpinnings. Look for the curious wooden galleries and check out the designer bar, SiSiSi, around on the less interesting facade at Diagonal 442. ✉ *Carrer de Còrsega 316. Closed to the public.*

★ ⑨ **Casa Vicens.** Antoni Gaudí's first important commission as a young architect was begun in 1883 and finished in 1885. In this work, Gaudí had still not succeeded in throwing away his architect's tools, particularly the T-square. The historical eclecticism (that is, borrowing freely from past architectural styles around the world) of the early Art Nouveau movement is evident in the Orientalist themes and Mudejar details lavished throughout the facade. Since it was commissioned by a ceramics merchant, this may be the explanation for the use of eyecatching colored ceramic tiles, which render nearly the entire facade into a striking checkerboard. Casa Vicens was the first time this technique, now omnipresent, was used in Barcelona. The chemaro palm leaves decorating the gate and surrounding fence are thought to be the work of Berenguer, while the comic iron lizards and bats oozing off the facade are Gaudí's playful nod to the Gothic gargoyle. Gaudí's second commission, built in 1885, was in the little town of Comillas in Santander, built for the Marquès de Comillas, Antonio López y López, a shipping magnate and the most powerful man of his time. Not surprisingly, the two houses bear a striking resemblance to each other. ⊠ *Carrer de les Carolines 24–26. Interior closed to the public.*

⑩ **Centre Moral Instructiu de Gràcia.** Another Berenguer creation (Gràcia is Berenguer country), this exposed-brick Mudejar facade is one of the few in Barcelona. The Centre Moral Instructiu was built in 1904 and still functions as a YMCA-like cultural institution of which Berenguer was president at one time. ⊠ *Carrer Ros de Olano 9.*

★ **Gran de Gràcia.** This central artery up through Gràcia would be a lovely stroll if the automobile and (worse) motorcycle din weren't so overpowering. (A tunnel would do the trick nicely.) However, many of the buildings along Gran de Gràcia are of great artistic and architectural interest, beginning with **Can Fuster,** at the bottom of Gran de Gràcia 2–4. Built between 1908 and 1911 by Palau de la Música Catalana architect Lluís Domènech i Montaner in collaboration with his son Pere Domènech i Roure, the building shows a clear move away from the chromatically effusive heights of Art Nouveau. More powerful, and somehow less superficial than much of Art Nouveau architecture, the building's impact comes more from structural elements such as the winged supports under the balconies or the floral base under the corner tower than from pure ornamentation. As you move up Gran de Gràcia, probable Berenguer buildings can be identified at No. 15; No. 23, with its scrolled cornice; and No. 35, No. 49, No. 51, No. 61, and No. 77. Officially attributed to a series of architects—since Berenguer lacked a formal degree (having left architecture school to become Gaudí's "right hand")—these buildings have long inspired debate over Berenguer's role in these Moderniste masterworks.

★ ㊤ **Mercat de la Llibertat.** This uptown version of the Rambla's Boqueria market is one of Gràcia's coziest spaces, a market big enough to roam in and small enough to make you feel at home. Built by Francesc Berenguer between 1888 and 1893, the Llibertat market reflects, in its name alone, the revolutionary and democratic sentiment strong in Gràcia's traditionally blue-collar residents. Look for Berenguer's decorative swans swimming along the roofline and the snails surrounding the coat of arms of the town of Gràcia. ⊠ *Carrer de les Carolines 24–26.*

⑩ **Mercat de la Revolucio.** Officially the Abaceria Central, the market got its early name from the nearby Plaça de la Revolució de Setembre de 1868 just a block away up Carrer dels Desamparats. Browse through and consider having something delicious such as a plate of wild mushrooms or a *tortilla de patatas* (potato omelet) at the very good bar and restaurant at the far corner on the lower east side.

★ ㊤ ㊔ **Parc Güell.** Güell Park is one of Gaudí's, and Barcelona's, most pleasant and stimulating places to spend a few hours. Whereas Gaudí's landmark Temple of the Sagrada Família (☞ The Eixample, *above*) can be exhaustingly bright and hot (though exciting) in its massive energy and complexity, Parc Güell is invariably light and playful, uplifting and restorative. Alternately shady, green, floral, or sunny, there's always a delicious corner here for whatever one needs. Named for and commissioned by Gaudí's main patron, Count Eusebio Güell, the park was originally intended as a hillside garden community based on the English Garden City model, centered, amazingly enough, on an open-air theater built over a covered marketplace. Only two of the houses were ever built, finally, as Barcelona's bourgeoisie seemed happier living closer to "town," and the Güell family eventually turned the area over to the city as a public park.

An Art Nouveau extravaganza with gingerbread gatehouses topped with, respectively, the hallucinogenic red-and-white fly ammanite wild mushroom (rumored to have been a Gaudí favorite) on the right and the *phallus impudicus* (no translation necessary) on the left, Parc Güell is a perfect visit for a sunny afternoon when the blue of the Mediterranean is best illuminated by the western sun. Other Gaudí highlights include the Room of a Hundred Columns—a covered market supported by tilted Doric-style columns, mosaic-encrusted buttresses, and guarded by a patchwork lizard—and the fabulous, serpentine, polychrome bench that snakes along the main square. Partly inspired by the profile rendered by one of Gaudí's assistants laying in a pool of plaster, the bench is an icon of the Moderniste movement, the most memorable creation of Gaudí assistant Josep Maria Jujol (who outdid himself here with the most colorful examples of *trencadís*, broken-mosaic work) and a perfect photoop. ✉ *Carrer d'Olot 3 (take metro to Lesseps; then walk 10 mins uphill or catch Bus 24 to park entrance).* ✆ *Oct.–Mar., daily 10–6; Apr.–June, daily 10–7; July–Sept., daily 10–9.*

★ Within Parc Güell, the **Gaudí Casa-Museu** occupies a pink, Alice-in-Wonderland house in which Gaudí lived with his niece from 1906 to 1926. Exhibits in this house museum include Gaudí-designed furniture, decorations, drawings, and portraits and busts of the architect. ✉ *Parc Güell (up hill to right of main entrance)*, ✆ *93/219–3811.* 💷 *450 ptas./€2.70.* ✆ *May–Sept., daily 10–8; Oct.–Feb., daily 10–6; Mar.–Apr., daily 10–7.*

96 **Plaça de la Virreina.** The much-punished and oft-restored church of Sant Joan de Gràcia stands where the Palau de la Virreina once stood, the mansion of the same Virreina (wife, in this case widow, of a viceroy) whose palace on the Rambla (☞ Palau de la Virreina *in* La Rambla, *above*) is now a prominent municipal museum and art gallery. The story of La Virreina, a young noblewoman widowed at an early age by the elderly Viceroy of Peru, is symbolized in the bronze sculpture in the center of the square portraying Ruth (of the Old Testament), represented carrying the sheaves of wheat she was gathering when she learned of the death of her husband, Boaz. Ruth, who remained loyal to her widowed mother-in-law, Naomi, is the Old Testament paradigm of wifely faith to her husband's clan, a parallel to La Virreina's lifelong devotion to the performance of good works with her husband's fortune.

The rectoral residence at the back of the church is the work of Gaudí's assistant Francesc Berenguer, whose buildings are sprinkled throughout Gràcia. Just across the street at Carrer de l'Or 44 is another Berenguer building, a giddily vertical Art Nouveau apartment house. The gigantic town house on the right side of Carre Torrijos is typical of the enormous upper Barcelona mansions constructed by late 19th-century- to early 20th-century textile barons and *indianos* (Catalans who had become wealthy in the New World). The house at 44 Carrer de l'Or was built in 1909 by Antoni Gaudí's right-hand man and perennial assistant Francesc Berenguer. Berenguer's role in Gaudí's work and within the Moderniste movement, despite his having left architecture school prematurely in order to work for Gaudí, was significant (if not decisive) and has been much studied and debated by architects and Art Nouveau scholars. Berenguer was a specialist in buildings with walls adjoining neighboring structures and the house at 4 Carrer de l'Or remains one of Berenguer's finest achievements, a vertical exercise with pinnacles at the stress lines over rich stacks of wrought-iron balconies. If Barcelona was Gaudí's sandbox, Gràcia was Berenguer's. Nearly every major building in Gràcia, including the Mercat de la Llibertat, is a Berenguer creation.

NEED A
BREAK? Gràcia is filled with cozy cafés, both indoors and out, but for the most classical Gràcia *terraza*, try the Plaça de Rius i Taulet, also known as the Plaça del Rellotge (Square of the Clock Tower), where the **Bar Candanchú** (⊠ Plaça de Rius i Taulet 9) runs tables until early morning. For a more delicious and elegant treat, **Botafumeiro,** just out on Gran de Gràcia (⊠ Gran de Gràcia 81), never disappoints.

⑨⑦ Plaça del Diamant. This little square is of enormous sentimental importance in Barcelona as the site of the opening and closing scenes in Mercé Rodoreda's famous novel entitled *Plaça del Diamant* (superbly translated into English by the late American poet and translator David Rosenthal as *The Time of the Doves),* the story of a young woman devoured by life and the Spanish Civil War. Colometa, the novel's protagonist, is portrayed in bronze caught in the middle of her climactic scream during which "a little bit of nothing trickled out of my mouth, like a cockroach made of spit . . . and that bit of nothing that had lived so long trapped inside me was my youth and it flew off with a scream of I don't know what . . . letting go?" The bronze birds represent the pigeons that Colometa spent her life obsessively breeding, while the male figure on the left pierced by bolts of steel is Quimet, her first love and husband, whom she met at a dance in this square and later lost in the war.

★ **⑩② Plaça Rius i Taulet.** Named for a memorable Gràcia mayor, this is the town's most emblematic and historic square, marked by the handsome clock tower in its center. The Gràcia Casa de la Vila (town hall) at the lower end of the square is yet another Francesc Berenguer opus; the clock tower, built in 1862, is just over 110 ft high. The symbol of Gràcia, the clock tower was bombarded by federal troops when Gràcia seceded from the Spanish state in 1870, 1873, 1974, and 1909. Always a workers' neighborhood and, as a result, prone to social solidarity and collective bargaining, Gràcia was mobilized by mothers who refused to send their sons off as conscripts to fight for the crumbling Spanish Imperial forces during the late 19th century, thus requiring a full-scale assault by Spanish troops to reestablish law and order. Today, sidewalk cafés prosper under the leafy canopy here, a good place for a refreshing stop.

⑨⑤ Plaça Rovira i Trias. This charming little square and the story of Antoni Rovira i Trias shed much light on the true nature of Barcelona's eternal struggle with Madrid and Spanish central authority. Take a careful look at the map of Barcelona positioned at the feet of the bronze effigy of the architect and urban planners near the center of the square and you will get an idea of what the city might have looked like if Madrid's (and the Spanish army's) candidate for the design of the Eixample in 1860, Ildefons Cerdá, had not been imposed over the plan devised by Rovira i Trias, initial and legitimate winner of the open competition for the commission.

Upper Barcelona: Sarrià and Pedralbes

Sarrià is a 1,000-year-old village that once overlooked Barcelona from the foothills of the Collserola. Gradually swallowed over the centuries up by the westward encroaching city, Sarrià has become a melange of petit bourgeois merchants, writers, artists, and a home for many Barcelona schools occupying what were once summer mansions for the city's commercial leaders. Santa Eulàlia, Barcelona's co-patroness, is always described as "the beautiful daughter of a wealthy Sarrià merchant" who fell afoul of Roman Consul Decius in the 4th century, a reminder of Sarrià's perennially well-off citizenry. J. V. Foix, famous Catalan poet who published in France throughout the Franco regime, is an honored citizen here, his descendants the proprietors of Sarrià's two famous Foix pastry shops. Now largely a pedestrian sanctuary, Sarrià still retains much of its village atmosphere just 15 minutes by the Generalitat train from the Rambla. The miniaturesque original town houses sprinkled through Sarrià are a reminder of the not-so-distant past when this enclave was an even more bougainvillea-festooned eddy at the edge of Barcelona's roaring urban torrent.

Pedralbes clings to the beginnings of the Collserola hills above Sarrià, a neighborhood of mansions scattered around the 14th-century Monestir de Pedralbes (Pedralbes Monastery) (now home to an important part of the celebrated Thyssen-Bornemisza Collection). Peripheral points of interest hereabouts include some of Gaudí's most memorable works, including Finca Güell on Avinguda de Pedralbes, Torre Bellesguard above Plaça de San Gervasio, and the Teresianas convent and school just above the intersection of General Mitre and Ganduxer; the Palau Reial de Pedralbes is a 20-minute walk downhill on the Diagonal (just behind the Finca Güell gate and the Cátdra Gaudí), while the Futbol Club Barcelona's monstrous, 100,000-seat Nou Camp sports complex and museum are another 20 minutes' walk down below the Hotel Princesa Sofia on the Diagonal.

Numbers in the text correspond to numbers in the margin and on the Sarrià and Pedrables map.

A Good Walk

Because the Monestir de Pedralbes closes at 2, the best way to explore this part of town is to first start with the monastery and then head back down into **Sarrià.** where you can browse and graze until 4 or 4:30. From Sarriá's Reina Elisenda train stop, it's a 20-minute walk or a 5-minute cab ride to the **Monestir de Pedralbes** ㉔. After a tour of the monastery and its Thyssen-Bornemisza Collection of paintings, take a walk down the cobblestone Baixada del Monestir alongside the sumptuously sculpted and sgraffito-covered El Conventet (Little Convent), named for an earlier Franciscan convent and one of the many luxurious—and private—mansions in this district, and cross to the Mató de Pedralbes restaurant (named for the *mató,* or cottage cheese, the Clarist nuns of Pedralbes were once famous for), where you might be tempted to have lunch at this excellent spot. Back up in Plaça del Monestir, walk east on Carrer del Monestir past the ancient ficus tree in the center of Plaça Jaume II and across Avinguda Foix into Carrer Ramon Miquel i Planes. A right on Sagrat Cor will take you down to the back of the **Sarrià market.** The Sarrià church and **Plaça Sarrià** ㉕ are just across Passeig Reina Elisenda. After touring Sarrià, where there are numerous fine lunch and dinner options, a short taxi ride will take you to **Finca Güell** ㉖ and its spectacular gate, home of the Cátedra Gaudí study center. From here, walk to the **Palau Reial de Pedralbes** ㉗ and its decorative arts collections, then perhaps athletically hike over to the **Camp Nou** ㉘ stadium—home of the famed FC Barcelona team, to catch a soccer match, or if your tastes run more to architecture, taxi over to the important Gaudí buildings at the convent and girls' school **Colegio de les Teresianas** ㉙ and the **Torre Bellesguard** ㉚.

TIMING

This is a three-hour outing, including at least an hour in the monastery. Count four or five with lunch included. The Monestir de Pedralbes closes at 2 PM, so go in the morning. Bar Tomás serves its famous potatoes

98

with *allioli* 1–4 and 7–10, another key timing consideration, while the Foix de Sarrià pastry emporium is open until 9.

Sights to See

⑩⑧ Camp Nou Stadium. If you're in Barcelona between September and June, go see the celebrated FC Barcelona club play soccer, preferably against Real Madrid (if you can get in) at Barcelona's gigantic stadium, the Camp Nou. Games are generally played by club (not national) teams Saturday night or Sunday afternoon at 5, but there may be King's Cup or international games during the week as well, usually on Wednesday. Ask your hotel concierge how to get tickets, or call the club in advance. The massive Camp Nou stadium seats 100,000 and fills almost to capacity. The museum has an impressive array of trophies and a five-screen video showing memorable goals in the history of one of Europe's most colorful soccer clubs. ⊠ *Arístides Maillol,* ☎ *93/330–9411.* ▣ *Museum 600 ptas./€3.61.* ☉ *Oct.–Mar., Tues.–Fri. 10–1 and 4–6, weekends 10–1 and 3–6; Apr.–Sept., Mon.–Sat. 10–1 and 3–6.*

⑩⑨ Colegio de les Teresianas. Built in 1889 for the Reverend Mothers of St. Theresa when Gaudí was in a relatively benign creative fervor and still occasionally using straight lines, this building showcases upper floors reminiscent of those in Berenguer's 44 Carrer de l'Or apartment house with its steep peaks and reiterative verticality. Hired to finish a job begun by another architect, Gaudí found his freedom of movement severely limited in this project. Gaudí fans especially admire the poetically simple parabolic arched hallway that the master created on the bottom floor; other characteristic Gaudí elements are the ceramic crosses on the building's four corners. Unfortunately, you can only study the Gaudí details on the exterior of the complex. ⊠ *Ganduxer 85,* ☎ *93/ 254–1670. Interior closed to the public. Two guided tour monthly Sat. 11 AM—call to confirm dates (free).*

106 **Finca Güell–Càtedra Gaudí.** Home of the Càtedra Gaudí, a Gaudí library and study center open to the public (curiosity is the only credential required), this tiny gatehouse with the fierce wrought-iron dragon made by Gaudí himself is surrounded by lovely ceramic mosaics. The garden inside is a lush oasis. To get there from Sarrià, walk through the park at the Casal de Sarrià at the western end of Vives i Tutó and the lovely Jardins de la Vil.la Amèlia and out Passeig Manuel de Girona to Avinguda de Pedralbes. The little street above the Finca Güell gatehouse is named for the American Gaudí scholar George R. Collins (1917–93). ⊠ *Av. Pedralbes 7,* ☎ *93/204–5250.* ⊙ *Weekdays 9–2.*

★ **104** **Monestir de Pedralbes.** Even without its Thyssen-Bornemisza Collection of Old Master paintings, this monastery is one of Barcelona's best semi-hidden treasures. Founded by Reina Elisenda for Clarist nuns in 1326, the convent has an unusual, three-story Gothic cloister, arguably the finest in Barcelona. The chapel has a beautiful stained-glass rose window and famous murals painted in 1346 by Ferrer Bassa, a Catalan much influenced by the Italian Renaissance. You can also visit the medieval living quarters. The monastery alone is a treat, but the **Thyssen-Bornemisza Collection,** installed in 1989 in what was once the dormitory of the nuns of the Order of St. Clare, sends it over the top. Surrounded by 14th-century windows and pointed arches, these canvases by Tiepolo, Canaletto, Tintoretto, Rubens, Velázquez, Zurbarán, and many others are a delight. Set it all to music with viola-da-gambista Jordi Savall's not infrequent early music concerts here and you're in for an unforgettable synaesthetic experience. ⊠ *Baixada Monestir 9,* ☎ *93/203–9282.* ▣ *Monastery and cloister 400 ptas./€2.40, Thyssen-Bornemisza Collection 400 ptas./€2.40, combined ticket 700 ptas./€4.21; free 1st Sun. of month.* ⊙ *Tues.–Sun. 10–2.* ✑

107 **Palau Reial de Pedralbes** (Royal Palace of Pedralbes). Built in the 1910s as the palatial estate of Count Eusebi Güell—one of Gaudí's most important patrons—this mansion was transformed into a royal palace by architect Eusebi Bona i Puig and completed in 1929. King Alfonso XIII, grandfather of Spanish king Juan Carlos I, visited the palace in the mid-1920s before its completion. In 1931 during the Second Spanish Republic the palace became the property of the municipal government and was made Museu de les Arts Decoratives (Decorative Arts Museum) in 1932. In 1936 the palace was used as the official residence of Manuel Azaña, last president of the Spanish Republic, and was the scene of the formal 1937 farewell tribute awarded volunteers of the International Brigades who fought for the Republic during the Spanish Civil War. Today, the palace houses both the **Museu de les Arts Decoratives** and the **Museu de la Ceràmica**. The collection of decorative arts comprises an array of palace furniture and antiques from the 15th through 20th centuries, while the ceramics display covers a wide sweep of Spanish ceramic art from the 12th century to the present, as well as ceramics by contemporary artists such as Miquel Barceló who showed here in summer 2000. The influence of Moorish design techniques in Spanish ceramics and decorative arts is carefully documented in a separate display. A good 30-minute forced march down from the Monestir de Pedralbes (☞ *above*), this is a good visit to combine with the Càtedra Gaudí study center (☞ above). The best way to walk there from Sarrià's Plaça de Sant Vicens is to cut across Major de Sarrià and Oriol Mestres to Fontcoberta, take a left and then a right on Vives i Tutó, and walk to the corner of Conde del Trinquet, where you can then go through the consecutive gardens of the Casal de Sarrià and the Jardíns de la Vil.la Amèlia, exiting into Passeig de Claudi Güell and cutting down to the end of Passeig Manuel Girona just across from the Càtedra Gaudí. After seeing Càtedra Gaudí, cut around the right side and walk along Carrer de Fernando Primo de Rivera, which runs along the garden walls of the palace, down to the main entrance on the Diagonal.

In addition, the palace is home to the **Museu de Ceràmica,** which makes a wide sweep of Spanish ceramic art from the 12th century to the present. The influence of Moorish design techniques in Spanish ceramics and decorative arts is carefully documented in a separate display. It's a 20-minute walk downhill from the monastery. ⊠ *Av. Diagonal 686,* ☎ *93/280–1621.* 🎟 *700 ptas./€4.21; free 1st Sun. of month.* ☺ *Daily 10–3.*

🔟 **Plaça Sarrià.** The 1,000-year-old village of Sarrià—today centered around **Plaça Sarria**—was once a cluster of farms and country houses overlooking Barcelona from the hills. It's now a quiet enclave at the upper edge of the roaring metropolis. Start your exploration at the main square, Plaça Sarrià, which hosts an antiques and crafts market on Tuesday morning, *sardana* dances on Sunday morning, and Christmas fairs in season. The Romanesque church tower, lighted a bright ocher at night, looms overhead. Across Passeig Reina Elisenda from the church, wander through the brick-and-steel **produce market** and the tiny, flower-choked **Plaça Sant Gaietà** behind it. Back in front of the church, cut through the Placeta del Roser to the left and you'll come to the elegant **town hall** in the Plaça de la Vila; note the buxom bronze sculpture of **Pomona,** goddess of fruit, by famed Sarrià sculptor Josep Clarà (1878–1958). After peeking in to see the massive ceiling beams (and very reasonable set lunch menu) in the restaurant Vell Sarrià, at the corner of Major de Sarrià, go back to the Pomona bronze and turn left into tiny Carrer dels Paletes (with its tiny saint-filled niche on the corner overhead to the right), which leads back to Major de Sarrià. Continue down this pedestrian-only street and turn left on bougainvillea-and honeysuckle-lined **Carrer Canet,** with its diminutive, cottagelike artisans' quarters. Turn right at the first corner on Carrer Cornet i Mas and walk two blocks down to Carrer Jaume Piquet.

A quick probe to the left will take you to No. 30, Barcelona's most perfect small-format **Moderniste house,** thought to be the work of no less than Palau de la Música architect Domènech i Muntaner, complete with faux-medieval upper windows, wrought-iron grillwork, floral and fruited ornamentation, and organically curved and carved wooden doors. The next stop down Cornet i Mas is Sarrià's prettiest square, **Plaça Sant Vicens,** a leafy space ringed by old Sarrià houses and centered on a statue of the village's patron, St. Vincent, bearing the millstone used to sink him to bottom of the Mediterranean after he was martyred in Valencia in 302 AD. Note the other versions of the saint, in the ceramic tiles and behind the ancient glass of the niche over the square's upper right-hand corner. Can Pau, the café on the lower corner with Carrer Mané y Flaquer, is the local hangout, a good place for coffee and tortilla and once a haven for such authors as Gabriel García Marquez and Mario Vargas Llosa, who lived in Sarrià in the early 1970s just as they were first becoming famous.

Other Sarrià landmarks to look for include the two **Foix** pastry stores, one at Plaça Sarrià 9–10 and the other on Major de Sarrià 57, above Bar Tomás. Both have excellent pastries, artisanal breads, and cold *cava.* The late J. V. Foix (1893–1987), son of the store's founders, was one of the great Catalan poets of the 20th century, a key player in keeping the Catalan language alive during the 40-year Franco regime. The Plaça Sarrià Foix, a good spot for homemade ice cream, has a bronze bust of the poet, whereas the Major de Sarrià location has a bronze plaque identifying the house as the poet's birthplace and inscribed with one of his most memorable verses: *Tota amor és latent en l'altra amor/tot llenguatge és saó d'una parla comuna/tota terra barega a la pàtria de tots/tota fe serà suc d'una mes alta fe.* (Every love is latent in the other love/every language is part of a common tongue/every country contributes to the fatherland of all/every faith will be the lifeblood of a higher faith). ⊠ *Plaça Sarrià (take Bus 22 from the bottom of Av. de Tibidabo, or the U-6 train on the FFCC subway to Reina Elisenda).*

NEED A
BREAK?

Bar Tomás, on Major de Sarrià on the corner of Jaume Piquet, is a Barcelona institution, home of the finest potatoes in town. Order the famous *doble mixta* of potatoes with *allioli* and hot sauce. Draft beer (ask for a *caña*) is the de rigueur beverage. This is a regular stop for everyone from King Juan Carlos to singer-songwriter Sam Lardner, Barcelona mayor Joan Clos to American philosopher Dan Dennett, who once sang "Oh Tell Me Why" there.

⑩ **Torre Bellesguard.** For Gaudí to the last drop, climb up above Plaça de la Bonanova to this private residence built in 1902 over the ruins of the summer palace of the last of the Sovereign Count-Kings of Catalan-Aragon realm known as the Corona d' Aragón (Crown of Aragón), Martí I l'Humà (Martin I the Humane), whose reign ended in 1410. Look for the stained-glass red and gold markings of the Catalan *senyera* (banner) on the tower, which is topped by the typical four-armed Greek cross favored by Gaudí. Since this is a private residence, the interior is unfortunately not viewable, though at the Càtedra Gaudí (☞ *below*) there are a number of photographic and analytical studies showing the architect's interior supporting arches in variegated sizes and shapes, probably the building's best feature. The Catalan Gothic reminiscences mixed with the Montserrat-ish massif exterior place Bellesguard (beautiful view) squarely in the Gaudí mainstream. ⊠ *Bellesguard 16–20.*

Tibidabo, Vallvidrera, and the Collserola Hills

Tibidabo is Barcelona'a traditional promontory, a romantic evening and late-night promenade overlooking the city and a nonpareil point from which to watch the Mediterranean produce Technicolor dawns and blazing sunrises. The Collserola hills, Barcelona's version of the Vienna Woods out to the northwest of the city, are visible rising verdantly behind the city. Honeycombed with well-kept trails, the Parc de Collserola is a vast (20,000 acre) forest and park beyond Tibidabo and Vallvidrera complete with wild boar and miles of wilderness. The offices of the Parc de Collserola authorities next to the Jacint Verdaguer museum at Vil.la Joana can supply detailed maps of this lush resource just 10 minutes by train from Sarrià. Vallvidrera perches at the pinnacle overlooking both the Montserrat massif to the west and Barcelona below to the east. Return to Barcelona either by walking the Carretera de les Aigües (Water Road), so named for the canals that once carried water into downtown Barcelona from the upper Llobregat river, or from Vallvidrera's Art Nouveau funicular station.

A Good Walk

At the top of Carrer de Balmes the U-7 FFCC Generalitat Tibidabo train's run from Plaça Catalunya ends at Plaça Kennedy. (Just imagine getting off with your skis and schussing back down to the palm tree–lined port before taking the subway back up for another run, as was necessitated during the legendary blizzard of 1954). The first building on the right as you start up Avinguda del Tibidabo is known as La Rotonda, notable for its Art Nouveau ceramic ornamentation on the upper part of the facade. The Tramvia Blau (Blue Trolley) sets out from just above La Rotonda and, passing the imposing white **Casa Roviralta–El Frare Blanc,** drops you at Plaça del Doctor Andreu, where the funicular climbs up to the heights of **Tibidabo.** Plaça del Doctor Andreu has several restaurants, the best of which is La Venta. From Tibidabo the road to the **Torre de Collserola** continues another 2 km (1 mi) over to **Vallvidrera,** where there are several good restaurants (such as Can Trampa in Plaça de Vallvidrera). From Vallvidrera, return to Barcelona via the funicular or on foot. The other way to approach is via the Baixador de Vallvidrera stop on the FFCC Generalitat railway line to San Cugat, Sabadell, or Terrassa. A five-minute walk up to the Jacint Verdaguer museum at **Vil.la Joana** will put you on well-marked trails through the Parc de Collserola. There are also trail markings to Vil.la Joana from the Torre de Collserola. The Barcelona train from the Baixador de Vallvidrera will drop you back in Plaça Catalunya in 20 minutes.

TIMING

This is a four-hour outing, just to Tibidabo, Vallvidrera, and back. Add an hour or two for lunch and another three for the trek out to Vil.la Joana and back by train. Walking from Vil.la Joana all the way to the end of the *rompeolas* (breakwater) in the port could be done in five hours.

Sights to See

Casa Roviralta– El Frare Blanc. Gaudí disciple Joan Rubió i Bellver, author of the Gran Via's Casa Golferichs, won the Barcelona architecture prize of 1913 with this hulking interplay of exposed brick and white surfaces. The house is traditionally known as *El Frare Blanc* (the white monk) for the *masía* (Catalan country house) that previously occupied the spot and served as home to a community of Dominican monks. Now the home of the Asador de Aranda restaurant, this is a place to keep in mind for a late-winter-afternoon roast after a hike in from beyond the Collserola hills. ⊠ *Av. Tibidabo 31,* ☎ *93/417–0115.*

Museu Verdaguer–Vil.la Joana Catalonian poet Jacint Verdaguer died in this house in 1902. The story of Verdaguer's reinvention of Catalan nationalism in the late 19th century, only for him eventually to die in disgrace, defrocked, and impoverished, is a fascinating saga (☞ the Close-Up box on Verdaguer, *above*). Considered the national poet of Catalonia and the most revered and beloved voice of the Catalan "Renaixença" of the 19th century, Verdaguer—universally known as *Mossen Cinto* (Mossen is Catalan for priest; Cinto is from Jacinto, Spanish for Jacint)—Verdaguer finally succumbed to tuberculosis and doctrinal religious troubles. Priest, poet, Pyreneist, and mystic, he was seen as a virtual saint and wrote works of great religious, telluric, and patriotic fervor such as *Idilis* and *Cants mistichs* as well his famous long masterpiece, *Canigó* (1886). In *La Atlantida* (1877), eventually to become a Manuel de Falla opera-oratorio, he wrote about prehistoric myths of the Iberian Peninsula and the Pyrenees. Verdaguer's death provoked massive mourning. His popularity was so enormous that violently anticlerical Barcelona anarchists in mid-uprising ceased fighting and stormed the churches to ring the bells on hearing the news of his death. The funeral was one of the greatest and most multitudinous events in Barcelona history, comparable only to Gaudí's in spontaneity and emotion.

Lines from his patriotic poem *Enyorança* (*Yearning*), which provides a glimpse into this romantic mind, are slowly and sonorously recited at Vil.la Joana every June 10 on the anniversary of his death as the last evening sun streams in through the clouds over the Montserrat massif to the west, setting for Verdaguerís immortal poem (and song) *Virolai.*

Sabéssiu lo catalá/sabríeu qué es enyorança/la malaltia dels cors/trasplantats a terra estranya . . . / . . . aqueix mal que sols té nom/en nostra llengua estimada/aqueixa veu dels ausents,/aqueix sospir de la pàtria/que crida sos fills llunyans/amb amorosa recança.

(If you knew Catalan,/you would know what yearning was,/the affliction of hearts/transplanted to foreign lands . . . / . . . that malady that only has a name/in our beloved tongue/the voice of those departed,/the sighing for the homeland/her distant sons lament/with loving sorrow.) ✉ *Crtra. de les Planes, Vallvidrera,* ☎ *93/204–7805.* 🎟 *Free.* ☉ *Oct.– Mar., Wed. 10–2, weekends 11–3; June–Sept., Wed. 10–2, Sat. 11–2 and 3–6, Sun. 11–3. Metro: FFCC de la Generalitat trains from Plaça Catalunya for Sant Cugat, Sabadell, or Terrassa.*

Tibidabo. One of Barcelona's two promontories—the other is Montjuïc (☞ *below*)—this hill bears a particularly distinctive name, generally translated as "To-Thee-I-Will-Give" and referring to the Catalan legend that this was the spot from which Satan showed Christ, and tempted him with, all the riches of the earth (namely, Barcelona below) "if thou will fall down and worship me" or, according to the Gospel according to St. Matthew, "Haec omnia Tibi dabo si cadens adoraberis me." When the wind blows the smog out to sea, the views from this 1,789-ft peak are legendary. The shapes that distinguish Tibidabo from below turn out to be a commercialized neo-Gothic church built by Enric Sagnier in 1902, a radio mast that used to seem tall, and— looking like something out of the 25th century—the 854-ft communications tower, the **Torre de Collserola** (☞ *below*), designed by Sir Norman Foster. There's not much to see here except the vista, particularly from the tower. Clear days are few and far between in 21st-century Barcelona, but if (and only if) you hit one, this excursion is worth considering. The restaurant **La Venta,** at the base of the funicular, is excellent and is a fine place to sit in the sun in cool weather (the establishment provides straw sun hats). The bar **Mirablau,** overlooking the city lights, is a popular hangout. ✉ *Take Tibidibo train (U-7) from Placa Catalunya; Buses 24 and 22 to Plaça Kennedy; or a taxi. At Av. Tibidabo, catch Tramvía Blau (the blue trolley), which connects with the funicular (☞ Getting Around in Barcelona A to Z, below) to the summit.*

Torre de Collserola. The Collserola Tower, which unkindly dwarfs the rest of the Tibidabo promontory, was designed by Norman Foster for the 1992 Olympics amid controversy over defacement of the traditional mountain skyline. A vertigo-inducing elevator ride takes you to the observation deck atop the tower, where you can drink in a splendid panorama of the city (when weather conditions allow). Take the funicular up to Tibidabo; from Plaza Tibidabo there is free transport to the tower. ✉ *Av. de Vallvidrera,* ☎ *93/406–9354.* 🎟 *600 ptas./€3.61.* ☉ *Wed.–Sun. 11–2:30 and 3:30–8.*

OFF THE
BEATEN PATH
Ⓒ

MUSEU DE LA CIÈNCIA – Young scientific minds work overtime in the Science Museum, just below Tibidabo—many of its displays and activities are designed for children ages seven and up. ✉ *Teodor Roviralta 55,* ☎ *93/212–6050.* 🎟 *600 ptas./€3.61.* ☉ *Tues.–Sun. 10–8. Metro: Avinguda de Tibidabo and Tramvía Blau halfway.*

Vallvidrera. This perched village is a quiet respite from Barcelona's headlong race. Oddly, there's nothing exclusive or upmarket, for the moment, about Vallvidrera, as most well-off *barcelonins* (as Gaudí and

Count Güell found out with Güell Park) prefer to be closer to the center of things. From **Plaça Pep Ventura,** in front of the Moderniste funicular station, there are superb views over some typical little Vallvidrera houses and the Montserrat massif hulking in the distance to the west. Vallvidrera can be reached from the Peu Funicular train stop and the Vallvidrera funicular, by road, or on foot from Tibidabo or Vil.la Joana. ⊠ *Plaça de Vallvidrera.*

Montjuïc

This hill overlooking the south side of the port is popularly said to have been named Mont Juif for the Jewish cemetery once located on its slopes, though a 3rd-century Roman document referring to the construction of a road between Mons Taber (around the Cathedral) and Mons Jovis (Mount of Jove) suggests that in fact the name derives from the Roman deity Jove, or Jupiter. Compared to the human warmth, hustle, and bustle of Barcelona, Montjuïc may feel a little like Siberia, but its Miró Foundation, the Romanesque collection of Pyrenean murals and frescoes in the Palau Nacional, the re-creation of the Moderniste masterpiece of the Mies van der Rohe Pavilion, and the lush gardens, Jardins de Mossèn Cinto Verdaguer, are all undoubtedly among Barcelona's must-see sites. The other Montjuïc events—the fortress, the Olympic stadium, Palau Sant Jordi, Poble Espanyol, and the Font Màgica (Magic Fountain)—are all interesting enough but are second-tier visits compared to Barcelona options such as Parc Güell and the Monestir de Pedralbes. The most dramatic approach to Montjuïc is by way of the cross-harbor cable car from Barceloneta or from the mid-station in the port; Montjuïc is normally accessed by taxi or Bus 61 (or on foot) from Plaça Espanya, or by the funicular that operates from the Paral.lel (Paral.lel metro stop, Line 3).

Numbers in the text correspond to numbers in the margin and on the Montjuïc map.

A Good Walk

Walking from sight to sight on Montjuïc is possible but not recommended. The walking tends to be on the tedious side, and you'll want fresh feet and backs to appreciate the museums and sights here, especially the Romanesque art collection in the Palau Nacional and the Miró Foundation.

The *telefèric* drops you at the Jardins de Miramar, a 10-minute walk from the Plaça de Dante. From here, another small cable car takes you up to the **Castell de Montjuïc** ⑪. From the bottom station, the **Fundació Miró** ⑫—a much-loved museum, with fine scenic vantage points, devoted to one of Barcelona's most celebrated modern artists—is just a few minutes' walk, and beyond are the **Estadi Olímpic** ⑬ (Olympic Stadium) and the Palau Sant Jordi. From the stadium, walk straight down to the Palau Nacional and its **Museu Nacional d'Art de Catalunya** ⑭—a colossal palace housing what is widely considered the finest collections of Romanesque art in the world, featuring murals and frescoes painstakingly removed from Pyrenean chapels and restored here. The **Museu d'Arqueologia** ⑮ is just down to east. From the Palau Nacional, a wide stairway leads down past the famous **Mies van der Rohe Pavilion** ⑯, leaving **Poble Espanyol** ⑰ 1 km (½ mi) up to the left, passes the **Plaça de les Cascades** ⑱ and the Font Màgic, and sends you through the Fira de Barcelona convention pavilions toward **Plaça de Espanya** ⑲.

TIMING

With unhurried visits to the Miró Foundation and the Romanesque exhibit in the Palau Nacional, this is a four- to five-hour excursion.

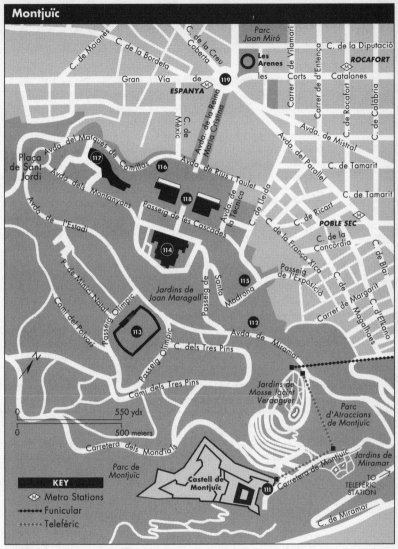

Have lunch afterward in the Poble Espanyol just up from Mies van der Rohe's Barcelona Pavilion or in the excellent restaurant at the Fundació Miró. Even better, find your way down into the Poble Sec neighborhood east of Montjuïc and graze your way back to the Rambla.

Sights to See

⑪⑪ **Castell de Montjuïc.** Built in 1640 by rebels against Felipe IV, the castle has been stormed several times, most famously in 1705 by Lord Peterborough for Archduke Carlos of Austria. In 1808, during the Peninsular War, it was seized by the French under General Dufresne. Later, during an 1842 civil disturbance, Barcelona was bombed from its heights by a Spanish artillery battery. The moat contains attractive gardens, with one side given over to an archery range, and the various terraces have panoramic views over the city and out to sea. The castle now functions as a **military museum** housing the weapons collection of early 20th-century sculptor Frederic Marès. ✉ *Carretera de Montjuïc 66,* ☎ *93/329–8613.* 🎫 *250 ptas./€1.50.* ☉ *Oct.–Mar., Tues.–Sat. 10–2 and 4–7, Sun. 10–2; Apr.–Sept., Tues.–Sat. 10–2 and 4–7, Sun. 10–8.*

★ ⑪③ **Estadi Olímpic.** The Olympic Stadium was originally built for the Great Exhibition of 1929, with the idea that Barcelona would then host the 1936 Olympics (ultimately staged in Hitler's Berlin). After failing twice to win the nomination, Barcelona celebrated the attainment of its long-cherished goal by renovating the semiderelict stadium in time for 1992, providing seating for 70,000. Next door and just downhill stands the futuristic **Palau Sant Jordi Sports Palace,** designed by the noted Japanese architect Arata Isozaki. The Isosazki structure has no pillars or beams to obstruct the view and was built from the roof down— the roof was built first, then hydraulically lifted into place. ✉ *Passeig Olímpic 17–19,* ☎ *93/426–2089.* ☉ *Weekdays 10–2 and 4–7, weekends 10–6.*

★ ⑪② **Fundació Miró.** The Miró Foundation was a gift from the artist Joan Miró to his native city and is one of Barcelona's most exciting showcases of contemporary art. The airy, white building, with panoramic views north over Barcelona, was designed by Josep Lluís Sert and opened in 1975; an extension was added by Sert's pupil Jaume Freixa in 1988. Miró's unmistakably playful and colorful style, filled with Mediterranean light and humor, seems a perfect match for its surroundings, and the exhibits and retrospectives that open here tend to be progressive and provocative, from Moore to Mapplethorpe. Look for Alexander Calder's fountain of moving mercury. Miró himself rests in the cemetery on Montjuïc's southern slopes. During the Franco regime, which he strongly opposed, Miró first lived in self-imposed exile in Paris, then moved to Majorca in 1956. When he died in 1983, the Catalans gave him a send-off amounting to a state funeral. ✉ *Av. Miramar 71,* ☎ *93/329–1908.* 🎫 *850 ptas./€5.11.* ☉ *Tues.–Wed. and Fri.–Sat. 10–7, Thurs. 10–9:30, Sun. 10–2:30.*

★ ⑪⑥ **Mies van der Rohe Pavilion.** The architectural masterpiece of the Bauhaus School and a virtual lodestone for Modernism, the legendary Pabellon Mies van der Rohe—the German contribution to the 1929 Universal Exhibition, reassembled between 1983 and 1986—remains a stunning "less is more" study in interlocking planes of white marble, green onyx, and glass. In effect, it is Barcelona's aesthetic antonym (possibly in company with Richard Meier's MACBA and the Mediterranean Gothic Santa Maria del Mar) for the hyper–Art Nouveau Palau de la Música and the city's myriad Gaudí spectaculars. Don't fail to note the matching patterns in the green onyx panels or the mirror play of the black carpet inside the pavilion with the reflecting pool outside, nor the iconic Barcelona chair designed by Ludwig Mies van der Rohe (1886–1969), reproductions of which have graced fancy Moderniste interiors around the world for decades. ⊠ *Av. Marquès de Comillas s/n,* ☏ *93/423–4016.* 🎟 *450 ptas./€2.70.* ☉ *Daily 10–8.*

⑮ **Museu Arqueològia.** Just downhill to the right of the Palau Nacional, the Museum of Archaeology holds important finds from the Greek ruins at Empúries, on the Costa Brava. These are shown alongside fascinating objects from, and explanations of, Megalithic Spain. ⊠ *Passeig Santa Madrona 39–41,* ☏ *93/423–2149.* 🎟 *450 ptas./€2.70.* ☉ *Tues.–Sat. 9:30–1 and 4–7, Sun. 9:30–1.*

★ ⑭ **Museu Nacional d'Art de Catalunya** (Catalonian National Museum of Art). Housed in the imposingly frescoed and columned **Palau Nacional,** this museum was built in 1929 and recently renovated by Gae Aulenti, architect of the Musée d'Orsay in Paris. Composing the world's finest collection of Romanesque and Gothic frescoes, altarpieces, and wood carvings, most of the art exhibited here was removed from small churches and chapels in the Pyrenees during the 1920s to save them from deterioration, theft, and art dealers. Most of the works, such as the famous *Pantocrator* fresco (a copy of which is now back in the church of Sant Climent de Taüll; ☞ Chapter 4), have been reproduced and replaced in their original homes, in answer to past critics who decried the removal en masse of so many art treasures from their intended church environments (initially done for safety's sake). The collection also contains works by El Greco, Velázquez, and Zurbarán. ⊠ *Mirador del Palau 6,* ☏ *93/423–7199.* 🎟 *950 ptas./€5.71; 550 ptas./€3.31 for temporary exhibits only.* ☉ *Tues.–Wed. and Fri.–Sat. 10–7, Thurs. 10–9, Sun. 10–2:30.*

⑱ **Plaça de les Cascades.** Upon leaving the Mies van der Rohe Pavilion (☞ *above*), you'll see the multicolor (at night) fountain in the Plaça de les Cascades. Stroll down the wide esplanade past the exhibition halls, used for Barcelona fairs and conventions, to the large and frenetic **Plaça d'Espanya.** Across the square is Les Arenes bullring, now used for theater and political rallies rather than bullfights. From here, you can take the metro or Bus 38 back to the Plaça de Catalunya.

⑲ **Plaça de Espanya.** This busy circle is a good place to avoid, but sooner or later you'll probably need to cross it to go to the convention center or to the Palau Nacional. Dominated by the so-called Venetian towers (they're actually Tuscan) built in 1927 as the grand entrance to the 1929 World's Fair, the fountain in the center is the work of Josep Maria Jujol, the Gaudí collaborator who designed the curvy and colorful benches in Parc Güell. The sculptures are by Miquel Blay, one of the master artists and craftsmen who put together the Palau de la Musica. The bullring, Les Arenes, is no longer used for tauromachy. On the corner of Carrer Llançà, just down to the right looking at the bullring, you can just get a glimpse of the kaleidoscopic lepidopteron atop the Art Nouveau Casa de la Papallona (House of the Butterfly).

☝ ⑰ **Poble Espanyol.** The Spanish Village was created for the 1929 Universal Exhibition. A sort of artificial Spain-in-a-bottle, with faithful reproductions of Spain's various architectural styles punctuated with boutiques, workshops, and studios, it takes you from the walls of Ávila to the wine cellars of Jerez de la Frontera. The liveliest time to come is at night, and a reservation at one of the half dozen restaurants gets you in for free, as does the purchase of a ticket for the two discos or the Tablao del Carmen flamenco club. ⊠ *Av. Marquès de de Comillas s/n,* ☏ *93/325–7866..* 🎟 *1,000 ptas./€6.01.* ☉ *Mon. 9–8, Tues.–Thurs. 9–2, weekends 9–4.*

DINING

Over the last quarter century Barcelona and Catalonia have undergone an important *renaixença* in all areas of cultural and artistic endeavor, the culinary arts perhaps foremost among them. Whereas in 1975 feeble faux-Castilian roasts and pseudo-Italian solutions were nearly all there was to be found beyond the staid classical canons of the international and France-mimetic confines of a few stuffy gourmet sanctuaries, new chefs such as Santi Santamaria and Ferran Adrià and a host of others have burst onto the scene with new energy and éclat informed by a nationalistic pro-Catalan intent. Barcelona now boils over with *cuina d'autor*—designer cuisine: chefs with original recipes—and a combination of traditional and experimental dining and decor that is a challenge (though a delicious one) to keep abreast of.

Whether it's a classical *lenguado a la plancha* (grilled sole) or a dark and savory *arroç negre amb sepia en su tinta* (black rice with squid in its ink), everything here comes loaded with taste (read salt, read garlic, read fresh, read hot). The new Mediterranean cuisine has been found to be so intrinsically good for health (stressing olive oil, garlic, wine, vegetables, fish) that nobody has time to worry about the taste-stealing restrictions (such as salt) that other, less pleasure-crazed cultures have embraced.

Be prepared for mouthwatering and tongue-twisting specialties such as the *minimandonguilles amb tomaquet concassé* (mini-meatballs with crushed tomato) and the *llom de xai al cardomom amb favetes a la menta* (lamb with cardamom and broadbeans with mint), or the Catalonia endemic *espardenyas* (sea slugs, so named for their resemblance to rope-soled espadrilles). Menus in Catalan are as musical as they are aromatic, with rare ingredients such as *salicornia* (seawort, or sea asparagus) with *bacalao* (cod) or fragrant wild mushrooms such as *rossinyols* (chanterelles) and *moixernons* (field agaric) accompanying dishes such *mandonguilles amb sepia* (meatballs with cuttlefish).

Barcelona restaurants are so many and so exciting that keeping up with them is an ongoing hobby for many Barcelona food lovers. Indeed, the main problem with food and wine in the city—perhaps an ironic one, in light of Spain's not-so-distant past—may be their very abundance. Dining heartily twice a day and taking full advantage of the tapas hour requires some management. The Spanish, looking forward to a substantial midday meal after having finished dinner late the previous night, breakfast on little more than coffee and a roll. Lunch, served between 2 and 4 in the afternoon—preceded by an *aperitivo*—is generally considered the main meal of the day. The workday lasts until at least 8, after which it's time for the itinerant *tapeo*. Finally, often after 10, comes dinner, which is often festive and can last until the wee hours. The traveler's key to surviving this delicious but demanding regimen is to partake zestily of tapas in the early evening—roam freely and you'll soon fill up on cleverly arrayed items from all four food groups. Above and after all, Spain is the ultimate moveable feast.

Barcelona's hotspots are changing quickly, with, for example, the two top restaurants of 1992 closed and gone, while places with names like Ot, Abac, Drolma, Folquer, Tram-Tram, Talaia Mar, and Acontraluz joining old favorites like Casa Leopoldo, Can Gaig, Cal Isidre, and Gorría in a constantly self-renewing succession of leapfrogging chefs and sous-chefs seeking the limelight.

Stick with local produce and local cuisine: Castilian specialties such as roast suckling pig, for example, are bound to taste better in Castile (where the best and freshest piglets prevail). Here, look instead for *mar i muntanya* (surf-and-turf) specialties such as rabbit and prawns, or dark meat with fruits or sweets, as in duck or goose with pears or prunes, or rabbit with figs. *Menús del día* (menus of the day) are good values, though they vary in quality and are generally served only at lunchtime. Restaurants usually serve lunch 1–4 and dinner 9–11; only a few places, notably Botafumeiro, Los Caracoles, and Set Portes, serve continuously from 1 PM to 1 AM. Tipping, though common, is not required; if you do tip, anywhere from 5% to 10% is perfectly acceptable. No one seems to care at all about tipping one way or the other, though gratitude is invariably expressed in one way or another and all parties seem to end up happier if a small gratuity is left. Note than many restaurants are closed during Holy Week, the week before Easter.

CATEGORY	COST*
$$$$	over 8,000 ptas./€48.08
$$$	5000–8,000 ptas./€30.05–48.08
$$	3000–5000 ptas./€18.03–30.05
$	under 3,000 ptas./€18.03

per person for a three-course meal, excluding drinks, service, and tax

Ciutat Vella (Old City): Barri Gòtic, El Rambla, Sanc Ponc

Ciutat Vella comprises the Rambla, Barri Gotic, Ribera, and Raval districts between Plaça de Catalunya and the port. Chic new restaurants and cafés seem to open daily in Barcelona's traditional Old Quarter.

$$$$ ✕ **Abac.** Xavier Pellicer, formerly with Santi Santamaria's Racó de Can Faves in Sant Celoni, is clearly headed for the stars after a brilliant opening in late 1999. In the tradition of Catalonia's finest restaurants, no detail is left to chance here. With carefully selected ingredients and innovative yet traditional recipes, this Catalan cuisine with international and cosmopolitan tendencies is all, in the end, "cuisine d'auteur," original Pellicer from soup to nuts: international and Catalan, traditional and daringly innovative. Try the *espardenyas con raviolis de enojo* (cuttlefish with fresh pasta ravioli stuffed with fennel). ⊠ *Rec 79–89,* ☎ *93/319–6600. Reservations essential. AE, DC, MC, V. Closed Sun. and Aug. No lunch Mon.*

$$$$ ✕ **Mey Hofmann.** This thickly vegetated dining room just up Argenteria from Santa Maria del Mar is a cooking academy and first-rate restaurant specializing in Mediterranean cuisine classified as *de creación*, meaning that they're always experimenting with new tastes and combinations. The young waiters and waitresses are chefs-in-training and usually encyclopedic about ingredients and preparations from aperitif wines to cheeses and desserts. ⊠ *Argenteria 74–78,* ☎ *93/319–5889. AE, DC, MC, V. Closed weekends.*

$$$$ ✕ **Passadis del Pep.** Hidden away through a tiny passageway off the Pla del Palau near the Santa Maria del Mar church, this lively bistro serves a rapid-fire succession of delicious seafood tapas and wine as soon you appear. Sometime late in the proceedings you may be asked to make a decision about your main course, usually a fish of one kind or another. You are free to stop at this point. Avoid *bogavante* (lobster) unless you're on an expense account. ⊠ *Pla del Palau 2,* ☎ *93/ 310–1021. AE, DC, MC, V. Closed Sun. and Aug. 15–31.*

$$$$ ✕ **Set Portes.** These "Seven Doors" near the waterfront hide a high-ceiling dining room, black-and-white marble floor, and mirrors aplenty. Going strong since 1836, this festive and elegant restaurant serves continuously from 1 PM to 1 AM, seven days a week. The cooking is Catalan, and the portions are enormous. Specialties are paella *de peix*

110

Barcelona Dining

(with fish) and *sarsuela Set Portes* (seafood casserole). ⊠ *Passeig Isabel II 14,* ☏ *93/319–3033. AE, DC, MC, V.*

$$$ ✕ **Can Isidre.** This small restaurant just inside the Raval from Avinguda del Paral.lel has a longtime following among Barcelona's artistic elite. Pictures and engravings, some original, by Dalí and other prominent artists line the walls. The traditional Catalan cooking draws on fresh produce from the nearby Boqueria and has a slight French accent. The homemade foie gras is superb. Come and go by cab at night; the area between Can Isidre and the Rambla is risky. ⊠ *Les Flors 12,* ☏ *93/441–1139. Reservations essential. AE, MC, V. Closed Sun., Holy Week, and mid-July–mid-Aug.*

$$$ ✕ **Casa Leopoldo.** Hidden away in the dark Raval on the west (right)
★ side of the Rambla, this excellent restaurant serves some of the finest seafood and Catalan fare in Barcelona. Since it's hard to find, the Gil family, now in its fourth generation here, will have you picked up at any hotel within city limits and driven to the door. Otherwise, approach along Carrer Hospital, take a left through the Passatge Bernardí Martorell, and go 50 ft right on Sant Rafael to the Gil front door. (Return the same way.) Rosa Gil speaks several languages, including English, and takes good care of her foreign guests. Try the *revuelto de ajos tiernos y gambas* (eggs scrambled with young garlic and shrimp) or the famous Catalan dish *cap-i-pota*, a stew of morsels of head and hoof of pork. The wine list offers an ample selection ranging from Albariños to Riojas, Costers de Segre, and Penedès. ⊠ *Sant Rafael 24,* ☏ *93/441–3014. AE, DC, MC, V. Closed Mon. No dinner Sun.*

$$$ ✕ **El Cafeti.** This romantic and graceful little hideaway at the end of the passageway in from Carrer Hospital is a candlelit and intimate bistro with an interesting menu encompassing a wide range of ingredients from foie gras to cod to game in season. Try the *ensalada tibia de queso de cabra* (warm goat cheese salad) or the *solomillo de corzo al foie* (roebuck filet mignon with foie gras). ⊠ *Hospital 99 (at the end of Passatge Bernardí Martorell),* ☏ *93/329–2419. AE, DC, MC, V. Closed Mon. No dinner Sun.*

$$$ ✕ **La Bona Cuina.** When the Madolell family converted their antiques business into a restaurant in the late 1960s, it soon gained respect for its neo-Baroque elegance, intimacy, and nouvelle Catalan cuisine. Fresh fish is the house specialty; try the *bacalao à la Cuineta* (cod with spinach, raisins, pine nuts, and white sauce). The location, overlooking the apse of the cathedral, is memorable. ⊠ *Pietat 12,* ☏ *93/268– 2394. AE, DC, MC, V.*

$$$ ✕ **Los Caracoles.** Just below the Plaça Reial, a wall of roasting chickens announces one of Barcelona's perennial favorites, especially for foreign visitors to the city. A walk through the kitchen into the restaurant is as exciting as anything that happens here. The walls are thick with photos of bullfighters and visiting celebrities who swarmed through the place during the '60s and '70s and continue to fill the restaurant day and night. The semiprivate dining room with gigantic antique sherry caskets, a wrought-iron candlelabra, and garlands of hanging garlic is the most evocative corner. *Tunas* (student vocalists in Renaissance costumes) are likely to serenade you at your table, while the open kitchen cranks out an eclectic but somewhat listless range of Castilian roasts, Mediterranean fish dishes, and, of course, *caracoles* (snails). ⊠ *Escudellers 14,* ☏ *93/302–3185. AE, DC, MC, V.*

$$–$$$ ✕ **Ca l'Estevet.** No wonder this place is an artist, student, journalist, and professorial favorite—it's just across the street from Barcelona's journalism school; around the block from Barcelona's premier liberal newspaper, *La Vanguardia*; around the corner from the MACBA (contemporary art museum); and only a five-minute haul from the Boqueria market on the Rambla. Estevet and family are charming (at least one waitress speaks English), and the carefully elaborated Catalan cuisine deserves to be taken very seriously, especially at these prices. This spot is unpretentious, lively, and tasty and offers top value. Try the asparagus cooked over coals, the *chopitos gaditanos* (deep-fried baby octopus), or the *magret de pato* (duck breast). The house wine is inexpensive, light, and perfectly acceptable. ⊠ *Valdoncella 46,* ☎ *93/302–4186. AE, DC, MC, V. Closed Sun.*

$$–$$$ ✕ **Café de l'Acadèmia.** With wicker chairs, stone walls, and background classical music, this place is sophisticated-rustic, and the excellent Catalan cuisine makes it more than a mere café. It's frequented by politicians from the nearby Generalitat. Be sure to reserve at lunchtime. ⊠ *Lledó 1,* ☎ *93/319–8253. AE, DC, MC, V.*

$$–$$$ ✕ **El Pebre Blau.** This handsome space, surrounded by centuries-old wooden doors and shutters, offers an ever-self-renewing selection of dishes collected from all over the Mediterranean. Every detail is cared for here with exquisite taste and judgment, a sybaritic bonanza on the site of the early baths (*banys vells*) of the waterfront district. ⊠ *Bany Vells 21,* ☎ *93/319–1308. AE, DC, MC, V. Closed midday.*

$$–$$$ ✕ **L'Ou Comballa.** Candelit romantic nooks and crannies, artisanal recipes researched and restored by culinary historian Teresa Ferri, all at excellent value: this little hideaway 50 ft from the lateral facade of the Santa Maria del Mar basilica is a gem. L'Ou Comballa ("the dancing egg" or, literally, "the egg how it dances") refers to the ancient Barcelona tradition of placing an egg atop the spurts of water from the city's fountains to celebrate Corpus Cristi every June. Dishes here range from Catalan to Turkish to Greek, but the highlights are the Moroccan or medieval Sephardic recipes painstakingly collected from around the Mediterranean over the last three generations of Ferri chefs. Choosing between L'Ou Comballa and its sister restaurant across the street is a tough but pleasant conundrum. Be sure to try the sephardic hen or the *amanidas mediterraneas* (Mediterranean salads). ⊠ *Bany Vells 20,* ☎ *93/310–5378. AE, DC, MC, V. Closed midday.*

$$–$$$ ✕ **La Flauta Mágica.** Specializing in dishes using only vegetarian and organically grown produce, this little spot near Santa Maria del Mar offers a unique range of fare. Meticulously selected and prepared ingredients from duck to soy bean make up an interesting menu with a fine selection of artisanally produced wines to go with it. The restaurant opens only in the evening from 9 to midnight. ⊠ *Bany Vells 18,* ☎ *93/268–4694. AE, DC, MC, V. No lunch.*

$$–$$$ ✕ **La Habana Vieja.** If you've got an itch for a taste of old Havana— *ropa vieja* (shredded beef) or *moros y cristianos* (black beans and rice) with *mojitos* (rum, mint, and sugar) or a round of *plátanos a punetazos* (punched plantains)—this is the place to come in Barcelona. The upstairs tables overlooking the bar are cozy little crow's nests, and the neighborhood is filled with quirky dives and saloons for before and after carousing. ⊠ *Bany Vells 2,* ☎ *93/268–2504. AE, DC, MC, V. Closed Sun.*

$$–$$$ ✕ **La Taxidermista.** Don't worry: no road kill is served here. Once a natural-science museum and taxidermy shop (Dalí once purchased 200,000 ants and a stuffed rhinoceros from this historic shop), this stylish place is the only recommendable restaurant in the sunny Plaça Reial. Interior decorator Beth Gali skillfully designed the interior around original beams and steel columns. Delicacies such as *bonito con escalivada y queso de cabra* (white tuna with braised aubergines and peppers and goat cheese) emerge from a kitchen run by Antoni Clapès, trained by Juan Marí Arzak, the famed chef based at his eponymously named spot in San Sebastian (☞ San Sebastian *in* Chapter 5). ⊠ *Plaça Reial 8,* ☎ *93/412–4536. AE, DC, MC, V. Closed Mon.*

$$–$$$ ✗ **Pou Dols.** Next to the early 16th-century Palau Centelles, this cooking academy and restaurant is a refreshing minimalist break (in design, not cuisine) from Barcelona's rich aesthetic diet of Gothic and Art Nouveau exuberance. After stepping across the glassed-over remains of the *pou dols* (freshwater well) at the door, be prepared for delicious specialties such as the *minimandonguilles amb tomaquet concassé* (mini-meatballs with crushed tomato) or the *llom de xai al cardomom amb favetes a la menta* (lamb with cardamom and broadbeans with mint). ⊠ *Baixada de Sant Miquel 6,* ☎ *93/412–0579. AE, DC, MC, V. Closed Sun. No lunch Sat.*

$$ ✗ **El Foro.** This blazing hotspot near the Born is always full to the rafters with ecstatic-looking young and not-so-young people. Painting and photographic exhibits line the walls, while meat cooked over coals, pizzas, and salads dominate the menu at this simple but lively restaurant and café. ⊠ *Princesa 53,* ☎ *93/310–1020. AE, DC, MC, V. Closed Mon.*

$$ ✗ **Gades.** For fondues of all descriptions and denominations, this medieval space converted to a modern restaurant near Passeig del Born is a good choice. Always filled with young couples and groups of savvy-looking international and Barcelona diners, the restaurant has ancient stone and brick walls and vaulted ceilings that are an ideal environment for good food, fine wines, and conversations lasting long into the wee hours. ⊠ *Carrer L'Esparteria 10,* ☎ *93/310–4455. AE, DC, MC, V. Closed Mon.*

$$ ✗ **Mon Obert.** This unusually quiet spot just off Carrer Escudellers offers a combination coffee house, bookstore, art gallery, and restaurant. The culinary creations of Xavier Estrany, an interesting selection of books to buy or read in situ, and painting or photographic exhibits on the walls, all in a peaceful refuge just a few steps off the roaring Rambla, add up to a successful experiment that is still largely undiscovered by all but a few *barcelonins.* ⊠ *Passatge d'Escudellers 5,* ☎ *93/301–7273. AE, DC, MC, V. Closed Sun.*

$ ✗ **Agut.** Wood paneling surmounted by white walls, on which hang
★ 1950s canvases, forms the setting for the mostly Catalan crowd in this homey restaurant in the lower reaches of the Gothic Quarter. Agut was founded in 1924, and its popularity has never waned—not least because the hearty Catalan fare offers fantastic value. In season (September–May), try the *pato silvestre agridulce* (sweet-and-sour wild duck). There's a good selection of wine, but no frills such as coffee or liqueur. ⊠ *Gignàs 16,* ☎ *93/315–1709. AE, MC, V. Closed Mon. and July. No dinner Sun.*

$ ✗ **El Convent.** Hidden away behind the Boqueria market, El Convent offers good value in a traditional setting. The Catalan home cooking, featuring such favorites as *faves a la catalana* (broad beans stewed with sausage), comes straight from the Boqueria. The intimate balconies and dining rooms have marble-top tables and can accommodate groups of 2 or 20. A bargain *menú del día* makes lunch the best time to come. ⊠ *Jerusalem 3,* ☎ *93/317–1052. AE, DC, MC, V.*

$ ✗ **Rita Blue.** This hotspot opens from midday (1 PM) to the wee hours (3 AM) and serves better than creditable Mediterranean cooking to a predominantly young clientele. Two steps from the Boqueria market across Carrer Hospital, the menu is market-driven and features whatever is seasonally best and freshest. Musical performances are offered on Sunday evenings. ⊠ *Plaça Sant Agustí 3,* ☎ *93/342–4086. AE, DC, MC, V.*

Barceloneta and Olympic Port

Barceloneta and the Olympic Port have little in common beyond their seaside location. The Olympic Port offers a somewhat massified and modern environment with a crazed disco strip, while Barceloneta is a more traditional maritime neighborhood.

$$$$ ✕ **Talaia Mar.** Generally understood as the finest restaurant in the Olympic Port, this bright spot has wonderful Mediterranean views and fresh sea produce as well. The taster's menu is a bargain, a good way to sample the chef's best work for little more than a regular meal would cost. ⊠ *Marina 16,* ☎ *93/221–9090. AE, MC, V.*

$$$–$$$$ ✕ **Can Majó.** Set on the beach in Barceloneta, Can Majó is one of
★ Barcelona's premier seafood restaurants. House specialties are *caldero de bogavante* (a cross between paella and lobster bouillabaisse) and *suquet* (fish stewed in its own juices), but whatever you choose will be excellent. In summer, the terrace overlooking the Mediterranean is the closest you can now come to the Barceloneta *chiringuitos* (shanty restaurants) that used to line the beach here. ⊠ *Almirall Aixada 23,* ☎ *93/221–5455. AE, DC, MC, V. Closed Sun.–Mon.*

$$$ ✕ **Antiga Casa Solé.** Just two blocks to the sea side of the charming Plaça de Sant Miquel, Barceloneta's prettiest square, this traditional Sunday midday pilgrimage occupies a characteristic waterfront house and serves fresh, well-prepared, and piping hot seafood of all kinds. Whether it's *lenguado a la plancha* (grilled sole) or the exquisite *arroç negre amb sepia en su tinta* (black rice with squid in its ink), everything here comes loaded with taste. In winter try to get close to the open kitchen for the aromas, sights, sounds, and heat. ⊠ *Sant Carles 4,* ☎ *93/221–5012. AE, DC, MC, V. Closed Mon. and Aug. 15–31. No dinner Sun.*

$$$ ✕ **Reial Club Marítim.** For sunset or harbor views, excellent maritime fare, and a sense of remove from the city, try Barcelona's yacht club, El Marítim, just around the harbor through Barceloneta. Highlights are *paella marinera* (seafood paella), *rodaballo* (turbot), *lubina* (sea bass), and *dorado* (sea bream). Ask for the freshest fish they have and you won't be disappointed. ⊠ *Moll d'Espanya,* ☎ *93/221–7143. AE, DC, MC, V. Closed Mon.*

$$$ ✕ **Tinglado Moncho's.** Part of the chain begun by the very successful Moncho of Gràcia's Botafumeiro, this relaxed harborside seafood spot can be counted on for dependably good, if not brilliant, interpretations of standard fish recipes from *besugo* (sea bream) to *dorada* (gilt-head bream) or *lenguado* (sole) as well as northern favorites such as *almejas con judias* (white beans and clams) or *judias pintas de Tolosa* (red beans from Tolosa stewed in blood sausage and chorizo). Open from noon until two in the morning, Moncho's is the best of the many similar spots lining the Olympic Port. ⊠ *Moll de Gregal 5–6,* ☎ *93/221–8383. AE, MC, V.*

$$–$$$ ✕ **Can Ramonet.** The oldest tavern in the port, founded in 1763, this singular flower-festooned house next to the Barceloneta market has barrel-top tables for tapas and regular tables for meals. Paella and seafood are strong suits; try the *arroz negro*—paella colored and flavored in cuttlefish ink. ⊠ *Carrer Maquinista 17,* ☎ *93/319–3064. AE, DC, MC, V. Closed Sun. and Mon.*

$–$$ ✕ **Can Manel la Puda.** First choice for a paella in the sun, year-round, is Can Manel, near the end of the main road out to the Barceloneta beach. Any time before 4 o'clock will do; it then reopens at 7. *Arroz a la banda* (rice with peeled shellfish) and paella *marinera* (with seafood) or *fideuà* (with noodles instead of rice) are all delicious. ⊠ *Passeig Joan de Borbó 60,* ☎ *93/221–5013. AE, DC, MC, V. Closed Mon.*

Eixample

Eixample dining, invariably upscale and elegant, ranges from traditional cuisine in Moderniste houses to designer fare in sleek minimalist-experimental spaces.

$$$$ ✕ **Beltxenea.** Long one of Barcelona's top restaurants, Beltxenea retains an intimate atmosphere in its elegant dining rooms. Carved wood columns in the hall, grand oak fireplaces, elegant Isabelline high-backed chairs, and red fringe–draped chandeliers all recall the past glories of this lovely town house. In summer you can dine outdoors in the formal garden. Chef Miguel Ezcurra's Basque cuisine is exquisite; a specialty is *merluza con kokotxas y almejas* (hake simmered in stock with clams and barbels). Try the house wines—all excellent. ⊠ *Mallorca 275,* ☎ *93/215–3024. Reservations essential. AE, DC, MC, V. Closed Sun. and Aug. No lunch Sat.*

$$$$ ✕ **Drolma.** Chef Fermin Puig has finally taken his well-deserved place
★   among Europe's gourmet elite. Named (in Sanskrit) for Buddha's female side, this intimate perch in the elegant Hotel Majestic (over the corner of Passeig de Gràcia and Valencia) catapulted to the top of Barcelona's gastronomical charts the minute it opened. Order the *menú de degustaciò* (taster's menu) and you might get pheasant cannelloni in foie-gras sauce smothered in fresh black truffles, or giant prawn tails in *trompettes de la mort* (black wild mushrooms) with *sôt-l'y-laisse* (free-range chicken nuggets). Fermin's *foie gras a la ceniza con ceps* (foie gras over wood coals with wild mushrooms)—a recipe rescued from a boyhood farmhouse feast—represents the blend of tradition and inspiration that is making this restaurant famous. ⊠ *Passeig de Gràcia 70,* ☎ *93/496–7710. Reservations essential. AE, DC, MC, V. Closed Sun. and Aug.*

$$$$ ✕ **Gorria.** Fermin Gorría's tried-and-true Basque formulae keep this Navarra (north-central Spain) outpost in Barcelona flourishing. Simple rank-and-file citizens of the menu such as *alubias estofadas* (kidney beans stewed with chorizo and blood sausage) are prepared and served to perfection along with roast suckling pig from Estella in southern Navarra or lamb from the Pyrenees. Navarra's position astride the Basque country uplands, the Ebro valley wine country, and the edge of the Castilian steppe is reflected in this hearty cuisine, surrounded by ancient wooden beams and stacks of wine barrels. ⊠ *Diputació 421,* ☎ *93/245–1164. Reservations essential. AE, DC, MC, V. Closed Sun. and Aug.*

$$$ ✕ **Can Gaig.** This traditional Barcelona restaurant is known for a bal-
★   anced and superb high quality in design, decor, *and* cuisine. Known for its market-fresh ingredients and cooking that is experimental yet based on ancient recipes from Catalan home cooking, the menu balances seafood and upland specialties, game, and domestic raw materials. Try the *perdiz asada con jamón ibérico* (roast partridge with Iberian bacon). ⊠ *Passeig de Maragall 402,* ☎ *93/429–1017,* 🖷 *93/429–7002. Reservations essential. AE, DC, MC, V. Closed Mon., Holy Week, and Aug.*

$$$ ✕ **Casa Calvet.** This Art Nouveau space in Antoni Gaudí's 1898–1900 Casa Calvet just a block down from the Ritz (☞ Lodging, *below*) is Barcelona's only opportunity to break bread in one of the great Moderniste's creations. The dining room is a graceful and spectacular design display featuring signature Gaudí ornamentation from looping miniparabolic door handles to polychrome stained glass, looping acid-engravings, and intricately carved wood in floral and organic motifs. The cuisine is light and Mediterranean with more contemporary than traditional fare. ⊠ *Casp 48,* ☎ *93/412–4012. AE, DC, MC, V. Closed Sun. and Aug. 15–31.*

$$$ ✕ **El Tragaluz.** *Tragaluz* means skylight—literally, "light-swallower"— and this Tragaluz is an excellent choice if you're still on a design high from Vinçón (☞ Shopping, *below*) or Gaudí's Pedrera. El Tragaluz is a sensory feast, with a glass roof that opens to the stars and slides back in good weather. The chairs, lamps, and fittings, designed by Javier

Mariscal (creator of 1992 Olympic mascot Cobi), all reflect Barcelona's passion for playful shapes and concepts. The sloping, sliding glass roof is ideal on moonlit summer nights, especially from the edge of the balcony, where you feel cozily ensconced in what seems like a post-modern treehouse. The Mediterranean cuisine is light and innovative. ⊠ *Passatge de la Concepció 5,* ☎ *93/487–0196. AE, DC, MC, V. Closed Jan. 5. No lunch Mon.*

$$$ ✗ **Jaume de Provença.** Locals come here because they've heard about the chef, Jaume Bargués, and can't wait to discover more of his haute-cuisine repertoire. Winners include *lenguado relleno de setas* (sole stuffed with mushrooms) and the *lubina* (sea bass) soufflé. Located in the Hospital Clinic part of the Eixample, the restaurant is done up in in modern black and bottle green. ⊠ *Provença 88,* ☎ *93/430–0029. Reservations essential. AE, DC, MC, V. Closed Mon., Aug., Holy Week, and Dec. 25–26. No dinner Sun.*

$$$ ✗ **L'Olivé.** Specializing in Catalan home cooking, this busy and attractive Eixample spot is always filled to the brim with clued-in diners having a great time. You soon see why: excellent food, hearty fare, smart ser-vice, and some of the best *pa amb tomaquet* (toasted bread with olive oil and squeezed tomato) in town. ⊠ *Muntaner 171,* ☎ *93/430–9027. AE, DC, MC, V. No dinner Sun.*

$$ ✗ **Mezzanine.** An excellent vegetarian choice in mid-Eixample, this ro-mantic spot offers full epicurean (albeit animal fat–free) sensuality. The *lasagna Mezzanina* is the pet offering of the house, a mainstay on the menu since the restaurant's opening in early 1999. Pasta filled with *bolog-nesa de soja* (soy bean–based bolognesa sauce) and candlelight with the good house wine make this a place to seek out at the corner of Provença and Aribau. ⊠ *Provença 236,* ☎ *93/454–8798. AE, DC, MC, V. Closed Sun.*

$ ✗ **La Tramoia.** This rollicking operation at the corner of Rambla de Catalunya and Gran Via gives marvelous tastes at low prices in a lively atmosphere. Try the onion soup or the *gambas al ajillo* (shrimp cooked in garlic and olive oil) and the *allioli. Tramoia* is Catalan for "back-stage" as well as "swindle," or the intrigue behind a deal, and here you're in the middle of both concepts: the place looks like backstage, and you can see the chef behind glass. ⊠ *Rambla de Catalunya 15,* ☎ *93/412–3634. AE, DC, MC, V.*

Gràcia

This exciting and cozy neighborhood is endowed with a wide range of restaurants encompassing the most gourmet cuisine in town, newer options with fine fare at affordable prices, and Basque taverns (with excellent northern beef specialities), all in a younger context made for quiet strolls and conversation.

$$$$ ✗ **Botafumeiro.** Barcelona's finest Galician restaurant is on Gràcia's
★ main thoroughfare. The mood is maritime, with white tablecloths and pale varnished-wood paneling, and the fleet of waiters will impress you with their soldierly white outfits and lightning-fast service. The main attraction is the *mariscos Botafumeiro,* a succession of myriad plates of shellfish. Costs can mount quickly. Try an assortment of *media racion* (half-ration) selections at the bar, where *pulpo a feira* (squid on potato), *jamón bellota de Guijuelo* (acorn-fed ham from a town near Salamanca), and *pan con tomate* (toasted bread with olive oil and tomato) make peerless late-night snacks. People-watching is tops, and the waiters are stand-up comics. ⊠ *Gran de Gràcia 81,* ☎ *93/218–4230. AE, DC, MC, V. Closed Mon. No dinner Sun.*

$$$$ ✗ **Jean-Luc Figueras.** Charmingly installed in the Gràcia town house that was once Cristóbal Balenciaga's studio, this exceptional place makes everyone's short list of Barcelona's best restaurants. The berry-pink walls,

polished dark-wood floors, and brass sconces make a rich and soothing setting for unforgettable Catalan cuisine with a French accent. Given the small extra cost, the luscious *menú de degustaciò* is, for value and variety, the best choice. This is Jean-Luc's third restaurant in Barcelona, and each has rocketed effortlessly to the top of the gourmet charts. Look for innovative interpretations such as the fried prawn with ginger pasta and mustard and mango sauce (but don't necessarily expect to find this on the menu—things change fast here). ⊠ *Carrer Santa Teresa 10,* ☎ *93/415–2877. Reservations essential. AE, DC, MC, V. Closed Sun. No lunch Sat.*

$$$ ✕ **El Racò d'en Freixa.** Chef Ramó Freixa, one of Barcelona's new culinary lights, is taking founding father José María's work to another level. His clever reinterpretations of traditional recipes, all made with high-quality raw ingredients, have qualified the younger Freixa's work as *cuina d'autor* (designer cuisine). One specialty is *peus de porc en escabetx de guatlle* (pig's feet with quail in a garlic-and-parsley gratin). ⊠ *Sant Elíes 22,* ☎ *93/209–7559. AE, DC, MC, V. Closed Mon., Holy Week, and Aug. No dinner Sun.*

$$$ ✕ **Ot.** Felip (a.k.a. "Flip") Planas and Oriol Lagé have formed a formidable culinary tandem in the Ot kitchen. The formula is unique: a set menu of one appetizer followed by two entrées, one fish and the other meat, and a selection of cheeses. This taster's menu is one of the best values in town. The menu changes every two weeks. If you're lucky you might score a *crema de alcachofas con su helado de lima y pimienta con gambas de Palamós* (cream of artichokes with lime and green pepper ice cream with Palamós shrimp), a hot-cold experiment characteristic of these two daring young chefs who delight in developing traditional recipes in exciting new ways. ⊠ *Torres 25,* ☎ *93/284–7752. AE, DC, MC, V. Closed Sun. No lunch Sat.*

$$–$$$ ✕ **Folquer.** This little hideaway in the bottom of Gràcia is a good way to end up a tour of this village-within-a-city. Offering one of the best-value taster's menus in Barcelona, this is a mini–gourmet restaurant that creatively prepares traditional Catalan specialties using first-rate ingredients. ⊠ *Torrent de l'Olla 3,* ☎ *93/217–4395. AE, DC, MC, V. Closed Sun. and Aug. 15–31. No lunch Sat.*

Sarrià-Pedralbes

For a cool summer evening breeze or a sense of village life in Sarrià, an excursion to the upper reaches of town (or, if you're at the Hotel Princesa Sofía or the Hotel Rey Juan Carlos, because you're close by) offers an excellent selection of restaurants.

$$$$ ✕ **Neichel.** Alsatian chef Jean-Louis Neichel is universally respected for such French delicacies as *ensalada de gambas al sésamo con puerros* (shrimp in sesame-seed sauce with leeks). The setting is the ground floor of a Pedralbes apartment block—mundane modernity compared to the cooking. ⊠ *Carrer Bertran i Rozpide 16 bis (off Av. Pedralbes),* ☎ *93/203–8408. Reservations essential. AE, DC, MC, V. Closed Sun., Jan. 1–6, Holy Week, and Aug. No lunch Sat.*

$$$$ ✕ **Via Veneto.** A delightful spot by any standard, this Belle Epoque standby may look excessively senior and serious, but it's still very much worth trying for some of the most inventive and carefully prepared international fare south of the Tour d'Argent. Dress up a little or you'll feel out of place. ⊠ *Ganduxer 10,* ☎ *93/200–7244. AE, DC, MC, V. Closed Sun. and Aug. 1–20. No lunch Sat.*

$$$–$$$$ ✕ **Tram-Tram.** At the end of the old tram line just uphill from the village of Sarrià, Isidre Soler and his stunning wife, Reyes, have put together one of Barcelona's finest and most original culinary opportunities. Try the *menú de degustaciò* (taster's menu) and you might be lucky enough to get marinated tuna salad, cod medallions, and venison filet

mignons, among other tasty creations. Perfectly sized portions and a clean and streamlined reinterpretation of space within this traditional Sarrià house—especially in or near the garden out back—make this a memorable meal. Reservations are a good idea, but Reyes can almost always invent a table. ⊠ *Major de Sarrià 121,* ☎ *93/204–8518. AE, DC, MC, V. Closed Sun. and Dec. 24–Jan. 6. No lunch Sat.*

$$$ ✕ **Acontraluz.** This stylish covered terrace in the leafy upper-Barcelona neighborhood of Tres Torres has a strenuously varied menu ranging from game in season, such as *rable de liebre* (stewed hare) with chutney, to the more northern *pochas con almejas* (beans with clams). All dishes are prepared with care and flair, and the lunch menu is a bargain. ⊠ *Milanesat 19,* ☎ *93/203–0658. AE, DC, MC, V.*

$$$ ✕ **El Asador de Aranda.** Designed by Art Nouveau architect Rubió i Bellver, this immense palace 1,600 ft above the Avenida Tibidabo metro station is a hike but worth remembering if you're in upper Barcelona. The acclaimed kitchen specializes in *cordero lechal* (roast lamb); try *pimientos de piquillo* (hot, spicy peppers) on the side. The ample dining room has a terra-cotta floor and is surrounded by a full complement of Art Nouveau ornamentation ranging from intricately carved wood trimmings to stained-glass partitions, acid-engraved glass, and Moorish archways. ⊠ *Av. del Tibidabo 31,* ☎ *93/417–0115. AE, DC, MC, V. Closed Holy Week and Sun. in Aug. No dinner Sun.*

$$$ ✕ **Satoru Miyano.** Japan discovered Barcelona, especially Gaudí, a long time ago, but Barcelona is just now discovering Japanese cuisine. One of the best two or three sushi spots in town, this clean-lined restaurant in upper Barcelona combines eastern and western culinary traditions with superb judgment and taste. The Mediterreanan sea and the Pacific Ocean meet deliciously here, with a varied selection of dishes from Spain, France, or Japan. ⊠ *Ganduxer 18,* ☎ *93/414–3104. AE, DC, MC, V.*

$$–$$$ ✕ **Vivanda.** Just above the Plaça de Sarrià, this leafy garden is especially wonderful between May and mid-October when outside dining, whether lunch or dinner, is a delight. The cuisine features Catalan specialties such as *espinacas a la catalana* (spinach with raisins, pine nuts, and garlic) and inventive combinations of seafood and inland products. ⊠ *Major de Sarrià 134,* ☎ *93/203–1918. AE, DC, MC, V. Closed Sun.*

$$ ✕ **El Mató de Pedralbes.** Named for the *mató* (cottage cheese) traditionally prepared by the Clarist nuns across the street in the Monestir de Pedralbes, this is a fine stop after touring the monastery, which closes at 2 PM, and has one of the most Catalan and best-value menus in town. Look for *sopa de ceba gratinée* (onion soup), *trinxat* (chopped cabbage with bacon bits), or *truite de patata i ceba* (potato and onion omelet). ⊠ *Obispo Català,* ☎ *93/204–7962. AE, DC, MC, V. Closed Sun.*

Outskirts of Barcelona

With the many fine in-town dining options available in Barcelona, any out-of-town recommendations must logically rank somewhere in the uppermost stratosphere of gastronomic excellence. These two, both rated among the top five or six establishments below the Pyrenees—one at the foot of Montseny, the other on the coast—undoubtedly do.

$$$$ ✕ **El Racó de Can Fabes.** Santi Santamaria's master class in Mediter-
★ ranean cuisine is well worth the 45-minute train ride (or 30-minute drive) north of Barcelona to Sant Celoni, a good jumping-off point for a Montseny hiking excursion. Internationally ranked as one of the three best restaurants in Spain (along with El Bullí in Roses and Arzak in San Sebastián), this sumptuous display of good taste and even better tastes is a must for anyone interested in fine dining. Every detail from the six different kinds of freshly baked bread to the anthological Catalan-French cheese selection rolled out near the end to the selection of

Havana cigars is done to perfection without losing Santi Santamaria's basic culinary philosophy: real food made from fine products superbly prepared. The taster's menu, as is usually the case in restaurants of this caliber, is the wisest solution. Catch a train at the RENFE station on Passeig de Gràcia or from Sants (the last train back is at 9:30, so this is a lunchtime-only transport solution). ⊠ *Sant Joan 6,* ☎ *93/867–2851. AE, DC, MC, V. Closed Mon., Feb. 1–15, and June 21–July 4. No dinner Sun.*

$$$$ ✕ **Sant Pau.** Carme Ruscalleda's place in Sant Pol de Mar is a scenic
★   40-minute train ride along the beach from Plaça Catalunya's RENFE station (look for the Calella train north), and the train drops you right at her door. It's one of Barcelona's best gourmet excursions. Increasingly hailed as one of Catalonia's top culinary artists, Ruscalleda has created a spot with a warm glow and a clean, spare look about it, with a glassed-over pool table, and drawings and paintings in pastels, set next to a garden overlooking the Mediterranean. Nearly every dish is a winner, ranging from appetizers like *salmonetes con aceitunas negras* (red mullet with black olives) with a "château" of tiny phyllo pasta, chicory lettuce, and a tarragon sauce to *vieiras* (scallops) with crisped artichoke flakes on slices of roast potato to main courses like *lubina* (sea wolf) on a bed of baby leeks and chard in a sauce of *garnatxa*, a sweet Catalan wine or the *butifarra de jabalá con piña y melocotón* (wild boar sausage with stewed pineapple and peach). Designer desserts include, for madame, the *misiva de amor* (love letter), a squarish pastry envelope with slivers of strawberry, raspberries, wild strawberries, blueberries, and julienned peaches, protruding from the "flap." Obviously, Ruscalleda whips up a taster's menu that you won't soon forget—follow her suggestions and those of her husband, Toni. ⊠ *Nou 10, Sant Pol de Mar,* ☎ *93/760–0662. AE, DC, MC, V. Closed Mon., Mar. 8–24, and Nov. 1–18. No dinner Sun.*

CAFÉS AND BARS

This is a city that may have more bars and cafés per capita—and a uniquely wide variety of same—than any other place in the world. In a country like Spain where it is important to give a sign that you are a man or woman of leisure—even in frantic, business-obsessed Barcelona—cafés serve an important function: safety valve, outdoor living room, meeting place, and a private cocktail pary to which everyone in the world is invited. Easily combining the Vienna coffee house (together but alone) concept with a natural southern European talent for joyful and boisterous improvisation, Barcelona owns a thousand intimate yet hyperactive and romantic nooks and crannies that seem ideally designed for lovers searching for the definitive connecting truth or for parties out for a good time.

Hangouts range from colorful tapas emporiums and sunny outdoor cafés to tea rooms and chocolaterias to a uniquely wide range of bars: *coctelerías* (cocktail bars), *whiskerias* (often singles bars with professional escorts), *xampanyerias* (champagne—actually *cava*, Catalan sparkling wine—bars), wine-tasting cellars, and beer halls. Even as this goes to print, new wine bars, cafés, music bars, and tiny live music clubs are scraping plaster from 500-year-old brick walls to expose lovely medieval structural elements that offer striking settings for postmodern people and conversations. Different bars and cafés close at a wide range of hours, though most of the hotspots in and around the Born are good until about 2:30 AM; for other after-hours options, *see* Nightlife and the Arts, *below.*

Cafés

Café de l'Opera. Directly across from the Liceu Opera House, this high-ceiling Art Nouveau interior has welcomed opera goers and performers for more than 100 years. It's a central point on the Rambla traffic pattern and de rigueur; locals and visitors alike know that if you're looking for someone, your quarry is likely to pass through this much-frequented haunt. ⊠ *Rambla 74,* ☎ *93/317–7585.* ⊘ *Daily 9:30 AM–2:15 AM.*

Café de la Princesa. One street in behind Carrer Montcada, this little boutique and café is a unique space dedicated to design, crafts, books, and a wide variety of wine and food tastings. Just the ancient walls, nooks, and crannies in this lovely spot merit a visit. ⊠ *Flassaders 21,* ☎ *93/268–2181.* ⊘ *Daily 9 AM–2 PM, 4:30–8.*

Café Paris. This popular café is always a lively place to kill some time. Everyone from Prince Felipe, heir to the Spanish throne, to poets and pundits of all spots and stripes can be spotted here in season. The tapas are excellent, the beer is cold, and the place is open 365 days a year from dawn to dawn. ⊠ *Carrer Aribau 184, at Carrer Paris,* ☎ *93/209–8530.* ⊘ *Daily 6 AM–2 AM.*

Café Viena. The rectangular perimeter of this inside bar is always packed with local and international travelers in a party mood. The pianist upstairs lends a cabaret touch. ⊠ *Rambla dels Estudis 115,* ☎ *93/349–9800.* ⊘ *Daily 9 AM–2 AM.*

Café Zurich. Ever of key importance to Barcelona rank-and-file society, this classic meeting point at the top of the Rambla is the city's prime meeting point. The outdoor tables offer peerless people-watching; the interior is high-ceilinged and elegant. ⊠ *Plaça Catalunya 1,* ☎ *93/317–9153.* ⊘ *Daily 9 AM–2 AM.*

Els Quatre Gats. Picasso staged his first exhibition at this legendary spot in 1899, and Gaudí and the Catalan impressionist painters Ramón Casas and Santiago Russinyol held meetings of their Centre Artistic de Sant Lluc in the early 20th century. Surrounded by colorful Toulouse-Lautrec-like paintings by Russinyol and Casas, the café offers variations of *pa torrat* (slabs of country bread with tomato, olive oil, and anything from anchovies to cheese to cured ham or omelets), while the restaurant serves the full gamut of fish and meat dishes. The café is a good place to read the paper and watch the crowd mill in and out, while the outside of the building, Casa Martí, by Moderniste master Puig i Cadafalch and sculptural detail by Eusebi Arnau, is the best part of all. ⊠ *Montsió 3,* ☎ *93/302–4140.* ⊘ *Daily 8 AM–1 AM.*

Espai Barroc. Filled with Baroque decor and music, this unusual "space" (*espai*) is in Carrer Montcada's most beautiful patio, the 15th-century Palau Dalmases, one of the many houses built by powerful Barcelona families between the 13th and 18th centuries. The stairway, decorated with a bas-relief of the rape of Europa and Neptune's chariot, leads up to the Omnium Cultural, an institution for the study and exhibition of Catalonian history and culture. The patio merits a look even if you find the café ambience too lugubrious. ⊠ *Carrer Montcada 20,* ☎ *93/310–0673.* ⊘ *Tues.–Sun. 8 PM–2 AM.*

Il Panetto. Il Panetto is wedged in beside the Roman walls to the left of the cathedral. Four or five cushions on the wall overlooking what was the moat are Il Panetto's most coveted seats, the other great people-watching spots being on the outside corner of the bar next to the street. Soups (especially leek and potato soup), gazpacho in summer, and sandwiches are house favorites. This is also a cool spot in summer for a morning coffee or an evening libation. ✉ *Plaça Ramon Berenguer el Gran 2,* ☎ *93/268–3004.* ⊙ *Daily 9 AM–1 AM.*

La Bodegueta. If you can find this dive (literally: it's a short drop below the level of the sidewalk), you'll find a warm and cluttered space with a dozen small tables, a few places at the marble counter, and lots of happy couples drinking coffee or beer, usually accompanied by the establishment's excellent *pa amb tomaquet* (bread with oil and tomato paste) and either Manchego cheese, Iberian cured ham, or *tortilla de patatas* (potato and onion omelet). ✉ *Rambla de Catalunya 100,* ☎ *93/215–4894.* ⊙ *Daily 8 AM–2 AM.*

La Cereria. Tucked in at the corner of Baixada de Sant Miquel and Passatge de Crèdit, this ramshackle little hangout has a charm all its own. The tables in the Passatge itself are shady and breezy in summer; look for the plaque at No. 4 commemorating the birth there of Catalan painter Joan Miró (1893–1983). ✉ *Baixada de Sant Miquel 3–5,* ☎ *93/301–8510.* ⊙ *Daily 10 AM–1 AM.*

La Confiteria. This beautifully restored bakery just off Avinguda del Paral.lel shows photographs, has live music on occasion, and serves drinks and light tapas in an intimate and artistic environment. ✉ *Sant Pau 128,* ☎ *93/443–0458.* ⊙ *Tues.–Sun. 9 AM–2 AM, Mon. 6 PM–2 AM.*

Laie Libreria Café. Much more than a bookstore, this café and restaurant serves dinner until one in the morning. Readings, concerts, and book presentations round out the ample program of events here. ✉ *Pau Claris 85,* ☎ *93/302–7310.* ⊙ *Mon.–Sat. 9 AM–1 AM.*

Schilling. Near Plaça Reial, Schilling is always packed to the point where you'll have difficulty getting a table. It's a good place for coffee by day, drinks and tapas by night. ✉ *Ferran 23,* ☎ *93/317–6787.* ⊙ *Daily 10 AM–2 AM.*

Venus. Pivotally placed on the corner of Comtessa de Sobradiel, Escudellers, and Avinyó, this cozy delicatessen, restaurant, and café is a perfect place to set up shop. The window overlooking Comtessa de Sobradiel seems ideally designed for reading, writing, and people-watching in the best tradition of the sidewalk café. ✉ *Avinyó 25,* ☎ *93/301–1585.* ⊙ *Daily 9 AM–2 AM.*

Coctelerías (Cocktail Bars)

Almirall. This Moderniste bar in the Raval is quiet, dimly lit, and dominated by an Art Nouveau mirror and frame behind the marble bar. It's an evocative spot, romantic and mischievous. ✉ *Joaquím Costa 33,* ☎ *93/302–4126.* ⊙ *Daily noon–2 AM.*

Boadas. A small, rather formal saloon near the top of the Rambla, Boadas is emblematic of the Barcelona *coctelería* concept, which usually entails a mixture of decorum and expensive mixed drinks amid wood and leather surroundings. ✉ *Tallers 1,* ☎ *93/318–9592.* ⊙ *Mon.–Sat. 12 AM–2 AM.*

Dry Martini Bar. The eponymous specialty is the best bet here, if only to partake of the ritual. This seems to be a popular hangout for mature romantics, husbands, and wives, though not necessarily each other's; it exudes a kind of genteel wickedness. ✉ *Aribau 162,* ☎ *93/217–5072.* ⊙ *Tues.–Sat. 12 AM–2 AM.*

El Born. This former codfish emporium is now an intimate haven for drinks, raclettes, and fondues. The marble cod basins in the entry and the spiral staircase to the second floor are the quirkiest details, but everything seems designed to charm and fascinate you in one way or another. ⊠ *Passeig del Born 26,* ☎ *93/319–5333.* ⊘ *Tues.–Sat. 12 AM– 2 AM.*

El Copetín. Right on Barcelona's best-known cocktail avenue, this bar has good cocktails and Irish coffee. Dimly lit, it's romantically decorated with a South Seas motif. ⊠ *Passeig del Born 19,* ☎ *93/317–7585.* ⊘ *Tues.–Sat. 6 PM–2 AM.*

Harry's. This is Barcelona's version of the "sank roo-do-noo" favorite that intoxicated generations of American literati, faux and otherwise, in Paris. ⊠ *Aribau 143,* ☎ *93/430–3423.* ⊘ *Mon.–Sat. 6 PM–2 AM.*

Miramelindo. The bar has a large selection of herbal liquors, fruit cocktails, pâtés, cheeses, and music, usually jazz. ⊠ *Passeig del Born 15,* ☎ *93/319–5376.* ⊘ *Mon.–Sat. 6 PM–2 AM.*

Tapas Bars

The *tapa* (literally, "lid")—originally a piece of cheese or ham covering a wayfarer's glass of wine and one of Spain's great contributions to world culinary culture—has not traditionally been Barcelona's strong suit. Even now, San Sebastián, Sevilla, Cadiz, Bilbao, and Madrid are all thought to be far ahead of Barcelona in tapa culture, but all this is changing: astute Catalans and Basques chefs are now making Barcelona into a booming tapa capital. Especially around Santa Maria del Mar and the Passeig del Born area, migratory wine tippling and tapa nibbling are prospering and proliferating. Beware of the tapas places along Passeig de Gràcia, which, while minimally acceptable, are somewhat massified and far from the city's best. The Sagardi chain is reliably good, as are the Lizarran taverns, both large-scale Basque operations that have managed to maintain quality.

Alex. This new tavern next to the Jamboree Jazz (☞ Jazz and Blues in Nightlife, *below*) club offers Basque *pinchos* (single tapas), cider, txakoli, and draught beer just two steps off the Rambla. ⊠ *Plaça Reial 16,* ☎ *93/318–6310.* ⊘ *Daily 9 AM–1 AM.*

Bar Tomás. Famous for its *patatas amb allioli* and freezing beer, this Sarrià classic is very much a place to seek out if you're in this part of town. Closed Wednesday (but open Sunday), the Iborra just behind on Carrer d'Ivorra is open when Bar Tomás is closed. ⊠ *Major de Sarrià 49,* ☎ *93/203–1077.*

Cal Pep. This lively hangout two minutes' walk east from Santa Maria del Mar toward the Estació de França has Barcelona's best and freshest selection of tapas, served piping-hot in a booming and boisterous ambience. ⊠ *Plaça de les Olles 8,* ☎ *93/319–6183.* ⊘ *Tues.–Sat. 1 PM–4 PM and 8–midnight, Mon. 8 PM–midnight.*

Ciudad Condal. A Barcelona hotspot always filled with a mature and discerning throng of hungry clients, this restaurant and grazing ground serves some of the city's finest tapas to a primarily well-to-do–looking crowd. ⊠ *Rambla de Catalunya 18,* ☎ *93/318–1997.* ⊘ *Daily 7:30 AM–1:30 AM.*

El Irati. This boisterous Basque bar between Plaça del Pi and the Rambla has only one drawback: it's narrow and hard to squeeze into. Try coming at 1 PM or 7:30 PM. The excellent tapas should be accompanied by txakolí. The tables in the back serve excellent full meals as well. ⊠ *Cardenal Casañas 17,* ☎ *93/302–3084.* ⊘ *Tues.–Sat. 12–12, Sun. 12–4.*

El Vaso de Oro. This little spot at the uptown edge of Barceloneta has become more and more popular over the last few years. If you can catch it when it's not crammed with customers, you're in for some of the

TAPAS: THE ULTIMATE MOVABLE FEAST

IT'S NO SECRET that travelers who have the good sense to hunt out local delicacies and to choose carefully the saloons and restaurants where they hang out can enjoy their trip to Spain for the food alone. This is especially true when it comes to that most Spanish of all creations—the *tapa* (hors d'oeuvre; derived from the verb *tapar*, meaning to cover). Just finding them, roving from tapas bar to tapas bar, can make dining a delightful adventure in Barcelona. The history of tapas goes back to the 781-year (7th-to-15th centuries) Moorish presence on the Iberian Peninsula. The Moors brought with them exotic ingredients such as saffron, almonds, and peppers; introduced sweets and pastries; and created refreshing dishes such as cold almond- and vegetable-based soups still popular today. The Moorish taste for small and varied delicacies has become Spain's best-known culinary innovation. The term itself is said to have come from pieces of ham or cheese laid across glasses of wine, both to keep flies out and to keep stagecoach drivers sober.

It is said that as far back as the 13th century, ailing Spanish king Alfonso X El Sabio ("The Learned") took small morsels with wine by medical prescription and so enjoyed the cure that he made it a regular practice in his court. Even Cervantes refers to tapas as *llamativos* (attention getters), for their stimulating properties, in *Don Quixote*. Often miniature versions of classic Spanish dishes, tapas allow you to sample a wide variety of food and wine with minimal alcohol poisoning, especially on a *tapeo*—the Spanish version of a pub crawl, though lower in alcohol and higher in protein: you walk off your wine and tapas as you move around.

In some of the more old-fashioned bars in Madrid and points south, you may be automatically served a tapa of the bar-man's choice upon ordering a drink—olives, a piece of cheese, a slice of sausage, or even a cup of hot broth. A few standard tapas to watch for: *calamares fritos* (fried squid or cuttlefish, often mistaken for onion rings), *pulpo feira* (octupus on slices of potato), *chopitos* (baby octopi), *angulas* (fantastically expensive, though delicious baby eels), *chistorra* (fried spicy sausage), *chorizo* (hard pork sausage), *champiñones* (mushrooms), *gambas al ajillo* (shrimp cooked in parsley, oil, and garlic), *langostinos* (jumbo shrimp or prawns), *patatas bravas* (potatoes in spicy sauce), *pimientos de Padrón* (peppers, some very hot, from the Galician town of Padrón), *sardinas* (fresh sardines cooked in garlic and parsley), *chancletes* (whitebait cooked in oil and parsley), and *salmonetes* (small red mullet).

Just to complicate things, the generic term *tapas* covers various forms of small-scale nibbling. *Tentempiés* are, literally, small snacks designed to "keep you on your feet." *Pinchos* are bite-size offerings impaled on toothpicks; *banderillas* are similar, so called because the toothpick is wrapped in colorful paper resembling the barbed batons used in bullfights. *Montaditos* are canapés, innovative combinations of delicacies "mounted" on toast; *raciones* (rations, or servings) are hot tapas served in small earthenware casseroles.

The preference for small quantities of different dishes also shows up in restaurants, where you can often order a series of small dishes *para picar* (to pick at). A selection of *raciones* or *entretenimientos* (a platter of delicacies that might range from olives to nuts to cheese, ham, or sausage) makes a popular starter for those dining in a group. The modern gourmet *menú de degustació* (taster's menu) is, in fact, little more than a succession of complex tapas.

When it Comes to Getting Local Currency at an ATM, Same Thing.

Whether you're in Yosemite or Yemen, using your Visa® card or ATM card with the PLUS symbol is the easiest and most convenient way to get local currency. For example, let's say you're in France. When you make a withdrawal, using your secured PIN, it's dispensed in francs, but is debited from your account in U.S. dollars. This makes it easy to take advantage of favorable exchange rates. And if you need help finding one of Visa's 627,000 ATMs in 127 countries worldwide, visit **visa.com/pd/atm**. We'll make finding an ATM as easy as finding the Eiffel Tower, the Pyramids or even the Grand Canyon.

It's Everywhere You Want To Be.®

SEE THE WORLD
IN FULL COLOR

Fodor's Exploring Guides bring all the great sights vividly to life with hundreds of photographs, fascinating historical background, and colorful anecdotes. Detailed maps and practical information keep you headed in the right direction.

Pair a **Fodor's** Exploring Guide with your trusted Gold Guide for a complete planning package.

best beer and tapas in town. ⊠ *Balboa 6,* ☎ *93/319–3098.* ⊙ *Daily 9 AM–12 AM.*

Euskal Etxea. Euskal Etxea is the best of the three Basque bars in or near the Gothic Quarter. The tapas and canapés will speak for themselves. An excellent and usually completely booked restaurant and a Basque cultural circle and art gallery round out this social and gastronomical oasis. ⊠ *Placeta de Montcada 13,* ☎ *93/310–2185.* ⊙ *Mon.–Sat. 9 AM–1 AM, Sun. 9 AM–4:30 PM.*

Jaizkibel. One of Barcelona's off-the-beaten-track secrets, this proto-Basque enclave is six blocks from the Sagrada Família, five from the Casa Macaia Fundació La Caixa art gallery and concert hall, three from the Monumental bullring, and just three from the Auditori, all proving this to be a handy place to work into an afternoon or evening at any of these spots. ⊠ *Sicília 180,* ☎ *93/245–6569.* ⊙ *Tues.–Sun. 8 AM–2 AM. Closed Aug.*

La Estrella de Plata. On its way to becoming a gourmet haven, this highly respected tapas bar is just across the Plaça de les Olles from Cal Pep (☞ *above*) and is a good alternative if the mob there is too daunting. ⊠ *Pla del Palau 6,* ☎ *93/319–7851.* ⊙ *Mon.–Sat. 10 AM–2 AM.*

La Palma. Behind the Placa Sant Jaume's *ajuntament* (city hall), toward the post office, is this cozy and ancient café with marble tables, wine barrels, sausages hanging from the ceiling, and newspapers to read. ⊠ *Palma Sant Just 7,* ☎ *93/315–0656.* ⊙ *Daily 8 AM–3 PM, 7 PM–10 PM.*

Lizarran. This chain of Basque tapa and *txikiteo* (from *txikito,* a small hit of wine) emporiums is all over town, but the one in Gràcia is a good solution for a stand-up dinner on your way to a movie at the nearby Verdi. Try the *tortilla de bacalao,* the codfish omelet, which they make to order. Try the txakolí, the tangy Basque wine. Another winner is the *cazuelita* (small earthenware dish) of *pochas con almejas* (beans and clams). ⊠ *Travessera de Gracia 155,* ☎ *93/810–1310.* ⊙ *Daily 9 AM–midnight.*

Moncho's Barcelona. One of José Ramón Neira's (a.k.a. Moncho) many establishments, including the upscale Botafumeiro (☞ Dining, *above*), this rangy bar and café serves very respectable *cazuelitas* (small earthenware casseroles) offering minitastes of Gallego and Catalan classics such as *alubias* (kidney beans), *lentejas* (lentils), or *calamares en su tinto* (squid stewed in its own ink). ⊠ *Travessera de Gràcia 44–46,* ☎ *93/414–6622.* ⊙ *Daily 12 AM–1:30 AM.*

Sagardi. This attractive, wood-and-stone cider house comes close to re-creating its Basque prototype. Cider shoots from mammoth barrels; hefty, piping-hot tapas make the rounds; and the restaurant prepares *txuletas de buey* (beefsteaks) over coals. ⊠ *Carrer Argenteria 62,* ☎ *93/319–9993.* ⊙ *Daily 1:30 PM–3:30 PM, 8 PM–12.*

Santa Maria. Combining a cutting-edge design environment with some ancient medieval stone walls and innovative tapa creations, Santa Maria is thriving. Leading chefs from Albert Adrià (Ferran's brother) to Mercabarna food guru Annette Abstoss are likely to turn up there for anything from *espardenyas* (sea slugs) to *escamarlans amb salicornia* (prawns with saltwort). ⊠ *Comerç 17,* ☎ *93/315–1227.* ⊙ *Tues.–Sat. 1:30 PM–3:30 PM, 8:30 PM–12:30. Closed Aug. 15–30.*

Taberne Les Tapes. Barbara and Santi, proprietors and chefs, offer a special 10-selection tapa anthology here, just behind the town hall and just seaward of Plaça Sant Jaume. Barbara, originally from Worcestershire, England, takes especially good care of visitors from abroad at this cozy groove of a place, known for its warm and cheery atmosphere. ⊠ *Plaça Regomir 4*, ☎ *93/302–4840*. ⊘ *Mon.–Sat. 9 AM–midnight. Closed Aug.*

Udala. This double-ended gem—restaurant at one end and tapas bar at the other—serves some of the best *montaditos* (canapés) and *cazuelitas* (little earthenware casseroles) in Barcelona. ⊠ *Sicília 202*, ☎ *93/245–2165*. ⊘ *Tues.–Sun. 8 AM–2 AM. Closed Aug.*

Xampanyerias, Cervecerias, & Wine Bars

Ateneu. Across the parking lot from the town hall in what was once the site of the Roman baths, this quiet restaurant-*enoteca* (wine library) offers a wide selection of wines and fine dining to go with them. ⊠ *Plaça de Sant Miquel 2 bis*, ☎ *93/302–1198*. ⊘ *Tues.–Sat. 1:30 PM–3:30 PM, 8:30 PM–12:30. Closed Sun.*

Bier Art. Barcelona's newest and most comprehensive beer garden is tucked behind the Santa Maria del Mar church and serves an endless variety of brews from the Finnish Lapin Kulta to the Belgian Delirium Tremens. The minimalist, clean-lined decor, perhaps an echo of the nearby early Catalan Gothic masterpiece, is as refreshing as the beer. ⊠ *Placeta Montcada 5*, ☎ *93/315–1447*. ⊘ *Tues.–Sun. 12:30 PM–4:30, 7:30–12:30 AM, Mon. 7:30 PM–12:30.*

El Xampanyet. Just down the street from the Picasso Museum, hanging *botas* (leather wineskins) announce one of Barcelona's liveliest and prettiest *xampanyerias*, stuffed to the gills most of the time. The house *cava* (cider) and *pan con tomate* (bread with tomato and olive oil) are served on marble-top tables surrounded by barrels and walls decorated with *azulejos* (glazed tiles) and fading yellow paint. ⊠ *Montcada 22*, ☎ *93/319–7003*. ⊘ *Tues.–Sat. 12–4 PM, 6:30 PM–12; Sun. 12–4.*

La Cava del Palau. Very handy for the Palau de la Música, this champagne bar serves a wide selection of *cavas*, wines, and cocktails, along with cheeses, pâtés, smoked fish, and caviar, on a series of stepped balconies adorned with shiny *azulejos*. ⊠ *Verdaguer i Callis 10*, ☎ *93/310–0938*. ⊘ *Daily 7 PM–2 AM.*

La Tinaja. Part wine bar, part tapas emporium, this handsome cavern just around the corner from that other tapas favorite, Cal Pep (☞ Tapas Bars, *above*), offers a good selection of wines from all over Spain and fine acorn-fed Iberian ham to go with it. The salads are also excellent, and the tone and tenor of the place are refined and romantic. ⊠ *Gran Via 702*, ☎ *93/265–0483*. ⊘ *Tues.–Sat. 12–4 PM, 6:30 PM–12.*

La Vinateria del Call. Just a block and a half from the cathedral cloister in the heart of the *call*, Barcelona's medieval Jewish quarter, this dark and candlelit spot serves wines, tapas, and full meals in an atmospheric environment. ⊠ *Sant Domènec del Call 9*, ☎ *93/302–6092*. ⊘ *Mon.–Sat. 6 PM–1 AM.*

La Vinya del Senyor. Ambitiously named "The Lord's Vineyard," this excellent wine bar directly across from the entrance to the lovely church of Santa Maria del Mar changes its list of international wines every fortnight. ⊠ *Plaça de Santa Maria 5*, ☎ *93/310–3379*. ⊘ *Tues.–Sun. 12–1 AM.*

Va de Vi. This beautifully restored (excavated, really) spot in the stables of what was once an aristocratic house is so entertaining to the eye it's hard to decide where to look. Meanwhile, the selection of wines (*Va de Vi* means "It's about wine") and artisanal cheeses and hams is first rate. ⊠ *Banys Vells 16*, ☎ *93/319–2900*. ⊘ *Daily 6 PM–2 AM.*

Xampú Xampany. This cava-tasting emporium on Gran Via is hot—always packed and booming—and a good way to try different kinds of Catalan sparkling wine. ⊠ *Gran Via 702,* ☎ *93/265–0483.* ☉ *Daily 6 PM–2 AM.*

LODGING

Barcelona's pre-Olympic hotel surge has been matched only by its post-Olympic hotel surge. New hotels are springing forth all over town while the old standards are frantically renovating to keep up. Architects Ricardo Bofill and Rafael Moneo have their hands full creating new and surprising lobbies, atriums, and halls while the in-house restoration industry is increasingly important, with gourmet options such as the Majestic's Drolma and the Condes de Barcelona's Thalassa at the forefront of the city's gastronomical elite. Barcelona and its bright and brisk hotel trade are many centuries removed from Miguel de Cervantes's early 16th-century description of the Catalan capital as "repository of courtesy, travelers' shelter . . .," but, as the author of *Don Quijote* discerned 400 years ago, Barcelona has a weakness for pampering and impressing visitors to its leafy streets and boulevards.

Hotels in the Gothic Quarter and along the Rambla are convenient for sightseeing and have plenty of old-world charm but, with notable exceptions, may be somewhat less lavish than some of the newer complexes out west on the Diagonal. Many Eixample hotels are set in late-19th- or early 20th-century town houses, often Moderniste in design, and offer midtown excitement and easy access to all of Barcelona. The Ritz, the Claris, the Majestic, the Condes de Barcelona, and the Colón probably best combine style and luxury with a sense of where you are, while the sybaritic new palaces such as the Arts, the Rey Juan Carlos I, the Hilton, and the Princesa Sofía cater more to business travelers seeking familiarity, convenience, and comfort. Smaller hotels like the San Agustín and the Mesón Castilla are less than half as expensive and more a part of city life, though they may also be noisier and less luxurious. Inexpensive options such as the Jardí and the Marina Folch are adequate and apt for combining tight budgets with decent lodging.

CATEGORY	COST*
$$$$	over 25,000 ptas./€150.25
$$$	20,000–25,000 ptas./€120.20–150.25
$$	14,000–20,000 ptas./€84.14–120.20
$	under 14,000 ptas./€84.14
All prices are for a standard double room, excluding tax.	

🕸 *following the text of a review is your signal that the property has a Web site, where you will find details and, usually, images; for a link, visit www.fodors.com/urls.*

Ciutat Vella (Old Town):
Barri Gòtic, El Rambla, Sanc Ponc, El Raval

Ciutat Vella comprises the Rambla, Barri Gòtic, Ribera, and Raval districts between Plaça de Catalunya and the port.

$$$$ 🏨 **Le Meridien.** English-owned and -managed, Le Meridien vies with the Rivoli Ramblas (☞ *below*) as the premier hotel in the Rambla area. Guest rooms are light, spacious, and decorated in pastels. The hotel hosts such music types as Michael Jackson and is very popular with businesspeople; fax machines and computers for your room are available on request. A room overlooking the Rambla is worth the extra

128

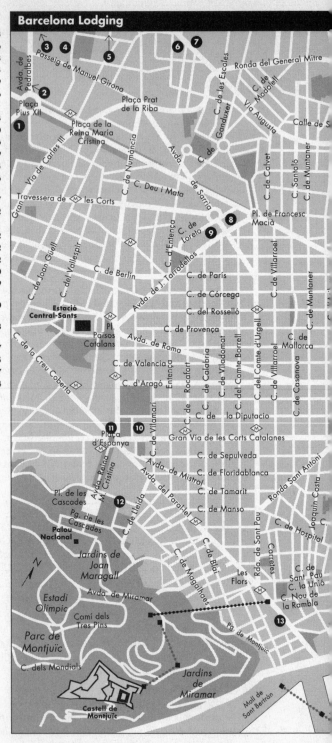

Barcelona Lodging

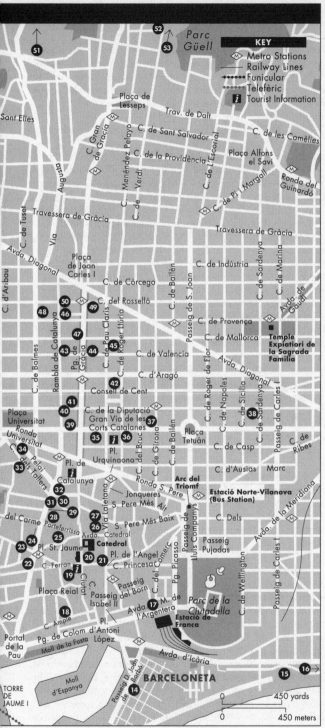

noise. ⊠ *Rambla 111, 08002,* ☎ *93/318–6200,* FAX *93/301–7776. 180 rooms, 26 suites. Restaurant, bar, parking (fee). AE, DC, MC, V.*

$$$–$$$$ 🛏 **Gran Hotel Barcino.** Appropriately named for the ancient Roman settlement of Barcelona that once surrounded this hotel (this site is about in the middle of where the Roman Forum once was), the Barcino offers nearly unparalleled ease for exploring the Gothic Quarter and Ribera. Rooms are small but well designed and furnished, and the concierge will advise you about not-to-miss events in either the City Hall or the Catalan seat of government, the Generalitat. ⊠ *Jaume I 6, 08002,* ☎ *93/302–2012,* FAX *93/301–4242. 53 rooms. Bar, breakfast room, cafeteria. AE, DC, MC, V.*

$$$ 🛏 **Citadines.** This new Rambla hotel is impeccably bright and modern, air-conditioned, soundproofed, and well equipped. Lodging ranges from one-room studios to apartments with sitting rooms. All have kitchenettes and small dining areas. The rooftop solarium offers panoramic views of Montjuïc and out over the port and into the Mediterranean. Across the way is the tower over the Poliorama theater, a station where George Orwell, author of *Homage to Catalonia,* was posted during internecine conflict within the Republican forces during the 1936–39 Spanish Civil War. Ask for a back room over Plaça Villa de Madrid for a quieter spot set over a leafy square with 3rd-century Roman tombs and roadway. ⊠ *Rambla 122, 08002,* ☎ *93/270–1111,* FAX *93/412–7421. 115 studios, 16 apartments. Breakfast room, kitchenettes, solarium, meeting rooms. AE, DC, MC, V.*

$$$ 🛏 **Colón.** There's something clubby about this elegant Barcelona
★   standby, which has a surprising charm and intimacy for its size. The front-desk staff always seems to know who you are. The location is ideal— directly across the plaza from the cathedral, overlooking weekend celebrations of the *sardana* (the Catalan folk dance), Thursday antiques markets, and, of course, the floodlit cathedral by night. Rooms are comfortable and tastefully furnished; try to get one with a view of the cathedral. The Colón was a favorite of Joan Miró, and for a combination of comfort, ambience, and location it may be the best hotel in Barcelona. ⊠ *Av. Catedral 7, 08002,* ☎ *93/301–1404,* FAX *93/317–2915. 130 rooms, 17 suites. Restaurant, bar, meeting rooms. AE, DC, MC, V.*

$$$ 🛏 **Meliá Confort Apolo.** This top hotel in one of Barcelona's most picturesque neighborhoods is just 300 yards from the port and handy to Montjuïc and the Fira de Barcelona. Completely overhauled and refitted with all of the latest gear from hair dryers to safes and minibars, this comfortable place is in the middle of the traditional cabaret and theater district, worlds apart (but only a 15-minute walk) from the Gothic Quarter. ⊠ *Av. del Paral.lel 57, 08002,* ☎ *93/443–1122,* FAX *93/443–0059. 290 rooms, 24 suites. Restaurant, breakfast room, in-room safes, minibars, parking (fee). AE, DC, MC, V.*

$$$ 🛏 **Mercure Barcelona Rambla.** The ornate, illuminated entrance takes you from the Rambla through an enticing marble hall; upstairs, you enter a sumptuous reception room with a dark-wood Art Nouveau ceiling. Guest rooms are modern, bright, and functional, and many overlook the Rambla, a dubious honor depending on your susceptibility to noise. Some of the back rooms overlook the moist and intimate, palm tree–shaded *jardín romántico* of the Ateneu Barcelonès, Barcelona's literary club and library, all to the tune of the hotel's waterfall, a welcome oasis reminiscent of the Rambla's early days as a spate river. ⊠ *Rambla 124, 08002,* ☎ *93/412–0404,* FAX *93/318–7323. 76 rooms. Bar, cafeteria, parking (fee). AE, DC, MC, V.*

$$$ 🛏 **Nouvel.** Centrally located just below Plaça de Catalunya, this hotel blends white marble, etched glass, elaborate plasterwork, and carved, dark woodwork in its handsome Art Nouveau interior. The rooms have marble floors, firm beds, and smart bathrooms. The narrow street is pedestrian-only and therefore quiet, but views are nonexistent. ⊠ *Santa Anna 18–20, 08002,* ☎ *93/301–8274,* FAX *93/301–8370. 69 rooms. Breakfast room. AE, MC, DC, V.*

$$$ 🏨 **Regencia Colon.** Tucked behind the Colon with just about every convenience the former offers (except the views of the cathedral and the clubby ambience) at half the price, the Regencia Colon is an option to consider seriously. In addition, it may be a little quieter back here where you're not listening to street minstrels through the night. Rooms are unexceptional, always impeccably clean, and the front desk works as well as or better than many three- and four-star hotels. ⊠ *Sagristans 13, 08002,* ☎ *93/318–9858,* FAX *93/317–2822. 55 rooms. Breakfast room, restaurant (no dinner). AE, DC, MC, V.*

$$$ 🏨 **Rialto.** When the Rialto expanded a few years ago and bought the house next door, it turned out to be the house around the corner in the Passatge del Crédito where Joan Miró was born. Now the Suite Miró offers a chance to sleep where the great Catalan painter was born and lived for many years. The hotel seems to have taken a leaf from the paradors' book, with subdued pine floors, white walls, and walnut doors. The rooms (ask for an interior one if street noise bothers you) echo this look, with heavy furniture set against light walls. There's a vaulted bar in the basement and a modern, mirrored *salón* off the lobby. ⊠ *Ferran 42, 08002,* ☎ *93/318–5212,* FAX *93/318–5312. 195 rooms, 3 suites. Restaurant, bar, cafeteria, lobby lounge. AE, DC, MC, V.*

$$$ 🏨 **Rivoli Ramblas.** Behind this upper-Rambla facade lies imaginative, state-of-the-art decor with marble floors. The guest rooms are elegant, and the roof-terrace bar has panoramic views. Try to get a back room over the Ateneu's palm trees and garden with the Rivoli's own cascades providing the water music. ⊠ *Rambla 128, 08002,* ☎ *93/302–6643,* FAX *93/317–5053. 87 rooms. Restaurant, spa, health club. AE, DC, MC, V.*

$$$ 🏨 **Suizo.** The Suizo's public rooms have elegant, modern seating and good views over the noisy square just east of Plaça del Rei. Guest rooms have bright walls and wood or tile floors. ⊠ *Plaça del Àngel 12, 08002,* ☎ *93/315–0461,* FAX *93/310–4081. 50 rooms. Restaurant, bar, cafeteria. AE, DC, MC, V.*

$$–$$$ 🏨 **Inglaterra.** A new partner in the Majestic group, this renovated neoclassical building welcomes all with a Moderniste stairway. Sleep new guest rooms have been decorated by Barcelona designer Josep Juan Pere in a Japanese-inspired style, featuring light colored wood and Asian motifs. The cafeteria-restaurant-library is an experimental multi-use space designed as an oasis-like refuge for rest and reflection at the edge of the Ciutat Vella. ⊠ *Pelai 14, 08001,* ☎ *93/505–1100,* FAX *93/505–1109. 55 rooms. Restaurant, bar, terrace-solarium. AE, DC, MC, V.*

$$–$$$ 🏨 **Park Hotel.** Across the street from the Estació de França and backing into some of Barcelona's prime art, architecture, and wine and tapa territory, this freshly renovated place is beginning to be heard from around Barcelona, especially since the opening of Abac, the gourmet restaurant under the hotel. The sleekly appointed rooms and modernized comforts of this modest but efficient hotel are looking better all the time. ⊠ *Av. Marquès de l'Argentera 11, 08003,* ☎ *93/319–6000,* FAX *93/319–4519. 87 rooms. Restaurant, bar, cafeteria. AE, DC, MC, V.*

$$ 🏨 **España.** If esthetics and authenticity mean more to you than comfort and practicality, this budget hotel built by no less than Lluís Domènech i Montaner, the greatest Art Nouveau architect of them all, might be the place. A stunning chimney in the breakfast room sculpted by Eusebi Arnau, murals in the dining room by Ramon Casas, and delicious details all around you, from the marble sink downstairs to the mosaic patterns on the landings, make this the best chance in Barcelona to actually live in a Moderniste masterpiece. The guest rooms themselves, though renovated recently, remain melancholy; the nearest

parking is behind the Boqueria or on the Rambla; and the hotel is at the edge of the raucous (though improving) Raval. ⊠ *Sant Pau 9–11, 08001,* ☎ *93/318–1758,* 𝐅𝐀𝐗 *93/317–1134. 85 rooms. Restaurant, breakfast room. AE, DC, MC, V.*

$$ ⊞ **Mesón Castilla.** A few steps up Carrer Tallers from the top of the Rambla, this little hotel is well positioned for exploring medieval Barcelona and the Moderniste Eixample. Just around the corner from Richard Meier's MACBA (Museu d'Art Contemporani de Barcelona) and the rest of the Raval, rooms here are quiet, comfortable, and generally flawless, especially considering the price. ⊠ *Valdoncella 5, 08001,* ☎ *93/318–2182,* 𝐅𝐀𝐗 *93/412–4020. 56 rooms. Bar, cafeteria. AE, DC, MC, V.*

$$ ⊞ **Metropol.** A block in from the port and midway between theRambla and Via Laetana, this modestly priced hotel offers numerousconveniences and a central location along with air-conditioning, a quiet street, and clean and cheerful guest rooms. A bright, upbeat lobby and sliding-glass entryway impart an accurate impression of the reigning esthetic here, while the police station next door makes street crime unlikely. ⊠ *Ample 31, 08002,* ☎ *93/310–5100,* 𝐅𝐀𝐗 *93/319–1276. 68 rooms. Bar, breakfast room.. AE, DC, MC, V.*

$$ ⊞ **San Agustín.** Just off the Rambla in the leafy square of the same
★ name, the San Agustín has long been popular with musicians performing at the Liceu opera house. Rooms are small but pleasantly modern, with plenty of fresh wood and clean lines. ⊠ *Plaça de San Agustí 3, 08001,* ☎ *93/318–1708,* 𝐅𝐀𝐗 *93/317–2928. 77 rooms. Bar, cafeteria. AE, DC, MC, V.*

$ ⊞ **Continental.** This modest hotel stands at the top of the Rambla, just below Plaça de Catalunya. Space is tight, but the rooms manage to accommodate large, firm beds. It's high enough over the Rambla to escape street noise, so ask for a room overlooking Barcelona's most emblematic street. This is a good place to read *Homage to Catalonia,* as George Orwell stayed here with his wife in 1937 after recovering from a bullet wound. ⊠ *Rambla 138, 08002,* ☎ *93/301–2570,* 𝐅𝐀𝐗 *93/ 302–7360. 35 rooms. Breakfast room. AE, DC, MC, V.*

$ ⊞ **Jardí.** Perched over the traffic-free and charming Plaça del Pi and Plaça Sant Josep Oriol, exterior rooms at this lovely budget hotel have pretty views of the Gothic church of Santa Maria del Pi from their own little balconies. Rooms can be noisy, especially in summer, when you'll want to leave the windows open due to the heat, although the air-conditioning scheduled (at press time) for fall of 2000 should have eliminated that problem. All rooms have modern pine furniture and small but new bathrooms. The in-house breakfast is excellent, and the alfresco tables at the Bar del Pi, downstairs, are ideal in summer. There are five floors—the higher, the quieter—and a new elevator. All in all, it's not the Ritz (☞ *below*), but it's a great value. ⊠ *Plaça Sant Josep Oriol 1, 08002,* ☎ *93/301–5900,* 𝐅𝐀𝐗 *93/318–3664. 40 rooms. Breakfast room. AE, DC, MC, V.*

Barceloneta

$$$$ ⊞ **Arts.** This luxurious Ritz-Carlton monolith—its 43 stories makes it one of Spain's tallest buildings—overlooks Barcelona from the new Olympic Port, providing unique views of the Mediterranean, the city, and the mountains behind. A short taxi ride from the center of the city, the hotel is virtually a world of its own, with three restaurants (one specializing in California cuisine), an outdoor pool, the Frank Gehry goldfish looming over the tropical waterfall in the car port, and the wonders of the beach nearby. If you want to enjoy modern Barcelona in all its glitz, this is a popular option. ⊠ *Carrer de la Marina 19–21, 08005,* ☎

93/221–1000, FAX *93/221–1070. 399 rooms, 56 suites. 3 restaurants, bar, pool, beauty salon, beach, parking (fee). AE, DC, MC, V.*

$$$ ⊞ **Barcelona Mar.** This recent addition to the Barcelona hotel scene is a dazzlingly modern operation run by the same chain that now owns the Barcelona Ritz (a.k.a. HUSA Palace). Just a five minute walk from the Nova Mar Bella beach and 10 minutes from the Olympic Port, this hotel option, with its offer of sun and sand, is nevertheless a good 15-minute taxi or subway ride from Barcelona's more traditional neighborhoods and sights. The contemporary design of the rooms—clean, streamlined, and impeccable—helps make up for this distance from Barcelona, as does the proximity of the waterfront. ⊠ *Carrer Provençals 10, 08019,* ☎ *93/266–5200,* FAX *93/266–5207. 75 rooms. Restaurant, bar, pool, parking (fee). AE, DC, MC, V.*

$ ⊞ **Marina Folch.** This little hideaway in Barceloneta is entirely new and has views over the port, an excellent restaurant downstairs, and a generous and caring family at the helm. Five minutes from the beach, it's a budget winner. ⊠ *Carrer Mar 16 pral., 08003,* ☎ *93/310–3709,* FAX *93/310–5327. 7 rooms. Restaurant. AE, DC, MC, V.*

Eixample

$$$$ ⊞ **Avenida Palace.** At the bottom of the Eixample, between the Rambla de Catalunya and Passeig de Gràcia, this hotel conveys elegance and antiquated style despite dating from only 1952. The lobby is a wonderful amalgam of Moderniste, art-deco, neo-baroque ornamentation, with curving staircases leading off in many directions. Everything is patterned, from the carpets to the plasterwork, a style largely echoed in the bedrooms, though some have been modernized and the wallpaper tamed. If you want contemporary minimalism, stay elsewhere. ⊠ *Gran Via 605–607, 08007,* ☎ *93/301–9600,* FAX *93/318–1234. 150 rooms, 10 suites. Restaurant, bar, health club. AE, DC, MC, V.*

$$$$ ⊞ **Claris.** Widely considered Barcelona's best hotel, the Claris is a fascinating mélange of design and tradition. The rooms come in 60 different modern layouts and designs, some with restored 18th-century English furniture, some with contemporary furnishings from Barcelona's endlessly playful legion of lamp and chair designers. Lavishly endowed with wood and marble, there is also a Japanese water garden, a rooftop pool, and two first-rate restaurants, one Catalan, the other (called La Beluga) dedicated to caviar. ⊠ *Carrer Pau Claris 150, 08009,* ☎ *93/ 487–6262,* FAX *93/215–7970. 106 rooms, 18 suites. 2 restaurants, bar, pool. AE, DC, MC, V.*

$$$$ ⊞ **Condes de Barcelona.** Reserve well in advance—this is one of
★   Barcelona's most popular hotels. The stunning, pentagonal lobby features a marble floor and the original columns and courtyard from the 1891 building. The newest rooms have hot tubs and terraces overlooking interior gardens. An affiliated fitness club around the corner offers golf, squash, and swimming. The restaurant, Thalassa, is excellent. ⊠ *Passeig de Gràcia 75, 08008,* ☎ *93/488–1152,* FAX *93/467–4785. 180 rooms, 8 suites. Restaurant, bar, parking (fee). AE, DC, MC, V.*

$$$$ ⊞ **Fira Palace.** This relatively new hotel has established itself among Barcelona's finest business and convention havens. Close to the Fira de Barcelona Convention Palace area that sprawls from Plaça Espanya east toward the steps up to the Palau Nacional, the hotel also offers easy access to Montjuïc and its attractions. Impeccably modern, it's a solid choice for generic creature comfort rather than local color. ⊠ *Av. Rius i Taulet 1, 08004,* ☎ *93/426–2223,* FAX *93/424–8679. 260 rooms, 16 suites. Restaurant, piano bar, pool, health club, parking (fee). AE, DC, MC, V.*

$$$$ 🏨 **Gran Hotel Catalonia.** This efficient new hotel just two blocks from Passeig de Gracia is comprehensively equipped with all of the most up-to-date equipment, from room safes to minibars and E-mail hook-ups. Rooms are conveniently soundproofed to combat the roaring traffic-flooded Balmes, and the hotel staff is extremely helpful with suggestions and arrangements. The rooms are cheery, ultramodern, streamlined, and bright, and the direct garage entrance will instantaneously solve your what-to-do-with-this-automobile problem. ✉ *Balmes 142, 08008,* ☎ *93/415–9090,* FAX *93/415–2209. 75 rooms, 10 suites. Restaurant, bar, cafeteria. AE, DC, MC, V.*

$$$$ 🏨 **Majestic.** With an unbeatable location on Barcelona's most stylish
★ boulevard, surrounded by fashion emporiums like Armani, Chanel, and Verino, the Majestic is a near-perfect place to stay. The building is part Eixample town house and part modern extension, but each room is stylishly decorated. The new restaurant, Drolma, is a destination in itself (☞ Dining, *above*). ✉ *Passeig de Gràcia 70, 08008,* ☎ *93/488–1717,* FAX *93/488–1880. 290 rooms, 20 suites. 2 restaurants, bar, pool, health club, parking (fee). AE, DC, MC, V.*

$$$$ 🏨 **Ritz.** Founded in 1919 by Caesar Ritz, this grande dame of Barcelona
★ hotels was restored to its former splendor in the mid-1990s. The imperial lobby is at once loose and elegant. Guest rooms contain Regency furniture, and some have Roman baths and mosaics. As for the price, you can almost double that of the nearest competitor. Service is generally excellent. ✉ *Gran Via 668, 08010,* ☎ *93/318–5200,* FAX *93/318–0148. 110 rooms, 12 suites. Restaurant, bar. AE, DC, MC, V.*

$$$–$$$$ 🏨 **Barcelona Plaza.** A standard business hotel, this well-operated place is efficient and well located for visitors to Barcelona participating in congresses at the Fira de Barcelona convention grounds. Also nicely placed for airport runs, this relentlessly modern place will take good care of you in its industrial, corporate, comfortable way. ✉ *Plaça Espanya 6–8, 08014,* ☎ *93/426–2600,* FAX *93/426–0400. 328 rooms, 10 suites. Restaurant, bar, cafeteria, outdoor hot tub, pool, parking (fee). AE, DC, MC, V.*

$$$–$$$$ 🏨 **Diplomatic.** This newly reopened star in Barcelona's Eixample district has exciting guest rooms designed in sweeping new contemporary lines and cool pastels. On the corner of Consell de Cent and just a block from Barcelona's busiest explosion of Moderniste architecture, the Manzana de la Discordia on Passeig de Gràcia, the hotel is also midway between the Eixample's two best *passatges* (passageways), Mendez Vigo and Passatge Permanyer. The restaurant, La Salsa, has acquired a serious following as has the Diplomatic, one of Barcelona's up and coming hotels. ✉ *Pau Claris 122, 08009,* ☎ *93/272–3810,* FAX *93/272–3811. 210 rooms. Restaurant, bar, meeting rooms, fitness room, sauna, outside pool, parking (fee). AE, DC, MC, V.*

$$$ 🏨 **Alexandra.** Behind a reconstructed Eixample facade, everything here is slick and contemporary. The rooms are spacious and attractively furnished with dark-wood chairs, and those that face inward have thatch screens on the balconies for privacy. From the airy, marble hall on up, the Alexandra is perfectly suited to modern martini sippers. ✉ *Mallorca 251, 08008,* ☎ *93/467–7166,* FAX *93/488–0258. 81 rooms. Restaurant, bar, parking (fee). AE, DC, MC, V.*

$$$ 🏨 **Calderón.** Ideally placed on the chic and leafy Rambla de Catalunya, this modern high-rise has a range of facilities normally found only in hotels farther out of town. Public rooms are huge, with cool, white-marble floors, and the bedrooms follow suit. Aim for one of the higher rooms, from which the views from sea to mountains and over the city are stunning. ✉ *Rambla de Catalunya 26, 08007,* ☎ *93/301–0000,* FAX *93/412–4193. 228 rooms, 25 suites. Restaurant, bar, 1 indoor pool, 1 outdoor pool, health club, free parking. AE, DC, MC, V.*

$$$ ⊞ **Cristal Palace.** Just off leafy Rambla Catalunya near the gardens of Barcelona's University, this newly renovated hotel is in the middle of the art gallery district and walking distance from the Rambla, the Ciutat Vella, and the Moderniste architecure of the Eixample. Guest rooms are fully modernized and decorated in wood, marble, and bright colors. ⊠ *Diputació 257, 08007,* ☎ *93/487-8778,* ⨋ *93/487-9030. 167 rooms. Restaurant, bar, parking (fee). AE, DC, MC, V.*

$$$ ⊞ **Gallery.** This modern hotel in the upper part of the Eixample, just below the Diagonal, offers impeccable comfort and service and a central location for middle and upper Barcelona. (In the other direction, you're only a half hour's walk from the waterfront.) It's named for its proximity to the city's prime art-gallery district, a few blocks away on Rambla de Catalunya and Consell de Cent. ⊠ *Rosselló 249, 08008,* ☎ *93/415-9911,* ⨋ *93/415-9184. 110 rooms, 10 suites. Bar, cafeteria. AE, DC, MC, V.*

$$$ ⊞ **Gran Hotel Havana.** This centrally located hotel is about equidistant from everything in Barcelona. Both a business and pleasure operation, the Havana may not remind you of the Greater Antilles, but the efficient service, the lofty patio with its rooftop skylight, and the bustling, busy feel of the place will help to boost your biorhythms to those of booming Barcelona. The air-conditioned, soundproofed rooms provide the refuge you will need from the roaring Gran Via. ⊠ *Gran Via 647, 08010,* ☎ *93/412-1115,* ⨋ *93/412-2611. 141 rooms. Restaurant, bar, exercise room, meeting rooms, parking (fee). AE, DC, MC, V.*

$$$ ⊞ **Regente.** Moderniste decor and copious stained glass lend style and charm to this smallish hotel. The public rooms are carpeted in a variety of patterns; guest rooms, fortunately, are elegantly restrained. The verdant roof terrace (with a pool) and the prime position on the Rambla de Catalunya seal the positive verdict. ⊠ *Rambla de Catalunya 76, 08008,* ☎ *93/487-5989,* ⨋ *93/487-3227. 79 rooms. Restaurant, bar, pool. AE, DC, MC, V.*

$$ ⊞ **Gran Via.** This 19th-century town house is a Moderniste enclave, with an original chapel, a hall-of-mirrors breakfast room, an ornate Moderniste staircase, and Belle Epoque phone booths. (To stay in character, go around the block to Gaudí's Casa Calvet, at No. 48 Carrer de Casp, for lunch or dinner.) Guest rooms have plain alcoved walls, bottle-green carpets, and Regency-style furniture; those overlooking the Gran Via itself have better views but are quite noisy. ⊠ *Gran Via 642, 08007,* ☎ *93/318-1900,* ⨋ *93/318-9997. 53 rooms. Breakfast room, parking (fee). AE, DC, MC, V.*

$$ ⊞ **Onix.** This modernized and renovated hotel just off the Gran Via near Plaça Espanya has many distinctly positive features: it's next to the Montjuïc convention center and Montjuïc's other attractions such as the Miró foundation and the Romanesque collection; Sants train terminal is a five-minute walk; it overlooks Barcelona's no-longer-in-use Les Arenes bullring as well as the leafy Parc Joan Miró; three buildings away is the Casa de la Papallona (House of the Butterfly), one of Barcelona's most spectacular Art Nouveau facades. Add to that the hotel's polyglot (English, French, Spanish) staff, fresh new rooms, and more than reasonable prices and the result is a definite success. ⊠ *Llançà 30, 08015,* ☎ *93/426-0087,* ⨋ *93/426-1981. 80 rooms. Breakfast room, parking (fee). AE, DC, MC, V.*

$-$$ ⊞ **Antibes.** Five minutes from Gaudí's Sagrada Família and across the street from Gorría, one of the finest Basque restaurants in town, this little hideaway has air-conditioned rooms with newly reformed bathrooms and a friendly and helpful staff. Walking distance from the Picasso Museum and the Barri de la Ribera, this Eixample address offers, along with economy, a handy vantage point from which to explore the northeastern part of the city. ⊠ *Diputació 394, 08013,* ☎ *93/232-*

*6211,*FAX *93/265–7448. 71 rooms. Bar,breakfast room, parking (fee). AE, DC, MC,V.*

$ 🏨 **Paseo de Gràcia.** Formerly a hostel, the Paseo de Gràcia has soft-color bedrooms with plain, good-quality carpets and sturdy wooden furniture. Add the location, on the handsomest Eixample boulevard, and you have a good uptown budget option. Some rooms, though not necessarily the newest, have balconies with views west over the city and the Collserola hills beyond. ✉ *Passeig de Gràcia 102, 08008,* ☎ *93/215–5828,* FAX *93/215–3724. 33 rooms. Bar, breakfast room. AE, DC, MC, V.*

Sarrià–Pedralbes

$$$$ 🏨 **Meliá Barcelona.** Redesigned by famous architect, urban designer, and city planner planner Oriol Bohigas in the mid-'80s, the Meliá's lobby has a waterfall second only to Niagara in water music, the hydraulic rush dominating the reception and the piano bar (aptly christened *Drinking in the Rain*). Rooms are functional and efficient if lacking in charm, and the hotel's location is convenient to none of the sights you have come to Barcelona to see. The hotel's famous brunches are gigantic feasts, though with Barcelona's myriad dining options it is a mystery how the responsible and clued-in visitor could possibly need, or survive, a major breakfast thrown in to the schedule. In any case, for breakfast-lovers: this is the best one in Spain (maybe Europe?). ✉ *Av. de Sarrià 50, 08029,* ☎ *93/410–6060,* FAX *93/321–5179. 300 rooms, 18 suites. Restaurant, bar, massage, sauna, exercise room, solarium. AE, DC, MC, V.*

$$$$ 🏨 **Princesa Sofia.** Long considered Barcelona's foremost modern hotel despite its slightly out-of-the-way location on Avinguda Diagonal, this towering high-rise offers a wide range of facilities and everything from shops to three different restaurants and the 19th-floor Top City, with breathtaking views. The guest rooms, decorated in soft colors, are ultracomfortable. ✉ *Plaça Pius XII 4, 08028,* ☎ *93/330–7111,* FAX *93/411–2106. 475 rooms, 30 suites. 3 restaurants, bar, indoor pool, pool, hair salon, sauna, health club, parking (fee). AE, DC, MC, V.*

$$$$ 🏨 **Rey Juan Carlos I–Conrad International.** Towering over the western end of Barcelona's Avinguda Diagonal, this skyscraper is an exciting commercial complex as well as a luxury hotel. Here you can buy or rent jewelry, furs, art, fashions, flowers, caviar, and even limousines. The lush garden, which includes a pond with swans, has an Olympic-size swimming pool, and the green expanses of Barcelona's finest in-town country club, El Polo, spread luxuriantly out beyond. There are two restaurants: Chez Vous serves French cuisine, and Café Polo has a sumptuous buffet as well as an American bar. ✉ *Av. Diagonal 661–671, 08028,* ☎ *93/364–4040,* FAX *93/364–4264. 375 rooms, 37 suites. 2 restaurants (3 in summer), 2 bars, pool, beauty salon, spa, health club, paddle tennis, 2 tennis courts, meeting rooms. AE, DC, MC, V.*

$$$–$$$$ 🏨 **Sansi Pedralbes.** This very contemporary polished-marble and black-glass box overlooking the gardens of the Monestir de Pedralbes may look out of place, but the views out into the Collserola hills and over Barcelona are splendid. Opened in spring of 2000, the hotel has rooms that are impeccable in equipment and design, while the air in this part of town can be a welcome relief from the steamy breath of portside Barcelona. For joggers it's only a 15-minute climb to the Carretera de les Aïgues (water road), Barcelona's best running track, across the side of the mountain behind the city. ✉ *Av. Pearson 1–3, 08034,* ☎ *93/206–3880,* FAX *93/206–3881. 60 rooms. Restaurant, bar, cafeteria, outdoor hot tub, pool, parking (fee). AE, DC, MC, V.*

$$$ 🏨 **Castellnou.** In leafy Tres Torres two steps from the train that can whisk you to the middle of town, next to the freeway to the Pyrenees, and handy to upper Barcelona's attractions in Sarrià, Pedralbes, and San Gervasio, this little gem has much to recommend it. The restaurant is intimate, but there are also many goods places to dine nearby. The service is warm and friendly and the rooms are new and impeccable. ✉ *Castellnou 61, 08017,* ☎ *93/203–0550,* FAX *93/205–6014. 49 rooms. Restaurant, breakfast room, meeting rooms. AE, DC, MC, V.*

$$$ 🏨 **Gran Derby.** This modern Eixample hotel is ideal for family use, composed entirely of suites, junior suites, and duplexes with sitting rooms. Decor reflects the local passion for innovation and design that is contemporary, sleek, and slick. Only the location is less than ideal; for sightseeing purposes, it's a bit out of the way, just below Plaça Francesc Macià, but a 20-minute march down the Diagonal puts you on Passeig de Gràcia. ✉ *Loreto 28, 08029,* ☎ *93/322–2062,* FAX *93/419–6820. 40 rooms. Bar, café, parking (fee). AE, DC, MC, V.*

$$$ 🏨 **Hesperia.** Well connected to downtown Barcelona by the comfortable Sarrià train, this is a modern, smoothly run hotel of complete dependability, set on a leafy street just a block up from Via Augusta. The rooms are medium to small in size but well designed and comfortable. The service is crisp and friendly, and the general demeanor of the place is smart and efficient. ✉ *Vergós 20, 08017,* ☎ *93/204–5551,* FAX *93/204–4392. 134 rooms. Restaurant, bar, breakfast room, parking (fee). AE, DC, MC, V.*

$$$ 🏨 **NH Pedralbes.** The two best things about this hotel are its location on the edge of leafy Sarrià and its manageable size. With only 30 rooms, the staff knows exactly who you are, and the general treatment of guests is light-years removed from the generic touch some of the larger establishments have trouble avoiding. Just a 10-minute walk from the Sarrià train (which can drop you in the center of town in a quarter of an hour) and only 20 minutes on foot from the Monestir de Pedralbes, these impeccably modern rooms are, if unremarkable, consistently reliable. ✉ *Fontcoberta 4, 08034,* ☎ *93/203–7112,* FAX *93/205–7065. 30 rooms. Restaurant, breakfast room, parking (fee). AE, DC, MC, V.*

$$$ 🏨 **Park Putxet.** Next to some of the jungliest parks and private enclaves in Barcelona, this hideaway in upper Barcelona has the advantage of being far enough from the Rambla to offer a sense of rest, relaxation, and refuge. Built on the high ground archaeological evidence has shown the earliest Iberian aboriginals also favored more than 3,000 years ago, today's recently reformed Park Putxet offers above-average comforts at a reasonable prices. Walking distance from Gràcia and just a few minutes by train or taxi from the center, this is a good choice if you'd prefer to be out of the middle of it all and like to walk. ✉ *Putxet 68, 08023,* ☎ *93/212–5158,* FAX *93/418–5817. 141 rooms. Restaurant, breakfast room, parking (fee). AE, DC, MC, V.*

$$$ 🏨 **Rubens.** A little out of the way above Plaça Lesseps, this recently renovated hotel offers easy access to Güell Park—just a few minutes' walk away—and a combination of taxi or public transport to downtown Barcelona. Rooms here are streamlined and furnished with attractive wooden furniture. The bar and restaurant are perfectly adequate for an evening at home in upper Barcelona. ✉ *Passeig de la Mare de Déu del Coll 10, 08023,* ☎ *93/219–1204,* FAX *93/219–1269. 139 rooms. Restaurant, breakfast room, parking (fee). AE, DC, MC, V.*

$$ 🏨 **Bonanova Park.** In a leafy corner of upper Barcelona nearSarrià this relaxed place provides relief from the downtown and midtown crush at a moderate cost. Several good restaurants are within walking distance, as are the metro stops of Sarrià and the green line's Maria Cristina. The rooms are bright and breezy and the predominantly residential neighborhood is quiet. ⊠ *Capità Arenas 51,08034,* ☎ *93/204–0900,*FAX *93/204–5014. 60 rooms. Bar,breakfast room. AE, DC, MC, V.*

$ 🏠 **Alberg Mare de Deu de Montserrat.** This may be just a youth hostel (which, in fact, has absolutely nothing against guests over 25, provided they take out an international youth hostel card—1000 ptas.—upon checking in), but it has a lobby that would put many of the luxury hotels in Barcelona to shame: a Moderniste tour de force featuring Moorish horseshoe arches and intricate polychrome marketry right out of the Arabian Nights and featured in several elegant art books about Barcelona. Once a grand mansion built for a rich family, the place now serves up beds that cost 2,500 ptas. for guests over 25; 1,900 ptas. if you're under 25, breakfast included. Despite the slight drawbacks of communal rooms and bathrooms, this is one of Barcelona's great bargains; the site is on a promontory overlooking the city near Gaudí's Güell Park. Bus 28 will take you from the Rambla to the door, while the nearest metro connection is the green line's Vallcarca station. The establishment closes its doors at midnight but opens them every 30 minutes thereafter to admit late arrivals, i.e. everyone. ⊠ *Passeig Mare de Deu del Coll 41–51,08023,* ☎ *93/210–5151,*FAX *93/210–0798. 223 beds in rooms of 6, 8, and 12. Restaurant, bar, cafeteria, parking (fee).AE, DC, MC, V.*

NIGHTLIFE AND THE ARTS

Daily events in the arts scene race headlong from 8 o'clock lectures and book presentations, *inauguraciones* (art show openings), *vernissages* (ditto), and events, to 9 o'clock concerts, theater, and dance events. And *then* sometime after 1 or 2 in the morning the nightlife kicks in—that is, early the next day for people with actual jobs and lives! Walking through Barcelona's Olympic Port music bar and disco row at midnight is like visiting a ghost town or a former movie set, but by 3 in the morning it's packed solid with humanity on fire for the Cubanas dancing on bars and tables all along the quai.

Barcelona's evening progression from art openings and concerts to tapa bars, music bars, and discos offers a ferocious volume and variety of options. From the early evening browsing and nibbling through the area around the Born to stand-up howling and imbibing at the Universal or Mas i Mas pub up above Travessera de Gràcia, or at the uptown terraces such as the Tres Torres, to the late live music at La Boîte, Bikini, or Luz de Gas to heavy-duty boogying at Luna Mora, Woman Caballero, or Otto Zutz, there are many ways and means to make it through to dawn in Barcelona with barely a pause to look at your watch.

To find out what's on, look in newspapers' *agenda* listings or the weekly *Guía Del Ocio,* available at newsstands all over town. *Activitats* is a monthly list of cultural events, published by the *ajuntament* and available from its information office in Palau de la Virreina (⊠ Rambla 99).

The Arts

Concerts

Catalans are great music lovers. Barcelona's most spectacular concert hall is that Moderniste masterpiece the **Palau de la Música** (⊠ Sant Francesc de Paula 2, ☎ 93/268–1000); the ticket office is open weekdays 11–1 and 5–8, Saturday 5–8 only. Performances run September–June, with Sunday-morning concerts at 11 a popular tradition. The calendar here is packed—everyone from Yo-Yo Ma to Madredeus to the Buena Vista Social Club performs here, while the house troupe is the

OBC Orquestra Simfònica de Barcelona i Nacional de Catalunya. Tickets range from 1,000 ptas./€6.01 to 15,000 ptas./€90.15 and are best purchased well in advance. The restored **Liceu** opera house on the Rambla is running a full season, though seats are expensive and hard to get. (Reserve well in advance) (☞ Opera, *below*). The **Auditori de Barcelona** (⊠ Lepant 150, near Plaça de les Glòries, ☎ 93/317–1096) schedules a full program of classical music with occasional jazz or pop concerts. Companies that perform here include the OBC (Orquestra Simfònica de Barcelona i Nacional de Catalunya) and the Orquestra Nacional de Cambra de Andorra. Watch especially for the Solistas del OBC, a series of free performances occasionally held in the town hall's opulent **Saló de Cent** (Plaça Sant Jaume s/n, ☎ 93/301–7775)—this is world-class chamber music in an incomparable setting. Barcelona's annual late-June–end-of-July summer arts festival **El Grec** offers a series of concerts, theater, and dance performances, many of them held outdoors in historic places such Plaça del Rei and the Teatre Grec, as well as in the Mercat de les Flors. Check listings for concerts at the intimate, 650-seat **Auditori Winterthur** (⊠ Av. Diagonal 547, behind L'Illa shopping mall, ☎ 93/290–1090), where you can often get interestingly close to major artists.

In late September, the **International Music Festival** (☎ 93/301–7775) forms part of the feast of Nostra Senyora de la Mercè (Our Lady of Mercy), Barcelona's patron saint. The main venues are Palau de la Música, Mercat de les Flors, and Plaça del Rei. Massively attended pop concerts are held in the Palau Sant Jordi on Montjuïc (⊠ Palau Sant Jordi, Passeig Olímpic 5–7, ☎ 93/426–2089). Barcelona's ever more successful **Festival de música antiga** (Early Music Festival) brings the best early music groups from all over Europe to town from late April to mid-May. Concerts are held all over town, though most lectures and performances are at the Centre Cultural de la Fundació "la Caixa" (⊠ Passeig de Sant Joan 108, ☎ 93/476–8600). Other prime spots for superb music surrounded by sublime architecture include the basilica of **Santa Maria del Mar,** the church of **Santa Maria del Pi,** the **Monestir de Pedralbes,** the medieval shipyards at **Reial Drassanes,** the **Saló del Tinell** in Plaça del Rei, the **Església de Sant Pau del Camp** in the Raval, the tiny **Església de Santa Anna** tucked in between Plaça Catalunya and Carrer de Santa Anna, the drop-dead wood-beamed Moderniste **Casa Golferichs** on Gran Via near Plaça Espanya, and even, very rarely, the **Real Círculo del Gran Teatre del Liceu,** Spain's oldest club and the only part of Barcelona's opera house to escape the 1994 holocaust. For details on concerts throughout the year, check the *agenda* page in either *La Vanguardia* or *El País* or call for cultural information at ☎ 93/316–2727 or ☎ 93/316–2740 to find out if and when events are taking place in these venues.

Dance

L'Espai de Dansa i Música de la Generalitat de Catalunya—generally listed as L'Espai, or "The Space" (⊠ Travessera de Gràcia 63, ☎ 93/414–3133)—is the prime venue for ballet and modern dance, as well as some musical offerings. **El Mercat de les Flors** (⊠ Lleida 59, ☎ 93/426–1875), near the Plaça de Espanya, is the more traditional setting for modern dance and theater. Cesc Gelabert, Mudanzas, Lanonima Imperial, and Mal Pelo are Barcelona's leading contemporary dance companies. **Teatre Tivoli** (⊠ Casp 10, ☎ 93/412–2063), **Teatre Victòria** (⊠ Av. Paral.lel 65–67, ☎ 93/443–2929), and **Teatre Apolo** (⊠ Av. Paral.lel 61, ☎ 93/441–9007) also stage dance spectacles ranging from flamenco to ballet to contemporary.

Film

Though some foreign films are dubbed, Barcelona has a full complement of original-language cinema; look for listings marked *v. o.* (*ver-
sión original*). The **Icaria Yelmo** (⊠ Salvador Espriu 61, near Carles I
metro stop) cinema complex in the Olympic Port now has the city's
largest selection of films in English. The **Filmoteca** (⊠ Av. Sarrià 33,
☎ 93/430–5007) shows three films daily in *v. o.*, often English. Recent releases are shown in *v. o.* at the **Verdi** (⊠ Verdi 32, Gràcia), **Arkadin**
(⊠ Travessera de Gràcia 103, near Gràcia train stop), **Capsa** (⊠ Pau
Claris 134), **Alex** (⊠ Rambla de Catalunya 90), **Rex** (⊠ Gran Via 463),
Casablanca (⊠ Passeig de Gràcia 115), and **Renoir Les Corts** (⊠ Eu-
geni d'Ors 12). For a semisecret movie theater offering double-feature
reruns for the price of one in v. o. (original sound track), seek out the
Maldá (⊠ Carrer del Pi 5), just a few steps from Plaça del Pi.

Flamenco

Barcelona is not richly endowed with flamenco haunts, as Catalans consider flamenco—like bullfighting—a foreign import from Andalusia.
El Patio Andaluz (⊠ Aribau 242, ☎ 93/209–3378) has flamenco shows
twice nightly (10 and midnight) and audiencé participation in the
karaoke section upstairs. **El Cordobés** (⊠ Rambla 35, ☎ 93/317–
6653) is the most popular club with tour groups. Other options include **El Tablao de Carmen** (⊠ Poble Espanyol, ☎ 93/325–6895) and
Los Tarantos (⊠ Plaça Reial 17, ☎ 93/318–3067). **Los Juaneles** (⊠ Al-
dana 4, ☎ 93/208–1389) is known for grass-roots, hard-core, pure gypsy
flamenco.

Opera

Restored to and beyond its former opulence, Barcelona's **Gran Teatre
del Liceu** is in full swing once again after its fall 1999 reopening (box
office: ⊠ Rambla 51–59, ☎ 93/486–9913, ✆). The season runs October–mid-July and includes a wide range of attractions, from 10 operas to 4 dance productions, 5 concerts, and 10–15 recitals; tickets range
from 1,000 ptas./€6.01 to 21,000 ptas./€126.21. There are also 11
small monographical concerts in the foyer designed to promote and
enhance comprehension of the operas performing during the season.
The *Sesiones Golfas* (After-hour Sessions) are a series of late-night (10
PM) entertainment events (for example, the music of Leonard Bernstein
in June 2001).

Theater

Barcelona *is,* to some degree, theater—a kind of ongoing street theater
where events and happenings are likely to surprise you at any moment.
La Fura dels Baus, for example, recently mobilized tug boats, booms of
a half-dozen freight derricks, the Mallorca ferry, and, of course, the new
drawbridge over the port itself, in an inaugural event that ended with
fireworks and acrobats on bungee cords throwing themselves into space.

In more classical theatrical endeavors, Els Joglars, Tricicle, Comediants, and La Cubana are sure to do something alarming to (or with)
their audiences every time out, while directors from Josep Maria Flotats
to transplanted Muscovite Boris Rotenstein reinterpret Pinter, Albee,
Wilde, Shakespeare, Molière, and Calderon in theaters all over town
in breakneck succession.

Most plays are performed in Catalan, though some are performed in
Spanish. Barcelona is well known for avant-garde theater and for
troupes that specialize in mime, large-scale performance art, and special effects (La Fura dels Baus, Els Joglars, Els Comediants). The city
also hosts a **Festival de Títeres** (Puppet Festival) in April.

The best-known theaters are the **Teatre Lliure** (✉ Montseny 47, Grà-cia, ☎ 93/218–9251), **Mercat de les Flors** (✉ Lleida 59, ☎ 93/318–8599), **Teatre Romea** (✉ Hospital 51, ☎ 93/317–7189), **Teatre Tívoli** (✉ Casp 10, ☎ 93/412–2063), and **Teatre Poliorama** (✉ Rambla Es-tudios 115, ☎ 93/317–7599). All stage a dynamic variety of classical, contemporary, and experimental theater.

Many of the older theaters specializing in big musicals (*Cats,* for one) such as Teatre Victòria, Teatre Apolo, and Teatre Arnau are along the Paral.lel. These include **Apolo** (✉ Paral.lel 56, ☎ 93/241–9007), **Teatre Arnau** (✉ Paral.lel 60, ☎ 93/441–4881), and **Victòria** (✉ Paral.lel 6769, ☎ 93/441–3979). The **Teatre Tívoli** (✉ Casp 8, ☎ 93/412–2063) also produces large-scale musicals. In July and August, an open-air sum-mer theater festival brings plays, music, and dance to the **Teatre Grec** (Greek Theater) on Montjuïc (✉ Rambla 99, ☎ 93/316–2700), as well as to Plaça del Rei, Mercat de les Flors, and other sites.

Nightlife

Cabaret

Near the bottom of the Rambla the minuscule **Bar Pastis** (✉ Santa Mònica 4, ☎ 93/318–7980) has live performances and every Edith Piaf song ever recorded. **Arnau** (✉ Paral.lel 60, ☎ 93/242–2804) is an old-time music hall that's still going strong as a venue for theatrical and musical events.

Casino

The **Gran Casino de Barcelona** (✉ Calle de la Marina, ☎ 93/225–7878), under the Hotel Arts, opens daily from 1 pm to 5 am, offering every-thing from slot machines to roulette, discotheque, floor shows, and restaurant.

Jazz and Blues

Try **La Cova del Drac** (✉ Vallmajor 33, ☎ 93/200–7032) or the Gothic Quarter's **Harlem Jazz Club** (✉ Comtessa Sobradiel 8, ☎ 93/310–0755), which is small but puts on atmospheric bands. **Jamboree Jazz & Dance-Club** (✉ Plaça Reial 17, ☎ 93/301–7564) is a center for jazz, rock, and flamenco. **La Boîte** (✉ Av. Diagonal 477, ☎ 93/419–5950) has an eclectic musical menu, as do **Luz de Gas** (✉ Muntaner 246, ☎ 93/209–7711) and **Luna Mora** (✉ next to the Hotel Arts, in the Olympic Port, ☎ 93/221–6161), offering everything from country blues to soul. The Palau de la Música holds an **international jazz festival** in November, and nearby Terrassa has its own jazz festival in March. The bustling **Blue Note** (☎ 93/225–8003), in the Port Vell's Maremagnum shop-ping complex, draws a mixture of young and not-so-young nocturnals to musical events and Wednesday-night buffets. Food and drinks are served until dawn, and credit cards are accepted.

Late-Night Bars

Barcelona's music bar and disco scene is an incandescent melange of dance and design, outrage, and eros. Catalunya's senses of humor and play begin about where Puritanical sensibilities call it a day, so don't be surprised to find topless dancers along the strip in the Olympic Port (or the stray couple up to some naughty things in phone booths or be-hind the curtains of photomatons). The eye-popping design of many of Barcelona's leading bars and discos can even distract you from the design of the fauna frequenting them, so be prepared for anything and everything.

Bar musical is Spanish for any bar with music loud enough to drown out conversation. The pick of these are **Universal** (✉ Marià Cubí 182–184, ☎ 93/200–7470), **Mas i Mas** (✉ Marià Cubí 199, ☎ 93/209–

4502), and that extravaganza of 1980s taste, **Nick Havanna** (⊠ Rosselló 208, ☎ 93/215–6591). **L'Ovella Negra** (⊠ Sitjàs 5, ☎ 93/317–1087) is the top student tavern. **Glaciar** (⊠ Plaça Reial 13, ☎ 93/302–1163) is *the* spot for young out-of-towners. The **Port Olímpic** is one solid *bar musical*, especially in summer and on weekends, as is **Port Vell**'s Maremagnum area.

For a more laid-back scene, with high ceilings, billiards, tapas, and hundreds of students, visit the popular **Velòdrom** (⊠ Muntaner 211–213, ☎ 93/230–6022)—with one of Barcelona's most evocative 1940ish interiors, it is located just below the Diagonal. Two blocks away is the intriguing *barmuseo* (bar-cum-museum) **La Fira** (⊠ Provença 171, ☎ 93/323–7271). Downtown, deep in the Barrio Chino, try the **London Bar** (⊠ Nou de la Rambla 34, ☎ 93/302–3102), an Art Nouveau circus haunt with a trapeze suspended above the bar. Other character bars to look for would include **Bar Almirall** (⊠ Joaquin Costa 33, ☎ 93/412–1535) and **Bar Muy Buenas** (⊠ Carme 63, ☎ 93/442–5053), or over by the Sagrada Família, the **Michael Collins Irish Pub** (⊠ Plaza Sagrada Família 4, ☎ 93/459–1964).

Nightclubs and Discos

Barcelona is so hot that it's hard to keep track of the haunts of the moment. Most clubs have a discretionary cover charge and like to inflict it on foreigners, so dress up and be prepared to talk your way past the bouncer. Any story can work; for example, you own a chain of nightclubs and are on a world tour. Don't expect much to happen until 1:30 or 2.

Tops for some time now is the prisonesque **Otto Zutz** (⊠ Lincoln 15, ☎ 93/238–0722), just off Via Augusta. **Woman Caballero** (⊠ Marqués de l'Argentera s/n, left side of Estació de Franca, ☎ 93/319–5356) is a new hot spot, as is **El Foro** (⊠ Princesa 53, ☎ 93/310–1020). The nearly classic **Up and Down** (⊠ Numancia 179, ☎ 93/280–2922), pronounced "Pen-*dow*," is another hot choice. **Bikini** (⊠ Deu i Mata 105, at Entença, ☎ 93/322–0005) will present you with a queue on festive Saturday nights. **Oliver y Hardy** (⊠ Av. Diagonal 593, ☎ 93/419–3181), next to the Barcelona Hilton, is more popular with the older set (i.e., you won't stand out if you're over 35); **La Tierra** (⊠ Aribau 230, ☎ 93/200–7346) and **El Otro** (⊠ Valencia 166, ☎ 93/323–6759) also accept postgraduates with open arms. **La Boîte Mas i Mas** (⊠ Av. Diagonal 477, ☎ 93/419–5950) has live music and a nice balance of civilization and insanity.

For one of Barcelona's most marvelous visual and aural treats, be sure to take yourself to the legendarily old-fashioned *sala de baile* (dance hall) **La Paloma** (⊠ Tigre 27, ☎ 93/301–6897), named after the haunting *habanera* song. This was the Studio 54 of its day—everyone from factory workers to jeweled princesses tangoed the night away in this gigantic, gilded ballroom (created by Salvador Alarma i Moragas in 1919), complete with opera-house chandelier and kitschy ceiling murals. With a big band playing tangos, the atmosphere adds up to an evening that's usually great fun; everyone comes here to celebrate old wedding anniversaries, new love affairs, and all manner of special events.

OUTDOOR ACTIVITIES AND SPORTS

Sports in Barcelona, especially spectator sports revolving around the world's wildest and wealthiest sports club, the Futbol Club Barcelona, is the most devastating and debilitating phenomenon to sweep the city since the 9th-century plague. The emcee of last year's Barcelona Poetry Festival's grand finale, for example, found it necessary to publicly thank the Barcelona soccer team for *not* reaching the European Cup 2000 finals, therefore permitting the festival's closing ceremony to have an audience. Where else in the world are even poets unabashed soccer fans?

A hundred years old in 1999, Barcelona's soccer club is Real Madrid's perennial nemesis (and vice-versa) as well as a sociological and historical phenomenon of deep significance in Catalonia. Supported by more than 200,000 quota-paying season ticket holders, FC Barcelona was the only legal outlet for Catalan nationalist sentiment during the 40-year Franco regime. Despite giant budgets and the world's best players, the Barcelona club's results, often as a result of what seemed to Catalans to be Madrid's and the central government's manipulation, never seemed to live up to full potential. This all changed after 1975, with Barcelona winning 4 consecutive league titles between 1990 and 1994 and 10 of the last 25. Nevertheless, Madrid's eight European cups (to Barcelona's one) are still a sore point for long-suffering Barcelona football fans.

On the participatory level, Barcelona, though less than obsessed with fitness (which they usually leave to a combination of walking, smoking, and boogying), offers an ever-increasing number of fitness clubs, squash courts, tennis courts, running and cycling trails, inline roller-skating excursions, golf courses, swimming pools, and sailing, windsurfing, and hiking options.

Beaches

Barcelona's beaches have improved and proliferated from Barceloneta north. At Barceloneta's south end is the Platja (beach) de Sant Sebastià, recently declared a nudist enclave, followed northward by the *platjas de* Barceloneta, Passeig Marítim, Port Olímpic, Nova Icaria, Bogatell, and Mar Bella. Topless bathing is common.

North of the City
North of Barcelona, the first beaches are Montgat, Ocata, Vilasar de Mar, Arenys de Mar, Canet, and Sant Pol de Mar, all accessible by train from the RENFE station in Plaça Catalunya. **Sant Pol** is our pick, with clean sand, a lovely old town, and **Sant Pau** (popularly called La Ruscalleda after its chef, Carmen Ruscalleda), one of the best restaurants in Catalonia. The farther north you go, toward the Costa Brava, the better the beaches.

South of the City
Ten kilometers (6 miles) south is the popular day resort **Castelldefels,** with a long, sandy beach and a series of handy and happening bars and restaurants. A 15-minute train ride from Plaça Catalunya's RENFE station to Gavà or Castelldefels deposits you on a 10-km (6-mi) beach for a superlative winter walk: From November through March the sun sets into the Mediterranean, thanks to the westward slant of the coastline here. There are several good places for lamb chops, *calçots* (spring onions), and paella; the best, **Can Patricio,** serves lunch until 4:30. **Sitges,** another 25 minutes south, has better sand and clearer water.

Bicycles and Inline Roller Skates

Cruising Barcelona on wheels whether by bike or skate is a good way to see a lot, save on transport and get good exercise in the bargain. For rentals of bicycles and skates try **BJ Motor** (⊠ Vallespir 20, ☎ 93/491–2293), **Escenic** (⊠ Marina 22, ☎ 93/221–1666), **Filicletos** (⊠ Passeig Picasso 40, ☎ 93/319–7885), **Icaria Esport** (⊠ Icaria 180, ☎ 93/221–1778), or **Rodats Inici** (⊠ Passeig Picasso 22, ☎ 93/319–7797).

Golf

Barcelona is 15–90 minutes away from many fine golf courses. Call ahead to reserve tee times.

Around Barcelona
Reial Club de Golf El Prat (⊠ El Prat de Llobregat, 08820, ☎ 93/379–0278), 36 holes. The greens fee at El Prat is 12,380 ptas./€74.41 on weekdays and exactly twice that on weekends and holidays. **Club de Golf de Sant Cugat** (⊠ Sant Cugat del Vallès 08190, ☎ 93/674–3958), 18 holes. **Club de Golf Vallromanes** (⊠ Vallromanes 08188, ☎ 93/568–0362), 18 holes. **Club de Golf Terramar** (⊠ Sitges, 08870, ☎ 93/894–0580), 18 holes.

Farther Afield
Club de Golf Costa Brava (⊠ La Masía, 17246 Santa Cristina d'Aro, ☎ 972/837150), 18 holes. **Club de Golf Pals** (⊠ Platja de Pals, 17256 Pals, ☎ 972/637009), 18 holes.

Health Clubs

For specifics, look in the *Páginas Amarillas/Pàgines Grogues* (*Yellow Pages*) under "Gimnasios/Gimnasis." We can recommend the **DiR** network of fitness centers, with addresses all over Barcelona (☎ 901/304030 for general information); the main branch is DiR Diagonal (⊠ Ganduxer 25–27, ☎ 93/202–2202). A day membership costs 1,900 ptas./€6.01 and includes aerobics classes and the use of a sauna, a steam room, a swimming pool, squash courts, and MTV. **Crack,** just off Passeig de Gràcia near the hotel Condes de Barcelona, is another winner, with a gym, a sauna, pool (summer only), squash courts, and paddle tennis; day membership here costs 2,000 ptas./€12.02, with a small supplement for the squash and paddle tennis courts (⊠ Pasaje Domingo 7, ☎ 93/215–2755).

Hiking

The **Collserola** hills behind the city offer well-marked trails, fresh air, and lovely views. Take the San Cugat, Sabadell, or Terrassa FFCC train from Plaça de Catalunya and get off at Baixador de Vallvidrera; the information center, 10 minutes uphill next to **Vil.la Joana** (now the Jacint Verdaguer Museum), has maps of this mountain woodland just 20 minutes from downtown. The walk back into town can take from two to five hours depending on your speed and the trails you choose. For information on hiking farther afield, including in the Pyrenees, contact the **Club Excursionista de Catalunya** (⊠ Paradis 10, ☎ 93/315–2311) or the **Associació Excursionista, Etnográfica i Folklorica** (⊠ Avinyó 19, ☎ 93/302–2730).

Swimming

Piscines Bernat Picornell (⊠ Av. del Estadi 30–40, ☎ 93/423–4041), on Montjuïc, is open daily from 7 AM to midnight, and the fee includes use of a sauna, gymnasium, and fitness equipment in addition to indoor and outdoor pools. Overlooking the beach from Barceloneta, the indoor pool at the **Club Natació de Barceloneta** (⊠ Passeig Joan de Borbó, ☎ 93/221–0010)—also known as Complex Esportiu Municipal Banys Sant Sebastiá—is open daily from 7 AM to 11 PM. Uphill from Parc Güell is the **Parc de la Creueta del Coll** (⊠ Castellterçol, ☎ 93/416–2625), which has a huge outdoor pool. In upper Barcelona **Parc Piscines i Esports** (⊠ Ganduxer 25–27, ☎ 93/201–9321) has both indoor and outdoor pools. All fees are around 1,000 ptas./€6.01 per day.

Tennis

The Olympic tennis facilities at **Vall d'Hebron** (✉ Pg. Vall d'Hebron 178–196, ☎ 93/427–6500) are open from 8 AM until 11 PM; clay costs 2,500 ptas./€15.03 per hour, hard courts 1,800 ptas./€10.82. **Complejo Deportivo Can Caralleu** (Can Caralleu Sports Complex), above Pedralbes, a 30-minute walk uphill from the Reina Elisenda subway stop (FFCC de la Generalitat), offers hard courts and clean air (☎ 93/203–7874). It's open daily 8 AM–11 PM and costs 1,250 ptas./€7.51 per hour by day, 1,600 ptas./€9.62 by night. The upscale **Club Vall Parc** (✉ Carretera de la Rabassada 79, ☎ 93/212–6789) is open daily 8 AM–midnight and charges 2,500 ptas./€15.03 per hour by day, 3,100 ptas./€18.63 by night.

Sailing and Windsurfing

On any day of the week in Barcelona you can see midday regattas taking place off the Barceloneta beaches or beyond the *rompeolas* (breakwater) on the far side of the port. For rentals of sailboats, power craft and windsurfing equipment, contact **Ronáutica** (✉ Moll de la Marina 11, Port Olimpic, ☎ 93/221–0380, FAX 93/221–0895) or **Proa 7** (✉ Consell de Cent 344, ☎ 93/487–0920).

SHOPPING

Shopping Districts

Shopping in Barcelona's design emporiums, fashion mills, and knick-knack shops is more like museum browsing than a buying spree, although it can, of course, be both. Places like Vinçon and BD delight the eye and stimulate the imagination nearly as quickly as they inhibit your credit card draw (design is expensive). Passeig de Gràcia is becoming known as one of the great shopping avenues in the world, while searching through Barcelona's antiques district along Carrer de la Palla (which follows the trace of the 4th century Roman walls) is always an adventure. The new shops opening daily around Santa Maria del Mar in the Barri de la Ribera range eclectically from Catalan and international design artifacts of all kinds to Moroccan ceramics to high fashion to nuts and spices, while the mega-stores in Plaça Catalunya, along the Diagonal, and in L'Illa farther west, are commercial free-for-alls offering everything under the sun and then some.

For high fashion, browse carefully through Passeig de Gràcia and the Diagonal between Plaça Joan Carles I and Plaça Francesc Macià. For a variety of music, books, sports, clothes, and food try L'Illa shopping center on the Diagonal west of Entença or El Triangle in Plaça Catalunya at the head of the Rambla. Antiques shopping alone could keep you booked solid in Barcelona, with some two dozen of the best shops in the Gothic Quarter, another 70 shops off Passeig de Gràcia in the Bulevard dels Antiquaris, and more in Gràcia and Sarrià.

Barcelona's prime shopping districts are the Passeig de Gràcia, Rambla de Catalunya, the Plaça Catalunya, Porta de l'Àngel, and Avinguda Diagonal up to Carrer Ganduxer. Farther out on the Diagonal is shopping colossus **L'Illa**, which includes **FNAC, Marks & Spencer,** and plenty of other consumer temptations. The **Maremagum** mall, in Port Vell, is another option. **Carrer Tuset,** north of the Diagonal, has lots of small boutiques. For affordable, old-fashioned, typically Spanish shops, prowl along **Carrer Ferran.** The area surrounding the **Plaça del Pi,** from the Boqueria to Carrer Portaferrissa and Carrer de la Canuda, has fashionable boutiques and jewelry and gift shops. The **Barri de la Ribera** around Santa Maria del Mar is increasingly filled with shops of all kinds. Check along

Carrer Banys Vells and, one street north of Carrer Montcada along Carrer Flassaders for design stores, jewelry and knickknacks of all kinds. Most stores are open Monday–Saturday 9–1:30 and 5–8, but some close in the afternoon. Virtually all close on Sunday.

Specialty Stores

Antiques

Barcelona's antiques shops and outlets are proliferating at a supply-defying pace. While the traditional stores are along Carrer de la Palla, Carrer del Pi, and Carrer dels Banys Nous in the Gothic Quarter, there are also a cluster of antiques stores on Passeig de Gràcia and new ones opening every day in upper Barcelona. The following are just a few standouts: **Carrer de la Palla** and **Carrer Banys Nous,** in the Gothic Quarter, are lined with antiques shops full of maps, books, paintings, and furniture. An **antiques market** is held every Thursday from 10 to 8, in front of the cathedral. The **Centre d'Antiquaris** (⊠ Passeig de Gràcia 55) contains 75 antiques stores. Try **Gothsland** (⊠ Consell de Cent 331) for Moderniste design. Find **La Maison Coloniale** (⊠ Sant Antoni Abat 61), near the Mercat de San Antoni. Once part of the Iglesia de Sant Antoni, the 15th-century stone vaulting overhead makes this one of Barcelona's most beautiful stores, while the colonial furniture includes many unusual gems. **Novecento** (⊠ Passeig de Gràcia 75) specializes in art and jewelry antiques. **Antiguedades J. Pla** (⊠ Aragó 517) buys and sells antiques of all kinds. **Alcanto** (⊠ Passeig de Gràcia 55–57) is a major clearinghouse for buying and selling a wide range of antiques. The neighborhood of **Sarrià** is becoming an antiquer's destination, with a plethora of shops along Cornet i Mas, Pedró de la Creu, and Major de Sarrià.

Art

There is a cluster of art galleries on Carrer Consell de Cent between Passeig de Gràcia and Carrer Balmes, and around the corner on Rambla de Catalunya, including **Galeria Joan Prats** (⊠ Rambla de Catalunya 54), **Ambit** (⊠ Consell de Cent 282), **Galeria Carme Espinet** (⊠ Balmes 86), **Sala Dalmau** (⊠ Consell de Cent 347), and **Sala Rovira** (⊠ Rambla de Catalunya 62). The nearby **Joan Gaspart Gallery** (⊠ Plaça Letamendi 1) is another important art gallery with a long tradition. Carrer Petritxol, which leads down into Plaça del Pi, is also lined with galleries, most notably the dean of them all, **Sala Parès** (⊠ Petritxol 5), and **Trama** (⊠ Petritxol 8). The Born and Santa Maria del Mar quarter is another art destination. Carrer Montcada has **Galeria Maeght** and others; Carrer Bany Vells, just one street south, has the lovely new **3 ART BCN** (⊠ Bany Vells 1). **Galeria Rosa Ventosa** is next to the church of Santa Maria del Mar (⊠ Sombrerers 1). **Galeria Verena Hofer** is at Plaça Comercial, across from the Born; and the ticking **Metrònom** (⊠ Carrer Fussina 4 is nearby at the uptown end of the Borne. Near Plaça del Pi, galleries line Carrer de la Palla, particularly **Sala d'Art Artur Ramón** (⊠ Carrer de la Palla 23) and **Galeria Segovia-Isaacs** (⊠ Carrer de la Palla 8). **La Rosa del Foc** (⊠ Rec 69), near the Born, specializes in photography exhibits. **Galeria Claramunt** (⊠ Ferlandina 27), next to the MACBA, is a good gallery to include in a pre- or- post-contemporary art outing. Other important spaces for seeing (not buying) local, contemporary art include **Fundació Caixa de Catalunya–La Pedrera** (⊠ Provença 261–265), **Fundació La Caixa–Centre Cultural** (⊠ Passeig Sant Joan 108), **Fundació La Caixa–Sala Montcada** (⊠ Carrer Montcada 14), and **Sala El Vienès-Casa Fuster** (⊠ Passeig de Gràcia 132).

Boutiques and Fashion

If you're into clothes and jewelry, you've come to the right place. Barcelona makes all the headlines on Spain's booming fashion front. **Chanel** (⊠ Passeig de Gràcia 70), **Giorgio Armani** (⊠ Av. Diagonal 620), **Loewe** (⊠ Passeig de Gràcia 35), and the other big names have shops along Passeig de Gràcia and Avinguda Diagonal. **El Bulevard Rosa** (⊠ Passeig de Gràcia 53–55) is a collection of boutiques with the very latest outfits; others are on the Diagonal between Passeig de Gràcia and Carrer Ganduxer. **Adolfo Domínguez,** one of Spain's top designers, is at Passeig de Gràcia 35 and Avinguda Diagonal 570; Toni Miró's two **Groc** shops, with the latest looks for men, women, and children, are at Muntaner 385 and Rambla de Catalunya 100. **David Valls,** at Valencia 235, represents new and young Barcelona fashion design, and **May Day** carries clothing, footwear, and accessories from the cutting edge. **Joaquim Berao,** a top jewelry designer, is at Roselló 277. **Forum Ferlandina** (⊠ Ferlandina 31), next to the MACBA, is where Beatriz Würsch designs and displays unusual and original jewelry.

Ceramics

Art Escudellers (⊠ Calle Escudellers 5), across the street from the restaurant Los Caracoles, has ceramics from all over Spain, with more than 140 different artisans represented and maps showing where the work is from. **Itaca** (⊠ Ferrán 26) has ceramic plates, bowls, and inspired objects of all kinds, including pottery from Talavera de la Reina and La Bisbal. The big department stores are also worth checking. For Lladró, try **Pla de l'Os** (⊠ Boqueria 3), just off the Rambla. Behind the Sarrià market on your way into bougainvillea-choked Plaça Sant Gaietá, have a look in at the ceramics store **Nica & Bet** (⊠ Pare Miquel de Sarrià 10), if only for a peek at the beautifully restored wooden doors.

Department Stores

The ubiquitous **El Corte Inglés** has four locations: Plaça de Catalunya 14, Porta de l'Angel 19–21, Avinguda Francesc Macià 58, and Avinguda Diagonal 617. **Marks & Spencer** is at the top of the Rambla on Plaça Catalunya and in the shopping mall **L'Illa,** west of Plaça Francesc Macià at Avinguda Diagonal 545, along with a full array of stores from Benetton to Zara. **Plaça Catalunya** now includes **FNAC** and **Habitat,** among other emporiums.

Design and Interiors

Some 50 years old, design giant **Vinçon,** at Passeig de Gràcia 96, has steadily expanded its chic premises through a rambling Moderniste house that was once the home of Moderniste poet-artist Santiago Rusiñol and the studio of his colleague, the painter Ramón Casas. It stocks everything from Filofaxes to handsome kitchenware. If for nothing else, come here to see one of Barcelona's most spectacular fireplaces, designed in wild Art Nouveau exuberance with a gigantic hearth that takes the form of a stylized face. A few doors up, at Passeig de Gràcia 102, is the upscale **Gimeno,** with elegant displays ranging from unusual suitcases to the latest in furniture design. **bd** (Barcelona design), at Carrer Mallorca 291–293, is a spare, cutting-edge home-furnishing store in another Moderniste gem, Doménech i Muntaner's Casa Thomas. **Habitat** has stores on Tuset at the Diagonal and in the new Plaça Catalunya Triangle complex behind Bar Zurich.

The area around the church of Santa Maria del Mar, an artisans' quarter since medieval times, is filling with cheerful design stores and art galleries. One of the best, **Testart Design,** at Argenteria 78, is owned and run by Matias Testart and Washington, D.C., native Natasha Chand.

Other browse-worthy shops include **Ici et Là,** across the square (⊠ Plaça Santa Maria del Mar 2), **Fem** (⊠ Palau 6, behind the *ajuntament*), **Papers Coma** (⊠ Montcada 20), and **Estudi Pam2** (⊠ Sabateret 1–3).

Food and Flea Markets

The **Boqueria,** on the Rambla between Carrer del Carme and Carrer de Hospital, is Barcelona's most colorful and bustling food market and the oldest of its kind in Europe. Open Monday–Saturday, it's most active before 3 PM. Other spectacular food markets include the two in Gràcia—**Mercat de la Llibertat** (near Plaça Gal.la Placidia) and the **Mercat de la Revolució** (on Travessera de Gràcia)—and the **Mercat de Sarrià** (near Plaça de Sarrià and the Reina Elisenda train stop). Barcelona's biggest flea market, **Els Encants,** is held Monday, Wednesday, Friday, and Saturday 8–7 at the end of Dos de Maig, on the Plaça de les Glòries (Metro: Glòries). The **Mercat Gòtic** fills the Plaça de la Seu, in front of the cathedral, on Thursday. **Sarrià**'s main square holds an antiques market on Tuesday. The **Sant Antoni** market, at the end of Ronda Sant Antoni, is an old-fashioned food, clothing, and used-book (many in English) market that's best on Sunday. On Thursday, a natural-produce market (honeys, cheeses) fills **Plaça del Pi** with interesting tastes and aromas, while neighboring Plaça Sant Josep Oriol hold a painter's market every Sunday. A stamp and coin market fills **Plaça Reial** on Sunday morning, along with another general craft and flea market near the Columbus monument at the port end of the Rambla.

Gourmet Foods

Casa Gispert (⊠ Sombrerers 23), on the inland side of Santa Maria del Mar, is one of the most aromatic and picturesque shops in Barcelona, bursting with spices, saffron, chocolates, and nuts. Other charming and fragrant saffron and spice shops include **Jobal** (⊠ Princesa 38) and **La Barcelonesa** (⊠ Comerç 27). Near Santa Maria del Mar, **Vila Viniteca** (⊠ Agullers 7) is one of the best wine stores in Barcelona, and the produce store across the way at Agullers 9 sells some of the prettiest cheeses around. **El Magnífico** (⊠ Argenteria 64) is famous for its coffees. **Tot Formatge** (⊠ Passeig del Born 13) has cheeses from all over Spain and the rest of the world. **La Casa del Bacalao** (⊠ Condal 8) specializes in salt cod and books of codfish recipes. **La Palmera** (⊠ Enric Granados 57) offers expert advice and a superb collection of wines, hams, cheeses, and olive oils. **Caelum** (⊠ Carrer de la Palla 8) sells a wide range of crafts and food products such as honeys and patés made in convents and monasteries from all over Spain. **Vilaplana** (⊠ Francesc Perez Cabrero) is famous in Barcelona for pastries, cheeses, hams, patés, caviars, and gourmet delicatessen items. **Foix de Sarrià** (⊠ Plaça Sarrià 9–10 and Major de Sarrià 57) is known for excellent pastries, breads, wines, cheeses, and cavas.

Miscellany

Lovers of fine stationery will linger in the Gothic Quarter's **Papirum** (⊠ Baixada de la Llibreteria 2), a tiny, medieval-tone shop with exquisite hand-printed papers, marbleized blank books, and writing implements. Lovely **La Manual Alpargartera** (⊠ Avinyó 7), just off Carrer Ferran, specializes in handmade rope-sole sandals and espadrilles. **Solé** (⊠ Carrer Ample 7) sells handmade shoes from all over the world. While in the area don't miss **La Lionesa,** just up the street at Ample 21, a picturesque old-time grocery store. Cutlery culture flourishes at the stately **Ganiveteria Roca** (⊠ Plaça del Pi 3) directly opposite the giant rose window of the Santa Maria del Pi church. If codfish recipes and general codfish lore are your thing, don't miss **La Casa del Bacalao** (⊠ Condal 8) just off Portal del Angel. **Eutherpe** (⊠ Elisabets 18) is a haven for lovers of early music near the MACBA. Don't expect to find any

Mozart here, or much of anything after Locatelli. **Otman** (⊠ Banys Vells 21, bis) has stores in Asilah, Morocco, and next to the Santa Maria del Mar basilica, this little slot is a find if you're looking for light, racy frocks, belts, blouses, or skirts.

BARCELONA A TO Z

Arriving and Departing

By Bus

Barcelona has no central bus station, but most buses to Spanish destinations operate from the **Estació Norte-Vilanova** (⊠ End of Av. Vilanova, a few blocks east of Arc de Triomf, ☎ 93/245–2528). Most international buses use the **Estació Autobuses de Sants** (⊠ Carrer Viriato, next to Sants train station, ☎ 93/490–4000). Scores of independent companies operate from depots throughout town (☞ Excursions *in* Guided Tours, *below*).

By Car

Arriving in Barcelona by car from the north along the A7 Autopista (freeway) or from the west along the A2 Autopista, you will encounter signs for the *Rondes* (ring roads) constructed for the 1992 Olympics. Ronda del Litoral will take you into lower Barcelona along the waterfront, while Ronda de Dalt (the upper Ronda) takes you along the edge of upper Barcelona to Horta, the Bonanova, Sarrià, and Pedralbes. For the center of town, take the Ronda Litoral and look for exits 21 (Paral.lel-Les Rambles) or 22 (Barceloneta-Via Laietana-Hospital de Mar). If you are arriving from the Pyrenees on the C1411/E-9 through the Tunel del Cadí, the Tunels de Vallvidrera will place you on the upper Via Augusta next to Sarrià, Pedralbes, and La Bonanova. The Eixample and Ciutat Vella are 10 to 15 minutes farther if traffic is fluid.

Don't be intimidated by driving or parking here. You can often find a legal and safe parking place on the street, and underground public parking is increasingly plentiful, easy, and inexpensive.

By Plane

All international and domestic flights arrive at the spectacular glass, steel, and marble **El Prat de Llobregat** airport, 14 km (9 mi) south of Barcelona, just off the main highway to Castelldefels and Sitges. For information on arrival and departure times, call **Iberia** (☎ 93/401–3131; 93/401–3535; 93/301–3993; 93/302–7656 for international reservations and confirmations). Most flights from the United States connect in Madrid; only Continental, Delta, Iberia, and TWA fly nonstop to Barcelona.

Check first to see if your hotel provides airport-shuttle service; otherwise, you can high-tail it into town via train, bus, taxi, or rental car.

BETWEEN THE AIRPORT AND DOWNTOWN

By Bus. The Aerobus leaves the airport for Plaça de Catalunya every 15 minutes (6 AM–11 PM) on weekdays and every 30 minutes (6:30 AM–10:50 PM) on weekends. From Plaça de Catalunya, it leaves for the airport every 15 minutes (5:30 AM–10:05 PM) on weekdays and every 30 minutes (6:30 AM–10:50 PM) on weekends. The fare is 500 ptas./€3.01.

By Car. Follow signs to the Centre Ciutat and you'll enter the city along Gran Via. For the port area, follow signs for the Ronda Litoral. The journey to the center of town can take anywhere from 15 to 45 minutes depending on traffic. Peak rush hours are between 7:30 and 9:30 in the morning, 1:30–2:30 in the afternoon, and 7–9 in the evening.

By Taxi. Cab fare from the airport into town is 2,500 ptas.–3,000 ptas.(€15.03–18.03).

By Train. The train's only drawback is that it's a 10- or 15-minute walk (with moving walkway) from your gate through the terminal and over the bridge. The train leaves the airport every 30 minutes between 6:12 AM and 10:13 PM, stopping first at the Estació de Sants, then at the Plaça de Catalunya, later at the Arc de Trionf, and finally at Clot. Trains going to the airport begin at 6 AM from the Clot station, stopping at the Arc de Triomf at 6:05 AM, Plaça de Catalunya at 6:08 AM, and Sants at 6:13 AM. The fare is 500 ptas./€3.01 on weekdays, 550 ptas./€3.31 on weekends and holidays.

By Train

Almost all long-distance and international trains arrive and depart from the **Estació de Sants** (⊠ Plaça dels Països Catalans s/n, ☎ 902/240202). En route to or from Sants, some trains stop at another station on **Passeig de Gràcia** (⊠ At Aragó, ☎ 902/240202). The Passeig de Gràcia station is often a good way to avoid the long lines that form at Sants during holidays. The **Estació de França** (⊠ Av. Marques Argentera s/n, ☎ 902/240202), near the port, handles certain long-distance trains within Spain and some international trains.

Getting Around

Modern Barcelona, above the Plaça de Catalunya, is built on a grid system. The old town, from the Plaça de Catalunya to the port, however, is a labyrinth of narrow streets, and you'll need a good street map to get around it. Most sightseeing can be done on foot—you won't have any choice in the Barri Gòtic—but you'll have to use the metro, buses, or taxis to link sightseeing areas. The T-Dia card costs 625 ptas./€3.76 and is valid for one day of unlimited travel on all subway, bus, and FFCC (Ferrocarriles de la Generalitat de Catalunya) lines. The 10-trip T-1 card costs 825 ptas./€4.96 and is valid for all bus, metro, and FFCC travel. When switching from the Metro line to the FFCC (or vice-versa), merely insert the card through the slot and the turnstile will open without charging you for a second ride provided less than an hour has elapsed since you punched in initially. Maps showing bus and metro routes are available free from booths in the Plaça de Catalunya; for general information on public transport, call 93/412–0000. General information is also available, though not necessarily in English, at 010. Turisme de Barcelona (☞ *below*) attends calls in English.

Turisme de Barcelona (Barcelona Tourism; ⊠ Plaça de Catalunya 17 bis, ☎ 906/301282) sells 24-, 48-, and 72-hour versions of the very worthwhile Barcelona Card. For 2,750, 3,250, or 3,750 ptas. (€16.53, 19.53, or 22.54), you get unlimited travel on all public transport as well as discounts at 27 museums, 10 restaurants, 14 leisure spots, and 20 stores. Other services include walking tours of the Gothic Quarter, an airport shuttle, a bus to Tibidabo, and the Tombbus, which connects key shopping areas.

By Boat

Golondrinas harbor boats make short trips from the Portal de la Pau, near the Columbus Monument. The fare is 750 ptas./€4.51 for a 30-minute trip. Departures are spring and summer (Holy Week through September), daily 11–7; fall and winter, weekends and holidays only, 11–5. It's closed December 16–January 2. For information call ☎ 93/442–3106.

By Bus

City buses run daily from 5:30 AM to 11:30 PM. The fare is 145 ptas./€0.87 (155 ptas./€0.93 Sunday and holidays); for multiple journeys purchase a Targeta T1, which buys you 10 rides for 875 ptas./€5.26 (like the metro's T2, plus buses). Route maps are displayed at bus stops. Note that those with a red band always stop at a central square—Catalunya, Universitat, or Urquinaona—and blue indicates a night bus. From June 12 to October 12 the Bus Turistic (9:30–7:30 every 30 minutes) runs on a circuit that passes all the important sights. A day's ticket, which you can buy on the bus, costs 1,400 ptas./€8.41 (925 ptas./€5.56 half day) and also covers the fare for the Tramvía Blau, funicular, and Montjuïc cable car across the port. The ride starts at the Plaça de Catalunya.

By Cable Car and Funicular

The Montjuïc Funicular is a cog railroad that runs from the junction of Avinguda Paral.lel and Nou de la Rambla to the Miramar station on Montjuïc (metro: Paral.lel). It operates weekends and holidays 11 AM–8 PM in winter, and daily 11 AM–9:30 PM in summer; the fare is 200 ptas./€1.20. A *telefèric* then takes you from the amusement park up to Montjuïc Castle. In winter the telefèric runs weekends and holidays 11–2:45 and 4–7:30; in summer, daily 11:30–9. The fare is 450 ptas./€2.70.

A Transbordador Aeri Harbor Cable Car runs between Miramar and Montjuïc across the harbor to Torre de Jaume I, on Barcelona's *moll* (quay), and on to Torre de Sant Sebastià, at the end of Passeig Joan de Borbó in Barceloneta. You can board at either stage. The fare is 850 ptas./€5.11 (1,000 ptas./€6.01 round-trip), and the car runs October–June, weekdays noon–5:45, weekends noon–6:15, and July–September, daily 11–9.

To reach the summit of Tibidabo, take the metro to Avinguda de Tibidabo, then the Tramvía Blau (350 ptas./€2.10 one-way) to Peu del Funicular, and finally the Tibidabo Funicular (450 ptas./€2.70 one-way) from there to the Tibidabo fairground. It runs every 30 minutes, 7:05 AM–9:35 PM ascending, 7:25 AM–9:55 PM descending.

By Metro

The subway is the fastest, cheapest, and easiest way to get around Barcelona. You pay a flat fare of 150 ptas./€0.90 no matter how far you travel, but it's more economical to buy a Targeta T2 (valid for metro and FFCC Generalitat trains, Tramvía Blau [blue tram], and the Montjuïc Funicular), which costs 875 ptas./€5.26 for 10 rides. The system runs 5 AM–11 PM (until 1 AM on weekends and holidays).

By Taxi

Taxis are black and yellow and show a green light when available for hire. The meter starts at 395 ptas./€2.37 (which lasts for six minutes), and there are supplements for luggage, night travel, Sunday and holidays, rides from a station or to the airport, and for trips to or from the bullring or a football match. There are cab stands all over town, and you can also hail cabs on the street. To call a cab, try 93/387–1000, 93/490–2222, or 93/357–7755, 24 hours a day.

Guided Tours

Turisme de Barcelona (Barcelona Tourism; ⊠ Plaça de Catalunya 17 bis, ☎ 906/301282) offers weekend walking tours of the Gothic Quarter (at 10 AM) for 1,000 ptas./€6.01.

Other urban tours are run by **Julià Tours** (⊠ Ronda Universitat 5, ☎ 93/317–6454) and **Pullmantur** (⊠ Gran Via 635, ☎ 93/318–5195). Tours

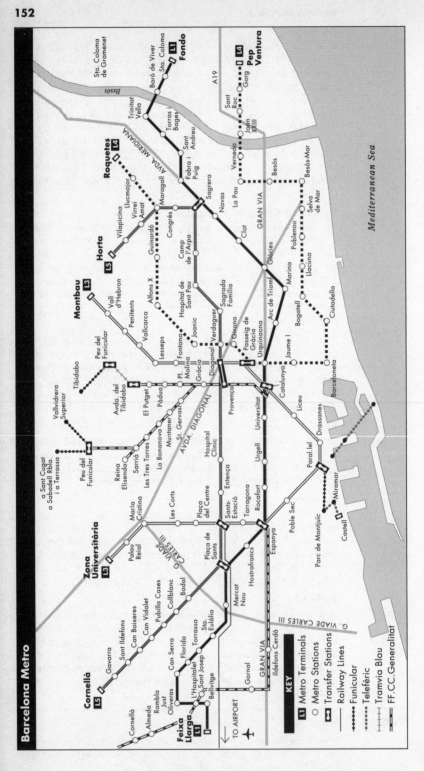

Barcelona Metro

leave from these offices, but you may be able to arrange a pickup at your hotel. Prices are 4,985 ptas./€29.96 for a half day and 12,750 ptas./€76.63 for a full day, including lunch.

Julià Tours and Pullmantur also run day and half-day excursions outside the city. The most popular trips are those to Montserrat and the Costa Brava resorts, the latter including a cruise to the Medes Isles.

Personal Guides

Contact **City Guides Barcelona** (☎ 93/412–0674), the **Barcelona Guide Bureau** (☎ 93/268–2422), or the **Asociación Profesional de Informadores Turísticos** (☎ 93/319–8416) for a list of English-speaking guides.

Special-Interest Tours

La Ruta del Modernismo (the Modernism Route), created by Barcelona's *ajuntament* (city hall), connects seven key Art Nouveau sites: Palau Güell, the Palau de la Música, the Fundació Tàpies, Casa Milà (La Pedrera), the Museu Gaudí (in the Parc Güell), the Museu d'Art Modern (in Ciutadella), and Gaudí's Sagrada Família church. Guided tours, some in English, are included at Palau Güell and the Palau de la Música. At Casa Milá there is one guided tour daily (6 PM weekdays, 11 AM weekends). At the Sagrada Família the guided tour costs extra. The route is headquartered at **Casa Amatller** (⊠ Passeig de Gràcia 41, ☎ 93/488–0139), open Monday through Saturday 10–7, Sunday 10–2. The price, 600 ptas./€3.61, gets you 50% discounts at all seven locations.

The bookstore in the **Palau de la Virreina** (⊠ La Rambla 99) rents cassettes whose walking tours follow footprints painted on sidewalks—different colors for different tours—through Barcelona's most interesting areas. The do-it-yourself method is to pick up the guides produced by the tourist office, *Discovering Romanesque Art* and *Discovering Modernist Art*, which have art itineraries for all of Catalonia.

Contacts and Resources

Bike Rental

Try **Bicitram** (⊠ Marquès de l'Argentera 15, ☎ 93/792–2841) and **Los Filicletos** (⊠ Passeig de Picasso 38, ☎ 93/319–7811). **Un Menys**—"One Fewer," in Catalan, meaning one fewer car on the streets of Barcelona—organizes increasingly popular outings that tack drinks, dinner, and dancing onto a gentle bike ride for a total price of about 5,000 ptas./€30.05. ⊠ Esparteria 3, ☎ 93/268–2105, FAX 93/319–4298. AE, DC, MC, V.

Car and Motorcycle Rental

Call **Atesa** (⊠ Muntaner 45, ☎ 93/323–0266), **Avis** (⊠ Casanova 209, ☎ 93/209–9533; Aragó 235, ☎ 93/487–8754); **Europcar** (⊠ Viladomat 214, ☎ 93/439–8403; Estació de Sants, ☎ 93/491–4822); **Hertz** (⊠ Tuset 10, ☎ 93/217–3248; Estació de Sants, ☎ 93/490–8662); or **Vanguard** (cars and motorcycles; ⊠ Londres 31, ☎ 93/439–3880).

Consulates

Canada (⊠ Via Augusta 125, ☎ 93/209–0634); **United Kingdom** (⊠ Av. Diagonal 477, ☎ 93/419–9044); **United States** (⊠ Passeig Reina Elisenda 23, ☎ 93/280–2227).

Emergencies

Tourist Attention, a service provided by the local police department, will offer assistance if you're the victim of a crime, seek medical or psychological help, or need temporary documents in the event of loss of the originals. English interpreters are on hand. ⊠ Guardia Urbana, Ramblas 43, ☎ 93/290–3440.

Other emergency services: **Police** (☎ 091; 092; main police station ⊠ Via Laietana 43, ☎ 93/301–6666). **Ambulance** (Creu Roja, ☎ 93/300–2020). **Hospital** (Hospital Clinic: ⊠ Villarroel 170, ☎ 93/454–6000 or 93/454–7000; metro: blue line to Hospital Clinic). **Emergency doctors** (☎ 061).

English-Language Bookstores

BCN Books (⊠ Aragó 277, ☎ 93/487–3455) is one of Barcelona's top stores for books in English. **El Corte Inglés** (⊠ Plaça de Catalunya 14, ☎ 93/302–1212; Av. Diagonal 617, ☎ 93/419–2828) sells English guidebooks and novels, but the selection is limited. For more variety, try the **English Bookshop** (⊠ Entença 63, ☎ 93/425–4466), **Jaimes Bookshop** (⊠ Passeig de Gràcia 64, ☎ 93/215–3626), **Laie** (⊠ Pau Claris 85, ☎ 93/318–1357), **La Central** (⊠ Mallorca 237, ☎ 93/487–5018), **Libreria Francesa** (⊠ Passeig de Gràcia 91, ☎ 93/215–1417), **Come In** (⊠ Provença 203, ☎ 93/253–1204), or **Llibreria Bosch** (⊠ Ronda Universitat 11, ☎ 93/317–5308; Roselló 24, ☎ 93/321–3341). The bookstore in the **Palau de la Virreina** (⊠ La Rambla 99, ☎ 93/301–7775) has good books on art, design, and Barcelona in general. **Altair** (⊠ Balmes 69–71, ☎ 93/454–2966) is an excellent travel and adventure bookstore with many titles in English.

Late-Night Pharmacies

Look on the door of any pharmacy or in any local newspaper under "*Farmacias de Guardia*" for the addresses of those open late at night or 24 hours. Alternately, dial 010.

Travel Agencies

American Express (⊠ Roselló 257, at Passeig de Gràcia, ☎ 93/217–0070). **Iberia** (⊠ Diputació 258, at Passeig de Gràcia, ☎ 93/401–3381; Plaça de Espanya, ☎ 93/325–7358). **Wagons-Lits Cook** (⊠ Passeig de Gràcia 8, ☎ 93/317–5500). **Bestours** (⊠ Diputació 241, ☎ 93/487–8580).

Visitor Information

The **Centre d'Informació Turistic de Barcelona** has two locations (⊠ Plaça de Catalunya 17 bis, ☎ 93/304–3421; Plaça Sant Jaume 1, ☎ 93/304–3421), both open Monday through Saturday 9–9 and Sunday 10–2. There are smaller tourist facilities at the **Sants** train station, open daily 8–8; the **Palau de la Virreina** (⊠ Rambla 99), open Monday–Saturday 9–9 and Sunday 10–2; and the **Palau de Congressos** (⊠ Av. María Cristina s/n), open daily 10–8 during trade fairs and conventions only.

Offices with information on Catalonia and the rest of Spain are at **El Prat Airport** (☎ 93/478–4704), open Monday–Saturday 9:30–8 and Sunday 9:30–3, and the **Centre d'Informació Turística** (⊠ Palau Robert, Passeig de Gràcia 107, at the Diagonal, ☎ 93/238–4000), open Monday–Saturday 10–7. For general information in English, dial 010.

From June to mid-September, **tourist information aides** patrol the Gothic Quarter and Ramblas area 9 AM–9 PM. They travel in pairs and are recognizable by their uniforms of red shirts, white trousers or skirts, and badges.

3 CATALONIA: THE COSTA BRAVA TO TARRAGONA

Is it the sun or the soil? The dreamy castle-capped peaks? The sapphire coves of the coast? Whatever the reason, Catalonia is adorned with magical places, most just a day-trip away from Barcelona. The star is the "Catalan Riviera"—the bewitching Costa Brava. Here, where Salvador Dalí once immortalized silvery-white sand beaches, getaways like Cadaqués sit on the brink of the bluest of Mediterranean seas. To journey back in time, discover inland Girona: a place of long history and—thanks to its Moorish baths, Romanesque abbeys, and medieval Jewish quarter—past glory. To the southwest of Barcelona, mountaintop Montserrat and the ancient Roman ruins of Tarragona also fascinate.

By James C.
Townsend

T HE PROBLEM OF TOURING CATALONIA—the province that comprises the northeast shoulder of Spain—is simplified by the fact that wherever you want to go, you start from Barcelona. Planes and ships set you down there, all roads and railways entering this corner of Spain are headed for Barcelona. There are not a half dozen different ways of setting out to explore Catalonia. There is one. But if Barcelona is the capital of Catalonia (to use the English spelling; it's Cataluña in Castilian, Catalunya in Catalan), it is too cosmopolitan, continental, and chic to be its "soul." To find the *real* Catalonia, you must simply remember that all roads lead *from* Barcelona and take to the hinterlands. And, in fact, many *Barcelonins* do exactly that. It is widely known that Barcelona is a city of second sons who left their countryside roots to seek fame and fortune in the metropolis. So it is not surprising that today even the city's hippest artists and most decidedly modern entrepreneurs still flee the capital every summer to return to their "roots"—the timeless inland villages and picturesque coastal hamlets of Catalonia.

In fact, mountain and sea—*muntanya i mar* in Catalan—are the two primal forces that define the spirit of Catalonia. With the Mediterranean on one side and the Pyrenees on the other, it is not surprising that legend ascribes the birth of Catalonia's very heart—the region known as the Empordà—to the love of a shepherd for a mermaid. The result, so to speak, scattered, with a generous hand, Catalonia's landscape with memorable sights and places. For starters, there is the Costa Brava, a celebrated resort area that extends along nearly a hundred miles of coast from Blanes, set at the mouth of the Tordera river some 40 mi north of Barcelona, up to Portbou on the French border. Crowded with fig trees and vineyards, cacti and mimosa, eucalyptus trees, pines, and birches, and its famous cork trees, set with Catalonia's most idyllic *platjes* (or beaches), often separated by rocky saleints threaded by *cales* (or creeks), indented by a 1,001 coves, and perfumed by the scents of lavender, thyme, and rosemary, this coast offers both hidden, unspoiled villages, like Calella de Palafrugell, and also, unfortunately, resort meccas like Lloret de Mar, overrun with people working on their nightclub "sun tan." But the glory of the Costa Brava Catalana—to use its full name—remains those villages and hamlets where the outside walls of houses, owing to phosphorus in the whitewash, glow like mother-of-pearl in the sun, and take on sharp, purple shadows. Such towns are a source of infinite enjoyment to anyone possessed of a fine eye for aesthetic beauty and for unexpected perspectives, so it's no wonder that the famous founder of Surrealism, Salvador Dali, adopted Cadaqués as a home base, or that another celebrated artist, Marc Chagall, found his "blue paradise" at Tossa del Mar. In unspoiled spots along this coast, lovely vacation motifs still reign: boats painted green and blue—the favorite color of Catalonia—drawn up on the sandy beach, women mending nets, wine being sipped in small bars and inns.

Those in search of more historical glamor and *mondanité* will want to head inland to one of the provincial capital of Girona, the biggest city of Northern Catalonia (75,000 population), and an amazing palimpset of many ages and styles, symbolized by its cathedral, first built in splendid Romanesque, transformed in willowy Gothic, then overlaid in florid Catalan Baroque. Arab, Christian, and Jewish communities all lived side by side in Girona, so visitors can wander down arcaded alleyways and along the waters of the Onyar river to discover not only the cathedral complex but the Banys Arabs (Arab Baths) and El Call, the most fully preserved historic Jewish neighborhood in

Spain—all three are remnants of Girona's medieval Golden Age. A university town, Girona is also home to fashionable cafés, fine bookstores, and a full cultural calendar. Not far away to its north lies another cultural must-do: Figueres and its spectacular Teatre-Museu Dalí, the leading shrine to the region's most famous native son.

Heading back south, enjoy some of Catalonia's amazing variety of landscapes in the rugged Montseny hills or the eery, volcanic Garrotxa region. To the northwest of Barcelona lies the most venerated pilgrimage spot in Catalonia, the "serrated mountain" shrine that is Montserrat—monastery of the La Moreneta ("The Black Virgin") and legendarily the site where Parsifal found the Holy Grail. Montserrat is as memorable for its setting as for its religious treasures, so all visitors will want to explore its strange, pink hills, jagged peaks, and crests dotted with hermitages (with funiculars offering breathtaking views). Heading southwest you'll find several other historic spiritual sanctuaries, including the Cistercian monasteries of Santes Creus and Santa Maria de Poblet, characterized by monolithic Romanesque architecture and beautiful cloisters. More worldly pleasures await along the Costa Daurada (the "Golden Coast") in the smart resort town of Sitges, while a stop in the city of Tarragona will bear ultimate witness to Catalonia's 2,000-year-old history, thanks to its famous ancient Roman ruins. Whether you're out to just enjoy a sunbeam on the Costa Brava or want to track down the trail of the Roman Emperors, be sure to enjoy some Catalan blackberries with several fresh oranges squeezed over them. After all, it's a treat "of ambrosial sweetness" that even the ancient Roman author Avienus recommended.

Pleasures and Pastimes

Beaches

As you eagerly approach the water line a thrill of excitement runs through your body as the cool sea breeze suddenly hits you after a hot drive. Wafts of salty essences combine with aromatic woody smells as your feet edge into the water. Jagged rocky cliffs shimmer around you and the deep blue of the Mediterranean sea extends to the horizon as sailboats and windsurf boards cut through the swells. On one of Europe's most famous resort coastlines, your expectations have been met. The fact remains, however, that much of this "rugged" coast is not given over to first-class beaches but sharp ridges that jut out creating deep coves or headlands where pine forest reaches the very edge of the water. Seek and you shall find, however, extensive sand beaches: at Blanes and Lloret, around the Bay of Roses, plus many secluded expanses of sand where people can, if so disposed, bask in the sun, alone and undisturbed.

The southern stretch of the Costa Brava begins at Blanes with five different beaches that run from Punta Santa Anna on the far side of the port—a tiny cove with a pebbly beach at the bottom of a chasm encircled by towering cliffs, fragrant pines, and deep blue-green waters—to the 2½ km (1 ½ mi) long S'Abanell beach, which draws the crowds. Two kilometers (1 ½ mi) up the coast comes Santa Cristina, where there is nothing better than to break for lunch and to enjoy a succulent fish paella at one of the beach's three *chiringuitos* (makeshift beach restaurants under awnings), especially at Joan and Maria Riera's very popular establishment. Note that parking is available at many beaches; you pay a small fee of 600 ptas./€3.61 per day, slightly below the going rate that is around 200 ptas./€1.20 per hour.

If you want nothing between you and the sun, head to the *cala* (cove) near Lloret de Mar called Boadella and reserved for nudists. Given the heavy tourist build-up, the beach that stretches along the promenade is Lloret de Mar's main attraction, but it's usually packed and you'll probably have to put up with your neighbor's boom box. At the northern end of this strand is Sa Caleta, a cove that offers more sheltered swimming. On the twisting, turning, and scenic road between Lloret and Tossa de Mar is the small pristine Cala Morisca (Moorish Cove). The main beach at Tossa de Mar is the Platja Gran (Big Beach) in front of the town beneath the walls, and just next to it is Mar Menuda (Little Sea), where a part of the film *Pandora and the Flying Dutchman* was shot. Small, fat, colorfully painted fishing boats—maybe the same ones that caught your dinner, are pulled up onto the beach—heightening the charm.

Which are the best beaches of the Costa Brava? That depends on what you are looking for. However, if you see a blue flag flying at a beach, you know it has received the approval of the European Environmental Education Foundation. One obvious beach rule: the closer they are to town, the more crowded they will be. The most popular beaches—in terms of size and beachgoers—are those at Platja d'Aro, L'Estartit, Lloret de Mar, Tossa de Mar, and Roses. All of these these fly blue flags. But the secret is to get to those beaches where few, if any, people go, such as the Cala del Senyor Ramon, between Sant Feliu de Guíxols and Tossa de Mar, or Platja Castell in Palamós. Other out-of-the-way beaches are Cala Montjoy and Cala Jóncols between Roses and Cadaqués. Ask the locals or do your own exploring, and when you find a pristine spot with no one around, don't tell anybody. Just dive into the crystalline waters and enjoy.

Dining

Home to El Bulli (☞ Roses, *below*)—where super chef Ferran Adrià is masterminding one of the most talked-about kitchens in the world today—filled with luxurious hotels, and with more than 2,000 years of culinary tradition behind it, Catalonia is a foodie's delight. Critic Ferran Agulló once said, "Catalan cuisine is essentially natural; it is not expensive, and it is easy." Chefs hold that the success of the local cuisine comes not only from the quality of the ingredients but from its great variety, which stems from the fact that there are so many geographical differences in a relatively small area. Fish from the Mediterranean, produce from the farmlands of the interior, and the robust cooking of lamb and game of the Pyrenees mountains all mean that just about any good restaurant can offer an excitingly varied menu.

Though some will disagree, many people will say that what is generally recognized as the Catalan cuisine of today originated in Girona, in the *comarca* (county) of the Alt Empordà, at the Motel (now Hotel) Ampurdán in Figueres, by the hand of the great chef Josep Mercader. Beginning first with French-influenced or "Spanish" cuisine, Mercader then simplified and creatively transformed traditional Catalan cuisine. Ever since his establishment opened in 1961, Mercader's influence has been felt all over Spain, and many restaurants in Girona have incorporated his recipes. His son-in-law, Jaume Subirós, continues and expands on the legacy.

The dish that best defines this area is the *platillo*. Difficult to define, the word is actually Castilian in origin and means "little plate." Some say these dishes were based on poor cuts or leftovers simmered with fresh seasonal vegetables. From the kitchen of Mercader emerged recipes such as the *platillo de pollastres amb bolets* (chicken with mushrooms), a recipe that specifically calls for range-fed chickens that have led a "happy life." Others hold that slow cooking and dramatic combinations rather than poverty of ingredients defines the *platillo*. Other dishes to look for are *ànec amb peres* (duck with pears); *conill amb prunes* (rabbit with prunes); *sèpia amb verdures* (cuttlefish with vegetables); *pesols amb sèpia* (peas with cuttlefish); and *sèpia amb tripa de bacallà* (cuttlefish with cod innards). All can make for a hearty and stimulating meal.

That Catalan staple, *pa amb tomàquet,* deserves a special mention. This consists of thick slices of bread, sometimes toasted, on which open tomatoes are rubbed, leaving the inner pulp. Sprinkled with olive oil and lightly salted, *pa amb tomàquet* is served to accompany countless Catalan dishes, cold cuts, anchovies and herrings. Look for it.

Of course, you cannot come to the Costa Brava and not try the fish. One of the best things to order is *suquet.* Originally, suquet was a very simple dish that fishermen made on their boats with little more than oil, water, onions, green peppers, garlic tomatoes, potatoes, and whatever portion of the catch was too rough and plain for sale. Today, it's an upscale dish and everybody has his or her own opinion about who makes it best. At the Big Rock restaurant (☞ Platja d'Aro, *below*), Carles Camós is said to make a seminal version. A highly prized fish is the *llobarro* (sea bass), and is best eaten with as few complications as possible, preferably grilled with a sprinkling of fennel and a tangy mayonnaise to dip in. Catalan writer Josep Pla, who wrote extensively on Catalan cuisine, regularly visited his friend Josep Mercader at the Hotel Ampurdán. Even in his dotage he could be seen ensconced at a table in the dining room of the hotel, beret perched on his head, shoveling flaky sea bass with fennel into his mouth, a half-filled bottle of Rioja claret wine by his wrist.

In December restaurants serve *El Niu* (the nest), a local casserole featuring cod, hake, cuttlefish, egg, and potatoes. From February through March the specialty is sea urchins, those spiny little creatures that cause excruciating pain when you step on one at the beach—but allow you to get back at them by eating their delicate pungent coral innards. A serving of a dozen sea urchins in a bar can cost 2,000 pesetas. However, over-fishing is threatening the sea urchin's survival (as many as 25,000 are pulled from the sea each week in winter-spring) and the Generalitat, the autonomous government of Catalonia, has been called upon to take measures for its protection. Whatever you opt for, follow the suggestions of the maitre d', who knows what is best back in the kitchen. Keep an eye out for the season of the year when you order and be ready for surprises on your palate—especially if you're lucky enough to snag a table at El Bullí.

CATEGORY	COST*
$$$$	over 6,000 ptas./€36.06
$$$	4,000–6,000 ptas./€24.04–36.06
$$	2,500–4,000 ptas./€15.03–24.04
$	under 2,500 ptas./€15.03
*per person for a three-course meal, excluding drinks, service, and tax		

Fiestas

Each town or village in Catalonia celebrates its yearly *Festa Major,* or festival, in honor of its patron saint. The dates of these festivities will vary but many of them are held at the height or end of summer. They are richly celebrated with dances, parades, athletic events, religious services, and general fun-making. The leading festivals, however, are the *verbenes,* the festivities of the Eves of St. John and St. Peter, on June 24 and 29, celebrated with thunderous fireworks and roaring bonfires that send flames leaping up high into the night sky, followed by riotous dancing till dawn. The biggest *verbena* welcomes the eve of *Sant Joan* (St. John) on June 24, or Midsummer Night's Eve. This celebration recalls the ancient pagan festivities of the summer solstice and the agricultural cycle of the birth and rebirth of the year. Nearly every town throws a party on this night and there are hundreds of private ones you just might get yourself invited to. Bring a bottle of *cava* (the native bubbly) and you'll be more than welcome. Just a few days later, June 29, is *Sant Pere* (St. Peter), the patron saint of fishermen. The fishermen of Roses invite all and sundry to a *suquet* (fish and potato soup) fueled with plenty of cold rosé wine.

Easter is the time for religious processions and performances, some dating back to the Middle Ages. A chilling reminder of the transience of life is the *Dansa de la Mort* (Dance of Death), on Holy Thursday (the Thursday before Easter Sunday) at Verges, 25 km (15 mi) south of Figueres. Men and boys dressed as skeletons maneuver eerily through the streets to the ominous beat of the drum. In the city of Girona, and other places, groups of men known as *manayes* dress up in uniforms of the Roman Legion and parade in military formation escorting the religious processions.

Lodging

Lodging on the Costa Brava ranges from the finest, most sophisticated hotels to spartan *pensions* that are no more than a place to sleep and change clothes between disco and beach. The better accomodations are usually well situated and have a splendid view of the seascape. There are plenty of comfortable hotels with no pretentions that offer a perfectly adequate stopover, rooms and dining included. If you are looking for quiet isolation, head inland and stay at one of the old reconverted *masies* (farmhouses) that are becoming increasingly popular and sought after. They are severely elegant and offer the highest luxury. If you intend on visiting during the high season (i.e., July and August), be sure to book reservations in advance at almost any hotel in this area, especially the Costa Brava, which remains one of the most popular summer resorts in Spain.

CATEGORY	COST*
$$$$	over 16,500 ptas./€99.17
$$$	9,500–16,500 ptas./€57.10–99.17
$$	6,000–9,500 ptas./€36.06–57.10
$	under 6,000 ptas./€36.06

All prices are for a standard double room, excluding service and tax.

✒ *following the text of a review is your signal that the property has a Web site, where you will find details and, usually, images; for a link, visit www.fodors.com/urls.*

Exploring Catalonia: The Costa Brava to Tarragona

Located in the northeast corner of the Iberian Peninsula, Catalonia spreads out north, south, and west of the city of Barcelona, over four provinces: Tarragona, Barcelona, and Girona—which run from south to north along the coastline of the Mediterranean Sea—and Lleida, which is landlocked. These four provinces are, in turn, subdivided into *co-marques,* or counties—for example, the Alt (upper) and Baix (lower) Empordà, in the upper northeast part of the province of Girona, both famed for their landscape and cuisine, are the names of two such co-marques. The capital is centered in Barcelona province, while just a day trip away (no destination is more than a five-hour excursion by bus) are a dazzling variety of sights. Moving north to Girona province you'll find both the Costa Brava—Spain's answer to the Cote d'Azur and the Amalfi Coast—and the historic city of Girona. To the west lies

Lleida province (mostly covered in Chapter 4), while Tarragona province is the most southerly, famous for its city of Tarragona.

A modern road network and an efficient railroad system connect the country from north to south and east to west. The A7 highway, which is a tollway, runs north from Barcelona to Girona, and south to Tarragona. To head west towards Lleida, and on to Madrid, you take the A7 south and turn west on to the A2 at L'Arboç. To get to Montserrat you take the A18. From Barcelona there are trains north and south along the coast and west inland. From the metropolis you can also drive just about anywhere in Catalonia in less than one day, even to the higher reaches of the Pyrenees mountains, but to get a good impression of the countryside a trip of several days is advisable. Catalonia is a geographically undulating country with a few interspersed mountain ranges such as the Montseny, just north of Barcelona; only the Pyrenees mountains are especially rugged. Here, roads twist and turn, and to get anywhere takes considerable time.

Numbers in the text correspond to numbers in the margin and on the Catalonia: Costa Brava to Tarragona map.

Great Itineraries

If you're out to explore Catalonia, who can resist waking up in Barcelona and not heading first to the Costa Brava? A trip up the coast will allow you to see a representative amount of Catalonia and get a real taste of the country. If you go all the way up to Port Bou at the French border you will have covered about half of the Catalan coastline. Five days is more than enough time to exhaustively discover the coast and have a full feast of the Costa Brava's fine beaches and coves before heading back to Barcelona or heading inland or out of Spain into France. If you decide to head south from Barcelona and visit the monasteries of Santes Creus and Poblet, Sitges, and Tarragona, the trip will be just as satisfying.

IF YOU HAVE 3 DAYS

Starting from Barcelona, the major urban area with the best communication links, make your first stop in the central Costa Brava at ⛨ **Tossa de Mar** ③, with its picturesque walled medieval town perched next to the sea. On your second day, drive inland and explore ⛨ **Girona** ㉑–㉚, with its Gothic cathedral and Jewish Quarter that still preserves an ancient atmosphere. On day three drive north to **Figueres** ⑲ and visit the Salvador Dalí Museum. Lunch at one of the town's many choice gourmet restaurants, and in the evening you can get back to Barcelona in under two hours down the A7 highway.

IF YOU HAVE 10 DAYS

With a week, you can contemplate seeing most of Catalonia's highlights. With the Costa Brava as your first destination, head out from Barcelona for the boisterous frenzy of ⛨ **Lloret de Mar** ②. Once that's out of your system, continue north the second morning along the coast taking in the charm of the many small *cales* (coves) along the way. Spend that night in walled and towered ⛨ **Tossa de Mar** ③, feasting at one of its fine seafood restaurants.For your third day journey inland to ⛨ **La Bisbal** ⑩ to check out its pottery and antiques stores and perhaps have lunch at the medieval village of Peratallada and staying at one of the ancient farmhouses-turned-luxury-hotels of the area such as Mas Torrent; a trip over to the Iberian ruins of **Ullastret** ⑪ is recommended.On the fourth morning, cruise along the coast to the stunning headland of Cap de Begur, the town of **L'Escala** ⑫, and the town of ⛨ **Roses** ⑯ on its famed bay. Make a must-stop at the Greek ruins of **Empúries** ⑬. Spend the fifth night in arty ⛨ **Cadaqués** ⑰ to savor the atmo-

Catalonia: The Costa Brava to Tarragona

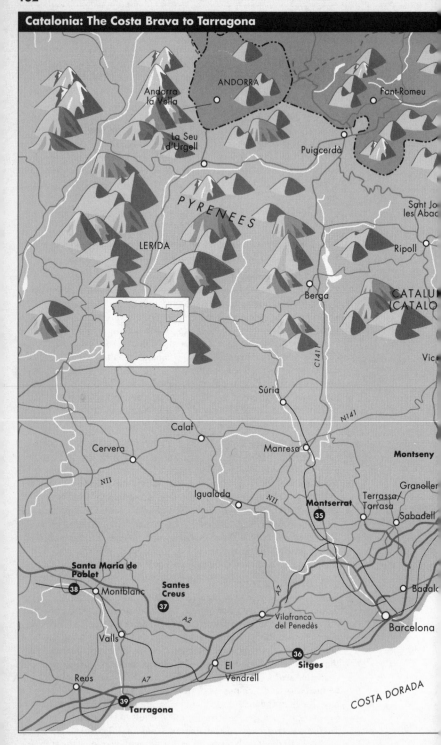

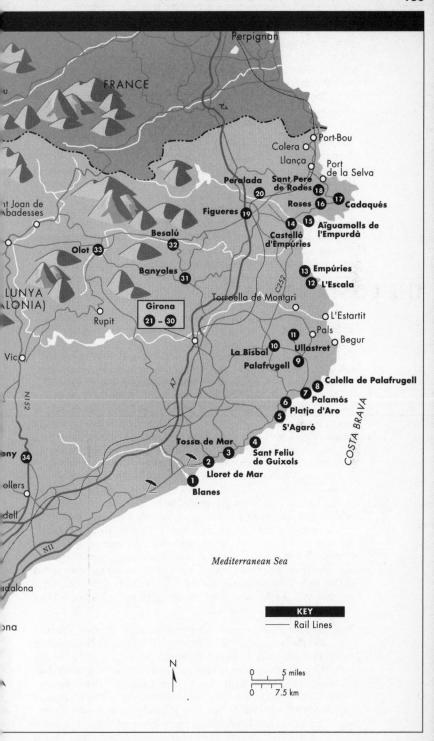

Perpignan

FRANCE

Port-Bou

Colera

Llança

Port
de la Selva

Peralada

Sant Pere
de Rodes

18

20

Roses

16

17 Cadaqués

Figueres

19

14

15 Aïguamolls de
l'Empurdà

Castelló
d'Empúries

Besalú

32

Olot **33**

Banyoles

31

13 Empúries

12 L'Escala

Torroella de Montgri

L'Estartit

Girona

21 – **30**

Rupit

Pals

Begur

11

Ullastret

La Bisbal **10**

9

Palafrugell

8 Calella de Palafrugell

7

Palamós

6

5 Platja d'Aro

S'Agaró

Tossa de Mar

4

3

Sant Feliu
de Guixols

2

34

Lloret de Mar

1

Blanes

Mediterranean Sea

COSTA BRAVA

KEY

— Rail Lines

N

0   5 miles

0   7.5 km

Vic

St Joan de
Abadesses

CATALUNYA
(CATALONIA)

N152

sphere that inspired Pablo Picasso and Salvador Dalí. On the sixth day, stop in **Figueres** ⑲, to visit the Dalí museum; then head south to the picturesque, history-rich city of ⛫ **Girona** ㉑- ㉚, worth a two-night stay. On the morning of the eighth day, get on highway A7 and point several hours south to sojourn in ⛫ **Tarragona** ㊴, visiting its extraordinary Roman ruins. On your ninth morning, head to the seaside resort of ⛫ **Sitges** ㊱. On your tenth day, before returning to Barcelona, recover from your tour by searching for peace and tranquility at the Benedictine monastery of **Montserrat** ㉟.

When to Tour Catalonia

Any time of the year is suitable to enjoy the beauty of the Costa Brava, but let's be honest: you want to do some serious sunning and swim in the Mediterranean Sea. Starting in June, the weather gets warm enough to take that first dip in the sea, though the water will still be cold. The weather keeps getting warmer until it peaks with torrid temperatures in late July and most of August. Late summer and early fall are perfect times to enjoy the Catalan bounty of seasonal mushrooms and game. Winters are usually brisk but stimulating and will offer many opportunities for taking long walks and visiting the cultural sights.

THE COSTA BRAVA

Fierce, virile, beautiful, pagan—but never dull—the Costa Brava is one of Spain's most bewitching places. The name means "rugged coast," a description first coined by Catalan writer Ferran Agulló Agull in 1905 and belied by its hospitality to visitors as one of Europe's most magnificently scenic coastlines, but not by its terrain, indented and capriously sketched with innumerable coves and little creeks, or *cales*. This is not a rectilineal coast, flat and sandy, where the ocean is allowed to break in all its fury. Hundreds of bays and peninsulas calm the waters before they hit land, allowing fishermen to make a living and also, in centuries gone by, Corsair pirates to gain plunder. When pirates plied the Mediterranean in the 16th and 17th centuries and threatened the Catalan coast, towns (carefully blended into the landscape as protective coloration) were built inland away from danger and the coastline was all but deserted. This threat was real. Miguel de Cervantes, the author of *Don Quixote,* was captured by Barbary pirates in 1575 and held for five years in Algiers (recent scholarship has concluded that he was captured on the Costa Brava's Bay of Roses). Today, of course, the only pirates are hotel owners, who make fortunes every summer from the bus loads of tour groups that swamp the Costa in high season. The coastline has triumphed: you can see a clear example of this at Port de la Selva, where the ancient village of Selva de Mar is several miles away from the coast while its fishing village of Port de la Selva has become the main attraction.

This Costa Brava is a comparatively recent discovery. The first "tourists" arrived at the beginning of the 20th century: well-to-do families from Barcelona, who came to escape the oven temperatures of the big city by bathing along the shore in best Victorian fashion. This *villegiature di Barcelona* was trailed, in turn, by artists and bohemians. Picasso, Marc Chagall, Santiago Rusiñol, and Salvador Dalí all came and were swiftly conquered by the coast's natural beauty as much as by the personal "handsomeness" of its inhabitants—Tossa del Mar once boasted a large colony of artists drawn by its Greek-profiled villagers—and the regional traditions. Today, different types of tourism have developed along the Costa Brava, one style aimed at mass tourism, at meccas like Lloret de Mar and Roses, one style found at more selective, family-oriented ports of call like Cadaqués and Tossa de Mar.

Ascending the coast of Northern Catalonia's Girona province—ranging from Blanes (40 mi north of Barcelona) to Portbou near the border with France—the Costa Brava is an unbroken series of inlets, bays, and coves, where a landscape of lush deep-green mountains serves as a backdrop to the rocky shore and aquamarine foreground of the coast and sandy beaches, many dotted by modern tourist developments. Inland, there is more tranquility with small towns and villages that remain relatively untouched. The landscape is one of carefully tended fields and orchards, vineyards and olive groves, and rolling, tree-covered hills. Here and there small fortified towns are a reminder of the age and turbulent history of these places that goes back to the Middle Ages or beyond and quickly inform the visitor why Catalonia acquired its name from the ancient Latin word, *Castellum*.

Setting out from Barcelona, it's not complicated to get to the Costa Brava or around the province of Girona. By road, take highway A7 north from Barcelona in the direction of France and get off at different exits depending on your final destination. You can also take national road N-II north, but it is heavily traveled, especially in the summer. The railroad travels north to the French border. Direct trains only stop at major towns. If you want to get off at a small town, be sure to take a local train; or take a fast direct train to, let's say, Girona, and wait for a local to go by.

Blanes

❶ *60 km (37 mi) north of Barcelona, 45 km (28 mi) south of Girona.*

The southernmost outpost of the Costa Brava, Blanes was first settled by Iberian tribes, followed by the ancient Romans. The town's **castle of Sant Joan,** on a mountain overlooking the town, goes back at least to the 11th century. The watchtower along the coastline was built in the 16th century to protect against incursions by Barbary pirates. If you fast-forward to the 20th century, you'll learn that Blanes was a flourishing town before the tourism boom of the late 1950s, with light industry (especially textiles) and a large fishing fleet. But its long beaches—the most southern of the Girona province—and adjacent coves, were just too perfect to be passed up by northern Europeans flocking to Spain in search of fine weather and low prices. Today, many travelers give the working port of Blanes a miss, but it's a must-do for greenthumbers, thanks to the presence of two celebrated botanical gardens, which attract more than 300,000 visitors each year. Terrace upon terrace of strange and exotic plants grip the steeply slanting hillside above

★ the sea at **Marimurtra,** the garden created by the German Karl Faust in 1928. It boasts more than 7,000 species, with the collection of cacti from the arid regions of South Africa and Central America especially notable. Poisonous, medicinal, and aromatic plants, ferns, evergreen, cork, and kermes or scarlet oak, conifers and vineyards, flourish in lush variety. ✉ *Jardí Botànic Marimurtra, Pg. Karl Faust, 10,* ☎ *972/ 330826.* ✇ *350 ptas./€2.10.* ☉ *Daily Apr.–Oct. 9–6; Nov.–Mar. 10– 5; weekends 10–2.*

★ The second famous botanical garden in Blanes is **Pinya de Rosa,** with some 4,000 species. Created in 1945 by industrial engineer Dr. Fernando Riviere de Caralt at the foot of the sea, it is noted for its collection of cacti (some as tall as 15 m), aloe, century, and yucca plants. American botanists consider its collection of more than 600 species of *Opuntia* (prickly pear) one of the finest in the world. In recognition for his contribution to botany, Dr. Caralt de Riviere's name was given to several discoveries of plant species, around the world, such as the *Aloe* *rivierei* discovered in North Yemen. ⊠ *Jardí Botànic Pinya de Rosa, Platja de Santa Cristina,* ☎ *972/355290.* ⌨ *350 ptas./€2.10.* ☉ *Daily 9–6.*

The summer event in Blanes that everyone waits for is the fireworks competition, held every night (at 10:30) from July 21 to 27, and coinciding with the town's yearly festival. The fireworks are launched over the water from a rocky outcropping in the middle of the seaside promenade known as Sa Palomera, while people watch from the beach and surrounding area as more gunpowder is burned in a half hour than at the battle of Trafalgar.

Launches (⊠ Crucetours, located on the harborfront, ☎ 972/372692 or 629/794-845) can take you up the coast to neighboring towns and beaches from May to the end of September.

Lloret de Mar

❷ *10 km (6 mi) north of Blanes, 67 km (42 mi) north of Barcelona, 43 km (27 mi) south of Girona.*

The Costa Brava officially begins at Lloret de Mar, but one look at it and you might be tempted to head back to Barcelona. Fairly destroyed by an attack of concretitis, the town is filled with tower hotels that fill with thousands of young people on a tight budget out to drink, dance, and work on a tan. Of course, if that is what you are looking for, this is the place. Swamped by faux English pubs and echt German biergartens, the town is now trying to give itself a face-lift: the old, white-elephant San Francisco hotel is slated for demolition, new pedestrian zones are on the drawing board, sidewalks are to be widened, and power and telephone lines to be buried. This will all help the town's cultural sites to be more prominent, including the Iberian ruins at Turó Rodó and the medieval castle of Sant Joan (both slated to be rehabilitated).

Two scenic delights lie on the outskirts of town. Between Blanes and Lloret is **Santa Cristina,** a sheltered sandy cove with an 18th-century chapel amidst soaring pine and eucalyptus trees that grow to the shore. One of the allegorical mural paintings by Joaquín Sorolla entitled *Catalunya* (on view at the Hispanic Society of America in New York City), was purportedly modeled in part on this landscape. Every July there is a pilgrimage by boat to the chapel.

In addition to the two botanical gardens at Blanes (☞ *above*), Lloret is home to the **Jardins de Santa Clotilde.** These were designed in 1919 by architect Nicolau Maria Rubió i Tudurí and are characterized by an emphasis on plants—flower lovers should look elsewhere. ⊠ *Ctra. de Blanes, Km 652,* ☎ *972/364735.* ⌨ *500 ptas./€3.01.* ☉ *Daily July–Oct. 4–8; Nov.–June 10–noon, 4–7.*

Dining and Lodging

$$$$ ✕▥ **Roger de Flor.** Resembling a dignified private villa, this much-enlarged older hotel stands out from the cookie-cutter concrete piles of Lloret. On the eastern edge of town, the hotel offers the finest panoramic views of any hotel in the vicinity (especially from its L'Estelat restaurant). Its gardens—set with a pool filled with pumped-in saltwater—are filled with geraniums, bougainvillea, and palms, and add an elegant touch to the combinations of traditional and contemporary architecture. The high-ceilinged, modern bedrooms are simple yet comfortable. ⊠ *Turó de l'Estelat, Apartat 66, 17320,* ☎ *972/364800,* ̄FAX̄ *972/ 371637. 87 rooms. Restaurant, pool, 2 tennis courts. AE, DC, MC, V. Closed Nov.–Mar.*

Nightlife

The top disco in town (although, at this writing, perhaps not the hottest), is the **St. Trop** (⊠ Baixada de la Riera 16, ☎ 972/365051).

Tossa de Mar

❸ *11 km (6mi) north of Lloret de Mar, 80 km (50 mi) north of Barcelona, 41 km (25 mi) south of Girona.*

Set around a blue buckle of a bay, Tossa del Mar is a symphony in two parts: the *Vila Vella,* or the Old Town—a knotted warren of steep, narrow, cobblestoned streets with many restored buildings (some dating back to the 14th century)—and the *Vila Nova,* or the New Town. The former is encased in medieval walls and towers, which can be rivaled only by those of Tarragona (☞ *below*), but the New Town is open to the sea and is itself a lovely district threaded by 18th-century lanes. Girdling the Old Town, located on the Cap de Tossa promontory that juts out into the sea, the 12th-century walls and towers at water's edge are Tossa's pride and joy, considered the only example of a fortified medieval town on the entire Catalan coast. Things may have changed since the days when Marc Chagall, the famous artist who vacationed here for four decades, called this his "blue paradise" and Ava Gardner arrived to film the Hollywood extravaganza, *Pandora and the Flying Dutchman,* but all in all, this beautiful village retains much of the magic of the unspoiled Costa Brava.

The Romans knew a good place when they saw it, as Turissa's (the name they gave Tossa del Mar) famous ancient villa, uncovered in 1914, proves. At *Els Ametllers* ("the almond trees"), near the back of the town and bounded on one side by Av. Pelegrí, are located the ruins of the **Vila Romana,** which include an oil press, warehouses, and several rooms with magnificent mosaic pavements (one of which bears the owner's name: *Salve Vitale*). Additional discoveries revealed a sunken swimming pool, a hot-air heating system, and a monumental fountain—all indications this family lived in imperial luxury. Unfortunately, the villa is still being excavated and is not open to public view; to see many of the excavated finds, however, visit the Museu Municipal, housed in a 12th-century Batlle palace; in addition to ancient Roman objects and mosaics, the museum has paintings by 19th-century Catalan painters and by Marc Chagall, Foujita, Masson, and others. ⊠ *Museu Municipal de Tossa de Mar, Placa del Pintor Roig i Soler 1,* ☎ *972/340709.* ⊡ *500 ptas./€3.01.* ☉ *Mid-June–mid-Sept., daily 10–10; mid-Sept.–mid-June, Tues.–Sun. 10–1:30 and 4–7.*

Hollywood buffs recall that the 1951 film chestnut, *Pandora and the Flying Dutchman*—directed by Albert Lewin and starring Ava Gardner, James Mason, and Spanish bullfighter Mario Cabrera (for whom Ava famously dumped Frank Sinatra)—was filmed in and around Tossa de Mar, called Puerto Esperanza in the film. The film opens with several fishermen speaking Catalan and pulling in a net with an unusual catch—the entwined bodies of a man and a woman. The ensuing film is a surrealistic fantasy about a man condemned for former sins to sail the seas eternally until he finds a woman who is willing to give her life for him. Brilliantly filmed in color, the movie left its mark on Tossa (50 years later there are still villagers who had bit parts or were extras in the movie, considered a sort of special fraternity). Tossa even has a statue to Ava Gardner on a terrace of the town's medieval walls, said to be a favorite spot of hers while she was making the film. What is compelling today about the film, however, are the location scenes on the then untouched, unblemished Costa Brava.

The main bus station (the local tourist office is conveniently located here) is on Plaça de les Nacions Sense Estat. Take Av. Ferrán and Avinguda Costa Brava to head down the slope to the waterfront and the Old Town, which is entered by the Torre de les Hores, and head to the Vila Vella's heart, the Gothic Church of Sant Vicenç. Then just saunter around and take a dip in the Middle Ages.

Dining and Lodging

$$$$ ✕ **La Cuina de Can Simon.** This elegantly rustic restaurant right beside Tossa del Mar's old walled city serves an elaborate, traditional cuisine with very up-to-date touches. The service is exquisite—when you first sit down you are served a complementary glass of *cava* and an apéritif; at dinner's end, tasty little pastries accompany coffee. ⊠ *Portal 24,* ☎ *972/341269. AE, DC, MC, V. Closed Jan. and Mon., except June 15–Sept. No dinner Sun.*

$$$ ✕ **Bahia.** Run for many years by sorely missed Camil.la Cruañas, who worked tirelessly to make the Costa Brava a hospitable destination for visitors, this place has long been an institution, with wonderful down-home cooking. Dishes such as *sim-i-tomba* (a kind of *suquet* typical of Tossa), brandade of cod, and great desserts were all revelations. Her recent passing away has left the restaurant in the hands of her sons who continue the tradition. ⊠ *Passeig del Mar 19,* ☎ *972/340322. AE, DC, MC, V.*

$$$$ 🏨 **Gran Hotel Reymar.** Built in the "Rationalist" style in the 1960s on
★ a spectacular rocky promontory at the edge of the sea—and just a 10-minute walk from the historic walls of the Old Town—this hotel's graceful lines contrast with the jagged rocks of its setting. Completely renovated in the 1990s, it has a fairly dazzling array of restaurants and bars. Rooms have satellite TV, marble-covered bathrooms, fine modern furniture, and seafront balconies. ⊠ *Platja de Mar Menuda s/n, 17320,* ☎ *972/340312,* 🆁🅰🆇 *972/341504. 166 rooms. 4 restaurants, 3 bars, 2 pools, tennis court, nightclub. AE, DC, MC, V. Closed Nov.–Apr.*

$$$ 🏨 **Hotel Diana.** Built by a disciple of the great Catalan architect Antoni Gaudí, this has a stunning Art Nouveau fireplace (which fetchingly incorporates a bust by Ferderic Marés of the wife of the man who originally built this villa)—one of the finest places on the Costa to cozy up with a glass of sherry and while the early evening away. Overlooking a beach, the hotel also features an enticing inner courtyard—a lush garden filled with palm trees, flowers, fountains, and many of the hotel's guests. ⊠ *Plaça de Espanya 6, 17320,* ☎ *972/341886,* 🆁🅰🆇 *972/341886. 21 rooms. AE, DC, MC, V. Closed Nov.–Apr.*

$$ 🏨 **Hotel Capri.** Maria Eugènia Serrat, who is a native Tossan, will pamper you at her small 22-room family hotel. Set on the beach in front of the town, with the medieval walls looming on the right, the hotel has a super location. Rooms are simply but elegantly decorated. ⊠ *Passeig del Mar 17, 17320,* ☎ *972/340358,* 🆁🅰🆇 *972/341552. 22 rooms. DC, MC, V. Closed Nov.–Mar.* 🍃

$$ 🏨 **Hotel Sant March.** This family hotel in the center of town, run by Francesc Zucchitello, is just two minutes from the beach. His wife and mother-in-law care for an interior garden that is the envy of many. All rooms open the garden—making for a much-appreciated oasis of tranquility in a sometimes hectic town. ⊠ *Av. del Pelegrí 2, 17320,* ☎ *972/ 340078,* 🆁🅰🆇 *972/342534. 29 rooms. DC, MC, V. Closed Oct.–Mar.* 🍃

Sant Feliu de Guíxols

④ *23 km (14 mi) north of Tossa de Mar, 100 km (62 mi) north of Barcelona, 37 km (23 mi) southeast of Girona.*

The next spot up the coast from Tossa del Mar is Sant Feliu de Guíxols, a fishing and shipping town set in a small bay. Handsome modernist mansions line the seafront promenade, recalling the town's former wealth from the cork industry. In front of the promenade there is an arching beach of fine white sand that leads around to the fishing harbor at its north end. Behind the promenade, a well-preserved old quarter of narrow streets and squares leads to a 10th-century gateway with horseshoe arches—all that remains of a pre-Romanesque monastery; nearby, a church still stands which combines Romanesque, Gothic, and Baroque styles. Here you will find the **Museu d'Història de la Ciutat** that exhibits local archaeological finds and displays on the cork and fishing industries.

Indeed, the next time you open a bottle of vintage champagne, you might say a little prayer for this venerable town. Surrounded by dark-green cork forests (as is much of northeastern Catalonia), it first found its place in the sun in the 17th century when French abbott Dom Pérignon, on a trip to the Benedictine monastery of Sant Pere de Rodes, 64 km (40 mi) north of here, discovered that the properties of cork allow it to contain the high pressure that builds up inside a champagne bottle. Before long, the cork forests of this town became famous, with the stripped bark of the cork oak (*quercus suber*) used to make cork stoppers (and other products such as insulation). Before the Dom's discovery, hemp plugs soaked in oil or wooden bungs had been used. At first, corks were made by hand, with each cork cut to shape by a craftsman (paid at a piecework rate, it was a good job and cork makers enjoyed a certain social standing). Eventually, of course, power-driven blades and punches took over, but not before founding the fortunes of many Sant Feliu de Guíxols residents. Vineyards, a staple crop in the Mediterranean region, were another important source of income, but the onset in the 19th century of the phylloxera germ caused an economic crisis and many *ganxons* (or natives of Sant Feliu de Guíxols), headed for America, especially New Orleans. Learn more about the town's cork and shipping trades at the **Museu d'Història,** which has interesting displays. ⊠ *Carrer Abadia s/n,* ☎ *972/821575.* ▭ *Free.* ☉ *Tues.–Sun. 11–2; June–Sept. 5–8, Oct.–May 6–9.*

Dining

\$\$ ✕ **Eldorado Petit.** This is the best restaurant in Sant Feliu de Guíxols and serves exquisite fish, with a grill-bar offering simpler, less expensive versions next door. Lluís Cruanyes is the chef. His philosophy is a winner: start with a good product and confuse it as little as possible. The restaurant was built thirty years ago, designed by furniture designer Jaume Tresserra, and today looks just as handsome as it did then. Start with sea cucumber with chantarelles and *ceps* sprinkled with garlic and parsley, followed by oven-baked sole with rosemary and potatoes. ⊠ *Rambla Vidal 23,* ☎ *972/321818. AE, DC, MC, V. Closed mid-Nov. and Wed. (Oct.–May).*

S'Agaró

★ ❺ *3 km (2 mi) north of Sant Feliu, 103 km (64 mi) north of Barcelona, 42 km (26 mi) south of Girona.*

S'Agaró is one of the Costa Brava's most elegant clusters of villas and seaside mansions, built up around S'Agaro Vell, a fashionably private development that often hosted the likes of John Wayne and Cole Porter. Set by the sea, S'Agaro itself offers a particularly delightful promenade walk along the sea wall from La Gavina—the noted hotel (☞ *below*), which presides over the community of S'Agaro Vell—to Sa Conca beach. S'Agaró Vell is one of the earliest examples in Spain of a tourist resort designed specifically as such. Located at the beach of Sant Pol, it was designed by poet and architect Rafael Masó i Valentí following to the fashionable style of the time known as *Noucentisme*—an alluring 1920s riff on the neoclassic style. The promoter was the visionary Josep Ensesa, son of a wealthy Girona industrialist who made his fortune in flour, and who, in the 1920s, created S'Agaró Vell as a luxury residential resort aimed exclusively at the pleasures of summer. Today, more than 50 homes—all designed in the well-proportioned, subdued lines that *Noucentisme* derived from Greek and Roman classical architecture—have been built; however, each abode cannot deviate from the basic style established by Masó.

Dining and Lodging

$$$$ ✕⊡ **L'Hostal de la Gavina.** The guestbook here is littered with famous
★ names, most of whom enjoyed their stay (Cole Porter broke into song in the lobby one early morning). These big rollers followed in the wake of young upper-class couples from Barcelona who began spending their honeymoons here in the 1930s (at least according to Catalan historian Glòria Soler's book on the tradition of summering in Catalonia, *L'Estiueig a Catalunya 1900–1950*. Inside the compound of S'Agaró Vell, on the eastern corner of Sant Pol beach, this hotel is a superb display of design and cuisine opened in 1932 by Josep Ensesa. On a clear summer evening its seven-arched loggia overlooking the sea is almost sublime. If you want complete comfort, superb dining, and tennis, golf, and riding nearby, and the last remnants of Costa Brava chic, stay here. ⊠ *Plaça de la Rosaleda s/n, 17248,* ☎ *972/321100,* ℻ *972/321573. 57 rooms, 17 suites. Restaurant. AE, DC, MC, V.*

Platja d'Aro

❻ *3 km (2 mi) north of Sant Feliu, 102 km (63 mi) north of Barcelona, 39 km (24 mi) southeast of Girona.*

Platja d'Aro has three kilometers of splendid beach to recommend it, though it is heavily built up. Like many other places on the coast, it was a knot of fishing shacks attached to the inland main town of Castell d'Aro, but tourist development did away with that.

Dining

$$$ ✕ **Big Rock.** One of the finest restaurants on the Catalan coast and very
★ reasonably priced, this is the domain of chef Carles Camós. Big Rock's cuisine is market-based and simple. It has a very popular fixed menu for 3,750 ptas./€22.54 that lets you choose from 20 entrées and 20 main dishes (and includes wine, dessert, and coffee), but everyone winds up ordering the *suquet* (Catalan fish and potato soup)—as famed food writer Coleman Andrews states in his book *Catalan Cuisine,* Camós sets the benchmark for this dish (for more on this dish, *see* Dining *in* Pleasures and Pastimes, *above*). ⊠ *Barri de Fanals 5,* ☎ *972/818012. AE, DC, MC, V. Closed Mon. and Dec. 25–Feb. No dinner Sun.*

$$ ✕ **Cal Rei.** In a 14th-century farmhouse in the neighboring village of Castell d'Aro, this spot serves a cuisine based on products bought at the market. Start with the zucchini pie with cream of cheese, then be sure to order the oven-baked cod. ⊠ *Barri de Crota 3,* ☎ *972/817925. AE, DC, MC, V. Closed Mon. in Jan.*

Nightlife

As a built-up center, Platja d'Aro has numerous nightclubs and discos. **Pach** (⊠ Avenida Sagar 179, ☎ 972/817637) is one of the most popular choices. The crowds also head to the **Paladium** (⊠ Barri Casavella s/n, ☎ 972/819152).

Palamós

❼ *109 km (68 mi) north of Barcelona, 46 km (29 mi) southeast of Girona.*

Facing south, Palamós is a working harbor town sited on a headland that protects it from the prevailing north wind. The town was founded in 1277 by the king of Aragon, Peter II, as a royal port, and the old quarter remains well-preserved, although its large walls (built in the 16th century as protection against pirates, including the notorious Turk Barbarossa) are no longer extant. With the second-largest fishing fleet on the Costa Brava, the **fish market** of Palamós is highly esteemed, its shrimp traditionally prized. Sleek sea bass, gargoyle-ish angler fish, hefty grouper, and colorful rock fish are auctioned at the local fish market, an exciting place to be in the early evening when the fishing boats begin to come in around six o'clock. If you would like to see what the Costa Brava looked liked before development, visit the beach

★ of **Castell** near Palamós. As the road to the beach emerges from a thick green Mediterranean forest of evergreen oak, pine, and spiny underbrush you are greeted by 250 m (280 yds) of wide sandy beach. At one end are several fishing shacks, with a couple of *xiringuitos* (makeshift restaurants under awnings) scattered along the beach. With no other buildings, let alone apartments or hotel in sight, it's no wonder Castell has been praised for its scenic beauty: American novelist Robert Ruark said of Castell, "There is no place in all the world with as much beauty and tranquility."

On the southern end of the beach overlooking the cove is **Mas Juny**, the (still privately owned) farmhouse that once belonged to Josep Maria Sert (1874–1945), the Catalan mural painter who was one of the most acclaimed painters of the 1930s and 1940s. With the money he received for decorating New York City's Waldorf-Astoria hotel he bought Mas Juny in 1929 for his 20-year-old, third wife, Rousadana (Roussy) Mdivani, of White Russian descent, and transformed this typical Catalan stone farmhouse into an elegant retreat. The Serts gave extravagant parties here, drawing the likes of Barbara Hutton, Marlene Dietrich, Baron Rothschild, and Coco Chanel. At the northern end of the beach, atop the rocky promontory of Agulla (Needle) del Castell, there are extensive partially excavated Iberian ruins. Unlike other Iberian remains that have been uncovered in urban settings, these are set in the natural habitat where these people lived 2,600 years ago.

Hidden in the woods behind the beach is a studio that painter Salvador Dalí designed and had built. It has an irregularly shaped door and is known as **La Barraca de la Porta Torta** ("the shack with the crooked door"). This small shack will be renovated in the future and incorporated into the Dalí route (Figueres, Port Lligat, and Púbol).

Recently, by public vote, the Catalan government purchased a part of the Castell area declared the Castell area as a "place of natural interest" with an eye to keeping developers out. To get there, take the road north from Palamós to Palafrugell and turn right to the beach about 2 km (1 mi) from town. This will bring you there in a few minutes. Arrive early as it gets crowded during the summer.

Calella de Palafrugell

❽ *120 km (74 mi) north of Barcelona, 44 km (27 mi) east of Girona.*

A pretty fishing village that still keeps some of its original charm, Calella de Palafrugell is especially popular for its July *habanera* song festival. With an arcaded seafront—called *Les Voltes* (the vaults)—and with fishing boats pulled up onto the beach, this is but the first of a series of small *cales* (coves) set with tiny fishing villages offering secluded places to bath, all worth a stop, if only to imagine what the Costa Brava was like before the tourist boom set in; other cales include Sa Riera, Aiguablava, Sa Tuna, Tamariu, and Llafranc. The sheer cliffs, transparent waters, and abounding vegetation found in this region make this the Costa Brava at its most quintessential.

Evidence of the isolation of this stretch of the coast is its own "language." Travelers will note the feminine article "Sa" or masculine "Es," as in Sa Riera or Es Pianc, in front of many place-names of the area—a feature of the *salat,* or salty, Catalan variant spoken along this coast. In earlier times locals rarely traveled inland and this isolation preserved this archaic "salty-speak," which natives of as far south as Tossa de Mar and as far north as Cadaqués continue to use in their daily speech.

This stretch of coast boasts the panoramic promontory **Cap Roig**, with views of the soaring Formigues (Ants) Isles, site of a decisive battle in 1285 where the Catalan fleet led by the great Catalan admiral Roger de Llúria destroyed the French fleet sailing to supply Philip the Bold's siege of Girona, therefore forcing the lifting of the siege and ending for many years French aspirations in the Mediterranean. Cap Roig is less than 2 km (1 mi) south of Callela de Palafrugell and makes for an enchanting half-hour walk.

Nightlife and the Arts

A throwback to the romantic 19th century is the persistence along the Costa Brava of the *habanera,* a musical lament strummed on a guitar in a swaying Cuban rhythm and sung mostly in Spanish, though some songs are in Catalan. Singing of longing for the homeland and the hard conditions of life in the colonies, these popular songs are performed by groups at events and clubs throughout the summer. You can catch them at many places, but especially at the Calella de Palafrugell *habanera* songfest, held on the first Saturday in July. The festival is held in the cozy *plaça* of Port Bo and tickets cost 2,500 ptas; for more information, contact the Calella de Palafrugell tourist office (☎ 972/614475).

Palafrugell

❾ *5 km (3 mi) west of Calella de Palafrugell, 123 km (76 mi) north of Barcelona, 39 km (24 mi) east of Girona.*

Departing from the coast to head inland some 4 km (2 mi), you'll reach Palafrugell, a busy market town that has preserved its Catalan flavor with the old streets and shops around its 16th-century church. Palafrugell is indelibly connected with the Catalan writer Josep Pla (1897–1981), who was a chronicler of daily life in Catalonia, especially of his home turf. His works can be considered as vast memoirs that cover a half century of Catalan life, seen through the eyes—sometimes ironic, and sometimes pained—of a man who laments the collapse of the rural world. Though he sided with the Franco regime during the Spanish civil war—something that was held against him by many Catalan intellectuals—he published his books in Catalan in 1947, something Franco frowned on. Pla is omnipresent in Palafrugell: bookstores, posters, even "Josep Pla" menus in restaurants. In an effort to expand the "resort" image of the Costa Brava, Palafrugell sponsors cultural events and festivals outside the summer season. The **Fundació Josep Pla** is the best place to get information on activities; there is a large library and a Josep Pla walk scheduled for Saturday morning. ⊠ *Carrer Nou 51,* ☎ *972/ 305577.* ◷ *Weekdays 9–1 and 5–8.*

La Bisbal

🔟 *8 km (5 mi) northeast of Palafrugell, 125 km (78 mi) north of Barcelona, 28 km (18 mi) east of Girona.*

From Palafrugell continue inland to La Bisbal, a town famous since the 16th century as a pottery-producing center. The land around the town conceals clay deposits from thousands of years of alluvial remains. Pottery shops line Carrer de l'Aigüeta, where you can find everything from the kitschy to the simply elegant. There are also antique shops where you can discover sought-after (and expensive) beautiful, old Catalan pottery. The best thing to do is to go directly to the pottery makers at several of the local factories, but the best outlet in town is **Terrisseria Salamó** (⊠ Carrer del Padró 54); for five generations this small craft center has been producing sets of china from the most traditional to the latest marbled designs.

Dining and Lodging

$$$$ ⭐ **Mas Torrent.** In the village of Torrent, but very close to La Bisbal, lies one of Spain's most refined retreats. A vision of easy-come elegance and rustic Catalan style, this reformed 18th-century *masia* is worthy of being featured in a sumptuous coffee-table art book—and, in fact, it once was. The panache carries over to its restaurant, decorated with place mats taken from the designs of Joan Miró, Antoni Tàpies, among other artists, and offering cuisine of the best of sea and land from the Baix Empordà. For total indolence, tempt yourself with the summer poolside buffet; the more active will utilize the sports facilites—golf, riding, deep-sea fishing for tuna, tennis, water sports—of the immediate region. The house has 10 suites and there are an additional 10 bungalows, each with their own terrace. ⊠ *Afores s/n, Torrent, 17123,* ☎ *972/303292,* ⅢⅩ *972/303293. 20 rooms. Restaurant, pool. AE, DC, MC, V.* 🐢

Ullastret

⓫ *6 km (4 mi) northeast of La Bisbal, 130 km (81 mi) north of Barcelona, 35 km (22 mi) east of Girona.*

Unaccustomed as we are to seeing massive Iberian stonework outside of Greek or Roman ruins, the vast dimensions of Ullastret can be an astonishing experience. Set in a tranquil rural setting about 2 km (1 mi) outside of the village of Ullastret, in the direction of Torroella de Montgrí, the archaeological site of Ullastret contains the remains of houses, temples, cisterns, grain silos, and burial sites. A sense of calm pervades the carefully tended and landscaped location, while soaring, fragrant cypress trees shade and cool.

The tribe that lived at Ullastret was the *Indiketes,* of the ancient Iberian race, already settled when the first Phoenician traders arrived in about 600 BC. Since the Greeks landed at nearby Empúries in about 630 BC, the temples located at the highest point of the village point to their Hellenizing influence. Start your visit by first following the outside wall, then enter the fortress through the main door. Once inside, walk among the houses and the streets that climb slowly to the top of the rise to the **Museu d'Arqueologia de Catalunya–Ullastret** (archaeological museum), whose collection of Attic (Athenian) pottery is illustrative of how Iberians acquired a civilizing polish from the Greeks. On the first Sunday of the month from May to September, a young woman called *Indiketa,* dressed in native Iberian costume, gives guided tours of the site at 11 and 12:30. With a prior reservation you can take this tour in English. ⊠ *Puig de Sant Andreu s/n,* ☎ *972/179058.* 🔁 *300* *ptas./€1.80.* ☉ *June 1–Sept. 30, Tues.–Sun. 10–8, Oct. 1–May 31, Tues.–Sun., 10–2 and 3–6.*

L'Escala

⑫ *10 km (6 mi) north of Ullastret, 135 km (84 mi) north of Barcelona, 39 km (24 mi) northeast of Girona.*

Set on the beautiful Bay of Roses, L'Escala faces north and feels the full effects of the *tramuntana* when it is blowing. With that in mind, and with more than a touch of irony, the Catalan writer Josep Pla said of L'Escala's natives, "The inhabitants of this village have, for the mere fact of living in it, a certain merit." Like many   others,   this fishing village has felt the effects of tourism—just look at all the tacky souvenir stands. But the beach, the fact that this is the best base to explore the ancient wonders of Empúries (☞ *below*), and L'Escala's divine anchovies make a trip worthwhile. Instead of shipping the local anchovies to the market, the fishermen of L'Escala kept these little treasures for themselves at home. In due time, these sublimely salted morsels were discovered by the earliest tourists; in due course what had been a cottage industry became a small industrial operation. Today, five shops have obtained quality certificates. Be sure to visit one—a slice of crisp toast with anchovies dripping olive oil, accompanied by a glass of cold, white wine, is just too good to pass up.

Dining and Lodging

$$ 🏨 **Nieves Mar.** This family hotel on the seafront is famous for its Ca la Neus restaurant, which offers up all the usual suspects: *suquet* (Catalan fish and potato stew), *llamantol al forn* (baked lobster), and *paella*. They also make a smashing *bouillabaisse*. The 10 suites and many of the guest rooms have fine views of the celebrated Bay of Roses. ⊠ *Passeig Marítim 8, 17130,* ☎ *972/770300,* 🆕 *972/773605. 65 rooms, 10 suites. AE, DC, MC, V. Closed Nov.–Mar.*

$$ ✕ **El Roser 2.** Set on the edge of town, and with all its tables looking out through the large picture windows onto the spectacular Bay of Roses, Roser 2 serves, for lack of a better word, nouvelle seafood cuisine. Salads include *gambes amb costelletes i formatge* (shrimp with rabbit ribs and cheese) and *barat amb melmelada de tomàquet* (mackerel with tomato jam). One of the most succulent dishes is *turbot rostit amb favetes a la catalana i espaguetis de calamar* (roasted turbot with little stewed *faves*—a lima-bean-like legume—and squid spaghetti). Ah, bliss! ⊠ *Passeig Lluís Albert 1,* ☎ *972/771102. AE, DC, MC, V. Closed Feb.* ✿

Empúries

★ ⑬ *1 km (½ mi north of L'Escala, 35 km (84 mi) north of Barcelona, 39 km (24 mi) northeast of Girona.*

The tourists that flock to the Costa Brava are only the most recent visitors to arrive here in the last 3,000 years. Back in the days when the *Odyssey* was the first travel guide book of note, the Greeks settled here from *Massalia* (modern Marseilles), for trading purposes, in the 6th century BC. Originally hailing from Phocaea in Ionia (today's western coast of Turkey), they set sail as part of the colonial expansion of the Greek city-states. They founded a city whose very name, Emporion or Emporium (which translates to "market"), symbolized prosperity, exports, and commerce, and whose site—on the south shore of the Bay of Roses, near L'Escala—was a promising one. Today, more than 2,500 years later, the importance of Empúries is that it is the only Greek city on the Iberian Peninsula that is still extant (others are known from written records but their exact location has never been established).

There are more than 30 acres of excavations to explore (including some beautiful mosaic floor remnants), a fascinating museum, and a scenic site backdropped by the sea.

When Scipio landed in Emporium in 218 BC he found a vigorous Greek settlement, comprising two towns: Paleopolis, the old city, and Neapolis, the new one. Paleopolis was where the modern walled village of Sant Martí d'Empúries is today (if you want a quick luncheon place, head here); once an island, it has been united to the mainland by the sedimentation of the river Ter whose mouth empties into the Bay of Roses. Some eighty years ago work on Neapolis was started by Barcelona archaeologists, and it brought to light much of Emporium's history. The peculiarity of Emporium was that it was two separate towns, housing Greeks and Iberians, with Greeks having access to the Iberian ghetto while Iberians were deprived of reciprocity—a situation probably due to security considerations given the bellicose nature of the locals. The arrangement—Greeks on the island, Iberians on the mainland—resulted in the latter having no direct access to the sea, which enabled the clever Greeks to monopolize trade and export. In time, however, the peaceful conditions of the place allowed the Greeks to move to the mainland where they founded Neopolis and continued their prosperous trade with the natives, attested by the abundant finds of Greek pottery in the surrounding area.

In 218 BC the Romans landed at Empúries as a result of the II Punic War against the Carthaginians (who were led by Hannibal), inaugurating a period of Roman occupation of the Iberian Peninsula that was to last for several centuries (and serve as the basis of the languages and culture of Spain and Portugal). The Romans added their own town to the place, rightly called, in the plural, Emporiae. Caesar erected a gymnasium there, as well as an amphitheatre (all these splendors vanished, sacked and destroyed by Norman invaders). Empúries eventually declined as other Roman cities, such as Tarragona, gained importance. It was abandoned in the 4th century AD and was lost from sight until its rediscovery in the 19th century.

Highlights of the site—keep in mind this doesn't look like a deserted Cecil B. De Mille movie set, since many structures only have their foundations extant—include the defensive walls, the open Agora marketplace, and the site of the Asklepion, the temple of the Greek god of medicine. In 1909, a statue of Asclepius was uncovered in a cistern in front of this temple, dated to the 4th century BC, and promptly moved to the Archaeological Museum in Barcelona (there are copies on site). Very recent excavations have uncovered the Roman baths of Empúries, but with only 10–15% of the Roman city as yet excavated. What you see today above ground is mostly the later Roman city, although the street grid is of the Greek settlement; beneath lies much of the Greek ruins, which will probably remain where they are. Further digging is likely to reveal important new discoveries in addition to the previously excavated goodies, including mosaic floors and phallic icons, that are now on view in the small **Museu d'Arqueologia** here. Enter the excavations from the seafront pedestrian promenade (which most people find by walking along the coast for 15 minutes from L'Escala or hopping the little Carrilet train that departs from L'Escala on the hour June 15 to September 15) from mid-June to mid-September; at other times, the only access is via a vehicle road of the main Figueres route. ⊠ *Museu d'Arqueologia de Catalunya–Empúries, Apt. 21, L'Escala,* ☎ *972/ 770208.* 🖾 *400 ptas./€2.40.* ⊘ *June–Sept., daily 10–8; Oct.–May, daily 10–6.* 🕭

Castelló d'Empúries

🔴 *11 km (7 mi) northwest of Empúries, 139 km (867 mi) north of Barcelona, 47 km (29 mi) northeast of Girona.*

From Empúries, the road heads inland about 2 km (1 mi), curving to avoid the marshlands of the Aïguamolls de l'Empordà, and continues on to Castelló d'Empúries, a town landmarked by the seignorial silhouette of the cathedral of Santa Maria of Castelló d'Empúries, which rises majestically above the Empordà plain. Castelló d'Empúries is fundamentally an agricultural town (but has an adjacent, self-contained, and not terribly appealing resort development on the Bay of Roses known as Empuriabrava). Castelló is a handsomely historic town with Gothic palaces and an intricate warren of cobbled streets; its heart is the Plaça dels Homes, where a tourist office can provide a town map. It is surrounded by marshes, lies several miles inland, and is now landlocked, but in the Middle Ages ships (and Viking raiders) sailed up the Muga river from the sea to dock here. The church of Santa Maria dates from the 13th and 14th centuries. Pride of place is given to the Romanesque bell tower and the portal sculpted with figures of the apostles and the Epiphany. Inside the spacious building is a fine 15th-century alabaster altar with delicate, highly detailed expressive figures. Seen from the fields out of town to the east of the cathedral—where there is an unobstructed view—Castelló d'Empúries makes for a majestic and solid picture.

Aïguamolls de l'Empordà

🔴 *Less than 1 km. (0.6 mi) from Castelló d'Empúries, 139 km (86 mi) north of Barcelona, 47 km (29 mi) northeast of Girona.*

It's almost a miracle that the **Parc Natural Aïguamolls de l'Empordà** has survived. Set beside the modern tourist resort of Empuriabrava—which was carved out of the same terrain in the mid-sixties—this parcel of land was next on the list for development when a popular conservation movement was founded in 1976 to save it. In 1983, the Catalan parliament declared the area a nature reserve and it has since become a haven for birds migrating from northern Europe to Africa. Thanks to this sanctuary the bird population of all the Empordà plain continues to prosper. Hundreds of species of birds flock here, including avocets, black-winged stilts, ringed plovers, common sandpipers, water rails, hoopoes, purple gallinules, rollers, marsh harriers, and Montagu's harrier. In addition, otters, marine cows, Camargue horses, and fallow deer have been reintroduced to this habitat. Fittingly, park administrators like to stress that silence is one of their finest assets. ⊠ *Carretera de Sant Pere Pescador,* ☎ *972/454222.* 🎫 *Free.* ☉ *Open daily during daylight hrs.* 🐾

Roses

🔴 *10 km (6 mi) north of Empúries, 153 km (95 mi) north of Barcelona, 56 km (35 mi) northeast of Girona.*

The opening lines of C.S. Forester's Horatio Hornblower novel *Flying Colours* read, "Captain Hornblower was walking up and down along the sector of the ramparts of Rosas, delimited by two sentries with loaded muskets, which the commandant had granted him for exercise. Overhead shone the bright autumn sun of the Mediterranean, hanging in a blue Mediterranean sky, and shining on the Mediterranean blue of Rosas Bay—the blue water fringed with white where the little waves broke against the shore of golden sand and grey-green cliff." It's not surprising Forester raised the curtain here, as the Golf de Roses has often been called the most splendid gulf on the Costa Brava. Today, you can still visit those ramparts—which circumvent the remains of the old Greek, Roman, and medieval cities of Roses—and take in the view of the town, picturesquely sitting at the head of the bay. Roses may not excel in scenic beauty any longer—many modern hotels, discos, and modern boats have intruded—but it's loaded with a heavy message of history.

Roses began as a Greek colony from the island of Rhodes (where its name derives from) and was a branch of the big Empúries settlement down the coast (☞ *above*). The Roman writer Cato states that the Greeks settled here in 776 BC, but archaeological excavations have not found any evidence earlier than 600 BC (still, the oldest coin ever found in Spain, a silver Greek drachma, was unearthed here). But the Greeks were simply the first in a long line of settlers. In fact, the historical concentration of civilizations inside Roses's **Ciutadella** (citadel) is unlike any in Spain. Within these walls, settlements of Greeks, Romans, and Visigoths followed each other in turn, with a residential quarter here up to the late 19th century. Inside the citadel is the Romanesque Benedictine **monastery and cloister of Santa Maria**, whose irregular pentagonal-shaped walls were begun in 1543 and designed by the engineer Pizano. Walls were important back then: much of Roses's strategic importance lay in the fact that its site offered a safe haven from the coast's blustery *tramuntana* wind, and ships would put in to wait for it to die down. An archaeologist gives free guided visits inside the Ciutadella on Sunday and Wednesday mornings at 11 AM in the winter and 10 AM in the summer; the *Ciutadella* is open to the public from 9 AM till dark.

Unfortunately, the little that remains of old Roses is swamped in the summer when the native population of 13,500 booms to 120,000. To serve these teeming numbers, the town has countless restaurants, discotheques, and amusement parks for the young. But almost everyone's main activity is going to the immense beaches that line the Bay of Roses and enjoying its stunning landscapes. If you head out along the coast between Roses and the next village to the north, Cadaqués, you'll discover an enchanting continuum of steep and bare rocky mountains covered with spiny underbrush. Although the hot Mediterranean sun beats down mercilessly in the summer, coves ringed by towering red pines dip into sheltered sandy beaches, allowing all to sunbathe, swim, and play. The last two coves before Cadaqués, Cala Montjoi and Cala Jònculs, are relatively free of development with only a couple of hotels and restaurants (one of them the famous **El Bulli**). Between these two inlets is the headland of Norfeu, with its jagged cliffs that tumble into the wine-dark sea at their feet. Motorboats and sailboats cruise busily along this coast in search of activity. The smart skippers anchor in the shelter of these coves to spend the day on the water. Then it's time to head back to Roses's marinas and party.

Dining and Lodging

$$$$
★ ✕ **El Bulli.** Spain's top restaurant and one of Europe's hottest culinary shrines, "The Bulldog" is under a state of siege, as foodies, celebrated chefs, and hordes of *Travel & Leisure* and *Gourmet* readers fight for reservations. No wonder—the word "innovative" falls far short of describing what goes on here, thanks to the chef Ferran Adrià. Whether you describe him as either a mad scientist, a poet, or a Dalí of the kitchen, Adrià makes your palate his playground with concepts like *escuma de fum* (foam of smoke)—no joke—and a bevy of other dazzling dishes. One memorable dinner began with peanut-honey brittle lollipops and ended with chocolate caramel tuiles garnished with pink peppercorns. Order the *Menú de Degustació* (taster's menu)—seven or eight "snacks," seven *tapes,* four main dishes, and three desserts (but some feasts can

go up to 35 "courses")—and you'll enjoy such startling combinations as pistachios in tempura, cauliflower couscous, and barnacles in tea. Many bites are delicious, others merely original, such as the *tortilla de patata* (potato and onion omelet), which you eat with a spoon from a martini glass, or *tagliatelle carbonara,* where the "pasta" is jellied chicken consomme, smothered in diced ham and Parmesan cheese. The only downsides are the tired decor—made up for by vistas of the pristine Cala Montjoi—and the tricky ride to the water's edge, best reached from Roses on a recently repaved road. If you're lucky you'll get the table in the kitchen and watch the wizards at work while you eat. Reservations weeks in advance are essential, especially because this restaurant is closed half the year (when Adrià heads back to Barcelona to work his private kitchen laboratory). Plan on spending 20,000 pesetas per person. ⊠ *Cala Montjoi, Roses,* ☎ *972/150457,* FAX *972/ 150717. Reservations essential wks in advance. AE, DC, MC, V. Closed Oct.–Apr. 1.* ☜

$$$$ 🏠 **Almadraba Park Hotel.** Sitting on a bluff overlooking the horseshoe-
★ shaped Cala Almadraba—a cove about a half mile wide, 4 km (2.5 mi) from Roses—set along a white-sand beach, and overlooked by scrub-covered hills, this stunning hotel is run by Jaume Subirós, proprietor of the Hotel Empordà. That Figueres hotel is considered the cradle of Catalan cuisine and the kitchen at the Almadraba offers the same level of gourmet cooking, so try to enjoy one of the fine rice dish specialities on the terrace with an incomparable view of the entire Bay of Roses. As for Almadraba, it's an Arabic word that means a bed where tuna are caught—in the 19th century, this cove used to be closed off with nets to catch the tuna migrating up the Catalan coast. There is a reproduction in the bar of Salvador Dalí's gory painting of this subject *La Pesca de les Tonyines.* The hotel's look and style? Think modern and angular.⊠ *Platja de l'Almadraba, 17480,* ☎ *972/256550,* FAX *972/256750. 60 rooms, 6 suites. AE, DC, MC, V. Closed mid-Oct.–mid-Mar.* ☜

$$$$ 🏠 **Vistabella.** This small elegant hotel, with an ambience of quiet simplicity, is placed high up on a cliff overlooking the cove of Canyelles Petites, 2.5 km (1.6 mi) up the coast from Roses. It has excellent service and includes an indoor swimming pool, its own beach, gym, sauna, solarium, paddle tennis, mini-golf, and water sports. Their kitchen is international. ⊠ *Av. Díaz Pacheco 26, 17480,* ☎ *972/ 256200,* FAX *972/253213. 23 rooms, 8 suites. AE, DC, MC, V. Mid-Oct.–mid-Mar.* ☜

$$ 🏠 **Canyelles Platja.** Located at the cove of Canyelles Petites, 2.5 km (1.6 mi) up the coast from Roses, this fully renovated hotel offers a wide array of features—even a supermarket and a bookstore. An underground passage leads directly from the hotel to the beach, where there is a snack bar. ⊠ *Av. Díaz Pacheco 7, 17480,* ☎ *972/256500,* FAX *972/256647. 100 rooms. AE, DC, MC, V. Closed Oct.–Mar.*

$$ 🏠 **Hotel Goya.** This family hotel in the center of Roses was one of the first hotels in town, and was run for many years by Teresa Mallol, a highly charismatic woman who made her guests feel completely at home. Now helmed by her son Albert Berta, the hotel, recently renovated, keeps welcoming guests back year after year. ⊠ *Riera Ginjolers, 17480,* ☎ *972/256123,* FAX *972/151461. 75 rooms. AE, DC, MC, V. Closed late Oct.–Easter.* ☜

Nightlife

Roses has a nifty Whitman's Sampler of nightspots, both hot and cool. The old favorites include the following. **Chic** (⊠ Ctra. Figueres s/n, ☎ ☎ 972/257051) is considered one of the top discos. For Flamenco— aimed for tourists and hybrid, not for the purist, but entertaining all the same—check out **El Patio Flamenco** (⊠ Ctra Roses s/n, ☎ ☎ 972/

257051). The castanets also click up a frenzy at **El Cortijo** (✉ Carrer Alhambra 47-49, ☎ 972/255316).

Cadaqués

★ ⓱ *17 km (11 mi) northeast of Roses, 167 km (104 mi) north of Barcelona, 70 km (43 mi) northeast of Girona.*

Cadaqués (pronounced cada-CASE) has been called the most beautiful village on the Costa Brava. Whether this is true or not it is certainly the most painted. Its jumble of white houses, roofed with red tiles, massed upon each other, and capped by the church of Santa Maria—which seems suspended in the air—has been daubed by hundreds of artists, some great and some not so great. A full list of the painters, writers, and artists who stayed here at one time or another would be encyclopaedic—Federico Garcia Lorca, Luis Buñuel, Marcel Duchamp, Salvador Dalí, John Cage, Pablo Picasso are just a few of the greatest names. Dalí—the founder of Surrealism and the man who gave us the *Persistence of Memory* (1931, Museum of Modern Art, New York City) and those melting watches—spent many childhood summers here, while Picasso may have been inspired by the boxlike, whitewashed houses of the Costa Brava (and France's nearby Vermeille Coast) to create Cubism. The earliest artist to set up his easel was the curmudgeon Eliseu Meifrén, whose masterly 1886 Impressionist seascapes first spread the allure of this village as a painter's delight. Today, Cadaqués has been discovered—the the horse-drawn carts that threaded their way up and down the mountain of El Pení have long ago been traded in for Mercedes; there are now more expensive art galleries than impoverished artists.

If you don't want to gallery-hop, head for the town's small museum, the **Museu Municipal d'Art,** which will entice art lovers with its collection of landscape (or should we say seascape) paintings inspired by Costa Bravan scenery. *Carrer Narcís Monturiol 15,* ☎ *972/258877.* ☉ *Easter–Nov. 1, 10:30–1:30.* ▣ *600 ptas./€3.61.*

The village is a labyrinth of steep and narrow pebble-paved streets lined with cubelike whitewashed houses. Its serpentine waterfront is lined with whitewashed private homes and inlets where small fishing boats have been pulled up onto the black slaty sand. The social center is the *rambla* crowded with outdoor cafés. When the sun goes down, these fill up with people having a few drinks before going off to dinner, then fill up again in the late hours with people as anxious to talk the night away as to catch the breezes off the sea. If you visit the Bar Melitón on this waterfront, you will see a plaque that commemorates the many hours Marcel Duchamp spent here playing chess.

Still off the beaten highway, Cadaqués can only be reached by one snaking road that travels over the Serra de Rodes range. It has always been difficult to reach Cadaqués—for years, villagers found it easier to sail to Italy and America than to travel to Fígueres, 30 km (19 mi) away (believe it or not, many couples had wedding pictures taken in Sardinia, as it was easier to sail there than to go to Figueres overland). Thanks to this seclusion, Cadaqués remains one of the most unspoiled and lovely towns of the coast.

★ Just one cove up the coast from Cadaqués—just a 15-minute walk away—is **Port Lligat,** where Salvador Dalí (1904–89) built his famous house in the 1930s, which became a love nest for him and his adored wife and model, Gala (who had left famed poet Paul Eluard to become Madame Dalí). Tour guides in English, French, and Catalan escort you through this abode and his many "wonders": the stuffed polar bear hung with turquoise jewels, the dismembered mannequins, the dressing area filled with photos of the artist and celebrities (Harpo Marx, among them), the bedroom with the panorama view over Cap de Creus, the easternmost point on the Spanish peninsula (Dali liked to boast he was the first man in Spain to see the sun every morning), and the swimming pool designed to look like either a phallus or the floor plan of the Alhambra (depending on who was asking the question). The view from the garden—which is full of amazing egg-shaped sculptures—will be familiar as it was a prevalent backdrop in Dalí's paintings. Note that the tour takes 40 minutes and must be booked in advance. ⊠ *Casa-Museu Salvador Dalí, Port Lligat,* ☎ *972/258063.* ☉ *By appointment, Mon.–Sat. 10:30–6. Closed mid-Jan.–mid-Mar.*

Dalí called **Cap de Creus**, the headland to the north, "a grandiose geological delirium"—a fairly apropos description since the rocky mineral formations of this cape twist and curl in the most extraordinary way, as if the earth had been convulsed, then wrung out and dropped into the sea and battered by surging waves. The area was declared a maritime and terrestrial natural park in 1998. To continue the Dalí theme, opt for a cruise out to Cap de Creus on the yellow boat *Gala,* now helmed by Senyor Caminada, the son of a longtime Dalí employee; it is moored at Port Lligat's shore and excursions are offered daily to the cape and back for about 1,000 ptas./€6.01 per person.

Dining and Lodging

$$$ ✕ **Es Trull.** On the harborside street in the center of town, this cedar-
★   shingled cafeteria is named for the ancient olive press that sits in its interior. It specializes in fish dishes such as *escórpora* (scorpion fish) and rice dishes, such as their star player, *arrós de calamar i gambes* (rice with squid and shrimp), or *arrós negre amb calamar i sèpia* (rice in ink of squid and cuttlefish), or *arrós amb lluç* (rice with hake). There are those who consider this the best kitchen in Cadaqués. ⊠ *Port Ditxós s/n,* ☎ *972/258196. AE, MC, V. Closed Nov.–Easter..*

$$ ✕ **Can Pelayo.** This family-run button of a place serves the best fish in town. It's hidden behind Plaça Port Alguer, a few minutes' walk south of the town center. ⊠ *Carrer Nou 11,* ☎ *972/258356. MC, V. Closed weekdays Oct.–May.*

$$ ✕ **Casa Anita.** Located on the street that leads to Port Lligat and Dalí's house, this tiny place offers a simple but generous cuisine. The crowd's *couleur locale* includes hippies, down-and-outs, beachcombers, and other riffraff on a very tight budget; in other words, this is a real find for the budgeteer, with food that is good, simple, and fresh. Try the salads and the sardine, mussel, and sea bass dishes, and get there early. ⊠ *Carrer Miquel Rosset 16,* ☎ *972/258471. AE, DC, MC, V. Closed for lunch Mon. Jan.–Mar.*

$$$$ ▥ **Playa Sol.** This hotel is in the cove of Es Pianc on the left side of the bay of Cadaqués as you face the sea, a five-minute walk from the village center. It's been open for 40 years and has the experience that comes with age. Boaties will love this place—all types of craft tie up here as Catalan writer Josep Pla spread its fame as the best place to drop anchor in the port of Cadaqués. ⊠ *Es Pianc 3, 17488,* ☎ *972/ 258100,* 𝔽𝔸𝕏 *972/258054. 50 rooms. AE, DC, MC, V. Closed mid-Dec.– mid-Feb.*

$$$ ▥ **Llané Petit.** On the right side of the bay of Cadaqués as you face the sea, this small hotel caters to people who want to make the most of their stay in the village and don't want to spend too much time in their hotel rooms. All of which is by way of saying that the ambience here is simple and serene—as is the cuisine, with lots of grilled meats and fish. ⊠ *Carrer Dr. Bartomeus 37, 17488,* ☎ *972/258050,* 𝔽𝔸𝕏 *972/ 258778. 37 rooms. AE, MC, V. Closed Dec. 10–25.*

Shopping

After all, didn't you come to Cadaqués to see, even purchase, some art? Cadaqués is all about art and there are quite a few galleries—most active from June through September, December, and Easter—worth visiting. The village social center, **L'Amistat** (✉ Dr. Trèmols 1, ☎ 972/258800) is a good place to start; in addition to being the place where villagers bide away their time playing cards and swapping tall tales, it regularly holds art exhibitions of local and international artists whose home is Cadaqués. **L'Ateneu** (✉ Av. Caritat Serinyana 8, ☎ 972/159209) is a non-profit organization that regularly exhibits Catalan, Spanish, and international artists; once a year they hold a three-day collective fund-raiser exhibition at the headland Cap de Creus. **Galeria 98** (✉ Riba Pitxot 4, ☎ 972/259025), as its name indicates, was founded in 1998 and has filled in the space left by the closing of several important galleries such as Bombelli and Elena Ramos. **Galeria de la Riba** (✉ Riba Pianc s/n, ☎ 972/159273) handles well-known Spanish, Catalan, and international artists. Opened in 2000, **Port Doguer** (✉ Guillem Bruguera 10, ☎ 972/258910) manages such established artists as the Moscardó brothers, Japanese painter Shigeyoshi Koyama, Sabala, Vilallonga, and Roca-Sastre, with exhibitions offered in a wonderful space—an old olive press. **Taller Fort** (✉ Hort d'en Sanés, ☎ 972/258549), which has been around for nearly 15 years, deals in international small-format art and also sponsors an annual painting competition.

Sant Pere de Rodes

★ ⓲ *18 km (11 mi) west of Cadaqués, 170 km (105 mi) north of Barcelona, 67 km (42 mi) northeast of Girona.*

Once commanding territory and power on both sides of the Pyrenees, the Benedictine monastery of Sant Pere de Rodes rises majestically on a steep mountainside overlooking Cap de Creus. The majesty of its architecture and the beauty of its view—which overlooks the entire Creus peninsula and the waters of the Mediterranean—make it a must-visit. Built in the 10th century, it is one of the finest examples of Romanesque architecture in Spain, with exceptional examples of masonry laid in the *opus spicatum* (herringbone) pattern. Particularly notable are the church, with its two-tiered ambulatory, the 12th-century bell tower, and defense tower. On the left-hand side of the church's altar as you go in is a winding stairway that leads to the second level; talk about claustrophobia—it's barely wide enough for one slender person. Also note the nave's 11th-century columns, decorated with wolf and dog heads.

Repeatedly sacked over the centuries, Sant Pere de Rodes lost most of its influence in the 18th century. Recently restored, the monastery will be the home of a study center for the Cap de Creus nature preserve. Located in the municipal limits of Port de la Selva, Sant Pere de Rodes can be reached from Vilajuïga or from Port de la Selva. The road winding up from Vilajuïga passes several groups of prehistoric dolmens, all conveniently indicated. Megaliths are very common in this area, 134 of them having been counted to date in the *comarca* (county) of the Alt Empordà alone, with new ones being discovered all the time. ✉ *Monestir de Sant Pere de Rodes, Port de la Selva, ☎ 972/387559. ☎ 600 ptas./€3.61; Tues. free. ☉ June–Sept., Tues.–Sun. 10–8; Oct.–May, Tues.–Sun. 10–5:30.* ✧

Figueres

🟤 *42 km (26 mi)north of Girona, 100 km (62 mi) north of Barcelona.*

Figueres is the capital of the *comarca* (county) of the Alt Empordà, the bustling county seat, as it were, of this predominantly agricultural region. Local people come from the surrounding area to shop at its many stores and stock up on farm equipment and supplies. But among the tractors and mule carts is the main reason tourists come to Figueres: the jaw-dropping Dalí museum, one of the most visited in Spain.

Painter Salvador Dalí is Figueres' most famous son. With a painter's technique that rivaled Jan van Eyck, a flair for publicity so aggressive it would put P. T. Barnum in the shade, and a penchant to shock (he designed the notorious scene of an eye being severed in Luís Bunuel's 1929 *Un Chien andalou,* loved telling people Barcelona's historic Gothic Quarter should be knocked down, and was given to create paintings with titles like *Two Pieces of Bread Expressing the Sentiment of Love*), Dalí scaled the ramparts of Art History as one of the foremost proponents of Surrealism, the esthetic movement launched in the 1920s by André Breton. His most lasting image were the melting watches (or, as cartoons in the newspapers would have it, "limp watches") of his iconic 1931 painting, *The Persistence of Memory.* Since he was born in Figueres (1904) and was to die here (1989), the artist decided to create a museum-monument to himself here during the last two decades of his life.

A museum was not big enough a word for Dalí, so he christened it the
★ the **Teatre-Museu Gala-Salvador Dalí.** Theater it is, as this was the old town theater, once reduced to a ruin in the Spanish civil war. Now topped with a glass geodesic dome and studded with Dalí's iconic egg shapes, the museum is a multilevel monument to his fertile imagination ("Beauty will be edible or not at all") and artistic creativity, set with gardens, ramps, and a spectacular drop cloth Dalí painted for the Les Ballets de Monte Carlo. Don't look for his greatest paintings here, although there are some memorable images, including *Gala at the Mediterranean,* which takes the body of Gala and morphs it into the image of Abraham Lincoln once you look through coin-operated viewfinders. The side-show image continues with other coin-operated pieces, including *Taxi Plujós* (water gushes over the snail-covered occupants sitting in a Cadillac once owned by Al Capone) and the Sala de Mae West, a trompe-l'oeil vision in which a pink sofa, two fireplaces, and two paintings become the face of La West. Fittingly, another "exhibit" on view is Dalí's own crypt; when his friends considered what flag to lay over his coffin at the lying in state, they decided to cover it with an embroidered heirloom tablecloth instead—Dalí would have liked this unconventional touch (if not the actual site: he wanted to be buried at his castle of Púbol next to his wife Gala, but the then mayor of Figueres took matters into his own hands). All in all, the museum is a piece of Dalí dynamite. ⊠ *Plaça Gala-Salvador Dalí 5,* ☎ *972/677500.* 🎫 *1,000 ptas./€6.01.* ☉ *Oct.– May, Tues.–Sun. 10:30–5:15; June–Sept., Tues.–Sun. 9–7:15.* 🐾

While Dalí was alive and active he frequented the Cafeteria Astòria at the top of the Rambla (still the center of social life in Figueres), signing autographs for tourists or just being Dalí: he once walked down the street with a French omelet in his breast pocket instead of a handkerchief. Along the Rambla you'll find the **Museu de l'Empordà,** whose collections range from the Roman to the Catalan Renaixença. ⊠ *Rambla 2,* ☎ *972/502305.* 🎫 *400 ptas./€2.40.* ☉ *July–Sept., Tues.–Sat. 10:30–2, 3:30–7, Sun. 11– 1:30; Oct.–June, Mon.–Sat. 11–1, 3–7, Sun. 11–1:30.*

Not far from the Museu de l'Empordà is the **Museu del Joguet de Catalunya,** where they like to say you will find the memories of your childhood. Doll collectors will be in heaven, with hundreds of antique dollies on display. The museum possesses collections of toys owned by, among others, Salvador Dalí, Federico García Lorca and Joan Miró. ✉ *Hotel de Figueres, Carrer de Sant Pere 1,* ☎ *972/504585.* ☉ *June–Sept. daily 10–1 and 4–7; Oct.–March, Tues.–Sat. 10–1 and 4–7; Sun. 11–1:30; closed Monday and Jan. 15–Feb. 15.*

If you happen to visit Figueres in winter, you just might catch the bizarre work of the man who frightens away the millions of starlings that sleep in the plantain trees on the Rambla at night. With a can fixed to one end of a long pole, he sets off thunderous firecrackers among the branches to frighten away these birds that leave the Rambla the worse for wear. Only in Figueres, Dalí's home town! Thursday is market day in Figueres and farmers gather at the top of the Rambla to do business and gossip, taking refreshments at cafés and discretely pulling out and pocketing large rolls of bills, the result of their morning transactions.

OFF THE
BEATEN PATH

Casa-Museu Castell Gala Dalí – If you've visited Figueres (☞ *above*) and Port Lligat (☞ *below*), you might like to do the third point of the Dalí triangle, as it is called, and pay a call on the castle of Púbol, where Dalí's wife Gala is buried in the crypt. The medieval castle—during the 1970s the residence of the painter's wife and at the beginning of the 1980s his own—has since 1996 been a museum; inside you can see the paintings and drawings that Dalí gave to Gala, as well as the elephant sculptures that adorn the garden, a collection of Gala's haute-couture dresses, and the furniture and many objects with which they decorated the house. Púbol, roughly between Girona and Figueres, is not easy to find. If you are coming by road on the A7 highway, exit at Girona Nord and take C255 district road to Palamós. Just after Bordils and the crossroads to Flaçà, turn right to La Pera and to Púbol. If you are coming from Figueres, follow the C252, and when you reach the Parlavà crossroads (traffic lights), turn right, putting you onto the C255. Turn right again and travel for about 2 km, when the road to La Pera and Púbol turns off on your left. If you are traveling by train, get off at the Flaçà station on the Barcelona-Portbou line of RENFE railways. Flaçà is about 4 km (2½ mi) from Púbol and you can walk or take a taxi. By bus the SARFA bus company has a stop in Flaçà and on the C255 road, some 2 km (1 mi) from Púbol. For information and bookings: ☎ 972/677500.

Dining and Lodging

$$$$
★

✕🏨 **Hotel Empordà.** Hailed as the birthplace of modern Catalan cuisine, this hotel and restaurant 1½ km (1 mi) north of Figueres on the NII is run by Jaume Subirós and is a pilgrimage destination for gourmets. The restaurant serves superb French, Catalan, and Spanish cooking in an elegant setting. For starters, opt for the *crema freda de meló amb flocs de pernil ibèric* (cold creme of melon with flakes of Iberian jam), followed by *terrina calenta de lluerna a l'oli de cacauet* (hot pot of gurnard fish in peanut oil) and, if it's winter, *llebre a la Royal* (boned hare cooked slowly in red wine). For dessert there is *gratinat de gerds al sabayon de garnatxa* (raspberries browned in *garnatxa* sabayon). The large plate glass window at the back of the restaurant looks out over verdant farmland and the Alberes mountain range in the distance. ✉ *Carretera NII, Figueres, 17600,* ☎ *972/500562,* 🆇 *972/509358. 42 rooms. AE, DC, MC, V.* ✍

$$
✕🏨 **Hotel Duran.** Once a stagecoach relay station, the Duran is now a well-known hotel and restaurant open every day of the year. Salvador Dalí had his own private dining room here, and you can still have dinner with the great surrealist, or at least with pictures of him. Try the *mandonguilles amb sepia a l'estil Anna* (meatballs and cuttlefish), a

mar i muntunya (surf-and-turf) specialty of the house. ☒ *Carrer Lasauca 5, 17600,* ☎ *972/501250,* ℻ *972/502609. 70 rooms. AE, DC, MC, V.*

Peralada

㉑ *12 km (7 mi) northeast from Figueres, 47 km (29 mi) north of Girona.*

Just a few miles northeast of Figueres, this small, quiet village has a fine glassware museum, a noted summer music festival, and—of all things—a Casino. The village's history goes back at least to the 9th century and the counts of Peralada, one of the noblest titles of Catalonia, originated here. Ramon Muntaner, the great 13th-century Catalan chronicler, was from Peralada and in his "Chronicle" describes how it was put to the torch in 1285 by the Almogàvers, Catalan soldiers of fortune who carved out an empire in Greece. Recent archaeological excavations have uncovered signs of this great fire. The town castle is the sight of the **Festival Internacional de Música,** a music festival held in the castle gardens every July and August. The world's finest artists perform here and original works are especially composed for this event. ☒ *Festival Internacional de Música–Castell de Peralada, 17491,* ☎ *93/2805868 or 972/538292,* ℻ *93/2038700 or 972/538515.* ☙

The **Museu del Castell de Peralada,** in the old Convent del Carme, houses the finest glassware museum in Spain, a library with over 70,000 volumes, and a wine museum. The park is one of the finest English-style gardens in the region, with a lake in which swans glide back and forth. ☒ *Plaça del Carme s/n,* ☎ *972/538125.* 🖼 *500 ptas./€3.01.* ☉ *Tours on the hr 10–noon, 4–7 (in English). Closed Mon. Sept. 16–June.*

Dining and Lodging

$$$$ 🏨 **Hostal de la Font.** Located in a former convent in the middle of Peralada, this is a delicious little place. Enric Serraplana, the proprieter, is also an antique dealer and the hotel shows this to effect. It has a beautifully decorated dining room with a communal table set for 16 at which all the guests can breakfast. ☒ *Carrer de la Font 15-19, 17491,* ☎ *972/ 538507,* ℻ *972/538506. 12 rooms. AE, MC, V.*

$$$ ✕ **Cal Sagristà.** Run by Enric Serraplana (his hotel is the Hostal de la Font, ☞ *above*), this fine place warmly greets you with aged bare-brick walls and contemporary paintings by artists such as Antonio Federico. Once a convent-school of the Augustine nuns—Sion, the woman in charge, attended school here—it gives onto an arbored terrace with a view encompassing the Alberes range and Puig Neulós, at 4,148 ft the highest point in the Alberes range and the easternmost major Pyrenean peak. For openers, the *amanida amb bolets confitats* (salad with preserved mushrooms) is a treat. Other delights include *magret de nec amb salsa de gerds* (duck magret with raspberry jam) and *cua de bou amb cebetes* (oxtail with shalots), all washed down with the local Castell de Peralada Blanco Seco. *Rodona 2,* ☎ *972/538301. AE, MC, V. Closed Nov. 15–Feb. 15 and Tues., except July–Aug.*

Nightlife and the Arts

The **Casino Castell de Peralada** occupies the Castell de Perelada, a 19th-century fairy tale re-creation with crenellated battlements of an original medieval castle. Games include French and American roulette, blackjack, and slot machines. A valid ID (proving you are over 21) is necessary for admission. ☒ *Castell de Peralada, Carrer Sant Joan s/n, 17491,* ☎ *972/538125.* 🖼 *550 ptas./€3.31.* ☉ *Fri.–Sat. 7 PM–5 AM; Sun. and holidays, 5 PM–4 AM; Mon.–Thurs., 7 PM–4 AM.* ☙

INLAND TO GIRONA

The ancient city of Girona, often ignored by visitors who bolt from its airport to the resorts of the Costa Brava (about an hour away), is an easy day trip from Barcelona, but it's more than that. Much of this city's charm comes from its narrow medieval streets, linked with frequent stairways, as required by the steep terrain. Historic buildings here include a magnificent cathedral (sitting atop 90 breathless steps), a Moorish-Romanesque Arab Bath, and an antique and evocative Jewish Quarter, at one time one of the most important in Europe before the Jews were expelled from Spain in 1492. Add in chic restaurants and a vibrant community of students and scholars (drawn by the local university), and you have a fascinating town worth a two- or three-day stopover. But if you're heading over from the Costa Brava, the first stop for most in the interior is the leading town of L'Emporda—that flat alluvial farming region that lies between the Ter and Muga rivers—Figueres, home of the celebrated Teatre-Museu Dali.

Northern Catalonia boasts the soft, green rolling hills of the Ampurdan farm country, the Alberes mountain range near the eastern tip of the Pyrenees—here, intrepid travelers can discover a region, which, studded with historic and picturesque towns such as Besalú, Olot, Rupit, and Vic, call to mind Italy's Tuscany or France's Lubéron. Sprinkled across these landscapes are charming *masies* (farmhouses) with austere, grayish or pinkish staggered-stone rooftops and ubiquitous square towers that make them look like fortresses. Even the tiniest village has its church, arcades square, and *rambla,* where villagers take their evening *passeig* (promenade). Around Olot, the volcanic region of the Garrotxa, with more than 30 now-extinct volcanoes (the last eruption was at least 9,500 years ago though experts say new activity cannot be discounted), is a striking landscape, with—amidst lush forests of beech, oak, and pine—barren moonscapes worthy of Star Wars. Heading back south to Girona, nature lovers can also make a stop at the Montseny wilderness park before entering the fray of Barcelona once again.

Girona

Numbers in the margin correspond to points of interest on the Girona map.

㉑ *97 km (60 mi) northeast of Barcelona.*

Girona (Gerona in Castilian), a city of more than 70,000 inhabitants, keeps intact the magic of its historic past. In fact, with its brooding hilltop castle, soaring cathedral, and dreamy riverside setting, it makes up a Paint-by-Numbers vision from the Middle Ages. Once called a "Spanish Venice"—quite inexcusably, for there are no real canals here, just the confluence of four rivers—the historic city is almost as evocative as that city on the lagoon. With El Call, the best-preserved Jewish community dating from the Middle Ages—and a Moorish-Romanesque Arab Baths, Girona not only excels in picturesque beauty but is also loaded with a heavy message of history: both its Jewish and Islamic communities thrived here for centuries. Today, as a university center, it deftly combines past and vibrant present—art galleries, chic cafés, and trendy boutiques have set up shop in many of the restored buildings of the old quarter.

The Romans founded Gerunda in the 1st century AD at a convenient ford that spanned the confluence of four rivers—the Ter, Onyar, Güell and Galligants. Nearby stone quarries supplied building material and the mountain on which the old city sits is known as *Les Pedreres*

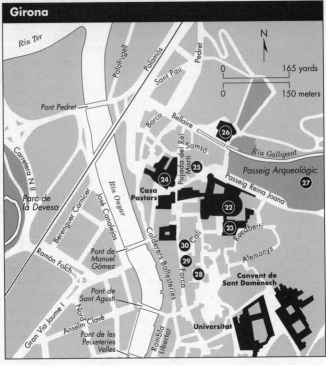

Girona

(quarry mountain). The old quarter of Girona, called the *Força Vella,* is built on the side of the mountain and is a tightly packed labyrinth of steep, narrow, cobblestone streets and fine buildings and monuments. You can still see vestiges of the Iberian and Roman walls in the cathedral square and in the patio of the old university. Head over from modern Girona (on the west side of the Onyar) to the old quarter on the east side. The main street of the old quarter is Carrer de la Força. It follows the old Via Augusta, the Roman road that connected Rome with its provinces.

The best way to get to know Girona is by walking along its cool, narrow, inviting streets. As you wander up and down the Força Vella, you will be repeatedly surprised by new discoveries. One of Girona's actual treasures is its setting, as it rises high above the Riu Onyar, where it merges with the Ter (which flows from a mountain waterfall that can be glimpsed in a gorge above the town). Regardless of your approach to the town, walk first along the west side banks of the Onyar, between the train trestle and the Plaça de la Independència, to admire an iconic view of the old town, drinking in pastel yellow, pink, and orange waterfront facades, their windows draped with a colorful array of drying laundry reflected in the shimmering river, and often adorned with fret-work grills of embossed wood or the delicate iron tracery of *reixes,* themselves hanging with vines and flowers. Cross the bridge over to the old city from under the arcades in the corner of the *Plaça de la Independència* and find your way to the tourist office, to the right at Rambla Llibertat 1. Then work your way up through the labyrinth of steep streets, using the cathedral's huge Baroque facade as a guide. Note that you can now purchase a **single-admission ticket** (good for one month) for all Girona museums at any town museum for 800 ptas./€4.81.

★ ② At the heart of the old city is Girona's **Catedral,** famous for its nave—at 75 ft, the widest in the world and the epitome of the spatial ideal of Catalan Gothic architects. Since the time when Charlemagne founded the original church in the 8th century, it has been through many fires, changes, destructions, and renovations, so you are greeted by a Rococo-era facade—"eloquent as organ music" and impressively set off by a spectacular flight of 17th-century stairs, which rises from its own plaça. Inside, three smaller naves were compressed into one gigantic hall by the famed architect Guillermo Bofill in 1416—typical of Catalan Gothic "hall" churches, this was made to facilitate preaching to crowds. The cathedral of Girona is now undergoing a complete restoration—its famous silver canopy, or *baldaquí* (baldachin), has now been restored and has recently been put back on view. Not on general view are the cathedral's red velvet pillows, used only for special occasions such as weddings (although a few are in place for celebrants of the Mass)—they were originally paid for in the 18th century by a duchess who calloused her knees in prayer. The oldest part of the cathedral remains the 11th-century Romanesque **Torre de Carlemany** (Charlemagne Tower).

The cathedral has an exquisite 12th-century cloister, which has an obvious affinity with the cloisters found in the Roussillon area of France; you can visit them with a ticket to the cathedral's **Museu Capitular,** or Tresor, indeed filled with treasures, including a 10th-century copy of Beatus's manuscript *Commentary on the Apocalypse*—one of the famous 10th-century manuscripts illuminated in the dramatically primitive, pre-Picassoian Mozarabic style—the Bible of Emperor Charles V, and the celebrated *Tapís de la Creació (Tapestry of the Creation),* considered by most experts to be the finest tapestry surviving from the Romanesque era (and in fact, thought to be the needlework of Saxons working in England). It depicts the seven days of the Creation of the World as told in Genesis in the primitive but powerful fashion of early Romanesque art, and looks not unlike an Asian mandala. It is made of wool with predominant colors of green, brown, and ochre; it once hung behind the main altar as a pictorial Bible lesson. The four seasons, the stars, winds, months of the year and days of the week, plants, animals, and elements of nature circle round a central figure, likening paradise to the eternal cosmos presided over by Christ whose penetrating gaze impassively watches the immutable wheel of time. In addition to its intrinsic beauty, along the bottom band (which appears to have been added at a later date) another significant detail is the depiction of two *iudeis,* or Jews, dressed in the round cloaks they were obliged to wear to set them apart from Christians. This scene is thought to be the earliest portrayal of a Jew known in Christian art. ✉ ☎ 972/214426. 🎟 *500 ptas./€3.01.* 🕐 *Oct.–Feb, Tues. to Sat, 10–2 and 4–6; March to June, Tues. to Sat, 10–2 and 4–7, July–Sept. 10–8; Sun. and holidays, 10–8; closed Mon.*

Housed in the Episcopal Palace (found on the eastern side of the cathedral), the **Museu d'Art** is Girona's main art museum, with an extensive collection, ranging from superb Romanesque *Majestats* (carved wood figures of Christ), reliquaries from Sant Pere de Rodes, and illuminated 12th-century manuscripts to paintings of the 20th-century Olot school of landscape. ✉ *Pujada de la Catedral 12,* ☎ *972/209536.* 🎟 *300 ptas./€1.80.* 🕐 *Tues.–Sat. 10–6, Sun. 10–2.*

After touring the cathedral complex, head back down the cathedral stairs—at the bottom looms the vast bulk of the church of **Sant Feliu,** landmarked by one of Girona's most distinctive belfries, topped by eight pinnacles. Today, one of Girona's most beloved churches, it was repeatedly rebuilt and altered over four centuries and stands today as an amalgam of Romanesque columns, Gothic nave, and Baroque facade. It was founded over the tomb of St. Felix of Africa, a martyr under Diocletian. ✉ *Pujada de Sant Feliu,* ☎ *972/201407.* ⊙ *Daily 9–10:30, 11:30–1, and 4–6:30.*

㉕ At the base of the cathedral's 90 steps, go left through the Sobreportes gate to the **Banys Arabs** (Arab Baths). In fact, the Arab baths are misnamed since they were actually built by Morisco craftsmen in the late 12th century, long after Girona's Islamic occupation (795–1015) had ended. Following the old Roman model that had disappeared in the West, the custom of bathing publicly may have been brought back from the Holy Land with the Crusaders. These baths are sectioned off into three rooms in descending order; a *frigidarium,* or cold bath, a square room with a central octagonal pool and a skylight with cupola held up by two stories of eight fine columns; a *tepidarium,* or warm bath; and a *caldarium,* or steam room, beneath which is a chamber where a fire was kept burning. Here the inhabitants of the old Girona came to relax, exchange gossip, or do business. We know from another public bath house in Tortosa, Tarragona, that the various social classes came to bathe by sexes on fixed days of the week; Christian men on one day, Christian women on another, Jewish men on still another, Jewish women (and prostitutes) on a fourth, Moslems, etc. ✉ *250 ptas./€1.50.* ⊙ *May–Sept., Tues.–Sat. 10–2 and 4–7, Sun. 10–2; Oct.– Apr., Tues.–Sun. 10–1.*

㉖ For more insight into Girona's history, head from the cathedral square, down Pujade Rei Marti and across the River Galligants to the church of **Sant Pere** (St. Peter; finished in 1131 and notable for its octagonal Romanesque belfry and the finely detailed capitals atop the columns in the cloister): next door is the **Museu Arqueològic** (Museum of Archaeology), which documents the region's history since Paleolithic times. ✉ *350 ptas./€2.10.* ⊙ *Church and museum daily 10–1 and 4:30–7.*

㉗ From the Museu Arqueològic you can head to the stepped **Passeig Arquaeològic,** which runs below the walls of the Old City, and which offers picturesque views from belvederes and watchtowers. From there, climb through the Jardins de la Francesa to the highest ramparts for a view of the town cathedral's famous 11th-century Romanesque Torre de Carlemany (Charlemagne Tower).

㉘ Girona is especially noted for **El Call,** its 13th-century Jewish Quarter, which can be found branching off Carrer de la Força, south of the Plaça Catedral. Jaume Riera i Sans, Director of the Archives of the Crown of Aragon, in Barcelona, and a Hebrew scholar, believes the word *call* (pronounced "kyle" in Catalan) is an old Catalan word meaning "narrow way or passage," derived from the Latin word *callum* or *callis.* Others suggest that it comes from the Hebrew word Qahal, meaning assembly or meeting of the community. Owing allegiance to the Spanish king (who exacted tribute for this distinction) and not to the city government, this once prosperous Jewish community—one of the most flourishing in Europe during the Middle Ages—was, at its height, a leading center of learning, with one of the most important schools of the Kabala (a body of mystical teachings of rabbinical origin from the 12th century, based on an esoteric interpretation of the Hebrew Scriptures) centered here. The most famous teacher of the Kabala from Girona was Mossé ben Nahman (also known as Nahmànides and by the acronym Ramban) who is popularly believed to be one and the same as Bonastruc ça Porta. ahmànides was the author of an important religious worked based on meditation and the reinterpretation of the Bible and the Talmud. According to the renowned Kabalistic scholar Gersholm C. Scholem, "In the history of the old Kabbalah, the Kabbalists of Girona were a group of epochal importance." The earliest presence of Jews in Girona is uncertain, but the first historical mention dates from 982, when a group of 25 Jewish families moved to Girona from nearby Juïgues, though Jews may have been already present in the region for several hundred years. Maria José Fuentes, professor of semitic philology at the University of Barcelona, has identified an amulet with the Star of David found at the ruins of Empúries that has been dated from the 2nd century AD.

Today the layout of El Call bears no resemblance to what this area looked like in the 15th century when Jews last lived here. Space was at a premium inside the city walls in Girona and houses were built higgledy-piggledy one atop the other. The narrow streets, barely wide enough for a single person to pass (they have now been widened slightly), crisscrossed one above the other. Evidence of the labyrinthlike layout of a few street ruts may still be seen inside the antique store Antiguitats la **29** Canonja Vella located in the **Placeta del Institut Vell,** located on Carrer de la Força. It is hear that you can also study a tar-blackened three-inch-long, half-inch-deep groove carved shoulder-high into the stone of the right door post as you enter. Few had ever noticed this small slot until the late scholar Eduard Tell correctly identified it as the placement of a *mezuzah,* a small case or tube of metal or wood in which a piece of parchment with verses from the Old Testament (declaring the essence of Jewish belief in one God), was placed within this slot and held there with tar. Every time someone went through the doorway this phylactery was touched as a sign of devotion. There is a second slot for another *mezuzah* inside this house on the door to the left as you enter in the same placement as the outside one. Very few examples of this article of worship are found elsewhere in Europe. A piece of parchment with the sacred verses was discovered in a nearby house (now in a private collection). ✉ *Carrer de la Força 33.*

30 The **Centre Bonastruc ça Porta,** at Carrer de la Força 8, is the lifeblood of the activities that refer to the recuperation of the Jewish heritage of Girona. Director Assumpció Hosta and her dedicated staff organize conferences, exhibitions, and seminars. Its newly enlarged **Museu de Història dels Jueus** (Museum of Jewish History) houses 21 stone tablets, one of the finest collections anywhere in the world of medieval Jewish funerary slabs, many with moving reverential inscriptions ("This stone is in memory of the honourable Estelina, wife of the illustrious Bonastruc Yosef; may she abide in the Garden of Eden. Amen."). These were recovered from the old Jewish cemetery of Montjuïc (which means "mountain of the Jews," the same as Montjuïc in Barcelona, where there was also a Jewish cemetery), revealed when the railroad between Barcelona and France was laid out in the nineteenth century. Its exact location, about one mile north of the city of Girona on the road to La Bisbal and known as *La Tribana,* is now being scientifically excavated by the use of sound waves and could well turn up additional material. The Centre Bonastruc ça Porta is also home to the Institut d'Estudis Nahmànides, with its extensive library on Judaica. ✉ *Carrer de la Força 8,* ☎ *972/276761.* ◻ *300 ptas./€1.80.* ☉ *May–Oct., Mon.–Sat. 10–8, Sun. 10–3; Nov.–Apr., Mon.–Sat. 10–6, Sun. 10–3.*

A five-minute walk uphill behind the cathedral leads to the **Torre de Gironella,** a tower several stories high surrounded by a park and marking the highest point in the Jewish Quarter. The tower was where Girona's Jewish community took refuge in early August of 1391, emerging 17 weeks later to find their houses in ruins. Even though Spain's official expulsion decree did not go into effect intil 1492, this attack effectively ended the Girona Jewish community. On December 20, 1998, the first Hanukkah celebration in 607 years took place in the gardens here, with representatives of the Jewish communities of Spain, France, Portugal, Germany, and the United States in attendance and Jerusalem's chief Sephardic rabbi, Rishon Letzion, presiding. It was an historic and moving event.

DINING AND LODGING

$$$$ ✕ **Albereda.** Excellent Catalan cuisine is served in a bright, if somewhat subdued, setting. Try the *galeta amb llagostins glaçada* (zucchini bisque with prawns). ⊠ *Carrer Albereda 7 bis,* ☎ 972/226002. *AE, DC, MC. Closed Sun.*

$$$$ ✕ **Celler de Can Roca.** With one Michelin star, this excellent restau-
★ rant, considered one of the eight or nine best in Spain, is a must stop for any self-respecting gourmet. You can survey the kitchen from the dining-room and watch chef Joan Roca create his masterful *arròs amb garotes i botifarra negre* (rice with urchins and black sausage), *cua de bou farcida amb foie gras* (oxtail stuffed with *foie gras*), and *bacallà amb espinacs i crema Idiazabal amb panses i pinyons* (cod with spinach and creme of Idiazabal cheese with raisins and pine nuts). For dessert try the *pastel calent de xocolata i gingebre* (hot chocolate cake with ginger) or jasmine tea ice cream. An awesome wine list awaits you. ⊠ *Carretera Taialà 40,* ☎ 972/222157. *AE, DC, MC, V. Closed Sun., Mon., and 1st two wks of July.*

$$–$$$ ✕ **Cal Ros.** Tucked under the arcades just behind the north end of Plaça
★ de la Llibertat, this historic place combines ancient stone arches with a crisp, contemporary decor and cheerful lighting. The cuisine is gamey and delicious: hot goat-cheese salad with pine nuts and *garum* (blackolive and anchovy paste dating back to Roman times), *oca amb naps* (goose with turnips), and a blackberry sorbet not to miss. ⊠ *Carrer Cort Reial 9,* ☎ 972/217379. *MC, V. Closed Mon. No dinner Sun.*

$$–$$$ ✕ **Penyora.** Here you'll find both good local fare and, if you order from the prix-fixe menu, a bargain. ⊠ *Carrer Nou del Teatre 3,* ☎ 972/218948. *AE, DC, MC. Closed Tues.*

$$$$ 🏨 **Carlemany.** Historic Girona has one foot firmly planted in the present, as the glittering modern edifice proves. In the center of the new city, the hotel's glass-encased façade overlooks an historic tower on a plaza, making for an impressive effect. The hotel hallways and rooms are hung with 100 original contemporary paintings and 40 lithographs. ⊠ *Plaça Miquel Santaló 1, 17002,* ☎ 972/211212, ℻ 972/214994. *87 rooms, 3 suites. AE, DC, MC, V.* 🍴

$$–$$$ 🏨 **Ultonia.** This central hotel is decorated with attractive wooden tables, paneling, and cupboards. ⊠ *Gran Via Jaume I 22, 17001,* ☎ 972/203850, ℻ 972/203334. *45 rooms. Coffee shop. AE, DC, MC, V.*

$ **Apartaments Històric Girona.** A suite of full apartments, these accom-
★ modations are located in a 9th-century house (actually, there are remnants of a 3rd-century Roman wall on the ground floor and in one of the apartments). One dining room even features a wall made in *opus spicatum* herringbone pattern, antedating Romanesque style. Casilda Cruz rents these apartments located in the Girona's old quarter for as many days as you'd like, from one day to one month, and they are even more enticing due to their bargain rates. ⊠ *Carrer Bellmirall 4A,* ☎ 972/223583. *5 apartments. AE, DC, MC, V.* 🍴

$ 🏨 **Bellmirall.** This pretty little hostel across the Onyar in the Jewish Quarter is charming and offers top value in the heart of Girona's most historic section. ⊠ *Carrer Bellmirall 3, 17001,* ☎ 972/204009. *7 rooms. AE, DC, MC, V. Closed Jan.*

Nightlife and the Arts

Girona is a university town so there's an especially lively night scene during the school year. Popular places for the young hip set include: **Platea** (⊠ Carrer Geroni Real de Fontclara 4, ☎ 972/227288); **Accés 21** (⊠ Carrer Bonaventura Carreres Peralta 7, ☎ 972/213708). The older crowd goes to **La Via** (⊠ Pedret 66, ☎ 972/410461), on the road going to Palamós. During the summer, the action is centered in **Les Carpes de la Devesa,** a park planted with huge plane trees on the other side of the Onyar river. From June to September 15, three awnings, or *carpes,* are set up in La Devesa for people to sit outside in the warm weather until the wee hours, enjoying drinks and listening to music. All Girona parties the summer away here.

Shopping

Girona has lots of good stores but here are some that are especially visiting. Don't forget—when your buying spree is over, repair to **La Vienesa** (⊠ Carrer La Pujada del Pont de Pedra 1, ☎ 972/486046) for some superb tea and pastries. If it's jewelry you're looking for, head to **Anna Casals** (⊠ Carrer Ballesteries 33, ☎ 972/410227). All manner of masks, dolls, pottery, and crafts are available at **La Carpa** (⊠ Ballesteries 37, ☎ 972/212002; candles are the specialty at **Karla** (⊠ Ballesteries 21, ☎ 972/227210). For design, plastic arts, restoration, interior decoration, religious paintings, and sculptures stop at **Dolors Turró** (⊠ Ballesteries 19, ☎ 972/410193). Two tempting food shops are **Gluki** (⊠ Argenteria 26, ☎ 972/201989), makers of chocolate since 1880, and **Turrons Candela** (⊠ Argenteria 3, ☎ 972/220938), which specializes in nougat.

For fine women's clothes the place to go is **Codina** (⊠ Carrer Santa Clara 24, ☎ 972/219880). Men will find fine garb at **Falcó** (⊠ Carrer Maluquer Salvador 16, ☎ 972/207156). Young people stock up for threads at **Desideratum** (⊠ Carrer Migdia 30, ☎ 972/221448). For shoes it's **Peacock** (⊠ Carrer Nou 15, ☎ 972/226848.

The best bookstore in Girona, with a large travel-guide section, and a small section of English fiction, is **Llibreria 22** (⊠ Carrer Hortes 22, ☎ 972/217295). For travel books and other editions in English, try **Ulysus** (⊠ Ballesteries 22, ☎ 972/221773).

Banyoles

 19 km (12 mi) north of Girona, 116 km (72 mi) from Barcelona.

Numbers in the margin correspond to points of interest on the Catalonia: Costa Brava to Tarragona map.

After visiting cosmopolitan Girona, escape into the Catalan countryside at Banyoles, known for its natural beauty of the **Estany de Banyoles,** the lake where rowing contests were held for the 1992 Olympic Games. In addition to Olympic-standard rowers, many other people come here to swim, row about the lake in boats, picnic along the shore, or fish for its famous carp. Although there is no Loch Ness monster here, reputedly there is a fabled carp said to be almost 100 years old called *La Ramona,* that weighs more than 15 kilos (33 lbs) and eats peanuts from your hand. You can try and spot her by renting a rowboat for 500 pesetas per hour per person, or taking the scenic cruiser around the lake for the same price. If she's swimming in the depths, forget abot it—legend has it this lake is so deep a young man dove in and came out in Majorca. The town of Banyoles itself has a graceful historic quarter, complete with the Monestir de Sant Esteve (usually locked, but ask around for admittance) and an arcaded Plaça Major. If you wish to stay over (most people make this a day-trip from Girona), inquire about accommodations at the local Turismo office at Passeig de la Industria 25.

The archaeological site of La Draga, situated next to the lake and a 10-minute walk from town, has revealed highly interesting finds. Neolithic lake dwellers made their home here and almost every season there are new discoveries. Catalan archaeologists working at this lakeshore site found a wooden tool at least 7,000 years old, the oldest wooden artifact ever found in the Mediterranean area, and one of the oldest in the world. Many of their finds are on view at the local **Museu d'Arqueològic.** At the museum you can also see the bones of ancient mastadons found in the area, and a copy of the famous Banyoles Jaw, discovered in 1887 and believed to be more than 100,000 years old, making it one of the earliest known human jawbones. Other regional treasures of natural history are on view at the Museu Municipal Darder d'Historia Natural on the adjacent Plaça dels Estudis. ⊠ *Plaça de Font 11, 17820,* ☎ *972/572361.* 🖼 *300 ptas./€1.80.* ☉ *Sept.–June, Tues.–Sat. 10:30–1:30 and 4–6:30, Sun. 10:30–2; July–Aug., 11–1:30 and 4–8, Sun. 10:30–2.*

Besalú

32 *25 km (15 mi) north of Banyoles, 34 km (21 mi) north of Girona.*

Besalú, once the capital of a feudal county that was part of Charlemagne's 8th- and 9th-century Spanish March, is 25 km (15 mi) west of Figueres on C260 and remains one of the most well-preserved and evocative medieval towns in Catalonia. This ancient town's most emblematic feature is its Romanesque **Pont Fortificat,** an 11th-century fortified bridge with crenellated battlements. Also, main sights are its two churches, Sant Vicenç (set on a café-lined and picturesque plaza) and Sant Pere, and the ruins of the convent of Santa Maria on the hill above town. The tourist office is in the arcaded Plaça de la Llibertat and can provide current opening hours for Sant Pere as well as keys to the *miqvé,* the unusual **Jewish baths** discovered in the 1960s.

There is another way to see the *miqvé* and the churches (usually closed otherwise): join the special guided tours—led by residents and some 30 costumed actors—of the historic quarter offered every Wednesday during July and August, which begin punctually at 11 PM at the entrance to the historic bridge. Just past the bridge, you nearly revert to the 11th century. Once in the quarter you are welcomed by a rabbi from the old Jewish community and shown the *miqvé,* where you can place a candle that floats in the waters. A walk through the **Call,** or Jewish Quarter, follows. A medieval "buffoon" then arrives, adding hilarity to the ambience. Laughter is followed by Gregorian chant, which can be heard in a visit to the church of Sant Pere, with a noted 13th-century ambulatory. The price for the tour is 1,500 pesetas, and tickets should be booked at the local tourist office (☎ 972/591240; open June through September only) on Plaça de la Llibertat, site of a Tuesday market.

Dining

$$$$ ✕ **Els Fogons de Can Llaudes.** In an 11th-century Romanesque chapel
★ that has been faithfully restored, proprietor Jaume Soler just won Spain's prestigious National Gastronomy Prize, and is teetering on the edge of a Michelin star. The *Menú de Degustació* (taster's menu) is recommended. Be sure to call ahead for reservations. ⊠ *Prat de Sant Pere 6,* ☎ *972/590858. MC, V. Closed Nov. 8–21 and Tues.*

Olot

③③ *21 km (13 mi) west of Besalu, 55 km (34 mi) northwest of Girona.*

Capital of the Garrotxa area, Olot is famous for its 19th-century school of landscape painters and has several excellent Art Nouveau buildings, including one with a facade by Domènech i Muntaner. The **Museu Comarcal de la Garrotxa** (County Museum of La Garrotxa) holds an important assemblage of *Modernismo* as well as sculptures by Miquel Blai, creator of the long-tressed maidens who support the balconies along Olot's main boulevard. ✉ *Carrer Hospici 8,* ☎ *972/279130.* ⧉ *450 ptas./€2.70.* ☉ *Mon. and Wed.–Sat. 10–1 and 4–7, Sun. 10–1:30.*

The villages of **Vall d'En Bas** lie south of Olot off Route A153. A new freeway cuts across this countryside to Vic, but you'll miss a lot by taking it. The twisting old road leads you through rich farmland past farmhouses whose dark wooden balconies are bedecked with bright flowers. Turn off for **Sant Privat d'En Bas** and **Els Hostalets d'En Bas.**

DINING AND LODGING

$$$ ✕ **Restaurante Ramón.** Ramón is so exclusive that he adamantly refuses to be in this book, so please don't let him see it. His restaurant, Olot's gourmet alcove par excellence, is the opposite of rustic: sleek, modern, refined, and international. Samples of the *cuina de la terra* (home cooking of regional specialties) include *patata de Olot* (potato stuffed with veal) and *cassoleta de judias amb xoriç* (white haricot beans with sausage). ✉ *Plaça Clarà 10,* ☎ *972/261001. Reservations essential. AE, DC, MC, V. Closed Thurs.*

$$$ 🏨 **Parador de Vic.** This quietly charming parador, also known as the Parador del Bac de Sau, is 14 km (9 mi) northeast of town off the Roda de Ter road past the village of Tavernoles. The views take in a stunning mountain and nearly lunar landscape over the Sau Reservoir. ✉ *Carretera Vic Roda de Ter, 08500,* ☎ *93/8887311. 36 rooms. Coffee shop, pool, tennis court. MC, V.*

$ 🏨 **La Perla.** Known for its friendly family ambience, this hotel is always Olot's first to fill up. On the edge of town toward the Vic Road, it's walking distance from two parks. ✉ *Av. Santa Coloma 97, 17800,* ☎ *972/262326,* 🆉 *972/270774. 30 rooms, 30 apartments. Restaurant, bar. MC, V.*

Montseny

③④ *75 km (47 mi) from Olot, 60 km (40 mi) north of Barcelona.*

Montseny is Barcelona's mountain retreat and refuge, a highland forest less than an hour north of the city, and the highest mountain range in Catalonia outside of the Pyrenees. Montseny's softly undulating slopes sweep up to the Massif's main peaks at Turó de l'Home (5,656 ft), les Agudes (5,633 ft), Matagalls (5,590 ft), and Calma i Puigdrau (4,455 ft). In the summer and in good weather they are a fairly easy climb. The view at the top of the Turó de l'Home can almost be described as overwhelming, stretching to the Pyrenees in the north and far past Barcelona in the south. Known as one of the great *pulmons* (lungs) of Europe for its forests of oxygen-producing beech, pine, oak, and fir trees, Montseny may, in the long run, be even more important to Catalonia's spiritual health than to its physical well-being. Repository of *seny,* which combats *rauxa* (impulsiveness)—the two polar opposites in the Catalan character—Montseny's mountain villages, such as Montseny itself, or Mosqueroles, Riells, Campins, Viladrau, and El Brull are rustic sanctuaries with delightful little inns and *masies* (farmhouses) to admire and to dine or stay in. It has been a protected park area since 1978 and that same year UNESCO included it within its MAB (Man and Biosphere) program of its world network of biosphere reserves. The *Servei de Parcs Naturals* (☎ 93/340-2541, www.diba.es/parcs/montseny/montseny.htm) organizes excursions along the many rivers and streams draining the Montseny Massif.

Dining and Lodging

$$$$ 🏨 **Hotel Monastir de Sant Marçal.** Jordi Tell runs this small, very exclusive hotel high up in the Montseny massif. Located in an 11th-century monastery with adjacent chapel (where mass can be celebrated), it offers a personalized sanctum sanctorum. Some visitors will appreciate its library; others, its private honey-based cosmetic line, *Sant Marçal del Montseny.* ⊠ *Carretera de Sant Celoni a Sant Marçal, Km 28, 08460, Montseny,* ☎ *93/8473043. 12 rooms. Restaurant, pool, beauty parlor, massage. AE, DC, MC, V.* 🐾

$$$ ✕🏨 **Can Barrina.** With splendid views over the Montseny Massif this classical country house, built in 1600 and restored in 1988, offers a menu strong on local products ranging from wild mushrooms such as *rossinyols* (chanterelles) and *múrgules* (morels) to wild boar, rabbit, duck, and venison. The roaring fireplace in the restaurant can be complemented by another in your room (if you can manage to secure either Rooms D or F) and in summer, the pool is welcome after a day of hiking the crests. ⊠ *Crtra. Palautordera, Km 1.2, south of Montseny,* ☎ *93/847–3065,* ℻ *93/847–3184. 14 rooms. AE, DC, MC, V.*

$$$ ✕🏨 **Can Marlet.** This ivy-covered stone hideaway near the village Riells offers excellent country cooking and cozy rooms for short escapes from Barcelona. Dinner by the fireplace after a fall hike through the Montseny beech forest might feature lamb, rabbit, or wild boar stew, all prominent features on the Can Marlet menu. ⊠ *Km 1.5 southeast of Riells,* ☎ *972/310023,* ℻ *972/870943. 11 rooms. AE, DC, MC, V. Closed Oct.–Mar. except weekends.*

SOUTHERN CATALONIA: MONTSERRAT TO TARRAGONA

The environs of Barcelona abound in places of great interest to both lovers of antiquity and of scenic landscapes—Sant Cugat del Vallés, with a lovely Benedictine abbey; Tarassa, the ancient Egara, which has charming examples of Romanesque architecture; Llobregat, with a Roman bridge. But the main ambition of many a tourist is to see the world-famous monastery of Montserrat, where medieval legend placed the Holy Grail (a claim contested by many other places!). From Montserrat you can move south of Barcelona and continue backward in time, with a time-out for a pleasure stop in Sitges, which is the prettiest and most popular resort in Barcelona's immediate environs, flaunting an excellent beach, a picturesque old quarter, and some interesting Moderniste bits. In from the coast lies the "Cistercian triangle," with two celebrated historic monasteries at Poblet and Santes Creus, with a walled town at Montblanc. Farther to the south, along the coast, the time machine zooms back to the days of ancient Rome when you arrive in Tarragona, in Roman times regarded as one of the Empire's finest creations; its wine was already famous and its population was the first *gens togata* in Spain, which conferred on them equality with the citizens of Rome. Roman relics, with the Circus Maximus heading the list, are still the stamp of Tarragona's grandeur, and to this the Middle Ages added wonderful city walls and citadels that fit the place like a glove.

Trains south from Barcelona take you to Sitges and Tarragona. A short railroad line serves Montserrat, taking you to Monistrol where you can catch the funicular to the monastery. If you're traveling southeast of Barcelona, to get to Sitges and Tarragona by road, your best bet is to take highway A16 south. You can also take one of the regular roads south, but again they are heavily traveled, particularly in the tourist season. If you are visiting the monasteries of Santes Creus and Poblet, take A7 south and turn west at L'Arboç. You will get to Montserrat by taking A18 west.

Numbers in the margin correspond to points of interest on the Catalonia: Costa Brava to Tarragona map.

Montserrat

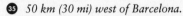 *50 km (30 mi) west of Barcelona.*

You don't have to be a believer to visit Montserrat. A nearly obligatory side trip from Barcelona is the shrine of *La Moreneta,* the Black Virgin of Montserrat, high in the mountains of the *Serra de Montserrat.* These weird, saw-tooth, phantasmagorical peaks have given rise to countless legends: Here St. Peter left a statue of the Virgin Mary carved by St. Luke, Parsifal found the Holy Grail, and Wagner sought inspiration for his opera. Whatever the truth of such mysteries, Montserrat is Catalonia's spiritual heartland. A monastery has stood on this site since the early Middle Ages, though the present 19th-century building replaced the rubble left by Napoléon's troops in 1812. Montserrat is the third most-visited tourist destination in Catalonia. Honeymooning couples flock here by the thousands seeking *La Moreneta's* blessing on their marriages. Twice a year, on April 27, Our Lady of Montserrat's name day, and September 8, that celebrates the *Verges trobades* (found virgins) of Catalonia, those statues of Our Lady discovered by shepherds in remote places and venerated all over the country, the diminutive statue of Montserrat's Black Virgin becomes the object of one of Spain's greatest pilgrimages.

While the Montserrat complex is vast, most architectural historians excoriate its modern renovation, bandying about adjectives like "ugly" and "wretched." Note, however, the Gothic portal of the Twelve Apostles. Of the monastery, only the basilica and museum are regularly open to the public. The **basilica** is dark and ornate, its blackness pierced by the glow of hundreds of votive lamps. Above the high altar stands the famous polychrome statue of the Virgin and Child, to which the faithful can pay their respects by way of a separate door (incidentally, the statue is black due to centuries of incense and candle smoke, not because the face and hands were ever painted black). Another treasure found here is the **Escolania,** the monastery's famous boys' choir, founded in the 13th century and noted for their rendition of the *Salve*—always a memorable experience. The boys receive intense musical training from an early age and a general education as well. Some boys later enter the monastery as monks while others move on to various professional activities, often with great success. At 1 PM daily they sing the *Salve regina* and the *Virolai,* the hymn of Our Lady of Montserrat. In the evening after vespers, at 7:10 PM, they sing, together with the monks, the *Salve montserratina,* alternating between polyphony and Gregorian chant. On Sunday and holidays they take part in the Mass at Montserrat and in vespers. In July and at Christmas the choir is away from Montserrat on vacation. The Escolania is one of the finest boys choirs in the world, regularly giving concerts on tour and recording music.

The monastery's **museum** has two sections: the Secció Antiga (open Tuesday–Saturday 10:30–2) contains old masters, among them paintings by El Greco, Correggio, and Caravaggio, and the amassed gifts to the Virgin; the Secció Moderna (open Tuesday–Saturday 3–6) concentrates on more recent artists. Visiting this art museum can be unsettling to those who expect Montserrat's monks to consecrated their lives to poverty and meditation. Of course, they have done so, but this impressive art collection is the result of private bequests. Xavier Busquets, one of Barcelona's most important architects, left many Impressionist and Modernist paintings to Montserrat on his death in 1990, including works by Monet, Sisley, Degas, Pissarro, Rouault, Sargent, Sorolla, and Zuloaga. Other donors have left examples by lesser-known masters of 19th- and 20th-century Catalan painting: Martí Alsina, Joaquim Vayreda, Francesc Gimeno, Santiago Rusiñol, Ramon Casas, Isidre Nonell, Joaquim Mir, Hermen Anglada-Camarassa, plus works by Picasso and Dalí.

But Montserrat is as memorable for its setting as for its artistic and religious treasures, so be sure to explore its strange, pink hills, many of whose crests are dotted with hermitages. The hermitage of **Sant Joan** can be reached by funicular. The views over the mountains to the Mediterranean and, on a clear day, to the Pyrenees, are breathtaking. Montserrat's rocky masses are of stone conglomerate, which, over thousands of years, have been molded into bizarre shapes by tectonic movements, climactic changes, and erosion. In the deep, humid shades between the stony outcroppings vegetation is exuberant. Nature lovers will relish traversing the many trails and paths that crisscross these formations; there are many routes good for short walks of a half day or more. Expert climbers will be challenged by the difficulty of the pinnacles and spires that rise at every turn, but play it safe—every year climbers are killed or injured. The countless legends that surround the monastery are undoubtedly rooted in the fantastic and strangely unreal appearance of these peaks of San Jerónimo, some of which jut up abruptly 3,725 ft above the valley of the River Llobregat and are outlined with monoliths which, from a distance, look like immense stone figures. Look especially for La Momia and her "daughter" La Momieta. El Massif de Sant Salvador crowns all. Also remarkable are the six colossal rocks called Les Santes Magdalenes, which have been compared to hashish visions, Henry Moore sculptures, and a Victorian tea party. In 1987, Montserrat's mountain range was declared a national park. On the night of June 9, 2000, Montserrat suffered a terrible rainstorm and flashflood. Damage to many dependencies of Montserrat was enormous. The very next day, work began to restore the damage, and by 2001 things should be back to normal again. Fortunately, the museum and the basilica were not damaged.

To get to Montserrat, follow the A2/A7 *autopista* on the new upper ring road (Ronda de Dalt), or from the western end of the Diagonal as far as Sortida (Exit) 25 to Martorell. Bypass this industrial center and follow signs to Montserrat. You can also take a train from Barcelona's Plaça Espanya metro station, which takes you to Monistrol de Montserrat, from where you can catch the funicular to the monastery, or a guided tour with Pullmantur or Julià. ☎ 93/877–7777. ☉ *Basilica: daily 6–10:30 and noon–6:30; museum: Secció Antiga Tues.–Sat. 10:30–2, Secció Moderna Tues.–Sat. 3–6.* ✍

Sitges

❸❻ *81 km (50 mi) southeast of Montserrat, 43 km (27 mi) south of Barcelona.*

This is no sleepy little village. In summer it's an action-packed town that never sleeps—its beaches are teeming and its nightlife, especially along Primer de Maig street, known as *"Carrer del Pecat"* (street of sin), is famous. The old part of the village still retains its narrow streets and cool, white fishermen's houses, while apartment developments spread in all directions.

Once a distant summer holiday resort, this beautiful but overgrown village has long been nicknamed *Blanca Subur* for its whitewashed houses. With its easily recognizable 18th-century Baroque-façaded parish church of Sant Bartomeu and Santa Tecla sitting on the promontory of La Punta over the sea—a scene endlessly painted by artists—Sitges has almost become a suburb of Barcelona. With the construction of the four-lane A16 highway, it's just a 20-minute commute away, and the train only takes about a half hour.

There's always been an artistic climate in Sitges. At the end of the 19th century followers of the *Modernista* movement flocked here by the hand of Santiago Rusiñol to celebrate the *Festes Modernistes,* a bonding of like-minded artists. American millionaire Charles Deering, heir to the farm-machinery fortune of his father William Deering, stayed here from 1910 to 1921 and was a friend of the *Modernistes,* playing a leading role in stimulating the arts in Sitges.

Natives of Sitges emigrated to America in the 19th century, especially to Cuba and Puerto Rico, many returning with great fortunes that they quickly spent on splendid homes that are still standing. You can see the elegant Vidal-Quardas homes at Carrer del Port Alegre 9 and Carrer Davallada 12, as well as many others around the town. February is Carnival time, and Sitges hosts thousands of visitors who come to see the parades and outrageous costumes. The large gay community of Sitges is especially visible at this time.

The most interesting museum here is the **Cau-Ferrat,** founded by the artist Santiago Rusiñol (1861–1931) and containing some of his own paintings together with two El Grecos. Connoisseurs of wrought iron will love the beautiful collection of *creus terminals,* crosses that once marked town boundaries. ✉ *Fonollar s/n,* ☎ *93/894–0364.* 💶 *500 ptas./€3.01; 1st Wed. of month free.* ☉ *Tues.–Sun. 10–2 and 5–9. Closed Mon.*

NEED A BREAK?	Linger over excellent seafood in a nonpareil sea-view setting at **Vivero.** ✉ *Passeig Balmins s/n,* ☎ *93/894–2149. Closed Tues. Dec.–May.*

En Route Upon leaving Sitges, make straight for the A2 *autopista* by way of Vilafranca del Penedès. Wine buffs may want to stop here to taste the excellent Penedès wines; you can tour and sip at the **Bodega Miguel Torres** (✉ Comercio 22, ☎ 93/890–0100). There's an interesting **Museu del Vi** (Wine Museum) in the Royal Palace, with descriptions of wine-making history. 💶 *500 ptas./€3.01.* ☉ *Tues.–Sun. 10–2 and 4–7.*

If you're traveling to Sitges by car, head southwest along Gran Via or Passeig Colom to the freeway that passes the airport on its way to Castelldefels. From here, the new freeway and tunnels will get you to Sitges in 20–30 minutes. Regular trains leave Sants and Passeig de Gràcia for Sitges; the ride takes half an hour. To get from Montserrat to Sitges you don't have to go back to Barcelona; take local road C1411 south from Montserrat to get on the autopista A7. Continue south on the A7 to Vilafranca del Penedès where you exit and take local road B211 to Sitges.

Dining and Lodging

$$$$ ✕ **La Nansa.** Located on a narrow street in the old quarter, this family restaurant, now in its fifth generation and run by Antoni Rafecas, has been open for 38 years and is famous for having brought back from

the last century *arròs a la sitgetana* (Sitges-style rice, a rice broth with meats and seafood). It also makes an award-winning suquet de lluerna (*suquet* of gurnard fish). For openers try their home-grown tangy *escabetx de bonítol* (pickled bonito). ⊠ *Carrer de la Carreta 24,* ☎ *93/8941927. AE, DC, MC, V.*

$$$$ 🏨 **Terramar.** This splendid old hotel is situated at the end of the long beachside promenade and has large balconied rooms with incredible views. Guests have a 50% discount at the golf course behind the hotel, one of the first golf courses to be constructed in Spain. ⊠ *Passeig Marítim 80, 08870,* ☎ *93/8940050,* 𝔽𝔸𝕏 *93/8945604. 204 rooms. Coffee shop. AE, DC, MC, V.*✍

Santes Creus

㊲ *50 km (31 mi) southwest of Sitges, 95 km (59 mi) west of Barcelona.*

Founded in 1157, **Santes Creus** is the first of the monasteries you'll come upon as A2 branches west toward Lleida. Three austere aisles and an unusual 14th-century apse combine with the newly restored cloisters and the courtyard of the royal palace. The cloister was designed by Reinard des Fonoll, probably an Englishman, who stayed on to live for 30 years at the monastery. The columns, originally a symbol of simplicity with leaf or plain motifs, are here a veritable zoo in stone where griffins, mermaids and all types of mythological animals accompany Adam and Eve, elephants, monkeys, dogs and lions. There is even the exotic face of a Viking and the Negroid features of the Green Man, the Celtic representation of nature. From Sitges, drive inland toward Vilafranca del Penedès and the A7 freeway. The A2 (Lleida) leads to the monasteries of Santes Creus and Poblet. To get to Santes Creus from Sitges, trains on the Lleida line go to L'Espluga de Francolí, 4 km (2½ mi) from Poblet. ☎ *977/638329.* ✉ *600 ptas./€3.61.* ☉ *Oct.–Mar., daily 10–1:30 and 3–6; Apr.–Sept., daily 10–1:30 and 3–7.*

Santa Maria de Poblet

★ **㊳** *25 km (19 mi) west of Santes Creus.*

This splendid Cistercian foundation at the foot of the Prades Mountains is one of the great masterpieces of Spanish monastic architecture. The cloister is a stunning combination of lightness and size; on sunny days the shadows on the yellow sandstone are extraordinary. Founded in 1150 by Ramon Berenguer IV in gratitude for the Christian Reconquest, the monastery first housed a dozen Cistercians from Narbonne. Later, the Crown of Aragón used Santa Maria de Poblet for religious retreats and burials. The building was damaged in an 1836 anticlerical revolt, and monks of the reformed Cistercian Order have managed the difficult task of restoration since 1940.

Today, monks and novices again pray before the splendid retable over the tombs of Aragonese rulers, restored to their former glory by sculptor Frederic Marés; sleep in the cold, barren dormitory; and eat frugal meals in the stark refectory. You can join them if you'd like—18 very comfortable rooms are available (for men only). Call Pare Benito (☎ 977/870089) to arrange a stay of up to 15 days within the stones and silence of one of Catalonia's gems.

There has always been a sharp rivalry between the monasteries of Montserrat and Poblet, often taking opposing sides in the many quarrels that plagued Catalonia in its history. The last coup may have been won by Poblet. In 1980, Josep Tarradellas, the first president of the restored Generalitat, Catalonia's autonomous government, left his library and papers to Poblet and not to Montserrat. To get to Poblet from Sitges, trains on the Lleida line go to L'Espluga de Francolí, 4 km (2½ mi) from Poblet. You can also stay with the train to Tarragona and catch a bus to the monastery (✉ Autotransports Perelada, ☎ 973/202058). *Reservations,* ☎ 977/870254. ✏ *500 ptas./€3.01.* ☉ *Guided tour daily 10–12:30 and 3–6 (until 5:30 Oct.–Mar.).*

Tarragona

❸❾ *50 km (30 mi) southeast of Poblet, 98 km (61 mi) southwest of Barcelona.*

Less than an hour from Barcelona, Tarragona offers a bracing mélange of fresh provincial capital. An ancient outpost of the Roman Empire, it remains a pungent fishing port, busy shipping harbor, and vibrant cultural center. The name Tarragona promises rich classical remains, and the city does not disappoint. As capital of the Roman province of Tarraconensis (from 218 BC), Tarraco, as it was then called, formed the empire's principal stronghold in Spain, and by the 1st century BC the city was regarded as one of the empire's finest urban creations. Its wine was already famous, and its people were the first in Spain to become Roman citizens. St. Paul preached here in AD 58, and Tarragona became the seat of the Christian Church in Spain until it was superseded by Toledo in the 11th century.

Entering the city from Barcelona, you'll pass the **triumphal arch of Berà**, dating from the 3rd century BC, 19 km (12 mi) north of Tarragona; and from the Lleida (Lérida) road, or *autopista,* you can see the 1st-century **Roman aqueduct** that helped carry fresh water 32 km (19 mi) from the River Gaià. Tarragona is divided clearly into old and new by the Rambla Vella; the old town and most of the Roman remains are to the north, while modern Tarragona spreads out to the south.

Start your tour of Tarragona at the acacia-lined Rambla Nova, at the end of which is a balcony overlooking the sea, the **Balcó del Mediterràni.** Walking uphill along the Passeig de les Palmeres, you'll arrive at a striking illustration of the dichotomy between ancient and modern.

★ The remains of Tarragona's **amphitheater** are visible down toward the sea; above stands the modern, semicircular Hotel Imperial Tarraco, artfully echoing the amphitheater's curve. Go down the steps to the amphitheater to see just how well preserved it is—you're free to wander through the access tunnels and along the seating rows. Sitting with your back to the sea, you might understand why Augustus favored Tarragona as a winter resort. In the center of the theater are the remains of two superimposed churches, the earlier of which was a Visigothic basilica built to mark the bloody martyrdom of St. Fructuós and his deacons in AD 259. ✏ *500-ptas./€3.01 pass valid for all of Tarragona's Roman remains and Casa Castellarnau.* ☉ *June–Sept., weekdays 9–8, weekends 9–3; Oct.–Mar., weekdays 10–1:30 and 3:30–5:30, weekends 10–2; Apr.–May, weekdays 10–1:30 and 3:30–6:30, weekends 9–3.*

Across the Rambla Vella from the amphitheater, students have excavated the vaults of the 1st-century Roman **Circus Maximus.** The plans just inside the gate show that the vaults now visible formed only a small corner of a vast arena (350 yards long), where 23,000 spectators gathered to watch chariot races. As medieval Tarragona grew, the city gradually swamped the Circus. ✏ *500-pta. pass valid for all of Tarragona's Roman remains and Casa Castellarnau.* ☉ *June–Sept., weekdays 9–8, weekends 9–3; Oct.–May, weekdays 10–1:30 and 4–6:30, weekends 10–2.*

Around the corner from the Circus Maximus, up Passeig Sant Antoni, is the former **Praetorium.** This towering building was Augustus's town house and is reputed to be the birthplace of Pontius Pilate. Its Gothic appearance is the result of extensive alterations in the Middle Ages, when it housed the kings of Catalonia and Aragon during their visits to Tarragona. The Praetorium is now the city's **Museu d'Història** (History Museum), with plans showing the evolution of the city. The museum's highlight is the **Hippolytus sarcophagus**, which bears a bas-relief depicting the legend of Hippolytus and Fraeda. 🖭 *500-pta. pass valid for all of Tarragona's Roman remains and Casa Castellarnau.* ☉ *June–Sept., weekdays 9–8, weekends 9–3; Oct.–May, weekdays 10–1:30 and 4–6:30, weekends 10–2.*

★ Next door to the History Museum, in a 1960s neoclassical building, is Tarragona's **Museu Arqueològic,** whose collection includes Roman statuary and such domestic fittings as keys, bells, and belt buckles. The beautiful mosaics include the Head of Medusa, famous for its piercing stare. Don't miss the video on Tarragona's history. 🖭 *350 ptas./ €2.10; free Tues.* ☉ *June–Sept., Tues.–Sat. 10:30–2 and 4–7, Sun. 10–2; Oct.–May, Tues.–Sat. 10–1:30 and 4–7, Sun. 10–2.*

Follow Passeig de Sant Antoni uphill from the museum (with the city walls on your left) to the ornately sculpted **Portal de Sant Antoni,** and enter the cobbled square. Walk down Carrer d'en Granada—past some lovely arched entryways—to Carrer Sant Bernat, where a right turn will take you into **Plaça del Forum,** once the seat of the provincial Roman authorities. At the far corner of the square you'll see signs for the **cathedral;** walk down Carrer de la Merceria and under the arcade on the right and you'll soon reach the stairway leading up into the **Pla de la Seu,** the cathedral square. The initial rounded placidity of the Romanesque apse, begun in the 12th century, later gave way to the spiky restlessness of the Gothic; the result is confused. If no mass is in progress, enter the cathedral through the cloister. The main attraction here is the altarpiece of St. Tecla, a richly detailed depiction of the life of Tarragona's patron saint. Converted by St. Paul and subsequently persecuted by local pagans, St. Tecla was repeatedly saved from demise through divine intervention. 🖭 *300 ptas./€1.80.* ☉ *Daily 10–1 and 4–7 (10–7 in summer).*

Back up Carrer Major toward the cathedral, Carrer Cavallers will take you down to the **Casa Castellarnau,** a Gothic *palauet,* or town house, built by Tarragona nobility in the 18th century. Now a museum, it features stunning decor from the 18th and 19th centuries. The last member of the Castellarnau family vacated the house in 1954. 🖭 *500-pta. pass valid for all Roman remains and Casa Castellarnau.* ☉ *Mon.–Sat. 10–1 and 4–7 (9–8 in summer), Sun. 10–2.*

At the end of Carrer Cavallers is the Plaça Pallol—**Les Voltes,** on the right, a Roman forum with a Gothic upper story added later, is one of the prettiest corners in Tarragona. Through the **Portal del Roser,** to the right, is the entrance to the **Passeig Arqueològic,** a path skirting the 3rd-century BC Ibero-Roman ramparts, built on even earlier walls of giant rocks. The glacis was added by English military engineers in 1707, during the War of the Spanish Succession. Look for the rusted bronze of Romulus and Remus.

Dining and Lodging

$$$ ✕ **Les Coques.** If you have time for only one meal in Tarragona, take it at this elegant little restaurant in the heart of historic Tarragona. The menu is bursting with both mountain and Mediterranean fare. Meat lovers should try the *costelles de xai* (lamb chops in a dark burgundy sauce); seafood fans should ask for *calamarsets* (baby calamari sautéed in olive oil, garlic, and secret seasonings). Reservations are recommended.

⊠ *Bajada Nueva del Patriarca 2 bis,* ☎ *977/228300. AE, DC, MC, V. Closed Sun. and July.*

$$ ✕ **Les Voltes.** Built into the vaults of the Roman Circus Maximus, this
★ out-of-the-way spot is certain to please hungry travelers lucky enough
to discover it. The hearty cuisine includes Tarragona specialties, mainly
fish dishes, as well as international recipes, with *calçotada* (spring
onions) in winter. ⊠ *Carrer Trinquet Vell 12,* ☎ *977/230651. DC, MC,
V. Closed July–Aug. No dinner Sun., no lunch Mon.*

$$$ 🏨 **Imperial Tarraco.** This large, white, half-moon hotel has a superb
position overlooking the Mediterranean. The large public rooms have
cool marble floors, black-leather furniture, marble-top tables, and
Oriental rugs. Guest rooms are plain but comfortable, and each has a
private balcony. Insist on a sea view. ⊠ *Passeig Palmeres, 43003,* ☎
977/233040, 🗇 *977/216566. 170 rooms. Restaurant, bar, pool, beauty
salon, tennis court, meeting rooms. AE, DC, MC, V.*

$$ 🏨 **Làuria** This is the most pleasant place to stay in downtown Tarragona.
Guest rooms are spacious and comfortable, and their terraces overlook
the serene pool and patio area, the Rambla Nova, or the sea. ⊠ *Rambla Nova 20, Tarragona 43004,* ☎ *977/236712,* 🗇 *977/236700. 72
rooms. Bar, breakfast room. AE, DC, MC, V.* ✎

$ 🏨 **España.** This modern town house offers comfort at a good price.
Guest rooms have white walls, shiny tile floors, and functional 1970s
furniture. Each exterior room has a balcony overlooking the Rambla.
⊠ *Rambla Nova 49, Tarragona 43003,* ☎ *977/232712. 40 rooms.
Breakfast room. AE, DC, MC, V.*

Nightlife and the Arts

Nightlife in Tarragona takes two forms: older and quieter in the upper
city, younger and more raucous down below. There are some lovely,
rustic bars in the Casc Antic, the upper section of old Tarragona. **Poetes** (⊠ Sant Llorenç 15), near the cathedral, is a *bar musical* (bar with
loud music, usually rock or blues) set in a bodega-like cellar. Quieter
talking-and-tippling spots include **El Càndil,** in the Plaça del Forum,
and **Museum.** There's another row of dining and dancing establishments
down in the new Port Esportiu, a newly built pleasure-boat harbor separate from the working port; young people flock here on weekends and
summer nights.

The **Teatre Metropol** (⊠ Rambla Nova 46, ☎ 977/244795) is Tarragona's center for music, dance, theater, and a variety of cultural events
ranging from *castellers* (human-castle formations) to folk dances.

Shopping

You have to haggle for bargains, but **Carrer Major** has some exciting
antiques stores. They're worth a thorough rummage, as the gems tend
to be hidden away. You can also try the shops just in front of the cathedral and in the Pla de la Seu; **Antigüedades Ciria** (⊠ Pla de la Seu 2)
has an interesting selection.

COSTA BRAVA TO TARRAGONA A TO Z

Arriving and Departing

By Bus

Buses to Lloret, Sant Feliu de Guíxols, Platja d'Aro, Palamós, Begur,
Roses, Cadaqués and other destinations on the Costa Brava are operated by **Sarfa** (⊠ Estació del Nord, Alí Bei 80, Barcelona, ☎ 93/265–
1158; Metro: Arc de Triomf). The bus line **Barna Bus** (☎ 93/232–0459)
overlaps and complements some of these destinations; It also leaves
from the same Estació del Nord station as Sarfa Buses. Buses can also

be caught at the Estació del Nord if you're heading south, to destinations like Tarragona and Sitges. **Teisa** handles buses inland from Girona city, and is located right next to the Girona train station (⊠ Estació d'Autobusos, Plaça d'Espanya s/n, Girona, ☎ 972/200275). Other bus transportation hubs are Lloret de Mar, Girona, and Figueres: **Lloret de Mar:** (⊠ Carretera Hostalric a Tossa s/n, ☎ 972/365788; **Girona:** (Plaça d'Espanya s/n, ☎ 972/212319); and **Figueres:** (⊠ Plaça Estació s/n, ☎ 972/673354).

For tours to Montserrat and south contact **Pullmantur** (⊠ Gran Via de les Corts Catalanes 635, ☎ 93/317–1297) or **Julià Tours** (⊠ Santa Eulàlia 178, L'Hospitalet de Llobregat, ☎ 93/402–6900).

By Car

The geographical proximity of the towns and villages of northeastern Catalonia and good roads make for easy access to the many sights and points of interest. From Barcelona, the fastest way to the Costa Brava is to start up the A7 *autopista* tollway toward Girona and then take Sortida (Exit) 10 for Blanes, Lloret de Mar, Tossa de Mar, Sant Feliu de Guíxols, S'Agaró, Platja d'Aro, Palamós, Calella de Palafrugell, and Palafrugell. Or continue north and get off at Sortida 6, the first exit after Girona, for the middle section of the Costa Brava; this will point you directly to the Iberian ruins of Ullastret. In the summer, coastal traffic can be slow and frustrating, and the roads tortuous. To reach the northern part of the Costa Brava, get off the A7 before Figueres at Exit 4, from where you can get to L'Estartit, L'Escala, Empúries, Castelló d'Empúries, Aïguamolls de l'Empordà, Roses, Cadaqués, Sant Pere de Rodes, and Port Bou.

To reach Sitges from Barcelona take the autopista A16 south along the coast, or take local road C246, while the A7 highway also runs south inland to Tarragona. To head west toward Lleida and the monasteries of Santes Creus, Poblet and the medieval town of Montblanc, and on to Madrid, you take the A7 south and turn west on to the A2 at L'Arboç. To get to Montserrat take highway A18.

By Train

The Spanish railroad company is called **RENFE,** which stands for *Red Nacional de Ferrocarriles de España*. Practically the entire Costa Brava, except Blanes, is *not* served directly by railroad, as the rail line runs far inland. If you plan on traveling by train to any town on the Costa Brava, check how close it is to the four hub towns of Caldes de Malavella, Girona, Flaçà, and Figueres. From one of these you can catch a bus or taxi to your destination. The train does serve the last three towns on the north end of the Costa Brava, Llançà, Colera and Port Bou. In the southern direction Sitges and Tarragona are also served directly by train.

Almost all long-distance and international trains leave from the **Sants-Estació** (⊠ Plaça dels Països Catalans s/n, ☎ 902/240202). En route to or from Sants, some trains stop at another station on **Passeig de Gràcia** (⊠ At Aragó, ☎ 902/240202). The Passeig de Gràcia station is often a good way to avoid the long lines that form at Sants during holidays. The **Estació de França** (⊠ Av. Marquès d'Argentera s/n, ☎ 902/240202), near the port, handles certain long-distance trains within Spain and some international trains.

By Plane

It may come as a surprise but Girona has an airport (☎ 972/186600), located about 6 mi south of the city in the town of Vilobí d'Onyar (Afores s/n). There is regular bus transportation from Girona airport to Girona city and vice versa. In addition to the major Spanish carrier **Iberia** (⊠

Plaça Marqués de Camps 8, Girona, ☎ 972/474192), Girona airport serves a large number of charter airlines, which are centralized under a single telephone number (☎ 972/186697) with the name Service Air.

Getting Around

By Boat

If you'd like to cruise in a small craft and get a view of the Costa Brava from the sea perspective there are many short-cruise lines along the coast. Visit the port area in any of the main towns and you will quickly spot these tourist cruise lines. **Blanes:** (✉ Bernat i Castañé, ☎ 972/355998). **L'Estartit:** Viatges Marítims Costa Brava (✉ Aquarium, ☎ 972/750880). **Roses:** Creuers Badia de Roses (✉ ☎ 972/255499); Roses Serveis Marítims (☎ 972/152426). Plan on spending 1,000 pesetas.

By Bus

Only Girona and Tarragona have a major municipal bus transportation service. Given its narrow streets, the old quarter of Girona does not run the bus service through its streets. City buses run daily from 7:00 AM to 10:00 PM. The fare is 125 ptas./€0.75 (130 ptas./€0.78 Sunday and holidays); for multiple journeys you can purchase a ticket for 10 rides for 1,000 ptas./€6.01 Route maps are displayed at bus stops. Tarragona, which is more spread out, also has an important municipal bus transportation service. City buses run daily from about 7:00 AM to after 10:00 PM. There are extra lines in summer that take travelers to the beaches. The fare is 110 ptas./€0.66; for multiple journeys you can purchase a ticket for 10 rides for 745 ptas./€4.48. Visit their useful website at http://www.fut.es/àemt/.

By Car

Setting out from Barcelona, it's not complicated to get to the Costa Brava or around the province of Girona. By road, take highway A7 north from Barcelona in the direction of France and get off at different exits depending on what your final destination is. This highway runs from about 10 to 30 miles inland from the coast and is the perfect feeder to the towns that sit along the sea. Highway exits are numbered in decreasing order as you travel north. If you prefer, you can also take national road N-II north, but it is heavily traveled, especially in the summer.

If you're heading for the southern part of the Costa Brava on highway A7, get off at exit 10 and take road GI-512 to Blanes. From there you can continue driving north along the coast to Lloret de Mar, Tossa de Mar, Sant Feliu de Guíxols, S'Agaró, Platja d'Aro, Palamós, Calella de Palafrugell, and Palafrugell. Here you will head inland for La Bisbal, and from there on to the city Girona. From Girona you can then aim for the inland towns of Banyoles, Besalú, Castellfollit de la Roca, and Olot.

If you want to go to the middle section of the Costa Brava, get off highway A7 at exit 6. This will point you directly to the Iberian ruins of Ullastret.

To get to the northern part of the Costa Brava get off highway A7 at exit 4. This will bring you to L'Estartit, L'Escala, Empúries, Castelló d'Empúries, Aïguamolls de l'Empordà, Roses, Cadaqués, Sant Pere de Rodes, Llançà, Colera, and Port Bou. Exit 4 will also take you directly to Figueres, Peralada, and the Alberes range. All the towns on the Costa Brava are interconnected by a regular road network that, take note, is very congested in the summer.

Many people live in Sitges and work in Barcelona, so it is a short commuter drive by highway A16 or local road C246. Tarragona is just over an hour's drive from Barcelona following highway A16.

By Train

The railroad travels north to the French border. A local line heads up the coast from Barcelona but but only takes you to Blanes; from there it turns inland and connects at Maçanet-Massanes with the main line up to France. Direct trains only stop at major towns, such as Girona, Flaçà, and Figueres. If you want to get off at a small town, be sure to take a local train; or you can take a fast direct train to, let's say, Girona, and get off and wait for a local to go by (the words for local, express, and direct, are basically the same in Spanish). The stop on the main line for the middle section of the Costa Brava is Flaçà, from where you can take a bus or taxi to your final destination. The northern section is covered by Figueres. Girona and Figueres are two towns with major bus stations that feed out to the towns of the Costa Brava. Trains south from Barcelona take you to Sitges and Tarragona. A short railroad line serves Montserrat, and takes you to Monistrol from where you can catch the funicular to the monastery.

Contacts and Resources

Bike Rental

Try **The World Rent a Bike** (⊠ Camprodon i Artesa 14, Lloret de Mar, ☎ 636/302112). For long-duration rental trips, check out **Cicles Empordà** (⊠ Av. Gola Estany 33, Roses, ☎ 972/152478).

Car Rental

Atesa: (⊠ Carretera Barcelona 204–206, Girona, ☎ 972/217274, 902/100101). **Avis:** (⊠ Barcelona 25, Girona,, ☎ 972/206933; ⊠ Enric Granados 24, Lloret de Mar, ☎ 972/373023; España 24, Sitges, ☎ 93/894–0287). **Europcar:** (⊠ Carrer del Freu s/n, L'Estartit, ☎ 972/751731; ⊠ Plaça de l'Estació s/n, Figueres, ☎ 972/673434; Carretera Blanes a Tossa s/n, Lloret de Mar, ☎ 972/363366). **Hertz:** (⊠ Plaça de l'Estació s/n, Girona, ☎ 972/210108; Plaça de l'Estació s/n, Figueres, ☎ 972/672801; Artur Carbonell 27, Sitges, ☎ 93/894–8986).

Emergencies

Police (☎ 091, national police; 092, municipal police; 088, Catalan police—Mossos d'Esquadra). **Ambulance** (Red Cross, ☎ 972/222222; ambulance pool, ☎ 972/505050). **Hospital** (Hospital de Girona, Doctor Josep Trueta: ⊠ Av. de França 60, ☎ 972/202700; Hospital de Figueres, Ronda Rector Arolas s/n, ☎ 972/501400). **Fire department** 085.

English-Language Bookstores

The best bookstore in Girona, with a large travel-guide section, and a small section of English fiction, is **Llibreria 22** (⊠ Carrer Hortes 22, ☎ 972/217295). For travel books and other editions in English, try **Ulysus** (⊠ Ballesteries 22, ☎ 972/221773). In Figueres, **Lara** (⊠ Joan Maragall 20, ☎ 972/501785) carries the latest books in Spanish, Catalan, and many in English.

Late-Night Pharmacies

Look on the door of any pharmacy or in any local newspaper under "Farmacias de Guardia" for the addresses of those open late at night or 24 hours. Alternately, dial 010.

Travel Agencies

Alfa Tours (✉ Plaça de Francesc Calvet i Rubalcaba 5, Girona, ☎ 972/220381). **The Foreign Office** (✉ Església 138, L'Estartit; **Crom Raid & Adventure** (✉ Av. de les Alegries 12, Lloret de Mar, ☎ 972/365412). **Viatges Berga** (✉ Carrer Sant Agustí 11, Tarragona,, ☎ 977/252610).

Visitor Information

The tourist offices you will find on the Costa Brava, inland, in Sitges and Tarragona, and at other locations, are very helpful and well-informed. Don't hesitate going to one if you have any problem or question about any of these Costa Brava places you will be visiting.

Blanes: (✉ Plaça de Catalunya s/n, ☎ 972/330348). **Cadaqués:** (✉ Cotxe 2-A ☎ 972/258315). **Lloret de Mar:** (✉ Plaça de la Vila s/n, ☎ 972/364735). **Palafrugell:** (✉ Plaça de la Església s/n, ☎ 972/611820). **Palamós:** (✉ Passeig de Mar s/n, ☎ 972/600550). **Platja d'Aro:** (✉ Mossèn Jacint Verdaguer 4, ☎ 972/817179). **Roses:** (✉ Av. de Rhode 101, ☎ 972/257331). **Sant Feliu de Guíxols:** (✉ Plaça Monestir s/n, ☎ 972/820051). **Tossa de Mar:** (✉ Av. de Pelegrí 25, ☎ 972/340108).

Girona tourist information office (✉ Rambla de la Llibertat 1, ☎ 972/226575) is open in the summer season Monday through Saturday, 8–8 (off peak season it closes from 2–4 PM), and Sunday from 9–2 PM. The **Figueres tourist information office** (✉ Plaça del Sol, s/n, ☎ 972/503155) is open Monday through Saturday, 8:30–8:30, Sunday, 9–3. The **Patronat de Turisme Costa Brava Girona** (☎ 972/208401), which is a consortium that groups all tourist activities in northeastern Catalonia, has a very useful website at www.costabrava.org.

4 THE PYRENEES

Historically both a barrier separating and a nexus connecting Europe with the Iberian Peninsula and North Africa, the Pyrenees have long been a source of fascination and magic for their many peoples and cultures. Spanning Spain's border with France from the Mediterranean to the Atlantic, the Catalonian, Aragonese, and Basque Pyrenees are a heady mixture of snow-capped mountains, green meadows, and remote valleys, filled with medieval villages and Romanesque art hidden away in chapels, churches, and monasteries. As gateways to the region, the proud flatland cities of Lleida and Zaragoza are rich havens for travelers on their way to or from the Pyrenees.

By George
Semler

T HE SNOWCAPPED PYRENEES separating the Iberian Peninsula
from the rest of the European continent have always been a magical realm, a source of legend and superstition, a breeder of myth
and mystical religious significance for nearly three millenniums of civilization. Along with the magic comes a surprising variety of ancient
cultures and languages, all Pyrenean and yet each one profoundly different from the next. And on a purely physical level, there are soft green
valleys along the bright rivers and granite and limestone heights of over
12,000 ft. To explore any of these valleys fully—the flora and fauna,
the local gastronomy, the peaks and upper meadows, the remote glacial
lakes and streams, the Romanesque art hidden in a thousand chapels
and hermitages—could take a lifetime. Each valley and village has its
store of lore and secrets. The Basque village of Zugarramurdi, for example, near the French border, burned Basque witches at the stake in
the early 17th century for holding orgiastic ceremonies in local caves
and still commemorates it all with an annual witches' dinner. San Juan
de Plan's present location is still attributed to the mysterious snake that
in the 13th century stole mother's milk and starved the village babies.
Clearly, this is a region that can cast a spell over the intrepid traveler
eager for discovery in this often overlooked stretch of earth.

Where to begin? The grassy crest of the Alberes range sweeping from
Le Perthus to the Mediterranean; the broad and sunny expanse of the
Cerdanya valley under the sheer rock walls of the Cadí; the Romanesque churches of the Noguera de Tor valley and the lake country above at Sant Mauricio; the towering heights of the Maladeta
massif; Ordesa National Park's Grand Canyon-like spaces; Hemingway's beloved Irati beech forest and river above Pamplona, and the
rolling moist green hills of the Baztán Valley in Pyrenean Navarra are
just a few of the most memorable points in this rich anthology of wilderness and civilization.

Each Pyrenean mountain system is drained by one or more rivers, forming some three dozen valleys between the Mediterranean and the Atlantic;
these valleys were all but completely isolated until around the 10th century. Local languages still range from Castilian Spanish to Euskera
(Basque), in upper Navarre; to dialects such as Grausín, Belsetán, Chistavino, Ansotano, Cheso, or Patués (Benasqués), in Aragón; to Aranés,
a dialect of Gascon French, in the Vall d'Aran; to Catalan at the eastern end of the chain from Ribagorça to the Mediterranean.

Over the centuries the Pyrenees have both joined and separated Spain
and the rest of Europe, keeping invaders at bay and, more recently, helping to create a trans-Pyrenean culture distinct from that of neighboring France. The earliest inhabitants of the prehistoric Pyrenees—originally
cave dwellers, later shepherds and farmers—saw their first invaders
when the Greeks landed at Empúries, in northern Catalonia, in the 6th
century BC. The seagoing Carthaginians colonized Spain in the 3rd century BC, and their great general Hannibal surprised Rome by crossing
the Oriental (eastern) Pyrenees in 218 BC. After defeating the Carthaginians, the Romans built roads through the mountains: Vía Augusta, from
Le Perthus to Barcelona and Tarragona; Strata Ceretana, through the
Cerdanya Valley and La Seu d'Urgell to Lleida; Summus Pyrenaecus (or,
as the Latin reflects, *Summus Portus,* or highest pass), at Somport, to
Jaca and Zaragoza; and the Via Lemovicensis from Bordeaux through
Roncesvalles to Pamplona, in the western, or Atlantic, Pyrenees.

After the fall of Rome, the Iberian Peninsula was the last of the empire to be overtaken by the Visigoths, who crossed the Pyrenees in AD

409. In the 8th century, the northern tribes then faced Moorish invaders from the south. Although Moorish influence was weaker in the Pyrenees than in southern Spain and only briefly pushed past the mountains into the rest of Europe, this region at the end of the first millennium was a crossroads of Arab, Greek, and European cultures. Toulouse was the melting pot of these influences, the medieval artistic and literary center. Christianity survived the Moors' invasion and occupation largely by fleeing to the hills and thus dotting the Pyrenees with Romanesque art and architecture. When Christian crusaders reconquered Spain, the Pyrenees were divided among three feudal kingdoms: Catalonia, Aragón, and Navarre, proud and independent entities with their respective spiritual "cradles" in the Romanesque mountain monasteries of Ripoll, San Juan de la Peña, and San Salvador de Leyre.

Throughout the centuries, the Pyrenees have remained a strategic factor to be reckoned with. The northbound Moorish empire on the Iberian Peninsula sputtered to a stop here. Charlemagne, probing south, lost Roland and his rear guard at Roncesvalles in 778, and his heirs lost all of Catalonia in 988. Napoléon never completed his conquest of the Iberian Peninsula largely because the Pyrenees presented insurmountable communication and supply problems. And Hitler was dissuaded by Franco from trying to use post–civil war Spain as a base camp for his African campaign, a decision that rendered the Pyrenees a path to freedom for Jews and *résistants* fleeing the Nazis.

The Pyrenees stretch 435 km (270 mi) along Spain's border with France. There are three main divisions: the Catalan Pyrenees from the Mediterranean to the Noguera Ribagorçana river, the central Pyrenees of Aragón extending west to the Roncal Valley, and the Basque Pyrenees, which fall gently westward through the Basque country to the Bay of Biscay and the Atlantic Ocean. The highest peaks are in Aragón—Aneto, in the Maladeta massif; Posets; and Monte Perdido, all of which are about 11,000 ft above sea level. Pica d'Estats (10,372 ft) is Catalonia's highest peak, while Pic D'Orhi (6,656 ft) is the highest in the Basque Pyrenees.

The routes suggested in this chapter are introductions to some of Spain's richest and most remote combinations of nature and mountain culture. The cities across the flatlands south of the Pyrenees—Barcelona, Lleida (Lérida, in Castilian Spanish), Huesca, Zaragoza, and Pamplona—make reliable gateways to and from the highland wilderness; a surprise snowfall in these mountains can bring a hiking or a road trip to an abrupt halt, sending motorists scurrying to lower and warmer climes.

Pleasures and Pastimes

Dining

Pyrenean cuisine is characterized by thick soups, stews, roasts, and the use of local ingredients prepared differently in every valley, village, and kitchen from the Mediterranean to the Atlantic. The three main culinary schools are those corresponding to the Pyrenees' three main regional and cultural identities—Catalan, Aragonese, and Basque—but within these are further subdivisions such as La Cerdanya, Vall d'Aran, Benasque, Roncal, and Baztán. Game is common throughout. Trout (once supplied by anglers, now often raised in lakes and ponds fed by mountain streams), wild goat, deer, boar, partridge, rabbit, duck, and quail are roasted over coals or cooked in aromatic stews called *civets* in Catalonia and *estofadas* in Aragón and Navarre. Fish and meat are often seared on slabs of slate (*a la llosa* in Catalan, *a la piedra* in Castilian Spanish). Wild mushrooms are a local specialty in season, as are wild asparagus, leeks, and herbs such as marjoram, sage, thyme, and rosemary.

CATEGORY	COST*
$$$$	over 6,000 ptas./€36.06
$$$	4,000–6,000 ptas./€24.04–36.06
$$	2,500–4,000 ptas./€15.03–24.04
$	under 2,500 ptas./€15.03

*per person for a three-course meal, excluding drinks, service, and tax

Fishing

Well populated with trout, Pyrenean streams provide excellent angling from the third Sunday in March to the end of August. Nearly all of the mountains' rivers and streams make fine cold-water fisheries, but the Segre, Aragón, Gállego, Noguera Pallaresa, Arga, and Esca are the most notable. Local ponds and lakes also tend to be rich in trout, providing a good way to combine hiking and angling. Call **Danica** (☎ 608/735376) for horse or helicopter tours with fly-fishing equipment included (for more information, *see* Fishing *in* the Pyrenees A to Z, *below*).

Hiking and Walking

Hiking and mountain climbing are fundamental Pyrenean activities in summer. Local and trans-Pyrenean trails crisscross the region, most with truly unforgettable views. Walking the often grassy crest of the range, with one foot in France and the other in Spain, is an exhilarating experience and well within the reach of the moderately fit. Try walking from Coll de Nuria to Ulldeter over the Sierra Catllar, above Setcases; scaling the Cadí over the Cerdanya; hiking over the Maladeta glacier to Aneto, the Pyrenees' highest peak; or, in autumn, hiking through the Irati beech forest, in upper Navarre. The Iparla Ridge walk, along the Navarre-France border crest, and the Alberes walk from Le Perthus out to the Mediterranean are two more favorite day hikes. Local *excursionista* (outing) clubs, especially the **Centre Excursionista de Catalunya,** in Barcelona (✉ Carrer Paradís 10, ☎ 93/315–2311), can help you get started; local tourist offices may also have brochures and rudimentary trail maps. You can also join equestrian trips, four-wheel-drive excursions to the upper Pyrenees, and horseback fly-fishing tours of the high streams and lakes from Llívia, in the Cerdanya. Wild-mushroom hunts in piny, hillside meadows are a way of life for many, combining walking, questing, and cooking. (Be 100% certain of any wild mushroom you consume; consult with an expert.)

Lodging

Most hotels in the Pyrenees feel informal and outdoorsy, with a large fireplace in one of the public rooms. Usually built of wood and slate under a steep roof, they blend with the surrounding mountains. Their comfortable, protected atmosphere reflects the tastes of the travelers, who are mostly skiers and hikers. Options include friendly family establishments such as the Güell, in Camprodón, and the Hotel Llívia, in the Spanish enclave of Llívia; grand-luxe places such as Torre del Remei in the Cerdanya Valley; rural accommodations in Basque *caseríos* (farmhouses) like the Iratxeko Berea in Vera de Bidasoa, on the upper reaches of Navarre's Bidasoa River; and town houses such as La Tuca, in Aragón's Canfranc ski station. The cities of the Pyrenees offer first-rate lodging options ranging from La Seu d'Urgell's Parador or its gourmet haven at El Castell to Baqueira's Tryp Royal Tanau, Lleida's Pirineos, Huesca's Pedro I de Aragón, or Jaca's Gran Hotel.

CATEGORY	COST*
$$$$	over 15,000 ptas./€90.15
$$$	10,000–15,000 ptas./€60.10–90.15
$$	6,000–10,000 ptas./€36.06–60.10
$	under 6,000 ptas./€36.06

All prices are for a standard double room, excluding service and tax.

✑ *following the text of a review is your signal that the property has a Web site, where you will find details and, usually, images; for a link, visit www.fodors.com/urls.*

Romanesque Art and Architecture

The treasury of Romanesque chapels, monasteries, hermitages, and cathedrals in these mountains is rich enough to organize many a trip around. The buildings are in various states of preservation; even a short hike may reveal the picturesque ruins of a 10th-century hermitage. Architectural sites to seek out include the tiny chapel at Beget, above Camprodón; the superb rose window and 50 carved capitals of the cathedral of Santa Maria, in La Seu d'Urgell; the matched set of churches and bell towers in the Noguera de Tor Valley, below the Vall d'Aran; the San Juan de la Peña and Siresa monasteries, west of Jaca; and the village churches of Navarre's Baztán Valley.

Winter Sports

Skiing is the main sport in the Pyrenees, and Baqueira-Beret, in the Vall d'Aran, is the leading resort. Thanks to increasing reliance on artificial-snow machines, there is usually fine skiing from December through March at more than 20 resorts—from Vallter 2000 at Setcases, in the Camprodón Valley, west to Isaba and Burguete, in Navarre. Although weekend skiing can be crowded in the eastern valleys, Catalonia's western Pyrenees, especially Baqueira-Beret, rank among Spain's best winter-sports centers and tend to have more breathing room. Cerler-Benasque, Panticosa, Formigal, Astun, and Candanchú are the major ski areas in Huesca. Numerous resorts offer helicopter skiing and Nordic skiing. Leading Nordic areas include Lles, in the Cerdanya; Salardú and Beret, in the Vall d'Aran; and Panticosa, Benasque, and Candanchú, in Aragón. Jaca, Puigcerdà, and Vielha have public skating sessions, figure-skating classes, and ice-hockey programs. The newspapers *El País, El Periódico de Catalunya,* and *La Vanguardia Española* print complete ski information every Friday in winter (☞ Outdoor Activities and Sports *in* the Pyrenees A to Z, *below*).

Exploring the Pyrenees

Traversing the Pyrenees from the Mediterranean to the Atlantic (or vice versa) is for mountain worshipers a pilgrimage of deep cultural and cosmic significance. It's a seven-week hike on foot, but you can make the crossing in 10–14 days by car. The main valleys are the Camprodón, Cerdanya, Aran, Benasque, Tena, Canfranc, Roncal, and Baztán.

Numbers in the text correspond to numbers in the margin and on the Catalan Pyrenees and the Central and Western Pyrenees maps.

Great Itineraries

Barcelona is the largest pre-Pyrenean base camp on the Spanish side. A trip through the Oriental Pyrenees (in the northeastern stretch of Spain) covers an important third of the chain. Five days is enough time to reach the Vall d'Aran and the Noguera de Tor Valley and its Romanesque churches before heading back to Barcelona or farther west or south; such a trip is probably the most cost-effective in terms of time, terrain, art, and architecture. A 10-day trip grants the satisfaction of a sea-to-sea crossing, but you'll spend the bulk of this time in your car.

IF YOU HAVE 3 DAYS

Start from Barcelona, the major urban area with the best communication links. Make your first stop in the mountains at the crisp, stony stream junction town of ⚎ **Camprodón** ①, then devote the rest of your stay to the wide and sunny Cerdanya Valley: Explore the Spanish enclave in France at ⚎ **Llívia** ⑧ the next day, and on day three drive west down the valley to the medieval mountain city of **La Seu d'Urgell** ⑫. Head back to Barcelona through the Cadí Tunnel.

IF YOU HAVE 5 DAYS

Starting from Barcelona or the Costa Brava, devote your first afternoon and night to ⚎ **Camprodón** ①. Explore the Cerdanya Valley and ⚎ **Llívia** ⑧ the next day, then head to ⚎ **La Seu d'Urgell** ⑫—climbing to the lofy "eagle's meadow," **Prat d'Aguiló** ⑪ on the way—for your third day and night. Spend your fourth day and night in the wintery Atantic valley of ⚎ **Vall d'Aran** ⑯–⑰, and your fifth day absorbing the Noguera de Tor Valley and its Romanesque churches. If you have time, go through pond and lake-dotted **Aigüestortes–Sant Maurici National Park** ⑭. Stop in **Zaragoza** ㉜, the capital of Aragón, on your way out of the mountains.

IF YOU HAVE 9 DAYS

With nine days, you can contemplate crossing the entire range. From Barcelona or the Costa Brava, the classic crossing begins with a symbolic wade in the Mediterranean at Cap de Creus (☞ Chapter 3), peninsular Spain's easternmost point, just north of Cadaqués; from which you cross westward to Fuenterrabía (☞ Chapter 5) to do likewise at the Cabo Higuer lighthouse on the Bay of Biscay. (Of course, you can also travel in the opposite direction, reversing the order of this chapter.) On the westbound trip, a day's drive up through Figueres and Olot (☞ Chapter 3) will bring you to ⚎ **Camprodón** ① and the surrounding unspoiled mountain towns, skiing, and wildlife. Stop next in ⚎ **Llívia** ⑧, moving on to the Cerdanya, the widest, sunniest valley in the Pyrenees. From there move westward through ⚎ **La Seu D'Urgell** ⑫ to **Aigüestortes–Sant Maurici National Park** ⑭, the ⚎ **Vall d'Aran** region and the winter-sports center Baqueira-Beret, near **Sarladú** ⑰. Stop in the Noguera de Tor Valley to see its Romanesque churches. Farther west, spend the next few days in the stately town of ⚎ **Benasque** ⑳, the ancient village of ⚎ **San Juan de Plan** ㉑, the restored medieval town of **Bielsa** ㉒, and the remote valleys of Upper Aragón, the ⚎ **Parque Nacional de Ordesa y Monte Perdido** ㉓, and ⚎ **Jaca** ㉔, the region's most important town. Finally, move through western Aragón into the Basque Pyrenees to visit the Irati Forest; go through the tunnel under the Velate Pass (or, more spectacularly, over the pass itself) to explore the **Baztán Valley** ㉛, and to follow the Bidasoa River down to ⚎ Fuenterrabía (☞ Chapter 5) and the Bay of Biscay.

When to Tour the Pyrenees

If you're a hiker, stick to the summer (June through September, with a definite emphasis on July), when the weather is better and there's less chance of a blizzard or lightning storm at high altitudes. October is an ideal time to enjoy the Pyrenees' still-green valleys and hunt for wild mushrooms. November brings colorful leaves, the last wild mushrooms, and the first frosts. The green springtime thaw, during which you can still ski on the snowcaps, is another spectacular season. For skiing, come between December and April.

THE CATALAN PYRENEES

Catalonia's easternmost Pyrenean valley, the Vall de Camprodón (Camprodón Valley), is still out of the way and hard enough to reach to have retained much of its original character. Whereas the Tunel del Cadí brought three million Barcelona residents within two hours of the Cardanya, the Capsacosta tunnel into the Camprodón valley only tempts some 70,000 Girona residents to take to the slopes. But the trip is well worth it, for the Camprodón valley has several exquisite towns and churches; a ski area; and, above all, mountains, such as the Sierra de Catllar, thick with boar, mountain goat, wild trout, snow partridge, and romantic majesty.

With two ski resorts—Vallter 2000 and Nuria at the eastern and western ends of the Pyrenees heights on the north side of the valley— the middle reaches and main body of the valley have remained pasturage for sheep, cattle, and horses and de facto natural parks, as yet undeclared but maintained as if they were by owners more interested in quality of life than in profits.

To reach the Vall de Camprodón from Barcelona you can take the N152 through Vic and Ripoll; from the Costa Brava go by way of either Figueres or Girona, Besalú, and the new Capsacosta tunnel. From France drive southwest through the Col (Pass) d'Ares, which enters the head of the valley at an altitude of 5,280 ft from Prats de Molló.

Camprodón

❶ *127 km (79 mi) northwest of Barcelona.*

Camprodón, the capital of its *comarca* (county), lies at the junction of the Rivers Ter and Ritort—both excellent trout streams. The rivers flow by, through, and under much of the town, giving it a waterfront character as well as a long history of flooding. The town owes much of its opulence to the summer folks from Barcelona who have built important mansions along the leafy promenade, **Passeig Maristany,** at the town's northern edge. Along with the church of **Sant Pere** (10th–11th centuries), Camprodón's best-known sight is the elegant **12th-century stone bridge** that broadly spans the River Ter in the center of town; its wide arch descends at a graceful angle from a central peak. The town is also known for its **sausages** of every imaginable size, shape, and consistency, and for its two cookie factories, Birbas and Pujol, locked in the embrace of eternal competition. (Birbas is better—look for the image of the bridge on the box.)

Lodging

$$ ▨ **Güell.** Owned and managed by the charming Güell family, this elegant glass, wood, and stone structure welcomes skiers and general enthusiasts to the Camprodón Valley. Rooms are simple but tasteful, with heavy, Pyrenean wood furniture. ✉ *Plaça d'Espanya 8, 17867,* ☎ *972/740011,* FAX *972/741112. 38 rooms. AE, DC, MC, V.*

Shopping

Don't miss **Cal Xec,** the sausage store at the end of the emblematic Camprodón Bridge. Along with every kind of charcuterie ever conceived, the shop sells Birbas and Pujol cookies.

En Route From Camprodón, take C151 north toward the French border at Col d'Ares and turn east toward Rocabruna, a village of crisp, clean Pyrenean stone at the source of the crystalline River Beget.

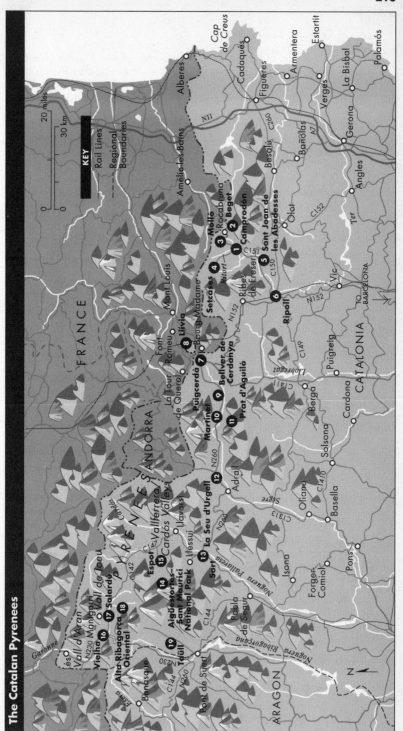

The Catalan Pyrenees

Beget

❷ *17 km (11 mi) east of Camprodón.*

The village of Beget, considered Catalonia's *més bufó* (cutest), was completely cut off from motorized transportation until the mid-1960s and was only connected to the rest of the world by asphalt roadway in 1980. Beget's 30 houses are eccentric stone structures with heavy wooden doors and an unusual golden tone peculiar to the Camprodón Valley. Graceful stone bridges span the stream in which protected trout feast. The 11th-century Romanesque church of **Sant Cristófol** has a diminutive bell tower and a famous 6-ft *Majestat*—a polychrome wood carving of Christ in a head-to-foot tunic—dating from the 12th or 13th century. This Romanesque-era sculpture type was particularly prized by Pyrenean parishes and this example offers a rare chance to see one in its original setting (many others were destroyed during the Spanish civil war). The church is usually closed, but townsfolk can direct you to the keeper of the key.

Dining

$$ ✕ **Can Po.** Perched over a deep gulley, Can Po serves first-rate cuisine in an ancient, ivy-covered, stone-and-mortar farmhouse. Specialties are *entrecot amb crema de ceps* (veal in wild-mushroom sauce) and *anec amb peras* (duck prepared with stewed pears). ⊠ *Carretera de Beget s/n, 17867,* ☎ *972/741045. AE, DC, MC, V. Closed Mon.–Thurs. mid-Sept.–mid-July.*

Molló

❸ *25 km (16 mi) northwest of Beget, 24 km (15 mi) south of Prats de Molló.*

Molló lies on route C151 on the Ritort stream toward Col d'Ares. Here you'll find the 12th-century Romanesque church of **Santa Cecilia,** a work of exceptional balance and simplicity. The delicate, Romanesque bell tower seems as naturally set into the building and the surrounding countryside as a Pyrenean mushroom.

Lodging

$$ 🏠 **François.** Just 500 yards from the center of town, this charming inn is a good base camp for hiking excursions to Beget and other points in the valley. The owners are patient and friendly, the rooms small but comfortable. ⊠ *Carretera Camprodón, 17868,* ☎ *972/130029,* ℻ *972/130029. 28 rooms. Restaurant, parking. AE, DC, MC, V.*

Setcases

❹ *11 km (7 mi) north of Camprodón, 91 km (56 mi) northwest of Girona, 15 km (9 mi) west of Molló.*

This tiny village is nestled at the head of the valley. Although Setcases (literally, "seven houses") is somewhat larger than its name would imply, the town has a distinct mountain spirit and a gravelly roughness, perhaps owing to the torrents flowing through and over its streets en route to the River Ter.

The **Vallter ski area,** above Setcases—built into a glacial cirque reaching a height of 8,216 ft—has a dozen lifts and, on very clear days, views east from the top all the way to the Bay of Roses on the Costa Brava.

On the road back down the valley from Setcases, **Llanars,** just short of Camprodón, has a 12th-century Romanesque church, **San Esteban,** of an exceptionally rich shade of ocher. The wood-and-iron portal depicts the martyrdom of St. Stephen.

Sant Joan de les Abadesses

⑤ *21 km (13 mi) southeast of Setcases, 14 km (9 mi) south of Camprodón.*

South of Camprodón, Sant Joan de les Abadesses—named for the 9th-century abbess Emma, daughter of Guifré el Pilós (Wilfred the Hairy), the founder of the Catalonian nation and medieval hero of the Christian Reconquest of Ripoll—is the site of the important 12th-century Romanesque church of **Sant Joan.** The altarpiece is a 13th-century polychrome wood sculpture of the Descent from the Cross, one of the most expressive and human of that epoch. The gesticulating, angled limbs of the carved figures seem to antecede, in their physical and emotional language, the anguish captured in Picasso's *Guernica* (historians now know that the artist was heavily influenced by Spanish Romanesque art). The town's arcaded **Plaça Major** has a medieval look and feel, and the **12th-century bridge** over the Ter is wide and graceful.

Ripoll

⑥ *105 km (65 mi) north of Barcelona, 65 km (40 mi) southeast of Puigcerdà.*

One of the first Christian strongholds of the Reconquest and a center of religious erudition during the Middle Ages, Ripoll is known as the *bressol* (cradle) of Catalonian nationhood. A dark, mysterious country town built around a **9th-century Benedictine monastery,** it was a focal point of culture throughout the Roussillon (French Catalonia and the Pyrenees) from the monastery's founding, in 888, until the mid-19th century, when Barcelona began to eclipse it for good.

The 12th-century doorway to the church of **Santa Maria** is one of Catalonia's great works of Romanesque art, designed as a triumphal arch. Its sculptures portray the glory of God and of all his creatures from the Creation onward. You can pick up a guide to the figures on the portal (crafted by stone masons and sculptors of the Roussillon school) in the church or at the information kiosk nearby. ⊠ *Cloister 350 ptas., museum 450 ptas./€2.10.* ⊘ *Tues.–Sun. 10–2 and 3–7.*

North of Ripoll, the **cogwheel train** from Ribes up to Nuria offers one of Catalonia's most unusual excursions. Known as the *cremallera* (zipper), the line was built in 1917 to connect Ribes with the **Santuari de la Mare de Deu de Núria** (Mother of God of Núria). The ride takes 45 minutes and costs 1,500 ptas./€9.02 round-trip. Núria, at an altitude of 6,562 ft at the foot of Puigmal, is a **ski area** and was the site of some of Spain's earliest ice-hockey activity in the 1950s.

The legend of **Núria,** a Marian religious retreat, is based on the story of Sant Gil of Nîmes, who did penance in the Núria Valley during the 7th century. The saint left behind a wooden statue of the Virgin Mary, a bell he used to summon shepherds to prayer, and a cooking pot; 300 years later, a pilgrim found these treasures in this sanctuary. The bell and the pot came to have special importance to barren women, who were believed to be blessed with as many children as they wished by placing their heads in the pot and ringing the bell, each peal of the bell meaning another child. ⊠ *Free.* ⊘ *Open daily except during mass.*

En Route From Ripoll, it's a 65-km (40-mi) drive on the N152 through Ribes de Freser and over the Collada de Toses (Tosses Pass) to Puigcerdà. Above Ribes, the road winds to the top of the pass over a sheer drop down to the Freser stream. Here, even during the driest months, emerald-green pastures remain moist in shaded corners—a sharp contrast to the shale and brown peaks above the timber line. In early spring the climate can range from showers down in Ribes to a blizzard up on the Tosses Pass.

This traditional approach to the Cerdanya has been all but replaced by the road through Manresa, Berga, and the Túnel del Cadí (Cadí Tunnel). Tosses was a barrier for centuries, until the railroad connected Puigcerdà to Barcelona in 1924. The 32 km (20 mi) of switchback curves between Ribes and La Molina kept many would-be travelers in Barcelona until the tunnel cut the driving time from three hours to two and all but eliminated the hazardous-driving factor.

LA CERDANYA

The Pyrenees' widest, sunniest valley—said to be in the shape of the handprint of God—is an Alpine paradise. High pastureland bordered north and south by snow-covered peaks, La Cerdanya starts in France, at Col de la Perche (near Mont Louis), and ends in the Spanish province of Lleida, at Martinet. Split into two countries and subdivided into two more provinces on each side, the valley is nonetheless a geographical and cultural unit with an identity all its own.

As the saying goes, "*Meitat de França, meitat d'Espanya, no hi ha altra terra com la Cerdanya*" ("Half France, half Spain, there's no country like the Cerdanya"): The Cerdanya straddles the border, which meanders through the rich valley floor no more purposefully than the River Segre itself. Residents on both sides of the border speak Catalan, a Romance language derived from early Provençal French, and regard the valley's political border with undisguised hilarity.

Unlike any other valley in the upper Pyrenees, this one runs east–west and thus has a record annual number of hours of sunlight. On the French side, two solar stations collect and store energy near Font Romeu, and a solar oven bakes ceramics in Mont Louis. France and Spain rub shoulders delightfully here—from your hotel in Puigcerdà you can head into the French town of Bourg-Madame for a morning *brioche au raisin* (raisin pastry) and a look at the trout in the Rahur river forming the border—then return to Spanish terra.

Puigcerdà

❼ *170 km (105 mi) north of Barcelona; 65 km (40 mi) northwest of Ripoll.*

Puigcerdà (*puig* means "hill"; *cerdà* derives from "Cerdanya") is the largest town in the valley. From the small piece of high ground upon which it stands, the views down across the meadows and up into the Pyrenees give a dizzying sense of simultaneous height and humility. Although parts of the town were blighted by bombing in the Civil War, there are sectors that retain a picturesque touch, making this a favorite with French day-trippers. The **Romanesque bell tower** and the **sunny sidewalk café** beside it are among Puigcerdà's prettiest spots, along with the Gothic church of **Santa Maria** and its long square, the **Plaça del Cuartel.** On Sunday, markets sell clothes, cheeses, fruits, vegetables, and wild mushrooms to shoppers from both sides of the border.

The **Plaça Cabrinetty,** with its porticoes and covered walks, has a sunny northeastern corner where farmers in for the Sunday market gather to discuss their lives and times. The square is protected from the wind and ringed by two- and three-story houses of various pastel colors, some with engraved decorative designs and all with balconies. From the lower end of Plaça Cabrinetty, Carrer Font d'en Llanas winds down to the *font* (spring), where "**Voldria** . . . " ("I wish . . . "), a haunting verse by the Cerdanya's greatest poet, Magdalena Masip (1890–1970), is inscribed on a plaque over the fountain: . . . *and I wish that I could have / my house beneath a fir tree / with all the woods for a garden / and*

all the sky for a roof. / And flee from the world around me / it over-
whelms me and confuses me / and stay quietly just there / drinking the
forest in great gulps / with clods of earth for a pillow / and a bed of
golden leaves . . . .

A 300-yard walk west from the *font* around the edge of town will bring
you to the stairs leading up from the train station to the balcony in
front of the town hall. From here, an ample view of the Cerdanya Valley stretches all the way past Bellver de Cerdanya down to the rock
walls of the Sierra del Cadí, at the end of the valley.

Le Petit Train Jaune (the little yellow train) leaves daily from Bourg-
Madame and from La Tour de Querol, both simple walks into France
from Puigcerdà. The border at La Tour, a longer but prettier walk, is
marked only by a stone painted with the Spanish and French flags. This
carrilet (narrow-gauge railway) is the last in the Pyrenees and is used
for tours as well as transportation; looking like something out of a Dr.
Seuss story, it winds through the Cerdanya to the walled town of Villefranche de Conflent. Popular with adults and children alike, the 63-
km (39-mi) tour can take most of the day, especially if you stop to browse
in Mont Louis or Villefranche. ⊠ *Boarding at SNCF stations at Bourg-*
Madame or La Tour de Querol. ☎ *3,500 ptas./€21.04 (175 frs.) per*
person, 2,500 ptas./€15.03 (125 frs.) per person in groups of 10 or
more, payable in French frs. only. ☉ *Schedule at Touring travel agency*
or Turismo office, Puigcerdà; or at RENFE station below Puigcerdà.

Dining and Lodging

$$–$$$ ✕ **La Tieta.** A 500-year-old town house built into the walls of Puigcerdàs,
La Tieta is one of the town's top restaurants. Its garden is an ideal place
for a late-night drink in summer. The menu features Cerdanya specialties
like *trinxat de Cerdanya* (a rib-sticking puree of cabbage and potatoes
with bits of fried salt pork or bacon) as well as roasts cooked over coals.
⊠ *C. Alfons I 45,* ☎ *972/880156. AE, DC, MC, V.*

$$ ✕ **Tapanyam.** Longtime restaurateur Pere Compte's new place is thriv-
ing. With live music every Saturday in summer, panoramic views of
the Pyrenees, excellent mountain cuisine, and fresh seafood, this friendly
spot is becoming a Puigcerdà standby. Decor is modern, with bay win-
dows overlooking the valley. ⊠ *Plaça d'Alguer 2,* ☎ *972/882360. AE,*
DC, MC, V.

$ ✕ **Madrigal.** This popular restaurant-bar near the town hall is the orig-
inal Compte establishment. The low-ceiling, wood-trim dining room
is filled with tables and benches. Selections include tapas and meals of
assorted specialties, such as *codorniz* (quail), *caracoles* (snails), *cala-*
mares a la romana (calamari dipped in batter), *albóndigas* (meatballs),
esqueixada (raw codfish with peppers and onion), and wild mushrooms
in season. ⊠ *Carrer Alfons I 1,* ☎ *972/880860. AE, DC, MC, V.*

$$$$ ✕🏨 **La Torre del Remei.** About 3 km (2 mi) west of Puigcerdà is this
★ splendid mansion, built in 1910 and brilliantly restored by José María
and Loles Boix of Boix (☞ Martinet, *below*). Everything about La Torre
del Remei is superb, from the general Belle Epoque luxury of the
manor house to the plush, tasteful rooms, heated bathroom floors, huge
bathtubs, and bottle of Moët & Chandon waiting on ice upon your
arrival. The restaurant serves top international cuisine with an emphasis
on local products such as lamb, trout, and game. Reserve well in ad-
vance. ⊠ *Camí Reial s/n, Bolvir de Cerdanya, 17463,* ☎ *972/140182,*
FAX *972/140449. 10 rooms, 1 suite. Restaurant, pool, 18-hole golf*
course, putting green. AE, DC, MC, V.

$$ 🏨 **Hotel del Lago.** This comfortable old favorite near Puigcerdà's emblematic lake is a graceful, tastefully appointed, and renovated series
of buildings built around a central garden. A two-minute walk from

the bell tower or the town market, it feels bucolic but is virtually in the center of town. ⊠ *Avda. Doctor Piguillem 7, 17520,* ☎ *972/ 881000,* FAX *972/141511. 13 rooms, 3 suites. Breakfast room, pool, parking. AE, DC, MC, V.*

$$ 🏨 **Hotel Prado.** On the edge of town on the road north to Llívia, the Prado is a warm and friendly place to stay in Puigcerdà, a local favorite for weddings and banquets run by a helpful and always pleasant family. The rooms are handsomely trimmed with alpine wood eaves and dormers, impeccably renovated and modernized. Surrounded, as the name Prado (meadow) suggests by fields and just a few minutes' walk across the border to the French town of Bourg-Madame, this is a good a lodging as any in the Cerdanya, especially for the value. ⊠ *Crtra, de Llívia, Km 1, 17520,* ☎ *972/880400,* FAX *972/141158. 54 rooms. Restaurant, bar, pool, parking. AE, DC, MC, V.*

Nightlife and the Arts

On weekends and holidays, clubs such as **N'Ho Sé, Transit,** and **Gatzara,** in Puigcerdà, and **De Nit,** 5 km (3 mi) from Puigcerdà (near Caixans, on the road to Alp), are filled till dawn with young French and Spanish night owls.

Shopping

Look for local specialties, such as herbs, goat cheese, wild mushrooms, honey, and basketry, in the Sunday markets held in most Cerdanya towns. Puigcerdà's **Sunday market** is as social as it is commercial; the long square in front of the church and former military barracks, known as the Plaça del Cuartel, fills with people and produce. In autumn, it's a great chance to learn about wild mushrooms of all kinds. If it's a horse you're shopping for, come to the annual **equine fair** in early November, a nonpareil opportunity to study both horses and horse traders.

Llívia

❽ *6 km (4 mi) northeast of Puigcerdà.*

A Spanish enclave in French territory, Llívia was marooned by the 1659 Peace of the Pyrenees treaty, which ceded 33 villages to France. Incorporated as a *vila* (town) by royal decree of Carlos V, who spent a night here in 1528 and was impressed by the town's beauty and hospitality, Llívia managed to remain Spanish. There are several interesting sights and some charming streets to discover. At the rise of the town, the 15th-century **fortified church** is an acoustic gem; see if anything sonorous is going on, especially during Llívia's summer music festival. The ancient pharmacy is now the **Museu Municipal**—founded in 1415, this is thought to be the oldest pharmacy in Europe. Its venerable dispensary has been reconstructed, and there are a variety of exhibits, ranging from herbal jars to centuries-old maps. The ticket includes entry to the 15th-century **Tour Bernat** tower adjoining the church. ⊠ *Carrer de l'esglesia,* ☎ *972/896313.* 💷 *350 frs.* ☉ *Mon.–Sat. 9–2 and 5– 8, Sun. 9–2.*

Look for the mosaic in the middle of town commemorating *Lampègia, princesa de la pau i de l'amor*—Princess of peace and of love, erected in memory of the red-haired Lampègia, daughter of the Duke of Aquitania and lover of Munuza, a Moorish warlord who governed the Cerdanya during the Arab domination. Munuza revolted against Emir Abderraman I and took the beautiful Lampègia for his wife, whereupon the Moorish leader sent his crack cavalry after the doomed couple who, fleeing, were trapped and captured in Planes. Munuza after being forced to witness the ravishing of the beautiful Lampègia at the hands of the Moorish cavalry captain was decapitated. Lampègia was sold into the harem of the Caliph of Damascus where she died of a broken heart before her father William IX of Aquitania, first Provençal poet, could ransom her freedom. Today only the mosaic in Llívia and the curious, tri-lobed chapel at Planes remain.

Dining and Lodging

$$ ✕ **Can Ventura.** Built into a 17th-century farmhouse, this superb
★ restaurant is the best around Puigcerdà for decor, cuisine, and value. Trout or beef cooked *a la llosa* (on slate) is a house specialty; the *entretenimientos* (a wide selection of hors d'oeuvres) are delicious. ⊠ *Plaça Major 1,* ☎ *972/896178. Reservations essential. MC, V. Closed Mon.–Tues.*

$$ ✕ **La Formatgeria de Llívia.** This unusual restaurant is built into a former cheese factory, part of which still functions while you watch. Just outside of town 1 km (½ mi) east of Llívia on the road to Saillagousse (France), chef-owners Marta Pous and Juanjo Meya have had great success with their fine local specialties, panoramic views south to Puigmal, and general charm and good cheer. ⊠ *Pla de Ro, Gorguja,* ☎ *972/ 146279. Reservations essential. MC, V. Closed Thurs.*

$$ ✕🖼 **Hotel de Llívia.** Here's an ideal family-run, no-frills, much-loved base of operations for anyone skiing or hiking in France, Andorra, *or* Spain. Hotel Llívia is owned and operated by the warm, generous Pous family, proprietors of Can Ventura (☞ *above*). A spacious place, with large fireplaces and a glass-walled dining room that's nearly as scenic as a picnic in a Pyrenean meadow, the hotel runs spontaneous shuttles to nearby ski resorts and can organize excursions as well as riding, hunting, or trout fishing. ⊠ *Avda. de Catalunya s/n, 17527,* ☎ *972/896000,* 🖷 *972/146000. 68 rooms, 10 apartments. Restaurant, pool, tennis court. DC, MC, V.*

Bellver de Cerdanya

★ ❾ *25 km (16 mi) west of Puigcerdà on N260.*

Bellver de Cerdanya has conserved its slate-roof and fieldstone Pyrenean architecture more successfully than many of the Cerdanya's larger towns. Perched on a promontory over the **River Segre,** which folds neatly around the town, Bellver is a mountain version of a fishing village— trout fishing, of course. The river is the town's main event; how much water is coming down—and whether it's low or high, muddy or clear, warm or cold—supplants the weather as a topic of conversation. Bellver's Gothic church of **Sant Jaume** and the arcaded **Plaça Major,** in the upper part of town, are lovely examples of traditional Pyrenean mountain-village design. South of the town is **Santa Maria de Talló,** a vast—it has been called the "Cathedral of the Cerdanya"—but rather unprepossessing Romanesque structure.

Dining and Lodging

$$ ✕🖼 **Bellavista.** Despite its location down on the main, heavily trafficked road between Puigcerdà and La Seu d'Urgell, this inn, run by a friendly family, is a great favorite for its simple Pyrenean cooking and its easy atmosphere. A few steps across the road from the river, this is a good choice for anglers (who need not, by the way, get up early: the water doesn't warm up enough to produce activity until noon, even in high summer). The rooms are beyond reproach, clean, and comfortable. Ask for a room on the back side away from the road. ⊠ *Crtra. Puigcerdà, Km 43, 25720,* ☎ *973/510000,* 🖷 *973/510418. 50 rooms. Restaurant, pool, 2 tennis courts. AE, DC, MC, V.*

$$ ✕🖼 **Fonda Biayna.** With woodsy decor and a provincial atmosphere,
★ this rustic little mountain retreat seems to have gotten happily stuck in an early Pyrenean time warp. The typical Catalan cuisine includes such gamey dishes as roast rabbit *allioli* (with a beaten sauce of gar-

lic and olive oil), *galtas de porc amb bolets* (pork cheeks with wild mushrooms), and *tiró amb naps i trumfes* (duck with turnips and potatoes). The guest rooms are simple, old-fashioned, and cozy. ✉ *Carrer Sant Roc 11 25720,* ☎ *973/510475,* 🖷 *973/510853. 16 rooms. Restaurant. AE, DC, MC, V.*

Martinet

❿   *10 km (6 mi) west of Bellver de Cerdanya on N260.*

The town of Martinet hasn't much to offer except Boix (☞ *below*), one of the best restaurants in the Pyrenees, and a few cozy watering spots that are hard to pass up in the heat of summer. For a course in trout economy, have a close look over the railing along the river just upstream from the junction of the Llosa and the Segre. Martinet's protected trout are famous in these parts: They dine from 1 to 4, when the sun slants in, cooks off aquatic-insect hatches, and illuminates every speckle and spot on these sleek leviathans.

For a spectacular excursion, drive or walk up the valley of the Riu Llosa into Andorra, or take the short but stunning walk from the village of **Aransa** to Lles: As you pull away from Aransa and onto an alpine meadow, the Cerdanya's palette changes with every twist of the trail. You'll even pass the ruins of a 10th-century hilltop hermitage. (The tourist office in La Seu d'Urgell has simple trail maps.) The village of **Lles** is a famous Nordic-skiing resort with miles of cross-country tracks.

Dining

$$$ ✕ **Boix.** The modern, Lego-block building doesn't look like much ★   from the outside, but this hotel restaurant in Martinet, 10 km (6 mi) west of Bellver, is something of an institution for fine Pyrenean cooking. José María Boix and his wife, Loles, (of Torre del Remei fame) are known for innovations on local, Catalan, and French cuisine, featuring *setas* (wild mushrooms) in season and such surprises as *magret de canard amb mel* (duck breast with honey). ✉ *Carretera N260, Km 204, 25724 Martinet,* ☎ *973/515050,* 🖷 *973/515065. AE, DC, MC, V.*

Prat d'Aguiló

★ **⓫**   *20 km (12 mi) north of Martinet up a dirt road that is rough but navigable by the average car. Follow signs for "Refugio Prat D'Aguilo."*

The spectacular Prat d'Aguiló, or Eagle's Meadow, is one of the highest points in the Cerdanya that you can access without either a four-wheel-drive vehicle or a hike. The winding, bumpy drive up the mountain takes about an hour and a half (start with ample fuel) and opens onto some excellent vistas of its own. From the meadow, a roughly three-hour climb to the top of the sheer rock wall of the Sierra del Cadí, directly above, reaches an altitude of nearly 8,000 ft. On a clear day you can see Puigcerdà and beyond; the River Segre seems no more than a thin, silver ribbon on the valley floor.

La Seu d'Urgell

★ **⓬**   *20 km (12 mi) south of Andorra la Vella, 50 km (30 mi) west of Puigcerdà past Bellver and Martinet along the River Segre.*

La Seu d'Urgell is an ancient town overlooking the snowy rock wall of the Sierra del Cadí. Its historical importance as the seat of the regional archbishopric since the Middle Ages (6th century) has left it with a rich legacy of art and architecture. The Pyrenean feel of the streets, with dark balconies and porticoes, overhanging galleries, and colonnaded porches—particularly **Carrer dels Canonges**—makes La Seu d'Urgell mysterious and memorable. Look for the medieval **grain measures** at the corner of Carrer Major and Carrer Capdevila. The tiny food shops on the arcaded Carrer Major are intriguing places to assemble lunch for a hike.

★ The 12th-century cathedral of **Santa Maria** is the finest cathedral in the Pyrenees. One of the most moving sights in northern Spain is that of sunlight casting the rich reds and blues of Santa Maria's southeastern rose window into the deep gloom of the transept. The 13th-century cloister is known for the individually carved, sometimes whimsical capitals on its 50 columns. (They were crafted by the same Roussillon school of masons who carved the doorway on the church of Santa Maria in Ripoll.) Don't miss either the haunting, 11th-century chapel of **Sant Miquel** or the **Diocesan Museum**, which has a striking collection of medieval murals from various Pyrenean churches and the colorful, 10th-century *Beatus de Lièbana* (an illustrated Mozarabic manuscript of the Apocalypse), along with a short film explaining the manuscript. Ask for the attractive and well-organized book detailing every local church on the entire Via Románica; it makes a lovely souvenir. ✉ *Cathedral, cloister, and museum 450 ptas./€2.70.* ☉ *Daily 9–1 and 4–8.*

Dining and Lodging

$$ ✕ **Cal Pacho.** Sample traditional local specialties at very reasonable prices in this dark, rustic spot, built in the typical Pyrenean style with stone and wood beams. Count on powerful *escudella* (mountain soup of vegetables, pork or veal, and noodles) in winter, and meat cooked over coals or on slate (*a la llosa*) year-round. ✉ *Carrer Lafont 11,* ☏ *973/ 352719. AE, DC, MC, V.*

$$$$ ✕⊞ **El Castell.** This wood-and-slate structure is one of the finest places
★ around Seu for both dining and lodging. Rooms on the second floor have balconies overlooking the river; those on the third have slanted ceilings and dormer windows. Suites tack on a salon. The restaurant specializes in mountain cuisine, such as *civet de jabalí* (wild-boar stew) and *llom de cordet amb trinxat* (lamb cooked over coals and served with puree of potatoes and cabbage). You need a reservation to stay overnight. ✉ *Carretera de Lleida (N260), Km 129, Apdo. 53, 25700,* ☏ *973/350704,* 🗚 *973/351574. 38 rooms, 4 suites. Restaurant. AE, DC, MC, V.*

$$$ ⊞ **Parador de la Seu d'Urgell.** For comfortable quarters right in town, don't hesitate to stay at the excellent parador, built into the 12th-century church and convent of Sant Domènec. The interior patio, the cloister of the former convent, is a lush and tranquil hideaway. Rooms are basic but warm-toned, and some look past the edge of town to the mountains. The small pool and the dining room have glass ceilings. ✉ *Carrer Sant Domènec 6, Lleida, 25700,* ☏ *973/352000,* 🗚 *973/352309. 77 rooms, 1 suite. Restaurant, indoor pool. AE, DC, MC, V.*

WESTERN CATALAN PYRENEES

"The farther from Barcelona, the wilder" is the rule of thumb and this is true of the western part of Catalonia. Three of the greatest destinations in the Pyrenees fall into this section: the Garonne-drained, Atlantic-oriented Vall d'Aran; the Noguera de Tor valley with its breathtaking Romanesque churches; and the Aigüestortes–Sant Maurici National Park with its network of pristine lakes and streams. The main geographical units in this section are the valley of the Noguera Pallaresa River, the Vall d'Aran headwaters of the Atlantic-bound Garonne, and the Noguera Ribagorçana River valley, Catalonia's western limit. The space in the middle of the rhombuslike area delimited by the roads C133, N230, and C144 contains the carefully maintained

Aigüestortes–Sant Maurici National Park, along with the Noguera de Tor Valley, with its matching set of gemlike Romanesque churches.

Sort

⑬ *From La Seu d'Urgell, take N260 toward Lleida, head west at Adrall, and drive 53 km (33 mi) over the Cantó Pass to Sort.*

Sort, the capital of the Pallars Sobirà (Upper Pallars Valley), is a center for skiing, fishing, and white-water kayaking. Don't be content with the Sort you see from the main road: One block back, the town is honeycombed with tiny streets and protected corners built against heavy winter weather. Sort is also the origin of the road into the unspoiled **Assua Valley**, a hidden pocket of untouched mountain villages, such as Saurí and Olp.

Dining

$ ✕ **Fogony.** If you hit Sort at lunchtime, come straight here for some bracing escudella or some roast lamb or goat before you head up into the high country. ⊠ *av. Generalitat 45,* ☎ *973/621225. MC, V. Closed Mon. except Aug.; closed Jan. 7–22.*

Aigüestortes–Sant Maurici National Park

⑭ *After Escaló, 12 km (8 mi) northwest of Llavorsí, the road to Espot and the Aigüestortes–Sant Maurici National Park veers west.*

Running water and the hydraulic cornucopia of high mountain terrain are the true protagonists in this wild domain of flower-filled meadows and woods in the shadow of the twin peaks of Els Encantats. More than 300 glacial lakes and lagoons (the beautiful Estany de Sant Maurici among them) as well as streams, waterfalls, and marshes make this rocky highland arcadia an aquatic symphony of everything from rills to rivers, tarns, pools, and brooks draining out to the two Noguera watercourses, the Pallaresa and the Ribagorçana, to the east and west.

The abundance of water is even more surprising surrounded by the bare rock walls carved out by the quaternary glacier that left these jagged peaks and moist pockets. The twin Encantats measure 9,065 ft and 9,035 ft respectively, while the Beciberri peak reaches 9,950 ft, the Peguera 9,709 ft, the Montarto 9,339 ft and the Amitges 8,745 ft.

The fauna and flora run a wide gamut from the soft lower meadows below 5000 ft to the highest crags at nearly double that height. Forested by pines, firs, beech, and silver birches, Aigües Tortes (which means "twisted waters") also has ample pastureland inhabited by Pyrenean chamois, capercaillie, golden eagle, and ptarmigan.

The dozen Aigües Tortes mountain refuges are the stars of the Pyrenees, ranging from the 12-bunk Beciberri, known as "the eagle's nest," the highest refuge or bivouac in the Pyrenees at 9,174 ft (brought in by helicopter in 1960), to the 80-bunk 7,326-ft Ventosa i Calvell refuge at the foot of Punta Alta. All of these mountain lodging places turn into hearty meeting points for tired and hungry hikers sharing trail tips and mountain lore between June and September.

Accessible either from the Noguera Ribagorçana valley and Bohi to the west or from the Noguera Pallaresa and Espot from the east, the park has strict rules: no camping, no fires, no vehicles beyond certain points, no loose pets. Access to the park is free; the dozen or so shelters equipped with bunks and mattresses provide overnight accommodations and excellent dining. For information and reservations contact the park administration (⊠ Camp de Mart 35, 25004, Lleida, ☎ 973/246650).

Lodging

The **Ernest Mallafré Refugio** (shelter) is at the foot of Els Encantats near Lake Sant Maurici (☎ 973/624009); the shelter sleeps 36 and is open February–December. The **L'Estany Llong Refugio** (☎ 973/690284), in the Sant Nicolau Valley, sleeps 57 and is open mid-June–mid-October.

Espot

⑮ *Next to the eastern entrance to Aigüestortes–Sant Maurici; 166 km (103 mi) north of Lleida; 15 km (9 mi) northwest of Llavorsí.*

Espot, which has a **ski area** (Super-Espot), nestles at the valley floor along a clear, aquamarine stream. The **Pont de la Capella** (Chapel Bridge), a perfect, mossy arch over the flow, looks as though it might have grown directly from the Pyrenean slate.

En Route From Esterri d'Aneu, C142 reaches the sanctuary of Mare de Deu de Ares, a hermitage and shelter, at 4,600 ft, and the Bonaigua Pass, at 6,798 ft. The latter offers a dizzying look back at the Pallars Mountains and ahead to the Vall d'Aran and the Maladeta massif beyond, shimmering white in the distance.

VAL D'ARAN AND ENVIRONS

The Vall d'Aran is at the western edge of the Catalan Pyrenees and the northwestern corner of Catalonia; from Esterri d'Aneu, the valley runs 46 km (29 mi) east to Vielha over the Bonaigua Pass. North of the main Pyrenean axis, it is the Catalan Pyrenees' only Atlantic valley, opening into the plains of Aquitania and drained by the Garonne, which flows into the Atlantic Ocean north of Bordeaux. The 48-km (30-mi) drive from the Bonaigua Pass to the Pont del Rei border with France follows the riverbed faithfully.

The valley's Atlantic personality shows in its climate—wetter and colder—and its language: The 6,000 inhabitants speak Aranés, a dialect of Gascon French derived from the Occitanian language group. With some difficulty, Aranés can be understood by speakers of Catalan and French. Originally part of the Aquitanian county of Comminges, the Vall d'Aran maintained feudal ties to the Pyrenees of Spanish Aragón and became part of Catalonia-Aragón in the 12th century. In 1389 the valley was assigned to Catalonia.

Neither as wide as the Cerdanya nor as oppressively narrow and vertical as Andorra, the Vall d'Aran has a sense of well-being and order, an architectural consonance unique in Catalonia. The clusters of iron-gray slate roofs, the lush vegetation, the dormer windows (a clear sign of French influence)—all make the Vall d'Aran a distinct geographic and cultural pocket that happens to have washed up on the Spanish side of the border. Hiking and climbing opportunities abound here. Guides are available year-round and can be arranged through the **tourist office** in Vielha (☎ 973/640110).

Vielha

⑯ *79 km (49 mi) northwest of Sort.*

Vielha (Viella, in Castilian Spanish), the capital of the Vall d'Aran, is a lively crossroads vitally involved in the Aranese movement to defend and reconstruct the valley's architectural, institutional, and linguistic heritage. The octagonal, 14th-century bell tower on the Romanesque

parish church of **Sant Miquel** is one of the town's trademarks, as is the
15th-century Gothic altar. The partly damaged 12th-century polychrome wood carving *Cristo de Mig Aran,* displayed under glass,
evokes a sense of mortality and humanity with a power unusual in medieval sculpture.

Dining and Lodging

$$$–$$$$ ✕ **Ca la Irene.** In nearby Arties, 6 km (4 mi) east of Vielha, this rustic
★ little place is known for fine mountain cuisine with a French flair. Three
tasting menus and gastronomic gems like poached foie gras in black truf-
fles and roast wild pigeon in nuts and mint make this place a must. ✉
Mayor 3, Hotel Valartiés, ☎ *973/644364,* 🗏 *973/642174. Reservations
essential. MC, V. Closed Mon. Nov.–Apr.; closed Oct. 15–Nov. 20.*

$$ ✕ **Era Mola.** Also known as Restaurante Gustavo y María José, this
★ restored stable with wood beams and whitewashed walls serves Aranese
cuisine with a French accent. The *confite de pato* (duck stewed with
apple) and *magret de pato* (breast of duck served rare with *carrade-
tas,* wild mushrooms from the valley) are favorites. ✉ *Carrer Marrech
14,* ☎ *973/642419. Reservations essential. MC, V. No lunch weekdays Dec.–Apr. except weekends and holidays.*

$$$ ✕🏨 **Parador Don Gaspar de Portolà.** Also known as the Parador de
Arties, this modern parador makes liberal use of glass and offers
panoramic views of the Pyrenees. Just 7 km (4 mi) from the Baqueira
ski slopes, it's big enough to be festive and small enough for intimacy.
✉ *Carretera Baqueira-Beret s/n, 25599,* ☎ *973/640801,* 🗏 *973/
641001. 54 rooms, 3 suites. Restaurant, bar, swimming pool, exercise
room, parking. AE, MC, V.*

$$$ ✕🏨 **Parador de Vielha.** This modern granite parador has a semicir-
cular salon with huge windows and spectacular views over the Maladeta
peaks. Rooms are furnished with traditional carved-wood furniture and
floor-to-ceiling curtains. The restaurant serves preponderately Catalan cuisine, such as *espinacas a la catalana* (spinach cooked in olive
oil with pine nuts, raisins, and garlic) or the restorative and powerful
olha aranesa (Aranese pot), a meat, vegetable, legume, and pasta soup
ideally conceived for this North Atlantic Pyrenean valley. ✉ *Carretera
del Túnel s/n, 25530,* ☎ *973/640100,* 🗏 *973/641100. 135 rooms.
Restaurant. AE, MC, V.*

$$ 🏨 **Pirene.** On the N230 road into Vielha from points south, this mod-
ern hotel commands some of the best views in town. Rooms are bright
and simply furnished. The cozy sitting room and the charming family
in charge make a stay here a delight. Book ahead during ski season: You're
15 minutes from the slopes. ✉ *Carretera del Túnel (N230) s/n, 25530,*
☎ *973/640075,* 🗏 *973/642295. 40 rooms. AE, DC, MC, V.* 🍴

Salardú

⑰ *9 km (6 mi) east of Vielha.*

Salardú is a pivotal point in the Vall d'Aran, a clearing house and jump-
ing off point for Tredós, the Montarto peak, the lakes and Circ de Colom-
ers, and the Aigüestortes national park, and the highland villages of
Unha and Montgarri. The town itself, with over 700 inhabitants, is
known for its steep streets, its 12th century Sant Andreu church, and
its fortified octagonally-based, 15th-century bell tower. The church's
Romanesque wood sculpture of Christ, protector of Salardú, is said
to have miraculously floated up the Garonne river.

OFF THE   The sanctuary of **Santa Maria de Montgarri** is 12 km (7 ½ mi) northeast
BEATEN PATH   of the town of Baguergue, which is 2 km north of Salardú. This partly ru-
ined 11th-century structure was once an important way station on the

route into the Vall d'Aran from France. The beveled, hexagonal bell tower and the rounded stones, which look like they came from a brook bottom, give the structure a stippled appearance not unlike that of a Pyrenean trout. Try to be there for the Romería de Nuestra Señora de Montgarri (Feast of Our Lady of Montgarri), on July 2, a country fair with dancing, game playing, and general carrying-on. Montgarrí is 14 km (6 mi) northeast of Salardú.

Dining and Lodging

$$$$ ✕⊞ **Tryp Royal Tanau.** This luxurious, sleek, and modern chalet hotel
★ 7 km (4 mi) east of Salardú has lifts directly up to the slopes and every possible comfort and amenity imaginable from gourmet cuisine and indoor and outdoor heated pools, Turkish baths, hydro-massage, and tanning lamps to jacuzzis or fitness machines, with prices to match. Undoubtedly the top skiing hotel in the Pyrenees (it's the only five-star establishment in the Vall d'Aran), this is the obvious place to ensure being thoroughly pampered between assaults on the snowy heights. The wood and sweeping glass construction makes you feel you're outdoors even when you're not, while the service and attention to detail in the hotel's restaurants, cafés and bars is impeccable. ⊠ *Carretera Baqueira-Beret, Km 7, 25598,* ☎ *973/644446,* ℻ *973/644344. 30 rooms, 15 apartments. Restaurant, pool, indoor and outdoor pools, parking. AE, MC, V.*

$$–$$$ ✕⊞ **Val de Ruda.** For more rustic and generally earthy surroundings,
★ this modern-traditional construction, one of the first skiing hotels— built in the traditional slate, wood, stone, and glass style of the Vall d'Aran—will take good care of you. A typical Casa Aranés constructed in 1982, the Val de Ruda is just 200 meters from the slopes and provides a cozy context of pine and oak-beamed warmth for après-ski and dinner. ⊠ *Baqueira, 25598,* ☎ *973/645258,* ℻ *973/645812. 34 rooms. Bar, restaurant, parking. AE, MC, V.*

$ ✕ **Casa Rufus.** Nestled in the tiny, gray-stone village of Gessa, between Vielha and Salardú, Casa Rufus is cozily furnished with pine and checked tablecloths. Rufus himself, who also runs the ski school at Baqueira, specializes in local country cooking; try the *conejo relleno de ternera* (rabbit stuffed with veal). ⊠ *Sant Jaume 8, Gessa,,* ☎ *973/645246 or 973/645872. MC, V. Closed May–July, Sept., Nov., and Sun.*

Outdoor Activities and Sports

Skiing, white-water rafting, hiking, climbing, parapenting, horseback riding, and fly-fishing are all available throughout the Vall d'Aran. The **Baqueira-Beret Estación de Esquí** (Baqueira-Beret Ski Station), visited annually by King Juan Carlos I and the royal family, offers Catalonia's most varied and reliable skiing. The station's 52 pistas cover a wide range of terrain and difficulty, from the gentle slopes of Beret to the more vertical runs in Baqueira. The Bonaïgua area is a mixture of steep and gently descending ski trails offering some of the longest and most varied runs in the Pyrenees, from forest tracks to open hillsides or jagged drops through rocky chutes and ravines. The internationally FIS-classified super-giant slalom run in Beret is Baqueira-Beret's star attraction, while the Hotel Pirene (HeliSwiss Ibérica; (☎ 973/645797) runs carefully guided helicopter outings to the surroundings peaks of Pincela, Areño, Parros, Mall de Boulard, Pedescals and Bassibe, among others. With a dozen restaurants and four children's areas scattered through the ski runs, you're never far from a bracing bowl of one thing or another, while the thermal baths at Tredós are just 4 km away. ⊠ *Salardú 25598,* ☎ *973/644455,* ℻ *973/644488. Barcelona office:* ⊠ *Passeig de Gràcia 2,* ☎ *93/318–2776,* ℻ *93/412–2942.*

For horseback riding, try the **Escuela de Equitación** (Crtra. de Francia, ☎ 973/642244). For climbing and "canyoning," call **Camins del Pirineu** (Av. Pas D'Arró 5, ☎ 973/642444). For adventure sports from white water rafting to kayaking to "canyoning" or quieter activities such as Romanesque chapel browsing or fly-fishing call **Deportur** (☎ 973/647045). For **golf** in Vall d'Aran, the recently opened Salardú golf course has nine challenging holes (☎ 619/739795). The **Palau de Gel de Vielha** (Av. de Garona 33, ☎ 973/642864) has a swimming pool, gymnasium, and saunas. For excursions through the upper reaches of the Vall d'Aran in four-wheel-drive vehicles call **Beraval** (☎ 973/641027). For fly-fishing permits and guides call the **Sociedad de Pesca de Vielha**(☎ 973/641824). The local tourist office can provide detailed information about many of these facilities.

La Pirena, the Pyrenean version of the dog-sledding Iditarod, rages through the Vall d'Aran in early February. The race runs from Panticosa, above Jaca, to La Molina, near Puigcerdà, February 1–15. For more information contact the tourist office in Jaca (☎ 974/360098).

Alta Ribagorça Oriental

⑱ *From Vall d'Aran take the 6-km (4-mi) Vielha tunnel to the Alta Ribagorça Oriental.*

This valley includes the east bank of the Noguera Ribagorçana River and the Llevata and Noguera de Tor valleys. The latter has the Pyrenees' richest concentration of medieval art and architecture.

From Vielha, route N230 runs south 33 km (20 mi) to the intersection with N260 (sometimes marked C144), which goes west over the Fadas Pass to Castejón de Sos. Four kilometers (2½ mi) past this intersection, the road up the Noguera de Tor Valley turns to the northeast, 2 km (1 mi) short of Pont de Suert.

The quality and unity of design apparent in the Romanesque churches along the Noguera de Tor River are the result of the sponsorship—and wives—of the counts of Erill. The Erill knights, away fighting Moors in distant theaters of the Reconquest, as the story goes, left their women behind to supervise the affairs of the home front, including the creation of places of worship. The women then brought in Europe's leading masters of architecture, masonry, sculpture, and painting to build and decorate series of churches. To what extent a single eye and sensibility was responsible for this extraordinarily harmonious and coherent set of chapels and churches may never be known, but they all clearly share certain characteristics: a miniaturistic tightness combined with eccentric or irregular design, and slender rectangular bell towers at once light and forceful, perfectly balanced against the rocky background.

Taüll

⑲ *58 km (36 mi) south of Vielha.*

A town of narrow streets and tight mountain design—wooden balconies, steep slate roofs—Taüll now has a **ski resort**, Boí Taüll, at the head of the Sant Nicolau Valley.

The three-naved Romanesque church of **Sant Climent,** at the edge of town, was built in 1123 and has a six-story belfry. The proportions, the Pyrenean stone, the changing hues in the light, and the general intimacy of the place create an exceptional balance and harmony. The church's murals, including the famous *Pantocrator,* the work of the "Master of Taüll," were moved to Barcelona's Museu Nacional d'Art de Catalunya (☞ Chapter 6) in 1922; you can see reproductions here. 🖼 *500 ptas./€3.01* ⊘ *Daily 9–2 and 4–8.*

Other important **churches** in Taüll include Sant Feliu, at Barruera; Sant Joan Baptista, at Boí; Santa Maria, at Cardet; Santa Maria, at Col; Santa Eulàlia, at Erill-la-vall; La Nativitat de la Mare de Deu and Sant Quirze, at Durro; Sant Llorenç, at Sarais; and Sant Nicolau, in the Sant Nicolau Valley, at the entrance to Aigüestortes–Sant Maurici National Park.

Dining

$$ ✕ **La Cabana.** This rustic place specializes in lamb and goat cooked over coals but also offers a fine *escudella* (sausage, vegetable, and potato stew) and an excellent *crema de carrerres* (cream of meadow mushroom) soup. ⊠ *Carretera de Taüll,* ☎ *973/696213. MC, V. Closed Mon. Dec.–Apr., May–June 23, and Oct.–Nov.*

ARAGÓN AND THE CENTRAL PYRENEES

The highest, ruggedest, wildest, and most spectacular range of the Pyrenees, the hump of "the dragon's back" is, perhaps unsurprisingly, the part in the middle farthest from sea level at either end. From Benasque on Aragón's eastern side to Jaca at the western edge are the great heights and most dynamic landscapes of Alto Aragón (Upper Aragón), the northern part of the province of Huesca, including the Maladeta (11,165 ft), Posets (11,070 ft), and Monte Perdido (11,004 ft) peaks, the three highest points in the Pyrenean chain.

Communications between the high valleys of the Pyrenees were all but nonexistent until the 19th century. Four-fifths of the region had never seen a motor vehicle of any kind until the early part of the 20th century, and the 150 km (93 mi) of border with France between Portalet de Aneu and Vall d'Aran had never had an international crossing. This combination of high peaks, deep defiles, and lack of communication has produced what were historically some of the Iberian Peninsula's most isolated towns and valleys. Today, numerous ethnological museums preserve evidence of a way of life that has nearly disappeared over the last 50 years. Residents of Upper Aragón speak neither Basque nor Catalan, but local dialects such as Grausín, Chistavino, Belsetá and Benasqués have more in common with each other and with Occitanian Langue d'Oc than with either modern Spanish or French. Furthermore, each valley has its own variations on everything from the typical Aragonese folk dance, the *jota* (such as Bielsa's Chinchecle), to cuisine, to the different kinds of folkloric costumes. The unspoiled setting is habitat for a wide variety of Pyrenean wildlife, including several strains of mountain goat, deer, and, above Jaca between Somport and the French Vall d'Aspe, the recently reintroduced Pyrenean brown bear.

Benasque

★ ⑳ *120 km (70 mi) northeast of Huesca, 79 km (49 mi) southwest of Vielha.*

Benasque, Aragón's easternmost town, has always been an important link between Catalonia and Aragón. This town of just over 1,500 people packs a number of notable buildings, including the 13th-century Romanesque church of **Santa Maria Mayor** and the ancient, dignified manor houses of the town's old families, such as the **palace of the counts of Ribagorza,** on Calle Mayor, and the **Torre Juste.** Take a walk around and peer into the entryways of these palatial digs; they're left open for this purpose.

The Central and Western Pyrenees

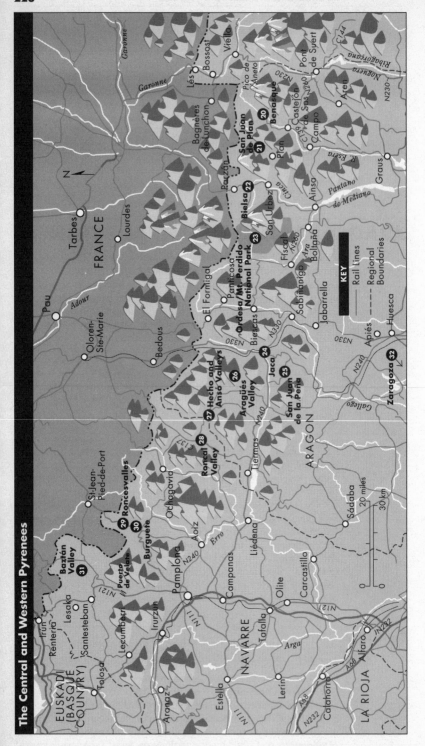

Anciles, 2 km (1 mi) south of Benasque, is one of Spain's best-preserved and -restored medieval villages, an excellent collection of farmhouses and *palacetes* (town houses). The summer classical-music series is a superb collision of music and architecture, and the village restaurant, Ansils, combines modern and medieval motifs in both cuisine and design.

The **Cerler ski area** (☎ 974/551012), 6 km (4 mi) from Benasque, covers the slopes of the Cogulla peak, east of town. Built on a shelf over the valley at an altitude of 5,051 ft, Cerler has 26 ski runs, three lifts, and a guided helicopter service to drop you at the highest peaks.

Dining and Lodging

$$ ✕ **Asador Ixarso.** Roast goat or lamb cooked over a raised fireplace in the corner of the dining room make this a fine refuge in chilly weather. The *revuelto de setas* (eggs scrambled with wild mushrooms) is superb, as are the salads. ⊠ *San Pedro 9, Benasque,* ☎ *974/552057. MC, V. Closed weekdays Sept. 15–Dec. 8 and Easter–June 29.*

$$ ✕ **Restaurante Ansils.** A rustic place ingeniously redesigned in glass, wood, and stone, Ansils specializes in local Benasqués dishes such as *civet de jabalí* (wild-boar stew) and *recau* (a thick vegetable broth). Holiday meals are served on Christmas and Easter. ⊠ *Anciles, Huesca,* ☎ *974/551150. AE, DC, MC, V. Closed weekdays Oct.–June.*

$$–$$$ ✕▦ **Gran Hotel Benasque.** This spacious new stone hotel is bracketed by the highest crests in the Pyrenees (Aneto and Posets) and serves as an impeccably comfortable base for exploring them. The decor and ambience are modern yet tasteful. The restaurant's mountain cuisine features *sopa Benasquesa* (a hearty highland stew) and *crepas Aneto* (crepes with ham, wild mushroom, and béchamel sauce). ⊠ *Carretera de Anciles 3, 22440,* ☎ *974/551011,* FAX *974/551509. 69 rooms. Restaurant, 2 pools, sauna, exercise room. AE, MC, V. Closed Nov.*

$$ ✕▦ **San Marsial.** Filled with antiques, ancient wooden doors, and artifacts, this comfortable inn also has one of Benasque's best restaurants. Try the lentil soup or the *caldereta de conejo* (rabbit stewed in almonds, olives, and bread crumbs). ⊠ *Carretera de Francia (C139) s/n, 22440,* ☎ *974/551616,* FAX *974/551623. 24 rooms. Restaurant, cafeteria. AE, DC, MC, V.*

En Route   South of Castejón de Sos, down the Esera Valley through the Congosto de Ventamillo—a sheer slice through the rock made by the Esera River—a turn west on N260 cuts over to Aínsa, at the junction of the Rivers Cinca and Ara.

San Juan de Plan and the Gistaín Valley

㉑ *14 km (8½ mi) east of Salinas.*

San Juan de Plan has become a treasury of local folklore. This detour begins with a well-marked road heading east of Salinas, 25 km (15 mi) north of Ainsa. The Cinqueta River drains the Gistaín Valley, flowing by or through the mountain villages of Sin, Señes, Saravillo, Serveta, and Salinas; the town of San Juan de Plan presides at the head of the valley, where an Ethnographic Museum, a weaving workshop, and an early music and -dance ensemble are the pride of the region. The **Museo Etnográfico** (⊠ Plaza Mayor s/n,, ☎ 974/506052) is a fascinating glimpse into the valley's way of life until as recently as 25 years ago. It's open daily 9–2 and 4–8, with an admission of 500 ptas./€3.01. Don't miss a tour of the town's weaving industry, **Artesanía Textil** (⊠ Las Gallerices s/n, 22367, ☎ FAX 974/506208), restored by Amanda Tyson, the town's resident American.

Dining and Lodging

$$ ✕⌧ **Casa la Plaza.** This charming spot, owned and run by the one-time mayor, has cozy rooms with original antique furniture. The restaurant serves very original interpretations of traditional Pyrenean dishes making abundant use of game and wild mushrooms. ⌧ *Plaza Mayor s/n, 22367,* ☎ *974/506052,* ⌧ *974/506052. 13 rooms. AE, DC, MC, V. Closed sporadically Oct.–May; call to confirm.*

Bielsa

🐼 *34 km (21 mi) northeast of Aínsa.*

Bielsa, at the confluence of the Cinca and Barrosa rivers, is a busy summer resort with some lovely mountain architecture and an ancient, porticoed town hall, one of the few buildings left standing after Franco's punitive post-combat bombing strike virtually destroyed the town in 1938. Northwest of Bielsa the **Monte Perdido glacier** and the icy **Marboré Lake** drain into the **Pineta Valley** and the Pineta Reservoir. You can take three- or four-hour walks from the parador up to Larri, Munia, or the Marboré Lake among remote peaks.

Dining and Lodging

$$–$$$ ✕⌧ **Parador de Bielsa.** This modern structure of glass, steel, and stone overlooks the national park (☞ *below*), the peak of Monte Perdido, and the source of the Cinca River. Rooms are decorated in bright wood, but the best part is your proximity to the park and the views. The restaurant specializes in Aragonese mountain dishes such as *pucherete de Parzán* (a stew with beans, sausage, and an assortment of vegetables). ⌧ *22350 Bielsa,* ☎ *974/501011,* ⌧ *974/501188. 24 rooms. Restaurant. AE, DC, MC, V.*

$$ ✕⌧ **Valle de Pineta.** This corner castle overlooking the river junction is the most spectacular refuge in town. The restaurant is excellent, the views without compare. Try for the top corner room, which looks up and down both valleys. ⌧ *Baja s/n, 22350,* ☎ *974/501010,* ⌧ *974/501191. 26 rooms. AE, DC, MC, V. Closed Nov.*

En Route   You can explore the **Valle del Cinca** from the river's source at the head of the valley above Bielsa. From Bielsa, drive back down to Aínsa and turn west on N260 (alternately marked C138) for Broto.

Ordesa/Monte Perdido National Park

🐼 *From Aínsa, turn west on N260 for the 53-km (33-mi) drive through Boltaña to Broto, Torla, and the Parque Nacional de Ordesa y Monte Perdido.*

En route to the park, **Broto** is a prototypical Aragonese mountain town with an excellent **16th-century Gothic church.** Nearby villages such as **Oto** have stately manor houses with classic local features: baronial entryways, conical chimneys, and wooden galleries. **Torla** is noteworthy for its mountain architecture and as the entry point to the park; it's a popular base camp for hikers.

The **Parque Nacional de Ordesa y Monte Perdido** is one of Spain's great underrated wonders, a domain many consider comparable to North America's Grand Canyon. The entrance lies under the vertical walls of the Mondarruego mountain source of the Ara River and its tributary, the Arazas, which forms the famous Ordesa Valley. The park was founded by royal decree in 1918 to protect the natural integrity of the Central Pyrenees, and it has expanded from 4,940 to 56,810 acres as provincial and national authorities have added the Perdido massif, the head of the Pineta Valley, and the Escuain and Añisclo canyons. Defined by the Ara and Arazas rivers, the Ordesa Valley is endowed with pine, fir, larch, beech, and poplar forests; lakes, waterfalls, and high mountain meadows; and protected wildlife, including trout, boar, chamois, and the *Capra Pyrenaica* mountain goat.

Hikes through the park (on well-marked and -maintained mountain trails) lead to waterfalls, caves, and spectacular observation points. The standard tour, a full day's hike (8 hours), leads from the parking area up the Arazas River, past the *gradas de Soaso* (Soaso risers; a natural stairway of waterfalls) to the *cola de caballo* (horse's tail), a lovely fan of falling water at the head of the Cirque de Cotatuero. A return walk on the south side of the valley to the Refugio de los Cazadores (hunters' hut) offers a breathtaking view followed by a two-hour descent back to the parking area. A few spots, while not technically difficult, may seem precarious. Information and guidebooks are available at the booth on your way into the park. The best time to come is from the beginning of May to the middle of November, but check conditions with regional tourist offices before driving into a blizzard in May or missing out on *el veranillo de San Martín* (Indian summer) in the fall.

En Route After exploring Ordesa, follow N260 (sometimes marked C140) west over the Cotefablo Pass from Torla to Biescas, which is set in the scenic Tena Valley, and continue on to Jaca.

Jaca

㉔ *Down the Tena Valley through Biescas, a westward turn at Sabiñánigo onto N330 leaves a 14-km (9-mi) drive to Jaca.*

Jaca, the most important municipal center in Alto Aragón (with a population of more than 15,000), is anything but sleepy. Bursting with ambition and blessed with the natural resources to fuel their relentless drive, Jacetanos are determined to host a Winter Olympics someday. An important stronghold during the Christian *Reconquista* of the Iberian Peninsula from the Moors, proud Jaca claims never to have bowed to the invaders and annually celebrates, on the first Friday of May, the decisive battle in which the appearance of a batallion of women with their hair and jewelry flashing in the sun intimidated the Moorish cavalry, producing a headlong retreat.

Praised down through history by the likes of 13th-century King Alfonso X el Sabio, 16th-century novelist Miguel de Cervantes and Nobel prize–winning 20th-century Spanish histologist Santiago Ramón y Cajal, Jaca was officially founded as a kingdom of its own, Jacetania, by King Sancho Ramíro in 1035.

As a cultural center, Jaca holds its own, hosting a Summer University, the Center for Pyrenean Studies, and a noted biannual **Pyrenean Folklore Festival,** held every July 15 to 30th in the Palacio de Congresos, Town Hall (✉ Calle Mayor, ☎ 974/355758), and other venues in Jaca; the festival is shared with Olorón-Sainte-Marie across the border in France: odd years in Jaca, even years in Olorón-Sainte-Marie. Other seasonal events revolve around sports, as Jaca is Northern Spain's winter sport capital (☞ Outdoor Activities and Sports, *below*).

NEED A BREAK? One of Jaca's most emblematic restaurants is **La Campanilla** (✉ Escuelas Pías 8, behind *ayuntamiento*). The baked potatoes with garlic and olive oil are an institution, unchanged for as long as anyone can remember.

Conquered and fortified by the Romans in the 4th centry as *Iacca*, former capital of the 11th-century kingdom of Jacetania, Jaca has perenially been an important stop on the pilgrimage to Santiago de

Compostela and a key Upper Aragón city. Starting at the cathedral, just inside the old part of town across from the Ciudadela fortress, the egg-shaped enclave of early Jaca can be strolled from stem to stern in twenty minutes. The 11th-century **Cathedral de Santa María,** one of the oldest in Spain, is notable for its historiated capitals, particularly the 11th-century depictions of the Sacrifice of Isaac and of King David and his musicians. The Museo Episcopal (Bishops' Museum) is filled with excellent Romanesque and Gothic murals. It's open daily 11–1:30 and 4:30–6:30; admission is 450 ptas./€2.70. ⊠ *Plaza de la Catedral s/n,* ☎ *974/355130.* ☉ *Daily 11–1 and 4–7. Closed Mon.*

The **Ciutadella** (citadel), in town, is a good example of 17th-century military architecture. It's open October–March, daily 11–2 and 4–5, April–September, daily 5–6. Admission is free. The **Rapitán Garrison,** outside town, is also known for its military architecture. It's open July–August, Monday to Saturday 5–8, Sunday 11–1, and admission is free. Other historic architecture to find and explore include the 15th-century **Torre del Reloj** (clock tower) with its Gothic windows and the plateresque doorway to the *Casa Consistorial*, an important example of 16th-century Renaissance civil construction and design.

The high, wild, and usually snowy **ski areas** of Candanchú and Astún are 32 km (20 mi) north on the road to Somport and the French border. In summer, a free guided tour covers the valley (the train ticket costs 450 ptas./€2.70) and the mammoth (and semiderelict) Belle Époque railroad station at the village of **Canfranc,** 25 km (15 mi) north of Jaca, surely the largest and most ornate building in the Pyrenees.

Dining and Lodging

$$ ✕ **La Cocina Aragonesa.** This Jaca mainstay is famous throughout Spain for its fresh and innovative dishes featuring game in season, including venison, wild boar, partridge, and duck. Try the partridge stuffed with foie gras. ⊠ *Cervantes 5,* ☎ *974/361050. AE, DC, MC, V. Closed Wed.*

$$ ✕ **La Tasca de Ana.** "Ana's Tavern" is a beauty and nearly anyone in Jaca will send you here for a meal composed of tapas of every variety, all superbly interpreted. Invent your own menu beginning with a round of olives and working through (for example) cured Iberian ham, cuttlefish, *albondigas* (meatballs), and *civet de jabalí* (wild boat stew), concluding with a cheese from the famous Roncal valley just to the west. ⊠ *Ramiro I 3,* ☎ *974/363621. AE, DC, MC, V. Closed Wed.*

$$ ✕ **El Fau.** Tucked sweetly under the cool and shady porticoes next to the cathedral, with excellent views of the south portal's capitals, El Fau is one of Jaca's best tapas and beer saloons, an ideal place, always booming, for a libation and a hot *cazuelita* (small earthenware casserole). ⊠ *Plaza de la Catedral 3,* ☎ *974/361719. AE, DC, MC, V. Closed Mon.*

$$–$$$ ✕🖪 **Gran Hotel.** This rambling hotel is central to life and tourism in Jaca. Done up in wood, stone, and glass, it has a garden and a separate dining wing. The comfortable rooms are furnished with rich colors and practical wood furniture. ⊠ *Paseo de la Constitución I, 22700,* ☎ *974/360900,* 🅵🅰🅇 *974/364061. 166 rooms. Restaurant, pool, meeting rooms. AE, DC, MC, V.*

$–$$ ✕🖪 **Hostal Somport.** This tidy little spot in the center of town halfway between the cathedral and the Town Hall is better than a good budget option. The rooms, beds, and baths are more than adequate and the location is an ideal crawling distance from the nearby taverns, saloons and music bars on Calle Gil Bergés. ⊠ *Calle Echegaray 11, 22700,* ☎ 🅵🅰🅇 *974/363410. 17 rooms. Restaurant. AE, DC, MC, V.*

Nightlife and the Arts

Discos such as **Dimensión** and **Oroel** are thronged with skiers and hockey players in season (October–April), but the main nocturnal attractions are the so-called *bares musicales* (music bars), usually less loud and smoky than the discos. Most of these are in the old part of Jaca, around Plaza Ramiro I and along Calle Gil Bergés and Calle Bellido.

Outdoor Activities and Sports

Jaca, over the last 25 years, has hosted the Winter Games of the Pyrenees and the World University Winter Games on numerous occasions. Either the National or the World Figure Skating Championships are held here nearly every year, and the national ice-hockey King's Cup is often played on Jaca's first-rate **Olympic-size ice rink** (⊠ Pista de Hielo, Av. Circunvalación s/n, ☎ 974/355306). For more information about outdoor sports in Jaca and environs, contact Transpirineos (⊠ Av. Regimiento de Galicia 2, ☎ 974/355306). Further information is available from the Jaca Tourist Office (⊠ Av. Regimiento de Galicia 2, ☎ 974/360098).

THE WESTERN AND BASQUE PYRENEES

San Juan de la Peña

㉕ *From Jaca, drive 11 km (6½ mi) west on N240 toward Pamplona to a left turn clearly signposted for San Juan de la Peña. From there it's another 11 km to the monastery.*

Before starting west through the Aragonese valleys of Hecho and Ansó, loop south to see the **Monasterio de San Juan de la Peña,** a site connected to the legend of the Holy Grail and another "cradle" of Christian resistance during the 700-year Moorish occupation of Spain. The site's origins can be traced to the 9th century, when a hermit monk named Juan settled here on the *peña* (cliff). A monastery was founded on the spot in 920, and in 1071 Sancho Ramirez, son of King Ramiro I, made use of this structure, which was built into the mountain's rock wall, to found the Benedictine Monasterio de San Juan de la Peña. The **cloister,** tucked under the cliff, dates from the 12th century and features intricately carved capitals depicting biblical scenes. ☎ 974/ 361476, ☒ 450 ptas./€2.70. ☉ *Oct.–mid-Mar., Tues.–Sun. 11–1:30 and 4–5:30; mid-Mar.–May, Tues.–Sun. 10–1:30 and 4–7; June–Sept., daily 10–noon and 4–8.*

En Route The Aragüés, Hecho, and Ansó are the last three valleys in Aragón. From Jaca, head west on N240 and take a hard right at Puente de la Reina (after turning right to cross the bridge) and continue north along the Aragón-Subordán River. The first right after 15 km (9 mi) leads into the Aragüés Valley along the Osia River to Aisa and then Jasa.

Aragüés Valley

㉖ *Aragüés del Puerto is 2 km (1 mi) from Jasa.*

Aragüés del Puerto is a tidy mountain village with stone houses and lovely little corners, doorways, and porticoes lovingly cared for by the ever-dwindling population of 154 inhabitants. The **Museo Etnológico** (Ethnological Museum) in an ancient chapel (ask for the caretaker at the town hall) offers a penetrating look deep into the past. From the document witnessing the 878 election of Iñigo Arista as king of Pamplona to the quirky manual wheat grinder the curios here are singular indeed, as are the baroque altar and pews on the ground floor. The distinctive folk dance in Aragüés is the *palotiau,* a special variation of the *jota* performed only in this village. Above Aragüés del Puerto are the twin peaks of **Bisaurín and Bernera,** two of the highest in the area at just under 9,000 ft each. Near the source of the River Osia, the Lizara **cross-country ski area** is in a flat expanse between the Aragüés and Jasa valleys. Look for the 3,000-year-old megalithic dolmens sprinkled across the flat along with the typical *labati* (huts for hay or for sheltering livestock). Following the river Osia and then the Articuso brook you will reach the glacial lagoon, the **ibón de Estanés** where legend has it that the beautiful Rosina perished in fleeing an ardent Moorish suitor.

Dining and Lodging

$ ✕ **Albergue Lizara.** This simple little spot on the way into town is the only game in town, but a good place for shelter and dinner if it's late in the day or you decide you want to explore the upper reaches or go cross-country skiing. Rooms are small but cozy and the Pyrenean cuisine is highland stick-to-your-ribs with no frills. ✉ *Calle Lizara s/n,* ☎ FAX *974/371519. 12 rooms (60 more beds in nearby dormitory). Restaurant. MC, V.*

Hecho and Ansó Valleys

㉗ *The Hecho Valley is 49 km (30 mi) west of Jaca. The Ansó Valley is 25 km (16 mi) west of Hecho.*

You can reach the Valle de Hecho by returning to the valley of the Aragón-Subordan and turning north again. The **Monasterio de San Pedro de Hecho,** above the town of Hecho, is the area's most important monument, a 9th-century retreat of which only the 11th-century church remains. *la Fabla Chesa,* a medieval Aragonese dialect descended directly from the Latin spoken by the Siresa monks, is thought to be the purest—that is, the closest to Latin—of all the Romance languages and dialects. The dialect has been kept alive in the Hecho Valley, especially in the works of the poet Veremundo Mendez Coarasa. The **Selva de Oza** (Oza Forest), at the head of the valley, is above the **Boca del Infierno** (Mouth of Hell), a tight draw where road and river barely squeeze through. Beyond the Oza Forest is a **Roman road** used before the 4th century to reach France through the Puerto del Palo (El Palo Pass)—one of the oldest routes across the border on the pilgrimage to Santiago de Compostela.

The Valle de Ansó is Aragón's western limit. Rich in fauna (mountain goats, wild boar, and even a bear or two), the Ansó Valley follows the Veral River up to Zuriza. Above Zuriza are three **cross-country ski areas,** known as the Pistas de Linza. Near Fago is the sanctuary of the **Virgen de Puyeta,** patron saint of the valley. Towering over the head of the valley is Navarra's highest point, the 7,989-ft **Mesa de los Tres Reyes** (Plateau of the Three Kings), named not for the Magi but for the kings of Aragón, Navarre, and Castile, whose 11th-century kingdoms all came to a corner here—allowing them to meet without leaving their respective realms.

Try to be in the town of **Ansó** on the last Sunday in August, when residents dress in their traditional medieval costumes and perform ancestral dances of great grace and dignity. From Ansó, head west to Roncal on the difficult but panoramic road through the Sierra de San Miguel.

Dining and Lodging

$$ ✕▥ **Gaby-Casa Blasquico.** Hecho's top restaurant, this diminutive gem is famous for carefully crafted Aragonese mountain cuisine. It's especially strong on game preparations, from wild boar to venison to partridge or migratory pigeon, but the menu includes a full range of lamb and vegetable dishes. Calling ahead is essential: Gaby will often open for anyone who reserves in advance, even if theoretically closed.

The six rooms for rent here are excellent value, comfortable and semisecret hideaways. ⊠ *Plaza Palacio 1,* ☎ *974/375007. 6 rooms. Restaurant. MC, V.*

$$ 🏨 **Usón.** For a base to explore the upper Hecho Valley or the Oza Forest, look no further. This friendly little Pyrenean inn will rent you a bike, get you a trout-fishing permit, or send you off in the right direction for a climb or hike. The restaurant, which serves primarily hotel guests, and is excellent. ⊠ *Carretera Selva de Oza (HU2131), Km 7, 22720,* ☎ *974/375358. 14 rooms. Restaurant. MC, V. Closed mid-Dec.–mid-Feb.*

Roncal Valley

㉘   *Take N240 from Jaca west along the Aragón River; a right turn north on NA137 follows the Esca River from the head of the Yesa Reservoir up the Roncal Valley.*

The Roncal Valley, the eastern edge of the Basque Pyrenees, is famous for its sheep's-milk cheese, Ronkari, and as the birthplace of Julián Gayarre (1844–90), the leading tenor of his time. The 34-km (21-mi) drive through the towns of **Burgui** and **Roncal** to **Isaba** winds through green hillsides and Basque *caseríos* housing farmers and their livestock. Burgui's red-tile roofs backed by rolling pastures contrast with the vertical rock and steep slate roofs of the Aragonese and Catalan Pyrenees; Isaba's wide-arched bridge across the Esca is a graceful reminder of Roman aesthetics and engineering techniques. Try to be in the Roncal Valley for El Tributo de las Tres Vacas (the Tribute of the Three Cows), celebrated every July 13 since 1375. The mayors of the valley's villages, dressed in distinctive traditional gowns, gather near the summit of San Martín to receive the symbolic payment of three cows from their French counterparts, in memory of the settlement of ancient border disputes over rights to high pastures and water sources. Feasting and celebrating follow. The road west (NA140) to Ochagavia through the Puerto de Lazar (Lazar Pass) has views of the Anie and Orhi peaks, towering over the French border.

Two kilometers (1 mile) south of Ochagavía, at Escároz, a small secondary roadway winds 22 km (14 mi) over the Abaurrea heights to Aribe, known for its triple-arched medieval bridge and ancient *horreo* (granary). A 15-km (9-mi) detour north through the town of Orbaiceta up to the headwaters of the Irati River, at the Irabia Reservoir, gets you a good look at the **Selva de Irati** (Irati Forest), one of Europe's major beech forests and the source of much of the timber for the fleet Spain commanded during her 15th-century golden age.

Roncesvalles

★ **㉙**   *2½ km (1½ mi) north of Burguete, 48 km (30 mi) north of Pamplona.*

Roncesvalles (Orreaga, in Euskera) is the site of the Colegiata, cloister, hospital, and 12th-century **chapel of Santiago,** the first Navarrese church on the Santiago pilgrimage route.

The **Colegiata** (Collegiate Church), built at the orders of King Sancho VII el Fuerte (the Strong), houses the king's tomb, which measures more than 7 ft long. The 3,468-ft Ibañeta Pass, above Roncesvalles, is one of the most beautiful routes into France. A stone **menhir** marks the traditional site of the legendary battle in *The Song of Roland* in which Roland fell after calling for help on his ivory battle horn. The well-marked eight-hour walk to or from St-Jean-Pied-de-Port is one of the most beautiful and dramatic sections of the entire pilgrimage.

Dining and Lodging

$$ ✕🏨 **La Posada.** This 17th-century building with a heavy stone entry is an ancient way station for pilgrims bound for Santiago de Compostela. The accommodations are simple but far more comfortable than the pilgrims' quarters in the neighboring Colegiata. ✉ *Carretera Pamplona–Francia (C135), Km 48, 31650,* ☎ *948/760225,* 🟥 *948/760225. 18 rooms. Restaurant. AE, DC, MC, V. Closed Nov.*

Burguete

③⓪   *2½ km (1½ mi) south of Roncesvalles, 120 km (74 mi) northwest of Jaca.*

Burguete lies between two mountain streams forming the headwaters of the Urobi River. The town was immortalized when Ernest Hemingway published *The Sun Also Rises,* in 1926, with its evocative description of trout fishing in an ice-cold stream above a moist Navarran village. Travelers to Burguete and Roncesvalles can feel securely bracketed between 11th-century French and 20th-century American literary classics.

Dining and Lodging

$$ ✕🏨 **Hostal Burguete.** This is the inn where Hemingway's character Jake Barnes spent a few days clearing his head in the cool streams of Navarre before plunging back into the psychodrama of the San Fermín festival and his impossible love with Lady Brett Ashley. It still works for this sort of thing, though there don't seem to be as many trout around these days. Good value and simple Navarran cooking make this a good place to stop for a meal or a night. ✉ *C. Única 51, 31540,* ☎ *948/760005. 22 rooms. Restaurant. MC, V. Closed Feb.–Mar.*

En Route   To skip Pamplona (☞ Chapter 3) and stay on the trans-Pyrenean route, continue 21 km (13 mi) southwest of Burguete on NA135 until you reach NA138, just before the town of Zubiri. A right turn takes you to Urtasun, where the small NA252 leads left to the town of Iragui and over the pass at Col d'Egozkue (from which there are superb views over the Arga and Ultzana River valleys) to Olagüe, where it connects with NA121 some 20 km (12 mi) north of Pamplona. Turn right onto N121A and climb over the Puerto de Velate (Velate Pass)— or, in bad weather or a hurry, go through the new tunnel—to the turn for Elizondo and the Baztán Valley, N121B.

Baztán Valley

③①   *80 km (50 mi) north of Pamplona.*

Tucked neatly over the headwaters of the Bidasoa River and under the peak of the 3,545-ft Garramendi mountain looming over the border with France, the rounded green hills of the Valle de Baztán make an ideal halfway stop between the rocky crags of the central Pyrenees and the flat expanse of the Atlantic Ocean, below. Each village in this enchanted Basque valley seems smaller and simpler than the next, with tiny clusters of whitewashed, stone-and-mortar houses with red-tile roofs grouped around a central *frontón* (handball court).

Dining and Lodging

$$ ✕ **Galarza.** This stone town house overlooks the Baztán River in the
★   town of Elizondo. The kitchen serves excellent Basque fare, with a Navarran emphasis on vegetables. Try the *txuritabel* in season (roast lamb with a special stuffing of egg and vegetables) or *txuleta de ternera* (veal raised in the valley). ✉ *C. Santiago 1,* ☎ *948/580101. MC, V.*

$ ✕🏨 **Fonda Etxeberria.** This tiny inn in the Baztán Valley town of
★   Arizcun is an old farmhouse with creaky floorboards and oak doors. The rooms are small but handsome, and although they share baths,

RONCESVALLES AND THE SONG OF ROLAND: EPIC SOAP OPERA

ON THE 15TH OF AUGUST 778, the legendary French warrior hero Roland— military commander of Brittany and nephew of the great Frankish Emperor Charlemagne—died, along with the entire rear guard of the Frankish army, in the Pyrenean pass of Roncesvalles, north of Pamplona. Ambushed by the Basques of Navarra in retaliation for the sacking of Pamplona, Roland's demise became legend through the *chansons de geste* (songs of deeds), the best of which was *La Chanson de Roland* (The Song of Roland), considered the beginning of French literature. The poem includes a surprising payload of the elements of modern psychodrama: a family inheritance feud, a jealous stepfather's rivalry, two friends' alter egos, a tragic hero with the fatal flaw of pride, a lovely maiden pining away . . . a ready-made movie script.

History's only documentary reference to Roland is one line written by the medieval Frankish scholar Einhard in his 9th-century biography of Charlemagne, identifying one Hruodlandus (Roland in Frankish), his rank of prefect of the borderlands of Brittany, and his death in combat in the Pyrenees. Written in assonant rhyme, *La Chanson de Roland* is famous for its unified theme, its vivid and direct voice, and its warlike tone—and its enthralling story. Roland is one of Charlemagne's 12 peers and a nephew (son of Charlemagne's brother Carloman who died in 771). Carloman's widow marries Ganelon, who, as Roland's jealous stepfather, treacherously arranges for Saracens (Mooors) to ambush Charlemagne's rear guard, commanded by Roland, accompanied by his friend Olivier and the Bishop Turpin. The Saracens attack; Roland is too proud to blow his ivory battle horn, Oliphant, to call for help. Olivier, always characterized as "sage" or wise, begs him to blow his horn and call for relief. The Franks put up heroic resistance; when Roland finally calls for help

it's too late and he dies. Charlemagne returns to his aid and defeats the Moors. Ganelon is subsequently executed, while in the aftermath Aude, Roland's true love, dies of a broken heart.

Medievalists still argue over the exact location of Roland's final battle. The simple menhir and sword engraved with the years 778 and 1967 (the year the monument was placed there) visible beside the road to Saint-Jean-Pied-de-Port in the Ibañeta pass have traditionally (and erroneously) been accepted as the site of the battle. But the well-marked GR 65 trail starting behind the Colegiata in the village of Roncesvalles is the ancient Roman and Santiago de Compostela pilgrim route and certainly the path Charlemagne's troops would have followed. This Roman route turns east at the Ibañeta pass and follows a narrow track for 4 kilometers, entering France through the Lepoeder Pass, and continuing through the Bentarte pass, where most modern scholars place the battle, 4 km (2.4 mi) from the monument. R.H. Bautier describes the terrain as an ideal site for an ambush: "The attack would have taken place on the slopes of Altobiszcar just before the Lepoeder pass. There, for some 700 meters, the trail borders the Barranco Urdanchaio precipice, a straight drop of 300 to 400 meters . . . a perfect spot for surprise. The Basque montagnards would have rushed suddenly, throwing the Franks into the ravine with no chance for defense. In addition, the hairpin turn in the trail would have allowed no visibility from the main body of Charlemagne's column of troops."

The true story of Roland's final battle will probably never be known for certain until archaeological excavations are permitted on the supposed battle sites. For the moment, Spanish authorities have preferred to allow the Roland legend to benefit from a certain ambiguity, shrouded in the mists of time in the grassy and silent mountain slopes above Roncesvalles.

the baths are palatial. The restaurant serves simple country dishes, such as bean stew and roast lamb. ⊠ *Next to frontón in Arizcun,* ☎ *948/ 453013. 16 rooms. Restaurant. MC, V.*

ZARAGOZA: CITY OF THE FLATLANDS

For travelers who are journeying on our trans-Pyrenean safari—outlined in the many pages above—the mountain ranges and valleys create a truly scenic route from east to west. For those who wish to more directly connect Barcelona to Bilbao, their route should follow the great highway system that connects Spain's Mediterranean and Atlantic coasts and which travels through the Aragónese flatlands: these highways—the A2, the A7, and the A68—provide northern Spain's transportion axis (☞ Barcelona to Bilbao: Main Highway Routes map, at the front of this book). While this route is much less scenic, it does offer along the way the largely undiscovered city of **Zaragoza** ㉜. Aragón's urban base, the urban outpost is not only a useful Pyrenean gateway, it is an important midstation for visitors making the Barcelona-Bilbao circuit. The city retains an authentic provincial character that is refreshingly original in postmodern Spain and, of course, remains helpful for people driven out of the Pyrenees by blizzards, buzzards, bears, or Basques . . . (à la Roland).

On the map, Zaragoza is 138 km (86 mi) west of Lleida, 307 km (190 mi) west of Barcelona, 164 km (102 mi) southeast of Pamplona, and 322 km (200 mi) northeast of Madrid; for location, see the Barcelona to Bilbao: Main Highway Routes map at the front of this book.

Despite its hefty size (population 600,000), this sprawling provincial capital remains relatively obscure and is in some ways an oasis of authenticity, a detour from the tourist track. Straddling Spain's greatest river, the mighty Ebro, 2,000-year-old Zaragoza holds an important legacy of everything from Roman ruins to Arab, Romanesque, Gothic-Mudejar, Renaissance, Baroque, neoclassical, and Art Nouveau architecture. Rated one of Spain's most desirable places to live for a variety of reasons (air quality, cost of living, population density), Zaragoza seems to breathe a quiet sense of self-contained well-being.

Hulking hugely on the banks of the Ebro, the **Basílica de Nuestra Señora del Pilar** (Basilica of Our Lady of the Pillar), affectionately known as "La Pilarica," is Zaragoza's symbol and pride. An immense Baroque and eclectic structure with no fewer than 11 tiled cupolas, La Pilarica is the home of the Virgen del Pilar, the patron saint not only of peninsular Spain but of the entire Hispanic world. The fiestas honoring this most Spanish of saints, the week of October 12, are events of extraordinary pomp and fervor, with processions, street concerts, bullfights, and traditional *jota* dancing. The cathedral was built in the 18th century to commemorate the appearance of the Virgin on a pillar (*pilar*), or pedestal, to Santiago (St. James), Spain's other patron saint, in the 9th century. La Pilarica herself resides in a side chapel that dates from 1754. The frescoes in the cupolas, attributed to the young Goya, are among the basilica's treasures. The **Museo Pilarista** holds drawings and some of the Virgin's jewelry. ▨ *Basilica free; museum, 175 ptas./€1.05.* ☯ *Basilica daily 5:45 AM–9:30 PM; museum, daily 9–2 and 4–6.*

Zaragoza's cathedral, **La Seo,** across the square from the basilica, is the city's bishopric, or diocesan *seo* (seat). An amalgam of architectures ranging from the Mudéjar brick-and-tile exterior to the Gothic altarpiece to exuberant, Churrigueresque doorways, the Seo nonetheless has an 18th-century Baroque facade that seems to echo those of La Pilarica. The **Museo de Tapices** within features medieval tapestries.

✉ *Cathedral free; museum 300 ptas./€1.85.* ☉ *Cathedral, Mon.–Sat. 10–2 and 4–8, Sun. 5–8; museum, Tues.–Sat. 10–2 and 4–6, Sun. 10–2.*

Not far away, the **Iglesia de la Magdalena** (Church of Mary Magdalene), next to the remains of the Roman forum, has an ancient, brick Mudéjar bell tower. Parts of the **Roman walls** are visible near La Pilarica, as is the medieval **Puente de Piedra** (Stone Bridge) spanning the Ebro. The **Lonja** (stock exchange), the Moorish **Aljafería** (jewel treasury), the **Mercado de Lanuza** (produce market), as well as the various **churches** in the old town—San Pablo, San Miguel, San Gil, Santa Engracia, San Carlos, San Ildefonso, San Felipe, Santa Cruz, and San Fernando—will guide you through this jumble of back streets.

The **Museo del Foro** displays remains of the Roman forum and the Roman sewage system, though the presentation is in Spanish only. Two more Roman sites, the thermal baths at Calle de San Juan y San Pedro and the river port at Plaza San Bruno, have recently been opened to the public. ✉ *Plaza de la Seo s/n,* ☎ *976/399752.* ✉ *500 ptas./€3.01.* ☉ *Tues.–Sat. 10–2 and 5–8.*

The **Museo Camón Aznar** (✉ C. Espoz y Mina 23, ☎ 976/397328) has a fine collection of Goya's works, particularly engravings. It's open Tuesday–Friday 9–2 and 6–9, weekends 9–2, and admission is 75 ptas./€0.75. The **Museo Provincial de Bellas Artes** (Provincial Museum of Fine Arts; ✉ Plaza de los Sitios 5, ☎ 976/222181) is also rich in Goyas; it's open Tuesday–Saturday 9–2 and 4–7, Sunday 9–2, and charges 350 ptas./€2.10. The **Museo Pablo Gargallo** (✉ Plaza de San Felipe 3, ☎ 976/392058) is dedicated to one of Spain's greatest modern sculptors, born near Zaragoza in 1881. Hours are Tuesday–Sunday 9–2 and 4–7, and admission is 350 ptas./€2.10.

Excursions from Zaragoza include Goya's birthplace at **Fuendetodos,** 44 km (27 mi) to the southeast, and **Belchite,** another 20 km (12 mi) east of Fuendetodos, the site of the deliberately untouched ruins of a town destroyed in one of the fiercest battles of the Spanish Civil War.

Dining and Lodging

$$ ★ ✕ **El Fuelle.** This old-town favorite is known for fine Aragonese cuisine, a lively ambience, and specialties like *judías blancas* (white beans), *migas* (a traditional dish of chorizo, peppers, and bread crumbs soaked in olive oil and garlic), and *patatas asadas* (roast potatoes), the most emblematic dish here. ✉ *Calle Mayor 58,* ☎ *976/398033. AE, DC, MC, V.*

$$ ★ ✕ **La Matilde.** Conveniently stationed near Zaragoza's spectacular Lanuza market, La Matilde is one of the city's most popular restaurants, justly famed for its *cocina de mercado*—cuisine prepared according to what's freshest and best in the market at the moment. ✉ *Calle Predicadores 7,* ☎ *976/441008. AE, DC, MC, V.*

$$ ✕ **La Venta del Cachirulo.** This roadhouse just outside Zaragoza is worth a trip for authentic Aragonese cooking and folklore, including occasional *jota* dancing, singing, and a generally rough-and-tumble approach to delicious food. *Borrajas con almejas* (kale with clams) and *pato con cerezas* (duck with cherries) are among the local dishes served. ✉ *Carretera Logroño (N232), Km 1,* ☎ *976/331674. AE, DC, MC, V. No dinner Sun., except Aug. 1–15.*

$$$–$$$$ ✕▣ **Tibur.** This small hotel overlooks the cathedral, the basilica, and the stock exchange from its perch less than 100 yards from the Ebro. The setting is discreet and charming, and while the rooms are not spacious, they're nicely decorated. The excellent restaurant, the Foro Romano, serves both international and Aragonese cuisine. ✉ *Plaza de la*

Seo 2, 50001, ☎ 976/202000, ℻ 976/202002. *50 rooms. Restaurant, bar, cafeteria. AE, DC, MC, V.*

THE PYRENEES A TO Z

Arriving and Departing

By Plane

Barcelona's international airport, **El Prat de Llobregat,** is the gateway to the Catalan Pyrenees. Airports at Girona, Zaragoza, Pamplona, Bilbao, and Fuenterrabía (Hondarribia) also serve the Pyrenees of Catalonia, Aragón, Navarra, and the Basque country. Traveling from Barcelona or Bilbao into the Pyrenees by air is probably less practical and more dangerous than it's worth, but there are airfields in Puigcerdà, La Seu d'Urgell, Vielha, and Jaca that handle charter aircraft.

By Train

The Pyrenees may be accessed by train from Barcelona, Lleida, and Zaragoza. Train connections from Bilbao, Logroño, and San Sebastián can only make it as far as Pamplona, from which only a change in Zaragoza will get you up to Jaca.

Getting Around

By Car

The best way to tour the Pyrenees, short of hiking, is by car. The most difficult road into the Catalan Pyrenees from Barcelona is over the Collada de Toses (Tosses Pass) to Puigcerdà, but it's free and the scenery is spectacular. Safer, faster, and more expensive but somewhat less scenic (though you will have a great view of the Montserrat massif) is the approach through the Cadí Tunnel. The wide, two-lane roads of the Cerdanya are generally new and well paved; as you move west, roads may be more difficult to navigate, but the N260 *Eje Pirenaico* (Pyrenean Axis) has improved trans-Pyrenean communications significantly over the last ten years.

Because of the forgiving and flexible late dinner hour on the Spanish side of the Pyrenees, it is highly recommended to make the crossing from west to east traveling primarily between late morning and dark when the westward falling sun will, instead of blinding you, spotlight scenery in extra sharp evening light. The main links on the N260 are Irún, Puerto de Velate, Burguete, Roncesvalles, Aribe, Isaba, Ansó, Hecho, Jaca, Sabiñanigo, Biescas, Aínsa, Campo, Castejón de Sos, and Pont de Suert. At Pont de Suert, leave the "official" N260 trans-Pyrenean route in favor of the higher and more interesting route north through the Tunel de Vielha on the N230, over the Bonaigua pass on C142 which becomes C147 through Llavorsí to Sort, to rejoin the N260 and continue east to Adrall, La Seu d'Urgell, Puigcerdà and Ripoll. From Ripoll, leave the N260 again and take the C151 up into Camprodón and Vall de Ter before backtacking through the Capsacosta tunnel to Olot to again rejoin the N260 to Besalú, Figueres, and Port de la Selva. From Port de la Selva, the N260 continues to the French–Spanish border at Port Bou and Cerbère, but the true trans-Pyrenean route is completed by driving east to Cadaqués and, finally, Cap de Creus, the Iberian Peninsula's easternmost point.

Many of the main obstacles to Pyrenean motoring (i.e., the high mountain passes) have been supplanted by tunnels over the past 20 years. The tunnels at Velate, Vielha, the Tunel del Cadí, and the Capsacosta tunnel linking Vall de Ter with Girona have opened the Pyrenees to mass tourism. The Bonaigua pass into the Vall d'Aran, which used to be closed from the year's first snowfall until late spring, is now kept open by the Generalitat de Catalunya. To check road conditions or confirm whether mountain passes are open, call the RACC, or Reial Automovil Club de Catalunya (☎ ☎ 93/495–5022) or the Dirección General de Tráfico (☎ ☎ 900–123505).

By Train

There are four railheads in the Pyrenees: the FFCC de la Generalitat cogwheel train to Nuria from Ribas de Freser off the Barcelona–Puigcerdà line; and the RENFE lines to Puigcerdà, in the Cerdanya, which passes through La Molina and goes on to La Tour de Carol; Pobla de Segur, in the Noguera Pallaresa Valley; and Canfranc, north of Jaca via Zaragoza, below the ski resorts of Candanchú and Astún.

Contacts and Resources

Emergencies

Red Cross—Cruz Roja in Spanish; Creu Roja in Catalan (☎ Girona: ☎ 972/200415; Lleida: ☎ 973/267011; Navarre: ☎ 948/226404). **Police** (☎ Girona: ☎ 972/201381; Lleida: ☎ 973/245012; Navarre: ☎ 948/237000).

Fishing

Ramón Cosiallf and **Danica** (☎ 608/735376) can take you fly-fishing anywhere in the world by horse or helicopter, but the Pyrenees are their home turf. For about 15,000 ptas./€90.15 a day (depending on equipment), you can be whisked to high Pyrenean lakes and ponds, streams, and rivers and armed with equipment and expertise. You can purchase fishing licenses for each autonomous region (Catalonia, Aragón, Navarre) at local rod-and-gun clubs (Asociaciones de Pesca and/or Caza). To avoid being caught without a fishing license with offices closed for the weekend, pick up season licenses (1,600 ptas./€9.62) in Barcelona at **ICONA** (⊠ Calle Sabino de Arana 24, across from the Hotel Princesa Sofía, near the FC Barcelona stadium, ☎ 93/409–2090, open weekdays 9–2). In Puigcerdá, licenses are available at the office of **Agricultura, Ramadería i Pesca** (⊠ Calle de la Percha 17, ☎ 972/880–515, open weekdays 9–2).

Golf

Camprodón has a nine-hole course, **Club de Golf de Camprodón** (☎ 972/130125). The Cerdanya has three golf courses, two near Puigcerdà: **Reial Club de Golf de la Cerdanya,** (☎ 972/141408); **Club de Golf de Fontanals** (☎ 972/144374), and a nine-hole course at Font Romeu **Club de Golf de Font Romeu** (☎ 05/683–1078) in France. Jaca and Benasque also have golf facilities; check with local tourist offices for details. Greens fees are generally between 4,000/€20.04 and 8,000 ptas./€48.08

Guided Tours

The **Touring** travel agency (☎ 972/880602 or 972/881450, FAX 972/881939) in Puigcerdà can help arrange routes, guides, horses, or four-wheel-drive vehicles for treks to upper lakes, peaks, and meadows. Local *excursionista* (outing) clubs, especially the **Centro Excursionista de Catalunya** in Barcelona (⊠ Carrer Paradís 10, ☎ 93/315–2311), can advise climbers and hikers.

Outdoor Activities and Sports

Jaca, Puigcerdà, and Vielha have excellent **ice rinks** (Jaca, ☎ 974/361032; Puigcerdà, ☎ 972/880243; Vielha, ☎ 973/642864). Spain's daily newspaper *El País* prints complete ski information every Friday in season; for up-to-the-minute information in Catalan and Spanish, contact the **hotline** in Barcelona (☎ 93/416–0194). For further information, contact the **Federació Catalana Esports d'Hivern** (Catalan Winter Sports Federation; ⊠ Carrer Casp 38, Barcelona, ☎ 93/302–7040). The best

12 ski stations in the Pyrenees are Vallter 2000 above Camprodón, La Molina and Masella in La Cerdanya, Llessui and Super-Espot in the Noguera Pallaresa valley, Baqueira-Beret in Vall d'Aran, Boí-Taüll in the upper Noguera Ribagorçana valley, Cerler in Aragón above Benasque, Formigal and Panticosa in the Tena Valley east of Jaca, and Candanchú and Astún north of Jaca.

For guides through the Aragonese Pyrenees, contact **Transpirineos** (⊠ Av. Regimiento de Galicia 2, Jaca, ☎ 974/364998). In Benasque, for rafting, parapenting, canyoning or for equipment and guides to scale Aneto, the Pyrenees highest peak, either on foot or on skis, call **Casa de la Montaña** ⊠ Av. de los Tilos s/n, Benasque, ☎ 974/552094). **Compañia de Guías de Benasque** (⊠ Av. de los Tilos s/n, Benasque, ☎ 974/551336) provides a full range of guided activities.

Visitor Information

Regional tourist offices: **Aragón** (⊠ Torreon de la Zuda, Glorieta de Pío XII, Zaragoza, ☎ 976/393537). **Barcelona** (⊠ Palau Robert, Passeig de Gràcia 107 [at Avda. Diagonal], ☎ 93/238–4000). **Girona** (⊠ Rambla de la Llibertat 1, ☎ 972/202679). **Lleida** (⊠ Plaça de la Paeria 11, ☎ 973/248120). **Navarre** (⊠ Duque de Ahumada 3, Pamplona, ☎ 948/211287).

Local tourist offices: **Aínsa** (⊠ Avda. Pirenaica 1, ☎ 974/500767). **Benasque** (⊠ Plaza Mayor 5, ☎ 974/551289). **Bielsa** (⊠ Plaza del Ayuntamiento, ☎ 974/501000). **Camprodón** (⊠ Plaça Espanya 1, ☎ 972/740010). **Jaca** (⊠ Avda. Rgto. Galicia, ☎ 974/360098). **Puigcerdà** (⊠ Carrer Querol 1, ☎ 972/880542). **La Seu d'Urgell** (⊠ Avda. Valira s/n, ☎ 973/351511). **Vielha** (⊠ Avda. Castiero 15, ☎ 973/640979).

5 BILBAO AND THE BASQUE COUNTRY

With the opening of the hyperbole-proof Bilbao Guggenheim museum, this former industrial giant has reinvented itself as the Athens of the Basque Country—a world apart with its own language, gastronomy, sports, and rural culture. From Bilbao to chic San Sebastián, the moist green hills and rugged coast of Euskadi are a succession of fresh redoubts. Nearby, Vitoria and the Plain of Alava lead into the Rioja Alavesa, while Navarra and La Rioja are richly endowed close cousins.

By George
Semler

TIME IN BILBAO MAY SOON NEED TO BE IDENTIFIED as BG or AG (Before Guggenheim, After Guggenheim). Never has a single monument of art and architecture so radically changed a city— or, for that matter, a nation, and in this case two: Spain and Euskadi. Architect Frank Gehry's stunning Museo Guggenheim, Norman Foster's sleek subway system, and the glass Santiago Calatrava footbridge, which allows pedestrians to all but walk on water, have all helped foment a cultural revolution in the commercial capital of the Basque Country. Although the inner city was most recently censed at 373,000, greater Bilbao (Bilbo, in Euskera, the native dialect) now encompasses almost 1 million inhabitants, nearly half the total population of the Basque Country and the fourth-largest urban population in Spain. The Basque Country's political and social conflict came to a temporary halt after the Guggenheiming of Bilbao. Never in the annals of urban renewal has a city, in one masterstroke, so comprehensively reinvented itself. Only recently a smoke-stained industrial soot-bowl—though never lacking a sparkling cultural and culinary tradition—Bilbao has made a brilliant investment in art and tourism, which in turn, revolutionized the city and led the entire Basque Country into a new era of economic and spiritual regeneration, suggesting that life can indeed imitate art (or at least an art museum).

Architect Frank Gehry's gleaming titanium whale hovering alongside the estuary of the Nervión river connects Bilbao's 700-year-old Casco Viejo (Old Quarter) with the 19th-century *Ensanche* ("Widening") and seems to collect and reflect light throughout Bilbao and all of the Basque Country. For starters, from the central atrium of the Guggenheim you can look both east up into Bilbao's most urban streets or above to the west where green hillsides, *caseríos* (farmhouses), and grazing livestock continue placidly about their age-old business. Meanwhile, churches in Bilbao's 700-year-old Casco Viejo are emerging from centuries of industrial grime, gleaming in the city's sudden resurgence, while parks and gardens are being reclaimed from what only recently were rusting shipyards and steel mills. Bilbao at the beginning of the 21st century seems a happy version of Hieronymous Bosch's *Garden of Earthly Delights* triptych—one of the greatest masterpieces on view in Madrid's Prado —as the green hills surrounding the city bustle with activity on dozens of levels, a virtual anthill of commerce and endeavor.

And as Bilbao goes, so goes Euskadi (the official name of the region known as the Basque Country). A land of steep green hillsides, fine mist—the legendary *siri-miri*—and russet farmhouse rooflines hugging the horizon, the semiautonomous Basque Country is the cradle of the linguistically mysterious, non–Indo-European language Euskera. With its rocky coastline and pre-Pyrenean uplands, Euskadi is a distinct national and cultural entity within Spain.

A country within a country, or a nation within a state (the semantics are much debated still), the Basque Country is only nominally Spanish. In contrast to the traditionally individualistic and passionate Latin peoples who have been their neighbors, the Basques have often been regarded as more collective-minded and practical. They are also known to love competition—it has been said that Basques will bet on anything that has numbers on it and moves. Such traditional rural sports as chopping mammoth tree trunks, lifting boulders, and scything grass reflect the timeless Basque attachment to the land and to farm life as well as an ingrained enthusiasm for feats of strength and endurance. Even poetry and gastronomy become contests in Euskadi, as *bertsolaris* (amateur poets) improvise duels of devastatingly witty verse and male-only gastronomic societies compete in cooking contests to see who can make the best *marmitako* (tuna and potato stew).

Basques come in different forms and phylla: there is the upland Basque, considered a purer strain, more mystical and less adulterated and cosmopolitan than the coastal Basque, which has been "tainted" by outside influences from the sea. Bilbao is the traditional *barrio industrial* (industrial neighborhood), while San Sebastián—that seaside resort once favored by crowned heads (and heads that were no longer crowned)—is the *barrio jardin* (garden neighborhood). The Basque from the Plain of Alava has a definite Castilian streak, while the Navarra Basque ranges from the proto-Basque of the Pyrenees to the Basque from Pamplona and points south, who isn't very Basque at all but a kind of Spanish-speaking northern Castilian. All in all, the question of Basque ethnic "purity" is an increasingly unpopular concept in this early 21st-century era of fusion, though the continuing reaction to 40 years of the same "internal exile" that Catalonia experienced—the suppression of a cultural identity—is understandable. Then again, in the words of Madrid poet Carlos Bousoño, "It is difficult to understand the cultural aspirations of a society that takes as a matter of pride the fact of having eluded the two most important civilizing and cultural events of the last 2,000 years: Romanization and Arabization."

The much-reported Basque independence movement is made up of a small but radical sector of the political spectrum. The underground organization known as ETA, or Euskadi Ta Askatasuna (Basque Homeland and Liberty), has killed more than 700 people in more than a quarter century of terrorist activity. Violence in the Basque Country has waxed and waned over the last decade, though the problem is extremely unlikely to affect the traveler.

The Basque Country, Bilbao especially, has traditionally had close connections with both Britain and the United States. Bilbao and its province, Vizcaya, were the source of most of the iron used by the English during the Industrial Revolution. Primarily an agricultural and fishing region of modest opportunity before industry made it a center of productivity on the peninsula, the Basque Country has long sent out waves of immigrants to the New World. Rare is the Basque without a wealthy family member who started out as a shepherd in Nevada or a pelota player in Miami. Perhaps as a result, Basques are unusually friendly to both Americans and Britons . . . friendlier, in fact, than they are to Spaniards from Madrid and points south, who are often suspected, at least until proven otherwise, of a touch of arrogance or a lack of respect for Basque culture and identity.

In the end, this entire region is packed with pleasures and treasures. Bilbao and the Basque Country, with part-Basque Navarra and La Rioja wine country thrown in, offer a wide range of geography as well as urban variety. From the industrial muscle and newfound artistic power of Bilbao to the grace and lightness of San Sebastián, from the classical sweep of Pamplona to Vitoria's weathered stone or Logroño's streets looking out on the fruited plains of the Ebro valley, the five main cities each have distinct characters to savor. The area's towns and villages offer an even wider selection of memorable spots: the landlocked schooner of Laguardia, peninsular Guetaria surrounded by the Bay of Biscay, the wide beachfront of Mundaca, Pyrenean Roncesvalles (☞ Chapter 4), and the highland refuge of La Rioja's Viniegra de Abajo are each radically different schemes, while the geographical gamut from Atlantic ocean to the Pyrenees or the Sierra de la Demanda peaks offer surfing, sailing, skiing, or mountain hiking all within a 100-mi radius.

Pleasures and Pastimes

Art and Architecture

Ever since the Bilbao Guggenheim eclipsed Madrid's Prado Museum as the most visited art venue on the Iberian Peninsula, visitors to the Basque Country are coming for much more than the coast and the cuisine. Along with the excellent art museums in Bilbao, San Sebastián and Vitoria and the Zuloaga museum in Zumaya, a series of must-see buildings, bridges, and even subways have popped up in the Basque cities. San Sebastián's Kursaal by Rafael Moneo is competing successfully with Santiago Calatrava's Zubi-Zuri footbridge, Norman Foster's subway system linking all of greater Bilbao, the Palacio Euskalduna music and convention hall by Federico Soriano and Dolores Palacios, as well as with Frank O. Gehry's Guggenheim. Meanwhile, new projects are on the way: both Calatrava and Gehry are designing futuristic houses and wine cellars for vintners in the Rioja Alavesa (the Basque part of La Rioja in the province of Alava north of the Ebro), while Bilbao's Abandoibarra project under the direction of architect Severino de Atxukaro will convert the riverside space between the Guggenheim and the Palacio Euskalduna into a series of gardens. The Abandoibarra plan will also connect the Universidad de Deusto with the left bank of the Nervión via a footbridge.

Beaches

West and north of Bilbao, the beaches at **Getxo, Gorliz,** and **Mundaca** (with its famous left-breaking surfing wave at the mouth of the Ría de Gernika) are all excellent. Farther east, the beaches at **Ea, Lequeitio, Ondarroa,** and **Motrico** are the most notable, while in the Province of Guipuzcoa, the smaller beaches at **Zumaya** and **Guetaria** are quiet and intimate except in August, when they may be crowded. **Zarauz,** west of San Sebastián, is another good choice with a huge expanse of sand. San Sebastián's most emblematic beach, **La Concha,** which curves around the bay along with the city itself, is scenic and clean, but it's packed wall-to-wall in the summer. **Ondarreta,** at the western end of La Concha, is often less crowded, and the relatively new and quiet beach on the northern side of the Urumea River, the **Playa de Zurriola,** the beach where surfers gather waiting for breakers, is wilder and lonelier. **Fuenterrabía,** the last stop before the French border, has a vast expanse of fine sand along the Bidasoa estuary.

Dining

Bilbao is so deeply, purely, and seriously gourmet that the legendary dean of Bilbao chefs, Genaro Pildaín of Guria, spends more time talking about his potato and leek soup than about truffles or foie or sturgeon roe. Long before the Guggenheim sprang to life like some wild titanium mushroom, those-in-the-know knew that downtown Bilbao concentrated some of the Basque Country's and Spain's most supreme and superb dining establishments. These are chefs who snicker a little about Catalonia's superstar chef Ferran Adrià and his Bullí restaurant; as one of them said: "Yes, well, my belief is that *everything* we serve here ought to be good." And master chef Jose María Arzak and the San Sebastián school are regarded as, though admirable, sadly tainted by the influence of nearby France.

Guria, Goizeko Kabi, Zortziko, El Perro Chico, Jolastoki, Mendigoikoa (only El Perro Chico has any Latin in it, so don't despair if this sounds like consonant soup): as you can tell from this list of top restaurants, wherever you go in Bilbao—even the lowliest tapas bar— there is a very high standard of culinary excellence in play, without which, as a result of the fierce competition, an eating establishment couldn't sell so much as a boiled egg. Meanwhile, Ander Calvo invents world championship gourmet sandwiches at his Taberna de los Mundos in the Ensanche and Santiago Ruiz Bombín puts up spotlight-enhanced *montaditos* (canapés) and *pinxitos* (tapas on toothpicks) that look as though they'd be more at home over in the fine-arts museum across the river.

The Basque cuisine in and around Bilbao and San Sebastián is generally considered the best food in Spain, combining the fresh fish of the Atlantic and upland vegetables, beef, and lamb with a love of sauces that is rare south of the Pyrenees—a result, no doubt, of Euskadi's proximity to France. The now 20-year-old *nueva cocina vasca* (new Basque cooking) movement has introduced exciting elements. In San Sebastián or Bilbao, as throughout Euskadi, it's nearly impossible to avoid a great meal. Specialties include *kokotxas* (nuggets of cod jaw), *besugo a la parrilla* (sea bream grilled over coals), *chuleta de buey* (garlicky beefsteak grilled over coals), and the deservedly ubiquitous *bacalao al pil-pil*—cod-flank fillets cooked very slowly in a boiled emulsion of garlic and gelatin from the cod itself, so that the oil makes a popping noise ("pil-pil") and a white sauce is created.

Though the local Basque wine, *txakolí,* a young, white brew made from tart green grapes, is a refreshing accompaniment for tapas and first courses, serious dining in the Basque Country is invariably accompanied by wines from La Rioja. Just an hour south of Bilbao, La Rioja and its wines are very much part of daily life throughout the Basque Country, especially in Bilbao, where one gets the impression that the vineyards are there specifically for the pleasure and greater glory of bilbainos and their culinary adventures.

Though La Rioja Alta produces the finest wines in Spain, purists insisting on sipping a Basque wine with their Basque cuisine could choose a Rioja Alavesa, from the north side of the Ebro. Navarre also produces some fine vintages, especially rosés and reds—and in such quantity that some churches in Allo, Peralta, and other towns were actually built with a mortar mixed with wine instead of water.

Though top restaurants are expensive in the Basque Country, some of what is undoubtedly Europe's finest cuisine is served here in settings that range from the traditional hewn beams and stone walls of old farmhouses to sleekly contemporary international restaurants all the way up to the Guggenheim itself, where San Sebastián superstar Martín Berasategui runs a dining room as superb as its habitat. But don't feel you need to go grand gourmet to dine well in the Basque Country; don't miss a chance to go to a *sidrería,* a typical Basque cider house (in Astigarraga, near San Sebastián, there are no fewer than 17), where *tortilla de bacalao* (codfish omelet) and thick *chuletas de buey* provide the traditional ballast for copious draughts of hard apple cider.

CATEGORY	MAJOR CITIES*	OTHER AREAS*
$$$$	over 8,000 ptas./ €48.08	over 6,000 ptas./ €36.06
$$$	5,000–8,000 ptas./ €30.05–48.08	4,000–6,000 ptas./ €24.04–36.06
$$	2,500–5,000 ptas./ €15.03–30.05	2,000–4,000 ptas./ €12.02–24.04
$	under 2,500 ptas./ €15.03	under 2,000 ptas./ €12.02

per person for a three-course meal, excluding drinks, service, and tax

Fiestas

Pamplona's **Feast of San Fermín** (July 6–14) was made famous by Ernest Hemingway in *The Sun Also Rises* and remains best known for its running of the bulls. The town's population triples that week, so reserve rooms well in advance. Bilbao's **Semana Grande** (Grand Week), in early August, is bigger than ever: Spain's largest bullfights of the season seem to stimulate appetites worthy of Bilbao's fine fleet of restaurants. West of Bilbao, Laredo's **Batalla de los Flores** (Battle of the Flowers) is held the last Friday in August. The coastal town of Lequeitio, east of Bilbao, is famous for its unusual September (1–18) **Fiestas de San Antolín,** in which (on September 5) men dangle from the necks of dead geese strung on a cable over the inlet. Closer to San Sebastián, in the first week of August, the fishing village of Guetaria celebrates **Juan Sebastián Elcano**'s completion of Magellan's voyage around the world. San Sebastián hosts a renowned **international film festival** in late September and celebrates its saint's day on January 19. San Vicente de la Barquera honors its patron saint with a famous maritime procession for **La Folía,** April 21. La Rioja's famous **Batalla del Vino** (Wine Battle), a free-for-all honoring the fruit of the vine, takes place in Haro on June 29. Vitoria's weeklong **Fiesta de la Virgen Blanca** (Festival of the White Virgin) celebrates the city's patron saint with bullfights, floral offerings, and general carousing beginning on August 4. The curious inaugural event involves the lowering of a dummy, an effigy named Celedón, from the San Miguel church to a house from which a similarly dressed man emerges, whereupon everyone lights a cigar.

Hiking and Walking

Well-marked footpaths wind through the Cordillera Cantábrica to the Pyrenees along the edge of the Basque coast, connecting towns, scaling mountains, and ambling from one fishing village to another. The air, color, and scenery far exceed anything you'll experience by car. Try the walks around Zumaya, or the walk over Jaizkibel between San Sebastián and the French border. The GR11 trail crosses the Pyrenees of Navarre, while the Camino de Santiago pilgrimage route crosses Navarre and La Rioja on its way west. Local tourist offices can usually suggest a variety of routes of your preferred length and intensity.

Lodging

Room rates can be astronomical in the big cities and surprisingly reasonable in more charming, if less luxurious, inns and farmhouses scattered around the hills and fishing towns. San Sebastián—long one of Spain's most fashionable resorts—is particularly pricey, especially in the summer, and Pamplona rates double or triple during the San Fermín fiesta in July. Reserve ahead in Bilbao, where the Guggenheim Museum is filling hotels, and nearly everywhere in summer. The quality of hotels, service, and connected restaurants is generally quite high. Another lodging option is a Basque-farmhouse stay booked through the Agroturismo lodging network; these are economical, authentic, and picturesque. Check with local tourist offices for details and availability.

CATEGORY	MAJOR CITIES*	OTHER AREAS*
$$$$	over 25,000 ptas./ €150.25	over 15,000 ptas./ €90.15
$$$	15,000–25,000 ptas./ €90.15–150.25	9,000–15,000 ptas./ €54.09–90.15
$$	10,000–15,000 ptas./ €60.10–90.15	6,000–9,000 ptas./ €54.09
$	under 10,000 ptas./ €60.10	under 6,000 ptas./ €36.06

All prices are for a standard double room, excluding breakfast and tax.

✎ *following the text of a review is your signal that the property has a Web site, where you will find details and, usually, images; for a link, visit www.fodors.com/urls.*

Sports and Outdoor Activities

Basques are as passionate about sports as they are about food, and you need not participate to catch the action. If you do want to get up and about, there's excellent skiing, sailing, surfing, windsurfing, and trout or Atlantic-salmon fishing in various parts of this rich terrain.

Pelota is the Basque national sport. Most towns have a local *frontón* (backboard or wall), where games normally start at 4 or 4:30 PM. Other traditional Basque rural sports (*herrikirolak*) include the tug-of-war and log-chopping, ram-butting, and scything competitions. The most idiosyncratic of the local contests is the *harrijasotazailes,* the raising of huge rocks by practiced stone-lifters. *Jai-alai* (a generic term for ball games from handball to *cesta punta,* played with wicker gloves), *estropadak* (whale-boat regattas), and horse races round out the ample sports menu. Watch for local postings or ask at the tourist office.

Athletic de Bilbao is the traditional local football giant, with San Sebastián's Real Sociedad just behind. Up-and-down first- and second-division teams also compete in Santander, Pamplona, Logroño, and Vitoria. Inquire at your hotel or the local tourist office about schedules and tickets. For more information, see the Close-Up Box on Basque sports, *below.*

Exploring Bilbao and the Basque Country

This chapter covers Bilbao and the three main provinces of Euskadi, the Basque Country: Bilbao and Vizcaya; San Sebastián and Guipúzcoa; and Vitoria, the Basque capital, and the province of Alava. Navarra, part Basque in its upper reaches, and La Rioja—the area's wine stash—are fundamental and closely linked neighbors. This compact and well-communicated corner of the Iberian Peninsula is 60 minutes wide, give or take a few, along some of the finest and most picturesque (no billboards allowed) freeways in the world, though the tiny byways and country roads make the best, if slowest, exploring routes. If you begin from Bilbao and circle out along the coast of Vizcaya and into the Basque hills, the beach resort of San Sebastián is less than an hour north while Pamplona and the Navarran Pyrenees are an hour northwest along the French border. Vitoria and La Rioja Alavesa are less than an hour inland from Bilbao, while Logroño and wine country are just over an hour west.

Numbers in the text correspond to numbers in the margin and on the Basque Country, Navarra, and La Rioja and the Bilbao maps.

Great Itineraries

On the map, this region may not look like it covers much ground, but the best roads for exploring are also the slowest. Moreover, each of the main entities—Vizcaya, Guipúzcoa, and Alava—has enough hills, streams, and villages for a lifetime of discovery once you've seen the cities of Bilbao, San Sebastián, and Vitoria.

Ten days to two weeks is a fair frame for this chapter, though you could happily spend most of that time span in the tiniest village or fishing port. In six days you can cover the high points and come away with some ideas for future visits. Three days is time enough for a taste.

IF YOU HAVE 3 DAYS

In three days you'll be hard-pressed to do justice to **Bilbao** ①–③⑦ or even the **Museo Guggenheim** ④ alone, but seeing the **Casco Viejo** ("old part") and the **Ensanche** ("Widening") and making a trip out to the Basque hills at **Axpe** ㊾ or the beach at **Mundaca** ㊷ is barely possible for the ambitious and tireless tourist avid for the full Bilbao treatment.

BASQUES: GONZO OVER GAMES

BASQUES COMPETE at virtually everything: cooking, poetry writing, eating, rowing, chopping, lifting, scything, horse racing, ox hauling, sheep herding, and—of course—all national and international team games such as football, rugby, basketball, field hockey, ice hockey, and team handball, among others. Basques will, more often than not, surprise you by playing and excelling at games they've never tried before. When ice hockey was introduced in the shadow of the Pyrenees in the early 1970s, Basques quickly established a lock on all the championships, competing against clubs with greater means and bigger budgets. No one remembers the last time either of the two major Basque football teams, Athletic de Bilbao and Real Sociedad, dropped down to second division. What's more, between the two teams, they won four consecutive league titles in the late '70s and early '80s.

Known for a hardy, rough-and-tumble nature, Basque sporting temperament is well typified in *Estropadak*, the annual whaleboat regattas, to which Basques from upland villages traditionally make 20-mi hikes to watch. Eight-oared sliding bench crews gliding along the Thames in sleek shells seem like lawn bowling compared to whaleboat racing in the swells of the open Atlantic. With one or more of the 13 oarsmen frequently dumped overboard, the regatta is spectacular enough to bring the entire San Sebastián fleet out to accompany the boats to the finish while thousands watch the spectacle from the shore.

Instinctively collective, Basques are good at team sports, and especially at defense, which is generally understood as the most difficult aspect of team games to develop. The Basque Country, famous for supplying Spanish first division football with legendary goaltenders, is known for its defensive ferocity, as demonstrated in the defense of their language and culture against Roman, Moorish, and Spanish imperialism. Basques are also known, in the sports world, for their keen sense of angles, acquired from the legendary ball games played against the wall, or *fronton*, in the center of every village. The game of *pelota* (ball), a descendant of the medieval *jeux de paume* (hand, or, literally "palm" games), is a mainstay of rural Basque culture, played in variations using different surfaces and equipment. The courts include the *place libre*, literally "free space," with a front wall; the *trinquet*, a room with a front wall as a backboard; and the *mur à gauche*, or "wall to the left," a three-walled court including front (*fronton*), side and back walls. Equipment covers a wide range of bats, baskets, gloves, rackets, and balls, but the most traditional is the *esku huska*, the bare hand. *Cesta punta*, the game the world knows as jai alai, is played with a curved and elongated leather and wicker glove (*xistera*). Small bats or paddles are used in the game of *pala*. Strung rackets are also used for certain types of pelota played against a fronton. Jai alai, the game best known outside the Basque Country (literal translation: *fiesta alegre*, or "joyous fiesta"), is played in a three-walled court between two, four, or six players using the xistera. The game is mesmerizing as a result of the speed of the ball in flight and the artistry of the players in figuring out where and how to play each shot.

As if all this weren't enough, cooking, versifying, rowing, and playing jai alai are just the tip of the *herri kirolak* (people's or rural sports) iceberg. *Aizkolari* chop wood in several different kinds of events; *trontzalariak* contests are about sawing the stuff; *harrijasotzaileak* hoist cubic, cylindrical, rectangular, or round stones of up to 700 lb up onto their shoulders; *gizon proba* (man test) is a stone-hauling event for men, not oxen. Journalist Joel Reingold once said that Basques will compete over and bet on anything that moves and has numbers on it. In a recent retraction, Reingold now admits his error: Basques compete over and bet on absolutely everything, numbers or not.

Then again, three days could be one in Bilbao, one in San Sebastián, and one in Pamplona (on the way east to Barcelona) in a pinch. For the Bilbao-based three-day attack, start with the **Guggenheim** ④ in the morning, visit the **Mercado de la Ribera** ⑧, and dive into the **Casco Viejo** for a tapa at Xukela and another at Victor Montes in **Plaza Nueva** ⑫ on your way across the Puente del Mercado to Perro Chico for lunch. In the afternoon, see more of the Guggenheim and eventually have dinner at Guria or Zortziko. On day two, see the **Museo de Bellas Artes** ③ and walk across the **Ensanche** for one of Ander Calvo's championship gourmet sandwiches at his Taberna de los Mundos before hopping the Eusko Tren from **Estación de Atxuri** ⑲ to **Bermeo** ㊶ and **Mundaca** ㊷ for sunset over the Urdaibai natural preserve at the mouth of the Ría de Guernica. The relentless will find a way to swing a late dinner at Goizeko Kabi. Day three would include a walk through the **Doña Casilda de Iturrizar park** ②, more Guggenheim, a look through the fascinating **Museo Vasco** ⑬, and a funicular ride to **Artxanda** ㉕ and El Txakolí de Artxanda for lunch overlooking the city. After more Guggenheim in the afternoon, a 30-minute drive will put you in **Axpe** ㊾ at Mendigoikoa for dinner, or if that seems like too much, try an in-town solution like Casa Rufo. If your three days are destined to include Bilbao, San Sebastián, and Pamplona, see the **Guggenheim** ④ and the Casco Viejo in Bilbao; the **Parte Vieja, Museo San Telmo,** and **La Concha** beach in **San Sebastián** ㊽; and, in **Pamplona** ㉛, the **Plaza del Castillo,** the **Iglesia de San Saturnino, Calle San Nicolás,** and the **Cathedral.**

IF YOU HAVE 6 DAYS

Bilbao ①–㊲ alone is at least a three-day exploration, with side trips even a week. Spend days one and two exploring the **Guggenheim** ④, the **Casco Viejo,** and the **Ensanche.** On day three, after a final shot at the Guggenheim, loop around the Basque coast, with lunch in Getxo at Jolastoki, to ▦ **Mundaka** ㊷. On day four reach ▦ **San Sebastián** ㊽ either via the Basque Coast and the fishing ports of **Elanchove** ㊹, **Lequeitio** ㊺, **Ondárroa** ㊻, **Zumaya** ㊶, and **Guetaria** ㊷ or through the Basque highlands and **Axpe** ㊾, **Elorrio** ㊼, **Oñate** ㊽, and the **Santuario de San Ignacio** ㊽ in Azpeitia. **San Sebastián** ㊽ merits much more than one night, so if you're tempted to throw out the rest of your itinerary and stay, don't blame us; it's been done before. If you can manage to leave, on day four try to swing north through Fuenterrabía (Hondarribia, in Basque, is what you're most likely to see on road signs) and drive through the Velate pass and the beautiful Baztan Valley to ▦ **Pamplona** ㉛. By evening of day five you can be perched over the Ebro River valley and La Rioja in ▦ **Laguardia** ㊻ and on day six you can explore **Haro** ㊽ and **Logroño** ㊽ on your way east for a night at the castle of ▦ **Olite** ㊽.

IF YOU HAVE 10–15 DAYS

▦ **Bilbao** ①–㊲ alone is at least a three-day exploration, with side trips even a week. Spend days one and two exploring the **Guggenheim** ④, the **Casco Viejo,** and the **Ensanche.** On day four, have a look through **Las Encartaciones** uplands west of Bilbao, before a final evening at the Guggenheim. On day five drive around the Basque coast, with lunch in **Getxo** ㊳ at Jolastoki, to ▦ **Mundaka** ㊷. On day six make it to ▦ **San Sebastián** ㊗, either via the Basque Coast and the fishing ports of **Elanchove** ㊹, **Lequeitio** ㊺, **Ondárroa** ㊻, **Zumaya** ㊶, and **Guetaria** ㊷ or through the Basque highlands and **Axpe** ㊾, **Elorrio** ㊼, **Oñate** ㊴, and the **Santuario de San Ignacio** ㊵ in Azpeitia. **San Sebastián** ㊗ is an easy place to stay for a while. Whenever you do manage to leave, after a foot and boat trip to **Pasajes to San Juan** ㊿ preferably, swing north through Fuenterrabía and drive through the Velate pass and the beautiful Baztan Valley to ▦ **Pamplona** ㉛. By evening of day seven or eight (or whatever it may have gotten to be) you can, having explored

The Basque Country, Navarra, and La Rioja

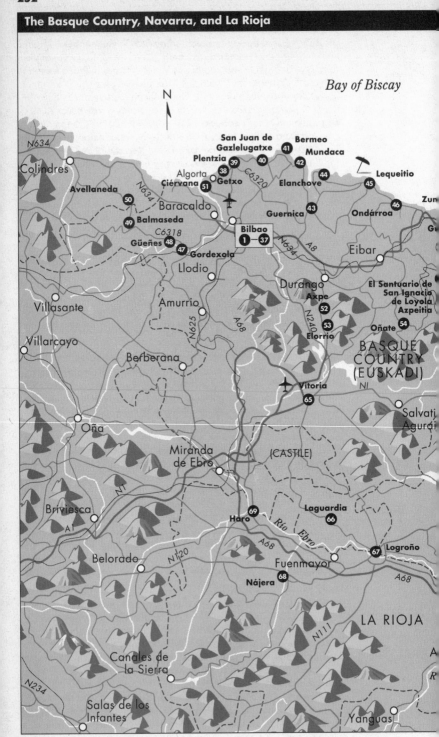

Bay of Biscay

N

Colindres
N634

Avellaneda
Ciérvana
Algorta
San Juan de Gazlelugatxe
Plentzia
Getxo
Bermeo
Mundaca
Elanchove
Guernica
Lequeitio
Ondárroa
Zun
Baracaldo
Balmaseda
Güeñes
Gordexola
Bilbao
Eibar
Llodio
Durango
Axpe
El Santuario de San Ignacio de Loyola Azpeitia
Villasante
Amurrio
Elorrio
Oñate
Villarcayo
Berberana
BASQUE COUNTRY (EUSKADI)
Vitoria
Salvati Agurai
Oña
Miranda de Ebro
(CASTILE)
Briviesca
Haro
Laguardia
Belorado
Fuenmayor
Logroño
Nájera
LA RIOJA
Canales de la Sierra
Salas de los Infantes
Yanguas

C6320
N634
A8
N240
NI
A68
N625
N1
A1
N120
A68
Río Ebro
N111
N234
C6318
N634

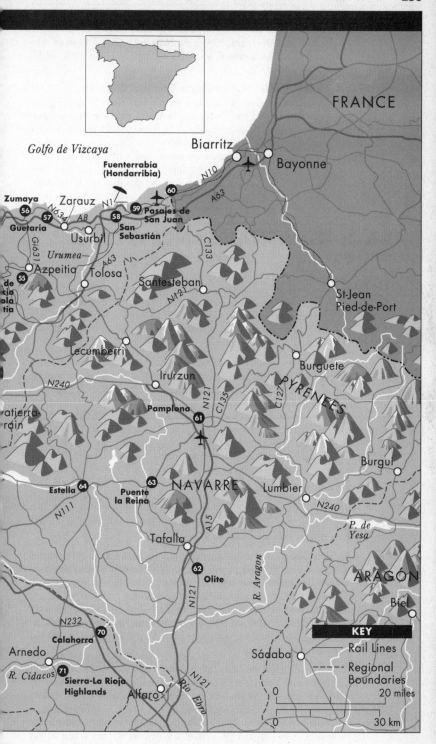

FRANCE

Golfe de Vizcaya

Biarritz

Bayonne

**Fuenterrabía
(Hondarribia)**

Zumaya Zarauz N1 **60**

56 **57** N634 A8 **58** **59** **Pasajes de
San Juan**

Guetaria Usurbil **San
Sebastián**

Gi631 A63 C133

Urumea

55 Azpeitia Tolosa

*de
io
ía* Santesteban

N121

St-Jean
Pied-de-Port

Lecumberri

Irurzun Burguete

N240 N121 C135 **PYRENEES**

*atierra-
ráin* **Pamplona** **61** C127

Burgui

Estella **64** **63** **NAVARRE** Lumbier

**Puente
la Reina** A15 N240

N111 *P. de
Yesa*

Tafalla **ARAGÓN**

62 **Olite** *R. Aragon* Biel

N232 N121

70

Calahorra Sádaba

Arnedo

R. Cidacos **71**

**Sierra-La Rioja
Highlands** Alfaro N121 *Río Ebro*

KEY
——— Rail Lines
- - - Regional Boundaries

0 _____ 20 miles

0 _____ 30 km

Vitoria ⑥, be perched over the Ebro River valley and La Rioja in ⊞ **Laguardia** ⑥. Next day tour the **Najerilla valley** all the way up to the Monasterio de Valvanera, exploring **Nájera** ⑦ and ⊞ **Haro** ⑥. On your way east see **Logroño** ⑥ and plan on a night at the castle of ⊞ **Olite** ⑥.

When to Tour Bilbao and the Basque Country

May–June and September–October are the best times to enjoy good weather and to avoid the tourist crush, which peaks in August. The Basque Country is characteristically rainy, especially in winter, though the rain here generally seems refreshing and cleansing rather than gloomy or depressing: the greenery seems to get brighter. Summer is temperate, fresh compared to most Iberian climes in July and August and the reason the Basque coast became famous as a summer watering spot. Extended daylight, an absence of crowds, and sweet temperatures make late May through June ideal.

BILBAO: THE RENAISSANCE CITY

The Bilbao Guggenheim ought to sell four-day passes. Between a careful exploration of the famous Gehry building, a leisurely perusal of the important modern permanent collection of art, a good look at whatever temporary exhibition is on display, and another day to wander back through works, nooks, or crannies of whatever you feel you need another hit of, you can easily spend this much time at the museum—with time off to explore the city, of course.

A good deal of time is beneficial, as it turns out, for Bilbao is a city with notable sights and attractions. Completely surrounded by the green hills of Artxanda, Bérriz, Abril, Artagan, Malmasin, Arnótegui, Pagasarri, Arraiz, and Cobetas, it is suddenly—*mirabile dictu*—more famous for its emblematic "Bilbao blue" skies of deep cerulean than for its dreary *siri-miri* drizzle or the rusting remains of its once opulent shipyards. Between global warming and the dazzling Guggenheim-generated optimism currently ranked somewhere between Transilium and Prozac on the anti-depressant hit parade, Bilbao—once written off as a dreary factory-ridden seaport—is now a city where walking through lush green parks, along the river, through art museums, and across architecturally poetic footbridges is more than an option. On the map, **Bilbao** ⑦ is located 607 km (376 mi) west of Barcelona, 100 km (62 mi) west of San Sebastián, and 305 km (189 mi) northwest of Zaragoza.

Though Bilbao's new attractions get more press, the city's old treasures still quietly line the banks of the rust-colored Nervión River. The Casco Viejo (Old Quarter)—also known as Siete Calles (Seven Streets)—is a charming jumble of shops, bars, and restaurants on the river's Right Bank above the Puente del Arenal. In the *Ensanche* ("Widening") on the Left Bank of the river, broad 19th-century boulevards such as Gran Vía (the main shopping artery) and Alameda Mazarredo are the city's more formal face.

Flaviobriga, as the Romans called what they described as a bustling hub filled with a remarkable quantity and quality of iron ore, women, and foodstuffs, has always been prosperous. Founded in 1300 by a Vizcayan noble, Diego López de Haro, earliest Bilbao was Spain's main northern port for the sheep's-wool exports that represented the Iberian Peninsula's most important source of medieval wealth. Later Bilbao became an industrial and mining center, thanks mainly to the abundance of minerals in the surrounding hills. An affluent industrial class grew up here, as did the working-class suburbs (like Portugalete and Baracaldo) that line the Margen Izquierda (Left Bank) of the Nervión estuary. Agriculture and fishing made way for shipbuilding, coal mining, and steel manufacturing, as Bilbao and the industrial revolution embraced each other in the 19th century. The Universidad Comercial de Deusto, founded by the Jesuit Order in 1886 was one of the first business management schools in the world, an academy for industrial leadership unparalleled in its time. Meanwhile, early banking moguls such as Carlos Jacquet and Pedro McMahon y Aguirre developed expertise and power in this area that led to the early Banco de Vizcaya and eventually to today's giant Banco de Bilbao-Vizcaya.

Over the course of the 20th century the iron and coal mines began to fail; by the '60s the heavy steel industry was becoming technologically obsolete, though by that time Bilbao's expertise in banking and commerce was solidly established. When steel giant Altos Hornos closed and the mills along the Nervió became a Basque version of Chicago's rust belt, business and commerce continued. Nevertheless, the numbers tell their story: Bilbao's population doubled between 1950 and 1975 but has remained static over the last quarter century.

Many of the wealthy left during those last 25 years, driven out by the fear of kidnapping and the extortion of the so-called revolutionary tax of the ETA (Euskadi Ta Askatasuna, or Basque Homeland and Liberty). The Right Bank suburb of Getxo, for instance, has been remarkable for its abandoned mansions, many of which are now being restored and revitalized as descendants of the original owners move back. Between the upsurge of ETA and the industrial "reconversion" (layoffs, or downsizing), Vizcaya was at a standstill until the early '90s when the Basque and Bilbao governments, along with Guggenheim Museum director Thomas Krens and architect Frank Gehry, concocted an unlikely scheme designed to inject new confidence and hope into an unraveling socioeconomic panorama.

A curious blend of London, Chicago, and Madrid, Bilbao has a brisk, big-city, heavy-industry, no-nonsense edginess until you get the hang of it. Even—maybe especially—gourmet dining is approached very seriously. Jorge Oteiza, legendary Basque sculptor and founder of the Escuela Vasca (Basque School)—the artistic movement that forged most of today's Basque artists—once answered, when asked where he was from, "From? Where's a person going to be from? Bilbao, of course. My native fishing village of Orio? From Orio is my childhood!"

Easy rides on a designer subway get you close to the beach at Getxo, while a picturesque train ride from the narrow-gauge Atxuri station through the Urdaibai natural park reaches Mundaca and Bermeo in under an hour. With the Vizcaya highlands a mere 30-minute drive from the center of town, the valleys of Atxondo and Las Encartaciones are Bilbao's backyard, honeycombed with vales and swales of nearly inconceivable greens punctuated with red-roofed *caseríos* (farmhouses).

Along the River Nervión

Walking the banks of the Nervión is a surprisingly beautiful and satisfying jaunt now that the estuary is peppered with some of the most-talked-about buildings in the world. After all, this was how—while out on a morning jog—the Guggenheim's director, Thomas Krens, first discovered the perfect spot for his project. From the Palacio Euskalduna to the colossal Mercado de la Ribera, with parks and green zones on either side of the river, Deusto University on the Right Bank, and, of course, the Guggenheim on the left, staying close to the river is a good idea that will get even better over the next few years when architect Cesar Pelli's Abandoibarra project fills in the half-mile between the Guggenheim and the Euskalduna bridge with a series of parks, the Deusto University library, a luxury hotel, and shops.

A Good Walk

Starting at the shiplike **Palacio de Euskalduna** ①—a music venue and convention hall—walk up through the botanical bonanza **Parque de Doña Casilda de Iturrizar** ② to Bilbao's excellent **Museo de Bellas Artes** ③, where the El Greco and Goya masterworks share wall space with lesser-known but wonderful painters like Sorolla and Zuloaga. Then walk through the modern (and as yet uncompleted) **Abandoibarra gardens,** or along Alameda Mazarredo, to the **Museo Guggenheim** ④— with luck the sun will be giving a shine to its titanium-covered walls. Continue on the river side of the Guggenheim up to and across Santiago Calatrava's **Puente de Zubi-Zuri** ⑤—another of Bilbao's new modernist landmarks—and past the **Ayuntamiento** ⑥ (city hall), to the linden tree–lined Paseo del Arenal. From there walk up the river past the **Teatro Arriaga** ⑦—a reconstructed Belle Epoque theater—and the **Mercado de la Ribera** ⑧ for a look at one of the largest covered food markets in Europe. From there, after having a good look at the church of **San Antón** ⑨, cross the river on the Puente de la Ribera and turn left for lunch at either **El Perro Chico** or just a *caldo* (broth) at **Bar Antonio** ⑩ at Calle Marjana 16.

TIMING

Depending on how long you spend snoozing in the grass in the park or browsing through the market, this is at least a three-hour walk. Add two to three hours for a Guggenheim visit.

Sights to See

⑥ **Ayuntamiento.** Near the Ayuntamiento bridge is the city hall, built by architect Joaquín de Rucoba, author of the Teatro Arriaga, in 1892 on the site of the San Agustín convent destroyed during the 1836 Carlist War. Sharing the same Belle Epoque style as the Teatro Arriaga, the Ayuntamiento, while no architectural feast, is characterized by the same brash, slightly aggressive attitude that most bilbainos confess to without embarrassment. The Salón Árabe, the interior of the building's highlight, was designed by the same architect who built the Café Iruña, as their mutual neo-Mudéjar motifs suggest. *Tours by special request to Ayuntamiento Public Relations,* ☎ *94/445–2828; tours 94/416–0022.* ☉ *Tours possible during normal hrs (weekdays 9–1 and 4:30–7) by special request to Ayuntamiento Public Relations.*

★ ⑩ **Bar Antonio.** This little gem (if it's still around: these last remnants of real life in Spain are sadly and rapidly disappearing in favor of more upscale, modern places), wedged into the corner of a little no-name square over the river, is one of the old guard and serves, among other things, *caldo* (broth), one of the best and best-value items you will find in Spanish cafés and taverns (usually from north of Madrid and in the winter). The WC (water closet, a.k.a. toilet) is another event every American traveler should experience. ⊠ *Calle Marjana 6,* ☎ *94/415–0817.*

⑧ **Mercado de la Ribera.** This triple-decker ocean liner with its prow headed down the estuary toward the open sea is one of the best markets of its kind in Europe, as well as one of the biggest, with more than 400 stands covering 37,950 square ft. Like the architects of the Guggenheim and the Palacio Euskalduna nearly 75 years later, the architect of the Mercado de la Ribera was not unplayful with this well-anchored ocean-going grocery store. From the stained-glass entryway over Calle de la

Ribera to the tiny catwalks over the river or the diminutive restaurant on the second floor, the market is a vital and inviting place to spend some time. Look for the farmer's market on the top floor, or stand in No. 121, with a brilliant display of, among other things, peppers, garlics, onions, beans, and snails. Down on the bottom floor, ask how fresh a fish is some morning and you might hear, "Oh, that one's not too fresh: last night." ⊠ *Calle de la Ribera 20,* ☎ *94/415–3136.* ☼ *Mon.–Sat. 8 AM–1 PM.*

★ ❸ **Museo de Bellas Artes** (Museum of Fine Arts). Don't let the Guggenheim eclipse this museum, considered one of the top five museums in a country that has a staggering number of great paintings and museums. Bilbao's Museum of Fine Arts is like a mini-Prado, with representatives from every Spanish school and movement from the 12th through the 20th centuries. The museum's fine collection of Flemish, French, Italian, and Spanish paintings includes works by El Greco, Goya, Velázquez, Zurbarán, Ribera, Gauguin, and Tàpies. One large and excellent section traces developments in 20th-century Spanish and Basque art alongside those of their better-known European contemporaries, such as Léger and Bacon. There's even a Mary Cassat, and there are several Sorollas. With the statue of famous Basque painter Ignacio de Zuloaga outside to greet visitors, this sparkling collection at the edge of the Doña Casilda Park and on the Left Bank end of the Deusto bridge is five minutes from the Guggenheim. Three hours might be barely enough to fully appreciate this international and pan-chronological painting course. Look especially for Zuloaga's famous portrait of La Condesa Mathieu de Moailles and Sorolla's portrait of Basque philosopher Miguel de Unamuno. ⊠ *Parque Doña Casilda Iturrizar,* ☎ *94/439–6060.* ▨ *600 ptas./€3.61; free Wed. (ask for "Bono Artean," the 900 ptas./€5.41 ticket good for both the Guggenheim and Bellas Artes.* ☼ *Tues.–Sat. 10–1:30 and 4–7:30, Sun. 10–2.*

★ ❹ **Museo Guggenheim Bilbao.** Covered with a photogenic 30,000 sheets of titanium, the Guggenheim opened in October 1997 and became Bilbao's main attraction overnight. The enormous atrium, more than 150 ft high, is connected to the 19 galleries by a system of suspended metal walkways and glass elevators. Vertical windows let you peep out at the undulating titanium flukes and contours of this beached whale every so often. With most of its works of modern art drawn from New York's Solomon R. Guggenheim Museum, the Bilbao Guggenheim is drawing visitors from all over the world, even neighboring France. Now in its third record-breaking year, this advance-overhype–defying phenomenon continues to delight all comers. Something about the place makes you want to know more—about everything. So don't fail to rent the "Acousticguide" (600 ptas./€3.61), the battery-operated telephone-like apparatus that will tell you exactly everything you always wanted to know about modern art, contemporary art, and the Guggenheim. The museum's architect, Frank Gehry, tells you about his love of fish (one of the inspirations for the design of the building), or how his creative process works, while you also get the low-down on many of the works in the collection (a Kokoschka painting entails a description of Alma Mahler's lethal romance with the painter).

The collection, described by director Thomas Krens as "a daring history of the art of the 20th century," consists of 242 works, 186 from New York's Guggenheim and 50 acquired by the Basque government. The second and third floors exemplify the original Guggenheim collection of Abstract Expressionist, Cubist, Surrealist, and geometrical works. Artists whose names are synonymous with the art of the 20th century (Kandinsky, Picasso, Ernst, Braque, Miró, Pollock, Calder,

Malevich) and European artists of the '50s and '60s (Chillida, Tàpies, Iglesias, Clemente, and Kiefer) are joined by contemporary figures (Nauman, Muñoz, Schnabel, Badiola, Barceló, Basquiat). The ground floor is dedicated to large-format and installation work, some of which—like Richard Serra's *Serpent*—was created specifically for the space it occupies. Claes Oldenburg's *Knife Ship,* Robert Morris's walk-in *Labyrinth,* and pieces by Beuys, Boltansky, Long, Holzer, and others round out the heavyweight division in and around what is now one of the largest galleries in the world.

In summer, at Christmas and Easter, and on weekends, long lines tend to develop. But between the playful clarinetist making a well-deserved killing on the front steps and the general spell of the place (who can be irked with *Puppy,* Jeff Koons's 40-ft-high postmod sculpture of a Westmoreland Terrier, covered with flowers, that stands in front of the building?) no one seems too impatient, but the way to avoid this line is to buy advance tickets from Servicaixa ATM machines or, in the Basque Country, the BBK bank machines. Failing that (sometimes they run out), go around at closing time and buy tickets for the next few days. This is one museum to splurge on. (For more on the building and its collection *see* the Close-up box, "The Silver Dream Machine: Museo Guggenheim Bilbao," *below.*) *Abandoibarra Etorbidea 2,* ☎ *94/435–9080.* 🖭 *1,200 ptas./€7.21.* ☉ *Tues.–Sun. 11–8.*

❶ Palacio de Euskalduna. Constructed to resemble a rusting ship in memory of the Astilleros Euskalduna (Basque-country shipbuilders) that operated shipyards here beside the Euskalduna bridge into the mid-'80s, this music venue and convention hall was officially opened in early 1999. Designed by Federico Soriano, Euskalduna is now Bilbao's main opera venue and home of the Bilbao Symphony Orchestra. The auditorium has a 2,200-person capacity and 71-stop organ, Spain's largest, offering a different tune and a big turnaround from the pitched battles waged here between workers, Basque nationalists, management, and police, as the shipyards laid off thousands. ✉ *Abandoibarra 4,* ☎ *94/403–5000,* 𝙵𝙰𝚇 *94/403–5001.* ☉ *Office Hours: Mon.–Fri. 9–2 and 4–7; box office noon–2 and 5–8:30, Sun. noon–2; guided tours Sat. at noon or by appointment (fax Departamento Comercial at 94/403–5001).* 🖭 *300 ptas./€1.80.*

❷ Parque de Doña Casilda de Iturrizar. Bilbao's main park, this lush collection of exotic trees, ducks and geese, fountains, falling water, and great expanses of usually lovers-littered lawn is a delight and a sanctuary from the hard-edged Ensanche, Bilbao's modern, post-1876 expansion. Doña Casilda de Iturrizar, a well-to-do 19th-century Bilbao matron, married a powerful banker and throughout her life used his wealth to support various cultural and beneficent institutions in Bilbao.

❺ Puente de Zubi-Zuri. "White bridge" in Euskera, Santiago Calatrava's signature span connects Campo Volantín on the Right Bank with the Ensanche on the left. Just a few minutes from the Guggenheim, Calatrava's playful seagull-shape bridge swoops brightly over the dark Nervión. The Plexiglas walkway suggests walking on water, though wear and tear have reduced the surface from transparent to a mere translucent. The new airport just west of Bilbao at Sondika, also designed by Calatrava, resembles a massive, white Air France Concorde and has already dubbed *La Paloma* (the dove), despite more closely resembling a snow goose poised for takeoff. Yet another Calatrava creation in Vizcaya, his bridge at Ondarroa completes this troika of gleaming white suspension exercises, all exploring the theme of flight.

THE TITANIUM DREAM MACHINE: MUSEO GUGGENHEIM BILBAO

I **F PICASSO'S** *Guernica* was the 20th century's most famous and embattled painting, Bilbao's Museo Guggenheim is arguably its most celebrated building: two all-time, world-class artistic phenomena located—or, in the case of Picasso, first inspired, within some 20 miles of each other. Described by Spanish novelist Manuel Vazquez Montalban as a "meteorite," the Guggenheim's eruption of light and titanium in the middle of what until very recently was the ruins of Bilbao's failed shipyards and steel industry has energized and reanimated this city in a dramatic and unprecedented way.

Traditionally considered the least attractive corner of the quadrangle it forms with Pamplona, San Sebastián, and Vitoria, Bilbao has in one master stroke become a stellar European destination: even neighboring France sends busloads of admiring visitors. All in all, this seems to be an urban Cinderella story without parallel.

How Bilbao and the Guggenheim met and meshed is in itself a saga: The Guggenheim's director, Thomas Krens, who was searching for the ideal emplacement for a major European museum (and having found nothing acceptable in Paris, Madrid, or elsewhere) accepted an invitation to Bilbao with low expectations. Seeking a center city space in a metropolis big enough to provide context but not so stacked with attractions as to overshadow the museum, Krens was out for a morning jog when he found it—the empty riverside lot once occupied by the Altos Hornos de Vizcaya steel mills. The site, at the heart of Bilbao's traditional steel and shipping port, was the perfect place for a metaphor for Bilbao's macro-reconversion from steel to titanium, from heavy industry to art, as well as a nexus between the early 14th-century Casco Viejo and the new 19th-century Ensanche and between the wealthy Right Bank and working class Left Bank of the Nervión.

Frank Gehry's gleaming brainchild, alternately hailed as "the greatest building of our time" (architect—and hypemeister— Philip Johnson), and "a miracle" (Herbert Muschamp, *New York Times*) has sparked a renaissance in the Basque country after more than a half century of troubles. In its first year, the Guggenheim attracted 1.4 million visitors, three times the number expected and more than what both Guggenheim museums in New York received together in the same period. Incredibly, the Guggenheim already holds the Spanish record for single-day visits to a museum (9,300).

The museum itself is every bit as dazzling as all the advance notice suggests. At once suggestive of a silver-scaled fish and a mechanical heart, Gehry's amalgam of titanium, limestone, and glass provides an ideal context for the contemporary and postmodern artworks it contains. The smoothly rounded jumble of surfaces and cylindrical shapes recall Bilbao's shipbuilding and steel-manufacturing past while using transparent and reflective materials to create a shimmering, futuristic luminosity. With the final section of the La Salve bridge spanning the Nervión folded into the structure, the Guggenheim serves both as a doorway to Bilbao and an urban forum: from the atrium you can see up into the center of the new part of town, across the river to the old city, and up onto the heights of Artxanda where livestock graze tranquilly along the green hillsides.

Most observers of the museum agree that Gehry has largely succeeded in his stated intent to build something as moving as a Gothic cathedral in which "you can feel your soul rise up," and to make it as poetically playful and perfect as the fish—as per Schubert's ichthylogical hommage in his famous "Trout Quintet"—he is known to admire: "I wanted it to be more than just a dumb building; I wanted it to move, to have a plastic sense of movement!". Perhaps even more important, the building, at the heart of the city, functions as a heart in the way that it pumps people through itself, and as the prime generator of Bilbao and the Basque country's economic and social renewal.

❾ San Antón. Both the church and bridge named for St. Anthony are emblematic symbols of Bilbao and appear on the municipal coat of arms. The original church was finished in 1433, though the structure underwent significant alterations up until the mid-17th century. The early bridge was swept away by an 1882 flood; its replacement, all but connected to the church, bears a pair of bas-relief wolves from the coat of arms of Don Diego López de Haro (from the Latin *lupus,* for wolf, as in López). ✉ *Calle de la Ribera s/n.*

★ **❼ Teatro Arriaga.** As exciting a source of Bilbao pride 100 years ago as the Guggenheim is today, this 1,500-seat theater was built between 1886 and 1890 when Bilbao's population was a mere 35,000, a gigantic per capita cultural investment by any standard. Always a symbol of Bilbao's industrial might and cultural vibrancy, the original "Nuevo Teatro" (New Theater) de Bilbao was a lavish Belle Epoque, neo-Baroque spectacular modeled after the Paris Opéra by architect Joaquín Rucoba (1844–1909). The theater was renamed in 1902 for the Bilbao musician thought of as "the Spanish Mozart," Juan Crisóstomo de Arriaga (1806–1826), a child prodigy born in the Casco Viejo (see the plaque at Calle Somera 12) who composed symphonies at the age of 11 and wrote an opera at 13. Arriaga enrolled in the Conservatory of Music in Paris at 16 where, after three years as a brilliant student, he became a professor shortly before his death of tuberculosis at the age of 19.

After a 1914 fire devastated the original theater, the new version opened in 1919. Following years of splendor, the Teatro Arriaga, along with Bilbao's economy, gradually lost vigor and closed down in 1978 for restoration work that was finally concluded in 1986. Now sharing the limelight with the Auditorio del Palacio de Euskalduna, the Arriaga stages opera, theater, concerts, and dance events throughout the season from September through June. Defying easy stylistic classification, the Teatro Arriaga's symmetry and formal repetition suggest Neoclassicism while its elaborate ornamentation defines the Belle Epoque style. Walk around the building to see the stained glass on its rear facade and the succession of exuberant, bare-breasted caryatids holding up the arches facing the river. ✉ *Plaza Arriaga 1,* ☎ *94/416–3333.*

El Casco Viejo

Walled until the 19th century, Bilbao's Casco Viejo ("old part," the city's oldest nucleus) is often synonymous with Siete Calles, so called for the original "seven streets" of proto-Bilbao in 1442. A finer distinction separates the Casco Viejo per se—the newer part of the old part of town around the 19th-century Plaza Nueva (New Square)—from the original 15th-century Siete Calles, the seven streets between the Santiago cathedral and the Mercado de la Ribera. Both parts of this warren of antiquity are filled with some of Bilbao's oldest and most charming architecture and ambience, all miraculously connected to modern Bilbao and, even the beach at Getxo, by Norman Foster's spotless *"fosterito,"* the streamlined subway stop across the square from the Museo Vasco, with its iron-age Mikeldi sculpture in the cloister, tidily spanning some 4,000 years of history.

A Good Walk

Starting at the church of **San Nicolás de Bari** ⑪, walk through Neoclassical 19th-century **Plaza Nueva** ⑫, with its ranks and rows of excellent cafés, restaurants, and tapas emporiums into Calle Sombrería where a left turn takes you into Calle de la Cruz; there the superb **Museo Vasco** ⑬—devoted to Basque archaeology and history—occupies one side of **Plaza Miguel de Unamuno** ⑭, with its bust of the great Basque philosopher, professor, and novelist in the center. At the far side of the square are the 313 stairs leading up to the Gothic (and later) **Basilica de Nuestra Señora de Begoña** ⑮, patron saint of Vizcaya, a much-cherished Bilbao emblem and cult. Passing the Baroque-era church of **Santos Juanes** ⑯ on Calle de la Cruz, continue to the **Portal de Zamudio** ⑰, more a tiny square than a street, from which a swing to the left leads into **Calle de la Somera** ⑱, the first, highest, and driest of the original seven streets. After a walk through Calle Somera past the Juan Crisóstomo Arriaga plaque at No. 12, cross to the church of **San Antón** ⑨ and walk left to the narrow-gauge railroad station, the **Estación de Atxuri** ⑲ and Plaza de la Encarnación and the 16th-century Basque Gothic **Convento de la Encarnación** ⑳. From here, return downriver past the Puente de Sant Antón to Calle Tenderia, where a right turn leads to the early 15th-century Gothic **Catedral de Santiago** ㉑, the oldest church in the Casco Viejo. From the cathedral, a few steps away on the corner of Calle de Perro and Calle Torres, is the **Palacio Yohn** ㉒ cultural center, with elements dating back to the 14th century. Directly across from the portal of the Palacio Yohn is a feast-day **paving stone** ㉓, marked with a star from which, as you face the Palacio Yohn and look up to the left, the Basilica de la Begoña is discernible towering in the distance over the Casco Viejo. From here walk down Calle Bidebarrieta to the **Biblioteca de Bidebarrieta** ㉔, a public library, concert hall, and heir to Bilbao's liberal intellectual tradition.

TIMING

This browsing and grazing itinerary is at least a three-hour project and probably ought to take four or five, depending on stops. Add two hours for a careful visit to the Museo Vasco.

Sights to See

⑮ **Basílica de Nuestra Señora de Begoña.** Bilbao's most cherished religious sanctuary, dedicated to the patron saint of Vizcaya, can be reached by the 313 stairs from Plaza de Unamuno or by the gigantic elevator looming over at Calle Esperanza 6 behind the San Nicolás church. The church's Gothic nave was begun in 1519 on the site of an early hermitage where the Virgin Mary was alleged to have appeared long before. Finished in 1620, the basilica was completed with the economic support of the shipbuilders and merchants of Bilbao, many of whose businesses are commemorated on the inner walls of the church. The high ground the basilica occupies was strategically important during the Carlist Wars of 1836 and 1873, and as a result, La Begoña suffered significant damage that was not restored until the beginning of the 20th century. Comparable in importance (if not in geographical impact) to Barcelona's Virgen de Montserrat (☞ Chapter 3), la Basílica de la Begoña is where the Athletic de Bilbao soccer team makes its pilgrimage, some of the players often barefoot, in gratitude for triumphs.

★ ㉔ **Biblioteca de Bidebarrieta.** This historic library and intellectual club was originally called "El Sitio" (the siege) in memory of Bilbao's successful resistance to the Carlist siege of 1876. Carlists, supporters of Fernando VII's brother, Don Carlos, over his daughter Isabella II as rightful heir to the Spanish throne, were conservative and clericalist, thus anathema to liberals, who refused them entry to their club after the war. The siege itself is understood to have been responsible for the invention of Bilbao's most famous codfish recipe, *bacalao al pil-pil,* when a local businessman who had ordered 20 o 22 (20 or 22) codfish took a mistaken delivery of 20,022 cod just as the siege locked into place. Using the abundant oil in stock and some culinary ingenuity, he managed to sell all the cod using this recipe. In the process, the cod merchant became wealthy, and Bilbao and bacalao al pil-pil were forever united. Now a municipal library, the Bidebarrieta's music auditorium is one of Bilbao's most beautiful venues and a spot to check for the infrequent performances held there. The reading rooms are open to the public, a good place to read newspapers, make notes, or just enjoy the historical echoes and overtones of the place. ⊠ *Calle Bidebarrieta 4,* ☎ *94/415–6930.* ☉ *Mon.–Fri. 8:30–8:30, Sat. 8:30–2.*

⑱ Calle de la Somera. The first, highest, and driest of the original seven streets—*Zazpikaleak,* in Euskera—Calle Somera would have been called High Street in early London. A mere three streets until 1375, the seven streets cut by *cantons* (narrow alleys) were in place by 1442. The original Siete Calles nearly formed a peninsula, as the Arenal and Plaza Nueva parts of the Casco Viejo were under water. Arenal means "sandy area" and was originally a sandy shore where the river deposited sediment in the eddy formed by the point of land at the end of Calle Santa María.

㉑ Catedral de Santiago (St. James's Cathedral). Bilbao's earliest church, this was a pilgrimage stop on the coastal route to Santiago de Compostela. Work on the structure began in 1379, but fire delayed completion of the structure until the early 16th century. The florid Gothic style with Isabelline elements is covered by a nave in the form of a Greek cross supported by ribbed vaulting resting on cylindrical columns. The notable outdoor arcade, or *pórtico,* was used for public meetings of the early town's governing bodies. ⊠ *Plaza de Santiago.*

⑳ Convento de la Encarnación. This square and early 16th-century convent, church, and museum are across from the Atxuri station just upstream from the Puente de San Antón. The Basque Gothic architecture gives way to Renaissance and Baroque ornamentation high on the main facade. The **Museo Diocesano de Arte Sacro** (Diocesan Museum of Sacred Art) occupies a carefully restored 16th-century cloister. The inner patio alone, ancient and intimate, more than amortizes the visit. On display are religious silverwork, liturgical garments, sculptures, and paintings dating back to the 12th century. ⊠ *Pl. de la Encarnación 9,* ☎ *94/ 432–0125.* 🎫 *Free.* ☉ *Tues.–Sat. 10:30–1:30 and 4–7, Sun. 10:30–1.*

⑲ Estación de Atxuri. Bilbao's narrow-gauge railroad station at Atxuri connects with Guernica, Mundaca, and Bermeo on the Basque coast, a spectacular ride through the Ría de Guernica that allows the best available views of the Urdaibai natural park (unless you're in a boat). The train to San Sebastián is another favorite excursion, chugging through villages such as Zumaya and Zarauz. You can even get off and walk for a few hours, catching a later train from another station. Narrow-gauge railways were the standard railroad in Vizcaya and in much of the north of Spain, owing to steep grades and tight quarters in general, as well as economics. Today there are only a few left. Check with the FEVE (Ferrocarriles Españoles de Via Estrecha) headquarters for information about the luxury Cantabrican Express that runs from San Sebastián to Santiago de Compostela with stops for wining, dining, and sightseeing.

★ ⑬ Museo Vasco (Museo Arqueológico, Etnográfico e Histórico Vasco) (Old Museum; Museum of Basque Archaeology, Ethnology, and History). One of the definitely-not-to-miss visits in Bilbao, this museum is housed in an austerely elegant 16th-century convent. The collection centers on Basque ethnography, Bilbao history, and comprehensive displays from the lives of Basque shepherds, fishermen and farmers. Highlights include *El Mikeldi* in the cloister, a pre-Christian iron-age stone animal representation that may be 4,000 years old; the room dedicated to Basque shepherds and the pastoral way of life; the *Mar de los Vascos* exhibit featuring whaling, fishing, and maritime activities; the second-floor pre-historic exhibit featuring a wooden harpoon recovered in the Santamamiñe caves at Kortezubi dated from the 10th century BC; and the third-floor scale model of Vizcaya province with the *montes bocineros* ("bugling mountains"), showing the five peaks of Vizcaya used for calling the dif-ferent *anteiglesias* (parishes) with bonfires or *txalaparta* (percussive sticks) to the general assemblies held in Guernica. One interesting Roman scouting report on *Flaviobriga* (the ancient Latin name for Bilbao's province), written in Latin, reads *Pomorum est eitam uberrimus proventus, ut nisi qui viderint praesentes, facile adduci non possint, ut credat* ("Flaviobriga has such a rich supply of apples that if those who saw them were not present, it would not be easy for them to believe us.") ⊠ *C. Cruz 4,* ☎ *94/415-5423.* 🎫 *300 ptas./€1.80; free Thurs.* ⏱ *Tues.–Sat. 10:30–1:30 and 4–7, Sun. 10:30–1.*

㉒ Palacio Yohn. This graceful and ancient building, oddly and erro-neously known as "La Bolsa" (the stock exchange)—though no exchange of stock has ever taken place here—is thought to be built over a 14th-century structure. Immigrants from Central Europe moved here in the 18th century and apparently set up such a thriving commercial enter-prise that it became known as "the exchange." The building takes its name from Leandro Yohn, one of the successful merchants. Now used for the Centro Cívico de la Bolsa, a municipal cultural center, the palace has medieval ceilings that are covered with graceful vaulting. ⊠ *Calle Pelota 10,* ☎ *94/416-3199.* ⏱ *Oct.–May, Mon.–Sat. 9–1:30 and 4–9; June–Sept., Mon.–Sat. 9–1:30.*

㉓ Paving Stone. Directly across from Palacio Yohn is a star-shaped de-sign on a paving stone, from which, looking up to the left, the Basílica de la Begoña is visible towering over the Casco Viejo. Every October 11 *txikiteros* celebrate the feast day of the Virgin of la Begoña here, dispensing *txikis* ("little ones," meaning shot glasses of wine) and dancing the honorary and athletic Aurresku.

⑭ Plaza Miguel de Unamuno. Named for Bilbao's all-time greatest in-tellectual, source of fame and fable throughout Spain and beyond, this plaza honors Miguel de Unamuno—a philosopher, novelist, professor, and wit as well as a man of character and temperament (an unusual combination). De Unamuno wrote some of Spain's most seminal works—including *Del sentimiento trágico de la vida en los hombres y los pueblos* (*The Tragic Sense of Life in Men and Nations*); his *Niebla* (Mist) has been generally accepted as the first existentialist novel, pub-lished in 1914 when Jean-Paul Sartre was nine years old. Unamuno was notorious for his aggressive and combative spirit. His life is filled with the kind of stories professors love to tell. For instance, when he was rector of the University of Salamanca at the age of 72 when the Spanish Civil War broke out in 1936, Unamuno sat seething through a graduation ceremony hijacked by Spanish Foreign Legion founder General Millan Astray. After the one-eyed, one-armed, battle-scarred Astray closed with his characteristic "Viva la Muerte!" (Long Live Death)—the Legionnaires' battle cry—Unamuno rose to his feet and delivered a vitriolic diatribe against the military rebellion ending with the famous "*Vencereis, pero no convencereis!*" (You may vanquish but you will not convince). The military contingent, outraged, reportedly might have lynched the old man if he hadn't been escorted home by Carmen Polo de Franco, wife of the Generalísimo himself. In another famous Unamuno story, a student, during a lecture in Spanish, corrected Unamuno's pronunciation of the word "Shakespeare." Unamuno (who spoke Greek, Arabic, French, and German as well) thanked the young man and delivered the rest of the lecture in perfect English. Physical Unamuno evidence in the Casco Viejo includes the philosopher's bust in Plaza de Unamuno, his birthplace at No. 7 Calle de la Cruz, and the nearby Filatelia Unamuno, a rare stamp emporium that is a favorite of collectors.

⑫ **Plaza Nueva.** This 64-arch Neoclassical plaza seems to be typical of every Spanish city from San Sebastián to Salamanca to Sevilla. With its Sunday morning market, its December 21 natural-produce Santo Tomás market, and its permanent tapas and restaurant offerings, Plaza Nueva is an easy place to spend a lot of time. It was finished in 1851 as part of an ambitious housing project designed to ease the demographic pressure on limited mid-19th-century Bilbao space. Note the size of the houses' balconies: it was the measure—the bigger, the better—of the social clout of their inhabitants. The tiny windows near the top of the facades were servants' quarters. The coat of arms at the head of the square was originally the Diputación, or provincial government office, but is now the **Academia de la Lengua Vasca** (Academy of the Basque Language). The coat of arms features the tree of Guernica, symbolic of Basque autonomy, while the two wolves are for Don Diego López de Haro (López–*lupus*–wolf). The bars and shops around the arcades include two versions of **Victor Montes** establishments, one for tapas and light formulas at Plaza Nueva 8 and the other for more serious sit-down dining at Plaza Nueva 2. The **Café Bar Bilbao**, at Plaza Nueva 6, also known as Casa Pedro, has wonderful photos of early Bilbao, while the **Argoitia** at No. 15 across the square has a nice angle on the midday sun and a coat of arms inside with the *zatzpiakbat* ("seven-one" in Basque), referring to the cultural unity of the three French and four Spanish Basque provinces.

⑰ **Portal de Zamudio.** This short street (one house) or small plaza is significant in the Casco Viejo as the first and most important entry through the walls of 15th-century Siete Calles. The upper street, Calle Somera, is early Bilbao's first and most important thoroughfare; Zamudio was the name of an important early noble Bilbao family whose house was near this entryway.

⑪ **San Nicolás de Bari.** Honoring the patron saint of mariners and early Bilbao's waterfront church, San Nicolás de Bari was built over an earlier eponymous hermitage and opened in 1756. With a powerful facade over the Arenal, originally a sandy beach, San Nicolás was much abused by French and Carlist troops throughout the 19th century. Sculptures by Juan Pascual de Mena adorn the inside of the church. Look for the oval plaque to the left of the door marking the high-water mark of the flood of 1983.

⑯ **Santos Juanes.** Distinguished for accumulating the deepest water of any building in the Casco Viejo during the disastrous 1983 flood, as can be witnessed by the water mark over 14 ft above the floor in the back of the church (to the left as you come in), this simple Baroque church was the first Jesuit building in Bilbao, built in 1604. Originally the home of the Colegio de San Andrés de la Compañía de Jesús (St. Andrew's School of the Order of Jesuits), the original school is now divided between the Museo Vasco and the church dedicated to both St. Johns, the Evangelist and the Baptist. The church's most important relic is what is reported and widely believed to be the largest existing piece of the cross, the *Relicario de la Vera Cruz* (Relic of the True Cross), a silver-plated cross containing the original fragment of the one used at Calvary to execute Jesus Christ in 33 AD.

Bilbao

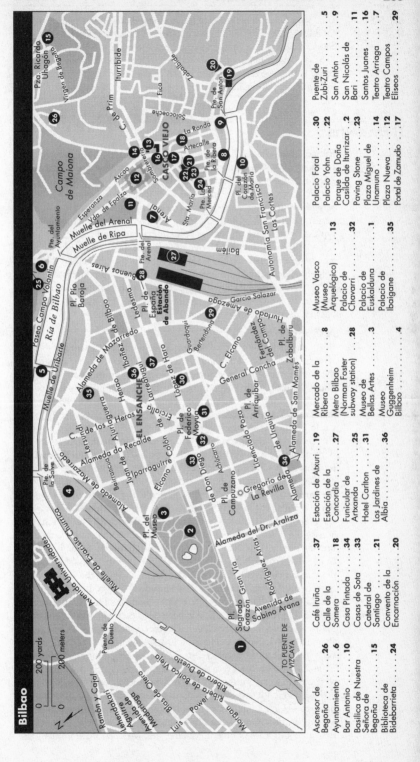

265

The **Funicular de Artxanda** and the **Ascensor de Begoña** are each popular Bilbao landmarks and routes connecting the Casco Viejo with points overlooking the city. The panorama from Artxanda is the most comprehensive view of Bilbao, and the various typical *asadors* (roasters) located here serve delicious beef or fish cooked over coals. La Basilica de la Begoña is the classic pilgrimage and site of weddings and christenings.

El Ensanche

Bilbao's busy Ensanche ("Widening") has a rhythm and timbre more redolent of Manhattan or London than of Paris or Barcelona. Once Bilbao "saltó el río" (jumped the river) from the Casco Viejo in 1876, the new city center became Plaza Moyúa—at the heart of the Ensanche—with the Gran Vía as the district's most important thoroughfare. The late-19th-century and early 20th-century architecture typical of this part of town is colossal, ornate, and formal with only a few eruptions into Art Nouveau. Bilbao expressed its euphoria and wealth in the Ensanche as Barcelona did in its famous Art Nouveau neighborhood, the *Eixample* (☞ Chapter 2), though the distinct tastes and sensibilities of Basques and Catalans are nowhere more manifest than in these two wildly divergent turn-of-the-20th-century urban developments.

A Good Walk

From the graceful railroad station **Estación de la Concordia** ㉗ (also known as Estación de Santander), as you overlook Teatro Arriaga from the Left Bank of the Nervión, it's just a two-minute walk around to **Plaza Circular,** with its monument to Don Diego López de Haro and its *fosterito,* the transparent tube leading into the **Metro Bilbao's Norman Foster subway station** ㉘. As you walk left up Hurtado de Amézaga, Calle Ayala is the first right, leading past the Iglesia del Sagrado Corazón to Alameda Urquijo. Take a left up Alameda Urquijo to Calle Bertendona and go left again to the curious facade of the **Teatro Campos Eliseos** ㉙. Crossing back over Alameda Urquijo and Calle Gardoqui, cut past the municipal library to the opulent government seat at **Palacio Foral** ㉚, built in 1900. From there it's just another two blocks to **Plaza Moyúa,** the hub of the Ensanche, where the **Hotel Carlton** ㉛ and the Flemish Renaissance–style **Palacio de Chavarri** ㉜ face each other across the colorful flower beds in the center of the circle. One block farther down Gran Vía are the colossal **Casas de Sota** ㉝—a 1919 block of apartments and offices—taking up an entire city block. At this point either cut over to Plaza de Indautxu for a look at the 1920s painted murals on the facade of the **Casa Pintada** ㉞ or go directly north on Ercilla to Plaza Dejado, turn left on Calle de los Heros, and right on Cosme Echevarrieta, to reach Alameda de Mazarredo and the surprising midtown *caserío* (country house), the **Palacio de Ibaigane** ㉟, once home to one of Bilbao's richest and most prominent citizens. From here, consider a stop at the little café at No. 12 overlooking Santiago Calatrava's Zubi-Zuri footbridge. From there continue along Alameda de Mazarredo to the next street on the left, **Calle Arbolantxa,** leading into a pretty little square with several inviting places, including the Café Antzokia. Back on Alameda de Mazarredo it's just another block to Plaza San Vicente and **Los Jardines de Albia** ㊱, one of the Ensanche's capital destinations and home of the landmark, neo-Mudejar **Café Iruña** ㊲.

TIMING
This is a three-hour tour, adding time for stops in cafés and shops.

Sights to See

③⑦ Café Iruña. Famous for its ambience and decor, the Iruña is an unavoidable and essential Bilbao haunt on the Ensanche's most popular garden and square, Los Jardines de Albia. The neo-Mudejar dining room overlooking the square is the place to be (if they try to stuff you in the back dining room, demur and come back another time). The bar has two distinct sections: the elegant side near the dining room where sculptor Lorenzo Quinn's bronze arm, a San Miguel commission, hoists a beer tankard at the center of the counter; and the older, more bare-bones Spanish side on the Calle Berástegui side with its plain marble counters and *pinchos morunos de carne de cordero* (lamb brochettes) as the house specialty. This place was founded by a Navarra restaurateur (Iruña is Euskera for Pamplona) in 1903; the Moorish decor in the dining room has been understood as an echo of the town hall's Salón Árabe (Arabian Hall). Hot with ambience from dawn until after midnight, the Iruña (with the permission of the Café Boulevard and La Granja) is Bilbao's most cosmopolitan café. ⊠ *Calle Berástegui 5,* ☎ *94/423–7021.*

③④ La Casa Pintada. Just off Plaza Indautxu, this unusual painted facade, formally known as **La Casa de los Aldeanos** (House of the Villagers), is a 1929 construction designed by the architect Adolfo Gil. The painted images evoke an idealized rural Vizcayan village, a pastoral paradise in the midst of Bilbao's industrial and urban austerity.

③③ Casas de Sota. This immense block of houses, offices, and apartments was built by Manuel María de Smith in 1919 and remains a good example of an early 20th-century bourgeois residence. The horizontal line of the red rooftops, arches, and galleries seem to reflect the Basque *caserío* (farmhouse) architecture translated to big-city splendor. ⊠ *Gran Vía 45.*

②⑦ Estación de la Concordia. Designed by the engineer Valentín Gorbeña in 1893 and finished by architect Severino Achúcarro in 1898, this colorful railroad station looks across the Nervión River to the Paris Opéra–inspired Teatro Arriaga, responding with its own references to the colonnaded Parisian Louvre. Considering the clearly defined Bilbao Anglophilia in nearly all aspects of daily life from soccer (coaches and style of play) to (until the late '70s) bobby-helmeted police, these two key France-inspired architectural gems are surprising, perhaps explainable only as rule-confirming exceptions. The peacock-fan-shape, yellow-and green-tiled entrance is the station's most spectacular feature, along with the immense stained-glass window over the access to the tracks in which all of the different facets of Vizcayan life and work are represented, from farmers and fishermen to factory workers and jai-alai players. Meanwhile, the graceful arch of the hangar over the tracks is typical of traditional railroad terminals around Europe.

③① Hotel Carlton. Bilbao's old-world favorite has hosted the famous over the last century from Orson Welles to Ernest Hemingway and Ava Gardner. Architect Manuel María de Smith based this project on the London hotel of the same name, while the stained glass in the oval reception area is a reduced version of the one in Nice's famous Hotel Negresco. The Carlton's bar, the Grill, has a particularly clubby English feel to it, surrounded by murals painted by hotel client Martinez Ortiz in 1947. The murals, representing an equestrian scene with horses and some 10 bourgeois figures, is remarkable for the detailed painting of every hand and each finger of the personae populating the walls.

③⑥ Los Jardines de Albia. A required stop in the Ensanche, one of the two or three places all bilbainos will insist you see, this green space in the concrete and asphalt surfaces of this part of town is especially welcome to locals and visitors alike. Overlooking the square is the lovely Basque Gothic **Iglesia de San Vicente Mártir,** its Renaissance facade facing its own Plaza San Vicente. The amply robed sculpture of the Virgin on the main facade, as the story goes, had to be sculpted a second time after the original version was deemed too scantily clad and more appropriate for a Venus than a Virgin). The Jardines de Albia are centered on the bronze effigy of writer Antonio de Trueba by the famous Spanish sculptor Mariano Benlliure (1866–1947), author of monuments to the greatest national figures of the epoch including the tenor Julián Gayarre (1844–90) (☞ Roncal Valley *in* Chapter 4). ⊠ *Calle Colón de Larreátegui s/n.*

28 **Metro Bilbao (Norman Foster subway station).** Metro Bilbao, the city's much-cherished subway system was designed by British architect Norman Foster—who founded his stellar modernist reputation with the pipe-and-conduit-covered Lloyd's building in London—and opened in November of 1995. The world's most recently completed underground subway system, it was also Bilbao's first metro and has become a source of great pride for bilbainos. Hardly necessary before Bilbao began to spread up and down the Nervión estuary, the Bilbao subway now connects Bolueta, upstream from the Casco Viejo, with Plentzia, a run of 30 km (19 mi). Oddly arriving from the right (either a Foster slip-up, another example of deliberate Bilbao Anglophilia, or someone's unremedied remedial reading glitch)—as opposed to standard subways and trains that arrive from the left and circulate on the right—the metro is invariably spotless and gleaming, graffiti are scarce, and most of the clients are well dressed and ride in a respectful silence.

Crossing under the riverbed twice—there is really no main hub, as the route follows a straight line (with Moyúa, dead center in the middle of Bilbao's Ensanche, or new part, the most central of the stops)—the subway runs from 6 AM to 11 PM and costs just under a dollar for a medium-distance trip, slightly longer for out-of-town destinations. Winner of the architectural Nobel Prize, the Brunel Prize of 1996, the metro in general and the Sarriko station in particular were designated as the prizewinning elements. The Sarriko station, the largest of all of the 23 stops, is popularly known as *El Fosterazo* (the Big Foster) whereas the others are *fosteritos* (little Fosters). The most spectacular are segmented glass tubes curving up from underground, such as those at Plaza Moyúa and Plaza Circular, widely thought to resemble transparent snails. The entire metro line is lineal, running down the Nervion estuary from above, or east of, the Casco Viejo, all the way to the mouth of the Nervion at Getxo, before continuing on to the beach town of Plentzia.

NEED A BREAK?   Founded in 1926, **Café La Granja** (⊠ Pl. Circular 3), near the Puente del Arenal, is a Bilbao classic. It retains its Old World ambience along with good coffee, beer, *tortilla de patata* (potato omelet), and a lunch menu.

32 **Palacio de Chavarri.** Victor Chavarri, a leading *prohombre* (captain of industry) of the last quarter of the 19th century, was a force in mining, industry, and every other area of Bilbao's economic and financial life. (His descendants are still prominent socialites in Madrid.) His Flemish Renaissance palace on Plaza Frederico de Moyúa was intended to recall the great industrialist's student epoch in Liège, Belgium. Built by the Belgian architect Paul Hankar in 1889, the ornate ochre structure is based on another Hankar building, the Hotel Zegers-Regnard in Brussels. Note that every set of windows is unique. ⊠ *Plaza de Federico Moyúa 5.*

③⑤ **Palacio de Ibaigane.** This graceful manor-house design is the only one of its kind left in Bilbao, an elegant and sweeping country house with classic *caserío* (farmhouse) details surrounded by the generally hard-edged Ensanche. Now the official seat of the Athletic de Bilbao soccer club, the house was originally the residence of the de la Sota family, whose most outstanding member, Ramón de la Sota, founded the company and became one of the most important shipbuilders in Europe. His company "Euskalduna" specialized in ship repair and opened shipyards in New York, London, Rotterdam, and Paris. Awarded the title "Sir" by Great Britain for his services to the Allied cause in World War I, de la Sota went on to found the Euskalerria Basque rights organization, which later joined forces with the Basque Nationalist party founded by Sabino Arana in the late 19th century. Because of his affiliation with Basque nationalism Sir Ramón de la Sota's properties and businesses were seized by the Franco regime following the end of the Spanish Civil War in 1939 and not returned to the family until 1973. ⊠ *Alameda de Mazarredo 15.*

③⓪ **Palacio Foral.** This intensely decorated facade just two blocks from Plaza Moyúa was built by architect Luis Aladrén as the seat of the *Diputación* (provincial government) in 1900. A manifestation of the bullish economic moment Bilbao was experiencing as the 20th century got under way, the building was much criticized for its combination of overwrought aesthetic excess on the outside and minimally practical use of the interior space. The 19th-century Venetian motifs of its halls and salons, the chapel, and the important collection of paintings and sculptures are the best reasons to see the inside of the building. ⊠ *Gran Vía 45.* ▣ *Free.* ⊙ *Weekdays 9–2 and 4–8.*

②⑨ **Teatro Campos Eliseos.** If you have come from Barcelona, this extraordinary facade may seem familiar. The wild Moderniste (Catalan Art Nouveau) excitement of the intensely ornate circular arch—nearly Plateresque in its intricate relief and relentless onslaught of decorative detail—is a marked contrast to the more sober and austere Bilbao interpretation of the turn-of-the-20th-century euphoria that convulsed both Basque and Catalan capitals. Predictably, bilbainos don't think very highly of this, to the Basque eye, exaggerated ornamentation. The theater is called Campos Eliseos after Paris's Champs-Elysées (another spasm of Francophilia in a town of Anglophiles), as this area of town was a favorite for early 20th-century fresh-air promenades. ⊠ *Calle Bertendona 12.*

OFF THE BEATEN PATH | The **Puente de Vizcaya**—commonly called the **Puente Colgante** (Hanging Bridge)—inaugurated in 1893, has been one of Bilbao's most extraordinary sights ever since it was built. The bridge, a transporter hung from cables, ferries cars and passengers across the Nervión, uniting two distinct worlds: exclusive, bourgeois Las Arenas and Portugalete, a much older, working-class town now filled with jobless steelworkers (Dolores Ibarruri, the famous Republican orator of the Spanish Civil War, known as *La Pasionaria* for her ardor, was born here). Portugalete is a 15-minute walk from Santurce, where the quayside Hogar del Pescador serves simple and ample fish specialties. *Besugo* (sea bream) is the traditional choice, but the fresh grilled sardines are hard to surpass. To reach the bridge, take the subway to Areeta, or drive across the Puente de Deusto, turn left on Avenida Lehendakari Aguirre, and follow signs for Las Arenas.

Dining and Lodging

$$$$ ✕ **Casa Rufo.** This charming and cozy series of nooks and crannies tucked into the back of a delicatessen is famous for its *txuleta de buey* (beef chops). Let the affable owners size you up and bring on what you need and desire; they seem to know. The house wine is an excellent *crianza* (two years in oak, one in bottle) from La Rioja, but the wine list offers a good selection of wines from Ribera de Duero, Somantano, and El Priorat as well. These people are into food and like to share it with you. ✉ *Calle Hurtado de Amézaga 5,* ☎ *94/443–2172. Reservations essential. AE, DC, MC, V. Closed Sun.*

$$$$ ✕ **Goizeko Kabi.** Here you can choose your own crab or crayfish. The dining rooms are of brick and wood accented by Persian rugs and chairs upholstered with tapestries. Chef Fernando Canales's creations include *láminas de bacalao en ensalada con pimientos rojos asados* (sliced cod in green salad with roasted red peppers) and *hojaldre de verdura a la plancha con manito de cordero* (grilled vegetables in puff pastry with leg of lamb). ✉ *Particular de Estraunza 4 y 6,* ☎ *94/442–1129. Reservations essential. AE, DC, MC, V. Closed Sun.*

$$$$ ✕ **Guggenheim Bilbao.** The opportunity to complement the visual feast offered by the Guggenheim with at least two more sensorial elements is one to take seriously. After all, this spot (overseen by Martín Berasategui) under the direction of chef Bixente Arrieta is on everyone's short list of Bilbao restaurants, as anyone will discover upon ordering *lomo de bacalao asado en aceite de ajo con txangurro a la donostiarra i pil-pil* (cod flanks in garlic oil with San Sebastián crab and emulsified juices)—a revolutionary approach to Bilbao's traditional codfish specialty. Diving into a postmodern lobster salad (with lettuce-heart shavings and tomatoes) at a corner table—the view overlooks the Nervión, the University of Deusto, and the green heights of Artxanda—should prove a perfect Bilbao moment. ✉ *Av. Abandoibarra 2,* ☎ *94/423–9333. Reservations essential. AE, DC, MC, V. No dinner Sun.*

$$$$ ✕ **Guria.** Genaro Pildain, the dean of Bilbao chefs, was born in Arakaldo,
★   with 125 inhabitants still the smallest village in Vizcaya province. Describing himself as "a failed carpenter," Pildain learned how to cook from his mother and talks more about his potato and leek soup than about truffles and Beluga caviar—and that makes most critics happy. With an innovative and streamlined approach to traditional Basque cooking, Guria dazzles with simplicity and perfection. Every ingredient and each recipe and *punto de cocción* ("cooking point," i.e. how much heat and when to get it out) is nonpareil. Asked for a comment on the culinary acrobats and magicians copping the headlines in Spain of late, Don Genaro says only that he believes that "everything" he serves should be good. His *alubias "con sus sacramentos"* (fava beans "with their sacraments," meaning chorizo and blood sausage) are reduced, deconstructed, to a superb puree. His *crema de puerros y patatas* (cream of potato and leak soup) is as pure and profound as his lobster salad with *perretxikos de Orduña* (small wild mushrooms known as St. George's or spring mushrooms). ✉ *Gran Vía 66,* ☎ *94/441–0543. Reservations essential. AE, DC, MC, V. No dinner Sun.*

$$$$ ✕ **Jolastoki.** The danger of listing this beautiful spot along with the beach town and suburb of Getxo is that visitors to Bilbao might lose sight of it among the in-town culinary surfeit and miss out on one of the best restaurants in Vizcaya and (who can doubt it?) the world. Begoña Beaskoetxea's graceful mansion is just a 20-minute ride on Bilbao's pride-and-joy Norman Foster subway. A seven-minute walk from the metro stop to Jolastoki (which means "place to play" in Basque) will place you at one of Bilbao's finest tables. The salmon (when there is salmon) is wild, from the nearby Cantabrian River Cares; you can

even read who caught it and using what kind of lure. The *pichon de bresse* (Bresse pigeon) is roasted in balsamic vinegar, dark, red, and fragrant. The *lubina al vapor* (steamed sea wolf) is as light as a soufflé while the salads are encyclopedic and delicate; the dessert of red fruits includes 11 varieties of fruit with a sorbet in a raspberry coulis. Afterward, you'll feel surprisingly viable, so take a walk through the Getxo fishing quarter and enjoy a swim at the beach. ✉ *Los Chopos 24,* ☎ *94/491–2031. Reservations essential. AE, DC, MC, V. Closed Sun.*

$$$$ ✕ **Zortziko.** This lovely place combines an ultramodern kitchen with a building that has been declared a historical monument. Try the *langostinos con risotto de perretxicos* (prawns with wild mushroom risotto) or the *suprema de pintada asada a la salsa de trufas* (guinea hen in truffle sauce). Chef Daniel García retains his ranking as one of the Basque region's culinary stars. ✉ *C. Alameda Mazarredo 17,* ☎ *94/423–9743. Reservations essential. AE, DC, MC, V. Closed Sun. and Aug. 25–Sept. 15.*

$$$ ✕ **Bermeo.** Named after the coastal village to the north (☞ *below*), this top restaurant specializes in fresh market cuisine and traditional Basque interpretations of fish, shellfish, and seafood of all kinds. Try the *rodaballo* (turbot) in vinaigrette sauce. ✉ *C. Ercilla 37,* ☎ *94/470–5700. Reservations essential. AE, DC, MC, V. Closed first 2 wks of Aug. No lunch Sat.*

$$$ ✕ **El Perro Chico.** Just across the tiny Puente de la Ribera footbridge
★ immediately below the hulking yellow market, this gem of a spot is a big favorite among the many global glitterati who have "discovered" and adopted post-Guggenheim Bilbao. Dennis Hopper, Jeremy Irons, Bilbao opera star María Bayo: the list is long. Frank Gehry is said to have discovered, on the walls here, "Bilbao blue"—the deep azure characteristic of the skies over Bilbao—and used it for the Guggenheim's office building to the right of the museum's main entrance. Chef Rafael García Rossi and ex–art gallery owner Santiago Diez Ponzoa run a happy ship here. Everything is terrific, but especially noteworthy are the *alcachofas con almejas* (artichokes with clams); the extraordinarily light *bacalao con berenjena* (cod with aubergines), in which the aubergine counters the normally heavy cod; and the dark and bitter combination of the *pato a la naranja* (duck à l'orange). ✉ *C. Aretxaga 2,* ☎ *94/415–0519. Reservations essential. AE, DC, MC, V. Closed Sun. No Mon. lunch.*

$$–$$$ ✕ **Matxinbenta.** Mixing Basque cooking with an international flair, this cozy spot offers innovative seafood dishes and roasts and prepares the most traditional specialties to perfection. Best in show goes to the *bacalao Matxinbenta con base vizcaina* (cod prepared on a red-pepper base *al pil-pil*). The railroad train or ocean liner decor (it's hard to be sure which) features separate glass compartments, which combats smoke poisoning while allowing you to ogle fellow diners freely without eavesdropping at the same time. The wine list is comprehensive, while the *delicia de verduras con foie* (mixed selection of vegetables with goose liver) is an anthological array of broccoli, spinach, carrots, and zucchini with a cream of tomato sauce. ✉ *Ledesma 26,* ☎ *94/424–8495. AE, DC, MC, V. Closed Sun.*

$$ ✕ **Gorrotxa.** Carmelo Gorrotxategui's fine eclectic menu mixes Basque,
★ French, and Castilian cuisines. The man can do anything from *foie gras con uvas* (goose liver with grapes) to lobster Thermidor to *chuleta de buey* (beefsteak). The *costillar,* roast rack of lamb with potatoes, will more than satisfy. The decor is English, with wood paneling and carpets. ✉ *Alameda Urquijo 30,* ☎ *94/443–4937. AE, DC, MC, V. Closed Sun., Holy Week, 1 wk in July, 1 wk in Aug.*

Bilbao Dining and Lodging

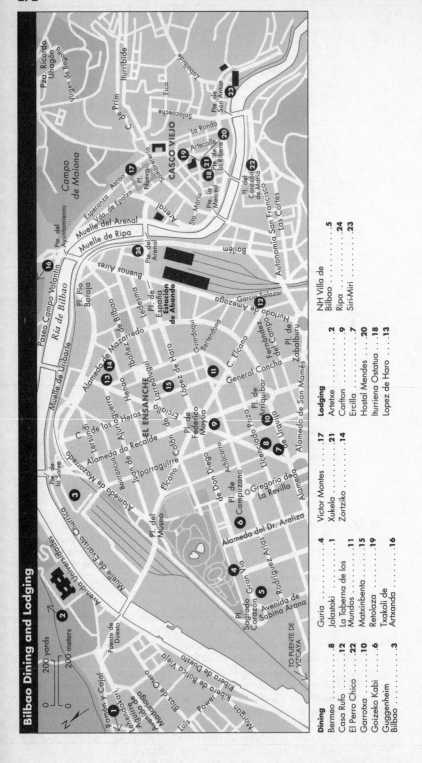

0 200 yards
0 200 meters

TO PUENTE DE
VIZCAYA

Dining
Bermeo **8**
Casa Rufo **12**
El Perro Chico **22**
Garrotxa **10**
Goizeko Kabi **6**
Guggenheim
Bilbao **3**

Guria **4**
Jolastoki **1**
La Taberna de los
Mundos **11**
Matxinbenta **15**
Retolaza **19**
Txakoli de
Artxanda **16**

Victor Montes **17**
Xukela **21**
Zortziko **14**

Lodging
Artetxe **2**
Carlton **9**
Ercilla **7**
Hostal Mendes **20**
Iturriena Ostatua . . . **18**
Lopez de Haro **13**

NH Villa de
Bilbao **5**
Ripa **24**
Siri-Miri **23**

$$ ✕ **Retolaza.** Bilbao has flocked to this traditional Basque restaurant since 1906. Operated by the third generation of its founding family, it has wood beams, low ceilings, and a reasonably intimate and serious feel. The classic Vizcayan fare includes *sopa de aluvias* (red beans and sausage) and *bacalao al pil-pil.* ✉ *Tendería 1,* ☎ *94/415–0643. AE, DC, MC, V. Closed July 24–Aug. 15. No dinner Sun.–Mon.*

$$ ✕ **La Taberna de los Mundos.** Ander Calvo won both first and second prizes in the World Championship sandwich competition held in Madrid in early 2000. His championship entry was a sandwich of melted goat cheese with garlic, wild mushrooms, and sweet red piquillo peppers on a bed of acorn-fed wild Iberian ham and slices of organically grown tomatoes on slipper bread. Clearly a genius, Calvo has been a food nut since his mother gave him a kitchen set at age four. His restaurants (he has two more in Bilbao and another in Vitoria) are much more than fast food—photography and art shows are mounted, travel and adventure lectures are offered, and a global interest is reflected in the name of the chain and in Calvo's obsession with early maps and navigational techniques. Don't miss this place, but avoid lunch (when lines form) unless you have a rock-solid reservation or come in at 1. ✉ *C. Luchana 1,* ☎ *94/416–8181. AE, DC, MC, V. Closed Mon. Sept. 15–June 15.*

$$ ✕ **Txakoli de Artxanda.** The funicular from the end of Calle Múgica y Butrón up to the mountain of Artxanda overlooking the city deposits you next to an excellent spot for a roast of one kind or another after a hike around the heights. Whether ordering lamb, beef, or the traditional Basque *besugo* (sea bream), you can't go wrong at this picturesque spot with unbeatable panoramas over Bilbao. ✉ *Monte Artxanda,* ☎ *94/445–5015. AE, DC, MC, V. Closed Mon. Sept. 15–June 15.*

$$ ✕ **Victor Montes.** A hot point for the daily *tapeo* (tapas tour), Victor
★ Montes is always crowded with congenial grazers. The well-stocked counter might offer anything from wild mushrooms to *txistorra* (spicy sausages) to *Idiazabal* (Basque smoked cheese) or, for the adventurous, *huevas de merluza* (hake roe), all washed down with splashes of Rioja, txakolí, or cider. For a table, reserve as far ahead as possible. ✉ *Plaza Nueva 8,* ☎ *94/415–7067. No dinner Sun.*

$$ ✕ **Xukela.** Santiago Ruíz Bombin never closes because he loves mak-
★ ing bits of food into spectacular and delectable paintings and watching his clients inhale them. With art gallery–quality lighting over his bar, the combinations of green and red peppers, truffles, red and black caviar, anchovies, parsley, thyme, and an endless list of other ingredients are here deployed much as a painter's palette dispenses pigments, with the important difference that in this art gallery you get to munch on and swallow the work. (Didn't you ever feel a desire to bite into a Boudin or a Manet or a Sorolla?) Prize-winning Bilbao tapa and *pintxo* (single tapa on a toothpick) artisan for 2000, this tapas sanctuary will spoil you for all the rest . . . but it's worth it. ✉ *Calle del Perro 2,* ☎ *94/415–9772.*

$$$$ ✕🏨 **Lopez de Haro.** Five minutes from the Guggenheim, Bilbao's only five-star hotel is becoming quite a scene now that the city is a bona fide nexus for contemporary art. The converted 19th-century building has an English feel and all the comforts your heart desires. The excellent restaurant, the Club Náutico, serves modern Basque dishes created by Alberto Vélez—a handy alternative on one of Bilbao's many rainy evenings. ✉ *Obispo Orueta 2, 48009,* ☎ *94/423–5500,* FAX *94/423–4500. 49 rooms, 4 suites. Restaurant, bar, cafeteria, exercise room, parking (fee). AE, DC, MC, V.*

$$$ ✕🏨 **Ercilla.** This modern hotel fills with the taurine crowd during Bilbao's Semana Grande in early August, partly because it's near the bullring and partly because it has taken over from the Carlton as the place to see and be seen. Impeccable rooms, facilities, and service underscore its reputation. This might not be the place to stay if you're looking for a quiet getaway. ⊠ *C. Ercilla 3739, 48009,* ☎ *94/470–5700,* ℻ *94/443–9335. 346 rooms. Restaurant, bar, cafeteria, parking (fee). AE, DC, MC, V.*

$$$ ✕🏨 **NH Villa de Bilbao.** If a bit impersonal and chilly at the front desk, this functional place offers a good number of pluses—including one of the greatest hotel breakfasts ever engineered, along with rooms that are comfortable and comprehensively equipped with everything from climate control to minibars. But the best thing about this cosmopolitan operation is its location near the Plaza del Sagrado Corazón at the far end of the Doña Casilda de Iturrizar park—a locations that akes this lush forest and meadow an unavoidable part of your day as you set out for the Guggenheim, the Museo de Bellas Artes, or any other point in Bilbao (the farthest of which is no more than a 45-minute hike away). Barely a hundred yards from the Palacio Euskalduna, three blocks from San Mamés soccer stadium, and two streets below the taverns of Licenciado Poza, this is a fine location from which to tackle Bilbao. ⊠ *Gran Vía, 48011,* ☎ *94/441–6000,* ℻ *94/441–6529. 139 rooms. Restaurant, bar, cafeteria, minibars, parking (fee). AE, DC, MC, V.*

$$$ 🏨 **Carlton.** The luminaries who have trod the halls of this grande dame include Orson Welles, Ava Gardner, Ernest Hemingway, Lauren Bacall, and most of Spain's great bullfighters. During the Spanish Civil War it was the seat of the Republican Basque government; later it housed a number of Nationalist generals. It remains elegant, well attended, and centrally located. ⊠ *Plaza Federico Moyúa 2, 48009,* ☎ *94/416–2200,* ℻ *94/416–4628. 148 rooms. Restaurant, bar, meeting rooms. AE, DC, MC, V.*

$$ 🏨 **Artetxe.** With rooms overlooking Bilbao from the heights of Artxanda, the Artetxe offers excellent value and a quiet setting surrounded by the green hills and meadows you see from the Guggenheim museum. Local *asadores* (restaurants specializing in meat or fish cooked over coals) are good dining options. What you lose here in big-city Bilbao urban you gain in good air and peace and quiet. Recently overhauled, this Basque farmhouse has all new fresh wood trimmings and young owners eager to make their inn a success. ⊠ *Camino de Berriz 112 (off Carretera Enékuri–Artxanda, Km 7), 48014,* ☎ *94/474–7780,* ℻ *94/474–6020. 12 rooms. Breakfast room. AE, DC, MC, V.*

$$ 🏨 **Siri-Miri.** A small, carefully run hotel near the Atxuri station and the Casco Viejo, this modest spot has perfectly nice rooms with views over some of Bilbao's oldest architecture. The buffet-style breakfast is excellent, and the owner and manager helpful with advice about your stay in Bilbao. ⊠ *Plaza de la Encarnación, 48006,* ☎ *94/433–0759,* ℻ *94/433–0875. 28 rooms. Breakfast room. AE, DC, MC, V.*

$–$$ 🏨 **Iturriena Ostatua.** This traditional Basque town house in Bilbao's old quarter has rough and heavy wooden beams that are a feast for the eyes. There are also stone walls, wood floors, and curios ranging from primitive tools to effigies of sheep and a portable combat confessional from the Spanish Civil War. Everything about the place, including the price, is superlative. ⊠ *Santa María Kalea 14, 48005,* ☎ *94/416–1500,* ℻ *94/415–8929. 21 rooms. Breakfast room. AE, DC, MC, V.*

$–$$ 🏨 **Ripa.** Overlooking the San Nicolas church and the Teatro Arriaga from the other (Ensanche) side of the Nervión river, this modest but charming hotel has guest rooms featuring wooden panels, floors and beds, and a quiet environment with neither the Casco Viejo's human uproar nor the Ensanche's traffic. Fifty meters from the train station, a ten-minute walk from the Guggenheim, and five minutes from the Mercado de la Ribera, this is arguably the best lodging value in town.

✉ *Calle Ripa 3, 48005,* ☎ *94/423–9677,* 🖷 *94/423–1816. 15 rooms. AE, DC, MC, V.*

$ 🔁 **Hostal Mendez.** This may be the best value in town, with small but impeccable and well-appointed rooms, some of which (Nos. 1 and 2) overlook the facade of the Palacio Yohn (pretty views but noisy at night: bring earplugs). A brace of handsome sculpted setters stands vigil at the bottom of lovely, creaky wood stairs. Fourth-floor rooms are even less expensive in this century-old walk-up building. ✉ *Santa María Kalea 13, 48005,* ☎ *94/416–0364. 12 rooms. AE, DC, MC, V.*

Cafés

Bilbao's many coffeehouses and bistros have long provided refuge from the siri-miri and steel mills outside. The top of the list is occupied by **Café La Granja** (✉ Plaza Circular 3)—opened in 1926, this landmark is a Bilbao mix of old-world panache and fine beers, coffees, and food, with the lunch menu a reasonably priced delight. You can also refuel at the enormous **Café Iruña** (✉ Jardines de Albia), another turn-of-the-20th-century classic, and the **Café Bulevard** (✉ Calle Arenal 3), Bilbao's oldest, dating back to 1871. **Café El Tilo** (✉ C. Arenal 1) may be the best of all, named for the linden tree typical of Bilbao and painted with original frescoes by Basque painter Juan de Aranoa (1901–1973). **Bar los Fueros** (✉ Calle de los Fueros 4), as much a watering hole as a café, is one of Bilbao's most authentic enclaves, perfect for an *aperitivo* or a nightcap. **Café y Té** (✉ Plaza Federico Moyúa 1) has a pleasant marble counter and a combination rural-urban aesthetic.

Nightlife and the Arts

The prized **Teatro Arriaga** (✉ Plaza Arriaga s/n, ☎ 94/416–3244) continues to stage ballet, theater, concerts, opera, and *zarzuela* (comic opera). Bilbao's Asociación Bilbaína de Amigos de la Opera (☎ 94/435–5100), with its resident Coro de Opera de Bilbao, stages eight operas annually, contracting leading opera companies from around the world. The **Palacio Euskalduna** (✉ Calle Abandoibarra 4, ☎ 94/330–8372) has largely replaced the Arriaga as Bilbao's top venue for ballet, opera, and classical music; it often hosts the Orquesta Sinfónica de Bilbao. Opera and zarzuela are also performed at the **Teatro Coliseo Albia** (✉ Alameda Urquijo 13, ☎ 94/415–3954); information is available at Rodríguez Arias 3 (☎ 94/415–5490). For jazz keep your eye on **Bilbaína Jazz Club** (✉ Calle Navarra s/n, ☎ 619–442320), where dinner is also served. **Bilborock** (✉ Muelle de la Merced 1, ☎ 94/415–1306) has top rock groups from Spain and abroad. **Café-Teatro Mistyk** (✉ Calle Ercilla 1, ☎ 94/423–6342) is the latest and hottest venue for an eclectic range of performances ranging from jazz to theater. **Kafe Antzokia** (✉ Calle San Vicente 2, ☎ 94/424–4625) is a hot multidisciplinary space with folk, rock, jazz, and pop performances. Bilbao hosts a **blues festival** in June, a **jazz festival** in July, and a **folk and Habaneras festival** in September; inquire at the tourist office (☞ Visitor Information *in* Bilbao and Basque Country A to Z, *below*), as venues change.

Bilbao's nightlife comes in various stages and levels of intensity. For relaxed, bar-to-bar, tavern-to-tavern wining and dining on the run, the earliest and healthiest phase of the project, the action begins in places such as the **Casco Viejo** and, in the Ensanche, along **Calle Licenciado Poza** where serious *poteo* (tippling), *txikiteo* (tippling), and *tapeo* (tippling and tapa grazing) continues late into most nights, especially Thursday to Sunday. After Athletic de Bilbao soccer victories in the San Mames stadium, known affectionately as La Catedral, "Poza arde" (Poza is burning), as the saying goes, meaning that the bars and taverns along Calle Licenciado Poza overflow with thirsty and celebratory soccer fans. After defeats, the mood is less euphoric, but Poza is still hot as a pistol. Other top bar-hopping zones include **Paseo del Arenal, Calle Ledesma,** and **Calle Elcano. Los Jardines de Albia,** with the **Café Iruña** in the forefront, is also a hub for a variety of cafés, bars, and taverns.

Stage two is more liquid. For straight-up cocktails, all hotel bars, especially the Carlton's (☞ Lodging, *above*), are excellent. Try **Bilbost** (✉ Plaza Pedro Eguillor 2) or **Old Tavern** (✉ Calle Rodríguez Arias 3).

"Pubs" in Spain, and especially Bilbao, are smokier, more musical places for drinking serious *"copas,"* which are understood as either beer or mixed drinks such as *cubatas* (Cuba libres, Coca-Cola and rum). Top pubs around Bilbao include **Azulito** (✉ Particular de Estraunza 1); **Beer House** (✉ Plaza de San Pedro 2); **Brick** (✉ Calle Elcano 29); **Galeón** (✉ Alameda Mazarredo 19); **Chaflan** (✉ Calle Colón de Larreátegui 15); the **Dubliners** (✉ Plaza de Moyúa 6); **Cotón Club** (✉ Alameda Gregorio de la Revilla 25); **Kiss** (✉ Elcano 29); **Magic** (✉ Calle Colón de Larreátegui 80); **Kilkenny Tavern** (✉ C/ Bertendonar 8); and **Whiskey Viejo** (✉ Calle Lersundi 5).

Stage three involves dancing at discos. The top current disco choices include **Columbus** (✉ Calle Urazurrutia s/n); **Palladium** (✉ Calle Iparraguirre 11); **Rock Star** (✉ Gran Vía 87); **Tiffanys** (✉ Calle Francisco Macià 11). For ballroom dancing try **Flash** (✉ Calle Telesforo de Aranzadi 4) and for salsa and Latin rhythms **Caché Latino** (✉ Calle Ripa 3); **Jaragua** (✉ Calle Ibañez de Bilbao 9); and **Pelícanos** (✉ Calle Mazarredo 20).

Shopping

Basque *txapelas* (berets) are famous worldwide and make fine gifts. Best when waterproofed, they'll keep you remarkably warm in rain and mist. Try **Sombreros Gorostiaga** (✉ C. Victor), in the old quarter, for the most famous line of berets, Elosegui. **Basandere** (✉ Iparraguire 4, ☎ 94/423–6386), just across from the Guggenheim, sells a wide range of quality artisanal products made in the Basque Country, as does **Spirit of Bilbao** (✉ Elcano 2). **Legendario** (✉ Iparraguirre 4), somewhat incongruously but happily, sells imported goods, including rum and tobacco, from Cuba. **Bilbao Goyoaga** (✉ Ribera 3, Getxo) makes and sells woodcarvings. **Kabi-Art** (✉ Avda. Cervantes 43) is a ceramicist, as is **Ortuzar Itziar** (✉ Estrada Hormaza 12, Getxo). **Tallerias San Antón** (✉ Zabalbide 7) is an artisanal glass cutter. For wines look for **El Rincón del Vino** (✉ Gral. Concha 1) or **Ibeas** (✉ Licenciado Poza 23). For fashions **Derby** (✉ Alameda Urquijo 6), **Javier de Juana** (✉ Gran Vía 24), **Otto Milano** (✉ Gregorio de la Revilla 1), **Zubiri** (✉ Ercilla 30), **Muselina** (✉ C. Colón de Larreátegui 41), and **Tisdana** (✉ Rodríguez Arias 21) are tops, along with **Smith & Smith** (✉ Telesforo Aranzadi 2), and **Class** (✉ Astarloa 5). For shoes, look for **La Palma** (✉ Correo 3) or **Ayestaran** (✉ Gran Vía 63). Top music stores include **Vellido** (✉ Plaza Moyua 4), **Long-Play** (✉ Gregorio de la Revilla 6), **Gordon** (✉ Autonomía 33), **Disco** (✉ Berastegui 1), **Jomadi** (✉ Autonomía 22), and **Vinilo** (✉ C. Colón de Larreátegui 22).

AROUND BILBAO:
SIDE TRIPS IN VIZCAYA

Around Bilbao are three suggested itineraries, one coastal and two inland. The coastal route begins west down the Nervión and swings around east to Urdaibai and, eventually, on to Guipúzcoa. One inland loop is west of Bilbao, while the other lies to the east. The coastal route around the edge of the Atlantic Bay of Biscay (Golfo de Vizcaya) northwest of Bilbao is a spectacular and uplifting blast of fresh north Atlantic air and ocean. Each village and beach has its own esthetic and character, whether a fishing port, surfing spot, or sandy expanse, and locals never tire of sampling the different tastes, ports, and seascapes of their Atlantic coast. The loop around the coast of Vizcaya begins at Getxo just down the Nervión estuary and runs around through Plentzia, Bakio, Bermeo, and Mundaca to Guernica at the beginning of the Urdaibai wetlands. The second section of Vizcayan coast begins beyond Urdaibai and includes Elanchove, Leikeitio, and Ondarroa before crossing into the neighboring province of Guipúzcoa beginning at Zumaia. Inland and upland Vizcaya includes the rustic wilderness villages of Las Encartaciones west of Bilbao and the velvety green Atxondo valley east of Durango up to Elorrio.

The Basque Coast

For refreshing Atlantic gulps of a variety of beaches, fishing ports, open ocean and green hills, take a drive around the coast of Vizcaya, first heading down the Nervión to Getxo and working around through Plentzia, Gorliz, Arminza, Bakio, San Juan de Gaztelugache, Bermeo, Mundaka, Guernica, Amorebieta and back to Bilbao. This is a trip that can take a day or week, depending on tastes and timetables. The next coastal tour would be out past Guernica to Kortezubi and Elantxobe, Leikeitio, Ondarroa and Markina, continuing on through Zumaya, Guetaria, Zarauz to San Sebastián, with a side trip up to the Santuario de Loyola and Oñate.

Getxo

38 *13 km (8 mi) northwest of Bilbao, 10 km (6 mi) southwest of Plentzia.*

Getxo, an early watering spot for the elite Bilbao industrial classes, along with its rambling mansions has five beaches (Areaga, Arenas, Arrigunaga, Aizkorre, and Barinatxe) and an ancient fishing port. In addition to the exquisite Jolastoki (☞ Bilbao Dining and Lodging, *above*), restaurants and hotels along the beaches here make good hideaways just a 20-minute (designer) subway ride from Bilbao.

Dining and Lodging

$$$ 🏨 **Los Tamarises.** This modern beachfront hotel has an excellent restaurant and offers a very different sun and sand experience than midtown life in Bilbao can provide. Getxo's assortment of churches, hermitages, windmills, and mansions, along with the tight, steep streets of the fishing quarter, can keep you busy and entertained, with the Guggenheim just a few minutes away. The hotel is a smoothly running operation that lives up to its reputation for comfort and attentive service. ✉ *Playa de Ereaga, 48990,* ☎ *94/491–0005,* 𝖥𝖠𝖷 *94/491–1310. 42 rooms. Restaurant, bar, free parking. AE, DC, MC, V.*

OFF THE
BEATEN PATH

Butrón – This late-19th-century castle (✉ Barrio Butrón s/n, Gatika, ☎ 94/615–1110; ⊙ daily 10:30–8, 🚇 in the village of Gatika (4 km or 2 mi east of Sopelana on BI3121) was restored during the 20th century on the site of a 13th-century fortification built by the notorious Butrón family, important protagonists of the bloody Guerra de Banderizos (Factional Wars) that swept the length and breadth of Vizcaya during the Middle Ages. The bottom 30 ft of the castle are from the original structure, but the rest is, though impressive, pure Walt Disney. The castle is open daily 10:30–8, and the admission charge is 700 ptas./€4.21 to visit castle, 900 ptas./€5.41 to visit the castle and private rooms.

Plentzia

③⑨ *10 km (6 mi) northeast of Getxo, 21 km (13 mi) north of Bilbao.*

Don't be surprised if you find yourself riding Bilbao's Norman Foster subway next to someone carrying a surfboard. Plentzia and its excellent beach at Gorliz on the eastern side of the Ría de Plentzia are easily reached by subway from downtown Bilbao.

Dining and Lodging

$$$ ⬚ **Uribe.** This little place in Plentzia's fishing port allows easy access to the beach—in fact, it's so near the water it's nearly like cruising without the motion sickness. You'll find no frills or restaurant, and rooms are small, but there are pleasant people to stay with and it's a short walk and a subway ride from the middle of Bilbao. ✉ *Erribera 13, 48620,* ☎ *94/677–4478,* ℻ *94/677–4461. 8 rooms. MC, V.*

En Route From Plentzia to Bermeo follow the scenic coastal BI3151 to Bakio, where the road becomes BI3101. Have a look at the 12th-century Ermita de San Pelayo just before rounding the corner over the tiny island and Ermita de San Juan de Gaztelugatxe far below.

San Juan de Gaztelugatxe

④⓪ *5 km (3 mi) northeast of Bakio, 12 km (7 mi) west of Bermeo.*

This nearly unbelievably picturesque hermitage clinging to its rocky promontory over the Bay of Biscay is exactly 231 steps up along a narrow corridor built into the top of a rocky ledge connecting what would otherwise be an island to the mainland. A favorite pilgrimage for bilbainos on holidays, the Romanesque chapel is said to have been used as a fortress by the Templars in the 14th century. This is reputedly a magic spot—literally: a complete walk around the bell tower is alleged to cure nightmares and insomnia, as well as to grant wishes.

Dining and Lodging

$$$ ⬚ **Ostatua Gaztelubegi.** The views from this popular little hotel and restaurant overlooking the hermitage of San Juan de Gaztelugatxe are some of the most panoramic and vertiginous anywhere along the Basque coast. The bar is always booming and the cuisine is simple Basque cooking from *alubias* to *besugo* (beans to sea bream). ✉ *Carretera BI3101, Km 3 (from Bakio), 48130,* ☎ *94/619–4924. 7 rooms. Restaurant. MC, V.*

Bermeo

★ ④① *30 km (18 mi) east of Plentzia, 3 km (2 mi) west of Mundaca.*

Bermeo claims the largest fishing fleet in Spain, comprising 62 long-distance boats of more than 150 tons and 121 smaller craft that specialize in hake. Bermeo was long a whaling port; in the 16th century local whalers had to donate the tongue of every whale to help raise money for the church. The town still has one of only two wooden-boat shipyards on the northern coast, and the boats that fill its harbor make a cheerful picture. Walk into Bermeo's central square and have a look at the lovely *Udaletxea* (town hall, in Euskera) with its prominent coat of arms and the curious sundials in almost perpetual shadow above the fountains dated 1745 at the building's eastern corner. The bandstand is the scene of summer concerts, while the church is notable for its bare wooden floors and its wooden choir loft. If you drive to the top of the windswept hill, there is a cemetery that overlooks the crashing waves below. Townspeople tend family tombs at sunset.

Bermeo's **Museo del Pescador** is the only museum in the world dedicated exclusively to the craft and history of fishermen and the fishing industry from whales to anchovies. The tower building that houses the museum, **La Torre de Ercilla,** was built by Alonso de Ercilla y Zuñiga (1533–1594), Bermeo native and Spanish epic poet and eminent soldier in the army of Felipe II. Ercilla's *La Araucana* is considered the finest epic poem in Spanish literature, an account of the conquering of Arauco (Chile). ⊠ *Torre de Ercilla,* ☎ *94/688–1171.* 🎟 *Free.* ☉ *Tues.–Sat. 10–1:30 and 4–7:30, Sun. 10–1:30.*

Dining

$$ ✕ **Jokin.** You have a good view of the *puerto viejo* (old port) from this cheerful, strategically located restaurant. The fish served comes directly off the boats in the harbor below. Try the *rape Jokin* (anglerfish in a clam and crayfish sauce) or *chipirones en su tinta* (small squid in its own ink) and, for dessert, the *tarta de naranja* (orange cake). ⊠ *Eupeme Duna 13,* ☎ *94/688–4089. AE, DC, MC, V. No dinner Sun.*

Mundaca

④② *45 km (28 mi) northeast of Bilbao.*

Mundaca (Mundaka, in Euskera) is a tiny town that draws surfers from all over the world, especially in winter, when the waves are some of the world's longest. The left-breaking roller that forms off the entrance to the Urdaibai natural preserve at the mouth of the Ría de Guernica is Europe's longest wave. The town itself is filled with houses bearing coats of arms and graceful summer houses. The Santa Catalina peninsula with its hermitage and the parish church with its Renaissance door are among Mundaca's prime architectural gems. Look for the **Mundaka Surf Shop** (⊠ Calle Surf 1, ☎ 94/687–6721, ℻ 94/687–7845), run by Australian Craig Jones, for surfing advice and equipment.

Dining and Lodging

$$ ✕ **Casino José Mari.** Built in 1818 as an auction house for the local fishermen's guild, this building, with wonderful views of Mundaca's beach, is now a local eating club. The public is welcome, and it's a prime lunch stop in summer, when you can sit in the glassed-in, upper-floor porch. Very much a local haunt, the club serves excellent fish caught, more often than not, by members. ⊠ *Parque Atalaya (in center of town),* ☎ *94/687–6005. Reservations not accepted. AE, MC, V.*

$$ 🏨 **Atalaya.** This 1911 landmark was converted very tastefully from a private house to a hotel. Guest rooms are charming and comfortable, and those upstairs have balconies with marvelous views. Room No. 12 is the best in the house. The breakfast room is cheerful and light. ⊠ *Itxaropen Kalea 1, Villa María Luísa Esperanza, 48360,* ☎ *94/687–6888,* ℻ *94/687–6899. 15 rooms. Bar, breakfast room. AE, DC, MC, V.*

En Route From Mundaca follow signs for Guernica, but don't fail to stop at the Mirador de Portuondo, a roadside lookout on the left (at Km 43 on BI635) as you leave town, for an excellent view of the estuary.

Guernica

④③ *15 km (9 mi) east of Bilbao.*

On Monday, April 26, 1937—market day—Guernica suffered history's second terror bombing against a civilian population (the first, much less famous, was against neighboring Durango, about a month earlier). The planes of the Nazi Luftwaffe were sent with the blessings of General Franco to experiment with saturation bombing of civilian targets and decimate the traditional seat of Basque autonomy in the bargain. Since the Middle Ages, Spanish sovereigns had sworn under the ancient **oak tree of Guernica** to respect Basque *fueros* (special local rights—just the kind of local autonomy inimical to the *generalísimo* and his "National Movement" of Madrid-centered Spanish unity). More than 1,000 people were killed in the bombing, and today Guernica remains a symbol of independence in the heart of every Basque, known to the world through Picasso's famous painting (now in Madrid's Centro de Arte Reina Sofía). For the story of the town and the painting, see the Close-Up Box, "*Guernica*: The Passionate Eye," *below*.

The city was destroyed—though the oak tree miraculously emerged unscathed—and has been rebuilt as a modern, unattractive place. One point of interest, however, is the stump of the sacred oak, which finally died several decades ago, in the courtyard of the **Casa de Juntas** (a new oak has been planted alongside the old one)—the object of many a pilgrimage. Nearby is the stunning estuary of the **Ría de Guernica,** a stone's throw from some of the area's most colorful fishing towns.

Dining and Lodging

$$ ✕ **Baserri Maitea.** Here's your chance to see the inside of one of the
★ Basque Country's traditional *caseríos* (farmhouses): this one is 300 years old. Strings of red peppers and garlic hang from wooden beams in the cathedral-like interior. Entrées include the *pescado del día* (fish of the day) and *cordero de leche asado al horno de leña* (milk-fed lamb roasted in a wood-burning oven). The pastries are homemade. ⊠ *BI635 to Bermeo, Km 2,* ☎ *94/625–3408. AE, DC, MC, V. No dinner Sun., except June–Sept.*

$ 🏨 **Boliña.** Not far from the remains of the famous oak in downtown
★ Guernica, the Boliña is pleasant, friendly, and modern, a good base for exploring the Vizcayan coast. Rooms are smallish but comfortable. ⊠ *Barrenkale 3, 48300,* ☎ FAX *94/625–0300. 16 rooms. Restaurant, bar. AE, DC, MC, V.*

En Route From Guernica, either head back to Bilbao or continue northeast toward Kortezubi on the BI638. For a rewarding side trip, turn left at Arteaga and follow the BI3237 around the east side of the Ría de Guernica and the Urdaibai nature preserve to Elanchove (Elantxobe, in Euskera). From there, drive the coast road through Ea and Ipaster to Lequeitio, one of the prettiest ports on the Basque coast.

OFF THE
BEATEN PATH
SANTIMAMIÑE CAVERNS – On the Kortezubi road 5 km (3 mi) from Guernica, the Santimamiñe Caverns (⊠ Barrio Basondo, Kortezubi, ☎ 94/625-2975) contain important prehistoric cave paintings. Guided visits are offered weekdays at 10:30, noon, 4, and 5:30, except holidays. Look for signs for the nearby **Bosque de Oma,** a forest of trees with vividly painted trunks created by Basque artist Agustín Ibarrola, a striking and successful marriage of art and nature.

Elanchove

🄴 *27 km (17 mi) from Bermeo.*

The tiny fishing village of Elanchove nestles among huge, steep cliffs, with a small breakwater protecting its fleet from the storms of the Bay of Biscay. The view of the port from the upper village is breathtaking. The lower fork in the road leads to the port itself.

The upper village is quite unaccustomed to tourists. Stop into the rustic **Bar Itxasmin,** which has a small restaurant; it's just off the plaza where the road ends.

GUERNICA: THE PASSIONATE EYE

IF HELEN OF TROY is history's most fought-over woman, capable of launching 1,000 ships and a 10-year war, Picasso's *Guernica* must stand as the most embattled painting. When the 56-year-old Picasso was commissioned by the struggling government of the Spanish Second Republic to create a work for the 1937 International Exposition in Paris, little did he imagine that the stark quasi-grisaille mural-sized image he produced in protest of the German Condor Legion's "experimental" bombing of an obscure Basque village would become one of the most famous and disputed works of art in history.

The rural market town of Guernica (now known as Gernika-Lumio), 20 km (12 mi) east of Bilbao, was already at the heart of Basque autonomy and identity as early as the 14th century when the feudal lords of Vizcaya swore on the legendary *Gernikako Arbola* (Tree of Guernica) to respect Basque *fueros,* or autonomous rights and privileges. When General Francisco Franco sent the German Condor Legion to Guernica to experiment with saturation bombing techniques, he undoubtedly knew that the strike would be triply devastating: a blow to Basque nationalism, a warning to neighboring Bilbao, and a demonstration of the consequences of supporting the Republic.

Tuesday, April 26, 1937, was market day in Guernica, and the town was filled with woman, children, animals, and farmers too senior to have been taken off to the front to fight for one side or the other, with or against Franco's recently launched Northern Campaign. By the time the un-opposed bombers had dropped their ordnance, more than 1,000 civilians lay dead or dying in and under the ruins of Guernica. The aftermath was confused as journalists spread the word and international outcry grew. The Condor Legion initially claimed innocence; later they would allege that planes returning from an aborted mission had mistakenly dumped ordnance. Not until the 60th anniversary of the event, on April 26, 1997, did German president Roman Herzog publicly and officially assume responsibility for the participation of German warplanes in the bombing of Guernica.

Meanwhile, Picasso's painting began its own travels and travails. As part of the Spanish Pavilion in the 1937 International Exposition in Paris, *Guernica* was not a great success. Nearly substituted at the last minute by a more upbeat and bellicose triptych, the nightmarish, mural-like panel in shades of black, white, and gray, far from featured in the exhibit, was used as a backdrop. In 1939, Picasso ceded it to New York's Museum of Modern Art in the name of the democratically elected Second Republican Government of Spain—stipulating, however, that the painting should one day be returned to Spain when it was returned to a democratic form of government. Over the following 30 years, Picasso's fame exploded and so did *Guernica*'s, not only as a work of art but as a symbol of Spain's continuing condition as a virtual hostage of a totalitarian regime.

Artistically, *Guernica* is widely considered to resemble a cubist remake of Goya's famous *Dos de Mayo* canvas with a similar interplay of darkness and fire; gaping, agonized mouths; and an analogous overall organization of pictoric space. The painting's main protagonists—bull, horse, woman, and warrior—share a common scream of horror. The animals are featured more powerfully than the humans, making the painting a semimythological symbol of universal suffering and cruelty. The light bulb overhead is considered a metaphor for modern technology, while the hand-held gas lantern refers to the eternal light of human understanding and traditional values.

When Franco died in 1975, two years after Picasso, negotiations with Picasso's heirs for the return of the painting to Spain were already under way. Today, it is on view at the Museo Reina Sofía and experts now consider *Guernica* too fragile to ever be moved again.

Dining and Lodging

$ ✕🏠 **Arboliz Jatetxea.** Set on a bluff overlooking the coast, about 2 km (1 mi) outside Elanchove on the road to Lequeitio, this rustic inn is a little far from the harborside bustle yet pleasant. Rooms are simple, modern, and well kept, and several have balconies. ✉ *Arboliz 12, Ibarranguelua 48311,* ☎ *94/627–6283. 9 rooms, 3 with bath. Restaurant. AE, MC, V.*

Lequeitio

45 *59 km (37 mi) east of Bilbao, 61 km (38 mi) west of San Sebastián.*

This bright little town is similar to Bermeo but has two wide, sandy beaches right by its harbor. Soaring over the Gothic church of Santa María (open for Mass only) is a graceful set of flying buttresses. Lequeitio is famous for its fiestas (September 1–18), which include a gruesome event in which men dangle for as long as they can from the necks of dead geese tied to a cable over the inlet while the cable is whipped in and out of the water by crowds of burly men at either end.

Ondárroa

46 *61 km (38 mi) east of Bilbao, 49 km (30 mi) west of San Sebastián.*

Farther east along the coast from Lequeitio, Ondárroa is another gem of a fishing town. Like its neighbors, it has a major fishing fleet painted various combinations of red, green, and white, the colors of the Ikurriña, the Basque national flag.

Note if you wish to continue directly along the Basque Coast in the direction of San Sebastiàn and not head inland on Vizcaya excursions, skip over the following Inland Vizcaya section and go directly to the town listing for Zumaya, *below.*

Inland Vizcaya

Excursions inland from Bilbao, as well as beautiful explorations of true upland Basque life, will give you the full sense of what Vizcaya is all about and where the produce that appears in Bilbao's exquisite menus comes from; the proximity of so much fertile farmland so close to such industrial urban development is startling. This Inland Vizcaya section comprises two main trips: one, to **Las Encartaciones,** 30 minutes west of Bilbao, a mountainous series of steep green hillsides, ravines, and villages. The second trip is to the east—the **Valle de Atxondo,** which rises up toward the limestone cliffs of Amboto, Vizcaya's magic mountain.

To make a loop through the valleys and villages of Las Encartaciones (so named for their medieval enrollment in a semiautonomous administrative "charter," or *carta*) leave Bilbao on the A8 Santander freeway and exit almost immediately on the BI636 for Sodupe and Balmaseda. Follow indications for Gordexola, 4 km (2 mi) south of Sodupe off BI636. From Gordexola, the tiny but well-paved BI3621 leads over a small mountain pass to rejoin the BI636. At the junction turn right to Güeñes 2 km (1 mi) east. From Güeñes return west to Balmaseda, from which the BI630 leads farther west into the Valle de Caranza, Vizcaya's western edge. To complete the loop, follow the BI2701 to Avellaneda (Urreztieta, in Euskera), Sopuerta, and Muskiz. From Muskiz drive along the estuary of the river Barbadún, under the A8 highway, to the beach at Arena and the fishing port of Ciérvana (Zierbena, in Euskera). From Ciérvana drive back upriver past Bilbao's new port area, Santurtzi, and Portugalete, or take the see-it-to-believe-it hanging bridge across to the Right Bank and Getxo.

Gordexola

47 *19 km (11 mi) southwest of Bilbao.*

Nestled in an elongated valley wedged between wooded heights, Gordejuela (Gordexola, in Euskera) is known for its numerous examples of the medieval Basque *casa-torre,* or fortified manor house, usually richly emblazoned with the family coat of arms over the main entryway and topped with a wooden porch or gallery under the eaves of the top floor. These farmhouse-fortresses are testimony to the factional feuds and clan warfare of the 14th and 15th centuries.

The many so-called *casas de los indianos* along the road were late-19th-century palaces built by *indianos,* the term used for fortune-seekers who had struck it rich in the New World (i.e., the Indies, as America was originally misunderstood to be) and came back to build luxurious mansions, marry the village beauty, found and finance the local school, and generally bask in their self-made glory.

The first Sunday in December the Fiesta de San Andrés in Gordexola is a classic country livestock and artisanal produce fair to keep in mind. The picturesque road over the pass to the next valley, the Kadagua River valley, passes the San Juan de Berbikiz hermitage 3 km (2 mi) from Gordexola. The "charter members" of Las Encartaciones met under the oak tree next to the hermitage.

Güeñes

48 *21 km (13 mi) southwest of Bilbao, 8 km (5 mi) west of Gordexola.*

Güeñes sits astride the Kadagua river, the spinal cord of Las Encartaciones running from above Balmaseda into the Nervión at Barakaldo. Güeñes highlights include the florid Gothic **Iglesia de Santa María** church with its pointed arch over an intricately sculpted door, and the ayuntamiento (town hall), which occupies the Villa Urrutia, an elaborate *indiano* palace. Drive up the left (north) bank of the Kadagua to see the **Palacio Tejada,** with its two giant coats of arms on the facade, before taking a small track to the right leading up to what is known as the **Palacio de las Brujas** and the **Casa Hurtado de Amézaga.** On the way into the village of Zalla, another track leads to Bolunburu, on the Kadagua River, where there are ruins of a *casa-torre* (house-tower), a mill, an iron ore furnace, and the tiny hermitage of **Ermita de Santa Ana.**

Dining and Lodging

$$ ✕ **Erreka Güeñes.** This little tavern and restaurant has a menu filled with Basque specialties with some dishes from the meseta of Castilla as well. Roast lamb is a local favorite, but look for migratory pigeon in season or out, as the game birds survive very successfully when vacuum-packed. ⌧ *Barrio Lasier s/n,* ☏ *946/690345. MC, V.*

Balmaseda

49 *30 km (13 mi) southwest of Bilbao, 9 km (5 mi) southwest of Güeñes.*

The oldest township in Vizcaya, founded 100 years before Bilbao in the late 12th century, Balmaseda celebrated its 800th anniversary in January 1999. An important stop on the route between the Cantabrian coast and the Castilian meseta, the Roman road between the important early port at Castro Urdiales and Herrera del Pisuerga passed through Balmaseda, making it the most important nucleus in Las Encartaciones. The Gothic **Iglesia de San Severino,** with Baroque details added in the 18th century, houses the intimate **Capilla del Santo Cristo** (Chapel of the Holy Christ), considered one of the gems of Basque Gothic architecture. The **Ayuntamiento** (town hall) is notable for its ground-floor *lonja* (exchange or market), which has so many arches it has been dubbed *la mezquita,* alluding to the forest of striped horseshoe arches in Cordoba's Mezquita. Don't miss **El Puente de la Muza**, a medieval toll bridge next to the San Juan church, with its tower used as a toll booth to charge admittance to the marketplace.

La Puchera Balmasedana (The Balmaseda Beanpot) is a local tradition descending from the railroad men who worked on the coal train to Bilbao and devised an ingenious method of using steam heat from the engine to cook *alubias con sus sacramentos* (kidney beans and their "sacraments": sausage, blood sausage, and fatback). Every October 23 this tradition is commemorated with a local *alubiada* (bean fest). Ask for directions to the famous *boina* (Basque beret) factory **La Encartada**, closed in 1992 after nearly 100 years of activity. The converted flour mill that supplied the electricity as well as all of the (now antique) British-made machinery used in the process are presently being restored as a museum. Balmaseda's Easter *Pasion Viviente* (Living Passion) is renowned throughout Spain; 500 actors re-create every moment of the last day of Christ from the Last Supper through Gethsemane, Calvary, and Golgotha.

Dining and Lodging

$$ ✕ **Abellaneda.** This is a good place for game, which runs wild and in great quantity throughout Las Encartaciones. If you see *jabalí con trompetas de la muerte* (wild boar with trumpets of death) on the menu, fear not: this is a lovely dark civet or stew made of wild boar and a delicious trumpet-shaped, black wild mushroom. ⊠ *La Cuesta 12,* ☎ *946/801674. MC, V.*

$$ ✕🔲 **San Roque.** This 17th-century convent was originally financed by a wealthy Balmaseda native, an *indiano* who lived in Panama. Consisting of the church, the convent (now the hotel), and a receiving area used by the municipality as a gallery for art shows or historical and ethnographical exhibits, this concentration of heavy stone arches and wooden overhead beams is a tempting spot to spend a night in, centuries removed from the crush and racket along the Nervión estuary. ⊠ *Campo de las Monjas 1, Balmaseda 48800 (leaving Balmaseda toward Burgos),* ☎ *946/102268,* FAX *946/102464. 17 rooms. Restaurant. AE, DC, MC, V.*

Avellaneda

🔟 *9 km (5 mi) north of Balmaseda, 6 km (4 mi) south of Sopuerta.*

From Balmaseda head south through Otxarán to Avellaneda, where the **Museo de las Encartaciones** in the ancient Casa de Juntas (Meeting House) displays documents, photographs, and artifacts revealing the history, customs, and traditions of Las Encartaciones. ⊠ *Casa de Juntas,* ☎ *946/504488.* ☉ *Sept. 15–May, Tues.–Sat. 10–2 and 4–6, Sun. 10–2; June–Sept. 15, Tues.–Sat. 10–2 and 5–7, Sun. 10–2.*

OFF THE BEATEN PATH   For an even wilder valley on Vizcaya's western edge, from Avellaneda continue farther west on the BI630 road to Carranza. In the Cantabrian enclave at Villaverde de Trucíos, look for the turnoff on BI2617 for **La Iglesia**, filled with noble houses, in one of which the Basque government of the Second Spanish Republic held its final meeting with Franco troops in hot pursuit late in the 1936–39 Spanish Civil War. The **Parque Ecológico de Vizcaya** offers a two-hour walk through a 49-acre park filled with Iberian fauna. The "subterranean cathedral" of the **Cueva de Pozalagua** is a karst, or limestone, cavern with spectacularly eccentric stalactites rising to the illuminated roof of the cave. For more serious

Bureau de change

Cambio

外国為替

In this city, you can find money on almost any street.

spelunking, rappel down into **La Torca del Carlista** to the largest underground cavern in Europe and one of the largest in the world, 1,650 ft long, 792 ft wide, and 446 ft high.

Ciérvana

51 *14 km (8 mi) north of Sopuerta, 21 km (13 mi) west of Bilbao.*

To complete the circle back into Bilbao continue north from Avellaneda through Sopuerta and Muskiz, past the Castillo de Muñatones, one of the biggest fortifications in Vizcaya, to the beach at La Arena, and then to the fishing port at Ciérvana. Along the quai, as in neighboring Santurtzi, fresh sardines cooked over coals and served with garlic and parsley provide a fragrant finale to this highland tour through Bilbao's little-known backyard.

$$ ✕ **Lazcano.** Overlooking the port with views out into the mouth of the Nervión, this excellent seafood preserve with its own live tank serves some of the freshest (and therefore best) fish in or around Bilbao. ⊠ *El Puerto,* ☎ *94/636–5032. MC, V.*

Axpe

52 *37 km (22 mi) east of Bilbao.*

Twenty minutes east of Bilbao on the San Sebastián freeway, turn southeast at Durango for the drive up into the **Atxondo Valley.** Turn right again for the village of Apatamonasterio and continue to Axpe where there are two graceful *caserios* serving excellent Basque fare. Back on the main road, continue on to Elorrio, last stop before the neighboring province of Guipúzcoa in upland Vizcaya. To reach Axpe drive east from Bilbao on the A8/E70 freeway toward San Sebastián. Get off at the Durango exit 31 km (19 mi) from Bilbao and take the BI632 road for Elorrio. At Apatamonasterio turn right onto the BI3313 and continue to Axpe.

The village of Axpe, in the valley of Atxondo, nestles under the limestone heights of Amboto, at 4,777 ft one of the four highest peaks in the Basque Country outside of the Pyrenees. Home of the legendary Basque mother of nature, Mari Urrika, or Mari Anbotokodama (María, Our Lady of Amboto), the spectral gray rockface of Amboto is a sharp contrast to the soft green meadows running up to the very foot of the mountain. According to Basque scholar and ethnologist José María de Barandiarán in his *Mitología Vasca (Basque Mythology),* Mari was "a beautiful woman, well constructed in all ways except for one foot, which was like that of a goat." Mari Anbotokodama's sons, Mikelatz and Atagorri, are, in Basque mythology, representations, respectively, of good and evil.

Dining and Lodging

$$ ✕ **Etxebarri.** A solid-looking wood-and-stone structure on Axpe's central square, this excellent country inn serves beef, alubias, and *chistorra* (spicy Basque sausage) that will stick to your ribs and, unforgettably, to your imagination as well. There's a contagious sense of well-being that pervades these Basque taverns and restaurants. Be sure to order some txakolí, lower in alcohol than aged wine but just as tart and refreshing. ⊠ *Plaza San Juan 1,* ☎ *94/658–3042. MC, V. No dinner Sun.– Mon.*

$$$–$$$$ ✕▥ **Mendigoikoa.** This handsome brace of stone farmhouses cling-
★ ing to the hillside over the village of Axpe are among Vizcaya's most exquisite hideaways. As one plaque on the outer wall of the restau-

rant attests, the King and Queen of Spain dined here with the Lehendakari (Basque president) Carlos Garaikoetxea in the early '80s. The lower of two farmhouses, Mendibekoa (lower mountain) has stunningly beautiful rooms, as well as restaurant space for breakfast and a glassed-in terrace overlooking the valley, while Mendigoikoa (upper mountain) is the restaurant. With a fire crackling in the far corner of the dining room and the heavy beams overhead, the *pichón de Navaz a la parilla* (Navaz pigeon cooked over coals) or the great *Txuletas de buey* (chunks of beef on the bone) taste as if they were grazing on this fragrant alpine hillside only moments ago. ⊠ *Barrio San Juan 33, Axpe 48290,* ☎ *94/682–0833,* FAX *94/682–1136. 12 rooms. Restaurant. AE, DC, MC, V.*

Elorrio

㊿ *3 km (2 mi) northeast of Axpe, 40 km (25 mi) east of Bilbao.*

Just another 3 km (2 mi) up the BI632 from the Apatamonasterio turnoff is the town of Elorrio, famous for its dense concentration of noteworthy medieval houses emblazoned with coats of arms and for its **Necropolis de Argiñeta**, on the edge of town next to the low-porched and rustic **Ermita de San Adrian**. The 23 pre-Christian stone tombs arranged under the oak trees around the hermitage include one dated 883, a mysterious and haunting glimpse of an early Basque civilization still being explored by archaeologists and ethnologists.

$$ ✕🖬 **Villa de Elorrio.** This cozy country inn is a handy place to spend a night or a week, surrounded by the Basque uplands, the Parque Natural de Urkiola, and the mountains of Oiz and Amboto on either side. Rooms are completely equipped with all the standard comforts and the restaurant serves simple but excellent Basque fare. ⊠ *Barrio San Agustín, Carretera de Durango, Km 1, Elorrio 48230,* ☎ *94/623–1555,* FAX *94/623–1663. 19 rooms. Restaurant. AE, DC, MC, V.*

Western Guipúzcoa

The province of Guipúzcoa, with San Sebastián as its capital and main city, begins between Elorrio and Mondragón and continues north to the French border along the Bidasoa river. Oñate, home of the medieval Basque university, is close to heart of Guipúzcoa and the fierce spirit of the mountain Basque, while the sequence of towns down toward and along the coast become progressively cosmopolitan as you move north along the coast.

Oñate

㊼ *40 km (25 mi) east of Elorrio, 74 km (46 mi) southwest of San Sebastián.*

Just across the Guipúzcoa provincial border, to the east of Elorrio, this little town with its medieval Sancti Spiritus university founded in 1540 and its numerous noble houses emblazoned with coats of arms is dear to the hearts of Basques. Aside from the astoundingly intricate Plateresque facade of the university, the town hall and the Gothic San Miguel church on the main square are noteworthy sights to see. The Basque Country's first university, where as many as 300 students studied in Latin from 1548 until 1901, was founded by the eminent local scholar and bishop Don Rodrigo Mercado Saez de Zuazola (1485–1548).

$$–$$$ ✕ **Iturritxo.** There are plenty of good restaurants in Oñate, but if you're looking for the best, this is the one to seek out. Put together by specialists in game in season and highland soups and bean stews that fortify the body and spirit on raw and rainy days in the Basque hills, this carefully prepared fare is never disappointing. ✉ *Atzeko 32,* ☎ *943/716078. AE, DC, MC, V. Closed Aug. 1–7. No dinner Mon., Tues.*

En Route Whether approaching from the upland redoubts of Oñate and Zumárraga or along the coastal road through Motrico and Deva, look for signs for Azpeitia and the sanctuary of one of Spain's greatest religious figures, St. Ignatius of Loyola, founder of the Jesuits and spiritual architect of the Catholic Reformation (also known as the Counter-Reformation). From either direction, the GI-631 takes you to Azpeitia and this colossal structure.

El Santuario de San Ignacio de Loyola, Azpeitia

★ ⑤⑤ *Azpeitia is 30 km (18 mi) northeast of Oñate, 44 km (27 mi) southwest of San Sebastián.*

El Santuario de San Ignacio de Loyola (Sanctuary of St. Ignatius of Loyola) was erected in honor of Iñigo Lopez de Oñaz y Loyola (1491–1556) after he was sainted as Ignacio de Loyola in 1622 for his defense of the Catholic Church against the tides of Luther's Reformation. The future founder of the Jesuit Order left his life as a courtier to join the army at the age of 26, but after being badly wounded in an intra-Basque battle he returned to his family's ancestral home, underwent a spiritual conversion, and took up theological studies. Almost two centuries later, Roman architect Carlos Fontana designed the basilica that would memorialize the saint after whom five universities in the United States and Canada and many others worldwide have been named. The structure is Baroque, and an exuberant, Churrigueresque Baroque at that—in contrast to the austere ways of Iñigo himself, who took vows of poverty and chastity after his conversion. The interior is richly endowed with polychrome marble, ornate altarwork, and a huge but delicate dome. The fortresslike tower house contains the room where Iñigo experienced conversion while recovering from his wound. His reputation as a "soldier of Christ" somewhat belies his teachings, which emphasized mystical union with God, imitation of Christ, human initiative, foreign missionary work, and, especially, the education of youth. ✉ *Crtra. Zumaya s/n,* ☎ *943/ 151792.* ☉ *Mon.–Sat. 9–2, 4–8; Sun. 9–2.*

$$ ✕🏨 **Arocena.** Just 8 km (5 mi) from Azpeitia and the Santuario de San Ignacio de Loyola, this is one of the many spa hotels to which Europeans flocked at the turn of the century. The Arocena has free bus service to the nearby springs, where medicinal waters are still used to treat liver-related diseases. Rooms facing away from the road have especially fine views of the mountains. The common rooms, including an elegant restaurant and lobby, faithfully retain the hotel's Belle Epoque flavor. ✉ *San Juan 12, Cestona 20740 (10 mins from sanctuary),* ☎ *943/ 147040,* 🅵🅰🆇 *943/147978. 109 rooms. Restaurant, bar, pool, tennis court, playground, chapel. AE, DC, MC, V.*

Zumaya

⑤⑥ *17 km (10 mi) north of Azpeitia, 14 km (8 mi) east of Ondarroa, 35 km (22 mi) west of San Sebastián.*

Zumaya, on the coast at the mouth of the Urola river, is a cozy little port and summer resort with the fjordlike estuary flowing back and forth, according to the tide, through town. Take a walk along the estuary and out to the point where you'll be looking out at open ocean. The walk from the Zuloaga Museum over the top through Azkizu to Guetaria is an excellent bracer for the appetite you'll want to have when you arrive there.

The **Museo Zuloaga,** on the N634 at the edge of town, has a fine collection of paintings by Goya, El Greco, Zurbarán, and others, in addition to the Basque Impressionist Ignacio Zuloaga—one of Spain's most celebrated early 20th-century painters (and longtime resident of Zumaya)—himself. ☒ ☎ 943/862341. ☜ 500 ptas./€3.01. ☯ Wed.–Sun. 4–8.

Dining and Lodging

$$ ✕ **Bedua.** Locals access this rustic gem by boat in the summer. A spe-
★ cialist in *tortilla de patatas con pimientos verdes de la huerta* (potato omelet with homegrown green peppers), Bedua is also known for *tortilla de bacalao* (codfish omelet), *chuleta de buey* (beefsteak), and fish of all kinds, especially *besugo* (sea bream). ☒ *Cestoa, Barrio Bedua (3 km [2 mi] up the Urola from Zumaya)*, ☎ 943/860551. MC, V.

Guetaria

57 *22 km (14 mi) west of San Sebastián.*

From Zumaya, the coast road and several good footpaths lead to Guetaria, known as *la cocina de Guipúzcoa* (the kitchen of Guipúzcoa province) for its surfeit of good restaurants and taverns. Guetaria was the birthplace of Juan Sebastián Elcano (1460–1526), the first circumnavigator of the globe and Spain's most emblematic naval hero: Elcano took over and completed Magellan's voyage after the latter was killed in the Philippines in 1521. The town's galleonlike **church,** with rough, sloping, wooden floors like the decks of a schooner, is officially classified as a National Monument. Across the street is the restaurant Iribar (☞ Dining, *below*), for food lovers nearly as important a site as the church and a great place for *besugo a la parrilla* (sea bream roasted over coals).

Zarauz, the next town, is another beauty, with a wide beach and numerous taverns and cafés.

Dining

$$ ✕ **Iribar.** The Iribar has been grilling fish and beef over coals outside the church for more than a half century (no doubt raising havoc at times with the fasting faithful within). While Kaia and Kai-pe, in the port, are also good places to dine, with views of the harbor's colorful fleet of fishing boats, the Iribar's warm family atmosphere makes it the best choice. ☒ *Kale Nagusia 38*, ☎ 943/140406. MC, V.

En Route Heading east toward San Sebastián, you have a choice of the A8 toll road or the coastal N634 highway. The former is a quick and scenic 44 km (27 mi), but the latter will take you through the village of Orio past a few more tempting inns and restaurants, not the least of which is the **Sidrería Ugarte,** in Usurbil.

SAN SEBASTIÁN TO FUENTERRABÍA

Graceful, chic San Sebastián invites you to slow down, stroll the beach for a while, and wander the exquisite streets comprising one of Spain's most famous and enchanting seaside resort towns. For an advance taste of the place, just open Hemingway's *The Sun Also Rises* to the part where Jake repairs to San Sebastián's La Concha beach after a wild San Fermín fest in Pamplona. East of the city, take the launch over to Pasajes de San Juan, from where Lafayette set off to help the colonial forces in the American Revolution. Victor Hugo spent a winter writing here. Just shy of the French border, you'll hit Fuenterrabía, a quaint and colorful port town.

San Sebastián

★ ⑤⑧ *100 km (62 mi) east of Bilbao.*

San Sebastián (Donostia, in Euskera) is a bright and elegant beach town arched around one of the finest urban strands in the world, **La Concha** (The Shell), so named for its almost perfect resemblance to the shape of a scallop shell. The best way to see San Sebastián is simply to walk around: The city is full of promenades and pathways, several leading up the hills that surround it. For a 7-km (4-mi) jaunt you can walk, without crossing a street, from the far end of the Zurriola beach in Gros to the Eduardo Chillida *Peine del Viento* (Wind Comb) sculpture at the western end of Ondarreta beach. Built for the enjoyment of both eye and spirit, San Sebastián is equally treasured for its gifts to the palate, and the only way to eat as much as you are going to want to is to hike and trek vigorously between meals.

The earliest records of San Sebastián date from the 11th century. A backwater for centuries, in 1845 the city had the good fortune to attract Queen Isabella II, who came seeking relief from a skin ailment in the icy Atlantic waters. Isabella was followed by much of the aristocracy of the time, and San Sebastián became a favored summer retreat for Madrid's well-to-do. The city is laid out in a remarkably modern way, with wide streets on a grid pattern, thanks mainly to the 12 different times it has been all but destroyed by fire. The last conflagration came after the French were expelled in 1813; English-Portuguese forces occupied the city, badly abused the population, and proceeded to torch the place. Today, San Sebastián is a seaside resort in a class with Nice and Monte Carlo and becomes one of Spain's more fashionable cities in the summer when French vacationers descend in droves. It is also, like Bilbao, an important cradle of Basque nationalist sentiment.

Nearly dead-center in the middle of the entrance to the bay, the tiny **Isla de Santa Clara** protects the city from Bay of Biscay storms, making La Concha one of the calmest beaches on Spain's entire northern coast. For added drama, a large hill dominates each side of the entrance, and a visit to **Monte Igueldo,** on the western side, is a must. (You can drive up for a toll of 175 ptas./€1.05 per person or take the *funicular*—cable car—for 200 ptas./€1.20 round-trip; it runs 10–8 June–Sept. 11–6 in Oct.–May, with departures every 15 minutes.) From the top, you get the remarkable panorama for which San Sebastián is famous: gardens, parks, wide tree-lined boulevards, Belle Epoque buildings, and, of course, the bay itself.

Every corner of Spain claims its distinctive culinary identity with great pride, but for sheer quality San Sebastián is in a league shared only with Bilbao. Long considered Spain's premier gourmet haven, San Sebastián is famous for its culinary excellence. Many of the city's restaurants—along with the two dozen or so private, all-male eating societies—are in the **Parte Vieja** (old quarter), on the east end of the bay beyond the elegant **Casa Consistorial** (City Hall) and formal **Alderdi Eder** gardens. City Hall began life as a casino in 1887; after gambling was outlawed early in the 20th century, the town council moved here from the **Plaza de la Constitución,** the old quarter's main square, now a hub for the *txikiteo,* the migrant grazing and tippling practiced nowhere with as much joy as here. For a lusty look at where all this provender comes from, don't miss **El Mercado de La Bretxa,** the open market where you might just run into José María Arzak or Pedro Subijana looking for just the right fish or wild mushroom to convert some pre-dawn fantasy into your lunch or dinner. San Sebastián's new concert hall, film society, and convention center, **Kursaal** (⊠ Av. Zurriola s/n, ☎ 943/003000), opened in 1999 to unanimous acclaim. Designed by the world-renowned Spanish architect Rafael Moneo, it is most frequently described as a pair of translucent rocks imbedded in the waterfront at the mouth of the Urumea River. Guided tours, 350 ptas./€2.10, are given daily at 11:30, 12:30, and 1:30.

Just in from the harbor, in the shadow of Monte Urgull, is the lovely Baroque church of **Santa María,** with a stunning carved facade featuring an arrow-riddled sculpture of (who else?) St. Sebastian. The interior is strikingly restful; note the ship above St. Sebastian high on the altar. Looking straight south from the front of the church, you can see the facade and spires of the **Catedral Buen Pastor** (Cathedral of the Good Shepherd) across town.

Museo de San Telmo occupies a 16th-century monastery behind the Parte Vieja to the right of the Santa María church. The former chapel, now a lecture hall, was painted by José María Sert (1876–1945), author of notable works in the Barcelona town hall, Vic Cathedral, London's Tate Gallery, and in New York City's Waldorf Astoria hotel. Sert's paintings here—in his characteristic monochromatic (camaieu) tones of gray, gold, violet, and earthy russets to enhance the sculptural power of his work—portray events from Basque history. Other key items are the discoidal steles used as funeral markers from prehistoric Basque history, ethnographical displays, and paintings by Zuloaga, Ribera, and El Greco. ⊠ *Plaza de Ignacio Zuloaga s/n,* ☎ *943/424970.* 🎟 *Free.* ☉ *Tues.–Sat. 10:30–1:30 and 4–8, Sun. 10:30–2.*

NEED A
BREAK?

Steps from the facade of Santa María, in the heart of the old quarter, the tiny café **Kantoi** (⊠ Calle Mayor 10) is an attractive place to grab a beverage among newspaper-reading young locals. Have a *chocolate con nata*—thick, dark hot chocolate with real whipped cream.

San Sebastián is divided by the **Urumea River,** which is crossed by three bridges inspired by late-19th-century French architecture. At the mouth of the Urumea, the incoming surf smashes the rocks with such force that white foam erupts to photogenic heights, and the noise is transfixing. From the far (northeastern) end of the Zurriola beach, red-and-white paint markings (indicative of long-distance hiking trails) will guide you three hours along the cliffs over the Bay of Biscay along ancient *calzadas* (paved tracks) thought to be either Roman or of the same epoch (1–4th centuries AD). This was the ancient coastal Camino de Santiago (Route of St. James) and will take you to the lighthouse at the mouth of the *pasajes* (straits) that lead into the industrial port at Renteria. From there you can walk in to Pasajes de San Pedro and take the tiny launch over the much-photographed Pasajes de San Juan (☞ *below*) for lunch at any one of several excellent restaurants.

OFF THE
BEATEN PATH

Chillida-Leku – Set in the Jauregui neighborhood of Hernani just 10 minutes south of San Sebastián, the recently opened Eduardo Chillida Sculpture Garden and Museum, is a must visit for those interested in contemporary art. Spain's most famous living artist, Chillida—the abstract sculptor whose Peine del Viento (Wind Comb) overlooks the San Sebastián harbor and whose work is found throughout Spain and the world—presents a comprehensive selection of his sculptures fetchingly displayed in a restored 16th-century Basque caserío farmhouse, and scheduled to change constantly as the artist completes and shows new pieces. ⊠ *Caserío Zabalaga, Barrio Jauregui 66,* ☎ *943/336006.* 🎟 *850 ptas./€5.11.* ☉ *Daily 10:30–2:00. Closed Tues.* ✍

Dining and Lodging

$$$$ ✕ **Akelarre.** This restaurant is on the slopes of Monte Igueldo, with spectacular views of both the bay and the city. Chef Pedro Subijana is known for top-level cuisine in every dish from lowly alubias to musky truffles, but look for his *lubina a la pimienta verde* (sea bass with green pepper) and such Basque classics as *calamares en su tinta* (squid in a sauce of its own ink). ⊠ *Barrio de Igueldo,* ☎ *943/212052 or 943/214086. Reservations essential. AE, DC, MC, V. Closed Mon., 1st 2 wks of June, and Dec. No dinner Sun.*

$$$$ ✕ **Arzak.** Renowned chef Juan Marí Arzak's intimate cottage on the
★ outskirts of San Sebastián toward Fuenterrabía is internationally famous, so reserve well in advance. The entire menu is a wonder, with traditional Basque preparations and more recent innovations. The pastries are supremely light and excellent. Prices are, of course, high, but no one who's ever dined here has been heard to question the price-to-value ratio. ⊠ *Alto de Miracruz 2,* ☎ *943/285593 or 943/278465. Reservations essential. AE, DC, MC, V. Closed Mon., last 2 wks of June, and 2 wks in Nov. No dinner Sun.*

$$$$ ✕ **Martín Berasategui.** This famous out-of-town gourmet sanctuary has
★ become even more prestigious since Martín Berasategui became the chef at the Bilbao Guggenheim as well. In fact, Berasategui's partner Bixente Arrieta runs the Guggenheim kitchen, so except for during gala events, you can count on the varsity chef's being in Lasarte. Home of San Sebastián's racetrack, Lasarte is 8 km (5 mi) south of town, an easy outing during the spring and summer racing season. Everything Berasategui serves or suggests is excellent, but one sure bet is the *lubina asada con jugo de habas, vainas, cebolletas, y tallarines de chipirón* (roast lubina with juice of fava beans, green beans, baby onions, and cuttlefish shavings). ⊠ *Loidi Kalea 4, Lasarte,* ☎ *943/366471. AE, DC, MC, V. Closed Mon. and mid-Dec.–mid-Jan. No lunch Sat., no dinner Sun.*

$$$–$$$$ ✕ **Urepel.** Both the cuisine and the interior design balance classic and contemporary elements in a felicitous way here. The *chicharro al escama dorada* (a skinned, deboned mackerel served under a layer of golden-brown sliced potatoes) is a typical Urepel invention. There is no head chef; the kitchen staff works as a team, in prototypically Basque egalitarian fashion. ⊠ *Paseo de Salamanca 3,* ☎ *943/424040. AE, DC, MC, V. Closed Sun. No dinner Tues.*

$$$ ✕ **Panier Fleuri.** One of the most select wine lists in Spain compliments the food here. Both are served in a sober dining room overlooking the crashing surf at the mouth of the Urumea River. Chef Tatus Fombellida is a winner of Spain's national gastronomy prize, no mean feat. Try his *faisán* (pheasant) or the *supremas de lenguado a la florentina* (sole baked with spinach and served with hollandaise sauce) and for dessert the lemon sorbet with champagne. ⊠ *Paseo de Salamanca 1,* ☎ *943/424205. Reservations essential. AE, DC, MC, V. Closed Wed., last 2 wks of Dec., 3 wks in June, and Christmas wk. No dinner Sun.*

$$ ✕ **Bar Ganbara.** This happening tapas bar near the Plaza de la Constitución has an ample selection of nibbles ranging from shrimp and asparagus to *jamón ibérico* (cured wild Iberian ham) on croissants to anchovies, sea urchins, and wild mushrooms in season. Proper meals are also served, with an emphasis on meats roasted over coals. ⊠ *C. San Jerónimo 21,* ☎ *943/422575. Closed Mon. No dinner Sun.*

$$ ✕ **Sidrería Petritegui.** For hearty dining and a certain amount of splashing around in hard cider, make this short excursion east of San Sebastián. Gigantic wooden barrels line the walls, while tables are piled with *tortilla de bacalao* (codfish omelet), *txuleta de buey* (thick chunks of beef), the smoky local sheep's-milk cheese from Idiazábal up toward the Sierra de Aralar south of Tolosa, and, for dessert, walnuts and *membrillo* (quince jelly). ✉ *Carretera San Sebastián–Hernani, Km 7, Astigarraga,* ☎ *943/457188. No credit cards. No lunch weekdays.*

$ ✕ **Casa Vallés.** Just a two-minute walk from the back of San Sebastián's cathedral, this fine little tapas bar and restaurant displays some 30 to 40 different freshly prepared and irresistible creations at midday and again in the early evening. Beloved by locals, it combines excellent food with great value. ✉ *Reyes Católicos 10,* ☎ *943/452210. AE, DC, MC, V. Closed Wed. and last 2 wks of June.*

$$$$ ⊡ **María Cristina.** The graceful beauty of the Belle Epoque is embodied in San Sebastián's top luxury hotel, which sits like the queen it's named after on the elegant west bank of the Urumea River. The grandeur continues in salons filled with Oriental rugs, potted palms, and Carrara marble columns, and in bedrooms to match. ✉ *Paseo República Argentina s/n, 20004,* ☎ *943/424900,* ℻ *943/423914. 139 rooms. Restaurant, bar, beauty salon, meeting rooms. AE, DC, MC, V.*

$$$ ⊡ **Londres y de Inglaterra.** This stately hotel has a privileged position on the promenade above La Concha. An old-world aesthetic informs the bright, formal lobby and continues throughout the hotel. The bar and restaurant face the bay, and guest rooms with bay views are the best in town. ✉ *Zubieta 2, 20007,* ☎ *943/426989,* ℻ *943/420031. 138 rooms, 7 suites. Restaurant, bar, minibars, casino, meeting rooms, parking. AE, DC, MC, V.*

$$ ⊡ **Aristondo.** This comfortable farmhouse 15 minutes above San Sebastián on Monte Igueldo is a scenic and economical place to stay while in Donosti. ✉ *San Martín 54 bis, 20007,* ☎ *943/215558,* ℻ *943/ 463914. 16 rooms. MC, V.*

$$ ⊡ **Bahía.** A two-minute walk from the beach, this hotel is small but appealing. It has a welcoming lobby, with a friendly minibar and salon, and its rooms are comfortable and modern. ✉ *San Martín 54 bis, 20007,* ☎ *943/469211,* ℻ *943/463914. 60 rooms. Bar. MC, V.*

Nightlife and the Arts

Glitterati arrive in San Sebastián for its **international film festival** in the second half of September (✪). Exact dates vary; ask the tourist office or read the local press for details and ticket information. The late-July **jazz festival** draws many of the world's top performers (✪). Most events for the film and jazz festivals are held in the Hotel Maria Cristina, the Teatro Victoria Eugenia, the Kursaal, and at other theaters around town. There's a varied program of theater, dance, and other events year-round at the beautiful **Teatro Victoria Eugenia** (✉ Reina Regente s/n, ☎ 943/481155 or 943/481160), as well as a complete program of events in the **Kursaal** (☎ 943/003000).

At night, look for *copas, potes* (both "drinks"), and general cruising in and around the **Parte Vieja.** The top disco is **Bataplan** (✉ Paseo de la Concha s/n, ☎ 943/485251) near the western end of La Concha.

Shopping

San Sebastian is nonpareil for stylish home furnishings and clothing. Wander **Calle San Martin** and the surrounding pedestrian-only streets to see what's in the windows. **Ponsol** (✉ C. Narrica 4, ☎ 943/420876) is the best place to buy Basque berets, called *boinas*; the Leclerq family has been hatting Donostiarras for three generations. Stop into **Maitiena** (✉ Avda. Libertad 32, ☎ 943/424721) for a fabulous selection of chocolates.

Pasajes de San Juan

59 *10 km (6 mi) east of San Sebastián.*

General Lafayette set out from Pasajes de San Juan (Pasaia Donibane, in Euskera) to aid the rebels in the American Revolution. There are actually three towns around the commercial port of Rentería: **Pasajes Ancho,** an industrial port; **Pasajes de San Pedro,** a large fishing harbor; and historic **Pasajes de San Juan.** This last is a tiny settlement of 18th- and 19th-century buildings along a single street fronting the bay's outlet to the sea. It's best reached by driving into Pasajes de San Pedro, on the San Sebastián side of the strait, and catching a launch across the mouth of the harbor (about 100 ptas./€0.60, depending on the time of day). The town is known for its three fine restaurants: Txulotxo, Casa Cámara (☞ Dining, *below*), and Artzape.

Dining

$$ ✕ **Casa Cámara.** Four generations ago, Pablo Cámara turned this old
★ fishing wharf on the narrows into a first-class restaurant. The dining room has lovely views and a central tank from which live lobsters and crayfish are hauled up for your inspection. Try *cangrejo del mar* (spider crab with vegetable sauce) or the superb *merluza con salsa verde* (hake in green sauce). ⊠ *Pasajes de San Juan,* ☎ *943/523699 or 943/ 517874. Reservations essential. AE, DC, MC, V. Closed Mon. No dinner Sun.*

Fuenterrabía

60 *12 km (8 mi) east of Pasajes.*

Fuenterrabía (Hondarribia, in Euskera) is the last fishing port before the French border. Lined with fishermen's homes and small fishing boats, the streets and harbor are a lively and colorful spot (almost as if the brightly painted houses were a terrestrial edition of the fishing fleet itself). Try to avoid weekends or holidays, when the place fills with visitors. If you have a taste for history, follow signs up the hill to the medieval bastion and onetime castle of Carlos V, now a national parador.

Dining and Lodging

$$$–$$$$ ✕ **Ramón Roteta.** Set in a beautiful old villa with an informal garden, this restaurant serves excellent food and is an easy choice for anyone staying at the parador. Sample the garlic and shrimp pastries or the rice with vegetables and clams. The pastries are homemade. ⊠ *Villa Ainara, C. Irún 2,* ☎ *943/641693. AE, DC, MC, V. Closed Tues. mid-June–mid-Sept. No dinner Sun.*

$$ ✕ **La Hermandad de Pescadores.** This centrally located "brotherhood" is owned by the local fishermen's guild and serves simple and hearty fare at reasonable prices. Try the *sopa de pescado* (fish soup) or the *almejas a la marinera* (clams in a thick, garlicky sauce). If you come outside peak hours (2–4 and 9–11), you'll find space at the long communal boards. ⊠ *Calle Zuloaga s/n,* ☎ *943/642738. AE, DC, MC, V. Closed Wed. No dinner Tues.*

$$$$ ▥ **Parador El Emperador.** Replete with suits of armor and other chivalric bric-a-brac, this parador occupies a superb medieval bastion that dates from the 10th century and housed Carlos V in the 16th century. Many rooms have gorgeous views of the Bidasoa River and estuary, dotted with colorful fishing boats. Reserve ahead and ask for one of the three "special" rooms, with canopied beds and baronial appointments; they're worth the moderate extra expense. ⊠ *Plaza Armas de Castillo, 20005,* ☎ *943/645500,* ℻ *943/642153. 36 rooms. Bar. AE, DC, MC, V.*

$ ⚏ **Caserío "Artzu."** This family barn and house, with its classic low, wide roofline, has been here in one form or another for some 800 years. Just west of the hermitage of Nuestra Señora de Guadalupe, 5 km (3 mi) above Hondarribia, Artzu offers modernized accommodations in an ancient *caserío* (farmhouse) overlooking the junction of the Bidasoa estuary and the Atlantic. ✉ *Barrio Montaña, 20280,* ☎ *943/ 640530. 6 rooms, 1 with bath. Restaurant. No credit cards.*

OFF THE BEATEN PATH | **Hendaye –** For a quick incursion into neighboring France, take the *navette* (shuttle launch) from Fuenterrabía across the estuary of the Bidasoa River to Hendaye Plage. Following the beach around to the right, connect up with the red-and-white paint markings indicating the trans-Pyrenean GR (Gran Recorrido or, in French, Grande Randonnée) trail and walk two hours up to the colorful mountain village of Biriatou, where, in summer, afternoon pelota games start at 6. From the Hendaye train station, get the local train back to Irún or San Sebastian.

En Route The fastest route from San Sebastián to Pamplona is the A15 Autovía de Navarra, which cuts through the Leizarán Valley and gets you there in about 45 minutes. Somewhat prettier, if slower and more tortuous, is the 134-km (83-mi) drive on C133, which starts out near the French border (and Fuenterrabía) and follows the Bidasoa River (the border with France) up through Vera de Bidasoa. When C133 meets N121 you can turn left up into the lovely Baztán Valley or right through the Velate pass to Pamplona.

NAVARRA

Composed largely of Basque stock, Navarra has always been, literally, a law unto itself, with its own kings, parliament, special rights, and system of taxation. Even granted some degree of autonomy under the Franco regime in return for adhesion to his cause (which the Caudillo's National Movement understood as that of religion, tradition, and the established order), Navarra first became independent in 824 when Basque chieftain Iñigo Aritza was named king of Pamplona, a title later expanded to include all of Navarra. Under Sancho III, who reigned from 1000 to 1035, Navarra reached its greatest power when Sancho married the Princess of Castille and ruled virtually all of Christian Spain. Bounced back and forth, though always as an independent realm, between France and Spain, Navarra didn't fully recognize the Spanish crown until 1839.

Bordering on the French Pyrenees to the north and the Ebro River to the south, Navarra is most Basque in its northern regions and progressively less so closer to its southern and eastern edges. This chapter will explore Pamplona and the southern part of Navarra, leaving the Baztán and Roncal valleys in the Pyrenees chapter (☞ Chapter 4). For a quick probe to the east to the fairy-tale castle at Olite, the route suggested here follows the Santiago de Compostela pilgrim trail through Puente la Reina and Estella and on toward Alava and the Basque capital at Vitoria.

Pamplona

 91 km (56 mi) southeast of San Sebastián.

Pamplona is known the world over for its running of the bulls, made famous by Ernest Hemingway in his 1926 novel *The Sun Also Rises.* The occasion is the festival of San Fermín, July 6–14, when Pamplona's population triples (along with hotel prices) and rooms must be reserved months in advance. Tickets to the bullfights (*corridas*), as opposed to the running (*encierro,* meaning "enclosing"), to which access is free, can be difficult to obtain. Every morning at 8 o'clock sharp a skyrocket is shot off, and the bulls kept overnight in the corrals at the edge of town are run through a series of closed-off streets leading to the bullring, a 902-yard dash. Running before them are Spaniards and foreigners feeling festive enough to risk a goring, most wearing the traditional white shirts and trousers with red neckerchiefs and carrying rolled-up newspapers. If all goes well—no bulls separated from the pack, no mayhem—the bulls arrive in the ring in under three minutes. The degree of peril in the *encierro* is difficult to gauge. Serious injuries occur nearly every day; deaths are rare but always a very real possibility. What's certain are the sense of danger, the mob hysteria, and the exhilaration. For a complete run-down on the technique, history, and legends surrounding Pamplona's main claim to fame, see the Close-Up Box, "Running with the Bulls," *below.*.

Founded by the Roman emperor Pompey as Pompaelo, or Pameiopolis, Pamplona was successively taken by the Franks, the Goths, and the Moors. The Pamplonicas managed to expel the Arabs temporarily in 750, when they put themselves under the protection of Charlemagne. But the foreign commander took advantage of this trust to destroy the city walls, so that when he was driven out once more by the Moors, the Navarrese took their revenge, ambushing and slaughtering the retreating Frankish army as it fled over the Pyrenees through the mountain pass of Roncesvalles in 778. This is the episode depicted in the 11th-century *Song of Roland,* although the French author chose to cast the aggressors as Moors. For centuries after that, Pamplona remained three argumentative towns until they were forcibly incorporated into one city by Carlos III (the Noble, 1387–1425) of Navarre.

Pamplona's **cathedral,** set near the portion of the ancient walls rebuilt in the 17th century, is one of the most important religious buildings in northern Spain thanks to the fragile grace and gabled Gothic arches of its cloister. Inside are the tombs of Carlos III and his wife, marked by an alabaster sculpture. The **Museo Diocesano** (Diocesan Museum) houses religious art from the Middle Ages and the Renaissance. ⊠ *C. Curia s/n.* 🎫 *Free.* ☉ *Cathedral daily; museum Tues.–Sat. 9–2 and 4–7, Sun. 9–2.*

On Calle Santo Domingo, in a 16th-century building once used as a hospital for pilgrims on their way to Santiago de Compostela, is the
★ **Museo de Navarra** (⊠ C. Jaranta s/n, ☎ 948/227831), with a collection of regional archaeological artifacts and historical costumes. The museum is open Tuesday–Saturday 9–2 and 5–7, Sunday 9–2, and admission is 350 ptas./€2.10 Pamplona's most remarkable civic building is the ornate, 18th-century **Ayuntamiento** (City Hall), on the Plaza Consistorial, which over the years has acquired a blackish color that sets off its gilded balconies. Stop in for a look at the wood-and-marble interior.

NEED A
BREAK?
Pamplona's gentry have been flocking to the ornate, French-style **Café Iruña,** in the central Plaza del Castillo, since 1888. The bar and salons are sumptuously paneled in dark wood. Beyond the stand-up bar is a bingo hall (you must be 18 to play). ⊠ *Plaza del Castillo 44,* ☎ *948/ 221801,* ☉ *Daily 5 PM–3 AM.*

One of Pamplona's greatest charms is the warren of small streets near the **Plaza del Castillo** (especially Calle San Nicolás), which are filled with restaurants, taverns, and bars. Pamplonicas are hardy sorts, well known for their eagerness and capacity to eat and drink.

RUNNING WITH THE BULLS

IN *THE SUN ALSO RISES,* Hemingway describes the Pamplona *encierro* (enclosing) in anything but romantic terms. Jake hears the rocket, steps out on his balcony (at La Perla, still available for a bird's eye view of the encierro), and watches the crowd run by: men dressed in the traditional San Fermin white with red sashes and neckerchiefs, those behind running faster, "some stragglers who were really running", then the bulls "running together". A perfect encierro: no bulls separated from the pack, no mayhem. "One man fell, rolled to the gutter, and lay quiet." A textbook move, and first-rate observation and reporting. (If the American killed in 1995 had "lay quiet," the bulls would have run by without a pause; the young man, however, tried to get up and was, as a result, gored to death. An experienced runner remains motionless, as fighting bulls respond only to movement.)

In the next encierro, a man is gored through and through and dies. The waiter at the Iruña café mutters "You hear? Muerto. Dead. He's dead. With a horn through him. All for morning fun. . . . " Despite this, generations of young Americans and other internationals have turned this barnyard bull management maneuver into the western world's most famous rite of passage. The idea is simple: six fighting bulls are guided through the streets by eight to ten *cabestros,* steers, (also known as *mansos,* meaning "tame"). The bulls are herded through the bullring to the holding pens from which they will emerge to be fought that afternoon. The course covers 848 meters in about 3 minutes over terrain of surprising variety. The Cuesta de Santo Domingo down to the corrals is the most dangerous part of the run, high in terror and low in elapsed time. The walls are sheer, and the bulls pass quickly. The fear here is that of a bull, as a result of some personal issue or idiosyncrasy, hooking along the wall of the Military Hospital on his way up the hill, forcing runners out in front of the speeding pack in a classic hammer and anvil movement. Mercaderes is next, cutting left for 104 meters by the town hall, then right up Calle Estafeta. The outside of each turn and the centrifugal force of 10,000 kilos of bulls and steers are to be avoided here.

Calle Estafeta is the bread and butter of the run, the longest (425 meters), straightest and least complicated part of the course. If the classic run, a perfect blend of form and function, is to remain ahead of the horns for as long as possible, fading to the side when overtaken, this is the place to try do it. The trickiest part of running with the bulls is splitting your vision so that with one eye you keep track of the bulls behind you and with the other you keep from falling over runners ahead of you. At the end of Estafeta the course descends left through the *callejón,* the narrow tunnel, into the bullring. The bulls move more slowly here, uncertain of their weak forelegs, allowing runners to stay close and even to touch their horns as they glide through the tunnel. The only uncertainty is whether there will be a *montón,* a pileup, in the tunnel or not. The most dramatic photographs of the encierro have been taken here, as the galloping pack slams through a solid wall of humanity.

Remember that the cardinal crime, punishable by a $1,000 fine, is to attempt to attract the bull, thus removing him from the pack and creating a deadly danger. There have been 13 deaths during this century, the last one on July 13th, 1995 when the 22 year-old American Peter Matthew Tassio was gored at the end of Calle Estafeta, dying almost immediately. "All for morning fun. . . . "

The central **Ciudadela,** an ancient fortress, is a parkland of promenades and pools. Walk through in late afternoon, the time of the *paseo* (traditional stroll), for a taste of everyday life here.

Dining and Lodging

$$$$ ✕ **Josetxo.** This warm, elegant family-run restaurant is one of Pamplona's finest. Specialties include *hojaldre de marisco* (shellfish pastry), *ensalada de langosta* (lobster salad), and *muslo de pichón relleno de trufa y foie*—pigeon stuffed with truffles and foie gras. ⊠ *Príncipe de Viana 1,* ☎ *948/222097. AE, DC, V. Closed Sun. except during San Fermín and Aug.*

$$$ ✕ **Hartza.** Archaic and elegant, this rustic place serves some of the most creative cuisine in Pamplona without omitting any of the hearty fare for which Navarre is known. Try the *oca con jugo de trufa y manzana* (goose with apple and truffles). ⊠ *Juan de Labrit 19,* ☎ *948/224568. AE, DC, MC, V. Closed Mon.; July 30–Aug. 24; and Dec. 24–Jan. 4. No dinner Sun.*

$$ ✕ **Erburu.** In the heart of the nightlife district, this dark, wood-beamed
★ restaurant is a true find, frequented by *pamplonicas* in the know. Come here to dine or just to sample tapas at the bar. Standouts are the Basque classic *merluza con salsa verde* (hake in green sauce) and any of a whole range of dishes made with *alcochofas* (artichokes). ⊠ *San Lorenzo 19–21,* ☎ *948/225169. AE, DC, MC, V. Closed Mon. and last 2 wks of July.*

$ ✕🏨 **Casa Otano.** This friendly, tumultuous hotel and restaurant is simple and well placed, right in the middle of the tapas-and-wine circuit and just a few paces from Pamplona's main square. The restaurant downstairs serves hearty Basque fare. The atmosphere is consistent with the madness that will be raging in the street if you come during San Fermín. ⊠ *San Nicolás 5, 31001,* ☎ *948/225095,* 🅵🅰🆇 *948/212012. 15 rooms. AE, DC, MC, V. Usually closed last 2 wks of July.*

$$$$ 🏨 **Los Tres Reyes.** Named for the three kings of Navarre, Aragón, and Castile—who, it was said, could meet at La Mesa de los Tres Reyes, in the Pyrenees, without stepping out of their respective realms—this modern glass-and-stone refuge operates on the same principle: come to Pamplona and find all the comforts of home. ⊠ *C. de la Taconera s/n, 31001,* ☎ *948/226600,* 🅵🅰🆇 *948/222930. 168 rooms. Restaurant, cafeteria, piano bar, pool, beauty salon, car rental. AE, DC, MC, V.*

$$–$$$$ 🏨 **Yoldi.** This hotel is always teeming with the somewhat snooty foreign *afición*—that is, old-hand bullfight fans. Still, anthropologically they're an interesting lot: knowledgeable-looking Hemingwayoids debating such taurine esoterica as the placement, angle, intent, and aesthetic of the third sword thrust on the second bull in the fifth *corrida* of the fourth *feria* of the last decade. If you're a member of People for the Ethical Treatment of Animals, stay away. ⊠ *Avda. San Ignacio 11, 31002,* ☎ *948/224800,* 🅵🅰🆇 *948/212045. 50 rooms. Bar, cafeteria. AE, DC, MC, V.*

$$–$$$ 🏨 **La Perla.** Hemingway watched his first running of the bulls here, from his balcony over Calle Estafeta. La Perla is the oldest hotel in town, though far from the best. The founder's son was a bullfighter, and the two bulls he killed before retiring preside over the salon. The timeless decor is simple but charming, straight out of *The Sun Also Rises*. Prices shoot up during San Fermín. ⊠ *Plaza del Castillo 1, 31001,* ☎ *948/ 227706,* 🅵🅰🆇 *948/211566. 67 rooms, 45 with bath. AE, DC, MC, V.*

Nightlife and the Arts

Pamplona has a thumping student life year-round. Summer brings a varied summer program of concerts, ballet, and *zarzuela*; contact the **Teatro Gayarre** (⊠ Avda. Carlos III Noble 1, ☎ 948/220139) for information. In August, the **Festivales de Navarra** bring theater and other events.

Shopping

Botas are the wineskins from which Basques typically drink at bull-fights or during fiestas. The art lies in drinking a stream of wine from a bota held at arm's length—without spilling a drop, if you want to maintain your honor (not to mention your shirt). You can buy botas in any Basque town, but Pamplona's **Anel** (⊠ C. Comedías 7) sells the best brand, Las Tres Zetas—"The Three Zs," written as ZZZ.

The **neckerchiefs** (pañuelos) worn for the running of the bulls are sold in various shops, as are *gerrikos*, the wide belts worn by Basque sportsmen during contests of strength, to hold in overstressed organs.

For sweets, try **Salcedo** (⊠ C. Estafeta 37), open since 1800, which invented and still sells almond-based *mantecadas* (powder cakes), as well as *coronillas* (delightful almond-and-cream concoctions). **Hijas de C. Lozano** (⊠ C. Zapatería 11) sells *café y leche* (coffee and milk) toffees that are prized all over Spain.

Olite

★ ⑥² *41 km (25 mi) south of Pamplona.*

Much of Olite is ancient and pleasant to walk through. The 11th-century church of **San Pedro** is interesting for its finely worked Romanesque cloisters and portal. The town's parador is part of a **castle** restored by Carlos III in the French style—a fantasy structure of ramparts, crenellated battlements, and watchtowers. You can walk the ramparts in the section not occupied by the parador. ⌨ *400 ptas./€2.40.* ☉ *Daily 10–2 and 4–5.*

Dining and Lodging

$$ ✕☲ **Parador Príncipe de Viana.** This parador is a series of towers, turrets, battlements, and ramparts, named for the grandson of Carlos III, who spent his life here. It's housed in part of Olite's castle complex, and the chivalric atmosphere is well preserved, with grand salons, secret stairways, heraldic tapestries, and the odd suit of armor. ⊠ *Pl. de los Teobaldos 2, 31390,* ☏ *948/740000,* ꜰꜰꜰ *948/740201. 43 rooms. Restaurant, bar. AE, DC, MC, V.*

Puente la Reina

⑥³ *31 km (19 mi) west of Olite, 24 km (15 mi) south of Pamplona.*

Puente la Reina is an important nexus on the Camino de Santiago: the junction of the two pilgrimage routes from northern Europe, one passing through Somport and Jaca and the other through Roncesvalles and Pamplona. A bronze sculpture of a pilgrim marks the spot. The graceful medieval bridge over the river Arga, one of the most emblematic images on the route, was built for pilgrims by Navarran king Sancho VII el Fuerte (the Strong) in the 11th century. The streets, particularly Calle Mayor, are lined with tiny, ancient houses. The church of **Santiago** (St. James), at the end of Calle Mayor, is known for its gold sculpture of the saint. The **Iglesia del Crucifijo** (Church of the Crucifix) has a notably expressive wooden sculpture of Christ on a Y-shaped cross, gift of a 14th-century pilgrim. Five kilometers (3 miles) east of here, the octagonal church of **Santa María de Eunate** was once used as a burial place for pilgrims who didn't make it. Six kilometers (4 miles) west of Puente la Reina, the church of **San Román,** in the carefully restored village of Cirauqui, has an extraordinarily beautiful carved portal.

Dining and Lodging

$$ **X⛭ Mesón del Peregrino.** A renowned haven for weary pilgrims, this rustic stone house just north of town is hard to pass up. The rooms are small but charming, and the cuisine features roasts, *menestra de verduras* (Navarran vegetable stew), and hearty bean-and-sausage–based soups. ⊠ *Carretera Pamplona–Logroño, Km 23, 31100,* ☎ *948/ 340075,* ⅲ *948/341190. 15 rooms. AE, DC, MC, V.*

Estella

ⓝ *19 km (12 mi) south of Puente la Reina, 48 km (30 mi) north of Logroño.*

Once the seat of the Royal Court of Navarre, Estella (Lizarra, in Euskera) is an inspiring stop on the Camino de Santiago. Its heart is the arcaded Plaza San Martín, its chief civic monument the 12th-century **Palacio de los Reyes de Navarra** (Palace of the Kings of Navarre). The town is laden with churches. The church of **San Pedro de la Rúa** has a beautiful cloister and a stunning carved portal; across the river Ega, the doorway to the church of **San Miguel** has fantastic relief sculptures of St. Michael the Archangel battling a dragon. The **Iglesia del Santo Sepulcro** (Church of the Holy Sepulchre) has a beautiful fluted portal. **Santa María Jus del Castillo,** converted from a synagogue in 1145, is the only vestige of Estella's medieval Jewish quarter. The nearby **Monasterio de Irache** dates from the 10th century but was later converted by Cistercian monks to a pilgrims' hospital. Next door is the famous brass faucet that supplies pilgrims with free-flowing holy wine.

VITORIA AND THE RIOJA ALAVESA

Medieval Vitoria, in the Basque province of Alava, is largely undiscovered by tourists, a stately town with a thousand wood-and-glass galleries tacked onto the facades of buildings. The weathered stone and noble coats of arms emblazoned on the mansions in the old part of town are some of the most impressive in all of Spain, not least for being found in what you would suspect might be an insignificant provincial backwater. The Rioja Alavesa and, in particular, the landlocked walled fortress of Laguardia rank among the Basque Country's most unforgettable destinations. Wine country from stem to stern, the Rioja Alavesa is famous for its full-bodied wines grown south of the Ebro, preferred over the lighter Rioja Alta brews by many wine buffs. The wine-growing towns of San Vicente de la Sonsierra and Elciego are rough and rustic yet emblazoned with the same impressive coats of arms you'll see in Vitoria.

Vitoria

★ ⓝ *93 km (58 mi) west of Pamplona, 115 km (71 mi) southwest of San Sebastián, 64 km (40 mi) southeast of Bilbao.*

Vitoria's standard of living has been rated the highest in Spain, based on such criteria as square yards of green space per inhabitant (14), sports and cultural facilities, and pedestrian-only zones. Capital of the Basque Country and its second-largest city after Bilbao, Vitoria (Gasteiz, in Euskera) is in many ways Euskadi's least Basque city. Neither a maritime nor a mountain enclave, Vitoria occupies the steppelike *meseta de Alava* (Alava plain) and functions as a modern industrial center with a surprisingly medieval Casco Antiguo (old quarter). Founded by Sancho el Sabio (the Wise) in 1181, the city was built largely of gray stone rather than sandstone; so Vitoria's oldest streets and squares from Spanish Middle Ages seem especially weathered, dark, and ancient.

Bordered by noble houses with covered arches and hundreds of white-trimmed glass galleries overlooking the square, the sloping **Plaza de la Virgen Blanca** occupies the southwest corner of old Vitoria. The monument in the center commemorates the Duke of Wellington's defeat of Napoléon's army here in 1813. The **Cafeteria de la Virgen Blanca** at the top left-hand corner of the square, with its giant wooden floorboards, is the spot to restore forces. The **Plaza de España,** just across the square past the monument and the handsome El Victoria café, is an arcaded Neoclassical square with the austere elegance typical of these formal 19th-century squares all over Spain. The **Plaza del Machete,** overlooking Plaza de España, is named for the sword used by medieval nobility to swear allegiance to the local *fueros,* or special autonomous Basque rights and privileges. A jasper niche in the lateral facade of the Gothic church of **San Miguel,** towering over Plaza del Machete, contains the Virgen Blanca (White Virgin), Vitoria's patron saint.

From the Plaza de la Virgen Blanca, Calle de Herrería follows the egg-shape outline left along the west side of the old city walls. Follow it to the **Palacio de los Alava Esquivel,** at the corner of Calle de la Soledad. Continuing north past the **Iglesia de San Pedro Apostol,** look for the house No. 27, across from the Cantón Anorbin, with elaborately sculpted engravings over the door. Don't miss the giant coat of arms on this building's far corner. The 15th-century **Torre de Doña Otxanda,** just before Calle de las Carnicerías, now houses the Museo de Ciencias Naturales (Museum of Natural Sciences). Ahead, in the Plazuela de Santo Domingo, are two more excellent coats of arms.

After turning the corner at the tip of the egg, across from Calle Txikitxoa, the ancient brick-and-wood house at Calle de la Correría 151 is **El Portalón,** a hostelry for 500 years and now an excellent restaurant (☞ *below*) and wine cellar. Across the street, the **Museo de la Arqueología** displays paleolithic dolmens, Roman art and artifacts, an ample inventory of medieval objects, and the famous *stele del jinete* (stele of the horseback rider), an early Basque discoidal tombstone. ⊠ *Calle Correria 116,* ☎ *0945/181922.* 🎫 *Free.* ☉ *Weekdays 10–2 and 4–6:30, Sat. 10–2, Sun. 11–2.*

Having come through Calle Txikitxoa, walk right up the Cantón de Santa María behind the cathedral, noting the tiny additions and accretions that have, over the centuries, been added to the back of Santa María's apse, clinging across corners and filling odd spaces. Walk down the ramplike Cantón Seminario and look carefully at the **ochre house at No. 14** on the corner of Correría and Cantón Apaizgaitegi. The main door nearest the corner has an elaborate coat of arms portraying lions and castles, once painted gold and purple, now faded. Equally faded helicoidal trim spirals around the corners of the house and around the coat of arms, while conch shells appear under scrolls below the windows.

The **Torre de los Hurtado de Anda** is across from the exquisitely sculpted Gothic doorway on the western facade of the **Catedral de Santa María.** Walk into the courtyard on the west side of this square and you'll find a surprising green space with the sculpted head of a fish protruding from the grass in front of an intensely sculpted door at the far right corner of the patio. Halfway down Calle Fray Zacarías Martinez is the 16th-century Renaissance **Palacio de Escoriaza-Esquibel,** with a lovely plateresque facade overlooking an open space. Down toward Plaza del Machete, on the corner of Calle Fray Zacarias Martinez (across from San Miguel), is the austere **Palacio Villa Suso,** built in 1538. Through Plaza del Machete to the left, the first street is Calle Cuchillería. At No. 24 Calle de la Cuchillería is the **Casa del Cordón,** a 15th-century structure with a 13th-century tower, is identifiable by the Franciscan *cordón* (rope) decorating one of the pointed arches on the facade. Farther down Calle Cuchillería, past interesting shops featuring antiques and home furnishings, is the 16th-century Palacio de Vendaña, at No. 58, with its powerfully emblazoned facade, home of the unique **Museo del Naiples "Fournier"** (Playing-Card Museum). The lovely Renaissance stairway inside is impressive, even if playing cards may not completely capture your imagination. ⊠ *Palacio de Vendaña, Calle Cuchilleria 54,* ☎ *0945/1819–20.* 🖾 *Free.* ☉ *Weekdays 10–2 and 4–6:30, Sat. 10–2, Sun. 11–2.*

Near the lush oasis at the **Jardines de la Florida** just south of Plaza de la Virgen Blanca are two museums. The **Museo Provincial de Armería** (Provincial Arms Museum) displays everything from prehistoric hatchets to 20th-century pistols and a sand-table reproduction of the 1813 battle between the Duke of Wellington and the French. ⊠ *Paseo Fray Francisco 3,* ☎ *0945/181925.* 🖾 *Free.* ☉ *Weekdays 10–2 and 4–6:30, Sat. 10–2, Sun. 11–2.* The **Museo de Bellas Artes** (Fine Arts Museum), with its Ribera, Zuloaga, and Picasso paintings, faces the Museo Provincial de Armería on Paseo Fray Francisco de Vitoria just south of the Jardines de la Florida park; the museum is closed for renovation during 2001–02. Next to the Museo de Bellas Artes is the **Ajuria-Enea Palace**, official seat of the Basque Government (no public visiting hours). ⊠ *Museo de Bellas Artes, Paseo Fray Francisco 8,* ☎ *0945/ 181918.*

Dining and Lodging

$$–$$$ ✕ **Asador Matxete.** In an unbeatable location in Vitoria's most historic square, this freshly designed space is built into ancient brick and stone overlooking some of the town's most characteristic wooden galleries stuck miraculously onto medieval stone buildings. The chefs here are specialists in roasts cooked over coals, so this is a perfect place for a taste of the Spanish meseta while still at the edge of the Basque Country. ⊠ *Plaza del Machete 4–5,* ☎ *945/131821. AE, DC, MC, V. No dinner Sun.*

$$–$$$ ✕ **El Portalón.** Between the dark, creaky wood floors and staircases
★ and the ancient beams, pillars, and coats of arms, this famous 15th-century inn seems too good to be true. The Basque touch with products from the Castilian *meseta* is at its best here. Try the *lomo de cebón asado en su jugo con puré de manzanas* (filet mignon with apple puree) or any of the *merluza* (hake) preparations. ⊠ *C. Correría 151,* ☎ *945/142755. AE, DC, MC, V. Closed Sun., Aug. 10–31, and Dec. 23–Jan. 5.*

$$$ ✕🏨 **Canciller Ayala.** This modern structure is handy for in-town comfort, just two minutes from the old quarter over the lush green Parque de la Florida. Rooms are bright, streamlined, and, if unremarkable, well beyond reproach. ⊠ *C. Ramon y Cajal 5, Vitoria 01007,* ☎ *945/130000,* ℻ *945/133505. 184 rooms. Restaurant, bar, parking. AE, DC, MC, V.*

$$$ ✕🏨 **Parador de Argómaniz.** Some 15 minutes east of Vitoria off the
★ N104 road toward Pamplona, this 17th-century palace has panoramic views over the Alava plains and retains a powerful sense of mystery and romance, its long stone hallways punctuated by imposing antiques. Rooms have polished wood floors and huge, terra-cotta-floored bathrooms; some have glass-enclosed sitting areas and/or hot tubs. The wood-beamed dining room on the top (third) floor makes breakfast or any other meal feel like a baronial feast. ⊠ *Carretera N-I, Km 363, Argómaniz 01192,* ☎ *945/293200,* ℻ *945/293287. 54 rooms. Restaurant, bar, free parking. AE, DC, MC, V.*

En Route Between Vitoria and Logroño, on the north bank of the Ebro River, is the wine-growing Rioja Alavesa region. Either sweep comfortably around on the Madrid road and approach from the west via Haro, Briones (where there is a lovely fortified medieval bridge over the Ebro), and San Vicente de la Sonsierra; or drive south on the slower and curvier A2124 through the Puerto de Herrera pass to the Balcón de La Rioja for a sweeping view of the Ebro Valley.

Laguardia

66 *66 km (40 mi) southeast of Vitoria, 17 km (10 mi) west of Logroño.*

Founded by the Navarran king Sancho Abarca in 908 to stand guard, as its name suggests, over Navarra's southwestern flank, Laguardia occupies a lofty promontory overlooking the Ebro River and the vineyards of the **Rioja Alavesa**—La Rioja wine country north of the Ebro in the Basque province of Alava. Flanked by the Sierra de Cantabria, Laguardia rises shiplike, its prow headed north, over the savory sea of surrounding vineyards. Ringed with walls, the dense concentration of emblazoned noble facades and stunning patios within the ramparts is all but without equal in Spain. The wine cellars and taverns of Laguardia are famous for serving excellent local reds, both *vino del año* (young wine of the year) and *crianzas* (aged three years), the full-bodied, delicate yet powerful wines of the south-facing vineyards on the north side of the Ebro.

Everything in Laguardia manages effortlessly and authentically to nourish your eyes, in all some 50 houses with coats of arms and medieval or Renaissance masonry. Starting from the town's 15th-century **Puerta de Carnicerías** or Puerta Nueva, the central portal opening out on the parking area on the east side of town, the first building inside is the original **16th-century town hall,** with its imperial shield of Carlos V. Farther into the square is the present town hall, built in the 19th century. An immediate right down Calle Santa Engracia will take you past a series of impressive facades and doorways. At **No. 25** the floor inside the portal is a lovely stone mosaic, while at **No. 19** a look inside behind the triply emblazoned 17th-century facade will reveal a stagecoach, floor mosaics, beams, and an inner porch (and, if you're lucky, the aroma of a potato-and-leek soup simmering in the kitchen). Nos. 9 and 15 both reveal interesting reliefs and masonry. La **Puerta de Santa Engracia,** with an image of the saint in an overhead niche, opens out to the right, while on the left at the entrance into Calle Víctor Tapia at **No. 17** is a coat of arms with the Latin *laus tibi* ("praise be to thee").

Laguardia's principal architectural gem is next: the unique (Spain's only) Gothic polychrome portal of the church of **Santa María de los Reyes.** The sculpted door, protected by a posterior Renaissance facade, is centered around a lovely and lifelike effigy of La Virgen de los Reyes (Virgin of the Kings), the most beautiful element in the entire tableau, sculpted in the 14th century and painted in the 17th by Juan Francisco de Ribero. Flanking the image of Santa María are the apostles and bibilical scenes.

From the church, swing around the prow of the ship, past the ornate castle and hotel El Collado, to the monument to the famous Laguardia composer of fables, **Felix María Samaniego** (1745–1801), heir to the tradition of Aesop and Lafontaine. Now sweep around through the park along the walls to the **Puerta de Págonos,** walk left past several emblazoned houses to Calle Págonos 13 where the *bodega* (wine cellar) of the **Posada Mayor de Migueloa** is usually in full cry. On your way through the building, don't fail to try a crianza and even a *cazuelita* (small earthenware serving dish) of something bracing like *patatas a la riojana* (potatoes with chorizo sausage) or *pochas con chorizo y cos-*

tilla (beans with sausage and lamb chop). Go through the corridor and you emerge in the Posada's beautiful entryway on Calle Mayor. Walk up to the left to the **Juanjo San Pedro Gallery** at Calle Mayor 1, always filled with interesting antiques and works of art, many of them by Juanjo San Pedro himself.

Other Laguardia sights not to miss include the 13th-century **Puerta de San Juan**, the only portal through the walls that maintains its original design; the oldest civic house in Laguardia at **No. 78** Calle Páganos; the **Panadería Torres** at Calle Félix Maria Samaniego 1 with its local specialties, the Española (a kind of madeleine) and the *hojaldre* (a biscuit); and the house where the fabulist Samaniego was born, at No. 28 Calle Mayor, now the **Estación de Enología** (Oenology Station), a technical laboratory supporting vintners.

Dining and Lodging

$$–$$$ ✕🏨 **Posada Mayor de Migueloa.** With a booming tavern on Calle Páganos (No. 38) and a passageway leading through to the stunning hotel and restaurant reception area on Mayor de Migueloa, this 17th-century palace deep in the medieval labyrinth of Laguardia has guest rooms with beautiful rough-hewn, original beams overhead. The innovative cooking ranges from beef with foie gras to *mollejas de cordero* (lamb sweetbreads) to *venado en salsa de miel y pomelo* (venison with a sauce of honey and grapefruit). The house *crianza* (wine aged in oak casks and in the bottle for at least three years) is excellent and the service is polished and encyclopedically well informed and helpful. ✉ *Mayor de Migueloa 20, 01300,* ☎ *941/121175,* 🆇 *941/121022. 8 rooms. Restaurant. AE, DC, MC, V. Closed Dec. 20–Jan. 20.*

$$ ✕🏨 **Marixa.** Food aficionados travel great distances to dine in Marixa's lovely restaurant, known for its excellent roasts, views, and value. The heavy, wooden interior is ancient and intimate, and the cuisine is Vasco-Riojano, combining the best of both worlds. Try the *menestra de riojana verduras* (a mixed-vegetable dish) or the *cordero asado a la parrilla* (lamb roasted over coals). The guest rooms are modern, cheery, and carpeted, with views over the medieval walls of Laguardia to the Ebro Valley beyond. ✉ *C. Sancho Abarca 8,* ☎ *941/600165,* 🆇 *941/ 600202. 10 rooms. AE, DC, MC, V. Closed mid-Dec.–mid-Jan.*

$$ ✕🏨 **Hotel Pachico.** This 120-year-old inn with a good and very popular restaurant offers brilliant views over the Sierra de Cantabria and the plains of Navarra to the east from its third-floor terraces. A no-frills but solid hotel with much tradition, this outpost of the Martinez brothers offers reliable service and a touch of what Laguardia is all about: non-pretentious authenticity and charm. ✉ *C. Sancho Abarca 20,* ☎ *941/600009,* 🆇 *941/600005. 24 rooms. AE, DC, MC, V. Closed mid-Dec.–mid-Jan.*

LA RIOJA

A diverse natural compendium of highlands, plains, vineyards, and the Ebro River basin, the producer of Spain's best wines is bordered by Navarra and Alava to the north and by Burgos, Soria, and Aragón to the south and east. The area's quarter of a million inhabitants are concentrated mainly along the Ebro in the cities of Logroño, Haro, and Calahorra, but the true treasures of La Rioja are in its mountains and along its river valleys.

La Rioja's culture and wines both combine Atlantic and Mediterranean influences, as well as Basque overtones and the arid ruggedness of Iberia's central *meseta*. Drained by the Rivers Oja (hence the name *río oja*), Najerilla, Iregua, Leza, and Cidacos, the La Rioja is com-

Close-Up

WATCH OUT, HERE HE COMES AGAIN!

THOUGHT YOU'D SEEN enough titanium for a lifetime? Close your eyes while driving through Elciego (literally, "blind man"), 3 km (2 mi) south of Laguardia, or you're in for a mini-Guggenheim surrounded by tempranillo grapevines. Frank Gehry's second contribution to the Basque Country's architectural patrimony was unveiled (scale model only, for the moment) in June 2000. Herederos del Marqués de Riscal, La Rioja Alavesa's most prestigious vintners, commissioned Gehry to design the new visitor center and headquarters for their vineyards in 1998. (The spokesman for the vineyard alleged that a 1929 vintage, the year of Gehry's birth, provided the decisive moment in the negotiations.)

Gehry's project consists of a building made of the yellow sandstone typical of traditional local architecture, covered with an undulating roof of steel and titanium sheets. The structure will occupy a hill overlooking the vineyard's manor house on the way into Elciego from Cenicero, across the Ebro River in Alava's neighboring community of La Rioja. Santiago Calatrava's building for Laguardia's Bodegas y Bebidas vintners, Rafael Moneo's creation in Oión, and French architect Philippe Mazières' CVNE (Cooperative Vinicola Norte de España) headquarters in Haro complete the four corners of spectacular contemporary architecture sprouting in northern Spain's wine country.

posed of the Rioja Alta (Upper Rioja), the moist and mountainous western end, and the Rioja Baja (Lower Rioja), the flatter and dryer eastern end, more Mediterranean in climate. Logroño, the capital, lies between the two. Occupied successively by Gascons, Romans, Moors, Navarrans, and Castilians, La Rioja was part of the Cantabrian duchy from 573 to 711. Asturian kings reconquered the region in 1023, and in 1076 Alfonso VI incorporated the region into the Crown of Castile. In the 15th and 18th centuries, La Rioja was part of Castile and Navarre and was later divided between the provinces of Burgos and Soria. La Rioja's original boundaries continued to be ignored throughout the 19th century, while petitions for *fueros* (special rights), such as those enjoyed by the Basques, were rejected. Finally, in 1980, the region regained the name La Rioja, and in 1982 it became a full-fledged Autonomous Community.

Logroño

🚲 *92 km (57 mi) southwest of Pamplona on N-III.*

La Rioja's capital is a busy city of 130,000 built over and around the Ebro River. A modern industrial center, Logroño has a lovely old quarter between its two bridges, bordered by the Ebro and the medieval walls. Breton de los Herreros and Muro Francisco de la Mata are the quarter's most characteristic streets, and La Rioja's four best religious structures are its dominant landmarks.

The 11th-century church of the **Imperial de Santa María del Palacio** is known as La Aguja (The Needle) for its pyramid-shape, 45-yard Romanesque-Gothic tower. The church of **Santiago el Real** (Royal St. James), reconstructed in the 16th century, is noted for its equestrian statue of the saint (also known as Santiago Matamoros—St. James the Moorslayer), which presides over the main door.

San Bartolomé is a 13th- to 14th-century French-Gothic church with an 11th-century Mudejar tower and an elaborately sculpted 14th-century Gothic doorway. The **Catedral de La Redonda** is a landmark for its twin Baroque towers.

Many of Logroño's monuments, such as the elegant **Puente de Piedra** (Stone Bridge), were built as part of the Camino de Santiago pilgrimage route. The **Puerta del Revellín,** the **Palacio del Espartero,** and the **medieval walls** are worth tracking down.

Near Logroño, the **Roman bridge** and the *mirador* (lookout) at **Viguera** are the main sights in the lower Iregua Valley. The **Castillo de Clavijo,** another panoramic spot, is where Spain's patron saint, Santiago (St. James), mounted on a white stallion, is believed to have helped the Christians defeat the Moors. The **Leza del Río Leza,** also known as the Cañón del Leza (Canyon of the Leza River), not far away, is La Rioja's most dramatic canyon.

An important wine-tasting and tapa-sampling center, **Calle Laurel** and the neighboring streets including Travesía del Laurel, Calle de San Juan, and Travesía de San Juan are collectively known as *el sendero de los elefantes* (the path of the elephants), an allusion to *trompas* (trunks), the Spanish expression for having a snootful. Each bar here is known for a specialty: Bar Soriano for its *"champis"* (*champiñones,* or mushrooms); Blanco y Negro for its *sepia* (cuttlefish); Casa Lucio for *migas de pastor* (bread crumbs with garlic and chorizo) or *embuchados* (crisped, sliced lamb tripe); or La Travesía for *tortilla de patatas* (potato omelet). Order a crianza and they'll break out the good glasses. A *cosechero* (wine of the year) is served in small shot glasses, while a *reserva* (specially selected grapes aged three years or more in oak and bottle) will elicit the snifters for proper swirling, smelling, and tasting.

Dining and Lodging

$$–$$$ ✕ **El Asador de Aranda.** The Castilian look and feel of this rustic place will remind you of the country inns and roadhouses of the meseta and how it must have felt to crowd in around a roast and a fire after a day at the reins of a stagecoach crossing from Barcelona to Madrid. Roast lamb is the specialty here, but *aluvias* (kidney beans) and *migas de pastor* (bread crumbs, garlic, sausage) will also be difficult to resist. ✉ *Republica Argentina 8,* ☎ *941/208125. AE, DC, V. No dinner Sun.*

$$ ✕ **El Cachetero.** Local dishes based on vegetables are the rule here, with roasts of goat and lamb also featured prominently. The cuisine is simple and homespun, and the raw materials are well known for freshness and seasonal relevance. ✉ *C. Laurel 3,* ☎ *941/228463. AE, DC, V. Closed Sun. and 1st 2 wks of Aug. No dinner Wed.*

$$$ ✕🏨 **Herencia Rioja.** This modern hotel near the old quarter has bright and comfortable rooms, a healthy buzz about it, and a fine restaurant. ✉ *Marqués de Murrieta 1, 26005,* ☎ *941/210222,* 🖷 *941/210206. 81 rooms, 2 suites. Restaurant, bar, cafeteria, exercise room. AE, DC, MC, V.*

$$$ ✕🏨 **Marqués de Vallejo.** A small but impeccable operation nicely positioned not far from the cathedral, this friendly family-run hotel is close to but not right in the middle of the tapa- and wine-tasting frenzy of Calle del Laurel. Nearby Plaza del Espolón has a subterranean parking lot where you can stash your vehicle. Rooms are small but clean and intimate, and Logroño's best features, from the Puente de Piedra (stone bridge) to the Baroque door of Santiago el Real, are all two steps from the hotel. ⊠ *Marqués de Vallejo 8, 26005,* ☎ *941/248333,* FAX *941/240288. 30 rooms. Bar, cafeteria. AE, DC, MC, V.*

La Rioja Alta

The Upper Rioja, the most prosperous part of the wine country, extends from the Ebro River to the Sierra de la Demanda. La Rioja Alta has the most fertile soil, the best vineyards and agriculture, the most impressive castles and monasteries, a ski resort at Ezcaray, and the historical economic advantage of being on the Camino de Santiago.

From Logroño drive 12 km (7 mi) west on route N120 to **Navarrete** to see its noble houses and the Baroque altarpiece in the Asunción church.

⓺ **Nájera,** 15 km (9 mi) west, was the court of the Kings of Navarre and capital of Navarre and La Rioja until 1076, when La Rioja became part of Castile and the residence of the Castilian royal family. The monastery of **Santa María la Real** (☎ 941/363650), "pantheon of kings," is distinguished by its 11th-century Claustro de los Caballeros (Cavaliers' Cloister), a Gothic nobles' cloister with lacy plateresque windows overlooking a grassy patio. The sculpted 12th-century tomb of Doña Blanca de Navarra is the monastery's most famous sarcophagus. For a walk through Nájera's best treasures, cross the bridge over the Najerilla (looking for trout if the water's clear: this is a no-kill section on what is arguably the best trout stream in Europe) into the old part of town and take the first left on Calle Mayor. Walk past the no-longer-functioning movie theater and concert hall with its fading painted facade and continue down to Santa María la Real with its silo-like corner turrets and *mozarabe* elements.**Santo Domingo de la Calzada,** 20 km (12 mi) west of Santa María la Real on N120, has always been a key stop on the Camino. Santo Domingo was an 11th-century saint who built roads and bridges for pilgrims and founded the pilgrims' hospital that is now the town's parador. The cathedral is a Romanesque-Gothic pile containing the saint's tomb, choir murals, and an elaborate walnut altarpiece carved by Damià Forment in 1541. The live hen and rooster in a plateresque stone chicken coop commemorate a legendary local miracle in which a pair of roasted fowl came back to life to protest the innocence of a pilgrim hanged for theft. Don't miss a stroll through the town's beautifully preserved medieval quarter.

Enter the **Sierra de la Demanda** by heading south 14 km (8½ mi) on LO-810. Your first stop is the town of **Ezcaray,** with its aristocratic houses emblazoned with family crests, of which the **Palacio del Conde de Torremúzquiz** (Palace of the Count of Torremúzquiz) is the most distinguished. Good excursions from here are the Valdezcaray winter-sports center; the source of the River Oja at Llano de la Casa; La Rioja's highest point, at the 7,494-ft Pico de San Lorenzo; and the Romanesque church of Tres Fuentes, at Valgañón.

The town of **San Millán de la Cogolla** is southeast of Santo Domingo de la Calzada. Take LO-809 southeast through Berceo to the Monasterio de Yuso, where a 10th-century manuscript on St. Augustine's *Glosas Emilianenses* is considered the first writing in Castilian Spanish. The nearby Visigothic Monasterio de Suso is where Gonzalo de Berceo, recognized as the first Castilian poet, recited his verse in the 13th century in *román paladino,* the Latin dialect that became the Castilian tongue and ultimately the language of more than 150 million people from the Mediterranean to the South China Sea.

⑥⑨ Haro, 49 km (30 mi) west of Logroño, is the wine capital of La Rioja. Its architectural highlights are the Flamboyant Gothic church of **Santo Tomás,** a single-nave structure from 1564, and the **Basílica de la Vega,** with a figure of the valley's patron saint, La Virgen de Valvanera. Haro's old quarter and ancient taverns are memorable, as are the cafés in the Plaza Mayor; local wines flow freely here, at local prices. Haro's wine makers have clustered their *bodegas* in the legendary *barrio de la estación* (train-station district) ever since the railroad first opened in 1863. Guided tours of these 100-year-old facilities and tasting sessions, some in English, can be arranged at the *bodegas* themselves or at the tourist office (☞ Close-up: Spain's Wine Country, *below*). The June 29 **Batalla del Vino** (Wine Battle) is a wet and epic brawl.

Dining and Lodging

$$ ✕ **Terete.** A favorite with locals, this rustic place has been roasting lamb in wood ovens since 1877. It has its own wine cellar, stocked with some of the Rioja's best. Try the *minestra de verduras* (vegetable stew). ✉ *C. Lucrecia Arana 17,* ☏ *941/310023. AE, DC, V. Closed Mon., 1st 2 wks of July, and last 2 wks of Aug.*

$$$ ✕🏠 **Hostería del Monasterio de San Millán.** Declared by UNESCO as patrimony of humanity, this magnificent inn occupying a wing of the Monasterio de Yuso (lower monastery) just 2 km (1 mi) from the Monasterio de Suso (upper monastery) is famous as the birthplace of the Castilian Spanish language destined to colonize and Christianize the globe from the Netherlands to the Philippines by the end of the 16th century. Rooms are elegant and somewhat austere, but the comforts are comprehensive and beyond reproach. ✉ *San Agustín 2, 26226,* ☏ *941/373277,* 🖷 *941/373266. 22 rooms. Restaurant, bar, cafeteria. AE, DC, MC, V.* ♨

$$$ ✕🏠 **Los Agustinos.** Haro's best hotel is built into a 14th-century monastery whose cloister (now a pleasant patio) is considered one of the best in La Rioja. Arches, a great hall, and tapestries complete the medieval look. ✉ *San Agustín 2, 26200,* ☏ *941/311308,* 🖷 *941/ 303148. 60 rooms. Restaurant, bar, cafeteria. AE, DC, MC, V*

La Rioja Baja

La Rioja's eastern area is more Mediterranean than Atlantic or Castilian in climate and vegetation, bordering the plains of Navarre, Soria, and Aragón. Its main river, the Cidacos, joins the Ebro at Calahorra (population 20,000), the region's largest city.

Lower Rioja has a number of key sights, including **Alfaro**'s medieval houses and church of San Miguel; **Arnedo**'s Monasterio de Vico; **Cornago**'s castle, with its four towers (three conical, one rectangular); **Igea**'s Palacio del Marqués de Casa Torre; and **Enciso**'s Parque Jurásico (Jurassic Park), with dinosaur tracks 150 million years old. Ten kilometers (6 miles) from Calahorra, there are castle ruins at **Quel. Autol** is the site of rock formations known as El Picuezo y La Picueza (roughly, Mr. and Mrs. Rockpile) for their resemblance to man and wife.

Calahorra

⑦⓪ *46 km (27½ mi) southeast of Logroño, 109 km (65½ mi) northwest of Zaragoza.*

The birthplace of Roman orator and rhetorician Quintilian (teacher of Tacitus), Calahorra was founded by the Romans 2,000 years ago. You can explore the town's Roman and medieval remains by following the tour posted near Calahorra's **Ayuntamiento** (Town Hall)—it covers the Quintilian monument, the Jewish quarter, and the medieval

LA RIOJA: WINE COUNTRY

THE EBRO RIVER basin has been an ideal habitat for grapevines since pre-Roman times. Rioja wines were first recognized in official documents in 1102, and exports to Europe flourished over the next several centuries. The phylloxera blight that ruined French vineyards in 1863 brought Spain both the expertise of Bordeaux vintners and an explosion in the demand for Spanish wine.

With its rich and uneroded soil, river microclimates, ocean moisture, and sun, La Rioja is ideally endowed for high-quality grapes. Shielded from the arid cold of the Iberian *meseta* (plain) by the Sierra de la Demanda and from the bitter Atlantic weather by the Sierra de Cantabria, Spain's prime wine country covers an area 150 km (93 mi) long and 50 km (31 mi) wide along the banks of the Ebro. The lighter limestone soils of the Rioja Alta (Upper Rioja)'s 50,000 acres produce the region's finest wines; the vineyards in the 44,000-acre Rioja Baja (Lower Rioja) are composed of alluvial and flood-plain clay in a warmer climate, ideal for the production of great volume.

The main grape of the Upper Rioja is the Tempranillo—so named for its early (*temprano*) ripening in mid-September—a dark, thick-skinned grape known for power, stability, and fragrance. Other varieties include the Mazuelo, used for longevity and tannin; and the Graciano, which lends aroma and freshness and makes high-quality wine. The Garnacha, the main grape of the Lower Rioja, is an ideal complement to the more acidic Tempranillo. The Viura, the principal white variety, is fresh and fragrant, often grown in the same vineyards with tempranillo and added to reds for acidity and freshness. Malvasía grapes stabilize wines that will age in oak barrels.

Rioja wines are categorized according to age. Garantía de Origen is the lowest rank, assuring that the wine comes from where it purports to come from and has been aged for at least a year. A Crianza wine has aged at least three years, with at least one spent in oak. A Reserva is a more carefully selected wine also aged three years, at least one in oak. Gran Reserva is the top category, reserved for extraordinary harvests aged for at least two years in oak and three in the bottle. Traditional Rioja wines are distinguished by the fact that most of it ages for a significant length of time in barrels made of old American oak, which is more porous, causing faster oxidation of the wine, which means more de facto aging in less time. Thus the traditional Rioja is deeper and smoother, oakier, whereas the new Riojas such as Roda or Reserva 904 spend less time in oak and consequently have a more complex structure with tastes of spices, flowers, and red fruits allowed to develop without being overpowered by heavy overtones of oak.

Wine and ritual overlap everywhere in La Rioja. The first wine of the year is offered to and blessed by the Virgin de la Valvanera on the Espolón de Logroño. Everything from the harvest and the trimming of the vines to the digging of fermentation pools and the making of baskets, barrels, and *botas* (wine skins)—even the glassblowing craft employed in bottle manufacture—takes on a magical, almost religious significance here in this hallowed Bacchian haven.

For a tour of vineyards and wine cellars, start with **Haro,** filled with both world-famous *bodegas* (wineries) and stunning noble architecture. Haro's *barrio de la estación* has all of La Rioja's oldest and most famous bodegas. Call the **Carlos Serres** winery (✉ San Agustín s/n, ☎ 941/311308) for a tour of the process. The **Muga** *bodega* (☎ 941/310498) welcomes tasters at just about any hour. Other visits in the Upper Rioja could include **Fuenmayor,** an historic wine-making center with a lovely old quarter; **Cenicero,** with several ancient bodegas; **Briones,** a perfectly preserved Renaissance town; **Ollauri,** home to a lovely cave bodega, "the Sistine chapel of the Rioja"; and **Briñas,** with a wine exhibit.

quarter along with the churches of San Andrés, Santiago, and San Celedonio. Ask for a map inside.

Calahorra's most important artistic and architectural riches are in the 12th-century **Catedral de Santa María,** on the site of what has been the regional bishopric since the 5th century. The building was restored in 1485 and completed in the 16th century. The choir is decorated with an intricately ornate screen; the Gothic side chapels and their altarpieces are spectacular; and the chapter room has sculpted alabaster saints as well as a Titian and a Zurbarán. The sacristy has a 15th-century monstrance known as El Ciprés (The Cypress), wrought in gold and silver. The **Museo Diocesano** (Diocesan Museum) displays Calahorra's finest art free of charge after the convent masses, until 1:30 PM; paid visits can be arranged by calling the museum's director, Don Angel Ortega (☎ 941/130098).

Dining and Lodging
$$ ✕ **La Taberna de la Cuarta Esquina.** This simple provincial tavern exemplifies the best of Spain: extraordinarily good and unpretentious food and service. Have a hearty roast or a *menestra de verduras* (vegetable stew). ⊠ *Cuatro Esquinas 16,* ☎ *941/310023. AE, DC, V. Closed Tues. and last 2 wks of July.*

$$$ ✕🏨 **Parador de Calahorra.** Calahorra's comfortable parador is the best place to spend a night in La Rioja's second city. The wooden, Castilian-style decor is elegant, and the restaurant serves typical Rioja home cooking, with a focus on roasts and fresh vegetables. ⊠ *Paseo Mercadal, 26500,* ☎ *941/130358,* 🕿 *941/135139. 60 rooms. Restaurant, bar, cafeteria. AE, DC, MC, V.*

The Sierra–La Rioja Highlands

71 The rivers forming the seven main valleys of the Ebro basin originate in the Sierra de la Demanda, Sierra de Cameros, and Sierra de Alcarama. These highlands have a character all their own.

The upper **Najerilla Valley** is La Rioja's mountain sanctuary and wildest corner, an excellent hunting and fishing preserve. The Najerilla River is a rich, weed-choked chalk stream and one of Spain's best trout rivers. The **Monasterio de Valvanera,** off C113 near Anguiano, is the sanctuary of the Virgen de la Valvanera, a 12th-century Romanesque-Byzantine wood carving of La Rioja's favorite icon, the Virgin and child. **Anguiano** is renowned for its Danza de los Zancos (Dance of the Stilts), held July 22, when dancers on wooden stilts run downhill into the arms of the crowd in the main square. At the valley's highest point are the Mansilla reservoir and the Romanesque **Ermita de San Cristóbal** (Hermitage of St. Christopher).

The upper **Iregua Valley,** off N111, has the prehistoric **Gruta de la Paz** caves at Ortigosa. The reservoir at **El Rasillo** is La Rioja's center for aquatic sports. **Villoslada del Cameros** is famous for its artisans, who make the region's traditional patchwork quilts, *almazuelas.* Climb to **Pico Cebollera** for a superb view of the valley. Work back toward the Ebro along the River Leza, through Laguna de Cameros and San Román de Cameros (known for its basket weavers), to complete a tour of the Sierra del Cameros.

The upper **Cidacos Valley** leads to the **Parque Jurásico** (Jurassic Park) at Enciso, famous for its dinosaur tracks. The upper Alhama Valley's main village is **Cervera del Río Alhama,** a center for handmade *alpargatas* (rope-sole shoes). Jews, Moors, and Christians lived here in harmony as long as 400 years after the Reconquest.

Dining and Lodging

$$ ✕🛏 **Venta de Goyo.** This cheery spot across from the mouth of the Urbión River at its junction with the Najerilla has wood-trimmed bedrooms with checkered bedspreads and an excellent restaurant where you can order game of different kinds or *alubias coloradas de Anguiano,* the small fava beans for which neighboring Anguiano is famous. A favorite of anglers and hunters in season, this cozy spot is like a private hunting lodge open to the public, the best of both worlds. ✉ *Crtra. LR-113, Km 24.6, Viniegra de Abajo 26323,* ☎ *941/378007,* FAX *941/ 378048. 22 rooms. Restaurant, bar, cafeteria. AE, DC, MC, V.*

$ ✕🛏 **Hospedería Nuestra Señora de Valvanera.** Built into the former monks' quarters of this 16th-century monastery built over a pre-Romanesque, 9th-century hermitage, this mountaintop hideaway tucked under La Rioja's highest peak, the 7,494-ft San Lorenzo, is an ideal base camp for hiking and getting well away from it all. The 12th-century Romanesque-Byzantine wood carving of the Virgen de Valvanera (Virgen of Valvanera) in the church is the object of the annual overnight 65 km (40 mi) pilgrimage from Logroño to the monastery every October 15 in celebration of the harvest home. Considered the ultimate power in the climate so crucial to the development of the all-important La Rioja grape harvest, La Virgen de la Valvanera is portrayed with a pomegranate symbolizing fertility and surrounded by grape vines. ✉ *Carretera LR-113, Km 24.6, Viniegra de Abajo 26323,* ☎ *941/377044,* FAX *941/ 377044. 28 rooms. Restaurant, cafeteria. AE, DC, MC, V.*

BILBAO, THE BASQUE COUNTRY, NAVARRA, AND LA RIOJA A TO Z

Arriving and Departing

By Boat

Santander is linked year-round to Plymouth, England, by a twice-weekly car ferry. For information, contact **Brittany Ferries** in Santander (✉ Paseo de Pereda 27, Santander 39002, ☎ 942/220000 or 942/214500) or Plymouth (✉ Millbay Docks, Plymouth PL1 3EW, U.K., ☎ 0990/360360), or travel agencies in either country. Book at least six weeks in advance in summer, as the 24-hour passages are often sold out. Another such option is the twice-weekly ferry between Bilbao and Portsmouth; contact **Ferries Golfo de Vizcaya** (✉ Cosme Etxevarrieta 1, Bilbao 48009, ☎ 94/423–4477, FAX 94/423–5496).

By Bus

Daily bus service connects the major cities to Madrid. San Sebastián and Bilbao are especially well served. In Madrid, call the bus company **Continental Auto** for information (☎ 91/533–0400), or go right to the station at Calle Alenza 20.

By Car

Driving is the best way to see this part of Spain. Barcelona and Bilbao are under six hours apart by highspeed motorway. Bilbao and San Sebastián are an hour apart; Vitoria and Bilbao, 40 minutes; Bilbao and Pamplona, 80 minutes; Bilbao and Logroño, 80 minutes.

By Plane

Sondika Airport (☎ 94/486–9301) is 11 km (7 mi) outside Bilbao. Iberia has regular connections from there to Madrid, Barcelona, France, and England. Smaller airports serve Santander, San Sebastián (at Fuenterrabía), Vitoria, and Pamplona, with less-frequent (twice-daily) service to Madrid and Barcelona.

By Train

Bilbao, San Sebastián, Pamplona, Vitoria, and Logroño are well served between each other and by direct trains from Barcelona's Sants station, Madrid's Chamartín Station and, with a change or two, by trains from virtually every major city in Spain. Call **RENFE** for information (☎ 902/24–0202).

Getting Around

By Bus

Bus service between the main cities and most smaller towns is comprehensive. Most have various bus companies leaving from different points in town. Ask at travel agencies, local tourist offices, or the following central bus stations: **Bilbao** (⊠ Gurtubay 1, ☎ 94/439–5205). **San Sebastián** (⊠ Sancho el Sabio 33, ☎ 943/463974). **Pamplona** (⊠ Calle Conde Oliveto 8, ☎ 948/223854). **Logroño** (⊠ Avda. España 1, ☎ 941/235983). **Vitoria** (⊠ Calle de los Herrán 27, ☎ 945/258400).

By Car

This pocket of Spain is superbly covered by freeways. Because rural landscapes and small towns are some of the main attractions, a car is the ideal mode of transportation. Some distances within the area: Santander–Bilbao, 107 km (66 mi); Bilbao–San Sebastián, 100 km (62 mi); San Sebastián–Pamplona, 91 km (56 mi); and Pamplona–Logroño, 92 km (57 mi).

By Train

Trains are not the ideal way to travel this region, but many cities are connected by rail. The principal train stations: **Bilbao** (⊠ Estación del Abando, C. Hurtado de Amezaga, ☎ 94/423–8623 or 94/423–8636). **San Sebastián** (⊠ Estación de Atotxa, Avda. de Francia s/n, ☎ 943/283089 or 943/283599; ⊠ RENFE office, C. Camino 1, ☎ 943/426430). **Pamplona** (⊠ On road to San Sebastián, ☎ 948/130202). **Logroño** (⊠ Pl. de Europa, ☎ 941/240202).

In addition, the regional train company **FEVE** (⊠ Estación de FEVE, next to Estación de Abando, Bilbao, ☎ 94/423–2266) runs a delightful narrow-gauge train that winds through stunning landscapes. From San Sebastián, lines west to Bilbao and east to Hendaye depart from the **Estación de Amara** (⊠ Pl. Easo 9, ☎ 943/450131 or 943/471852).

Contacts and Resources

Consulates

United Kingdom (⊠ C. Alameda Urquijo 2, 8th floor, Bilbao, ☎ 94/415–7600 or 94/415–7722).

Emergencies

Policia (Police): ☎ 092. **Bilbao Urgencias/Ambulance:** ☎ 94/410–0000. **Bilbao Hospital:** ☎ 94/441–8800.**Fire:** ☎ 080. **Emergency:** ☎ 112.

Guided Tours

Bilbao Paso a Paso (⊠ Cocherito de Bilbao 20, Ofic. 5, ☎ 94/473–0078, FAX 94/412–2633). Travel agents and tourist offices in the major cities can suggest tours offered by local firms, guides, and interpreters.

Jai-Alai

The best local *frontón,* from which the finest players depart for Miami and other jai-alai centers in the United States, is **Guernica Jai-Alai** (⊠ Calle Carlos Gangoiti 14, ☎ 94/625–6250); games are held on Mondays at 5 PM. **Durango Ezkurdi Jai Alai** (⊠ Plaza Ezkurdi s/n, ☎ no phone; call central Jai-Alai information, 94/625–6250) holds pelota and cesta punta matches all year on Mondays at 5 PM in Durango, 20 minutes northeast of Bilbao. **Markina** (✉ El Prado s/n, ☎ no phone; call 94/625–6250), dubbed *"la Universidad de la Pelota"* (Pelota U.) for the number of championship players produced there, is a pelota pilgrimage for enthusiasts. In Pamplona, try **Euskal Jai Berri** (✉ Crtra. N240 km. 6 km (Huarte), ☎ 948/331159); matches on Thursdays and weekends. In San Sebastián, **Galarreta Jai-Alai** ✉ Barrio Jauregui s/n, Hernani, Crtra. N240, km 3, ☎ 943/551023) is the place; matches on Thursdays and weekends.

Visitor Information

General information and pamphlets on all three Basque provinces (Alava, Vizcaya, and Guipúzcoa) are available at the Basque government building in **Vitoria** (✉ Parque de la Florida, ☎ 945/131321) and the tourist office in **San Sebastián** (✉ C. Fueros 1, ☎ 943/426282).

In **Bilbao,** the main regional and city tourist office (✉ Paseo de Arenal, ☎ 94/479–5770) is extremely helpful, providing free maps and brochures on the city and the rest of País Vasco. Ask for the Bilbao Guide, a free bimonthly magazine with complete event listings. Bilbao's other tourist office (✉ Avda. Abandoibarra 2, ☎ no phone) is cleverly located just outside the Museo Guggenheim; inside are a model and computer-generated images of what Bilbao will look like in five or six years if all goes well with the Ría 2000 project. There's also another information office in Bilbao's airport.

Other municipal tourist offices: **Fuenterrabia (Hondarribia)** (✉ Javier Ugarte 6, ☎ 941/291260). **Guernica** (✉ Artekale 5, ☎ 94/625–5892). **Guetaria** (✉ Parque Aldamar 2, ☎ 943/140957). **Haro** (✉ Plaza Monseñor Florentino Rodríguez, ☎ 941/303366). **Laguardia** (✉ Sancho Abarca s/n, ☎ 941/600845). **Logroño** (✉ Miguel Villanueva 10, ☎ 941/291260). **Mundaca** (✉ Txorrokopunta 2, ☎ 94/617–7201). **Oñate** (✉ Foruen Enparantza 4, ☎ 943/783453). **Pamplona** (✉ Duque de Ahumada 3, ☎ 948/220741). **San Sebastián** (✉ Reina Regente s/n, ☎ 943/481166). **Vitoria** (✉ Edifício Europa, Avda. Gasteiz, ☎ 945/161598).

6 BACKGROUND AND ESSENTIALS

Gothic to Gaudí:
The Architecture of Barcelona

Books and Videos

Spanish Vocabulary

GOTHIC TO GAUDÍ:
THE ARCHITECTURE OF BARCELONA

"OH HAPPY THE CITY with a mountain beside it, for it can admire itself from on high," extolled 19th-century Barcelona poet Joan Maragall. Anyone who has seen Barcelona from the heights of Tibidabo, with the city all spread out and glittering along the Mediterranean will find it easy to agree. But Barcelona is just as spectacular up close. Like those convex mirrors that reflect, in miniature, a drawing room in all its details, Barcelona's architectural splendors reflect twenty centuries of history. A tour through the city streets will reveal a dizzying array of architectural styles covering 2,000 years of construction from classical Roman, Romanesque, Gothic, Renaissance, Baroque, Neoclassical, Victorian, and Moderniste (Art Nouveau) to the rationalist, minimalist, and post-modern solutions of contemporaries such as Richard Meier, Santiago Calatrava, and Rafael Moneo. There's even a gilt-scaled Frank Gehry goldfish presiding over the Olympic Port, Barcelona's own tiny fragment of Bilbao's famous Guggenheim Museum. (Bilbao has a puppy; Barcelona, a minnow). Indeed, Barcelona owes much of its allure to the diversity of its many styles and esthetics, each of which has its own fervent fans and followers.

Well known for an irrepressible drive for wealth and power, contemporary Barcelona is also dedicated to the creation of a humane urban environment. Whether or not Barcelona put art—that is, painting and sculpture—at the top of its list, the quality and eclat of its architecture and interior design—arts that have a "use"—have always been prime concerns. A business-driven city, Barcelona has historically been as restless for new styles as for commerce. Relentlessly dynamic and chronically in love with novelty, Barcelona has boldly and repeatedly redesigned itself, whether the century was the 2nd, 12th, or 20th. It is no coincidence that the city's most iconic style—Catalan Modernisme—is best known as Art Nouveau. Barcelona's leaders, poets, movers, and shakers were quick to accept the most recent architectural innovations, be they Gothic, Moorish, or Minimalist. Love of the past may be enough in the rest

of Spain—but not in Barcelona. As each age destroyed old relics and demolished historic sectors, they also created new palaces, churches, and monuments, as one adds a chapter to a book. The result is that in Barcelona your eyes are never bored, as you move from the 4th to the 19th century in a few steps. Barcelona's fascination with new solutions and the stylistic vanguard (even the city's main newspaper is appropriately entitled *La Vanguardia*) has been a key factor in the ongoing revitalization that has made it one of the oldest cities in Spain.

If Barcelona can be said to have two sets of architectural opposites encompassing polar extremes of taste and style, the Moderniste Palau de la Música and the minimalist Mies van der Rohe Pavilion would be the secular set, while the liturgical pair might be Gaudí's Art Nouveau interpretation of the Bible, the Temple Expiatori de la Sagrada Família, and the immaculately clean-lined 14th-century early Catalan Gothic basilica of Santa Maria del Mar. Or maybe there are three, including Richard Meier's rationalist Museu d'Art Contemporani de Barcelona and Gaudí's organically rippling-around-the-corner Pedrera apartment block. Or even four, with Arata Isozaki's spacious Palau Sant Jordi stadium and the Romanesque Marcús chapel, a hundred of which could fit inside of Isozaki's gargantuan Olympic sports arena and concert hall. Either way, in between and all around, Barcelona's architectural offering is both vast and varied.

Beginning at the beginning, the still-standing and exposed remnants of Roman Barcelona are scattered around and through the high ground around the cathedral, which stands on early Barcelona's Acropolis-like Mons Taber. From directly in front of the cathedral steps, two cylindrical corner watch towers in Plaça Nova (on the far right) stand next to a section of the 2nd-century AD aqueduct that carried water into Barcelona from the Pyrenees. Perfectly preserved fluted columns are at Carrer Paradis 4, the remains of the 2nd-century Roman Temple of Augustus. Most interesting of all is Carrer Avinyó 19, where you can walk between the 1st-century enclosure and the hastily assembled 4th-century defensive wall, even sensing the emotions of the Roman colonists who put it together in the helter-skelter use of carved stones from other structures in a race to erect the walls before the next wave of Visigoths came over the horizon (☞ see the Close-Up box: Colonia Favencia Julia Augusta Paterna Barcino, *in* Chapter 2).

The pre-Romanesque 12th-century Església de Sant Pau del Camp in the Raval at the end of Carrer de Sant Pau is the next link. With decorative elements in the main door from as far back as the 10th century, Sant Pau del Camp's hulking mastodonic attitude is characteristic of early Romanesque structures and Christianity's (and humanity's) defensive posture as civilization emerged from the Dark Ages. The cloister of Sant Pau del Camp, universally described as an oasis, is a delicious gem: silent, shady, verdant and moist. The little-known 12th-century Església de Santa Anna just off Carrer Santa Anna is Barcelona's other early Romanesque gem, along with two chapels, the barely discernible Capella de Sant Llatzer on Plaça del Pedró and the Capella d'en Marcús at the beginning of Carrer Montcada, both built in the 12th century.

Gothic Barcelona begins with the 14th-century Santa Maria del Mar and ends with the 20th-century neo-Gothic facade of the Catedral de la Seu, the city's main cathedral. Strictly speaking and all posterior restoration, rebuilding, and imitation notwithstanding, Barcelona's Gothic architecture materialized between the 14th and the 16th centuries and is the city's most prevalent style short of 19th-century Catalan Modernisme. The so-called Barri Gòtic, the area around the cathedral, is, along with the Gothic and Renaissance palaces along Carrer de Montcada and Santa Maria del Mar in the Barrio de la Ribera, the main treasury for Barcelona's Gothic structures, with the spiky, soaring cathedral as its most striking example of Flamboyant Gothic. Early or Mediterranean Gothic churches such as Sant Maria del Mar, Santa Maria del Pi, the monastery and church of Santa Maria de Pedralbes, and the Iglesia de Sants Just i Pastor just behind Plaça Sant Jaume are among Barcelona's best examples of early Gothic, while the lateral facades of both the Generalitat and the Ayuntamiento (city hall) remain Gothic even though their main fa-

cades have been covered with the neoclassical symmetry required by mid-18th-century tastes and trends. La Llotja, Barcelona's maritime exchange, is another Gothic gem, especially its Sala Gòtica, or Gothic Hall. The facade suffered reforms, becoming neoclassical between 1794 and 1802. Drassanes, the medieval shipyards, built between the 14th and 17th centuries, is yet another Gothic masterpiece with its tremendous barrel vaults, while the Saló del Tinell in the Palau Reial Major (1370) is another of the Gothic Quarter's best Gothic spaces.

The Renaissance caught Barcelona in a period of political and economic decline, leaving little architecture of note. Still, the Palau del Lloctinent (1557) behind the cathedral and the Italian Renaissance–style main facade of the Generalitat, built in 1596, were erected before Baroque convents and churches began to appear in the early 18th century. Along the Rambla, the Betlem church was completed in 1729, while the churches of La Mercé (1775), Sant Felip Neri (1752), and Sant Miquel del Port (1755) in Barceloneta completed Barcelona's set of not especially lavish or interesting Baroque works.

Neoclassical facades, squares, and buildings became fashionable in Barcelona in the late 18th century after the Rambla was converted into a mid-city promenade by the demolition of the city's second set of ramparts. The Palau Moja and the Palau de la Virreina, facing each other across the Rambla de les Flors, were completed in the late 1770s while the sgraffiti-rich Casa Gremial dels Velers o de la Seda went up in 1763. The demise of the convents along the Rambla led to the construction of the neoclassical Plaça Reial (1848) by Francesc Daniel Molina, who had previously built a similar square in the Plaça de Sant Josep, now the site of the Boqueria market, between 1836 and 1840. (Close inspection will reveal the Doric columns around the edges of the market, now undergoing reforms designed to liberate the original square from the market.) Other neoclassical touches in Barcelona include the facades of the Town Hall and the Llotja and the covered porticoes of the Porxos d'en Xifré (1836) across Marquès d'Argentera from La Llotja.

Neoclassical symmetry and Ildefons Cerda's new post-1860 grid plan for Barcelona's *ensanche* ("widening"; *eixample* in Catalan) set the stage for what was to become Barcelona's signature architectural event, Art Nouveau or *modernisme,* most of which was built in the 20-year period between 1888 and 1908. Excluded by early trade agreements from central, southern, and western Spain's commerce with (plunder of) the New World, Barcelona had developed into a formidable industrial power ranking just after Great Britain, Germany, and Russia by the mid-19th century. Catalonia's prosperity led to a resurgence of Catalan nationalism, all of which received Modernisme like a spark falling into dry tinder. The 1890–93 period of frenzied economic growth popularly known as the *febre d'or* (gold fever) was the high water mark of this ebullient era, resulting in much of the Eixample's moderniste architecture.

Often erroneously described as a "disciple" of the celebrated Antoni Gaudí, Lluís Domènech i Montaner (1850–1924) was, in fact, two years older and Barcelona's earliest pioneer of Art Nouveau architecture. Antoni Gaudí (1852–1926) and José Puig i Cadafalch (1867–1956) complete the triumvirate of the leading Moderniste architects, with Joan Rubió i Bellver (1871–1952), Enric Sagnier i Villavecchia (1858–1931), Jeroni Granell i Manresa (1864–1923), Josep Maria Jujol (1879–1949), and Gaudí's assistant Francesc Berenguer i Mestres (1866–1914) also contributing significantly to the movement. But it was Domènech i Montaner, in 1878 at the age of 28, who published a manifesto exhorting Catalan architects to "search for a national architecture." It was Domènech i Montaner's café and restaurant, the Ciutadella's Castell dels Tres Dragons, built for the 1888 Universal Exhibition, that definitively launched the movement and opened the pandora's box of the Catalan Moderniste imagination. Innovator of the *obra total* (comprehensive workmanship) concept in which architects, painters, glassworkers, ceramicists, and ironworkers all worked together in the Arts and Crafts tradition established by Englishman William Morris, Domènech i Montaner left his works throughout the Eixample, at the Hospital de Santa Pau, and, most famously of all, at the Palau de la Música Catalana.

Barcelona's Moderniste architecture exploded throughout the Eixample and beyond in Gràcia and Sarrià as well. If no architect has ever so thoroughly marked a metropolis as Gaudí has Barcelona, it is also true that no architectural movement, much less one so extravagant and extraordinary, has ever so extensively hijacked a single city. Originally embraced as a "national architecture" exuberantly expressed by the Catalan bourgeoisie, the Modernisme fervor soon began to abate as tastes changed, and by the time of the 1929 Universal Exposition, had become a major municipal embarrassment. In journalist Carlos Soldevila's 1929 guidebook entitled "The Art of Showing Barcelona" he apologizes to the prospective visitor that the city "has suffered the misfortune of building a good part of the Eixample under the influence of the so-called Modernisme." A movement to have the Palau de la Música torn down described what is now hailed as "the flagship of Modernisme" as "a monument to the ostentatious vanity of an era of great hopes and illusions" and proposed, at the very least, radical reforms in the interior. In 1932, a prominent Barcelona art critic suggested that the Town Hall require "all Barcelona owners to eliminate the tribunes, finishes, and artistic facades of their *modern style* facades thus suppressing the trashy ornamentation that fouls the architecture of the building."

As Catalonia's fortunes waxed and waned, so did those of Modernisme. After the Spanish civil war ended in 1939 and Catalonia's 40 years of "internal exile" began, Modernisme, along with other manifestations of Catalonia's cultural identity (such as the right to publish in or even publicly speak the language, or to christen babies with traditional family Catalan names), was suppressed. Many buildings fell to the wrecker's ball, Doménech i Montaner's International Hotel on the Moll de la Fusta among them. Puig i Cadafalch's Casa Llorach and his Casa Trinxet, among others, were demolished; yet others were saved only through popular pressure organized by architects, artists, journalists, and historians. The official aesthetic of the Franco regime fell somewhere between clerical black and white, military olive drab, and the arid and austere buffs and browns of the Castilian meseta that Antonio Machado immortalized in verse. Modernisme, like the work of Joan Miró and Salvador Dalí, touched some playful nerve in the Catalonian sensibility, and as such, it became the official enemy of the state. Even Dalí referred to Art Nouveau as "very creative bad taste" while the now-revered journalist Josep Pla (who once wrote that the Sagrada Família reminded him of "a bunch of immense chicken guts") wrote that the Palau de la Música was "horrible and indescribably ugly" and complained bitterly of having to listen to music "*amb els ulls tancats*"—with his eyes closed.

So it was that throughout the middle part of the 20th century Modernisme was regarded by the rest of Spain and by much of the world at large (and by many Catalans as well) as a manifestation of some quirky and cartoonish tendency in the national *Zeitgeist* better left hidden under layers of soot. Even as late as 1975, the year of Franco's death, Barcelona's Art Nouveau patrimony was regarded warily. Since the democratic transition and the resurgence of Catalan nationalism, Modernisme has been resuscitated as the apex and epitome of all that is most creatively and characteristically Catalan, a curious leapfrogging effect of politics and aesthetics that now appears to have definitively decided in favor of Modernisme.

Barcelona architecture after Art Nouveau stumbled through *Noucentisme* ("ninehundredism"), an attempt to return to a more sober and classical canon, though little of note appeared other than the structures created for the 1929 International Exposition: the Venetian Towers, Poble Espanyol, Olympic Stadium, Fuentes de Montjuïc, and the Palau Nacional, all between Plaça d'Espanya and the top of Montjuïc. The 1929 Exposition did, however, bring one of the century's most important buildings to Barcelona, Miës van der Rohe's Barcelona Pavilion, part of the German Pavilion, a radically new approach to the use of space up to that time. Especially in the context of Moderniste Barcelona's lush urban landscape, "less is more" must have seemed, at the time, next to nothing.

Josep Lluís Sert, a Le Corbusier colleague and disciple, was Barcelona's most important architect during the 1930s, with his Casa Bloc—the first workers' housing south of the Pyrenees—built in the northeastern suburb of San Andreu in 1932 in coordination with the architectural cooperative GATCPAC. Sert went on to build his rationalist Dispensari Antituberculós at Carrer Torres i Amat in 1935, and the Joieria Roca, a jewelry store at the intersection of Gran Via and Passeig de Gràcia. After building the pavilion for the Spanish Republic at the 1937 Paris Exhibition (the same one for which Picasso was commissioned to paint his *Guernica*), Sert's next, final, and most important contribution to the Barcelona cityscape was the Fundació Joan Miró on Montjuïc, built after years of exile to honor his close friend Joan Miró, a bright and luminous series of orderly yet natural spaces.

At the end of the Franco regime in 1975, Barcelona embarked on its award-winning (Harvard's 1990 Prince of Wales Prize) urban renewal project, initially concentrating on filling open spaces with parks or the controversial *plaças duras* ("hard squares"), stark, clean-lined, open spaces such as the Parc Joan Miró and the Parc de l'Espanya Industrial next to Sants railroad station.

The 1992 Olympic Games provided further impetus for Barcelona's renewal. Along with the Rondas, or ring roads, the Villa Olímpica extended Cerdá's grid plan all the way northeast on the Diagonal to the Mediterranean. The Montjuïc Olympic site refurbished the original 1920 Olympic Stadium and constructed Arata Isozaki's colossal Palau Sant Jordi. Elsewhere in Barcelona, American architect Richard Meier's MACBA (Museu d'Árt Contemporani de Barcelona) is splashing light and symmetry into a traditionally dark and steamy neighborhood, while Piñón and Vilaplana's CCCB (Centre de Cultura Contemporani de Barcelona) next door ingeniously restores a medieval convent and adds a glass reflecting wall that seems to pluck Montjuïc and the Mediterranean from outer space miraculously into the patio. Rafael Moneo's rationalist woodpaneled Auditori and Ricardo Bofill's Parthenon-under-glass, the post-neoclassical Teatre Nacional near the eastern end of the Diagonal, along with Norman Foster's Torre de Collserola on Tibidabo and Santiago Calatrava's Torre de Calatrava in the middle of the Olympic Ring on Montjuïc, both of which were controversial, complete Barcelona's set of recent landmarks. Meanwhile the Palau de la Música is shedding, peeling away, the ugly church that some determined citizen attempted to cover it up with during the early

20th century, and the Sagrada Família steams toward a conclusion, some 50 years hence, that will nearly double its height and mass and require the demolition of several apartment buildings to open up an eastern approach to its main facade. Then, as now, it will persevere and continue to fascinate as the most striking element in Barcelona's ever-changing architectural kaleidoscope.

–George Semler

BOOKS AND VIDEOS

Books

Miguel de Cervantes described Barcelona in *Don Quijote de la Mancha* as "archive of courtesy and balm to the weary stranger." That is just one of the most memorable soundbites written about this great metropolis; you'll find many more in an array of books about the city. Pride of place goes to Robert Hughes's somewhat bombastic and personal take on Barcelona in his title of the same name. Colm Toibin's *Homage to Barcelona* is a good and informative read while George Orwell's *Homage to Catalonia* offers a wry and clear-headed account of Barcelona at the beginning of the Spanish Civil War. If you want to read more of our imimitable author, George Semler, he has also written a hands-on, witty, whimsical, and anecdotal tour of his home base, *Barcelonawalks,* which covers five of the city's most historic neighborhoods.

Mercé Rodoreda's moving novel *La Plaça del Diamant,* (translated by the late David Rosenthal as *The Time of the Doves*) begins and ends in Gràcia's square of the same name—a stream of consciousness immersion into the heart and mind of a young woman struggling to survive the Spanish Civil War and, in a greater sense, life's heartbreaks in general. Rodoreda's *My Christina and Other Stories,* also translated by Rosenthal, is a collection of short stories many of which are set in and around Barcelona. Richard Schweid's *Jews, Transvestites, and an Olympic Season,* published in 1994, is a quirky but fascinating look at two of Barcelona's minorities around the time of the 1992 Olympic Games. Barcelona novelist Manuel Vázquez Montalban's *Barcelonas* was translated by Andy Robinson in 1992, a dense and comprehensive take on Barcelona's past and present, while the same author's *Barcelona Fuente a Fuente* (Barcelona, Fountain to Fountain) is a cruise around the city from one neighborhood fountain to the next. *Barcelona Modernista,* by Eduardo and Cristina Mendoza, is an excellent study of the city during its late 19th-century economic and architectural heyday. *Walks in Picasso's Barcelona* by Mary Ellen Jordan Haight cruises much more than the great artist's favorite haunts. The late Nestor Lujan's *20 Segles de Cuina a Barcelona, de les ostres de Barcino als restaurants d'avui* (20 Centuries of Barcelona Cuisine from the Oysters of Barcino to the Restaurants of Today) is a comprehensive and amusing study of the history of the city's gastronomical life, while the hands down best title in the 1,423-title Amazon.com list of books on Barcelona is Emili Teixidor's *Sic Transit Gloria Swanson i altres narracions* (Sic Transit Gloria Swanson and Other Stories).

Ernest Hemingway's *The Sun Also Rises,* published in 1926, remains the best account of Pamplona's San Fermin festival ever written. Jake's fishing trip to northern Navarra's village of Burguete is also a gem, as is the description of swimming off San Sebastián's La Concha beach. With the upcoming anniversary celebrations of Antoni Gaudí, the architect's many legendary Barcelona buildings are being honored in a slew of new art books. Among them *Gaudí: Master Architect* (Abbeville) by Juan Nonell; *Gaudí: The Man and the Work* (Bullfinch Press) by Juan Bergos Marso et al.; *Gaudí of Barcelona* (Rizzoli) by Mella Levick and Lluis Permanyer; *Gaudí* (Taschen) by Rainer Zerbst; and *Barcelona Art Nouveau* (Rizzoli) by Lluis Permanyer. For a delightful and magisterial pictorial tour of many of Barcelona's most famous buildings, be sure to read *Inside Barcelona* (Phaidon) by Josep M. Botey.

Videos

Whit Stilman's *Barcelona* and Pedro Almodovar's *All About my Mother* are the two most recent Barcelona-based motion pictures to gain international acclaim, while the Costa Brava played a starring role, along with James Mason and Ava Gardner, in the 1951 Hollywood flick, *Pandora and the Flying Dutchman.*

SPANISH VOCABULARY

Words and Phrases

When touring from Barcelona to Bilbao, travelers can be faced with a daunting array of languages and dialects, from Barcelona's Catalan Spanish to Bilbao's Basque dialect—so daunting an array that most Spaniards are grateful if travelers simply make an effort to use phrases in the most widely known form of Spanish—Castilian Spanish, which you will find in the following vocabulary pages. Still and all, there are many other languages: from Galicia in Spain's northwestern corner to Catalonia's Cap de Creus, the Iberian Peninsula's easternmost point, some fourteen recognized dialects are spoken across the north of Spain: Gallego; Lengua Asturiana (Bable); Basque (Euskera); Pyrenean dialects such as Béarnais and Toy on the French side of the border; Aragonese dialects such as Belsetan, Chistavino, and Patués; Castilian Spanish; Occitanian, Gascon French, Aranés, and Catalan. If you wish to begin communicating in the two leading regional dialects—Catalan and Euskara—here are some important phrases to keep in mind. After the English meaning, the Catalan, then Euskara equivalencies are then given.

My name is . . . (Em dic. . . . /Ni . . . naiz); Hello, how are you? (Hola! Com va això?/Kaixo, zer moduz?); I'm very well, and you? (Molt beá. A vostè?/Ni oso ondo, eskerrik asko); Good morning (Bon dia/Egun on); Good afternoon (Bona tarda/Arratsalde on); Goodnight (Bona nit/Gabon); Welcome (Benvingut(s)/Ongi estorri); Hello (Hola!/Kaixo!); Bye (Adéu/Agur); See you later (A reveure/Geroarte); How are you? (Com va?/Zer moduz?); Very well (Molt bé/Oso ondo); Thank you (Gràcies/Eskerrik asko); Don't mention it (De res/Es horregatik); Please (Si us plau/Mesedez); Excuse me (Perdó/Barkatu); Yes (Sí/Bai); No (No/Ez); What is this? (Que es això?/Zer da Hau?); How much is this? (Cuan val?/Zenbat da?); Good morning, where is the tourist office? (Bon dia, on es l'oficina de Turisme?/Egun on, non dago turismo bulegoa?); Straight (Tot recte/Zuzen); To the left (A l'esquerre/Ezkerretara); To the right (A la dreta/Eskubitara); Bank (Banc/Banketxea); Bookshop (Llibreria/Liburudenda); Art Gallery (Sala d'Exposicions/Erakusgela); Bus stop (Parada d'autobus/Autobus geltokia); Train station (Estació de tren/Tren geltokia); Hospital (Hospital/Ospitalea); Hotel (Hôtel/Hotela).

	English	Spanish	Pronunciation
Basics			
	Yes/no	Sí/no	see/no
	Please	Por favor	pohr fah-**vohr**
	May I?	¿Me permite?	meh pehr-**mee**-teh
	Thank you (very much)	(Muchas) gracias	(**moo**-chas) **grah**-see-as
	You're welcome	De nada	deh **nah**-dah
	Excuse me	Con Permiso/perdón	con pehr-**mee**-so/ pehr-**dohn**
	Pardon me/ what did you say?	¿Perdón?/Mande?	pehr-**dohn**/**mahn**-deh
	Could you tell me . . . ?	¿Podría decirme . . . ?	po-**dree**-ah deh-**seer**-meh
	I'm sorry	Lo siento	lo see-**en**-to
	Good morning!	¡Buenos días!	**bway**-nohs **dee**-ahs

Good afternoon!	¡Buenas tardes!	**bway**-nahs **tar**-dess
Good evening!	¡Buenas noches!	**bway**-nahs **no**-chess
Goodbye!	¡Adiós! ¡Hasta luego!	ah-dee-**ohss** **ah**-stah-**lwe**-go
Mr./Mrs.	Señor/Señora	sen-**yor**/sen-**yohr**-ah
Miss	Señorita	sen-yo-**ree**-tah
Pleased to meet you	Mucho gusto	**moo**-cho **goose**-to
How are you?	¿Cómo está usted?	**ko**-mo es-**tah** oo-**sted**
Very well, thank you.	Muy bien, gracias.	**moo**-ee bee-**en**, **grah**-see-as
And you?	¿Y usted?	ee oos-**ted**
Hello (on the phone)	Diga	**dee**-gah

Numbers

1	un, uno	oon, **oo**-no
2	dos	dohs
3	tres	tress
4	cuatro	**kwah**-tro
5	cinco	**sink**-oh
6	seis	saice
7	siete	see-**et**-eh
8	ocho	**o**-cho
9	nueve	new-**eh**-veh
10	diez	dee-**es**
11	once	**ohn**-seh
12	doce	**doh**-seh
13	trece	**treh**-seh
14	catorce	ka-**tohr**-seh
15	quince	**keen**-seh
16	dieciséis	dee-**es**-ee-**saice**
17	diecisiete	dee-**es**-ee-see-**et**-eh
18	dieciocho	dee-**es**-ee-**o**-cho
19	diecinueve	dee-**es**-ee-new-**ev**-eh
20	veinte	**vain**-teh
21	veinte y uno/ vientiuno	**vain**-te-oo-noh
30	treinta	**train**-tah
32	treinta y dos	train-tay-**dohs**
40	cuarenta	kwah-**ren**-tah
50	cincuenta	seen-**kwen**-tah
60	sesenta	sess-**en**-tah
70	setenta	set-**en**-tah
80	ochenta	oh-**chen**-tah
90	noventa	no-**ven**-tah
100	cien	see-**en**
200	doscientos	doh-see-**en**-tohss
500	quinientos	keen-**yen**-tohss
1,000	mil	meel
2,000	dos mil	dohs meel

Days of the Week

Sunday	domingo	doh-**meen**-goh
Monday	lunes	**loo**-ness
Tuesday	martes	**mahr**-tess
Wednesday	miércoles	me-**air**-koh-less
Thursday	jueves	hoo-**ev**-ess
Friday	viernes	vee-**air**-ness
Saturday	sábado	**sah**-bah-doh

Useful Phrases

Do you speak English?	¿Habla usted inglés?	**ah**-blah oos-**ted** in-**glehs**
I don't speak Spanish	No hablo español	no **ah**-bloh es-pahn-**yol**
I don't understand (you)	No entiendo	no en-tee-**en**-doh
I understand (you)	Entiendo	en-tee-**en**-doh
I don't know	No sé	no seh
I am American/British	Soy americano (americana)/inglés(a)	soy ah-meh-ree-**kah**-no (ah-meh-ree-**kah**-nah)/ in-**glehs**(ah)
My name is . . .	Me llamo . . .	may **yah**-moh
Yes, please/No, thank you	Sí, por favor/No, gracias	**see** pohr fah-**vor**/ no **grah**-see-ahs
Yesterday/today/tomorrow	Ayer/hoy/mañana	ah-**yehr**/oy/mahn-**yah**-nah
This morning/afternoon	Esta mañana/tarde	**es**-tah mahn-**yah**-nah/**tar**-deh
Tonight	Esta noche	**es**-tah **no**-cheh
This/Next week	Esta semana/la semana que entra	**es**-teh seh-**mah**-nah/lah seh-**mah**-nah keh **en**-trah
This/Next month	Este mes/el próximo mes	**es**-teh mehs/el **prok**-see-moh mehs
How?	¿Cómo?	**koh**-mo
When?	¿Cuándo?	**kwahn**-doh
What?	¿Qué?	keh
What is it?	¿Qué es esto?	keh es **es**-toh
Why?	¿Por qué?	por **keh**
Who?	¿Quién?	kee-**yen**
Where is . . . ?	¿Dónde está . . . ?	**dohn**-deh es-**tah**
the train station?	la estación del tren?	la es-tah-see-**on** del **train**
the subway station?	la estación del metro?	la es-ta-see-**on** del **meh**-tro
the bus stop?	la parada del autobus?	la pah-**rah**-dah del oh-toh-**boos**
the bank?	el banco?	el **bahn**-koh
the hotel?	el hotel?	el oh-**tel**
the post office?	la oficina de correos?	la oh-fee-**see**-nah deh koh-**reh**-os
the museum?	el museo?	el moo-**seh**-oh
the hospital?	el hospital?	el ohss-pee-**tal**

the bathroom?	el baño?	el **bahn**-yoh
Here/there	Aquí/allá	ah-**key**/ah-**yah**
Open/closed	Abierto/cerrado	ah-bee-**er**-toh/ ser-**ah**-doh
Left/right	Izquierda/derecha	iss-key-**er**-dah/ dare-**eh**-chah
Straight ahead	Todo recto	**toh**-doh-**rec**-toh
Is it near/far?	¿Está cerca/lejos?	es-**tah sehr**-kah/ **leh**-hoss
I'd like . . .	Quisiera . . .	kee-see-**ehr**-ah
a room	un habitación habitación	**oo**-nah ah-bee- tah-see-**on**
the key	la llave	lah **yah**-veh
a newspaper	un periódico	oon pehr-ee-**oh** dee-koh
a stamp	un sello	**say**-oh
How much is this?	¿Cuánto cuesta?	**kwahn**-toh **kwes**-tah
A little/a lot	Un poquito/ mucho	oon poh-**kee**-toh/ **moo**-choh
More/less	Más/menos	mahss/**men**-ohss
I am ill	Estoy enfermo(a)	es-**toy** en-**fehr**- moh(mah)
Please call a doctor	Por favor llame un medico	pohr fah-**vor** ya- meh oon **med**-ee-koh
Help!	¡Ayuda!	ah-**yoo**-dah

On the Road

Avenue	Avenida	ah-ven-**ee**-dah
Broad, tree-lined boulevard	Paseo	pah-**seh**-oh
Highway	Carretera	car-ray-**ter**-ah
Port; mountain pass	Puerto	poo-**ehr**-toh
Street	Calle	**cah**-yeh
Waterfront promenade	Paseo marítimo	pah-**seh**-oh mahr-**ee**-tee-moh

INDEX